UNDERSTANDING COMPUTERS:
TODAY AND TOMORROW

10th Edition

INTRODUCTORY

DEBORAH MORLEY
CHARLES S. PARKER

THOMSON
COURSE TECHNOLOGY

Australia • Canada • Mexico • Singapore • Spain • United Kingdom • United States

THOMSON

COURSE TECHNOLOGY

Understanding Computers: Today and Tomorrow, 10th Edition
is published by Course Technology.

Managing Editor:
Rachel Goldberg

Senior Product Manager:
Amanda Young Shelton

Senior Product Manager:
Kathy Finnegan

Product Manager:
Karen Stevens

Product Manager:
Brianna Germain

Associate Product Manager:
Emilie Perreault

Editorial Assistant
Abbey Reider

Marketing Manager:
Brian Boyle

Developmental Editor:
Pam Conrad

Product Manager:
Melissa Hathaway

Production Editor:
Jennifer Goguen

Composition:
GEX Publishing Services

Text and Cover Designer:
Janet Lavine

In today's computer-oriented society, computers and technology impact virtually everyone's life. *Under-standing Computers: Today and Tomorrow, 10th Edition* will ensure that students are current and informed in order to succeed in our technocentric society. With this new edition, students will not only learn about relevant cutting-edge technology trends, but they will also gain a better understanding of technology and technology-related issues. This information will give students the understanding they need to succeed in today's world.

This non-technical, introductory text explains in straightforward terms the importance of learning about computers, the various types of computer systems and their components, the principles by which computer systems work, the practical applications of computers and related technologies, and the ways in which the world is being changed by computers. The goal of this text is to provide the reader with a solid knowledge of computer basics, an understanding of the impact of our computer-oriented society, and a framework for using this knowledge effectively in their lives.

KEY FEATURES

Based on the fundamental chapters of the 16-chapter Comprehensive version of *Understanding Computers: Today and Tomorrow, 10th Edition* text, this 9-chapter Introductory version is current and comprehensive. Flexible organization and an engaging presentation combine with learning tools in each chapter to help the reader master important concepts. Numerous marginal notations lead students to the Understanding Computers Web site where they can access new Further Exploration Links, as well as new Student Edition Labs, Crossword Puzzles, Online Study Guides, and Online Quizzes. Boxed features on a variety of topics provide insight on current issues of interest.

Currency
The state-of-the-art content of this book and its Web site reflect the latest technologies, trends and classroom needs. Throughout the writing and production stages, enhancements were continually being made to ensure that the final product would be as current as possible.

Comprehensiveness and Depth
Accommodating a wide range of teaching preferences, *Understanding Computers: Today and Tomorrow, 10th Edition* provides comprehensive coverage of traditional topics while covering hot topics such as wireless Internet and wireless networking; portable PCs and mobile devices; new and emerging types of hardware and technology; global computing issues; and computer sabotage, spyware, hacking, Web browsing privacy, and other timely societal issues related to security and privacy.

Readability

We remember more about a subject if it is presented in a straightforward way and made interesting and exciting. This book is written in a conversational, down-to-earth style—one designed to be accurate without being intimidating. Concepts are explained clearly and simply, without the use of overly technical terminology. Where complex points are presented, they are explained in an understandable manner and with realistic examples from everyday life.

Chapter Learning Tools

1. **Outline, Learning Objectives, and Overview:** For each chapter, an **Outline** of the major topics to be covered, a list of student **Learning Objectives**, and a **Chapter Overview** helps instructors put the subject matter of the chapter in perspective and lets students know what they will be reading about.

2. **Boldfaced Key Terms and Running Glossary:** Important terms appear in boldface type as they are introduced in the chapter. These terms are defined at the bottom of the page on which they appear and in the end-of-text glossary.

3. **Chapter Boxes:** In each chapter, a **Trend** box provides students with a look at current and upcoming developments in the world of computers; an **Inside the Industry** box provides insight into some of the personalities and practices that have made the computer industry unique and fascinating; and a **How It Works** box explains how a technology or product works in more detail than covered in the chapter. Periodic **Campus Close-Up** boxes take a look at how computers and technology are being used at colleges or other educational facilities.

TIP

4. **Marginal Tips:** New **Tip** marginal icons provide students with additional information about a common problem or misconception, such as common terminology mistakes, or present students with an interesting additional fact or statistic related to the chapter content.

5. **Illustrations and Photographs:** Instructive, current full-color illustrations and photographs appear throughout the book to help illustrate important concepts. Figures and screen shots are carefully annotated to convey important information.

6. **Summary and Key Terms:** The end-of-chapter material includes a concise, section-by-section **Summary** of the main points in the chapter. The chapter's Learning Objectives appear in the margin next to the relevant section of the summary so that students are better able to relate the Learning Objectives to the chapter material. Every boldfaced key term in the chapter also appears in boldface type in the summary. A matching exercise of selected **Key Terms** helps students test their retention of the chapter material.

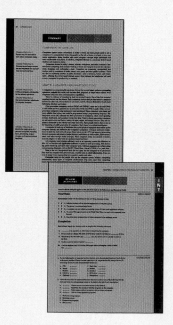

7. **Review Activities and Projects:** End-of-chapter activities allow students to test themselves on what they have just read. A **Self-Quiz** (with the answers listed at the end of the text) consists of ten true-false and completion questions. Five to eight additional easily graded matching and short-answer **Exercises** are included for instructors who would like to assign graded homework. End-of-chapter **Projects** require students to extend their knowledge by doing research beyond merely reading the book. Organized into six types of projects (Hot Topics, Short Answer/Research, Hands On, Writing About Computers, Presentation/Demonstration, and Interactive Discussion), the projects feature complete explicit instruction so that students can work through them without additional directions from instructors. Special icons denote projects that are written as group projects or that require Internet access.

8. **Understanding Computers Web Site:** Throughout the chapter, **Further Exploration** marginal icons direct students to the Understanding Computers Web site where they can access collections of links to Web sites containing more in-depth information on a given topic from the text. At the end of every chapter, students are directed to the Understanding Computers Web site to access the **Student Edition Labs** that are relevant to that chapter. The Web site also includes an **Online Study Guide**, **Online Glossary**, **Online Quizzes**, and **Crossword Puzzles**.

References and Resources Guide

A new 24-page **Reference and Resources Guide** brings together in one convenient location a collection of computer-related references and resources. The References and Resources Guide includes a computer history timeline, as well as additional coverage of numbering systems, coding charts, CPU characteristics, and Web searching techniques. It also includes a Web Guide, a Guide for Buying a PC, and Self-Quiz Answers.

NEW TO THIS EDITION

Increased Coverage of Societal Issues

Appearing in chapter boxes and in end-of-chapter projects, timely societal topics—such as Web browsing privacy, network security issues, e-mail hoaxes, digital copy protection, biometric input devices, electronic paper, spyware, hacking, and computer sabotage—are woven into the text.

New References and Resources Guide

New **24-page References and Resources Guide** at the end of the book provides students with a collection of reference material that can be used outside the classroom, such as a PC buyer's guide, Web searching tips, Web guide, and coding charts for ASCII, EBCDIC, and Unicode. This new References and Resources Guide incorporates some content from the 2003 Enhanced Edition's **Chapter 16, You and Your PC.** Most of the remaining content from that chapter has been integrated into other chapters in the text.

Expanded End-of-Chapter Material

Each chapter now has a total of 12 **End-of-Chapter Projects** including a new **Hot Topics** project, which has students research an emerging trend, and an additional **Hands-On** Internet project, which requires students to use the Web to research a particular topic or perform a specific online activity. So that instructors can easily determine which projects require Internet access before assigning them, these projects are denoted with a special marginal icon. Additionally, projects that could be used as a group activity are similarly denoted with a different marginal icon.

We have also increased the number of **Exercises** to between five and eight per chapter. These exercises are especially helpful for those instructors who like to assign graded homework. Answers to these exercises are included in the Instructor support materials.

New Web Site Content

The **Understanding Computers Web site** has been completely updated to include new **Further Exploration** links, interactive **Crossword Puzzles**, **Online Quizzes**, an **Online Glossary**, and a **Web Guide**. Additionally, **Online Study Guides** tailored for each chapter include a chapter outline with study tips. The new interactive **Student Edition Labs** that are referenced in each chapter are also available through the Understanding Computers Web site. To learn more about these Student Edition Labs, go to page IX.

STUDENT AND INSTRUCTOR SUPPORT MATERIALS

Understanding Computers: Today and Tomorrow, 10th Edition is available with a complete package of support materials for instructors and students. Included in the package are the Understanding Computers Web site, Instructor's Resources available both on CD-ROM and online, and SAM Computer Concepts.

The Understanding Computers Web Site

The Understanding Computers Web site located at:

http://www.course.com/uc10

provides media-rich support for students, including the following resources:

FURTHER EXPLORATION

▼ Further Exploration—links to Web sites with more in-depth information on a given topic from the text.

▼ Student Edition Labs—provides students with a series of multimedia-enhanced labs that help them learn through dynamic observation, step-by-step practice, and challenging review questions.

▼ Interactive Crossword Puzzles—crossword puzzles that incorporate the key terms from each chapter.

▼ Online Study Guide, Online Quizzes, and Online Glossary—provide students with study tips and an editable chapter outline where they add their own notes, plus an online quiz and an online glossary for that specific chapter.

▼ Web Guide—provides students with categorized and regularly updated links to the Web's most useful sites.

Student Edition Labs

New Web-based Student Edition Labs allow your students to master hundreds of computer concepts including input and output devices, file management and desktop applications, computer privacy, virus protection, and much more. Featuring up-to-the-minute content, eye-popping graphics, and rich animation, the highly interactive Student Edition Labs help students learn through dynamic observation, step-by-step practice, and challenging review questions. Access the free Student Edition Labs from the Understanding Computers Web site at www.course.com/uc10.

Student Edition Labs currently include:

- Using Input Devices
- Peripheral Devices
- Using Windows
- Working with Graphics
- Working with Audio
- Working with Video
- Word Processing
- Spreadsheets
- Databases
- Presentation Software
- Maintaining a Hard Drive
- Managing Files and Folders
- Binary Numbers
- Understanding the Motherboard
- Installing and Uninstalling Software
- Protecting your Privacy Online
- Keeping Your Computer Virus Free
- E-mail
- Creating Web Pages
- Connecting to the Internet
- Getting the Most out of the Internet
- Backing up Your Computer
- Visual Programming
- Advanced Spreadsheets
- Advanced Databases
- Networking Basics
- E-Commerce
- Web Design Principles
- Project Management
- Wireless Networking

Interactive glossary terms expand on key concepts.

Hands-on practice reinforces important topics.

Instructor Resources

Course Technology instructional resources and technology provide instructors with a wide range of tools that enhance teaching and learning. These tools can be accessed from the Instructor Resources CD or at www.course.com.

Electronic Instructor's Manual

The Instructor's Manual is written to provide instructors with practical suggestions for enhancing classroom presentations. For each of the 16 chapters of the text, the Instructor's Manual provides the following:

- ▼ **Instructor Notes** provide a summary of the chapter as well as suggestions for key points to cover in a lecture.

- ▼ **Troubleshooting Tips** are short tips included periodically throughout the Instructor Notes.

- ▼ **Quick Quizzes** are included for select topics in the chapter, and include one Multiple Choice, one True/False and one Short Answer question.

- ▼ **Classroom Activities** are in-class activities, which reinforce concepts and skills relevant to the topic at hand.

▼ **Discussion Questions** are thought provoking questions that can be used to involve students in the lecture.

▼ **Key Terms** are important terms covered in the chapter that students should know.

▼ **Chapter Quiz** consists of 10 objective questions and may be reproduced to distribute to students for additional homework or an in-class quiz.

ExamView

This textbook is accompanied by ExamView, a powerful testing software package that allows instructors to create and administer printed, computer (LAN-based), and Internet exams. ExamView includes over 2,400 questions that correspond to the topics covered in this text, enabling students to generate detailed study guides that include page references for further review. The computer-based and Internet testing components allow students to take exams at their computers, and also save the instructor time by grading each exam automatically.

PowerPoint Presentations

This book comes with Microsoft PowerPoint slides for each chapter. These are included as a teaching aid for classroom presentation, to make available to students on the network for chapter review, or to be printed for classroom distribution. Instructors can customize these presentations to cover any additional topics they introduce to the class.

Tabbing Guide

The tabbing guide can be used to show how and where this textbook has been updated for this edition. Page references are included to make planning a class easier for the instructor.

BlackBoard and WebCT Content

We offer a full range of content for use with BlackBoard and WebCT to simplify the use of Understanding Computers in distance education settings.

SAM Computer Concepts

Add more muscle and flexibility to your course with SAM (Skills Assessment Manager) Computer Concepts! SAM Computer Concepts adds the power of skill-based assessment and the award-winning SAM classroom administration system to your course, putting you in control of how you deliver exams and training.

By adding SAM Computer Concepts to your curriculum, you can:

- ▼ Reinforce your students' knowledge of key computer concepts with hands-on application exercises.

- ▼ Allow your students to "learn by listening" with access to rich audio in their Student Edition Labs.

- ▼ Build hands-on computer concepts exams from a test bank of more than 200 skill-based concepts tasks.

- ▼ Schedule your students' concepts training and testing exercises with powerful administrative tools.

- ▼ Track student exam grades and training progress using more than one dozen student and classroom reports.

Teach your introductory course with the simplicity of a single system! You can now administer your entire Computer Concepts and Microsoft Office course through the SAM platform. For more information on the SAM administration system, SAM Computer Concepts and other SAM products, please visit http://www.course.com/sam.

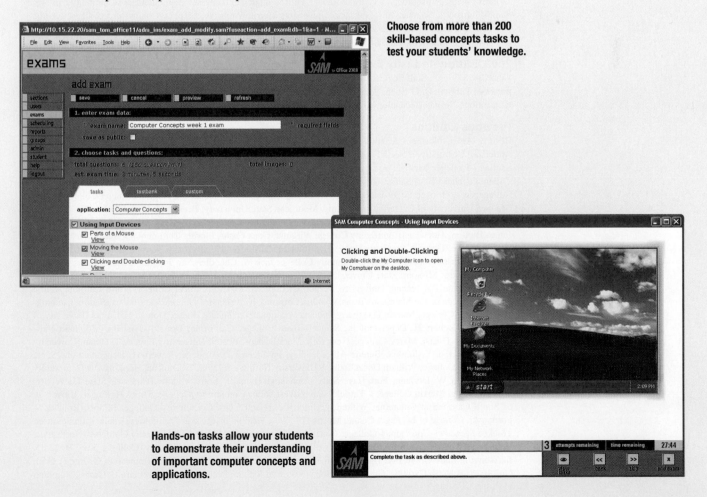

Choose from more than 200 skill-based concepts tasks to test your students' knowledge.

Hands-on tasks allow your students to demonstrate their understanding of important computer concepts and applications.

ACKNOWLEDGEMENTS

The following past and present educational and industry expert reviewers of this text deserve a special word of thanks for their thoughtful suggestions that have helped to define and improve the quality of this text over the years.

10th Edition–Educational Reviewers

Fariba Bolandhemat, Santa Monica College; Jackie Dennis, Prairie State College; Mike Doroshow, Eastfield College; John Dunn, Palo Alto College; Alyse Hollingsworth, Brevard College; John Jasma, Palo Alto College; Donna Madsen, Kirkwood Community College; Dixie Mercer, Kirkwood Community College; Savitha Pinnepalli, Louisiana State University; Allanagh Sewell, Southeastern Louisiana University; David Spaisman, Katherine Gibbs; Elizabeth Spooner, Holmes Community College

10th Edition–Industry Expert Reviewers

Jeremy Bates, Multimedia Developer, R & L Multimedia Developers; Charles Hayes, Product Marketing Manager, SimpleTech, Inc.; Rick McGowan, Vice President & Senior Software Engineer, Unicode, Inc.; Russell Reynolds, Chief Operating Officer & Web Designer, R & L Multimedia Developers; Rob Stephens, Director, Technology Strategies, SAS; Dave Stow, Database Specialist, OSE Systems, Inc.

2003 Enhanced Edition–Educational Reviewers

Beverly Amer, Northern American University; Cesar Marron, University of Wyoming; David Womack, University of Texas, San Antonio

2002 Edition–Educational Reviewers

Beverly Amer, Northern Arizona University; Chris Brown, Bemidji State University; Joann C. Cook, College of DuPage; Terry Felke, WR Harper College; Janos T. Fustos, Metropolitan State; Jim Hanson, Austin Community College; Richard Kiger, Dallas Baptist University; James Lasalle, University of Arizona; Paul Lou, Diablo Valley College; Kent Lundin, Brigham Young University-Idaho; Donna Madsen, Kirkwood Community College; Randy Marak, Hillsboro CC; Joseph D. Oldham, University of Kentucky; Lisa B. Perez, San Joaquin Delta College; Delores Pusins, Hillsborough CC; Mike Rabaut, Hillsborough CC; Tim Sylvester, Glendale Community College; Semih Tahaoglu, Southeastern Louisiana University; Merrill Wells, Red Rocks Community College; George Woodbury, College of the Sequoias; Nan Woodsome, Araphoe Community College; Israel Yost, University of New Hampshire; Vic Zamora, Mt. San Antonio College

2002 Edition–Industry Expert Reviewers

Alan Charlesworth, Staff Engineer, Sun Microsystems; Khaled A Elamrawi, Senior Marketing Engineer, Intel Corporation; Timothy D. O'Brien, Senior Systems Engineer, Fujitsu Software; John Paulson, Manager, Product Communications, Seagate Technology; Omid Rahmat, Editor in Chief, Tom's Hardware Guide www.tomshardware.com

Previous Editions

Beverly Amer, Northern Arizona University; James Ambroise Jr., Southern University, Louisiana; Virginia Anderson, University of North Dakota; Robert Andree, Indiana University Northwest; Linda Armbruster, Rancho Santiago College; Michael Atherton, Mankato State University; Gary E. Baker, Marshalltown Community College; Richard Batt, Saint Louis Community College at Meremec; Luverne Bierle, Iowa Central Community College; Jerry Booher, Scottsdale Community College; Frederick W. Bounds, Georgia Perimeter College; James Bradley, University of Calgary; Curtis Bring, Moorhead State University; Brenda K. Britt, Fayetteville Technical Community College; Cathy Brotherton, Riverside Community College; Janice Burke, South Suburban College; James Buxton, Tidewater Community College, Virginia; Gena Casas, Florida Community College, Jacksonville; Thomas Case, Georgia Southern University; John E. Castek, University of Wisconsin-La Crosse; Mario E. Cecchetti, Westmoreland County Community College; Jack W. Chandler, San Joaquin Delta College; Jerry M. Chin, Southwest Missouri State University; Edward W. Christensen, Monmouth University; Carl Clavadetscher, California State Polytechnic University; Vernon Clodfelter, Rowan Technical College, North Carolina; Laura Cooper, College of the Mainland, Texas; Cynthia Corritore, University of Nebraska at Omaha; Sandra Cunningham, Ranger College; Marvin Daugherty, Indiana Vocational Technical College; Donald L. Davis, University of Mississippi; Robert H. Dependahl Jr., Santa Barbara College, California; Donald Dershem, Mountain View College; John DiElsi, Marcy College, New York; Mark Dishaw, Boston University; Eugene T. Dolan, University of the District of Columbia; Bennie Allen Dooley, Pasadena City College; Robert H. Dependahl Jr.; Santa Barbara City College; William Dorin, Indiana University Northwest; Jackie O. Duncan, Hopkinsville Community College; John W. Durham, Fort Hays State University; Hyun B. Eom, Middle Tennessee State University; Michael Feiler, Merritt College; J. Patrick Fenton, West Valley Community College; James H. Finger, University of South Carolina at Columbia; William C. Fink, Lewis and Clark Community College, Illinois; Ronald W. Fordonski, College of Du Page; Connie Morris Fox, West Virginia Institute of Technology; Paula S. Funkhouser, Truckee Meadows Community College; Gene Garza, University of Montevallo; Timothy Gottleber, North Lake College; Dwight Graham, Prairie State College; Wade Graves, Grayson County College; Kay H. Gray, Jacksonville State University; David W. Green, Nashville State Technical Institute, Tennessee; George P. Grill, University of North Carolina, Greensboro; John Groh, San Joaquin Delta College; Rosemary C. Gross, Creighton

University; Dennis Guster, Saint Louis Community College at Meremec; Joe Hagarty, Raritan Valley Community College; Donald Hall, Manatee Community College; Sallyann Z. Hanson, Mercer County Community College; L. D. Harber, Volunteer State Community College, Tennessee; Hank Hartman, Iowa State University; Richard Hatch, San Diego State University; Mary Lou Hawkins, Del Mar College; Ricci L. Heishman, Northern Virginia Community College; William Hightower, Elon College, North Carolina; Sharon A. Hill, Prince George's Community College, Maryland; Fred C. Homeyer, Angelo State University; Stanley P. Honacki, Moraine Valley Community College; L. Wayne Horn, Pensacola Junior College; J. William Howorth, Seneca College, Ontario, Canada; Mark W. Huber, East Carolina University; Peter L. Irwin, Richland College, Texas; Nicholas JohnRobak, Saint Joseph's University; Elizabeth Swoope Johnson, Louisiana State University; Jim Johnson, Valencia Community College; Mary T. Johnson, Mt. San Antonio College; Susan M. Jones, Southwest State University; Amardeep K. Kahlon, Austin Community College; Robert T. Keim, Arizona State University; Mary Louise Kelly, Palm Beach Community College; William R. Kenney, San Diego Mesa College; Richard Kerns, East Carolina University, North Carolina; Glenn Kersnick, Sinclair Community College, Ohio; Gordon C. Kimbell, Everett Community College, Washington; Mary Veronica Kolesar, Utah State University; Robert Kirklin, Los Angeles Harbor Community College; Judith A. Knapp, Indiana University Northwest; James G. Kriz, Cuyahoga Community College, Ohio; Joan Krone, Denison University; Fran Kubicek, Kalamazoo Valley Community College; Rose M. Laird, Northern Virginia Community College; Robert Landrum, Jones Junior College; Shelly Langman, Bellevue Community College; James F. LaSalle, The University of Arizona; Linda J. Lindaman, Black Hawk College; Chang-Yang Lin, Eastern Kentucky University; Alden Lorents, Northern Arizona University; Paul M. Lou, Diablo Valley College; Deborah R. Ludford, Glendale Community College; Barbara J. Maccarone, North Shore Community College; Donna Madsen, Kirkwood Community College; Wayne Madison, Clemson University, South Carolina; Donna L. Madsen, Kirkwood Community College; Kathryn A. Marold, Ph.D., Metropolitan State College of Denver; Randy Marak, Hill College; Gary Marks, Austin Community College, Texas; Ed Martin, Kingsborough Community College; Vickie McCullough, Palomar College; James W. McGuffee, Austin Community College; James McMahon, Community College of Rhode Island; William A. McMillan, Madonna University; Don B. Medley, California State Polytechnic University; John Melrose, University of Wisconsin–Eau Claire; Mary Meredith, University of Southwestern Louisiana; Marilyn Meyer, Fresno City College; Carolyn H. Monroe, Baylor University; William J. Moon, Palm Beach Community College; Marilyn Moore, Purdue University; Marty Murray, Portland Community College; Don Nielsen, Golden West College; George Novotny, Ferris State University; Richard Okezie, Mesa Community College; Dennis J. Olsen, Pikes Peak Community College; Bob Palank, Florissant Community College; James Payne, Kellogg Community College; Robert Ralph, Fayetteville Technical Institute, North Carolina; Herbert F. Rebhun, University of Houston–Downtown; Arthur E. Rowland, Shasta College; Kenneth R. Ruhrup, St. Petersburg Junior College; John F. Sanford, Philadelphia College of Textiles and Science; Carol A. Schwab, Webster University; Larry Schwartzman, Trident Technical College; Benito R. Serenil, South Seattle Community College; Tom Seymour, Minot State University; John J. Shuler, San Antonio College, Texas; Gayla Jo Slauson, Mesa State College; Harold Smith, Brigham Young University; Willard A. Smith, Tennessee State University; Timothy M. Stanford, City University; Alfred C. St. Onge, Springfield Technical Community College, Massachusetts; Michael L. Stratford, Charles County Community College, Maryland; Karen Studniarz, Kishwaukee College; Sandra Swanson, Lewis &Clark Community College; William H. Trueheart, New Hampshire College; Jane J. Thompson, Solano Community College; Sue Traynor, Clarion University of Pennsylvania; James D. Van Tassel, Mission College; James R. Walters, Pikes Peak Community College; Joyce V. Walton, Seneca College, Ontario, Canada; Diane B.Walz, University of Texas at San Antonio; Joseph Waters, Santa Rosa Junior College, California; Liang Chee Wee, University of Arizona; Fred J. Wilke, Saint Louis Community College; Charles M. Williams, Georgia State University; Roseanne Witkowski, Orange County Community College; James D. Woolever, Cerritos College; Patricia Joann Wykoff, Western Michigan University; A. James Wynne, Virginia Commonwealth University; and Robert D. Yearout, University of North Carolina at Asheville.

We would also like to thank the people on the Course team—their professionalism, attention to detail, and enormous enthusiasm makes working with them a pleasure. In particular, we'd like to thank Rachel Goldberg, Amanda Young Shelton, Melissa Hathaway, Pam Conrad, and Jennifer Goguen for all their ideas, support, and tireless efforts during the design, writing, rewriting, and production of this book. Thanks to Marc Ouellette for managing the development of the Understanding Computers Web site, Emilie Perreault and Brianna Germain for managing the Instructor's Resource package, Abbey Reider for all her assistance, and Brian Boyle for his efforts on marketing this text. Thanks also to Kristen Duerr and Kathy Finnegan.
We are also very appreciative of the numerous individuals and organizations that were kind enough to supply information and photographs for this text.

Deborah Morley
Charles S. Parker

We sincerely hope you find this book interesting, informative, and enjoyable to read. If you have any suggestions for improvement, or corrections that you'd like to be considered for future editions, please send them to deborah.morley@thomson.com.

BRIEF CONTENTS

Preface

MODULE Introduction 1
Chapter 1
Introduction to the World of Computers 3
Chapter 2
Using Your PC, Windows, and the Web 39

MODULE Hardware 85
Chapter 3
The System Unit: Processing and Memory 87
Chapter 4
Storage 133
Chapter 5
Input and Output 173

MODULE Software 219
Chapter 6
System Software: Operating Systems and
Utilities 221
Chapter 7
Application Software 261

MODULE Networks and the Internet 309
Chapter 8
Computer Networks 311
Chapter 9
The Internet and World Wide Web 363

References and Resources Guide R-1

Credits C-1

Glossary/Index I-1

CONTENTS

Preface v

MODULE Introduction 1
Chapter 1 Introduction to the World of Computers 3
Overview 4
Computers in Your Life 4
> Why Learn About Computers? 4
> Computers in the Home 5
> Computers in Education 6
> Computers in the Workplace 7
> Computers on the Go 8
What Is a Computer and What Does It Do? 9
> Computers Then and Now 10
> Hardware 12
> Software 14
> Data and Information 16
> Computer Users and Professionals 16
Computer Networks and the Internet 17
> The Internet 18
> Accessing a Network 18
Computers to Fit Every Need 19
> Mobile Devices 19
> Personal Computers 19
> Midrange Servers 26
> Mainframe Computers 27
> Supercomputers 27
Computers and Society 28
> The Information Age and the New Information Revolution 28
> Benefits of a Computer-Oriented Society 29
> Risks of a Computer-Oriented Society 29

Summary 30
Key Terms 32
Review Activities 33
Projects 35

TREND Wearable PCs 9
HOW IT WORKS Setting Up a New PC 21
INSIDE THE INDUSTRY PC Modding 22
CAMPUS CLOSE-UP Wired Med Students 24

Chapter 2 Using Your PC, Windows, and the Web 39
Overview 40
Starting Your Computer: The Boot Process 40
Using the Windows Operating System 41
> The Windows Interface 41
> Opening Windows and Starting Programs 47
> Manipulating Windows 48
> Shutting Down the Computer 51

Using the Internet and World Wide Web 51
> What are the Internet and World Wide Web? 51
> What Is a Browser? 52
> Accessing the Internet 52
> Internet Addresses 54
> Surfing the Web 58
> Using Bookmarks and the History List 62
> Searching the Web 63
E-Mail and Other Types of Online Communications 65
> Sending E-Mail 68
> Receiving E-Mail 68
> Managing E-Mail 68
> Discussion Groups, Chat, Instant Messaging, and More 70
> Netiquette 71
Societal Implications of Cyberspace 72
> Security 72
> Privacy 73
> Differences in Online Communications 73
> The Anonymity Factor 73
> Information Integrity 75

Summary 76
Key Terms 78
Review Activities 79
Projects 81

TREND E-Mail Hoaxes 57
HOW IT WORKS Video E-Mail 67
INSIDE THE INDUSTRY Emoticons and Acronyms: Expressing Yourself Online 74

MODULE Hardware 85
Chapter 3 The System Unit:
Processing and Memory 87
Overview 88
Data and Program Representation 88
> Digital Data Representation 88
> Representing Numerical Data: The Binary Numbering System 89
> Coding Systems for Text-Based Data 90
> Coding Systems for Other Types of Data 92
> Representing Programs: Machine Language 95
Inside the System Unit 95
> The Motherboard 96
> CPU 96
> Memory 100
> Buses 104
> Expansion Slots and Cards 106
> Ports 108

How the CPU Works 111
> Typical CPU Components 112
> The System Clock and the Machine Cycle 113
Making Computers Faster Now and in the Future 115
> Speeding Up Your System Today 115
> Strategies for Making Faster Computers 118
> Future Trends 122
Summary 124
Key Terms 126
Review Activities 127
Projects 129

HOW IT WORKS MP3 Compression 94
TREND Unusual Uses for Computer Chips: Smart Bullets, Smart Tennis Shoes, and High-Tech Pets 99
INSIDE THE INDUSTRY Non-Volatile Memory 101

Chapter 4 Storage 133
Overview 134
Properties of Storage Systems 134
> Storage Devices and Media 134
> Non-Volatility 135
> Removable vs. Fixed Media 135
> Random vs. Sequential Access 135
> Logical vs. Physical Representation 136
Magnetic Disk Systems 137
> Floppy Disks and Drives 138
> High-Capacity Removable Magnetic Disks and Drives 140
> Hard Disk Drives 140
Optical Disc Systems 150
> Read-Only Discs: CD-ROM and DVD-ROM Discs 152
> Recordable Discs: CD-R, DVD-R, and DVD+R Discs 153
> Rewritable Discs: CD-RW, DVD-RW, DVD+RW, DVD-RAM, and Blue Laser Discs 154
Other Types of Storage Systems 154
> Magneto-Optical Discs 154
> Flash Memory Media 155
> Magnetic Tape Systems 158
> Remote Storage Systems 159
> Smart Cards 159
> Holographic Storage 161
Comparing Storage Alternatives 162
Summary 164
Key Terms 166
Review Activities 167
Projects 169

INSIDE THE INDUSTRY Data Recovery Experts 144
HOW IT WORKS Business Card CDs 151
TREND Digital Copy Protection 155
CAMPUS CLOSE-UP Penn State ID+ Smart Cards 162

Chapter 5 Input and Output 173
Overview 174
Input and Output 174
Keyboards 174
Pointing Devices 176
> Mice 176
> Electronic Pens 177
> Touch Screens 180
> Other Pointing Devices 181
Scanners and Related Devices 181
> Scanners 183
> Optical Mark Readers (OMRs) 185
> Bar-Code Readers 185
> Optical Character Recognition (OCR) Devices 187
> Magnetic Ink Character Recognition (MICR) Readers 187
Biometric Input Devices 189
Multimedia Input Devices 191
> Digital Cameras 191
> Audio Input Devices 193
Display Devices 195
> Display Device Characteristics 195
> CRT Monitors 197
> Flat-Panel Displays 197
> Smart Displays 198
> HDTV Monitors 198
> Data and Multimedia Projectors 199
> Emerging Display Technologies and Applications 199
Printers 200
> Printer Characteristics 200
> Laser Printers 204
> Ink-Jet Printers 205
> Special-Purpose Printers 206
> Fax Machines and Multifunction Devices 208
Multimedia Output Devices 208
> Speakers 208
> Voice-Output Systems 209
Summary 210
Key Terms 212
Review Activities 213
Projects 215

INSIDE THE INDUSTRY RFID: The Smart Bar Code 188
HOW IT WORKS Face Recognition 190
CAMPUS CLOSE-UP Smart Classrooms 201
TREND Electronic Paper 202

MODULE Software 219
Chapter 6 Systems Software: Operating Systems and Utilities 221

Overview 222
System Software vs. Application Software 222
The Operating System 223
> Functions of an Operating System 224
> Processing Techniques for Increased Efficiency 227
> Differences Among Operating Systems 230
Operating Systems for Desktop
  PCs and Servers 232
> DOS 233
> Windows 234
> Mac OS 237
> UNIX 237
> Linux 238
> NetWare 239
> OS/2 and OS/2 Warp 240
> Solaris 240
Operating Systems for Handheld PCs and Mobile
  Devices 240
> Embedded and Mobile Versions of Windows 240
> Palm OS 242
> Symbian OS 242
Operating Systems for Larger Computers 242
Utility Programs 243
> File Management Programs 243
> Antivirus Programs 246
> Diagnostic and Disk Management Programs 246
> Uninstall Utilities 247
> File Compression Programs 248
> Backup and Recovery Utilities 248
> Encryption Programs 250
> Network and Internet Utilities 250
The Future of Operating Systems 251

Summary 252
Key Terms 254
Review Activities 255
Projects 257

INSIDE THE INDUSTRY Linux Desktops:
  The Wave of the Future? 239
TREND Smart Cars 241
HOW IT WORKS Downloading and
  Installing Programs 245

Chapter 7 Application Software 261
Overview 262
The Basics of Application Software 262
> Types of Application Software 262
> Ownership Rights and Delivery Methods 263
> Software Suites 266
> Object Linking and Embedding (OLE) 268
> Desktop vs. Handheld PC Software 269
> Getting Help 270

Word Processing Concepts 271
> What Is Word Processing? 271
> Creating and Editing a Word
  Processing Document 272
> Formatting a Document 273
> Graphics, Tables, and Templates 275
> Word Processing and the Web 275
Spreadsheet Concepts 276
> What Is a Spreadsheet? 276
> Creating and Editing a Worksheet 276
> Formatting a Worksheet 279
> Charts and What-If Analysis 280
> Spreadsheets and the Web 281
Database Concepts 281
> What Is a Database? 281
> Creating a Database 282
> Modifying a Database 283
> Queries and Reports 284
> Databases and the Web 285
Presentation Graphics Concepts 285
> What Is a Presentation Graphic? 285
> Creating a Presentation 286
> Enhancing and Finishing a Presentation 287
> Presentation Graphics and the Web 288
Graphics and Multimedia Concepts 288
> Multimedia Applications 289
> Types of Graphics and Multimedia Software 291
> Graphics, Multimedia, and the Web 296
Other Types of Application Software 297
> Desktop and Personal Publishing Software 297
> Accounting and Personal Finance Software 298
> Educational, Entertainment, and
  Reference Software 298
> CAD and Other Types of Design Software 298
> Project Management Software 298

Summary 300
Key Terms 302
Review Activities 303
Projects 305

INSIDE THE INDUSTRY Jellyvision's Interactive Conver-
  sation Interface (iCi) 291
HOW IT WORKS Creating a Custom Music CD 295
TREND Spyware 299

MODULE Networks and the Internet 309
Chapter 8 Computer Networks 311
Overview 312
Networking and Communications Applications 312
> Wireless Phones 313
> Paging and Messaging 313
> Global Positioning Systems (GPSs) 314
> Satellite Radio 314

> Online Conferencing 314
> Collaborative Computing 315
> Telecommuting 316
> Telemedicine 316
What is a Network and How Does it
Transmit Data? 317
> Data Transmission Characteristics 317
> Wired vs. Wireless Connections 320
> Wired Network Transmission Media 320
> Wireless Network Transmission Media 322
Types of Networks 327
> Network Topologies 327
> Network Architectures 328
> LANs, WANs, and Other Types of Networks 329
Networking Hardware 331
> Network Adapters 331
> Modems 332
> Hubs, Switches, and Other
Networking Hardware 334
Communications Protocols 336
> Ethernet 336
> Token Ring 337
> TCP/IP 337
> 802.11 (Wi-Fi) 338
> Bluetooth 341
> Wireless Application Protocol (WAP) 342
> Other Networking Protocols 342
Network Security Issues 344
> Unauthorized Access and Use 344
> Computer Sabotage 349
Summary 354
Key Terms 356
Review Activities 357
Projects 359

INSIDE THE INDUSTRY Presence Technology 326
HOW IT WORKS Setting Up a Home Network 340
TREND Personal Biometrics: Finger Payment Systems 349

Chapter 9 The Internet and World Wide Web 363
Overview 364
Evolution of the Internet 364
> From ARPANET to Internet2 365
> The Internet Community Today 367
> Myths About the Internet 370
Getting Set Up to Use the Internet 371
> Type of Device 371
> Type of Connection and Internet Access 372
> Selecting an ISP and Setting Up Your PC 377
Searching the Internet 379
> Search Sites 379
> Search Strategies 381
> Evaluating Search Results 384
> Citing Internet Resources 385

Beyond Browsing and E-Mail 385
> Online Financial Transactions 385
> Online Entertainment 388
> Online News and Research 396
> Online Education 397
> Peer-to-Peer File Sharing 401
Censorship and Privacy Issues 401
> Censorship 402
> Web Browsing Privacy 402
> E-Mail Privacy 407
The Future of the Internet 407
Summary 408
Key Terms 410
Review Activities 411
Projects 413

TREND Aircraft-Based Internet: Broadband of the
Future? 375
INSIDE THE INDUSTRY The Napster Controversy 391
HOW IT WORKS Video-on-Demand 394

References and Resources Guide R-1
Computer History Timeline R-2
A Look at Numbering Systems R-7
> The Decimal and Binary Numbering System R-7
> The Hexadecimal Numbering System R-7
> Converting Between Numbering Systems R-8
> Computer Arithmetic R-9
> Using a Scientific Calculator R-10
Coding Charts R-11
> ASCII and EBCDIC R-11
> Unicode R-12
CPU Characteristics R-13
Guide to Buying a PC R-14
> Analyzing Needs R-14
> Listing Alternatives R-15
> System Troubleshooting and Upgrading R-17
Web Guide R-19
Web Searching Tips: A Closer Look at Google R-23
> Google Search Options R-23
> Google Advanced Search R-23
> Other Google Tools R-24
Answers to Self-Quiz R-25

Credits C-1

Glossary/Index I-1

MODULE
INTRODUCTION

We live in an age of *computers*. Businesses, government agencies, and other organizations use computers and related technologies to handle tedious paperwork, provide better service to customers, and assist managers in making good decisions. Individuals use computers for such activities as paying bills, shopping, managing investments, communicating with others, preparing taxes, playing games, researching products, listening to music, and exchanging electronic photos and greeting cards. Because of their growing prominence in our society, it is essential to know something about computers and what they can be used for today.

This module introduces you to computers and some of their uses. Chapter 1 helps you to understand what computers are, how they work, how people use them, and presents important terms and concepts that you will encounter throughout this text and in discussions about computers with others. Chapter 2 delves into how to use a computer to perform basic tasks and to access resources on the *Internet* and *World Wide Web*. Although the Internet and World Wide Web are covered in more detail in Chapter 9, Chapter 2 is intended to give you the knowledge, skills, and tools necessary to access the World Wide Web for research purposes and to complete the online exercises and activities that accompany this textbook.

INTRODUCTION

Chapter 1 Introduction to the World of Computers 3

Overview 4

Computers in Your Life 4

What Is a Computer and What Does It Do? 9

Computer Networks and the Internet 17

Computers to Fit Every Need 19

Computers and Society 28

Chapter 2 Using Your PC, Windows, and the Web 39

Overview 40

Starting Your Computer: The Boot Process 40

Using the Windows Operating System 41

Using the Internet and World Wide Web 51

E-Mail and Other Types of Online Communications 65

Societal Implications of Cyberspace 72

CHAPTER 1

OUTLINE

Overview

Computers in Your Life
Why Learn About Computers?
Computers in the Home
Computers in Education
Computers in the Workplace
Computers on the Go

What Is a Computer and What Does It Do?
Computers Then and Now
Hardware
Software
Data and Information
Computer Users and Professionals

Computer Networks and the Internet
The Internet
Accessing a Network

Computers to Fit Every Need
Mobile Devices
Personal Computers
Midrange Servers
Mainframe Computers
Supercomputers

Computers and Society
The Information Age and the New
Information Revolution
Benefits of a Computer-Oriented Society
Risks of a Computer-Oriented Society

Introduction to the World of Computers

LEARNING OBJECTIVES

After completing this chapter, you will be able to:

1. Explain why it's essential to learn about computers today.

2. Discuss several ways computers are integrated into our business and personal lives.

3. Define a computer and describe its four primary operations.

4. List some important milestones in computer evolution.

5. Identify the major parts of a personal computer, including input, processing, output, storage, and communications hardware.

6. Describe the purpose of a network and what the Internet is.

7. List the five basic types of computers, giving at least one example of each type of computer and stating what that computer might be used for.

8. Discuss the societal impact of computers, including some benefits and risks related to their prominence in our society.

Computers and other forms of technology have a big impact on our lives. Computers keep track of bank transactions and credit-card purchases. They control the satellites that are crucial to our nation's defense and they enable us to send people and equipment into space. Computers direct production in factories and provide business executives with the up-to-date information they need to make decisions. They also allow us access to the *Internet* to obtain information, listen to music and experience other types of online entertainment, and communicate with others. In addition to the *general-purpose computers* used by individuals at home and at work, there are special-purpose, *embedded computers* found in watches, televisions, phones, fax machines, kitchen appliances, exercise equipment, and many other everyday devices. In short, computers and computing technology are used in virtually an endless number of ways.

Fifty years ago, computers were part of an obscure technology that interested a handful of scientists. Today, they are an integral part of our lives. Experts call this trend *pervasive computing,* in which few aspects of daily life remain untouched by computers and computer technology. Pervasive computing—also referred to as *ubiquitous computing*—goes beyond traditional computer use. Instead, it foreshadows a future in which computers are virtually everywhere and practically any device may contain embedded computing technology to give it additional functions or to enable it to communicate with other devices on an on-going basis. Because of the prominence of computers in our society, it is important to understand what a computer is, a little about how it works, and the implications of living in a computer-oriented society.

This book is a beginner's guide. It will give you a comprehensive introduction to the field of computers and provide you with a solid foundation for future study. It will also provide you with the basic knowledge you need to understand and use computers in school, on the job, and in your personal life. Today, many jobs depend heavily on computer-based information, and your success in the workplace may depend on your ability to manage that information and use it to make effective decisions.

This chapter first examines what computers do and how they work. You will learn the correct terminology to use when discussing computers and computer components. A later section looks at the various categories of computers that today's users may encounter. The chapter closes with a look at the societal impact of computers. Most of the computer concepts introduced in this chapter are discussed in more detail in subsequent chapters of this text. ■

COMPUTERS IN YOUR LIFE

Why Learn About Computers?

Prior to about 1980, computers were large and expensive, and few people had access to them. The average person didn't need to know how to use a computer for his or her job and it was uncommon to have a computer at home. Furthermore, the use of computers generally required a lot of technical knowledge. Most computers used in organizations were equipped to do little but carry out high-volume paperwork processing, such as issuing bills and keeping track of product inventories. Most ordinary working people were

unfamiliar with computers and there were few good reasons or opportunities for learning how to use them.

Suddenly, in the early 1980s, things began to change. *Microcomputers*—inexpensive personal computers that you will read about later in this chapter—were invented and computer use increased dramatically. Today, an estimated 60% of all U.S. households own a personal computer and most individuals use a computer of some sort or another on the job. Whether you become a teacher, attorney, doctor, salesperson, professional athlete, manager, executive, or skilled tradesperson, you will likely use a computer to obtain and evaluate information and to communicate with others. Today's computers, with their almost dizzying speeds and high levels of accuracy and reliability, are very useful tools for these purposes; they are also continually taking on new roles in our society.

Just like you can learn to drive a car without knowing much about car engines, you can learn to use a computer without a complete understanding of the technical details of how a computer works. However, a little knowledge gives you a big advantage. Knowing something about cars can help you to make wise purchases and save money on repairs. Likewise, knowing something about computers can help you buy the right one for your needs, use it for maximum benefit, and have a much higher level of comfort and confidence along the way. Therefore, **computer literacy**—knowing and understanding the basics of computers and their uses—is essential today for everyone. The next few sections illustrate how computers are used in the home, at school, in the workplace, and other places in our society.

Computers in the Home

Home computing (see Figure 1-1) has increased dramatically over the last few years as computers and Internet access have become less expensive and an increasing number of computer-related consumer activities have become available. Use of the Internet at home to exchange *e-mail* (electronic messages), shop, *download* music and software, research products, pay bills, manage investments, play games, and so forth has grown exponentially. It is estimated that over 40% of all Americans have home Internet access and, on average, Americans spent 157 hours using the Internet at home in 2002. Most Internet access takes place through a personal computer, although some individuals use a Web-enabled cellular phone or an *Internet appliance*—an easy-to-use device designed for specific Internet

> **FIGURE 1-1**
> **Computer use at home.**

HOME OFFICE
Many people today use a computer to work from home on a part-time or full-time basis.

REFERENCE AND COMMUNICATIONS
Many individuals today have access to the Internet at home; retrieving news and other useful information, as well as exchanging e-mail, are popular home computer activities.

SMART HOMES AND APPLIANCES
Smart homes use a computer to facilitate home networking and to control household appliances, security, and media systems. Smart appliances (such as the smart refrigerator shown here) are regular appliances with some type of computer technology built in.

EDUCATION AND ENTERTAINMENT
For both children and adults alike, computers and the Internet offer a host of educational and entertainment activities, such as gaming, video-on-demand, music downloads, and more.

>**Computer literacy.** The knowledge and understanding of basic computer fundamentals.

tasks, such as accessing the Internet or exchanging e-mail—instead. These appliances sometimes incorporate the roles of more than one traditional appliance, such as the telephone or television, in addition to their computing capabilities—a trend referred to as *convergence*. Another growing use of computers at home is in the home office. With the ability to communicate with others via e-mail, fax, telephone, and other methods, more and more people are doing some type of work at home. From taking work home in the evening, to *telecommuting* part-time or full-time, to working entirely from home as a consultant or other self-employed individual, home computing for work purposes is increasing rapidly.

It is also becoming possible to have a *smart home* in which household tasks (such as watering the lawn, turning on and off the air conditioning, making coffee, monitoring the security of the home and grounds, and managing Internet access) can be controlled by a main home computer. *Smart appliances*—traditional appliances with some type of computer or communications technology built in—are expected to be even more prominent in the future.

Computers in Education

Today's youths could definitely be called the computing generation. Unlike baby boomers who may have been introduced to computers at college or on the job and older Americans who may never have used a computer until after retirement, if at all, many of today's young people have been brought up with computing technology. From video games to computers at school and home, most children and teens today have been exposed to computers and related technology all their lives. In fact, a 2001 report from the U.S. Census Bureau stated that approximately 65% of U.S. children live in a home with a computer, and about 90% use a computer at school. According to the report, while the *digital divide* (the gap between those who have access to technology and those who don't) still exists, "schools level the playing field by giving computer access to children who have none at home." Although the amount of computer use varies from school to school, many elementary and most secondary schools now have computers either in the classroom or in a computer lab; virtually all colleges have some sort of computing facility available for student use (see Figure 1-2).

With the increased availability of computers and Internet access in K–12 schools, the emphasis on computer use has evolved from straight drill-and-practice programs to using the computer as an overall student-based learning tool. Today, students use educational games and other educational software to enhance learning; productivity software—such as *word processors* and *presentation graphics programs*—for creative writing and preparing class presentations; and the Internet for research. Many teachers use a computer to create lesson plans, as well as to submit required school information, such as attendance and grade reports.

> **FIGURE 1-2**
> **Computer use in education.**

COMPUTER LABS
Many students today have access to computers in a school computer lab.

CLASSROOMS
Some classrooms today have computers or computer connections to enable students to use computers during class for note-taking, research, online testing, and more.

PRESENTATIONS
Using computers and projection equipment, both students and teachers can deliver effective classroom presentations.

At colleges and universities, computer use is typically much more integrated into daily classroom life than in K–12 schools. Computers are commonly found in classrooms, computer labs, dorms, and libraries. Students may be expected to use the Internet for research, to prepare computer-based papers and classroom presentations, and to access online course materials. In fact, some institutions require a computer for enrollment, and, increasingly,

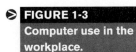

FIGURE 1-3
Computer use in the workplace.

instructors use computers to prepare and deliver classroom presentations and lectures. Many colleges also use computers to facilitate *distance learning*—a fast-growing alternative to traditional classroom learning in which students participate from their current location instead of physically going to the educational institution. Distance learning students can do coursework and participate in class discussions from home, work, or wherever they happen to be at the moment, which gives these students greater flexibility to schedule class time around their personal, family, and work commitments. Distance learning also allows students to take courses when they are not physically located near an educational institution.

Computers in the Workplace

Although computers have been used in the workplace for years, their role is continually evolving. Originally just a research tool for computer experts and scientists, and then a productivity tool for office workers, the computer today is used by all types of employees in all types of businesses—from the CEO of a multinational corporation, to the check-out clerk at the grocery store, to the traveling sales professional, to the auto mechanic at the local garage. The computer has become a universal tool for decision-making, productivity, and communications (see Figure 1-3). One of the fastest growing new uses for workplace computing is in the service industry, in which service professionals—such as food servers, repair technicians, and delivery people—use computers to record customer orders and other customer information, prepare bills, and capture authorizing customer signatures.

Some of the most common uses of computers in the workplace—such as *communications*, *productivity software*, *source data automation*, *point-of-sales systems*, *electronic data interchange* (*EDI*), and *e-commerce*—are discussed in later chapters of this book.

PERSONAL PRODUCTIVITY
Many business professionals today have a work computer to prepare written documents, commmunicate with others, maintain schedules, and perform Internet tasks.

PRESENTATIONS
Computers are commonly used today to create and give business presentations to both large and small audiences.

CUSTOMER SERVICE
Service professionals frequently use computers to record orders, prepare bills, and store authorizing customer signatures.

COMMUNICATIONS
Handheld computers are commonly used by employees who need to record data or need to access data located on the Internet or company network, while they are away from their desks.

Computers on the Go

In addition to being found in the home, at school, and in the workplace, most people encounter and use all types of computers in day-to-day life—from using an ATM machine to deposit or withdraw money from a bank account, to entering desired workout data into a smart treadmill or stationary bike at a local gym, to using a portable navigation system while traveling or hiking. As they become more and more integrated in our society, computers are also becoming less visible and more easy to use. For example, computerized *kiosks*—small self-service electronic booths providing information or other services to the public—usually include a screen that is touched with the finger to select options and request information. Kiosks are commonly found in hotels, conference centers, retail stores, and other public locations to allow consumers to look up information or purchase products. Some special types of kiosks allow people to download specific information (such as sporting event statistics and programs for cultural events or trade shows) wirelessly to their handheld computers; others allow individuals to copy and enlarge color photographs or print photos taken with a *digital camera*.

For Internet access while on the go, computers are increasingly being found in a wide variety of public locations, such as libraries, airports, health clubs, coffee houses, hotels, taxis, and restaurants. Some of these locations charge for access; others offer free access as a courtesy to customers, such as the unlimited access some hotels offer guests or the free access some McDonald's locations offer customers making a minimum purchase. It is also becoming increasingly common for individuals to carry Web-enabled cell phones, pagers, handheld computers, or similar portable devices to remain electronically in touch with others and to obtain stock quotes, driving directions, airline flight updates, and other needed information while on the go (see Figure 1-4). Some computers can even be worn on the body, as discussed in this chapter's Trend box.

➤ FIGURE 1-4
Computer use while on the go.

SELF-SERVICE KIOSKS
Computerized kiosks are widely available to view conference or bridal registry information, create greeting cards, print photographs, order products or services, and more.

PORTABLE COMPUTERS
Many people today carry a portable computer with them at all times or when they travel to remain in touch with others and to access Internet resources.

GPS RECEIVERS
Global positioning capabilities built into cars, portable computers, and handheld GPS receivers show users their exact geographical location, usually for navigational purposes.

HOTELS, RESTAURANTS, AND INTERNET CAFÉS
Many hotels and restaurants offer wired or wireless Internet access to their customers; Internet cafés, such as this one in Europe, provide fee-based Internet access by the minute or hour.

TREND

Wearable PCs

Like most other electronic devices, computing devices are shrinking. For example, the same computing power that formerly required an entire room of electronics and machinery now fits into a computer that can be held in the palm of a hand. As computer components get smaller, the possibility of creating PCs that can be worn on the body or embedded in clothing becomes more plausible. Already we have watches that can perform some of the functions found on handheld PCs; some of these watches can be used to exchange e-mail and other types of electronic messages, display *GPS* (global positioning system) navigational readings, take digital photographs, or play MP3 files. Web-enabled cell phones and portable PCs that fit into a pocket can provide full Internet capabilities.

Going a step further is the truly *wearable PC*. In a work-oriented wearable PC, the central processing unit (CPU) and hard drive are contained in a small unit, which is typically worn on a belt. A *microdisplay*—a tiny display screen often fitted into glasses or goggles—is used to display images close to the eye, which simulates viewing them on a large monitor. Instructions can be entered into the PC by using a wrist-worn keyboard or through a voice-input system. Wearable PCs are currently used by workers in a variety of industries, such as warehouse and construction workers, police and fire personnel, delivery and other types of service workers, telephone repair personnel, and other positions for which hands-free computing and communication is an advantage (see the accompanying photo). For business travelers, a wearable PC is much easier to carry around and use on a cramped airplane than a notebook PC; the eyepiece screen also allows one to work privately on documents in public places.

Wearable PCs designed for consumer use are also beginning to become available. One unit, about the size of a Walkman,

A wearable PC gives workers hands-free access to data and communications.

is designed to slip into a coat pocket or be worn on a belt and contains a CPU, memory, and an external port to connect other devices, just like a conventional PC. This PC runs a version of the Windows operating system software and comes with mobile versions of Pocket Word, Pocket Outlook, Internet Explorer, Windows Media Player, and other widely used software.

Some of the limitations of wearable PCs at the present time are limited battery life; corded connections between the system unit, eyepiece, and other components; unfamiliar appearance; and less-than-perfect voice-input systems. However, as PC components and related technology continue to shrink and as technology improves, we all may end up with a ready-to-wear PC.

WHAT IS A COMPUTER AND WHAT DOES IT DO?

A **computer** can be defined as a programmable, electronic device that accepts data, performs operations on that data, presents the results, and can store the data or results as needed. Being *programmable*, a computer will do whatever the instructions—called the *program*—tell it to do. The programs used with a computer determine the tasks the computer is able to perform.

>**Computer.** A programmable, electronic device that accepts data input, performs operations on that data, and presents and stores the results.

The four operations described in this definition are more technically referred to as *input*, *processing*, *output*, and *storage*. These four primary operations of a computer can be defined as follows:

▼ **Input**—entering data into the computer.

▼ **Processing**—performing operations on the data.

▼ **Output**—presenting the results.

▼ **Storage**—saving data, programs, or output for future use.

For example, let's assume that we have a computer that has been programmed to add two numbers. As shown in Figure 1-5, *input* occurs when data (in this example, the numbers 2 and 5) is entered into the computer; *processing* takes place when the computer program adds those two numbers; and *output* happens when the sum of 7 is displayed on the monitor. The *storage* operation occurs any time the data, program, or output is saved for future use.

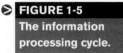

FIGURE 1-5
The information processing cycle.

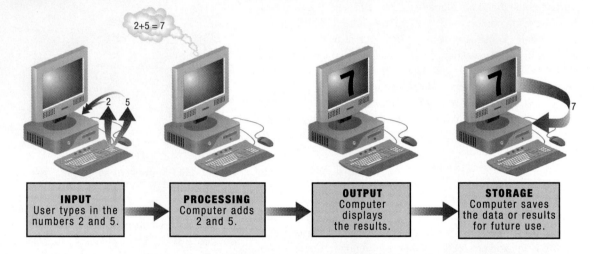

INPUT	PROCESSING	OUTPUT	STORAGE
User types in the numbers 2 and 5.	Computer adds 2 and 5.	Computer displays the results.	Computer saves the data or results for future use.

This progression of input, processing, output, and storage is sometimes referred to as the *IPOS cycle* or the *information processing cycle*. In addition to these four main computer operations, today's computers also typically perform communications functions, such as retrieving data from the Internet or other network, or sending a file or e-mail message to another computer. Therefore, *communications*—technically an input or output operation, depending on which direction the information is going—is sometimes considered the fifth primary computer operation.

Computers Then and Now

The basic ideas of computing and calculating are very old, going back thousands of years. However, the computer in the form we recognize it today is a fairly recent invention. In fact, personal computers have only been around since the late 1970s. The history of computers is often referred to in terms of *generations*, with each new generation characterized by a major technological development. The next sections summarize some early calculating devices and the different computer generations.

>Input. The process of entering data into a computer; can also refer to the data itself. **>Processing.** Performing operations on data that has been input into a computer to convert that input to output. **>Output.** The process of presenting the results of processing; can also refer to the results themselves. **>Storage.** The operation of saving data, programs, or output for future use.

Pre-Computers and Early Computers (before approximately 1945)

Experts believe ancient civilizations had the ability to count and compute, based on archeological finds such as notched bones, knotted twine, and hieroglyphics. The *abacus* is considered by many to be the earliest recorded calculating device. Believed to have been invented by the Babylonians sometime between 500 B.C. and 100 B.C., the abacus and similar types of counting boards were used solely for counting.

Other early computing devices include the *slide rule*, the *mechanical calculator*, and Dr. Herman Hollerith's *Punch Card Tabulating Machine and Sorter*. This device (see Figure 1-6) was the first electromechanical machine that could read *punch cards*—special cards with holes punched in them to represent data. Hollerith's machine was used to process the 1890 U.S. Census data and was able to complete the task in two and a half years, instead of the decade it usually took to process the data by hand.

First Generation (approximately 1946–1957)

The first computers were enormous, often taking up entire rooms. They were powered by *vacuum tubes*—glass tubes that look similar to large cylindrical light bulbs—that needed replacing constantly, required a great deal of electricity, and generated a lot of heat. *First-generation* computers could only solve one problem at a time, and needed to be physically rewired to be reprogrammed. Usually paper punch cards and paper tape were used for input, and output was printed on paper.

Two of the most significant examples of first-generation computers were *ENIAC* and *UNIVAC*. ENIAC (see Figure 1-6) was the world's first large-scale, general-purpose computer and was developed for the U.S. Army. UNIVAC was the first computer to be mass produced for general commercial use and was used to analyze votes in the 1952 U.S presidential election. Interestingly, its correct prediction of an Eisenhower victory only 45 minutes after the polls closed wasn't publicly aired because the results weren't trusted.

Second Generation (approximately 1958–1963)

The *second generation* of computers began when the *transistor*—a small device made of semiconductor material that can act like a switch to open or close electronic circuits—started to replace the vacuum tube. Transistors allowed computers to be physically smaller, more powerful, cheaper, more energy-efficient, and more reliable than in the

> **FIGURE 1-6**
> A brief look at computer generations.

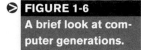

PRE-COMPUTERS
Dr. Herman Hollerith's Punch Card Tabulating Machine and Sorter is an example of an early computing device. It was used to process the 1890 U.S. Census in about one-quarter of the time usually required to tally the results by hand.

FIRST GENERATION
First-generation computers, such as ENIAC shown here, were large, bulky, used vacuum tubes, and had to be physically wired and reset to run programs.

SECOND GENERATION
Second-generation computers, such as the IBM 1401 mainframe shown here, used transistors instead of vacuum tubes so they were physically smaller, faster, and more reliable than earlier computers.

THIRD GENERATION
The integrated circuit marked the beginning of the third generation of computers. These chips allowed the introduction of smaller computers, such as the DEC PDP-8 shown here, which was the first commercially successful minicomputer.

FOURTH GENERATION
Fourth-generation computers (such as the original IBM PC shown here) are based on microprocessors. Most of today's PCs fall into this category.

TIP

For a more detailed timeline regarding the development of computers, see the "Computer History Timeline" located in the References and Resources Guide at the end of this text.

past. Typically data was input on punch cards and magnetic tape, output was on punch cards and paper printouts, and magnetic tape and disks were used for storage (see Figure 1-6). *Programming languages* (such as *FORTRAN* and *COBOL*) were also developed and implemented during this generation.

Third Generation (approximately 1964–1970)

The replacement of the transistor with *integrated circuits* (*ICs*) marked the beginning of the *third generation* of computers. Integrated circuits incorporate many transistors and electronic circuits on a single tiny silicon *chip*, allowing computers to be even smaller and more reliable than in earlier generations. Instead of punch cards and paper printouts, keyboards and monitors were introduced for input and output; magnetic disks were typically used for storage. The introduction of the computer *operating system*—programs that control and direct the computer—during this generation meant that operators no longer had to manually reset relays and wiring. An example of a third-generation computer is shown in Figure 1-6.

Fourth Generation (approximately 1971–present)

The ability to place an increasing number of transistors on a single chip led to the invention of the *microprocessor* in 1971, which ushered in the *fourth generation* of computers. In essence, a microprocessor contains the core processing capabilities of an entire computer on one single chip. The original IBM PC (see Figure 1-6) and Apple Macintosh, and most of today's modern computers, fall into this category. Computers in this generation typically use a keyboard and mouse for input; a monitor and printer for output; and magnetic disks and optical discs for storage. This generation also witnessed the development of *computer networks* and the Internet.

Fifth Generation (now and the future)

Although some people believe that the *fifth generation* of computers has not yet begun, most think it is in its infancy. This generation has no precise classification and some experts disagree with one another about its definition, but one common opinion is that fifth-generation computers will be based on *artificial intelligence*, in which computers can think, reason, and learn. Voice recognition will likely be a primary means of input, and computers may be constructed differently than they are today, such as in the form of *optical computers* that can compute at the speed of light.

FURTHER EXPLORATION

For links to further information about the history of computers, go to www.course.com/uc10/ch01

Hardware

The physical parts of a computer (shown in Figure 1-7 and discussed next) are collectively referred to as **hardware**; the instructions or programs used with a computer—called *software*—are discussed in a later section.

Hardware components can be *internal* (located inside the main box or *system unit* of the computer) or *external* (located outside of the system unit). External hardware components plug into connectors called *ports* located on the exterior of the system unit, unless they are wireless devices. There are hardware devices associated with each of the five computer operations previously discussed (input, processing, output, storage, and communications), as summarized in Figure 1-8.

>**Hardware.** The physical parts of a computer system, such as the keyboard, monitor, printer, and so forth.

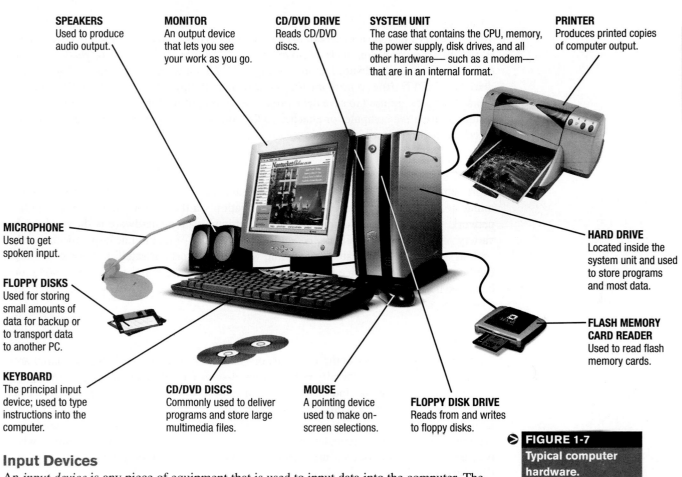

SPEAKERS
Used to produce audio output.

MONITOR
An output device that lets you see your work as you go.

CD/DVD DRIVE
Reads CD/DVD discs.

SYSTEM UNIT
The case that contains the CPU, memory, the power supply, disk drives, and all other hardware— such as a modem— that are in an internal format.

PRINTER
Produces printed copies of computer output.

MICROPHONE
Used to get spoken input.

FLOPPY DISKS
Used for storing small amounts of data for backup or to transport data to another PC.

KEYBOARD
The principal input device; used to type instructions into the computer.

CD/DVD DISCS
Commonly used to deliver programs and store large multimedia files.

MOUSE
A pointing device used to make on-screen selections.

FLOPPY DISK DRIVE
Reads from and writes to floppy disks.

HARD DRIVE
Located inside the system unit and used to store programs and most data.

FLASH MEMORY CARD READER
Used to read flash memory cards.

> **FIGURE 1-7**
> **Typical computer hardware.**

Input Devices

An *input device* is any piece of equipment that is used to input data into the computer. The most common input devices today are the *keyboard* and *mouse* (shown in Figure 1-7). Other possibilities include *image* and *bar-code scanners*, *joysticks*, *touch screens*, *digital cameras*, *electronic pens*, *touch pads*, *fingerprint readers*, and *microphones*. Input devices are discussed in more detail in Chapter 5.

Processing Devices

The main *processing device* for a computer system is the *central processing unit (CPU)*—a chip and related components located inside the system unit that performs the calculations and comparisons needed for processing, as well as controls the computer's operations. For these reasons, the CPU is often considered the "brain" of the computer. Also involved in processing are various types of *memory*—temporary holding places that the computer can use to store data and instructions when it is working with them. Memory is located within the system unit that houses the CPU and other components. The CPU, memory, and processing are discussed in more detail in Chapter 3.

Output Devices

An *output device* presents the results of processing to the user, most of the time on paper (via a *printer*) or on the computer screen or *monitor*, as shown in Figure 1-7. Other possible output devices are *speakers*, *headphones*, and *data projectors* (which project computer images onto a projection screen). Output devices are covered in more detail in Chapter 5.

INPUT	OUTPUT
Keyboard	Monitor
Mouse	Printer
Microphone	Speakers
Scanner	Headphones
Digital camera	Data projector
Electronic pen	
Touch pad	**STORAGE**
Joystick	Hard drive
Fingerprint reader	Floppy disk
	Floppy disk drive
PROCESSING	CD/DVD disc
CPU	CD/DVD drive
	Flash memory card
COMMUNICATIONS	Flash memory drive
Modem	Flash memory card reader

> **FIGURE 1-8**
> **Examples of common hardware by operation.**

Storage Devices

Storage devices include a variety of *drives* and other types of hardware used to access data stored on *storage media*, such as *floppy disks*, *CD discs*, *DVD discs*, or *flash memory cards*. The storage hardware featured in Figure 1-7 includes a *hard drive*, a *floppy disk drive*, a *CD/DVD drive*, a *flash memory card reader*, floppy disks, and CD or DVD discs. Storage devices are used to save data, programs, or output for future use and can either be installed inside the computer or attached to the computer as an external device. Storage is discussed in more detail in Chapter 4.

Communications Devices

Most computers today have some type of *communications device* to allow the user to communicate with others and access remote information via the Internet or another computer network. One of the most common types of communications hardware is the *modem*. A variety of modems are available, depending on the type of communications media used, such as a telephone line, cable connection, wireless network, or satellite. Another widely used communications device is the *network adapter*, used to connect a PC to a home or business network. Communications hardware and computer networks are covered in Chapter 8.

Software

The term **software** refers to the programs or instructions used to tell computer hardware what to do. Software is generally purchased on disk or CD, although many programs can be downloaded from the Internet instead. In either case, once the program has been obtained, it needs to be *installed* on a computer before it can be used. A newer alternative is running programs via the Internet without installing them on your computer. Instead, the programs are located on computers belonging to *application service providers* (*ASPs*) who typically charge a fee for their use. Installing and using software programs is discussed in Chapters 6 and 7.

Since computers cannot yet run programs written in ordinary English, all software programs are created using a *programming language*—a set of codes or commands that the computer system can read and use. Programming languages come in many varieties—*BASIC*, *Visual Basic*, *Pascal*, *COBOL*, *C++*, and *Java* are a few you may have heard of. Some languages are traditional programming languages for developing applications; others are designed for use with Web pages or multimedia programming. Programming languages are discussed in detail in Chapter 13.

Computers use two basic types of software: *system software* and *application software*. The differences between these types of software are discussed next.

System Software

The programs that allow a computer to operate are collectively referred to as **system software**. One of the most important pieces of system software is the *operating system*, which starts up the computer and controls its operation, such as setting up new hardware and allowing users to run other types of software and manage documents stored on their computers. Without an operating system, a computer can't function at all. Common operating systems are *Windows*, *Mac OS*, and *Linux*. Chapter 6 of this text covers system software in detail.

>**Software.** The instructions, also called computer programs, that are used to tell a computer what it should do. >**System software.** Programs, such as the operating system, that control the operation of a computer and its devices, as well as enable application software to run on the PC.

Application Software

Application software consists of programs designed to perform specific tasks or applications, such as computing bank-account interest, preparing bills, creating letters, preparing budgets, managing inventory and customer databases, playing games, scheduling airline flights, viewing Web pages, recording or playing CDs, and exchanging e-mail. Some examples of common types of application software are illustrated in Figure 1-9; application software is discussed in greater detail in Chapter 7.

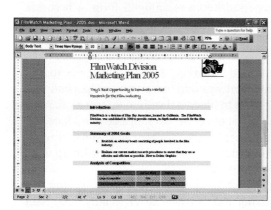

WORD PROCESSING PROGRAMS
Word processing programs are used to create written documents, such as reports, letters, and memos.

GAMES
Computer games are available for both kids and adults for educational and/or entertainment purposes.

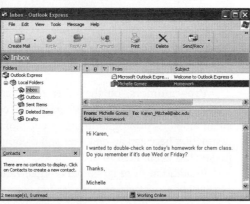

> **FIGURE 1-9**
> **Application software.** Application software can help individuals work more productively at their jobs, as well as provide entertainment.

MULTIMEDIA PROGRAMS
Multimedia programs are used to perform tasks such as playing music or video clips stored on a computer, CD, or Web page; listening to Internet radio stations; creating audio CDs; or transferring home movies to DVD discs.

E-MAIL PROGRAMS
E-mail programs are used to compose, send, receive, and manage electronic messages sent over the Internet or a private network.

WEB BROWSERS
Web browsers allow users to view Web pages and other information located on the Internet.

>**Application software.** Programs that enable users to perform specific tasks on a computer, such as writing a letter or playing a game.

Data and Information

To produce results, a computer inputs **data** and processes it. Almost any kind of fact or set of facts can become computer data—the words in a letter to a friend, the text and pictures in a book, the numbers in a monthly budget, a photograph, a song, or the facts stored in a set of employee records. Data can exist in many forms, such as data representing *text* (words or other data consisting of standard alphabetic, numeric, and special characters), *graphics* (illustrations or photographs), *audio* (sound, such as music or voice), and *video* (live video or video clips). When data is processed into a meaningful form, it becomes **information**.

Information is frequently generated to answer some type of question. A computer user might want to know, for example, how many of a firm's employees earn more than $100,000, how many seats are available on a particular flight from Los Angeles to San Francisco, or what Mark McGwire's home-run total was during a particular baseball season. Of course, you don't need a computer system to process data into information. Anyone can go through an employee file and make a list of people earning a certain salary. By hand, however, this work would take a lot of time, especially for a company with thousands of employees. Computers, however, can perform such tasks almost instantly with accurate results because of their extremely fast processing speeds.

Conversion of data into information is called a variety of terms, one of which is *information processing*. Information processing has become an especially important activity in recent years because the success of many businesses depends heavily on the wise use of information and computers have become a vital information processing tool. Because better information often improves employee decisions and customer service, many companies today regard information as among their most important assets and consider the creative use of information a key competitive strategy.

Computer Users and Professionals

In the early days of computing, a clear distinction separated the people who made computers work from those who used them. This distinction remains, but as computers become more available and easier to use, the line is blurring.

Computer users, or *end users*, are the people who use a computer to obtain information. They include the accountant electronically filing a client's taxes, the office worker using a word processing program to create a letter, and the shop-floor supervisor using a computer to check and see whether workers have met the day's quotas. Children playing computer games and people bidding at an *online auction* over the Internet are also considered computer users.

Programmers, on the other hand, are computer professionals whose primary job responsibility is to write the programs that computers use. Although a few end users may do small amounts of programming to customize the software on their desktop computers, the distinction between an end user and a computer professional is based on the work that the person has been hired to do.

In addition to programmers, organizations may employ other computer professionals. For instance, *systems analysts* design computer systems to be used within their companies. *Computer operations personnel*, in contrast, are responsible for the day-to-day operations of large computer systems. Computer operations personnel are also often employed to help train users or assist them with their desktop computers, and to troubleshoot user-related problems. Computer professionals and computer careers are discussed in more detail in Chapter 12.

>**Data.** Raw, unorganized facts. >**Information.** Data that has been processed into a meaningful form. >**Computer user.** A person who uses a computer. >**Programmer.** A person whose primary job responsibility is to write, maintain, and test computer programs.

COMPUTER NETWORKS AND THE INTERNET

A **computer network** links computers together so that users can share hardware, software, and data, as well as electronically communicate with each other (see Figure 1-10). As illustrated in this figure, many networks use a *network server* to manage the data flowing through the network devices. Network servers are powerful computers that manage the resources on a network. For example, they might control access to shared printers and other hardware, as well as to shared programs and data. The other computers on a network that access network resources through the network server are called *clients*. Chapter 8 discusses networks in greater detail.

Computer networks exist in many sizes and types. For instance, a home network might connect two computers inside the home to share a single printer and Internet connection and to exchange files. A small office network of five or six computers might be used to enable workers to access the company database, communicate with other employees, and access the Internet. A large corporate network might connect all of the offices or retail stores in the

FIGURE 1-10
Example of a computer network.

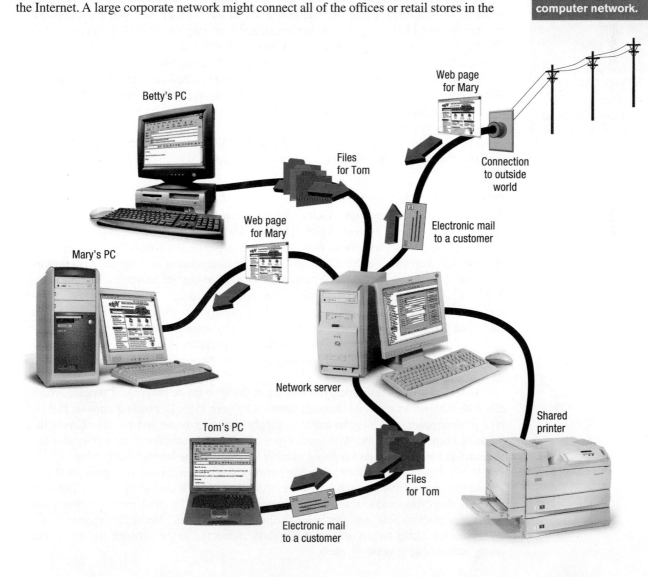

Betty's PC

Files for Tom

Web page for Mary

Web page for Mary

Mary's PC

Electronic mail to a customer

Connection to outside world

Network server

Tom's PC

Electronic mail to a customer

Files for Tom

Shared printer

>**Computer network.** A collection of computers and other hardware devices that are connected together to share hardware, software, and data, as well as to communicate electronically with one another.

corporation, creating a network that spans several cities or states. A public wireless network—such as those available at some coffee houses, restaurants, public libraries, and parks—might be used to provide Internet access to customers or the general public.

The Internet

The **Internet** is the largest and most well-known computer network in the world. It is technically a network of networks, since it is comprised of thousands of networks that can all access each other via the main *backbone* infrastructure of the Internet. Typically, individuals connect to the Internet through their *Internet service providers (ISPs)*—companies who provide Internet access, usually for a fee. ISP computers are continually connected to the Internet, so once users connect to their ISPs, they have access to the entire Internet. In other words, ISPs provide an *onramp* to the Internet for their subscribers. Connecting to the Internet is discussed in more detail in Chapter 2.

Millions of computers of all sizes, millions of people from all walks of life, and thousands of organizations worldwide are connected to the Internet. The two most common Internet activities today are exchanging e-mail and accessing the *World Wide Web* (*WWW*). The World Wide Web consists of a huge collection of *Web pages* that are available over the Internet. There are Web pages for virtually any topic. You can find Web pages that provide product information, current news and weather, airline schedules, government publications, music downloads, maps, telephone directories, movie trailers, and so forth. You can also use Web pages to shop, bank, buy and sell stock, and perform other types of online financial transactions.

The basics of using the Internet and World Wide Web are covered in Chapter 2; a more detailed discussion of the Internet is presented in Chapter 9.

Accessing a Network

To access a computer network (such as a home network, company network, or the Internet), you need either a modem (which typically sends and receives data over telephone or cable lines) or some other type of network adapter to physically connect your computer to the network. Software—either built into your operating system or a separate networking program—will allow you to *log on* to the network and access its resources. To log on to a home or corporate network, an identification number or name (often called a *user ID* or *login ID*) and a password are usually required—typically you will be asked to supply them each time you turn on the computer. After providing the correct information, you will have access to network resources and you can select the program you want to run, just as you would with a *stand-alone* (non-networked) computer. Accessing networks is discussed in more detail in Chapter 8.

To access Internet resources, you must open the appropriate program or programs (usually a *Web browser* or special program supplied by your ISP). Depending on your ISP and type of connection, you may be asked to supply your user name and password, as with a home or corporate network. With some types of Internet connections, your computer also needs to dial an appropriate telephone number to complete the Internet connection.

When a person, computer, or other network component (such as a printer) is connected to and available through a network, that component is said to be *online*. The word *online* is also often used to refer to tasks performed over the Internet, such as *online banking*, *online stock trading*, and just being "online to the Internet." Network components that are *offline* are either turned off or not currently connected to the network and so are currently unavailable to network users.

>**Internet.** The largest and most well-known computer network, linking millions of computers all over the world.

COMPUTERS TO FIT EVERY NEED

The types of computers available today vary widely from those small enough to fit in your pocket that do a limited number of tasks, to powerful *desktop computers* used for home and business, to the super-powerful computers used to control the country's defense systems. Computers are generally classified in one of five categories, based on size, capability, and price.

▼ *Mobile devices*—cellular phones, pagers, and other communications devices with computer or Internet capabilities built in.

▼ *Personal computers*—conventional *desktop*, *notebook*, *tablet*, and *handheld computers*.

▼ *Midrange servers*—computers that host data and programs available to a small network of users.

▼ *Mainframe computers*—powerful computers used to host a large amount of data and programs available to a large network of users.

▼ *Supercomputers*—extremely powerful computers used for complex computations and processing.

In practice, classifying a computer into one of these five categories is not always easy or straightforward. For example, the distinction between some mobile devices and some handheld computers is blurring as their capabilities converge, and while the Apple G4 computer is marketed as a very high-end personal computer, it is sometimes classified as a supercomputer because of its speed and processing power. In addition, technology changes too fast to have precisely defined categories. Instead, these five categories are commonly used to refer to groups of computers designed for similar purposes.

Mobile Devices

A **mobile device** is loosely defined as a very small device—usually based on a wireless phone, pager, or similar communications device (see Figure 1-11)—that has some type of computing or Internet capability built in. If the device is based on a wireless phone (such as a cellular phone), it is sometimes referred to as a *smart phone*; if based on a pager, it can be called a *smart pager*. Generally speaking, the computing capabilities of these devices at the present time are fairly limited. They are primarily designed to access the Web and e-mail wirelessly, in addition to their regular communications capabilities. Because of their small screen and keyboards (if the device contains a keyboard at all), today's mobile devices are most appropriate for individuals wanting constant e-mail and messaging ability—as well as occasional updates on stock prices, weather, directions, and other timely information—rather than general Web browsing and computing.

Personal Computers

A technological breakthrough in the early 1970s allowed the circuitry for an entire CPU to fit on a single silicon chip smaller than a dime. These computers-on-a-chip, or *microprocessors*, could be mass-produced at a very low cost. Microprocessors were quickly integrated into all types of products, leading to powerful handheld calculators, digital watches, electronic toys, and sophisticated controls for household appliances such as microwave ovens and automatic coffeemakers. Microprocessors also created the possibility of building inexpensive computer

> **FIGURE 1-11**
> **Mobile devices include smart phones (top) and pagers (bottom).**

>**Mobile device.** A very small device, usually based on a wireless phone or pager, that has some type of computing or Internet capability built in.

TIP

The term "PC" is typically used to refer only to IBM-compatible computers; personal computers manufactured by Apple are usually called "Macs."

> FIGURE 1-12
Typical desktop PC case styles.

DESKTOP CASE

TOWER CASE

ALL-IN-ONE CASE

systems small enough to fit on a desktop, inside a briefcase, or even inside a shirt pocket. These small computer systems, designed to be used by one person at a time, are called **microcomputers** or **personal computers (PCs)**.

PCs are widely used in homes, small businesses, and large businesses alike. For instance, an individual might use a PC at home to play games, pay bills, prepare his or her taxes, exchange e-mail, and access Web pages. A small business might use its PCs for a variety of computing tasks, including tracking merchandise, preparing correspondence, billing customers, responding to customer e-mails, updating the company Web site, and completing routine accounting chores. A large business might use PCs as productivity tools for office personnel and as analysis tools for decision makers, to name just two important applications. Office PCs are also commonly connected to a company network to provide access to company files, as well as the network's Internet connection.

Personal computers typically cost between $500 and $2,500 and usually conform to one of two standards: *PC-compatible* or *Macintosh*. PC-compatibles (sometimes referred to as *Windows PCs* or *IBM-compatible PCs*) evolved from the original IBM PC—the first PC widely accepted for business use—and are by far the most common type of personal computer used today. In general, PC-compatible hardware and software are compatible with all brands of PC-compatible computers—such as those made by IBM, Dell, Hewlett-Packard, NEC, Acer, and Gateway. These PCs typically run the Windows operating system. In contrast, computers conforming to the Macintosh standard are made by Apple, use the Mac OS operating system, and typically use different hardware and software than PC-compatible computers. Although PC-compatible computers are by far the most widely used, the Mac is traditionally the computer of choice for artists, designers, and others who require advanced graphics capabilities. Recently, the modern look of Apple's iMac desktop computer and iBook notebook computers has appealed to young computer buyers. Because there are virtually no Macintosh-compatible computers on the market to help drive down the price, expect to pay more for a Mac than for a PC-compatible computer with comparable hardware. Deciding between these two types of personal computers typically depends on what the computer will be used for and if there are any other PCs, such as a school or office computer, with which it needs to be compatible.

For a brief introduction to the steps involved with setting up a new PC, see the How it Works box.

Desktop PCs

Conventional PCs are often referred to as **desktop computers** because the complete computer system (system unit, monitor, keyboard, mouse, and so forth) fits on or next to a desk. As shown in Figure 1-12, a desktop PC can have a *desktop case* that is designed to be placed horizontally on a desk's surface with the monitor sitting on top of the system unit, or a *tower case* that is designed to rest vertically, typically on the floor. *All-in-one* desktop PCs incorporate the monitor and system unit into a single package. While the conventional appearance of a desktop PC is a fairly large white or black box, desktop PCs are getting smaller (at least one PC maker has created a complete Windows-based PC that is about the size of a paperback book) and are now available in a variety of colors and designs. For a look at a new industry trend—*PC modding*—see the Inside the Industry box.

>**Microcomputer.** A computer system based on a microprocessor, designed to be used by one person at a time; also called a personal computer or PC. >**Personal computer (PC).** Another name for microcomputer. >**Desktop computer.** A PC designed to fit on or next to a desk.

HOW IT WORKS

Setting Up a New PC

Before setting up a new PC, it is a good idea to give a little thought to its location. It should be close to a telephone jack, network jack, or exterior modem (if any of these are needed), and it should have its own power outlet. In addition, the location should have enough room for ventilation around the system unit and it should not be in direct sunlight. Although set-up procedures vary from system to system, the basic steps involved with setting up a typical PC are shown in the accompanying figure and described next.

First, carefully unpack the components for your new PC and locate all components, cables, manuals, and power cords. Using either the installation manual or a reference card containing specific directions for connecting the different parts of your computer system, plug the cables for the keyboard, mouse, monitor, and so forth into the appropriate ports on the exterior of the system unit. Pay attention to the color-coding or labeling system for the ports and plugs that is often included on new computer systems to make sure you get all the components connected correctly. Plug the power cables for the system unit,

monitor, and all other powered devices into a surge protector, and then plug the surge protector into the wall outlet as the last step of the setup process to avoid the PC starting up before you're ready.

After your system is up and running, you can install any additional software you have obtained, set up your Internet or network connection, and customize the desktop display. Be sure to use your operating system's backup feature to back up the entire system once it is completely ready to go so you can restore it at a later time if a problem occurs with your PC (you will need to continue to back up your data periodically so it won't be lost if you have to restore your PC using the system backup). Some operating systems, such as Windows XP, also automatically create *restore points* to which your computer settings can be rolled back if there is ever a problem with your computer. Even though using the operating system's system restore option usually doesn't alter your data files, it is still good practice to backup your data on a regular basis. You will also want to back up any application software that was preinstalled on your PC but not supplied on disc. Some PCs include some type of "Make discs" option to easily perform this task.

1. Unpack all components and locate the installation guide to refer to during the setup process.

2. Plug in all cables (for the monitor, mouse, keyboard, printer, speakers, etc.) into the appropriate port on the system unit. For speakers, usually just one speaker is connected to the system unit; the second speaker connects directly to the first speaker.

For conventional modems, the cord from the telephone wall jack is plugged into the appropriate port on the system unit; the second telephone port on the PC can be used for a telephone, if desired.

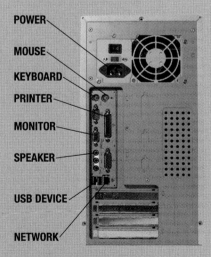

POWER
MOUSE
KEYBOARD
PRINTER
MONITOR
SPEAKER
USB DEVICE
NETWORK

5. Back up your PC and any programs that were pre-installed on your PC but not supplied on disc. Store the discs in a safe place and enjoy your new PC!

4. Install any additional software you have obtained, set up your Internet or network connection, and customize the desktop display.

3. Plug all power cords (for the system unit, monitor, printer, scanner, powered subwoofer, etc.) into a surge suppressor, then turn the power on.

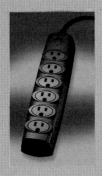

INSIDE THE INDUSTRY

PC Modding

Similar to hot-rodders, who create custom cars, *PC modders* modify high-performance PCs into functional works of art. Often the goal is a case design that reflects the modder's personality or interests; other reasons to modify a PC include souping it up to increase its functionality for specific power-hungry tasks, such as PC gaming.

Most PC modders build their PCs completely from the ground up, beginning with the motherboard and adding the newest and fastest components. Although most modified PCs still contain similar components to conventional PCs (such as a motherboard, hard drive, expansion cards, RAM, cabling, fans, and more), often the components need to be connected in an unconventional manner to fit inside the desired case design. Some interesting case components used by PC modders

include furniture, BBQs, toys, fish tanks, old radios, coffeemakers, model cars (see the accompanying figure), and custom-made fiberglass and acrylic cases. Often custom cutouts and lighting add to the overall effect and custom paint jobs are the norm. Some PC modders create PCs just for their own enjoyment or to display at shows; others sell their creations to friends or as a business. Companies that sell PC modding supplies (such as clear cases, glow-in-the-dark cables, fan sculptures, windows, and water cooling systems) also sometimes sell kits for the beginning modder; finished premodded PCs can often be purchased from specialty companies and some individuals. While not everyone may be ready for a PC that looks like the Starship Enterprise or a LEGO® creation, with the increased amount of time people are spending with their PCs, it is becoming more common to want a computer that's fun to look at.

All three of these modified PCs are fully-functioning computers.

Portable PCs

Smaller **portable PCs** are designed to be easily carried around, such as in a carrying case, briefcase, purse, or pocket, depending on their size. Portable computers are essential for many workers, such as salespeople who need to make presentations or take orders from clients off-site, agents who need to collect data at remote locations, and managers who need computing and communications resources as they travel. Wearable PCs are available for workers who need computer access but don't have their hands free. Increasingly, individuals are buying portable PCs as their primary computer and some experts predict that

>**Portable PC.** A small personal computer, such as notebook, tablet, or handheld PC, designed to be carried around easily.

portable PC sales will surpass desktop PC sales within the next few years. Several different types of portable PCs are illustrated in Figure 1-13 and discussed next.

Two types of portable PCs that are about the size of a standard paper notebook are *notebook computers* and *tablet PCs*. Both are designed for users who need a fully-functioning computer that they can easily take with them wherever they go, but the two types of PCs have different physical characteristics.

Notebook computers (sometimes called *laptops*) are fully-functioning computers that open to reveal a screen and keyboard. Although some notebooks have a swivel screen for easier reading or business presentations and others fold shut an additional time to make them pocket-sized, most notebooks follow the traditional *clamshell* design in which the monitor is on the inside top half of the PC and the keyboard is on the inside bottom half.

Tablet PCs can use either a *slate* or a *convertible tablet PC* design. Slate tablets include what looks like just the top half of a notebook PC. Typically slate tablets are not used with a keyboard; instead a finger or special electronic pen is touched to the screen to provide input. Newer *convertible tablet PCs* are essentially a combination of a notebook and tablet PC. In its notebook format, a convertible tablet PC is used just the same as a notebook PC, with keyboard input. When the screen is rotated and then closed with the screen facing out, the device resembles a slate tablet PC and only pen or touch input is used. Both notebook and tablet PCs today usually come with communications capabilities built in, so the PCs can be easily connected to an office network or the Internet. Although similar in capabilities to their desktop cousins, notebooks and tablet PCs tend to cost more, have smaller screens, and use denser keyboard arrangements (if a keyboard exists). Most notebooks can run on either batteries or electricity, but some tablet PCs use battery power only. Both notebooks and tablets also tend to use alternative pointing devices (such as an electronic pen or touch pad) instead of a mouse.

FURTHER EXPLORATION

For links to further information about PCs, go to
www.course.com/uc10/ch01

❯ FIGURE 1-13
Portable computers come in a variety of sizes and configurations.

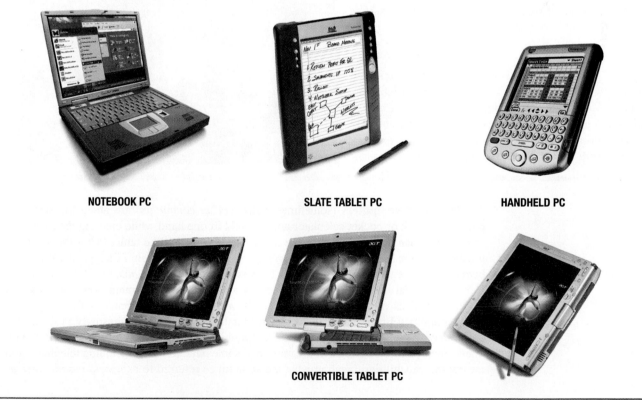

NOTEBOOK PC

SLATE TABLET PC

HANDHELD PC

CONVERTIBLE TABLET PC

>**Notebook computer.** A fully functioning portable PC that opens to reveal a screen and keyboard. >**Tablet PC.** A portable PC about the size of a notebook that is designed to be used with an electronic pen.

CAMPUS CLOSE-UP

Wired Med Students

From Stanford University to the University of Florida, medical students are going high-tech. Although some medical schools strongly recommend that their med students acquire a handheld PC, others–such as UCLA and University of Buffalo–require their use.

Medical students today commonly use handheld PCs to access class-specific materials, medical dictionaries, and drug databases, as well as to contact classmates, instructors, and administrators. Students can also view electron microscope images, CT-scans, and X-rays that have been converted to a high-resolution format readable by the PDA. Residents can view and update patient files, as well. Because information is entered directly into the computer system via the handheld PC, input errors can be reduced. In addition, since physicians can access any patient's record at any time, using a handheld PC can be an immense time-saver. For example, one family practice center in Oregon recently supplied PDAs to its physicians and residents for patient data access and found that the time required for reviewing charts, lab results, and other data dropped from 6.3 hours per week to 2.7 hours per week per physician–less than half the time it took before.

Although a little slow to embrace handheld PCs in the past, the medical community is quickly catching up. Scores of new applications–such as medical calculators, patient record systems, drug reference systems, prescription software, and diagnostic software–are rapidly changing the practice of medicine. In addition to saving a physician time and alleviating errors due to misreading a doctor's handwriting, handheld PCs can also automatically check patient records for such things as previous symptoms, drug interactions, and insurance coverage when the physician enters in a diagnosis or prescription. When doing rounds in the hospital, chart information can be entered into the portable PC and simultaneously transmitted wirelessly to the hospital's computer. At the end of the day, the same information can also be uploaded to the main computer at the physician's office to update the patient records located there.

Despite the late start, handheld use in the medical community is likely to explode in the near future. The portability factor, along with the trend of hospitals, pharmaceutical companies, and other organizations handing out free or low-cost devices to doctors, all point to massive increased growth in this area. Thanks to handheld PCs and prescription software, even one of the oldest standing doctor jokes–illegible handwriting–may soon become irrelevant.

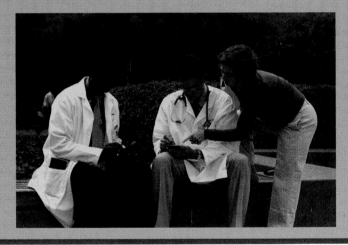

Handheld computers (sometimes called *pocket computers*) are about the size of a paperback book or pocket calculator and are held in one hand while entering data with the other. Many handheld PCs don't have a keyboard; instead—like tablet PCs—the screen is touched with the finger or electronic pen to provide input. Handheld PCs typically run off of batteries and are sometimes referred to as *personal digital assistants*, or *PDAs*, since they provide personal organizer functions such as a calendar, appointment book, and address book, as well as messaging, electronic mail, and other communications functions. The recent improved functionality of handheld PCs has made them increasingly practical for day-to-day tasks. In fact, handheld PCs and mobile devices have begun to converge, with many smart phones offering PDA features and some handheld PCs including telephone and messaging capabilities, creating what are sometimes referred to as *hybrid mobile devices*

>**Handheld computer.** A portable PC about the size of a paperback book or pocket calculator.

or *hybrid PDAs*. There are slip-on keyboards available for smart phones and handheld PCs for easier data entry and many PDAs include a built-in speakerphone or a headset jack, enabling the device to be used to take notes or look up information during a phone call. For a look at how PDAs are being used by medical students, see the Campus Close-Up box.

With the increasing use of portable computers, sharing information and synchronizing data between a portable computer and a primary desktop computer at home or in the office is becoming an important consideration. There are a variety of options, depending on the types of computers being used. Some handheld PCs come with a cradle that attaches via a cable to the user's primary PC. After inserting the handheld PC into the cradle, the data on the two PCs can be updated. Other portable PCs come with *infrared* capabilities that allow you to "beam" data from that device to your primary PC. Still others can store data on flash memory cards, which can then be inserted into a desktop PC's flash memory card reader to retrieve the data. With *wireless networking* technology, it is also possible for portable and desktop PCs to be in communication with each other and to synchronize data whenever they are within a particular range.

Although desktop PCs are still the norm for stationary home and office setups and are less expensive than comparable notebooks or tablets, today's notebooks are powerful enough that they can be used as an individual's sole computer. For users who prefer the features of a desktop computer but who must have a portable computer to use while on the go, notebook and tablet PCs can be made to work like a desktop computer through the use of a *docking station*—a device with *peripheral devices* (such as a monitor, keyboard, mouse, and printer) always attached. Docking stations typically have a slot or connector to attach the portable PC to the docking station; as soon as the PC is connected to the docking station, it can be used as a regular desktop PC by using the peripheral devices attached to the docking station.

Network Computers, Thin Clients, and Internet Appliances

Most personal computers sold today are sold as stand-alone, self-sufficient units that are equipped with all the necessary hardware and software to operate independently. In other words, they can perform input, processing, output, and storage without being connected to a network, although they can be networked if desired. In contrast, a device that must be connected to a network to perform processing or storage tasks is referred to as a *dumb terminal*. Somewhere between a PC and dumb terminal are devices that may be able to perform a limited amount of independent processing, but are designed to be used with a network. Two examples of these are *network computers* and *Internet appliances*.

Network computers (**NCs**)—more commonly called **thin clients** today—are designed to be used in conjunction with a company network (see Figure 1-14). Instead of

TIP

If you are considering buying a PC, refer to the "Guide for Buying a PC" located in the References and Resources Guide at the end of this book.

❯ **FIGURE 1-14**
Network computers (thin clients) and Internet appliances are designed to be used only with company networks or the Internet.

NETWORK COMPUTER

STAND-ALONE INTERNET APPLIANCE

SET-TOP BOX INTERNET APPLIANCE

>**Network computer (NC).** A PC designed to access a network for processing and data storage, instead of performing those tasks locally.
>**Thin client.** Another name for network computer.

using their own local disk drives for storage and their own CPUs for processing, these computers typically utilize a network server for those tasks. The primary advantage of thin clients is lower cost. Disadvantages include having limited or no local storage and not being able to function as a stand-alone computer when the network isn't working.

Network computers or other devices designed primarily for accessing Web pages and/or exchanging e-mail are called **Internet appliances** (sometimes also referred to as *information appliances* or *Web pads*). As shown in Figure 1-14, these devices can take on a variety of configurations. Some look like a small PC but cannot run any software other than their Web browser or e-mail programs; others take the form of a *set-top box* that connects to a TV. Some Internet appliances automatically log on to the Internet on a regular basis to check for new e-mail; others may automatically download other types of specified information (such as news, stock quotes, or sports scores) periodically, as directed by the user. Because Internet appliances usually have no other function than Internet access, have limited local storage, and may not be able to be connected to a printer, they cannot be used as general-purpose PCs. Although many Internet appliances have been discontinued shortly after their release, some experts view this as a still-growing area for consumer use—especially for individuals who don't want or need a conventional home PC. Others expect that low-end portable PCs or the emerging *digital media* units (devices that connect to a home's TVs, PCs, and sound system equipment via a home network to provide access to the Internet, stored media files, and recorded TV shows or movies), may eventually fulfill this role.

Midrange Servers

Midrange servers—called *minicomputers*, *minis*, or *midrange computers* in past years—are medium-sized computers used to host programs and data for small networks. Typically larger and more powerful than a desktop PC, midrange servers are usually located in a closet or other out-of-the way place and can serve many users at one time. Users connect to the server through a network, using their regular PC, a network computer, or a dumb terminal consisting of only a monitor and keyboard (as in Figure 1-15). Midrange servers are commonly used in small- to-medium-sized businesses, such as medical or dental offices.

> **FIGURE 1-15**
> **Midrange servers.** Midrange servers are used to host data and programs on a small network. Users connect to the server using PCs, network computers, or dumb terminals; the actual server (right) would typically be stored in a nearby closet or other out-of-the way place.

Mainframe Computers

The **mainframe computer** (see Figure 1-16) is the standard choice for most large organizations—such as hospitals, universities, large businesses, banks, and government offices—that need to manage large amounts of centralized data. Larger, more expensive, and more powerful than midrange servers, mainframes usually operate 24 hours a day, serving thousands of users connected to the mainframe via PCs, network computers, or dumb terminals, similar to midrange server users. During regular business hours, a mainframe runs multiple programs as needed to meet the different needs of its wide variety of users. At night, it commonly performs large processing tasks, such as payroll and billing. Today's mainframes are sometimes referred to as *high-end servers* or *enterprise-class servers*.

Supercomputers

Some applications require extraordinary speed, accuracy, and processing capabilities—for example, sending astronauts into space, controlling missile guidance systems, forecasting the weather, exploring for oil, and assisting with some kinds of scientific research. **Supercomputers**—the most powerful and most expensive type of computer available—were developed to fill this need. Some relatively new supercomputing applications include hosting extremely complex Web sites and decision-support systems for corporate executives and three-dimensional applications, such as 3D medical scans and architectural modeling. Unlike mainframe computers, which typically run multiple applications simultaneously to serve a wide variety of users, supercomputers generally run one program at a time, as fast as possible.

> **FIGURE 1-16**
Mainframe computers. Mainframes are frequently used by large businesses, schools, and hospitals to maintain records and other types of shared data; users connect to the mainframe via PCs, network computers, or dumb terminals.

Conventional supercomputers can cost several million dollars each. Over the past few years, it has become more common to build less-expensive supercomputers by connecting hundreds of smaller computers—typically high-end personal computers or midrange servers—into a *cluster* that acts as a single computer. The computers in the cluster often contain several CPUs each and are dedicated to processing cluster applications. The resulting supercomputer is often referred to as a *massively parallel processor* (*MPP*) computer. For example, one of the fastest supercomputers in the world, NEC's Earth Simulator (shown in Figure 1-17), contains a total of 640 computers containing 8 CPUs each for a combined total of 5,120 CPUs. It cost approximately $400 million, can perform about 40 trillion calculations per second, requires the floor space of four tennis courts, and is used primarily to simulate various global environmental phenomena such as global warming, the El Niño effect, and atmospheric and marine pollution, as well as to predict environmental changes on Earth.

A related process is *grid computing*—a recent trend of utilizing the unused processing power of a large number of computers connected through the Internet to work together on a single task on demand. For instance, consumers can volunteer their PCs to be used for scientific or medical research purposes via the Internet and their PCs' processing power

---

>**Mainframe computer.** A computer used in large organizations (such as hospitals, large businesses, and colleges) that need to manage large amounts of centralized data and run multiple programs simultaneously. >**Supercomputer.** The fastest, most expensive, and most powerful type of computer.

> **FIGURE 1-17**
The Earth Simulator supercomputer. Supercomputers are used for specialized situations for which immense processing speed is required.

will be tapped when needed by the research organization. New grid computing services are beginning to be offered to provide companies with immense processing power on demand, similar to the way electricity is delivered as it is needed. For instance, Gateway recently began selling the processing power derived from a grid of nearly 8,000 PCs located in its stores. Businesses or organizations can purchase supercomputer-level processing power from Gateway's grid when it is needed.

COMPUTERS AND SOCIETY

The vast improvements in technology over the past decade have had a distinct impact on the way we live today. At both home and work, computers impact our lives. They have become indispensable tools in our homes and businesses, and related technological advancements have changed the way our everyday items—cars, microwaves, coffee pots, exercise bikes, telephones, and more—look and behave. In fact, we may use a computer or computerized device without even realizing that a computer is involved. As our computers and everyday devices become smarter, they tend to do their normal jobs faster, better, and more reliably, as well as take on additional functions to help us in our busy lives. In addition to affecting individuals, computerization and advancing technologies have changed our society as a whole. Without computers, banks would be overwhelmed by the job of tracking all the transactions they process, moon exploration and the space shuttle would still belong to science fiction, and scientific advances such as DNA analysis and gene mapping would be non-existent. In addition, we as a society are getting used to everyday activities—shopping, banking, travel, and so on—becoming more and more automated. We are also becoming accustomed to having fast and easy access to an increasing amount of information.

The Information Age and the New Information Revolution

The prominence of information technology over the past few decades has resulted in this time period being referred to as the *information age*. Now, according to many experts, we are entering a new *information revolution*. Some believe that the last major information revolution was the invention of the printing press in the mid-1450s; today's information revolution is tied to the vast amount of information accumulated and distributed via the Internet. As discussed next and throughout this text, the availability of this huge collection of information has a great deal of advantages, but it has some disadvantages, as well.

Benefits of a Computer-Oriented Society

The benefits of having such a computer-oriented society are numerous, as touched on throughout this chapter. The capability to design, build, and test new buildings, cars, and airplanes before the actual construction begins helps professionals create safer end products. Technological advances in medicine allow for earlier diagnosis and more effective treatment of diseases than ever before. The benefit of beginning medical students performing virtual surgery using a computer instead of performing actual surgery on a patient is obvious. The ability to shop, pay bills, research products, participate in online courses, and look up vast amounts of information 24 hours a day, 7 days a week, 365 days a year via the Internet is a huge convenience. In addition, a computer-oriented society generates new opportunities. For example, advanced technologies, such as speech recognition software and Braille keyboards, enable physically- or visually-challenged individuals to perform necessary job tasks and communicate with others.

In general, technology has also made a huge number of tasks in our lives go much faster. Instead of a long delay for a credit check, you can be approved for a loan or credit card almost immediately. Documents and photographs can be e-mailed or faxed in mere moments, instead of waiting at least a day for them to be physically mailed. And you can download information, programs, music files, and more on demand when you want or need them, instead of having to order them and then wait for delivery.

Risks of a Computer-Oriented Society

Although there are a great number of benefits from having a computer-oriented society and a *networked economy*, there are risks as well. A variety of problems have emerged in recent years, ranging from stress and health concerns, to personal security and privacy issues, to ethical dilemmas. Many of the security and privacy concerns stem from the fact that so much of our personal business takes place online—or at least ends up as data in a computer database somewhere—and the potential for misuse of this data is enormous.

Another concern is that we may not have had time to consider all the repercussions of collecting such vast amounts of information. Some people worry about creating a "Big Brother" situation, in which the government or another organization is watching everything that we do. Although the accumulation and distribution of information is an important factor of our networked economy, it is one area of great concern to many individuals.

These types of concerns are serious and worthy of much more discussion. Consequently, subsequent parts of this book will delve into issues and technology related to security, privacy, intellectual property rights, ethics, health, access, the environment, and more in relation to computer and technology use.

SUMMARY

COMPUTERS IN YOUR LIFE

Computers appear almost everywhere in today's world, and most people need to use a computer or a computerized device frequently on the job, at home, at school, or in a consumer application. Being familiar with basic computer concepts helps individuals feel more comfortable using them. In addition, **computer literacy** is a necessary skill for most students and employees today.

Computers abound in today's homes, schools, workplaces, and other locations. Common home computing tasks include working at home and using the *Internet* for entertainment, shopping, and exchanging *e-mail*. Computers are commonly incorporated into devices used by consumers in banks, stores, cars, gyms, and other public locations. There are also an increasing number of public locations—such as libraries, hotels, and restaurants—offering free or fee-based Internet access. Most students and employees will need to use a computer for productivity or research.

WHAT IS A COMPUTER AND WHAT DOES IT DO?

Chapter Objective 3:
Define a computer and describe its four primary operations.

Chapter Objective 4:
List some important milestones in computer evolution.

A **computer** is a *programmable* electronic device that accepts **input**; performs **processing** operations; **outputs** the results; and can **store** data, programs, or output when needed. Most computers today also have *communications* capabilities.

There is evidence of counting far back in recorded history. One of the first recorded counting devices was the *abacus*. Early computing devices that pre-date today's computers include the *slide rule*, the *mechanical calculator*, and Dr. Herman Hollerith's *Punch Card Tabulating Machine and Sorter*.

First-generation computers, such as *ENIAC* and *UNIVAC*, came out in the mid-1940s to mid-1950s and were powered by *vacuum tubes*. In the late 1950s to early 1960s, *second-generation* computers using *transistors* were introduced. These computers were faster and more reliable than before, and could be programmed using a *programming language*. The *integrated circuit (IC)* initiated the *third generation* of computers, which used operating systems, keyboards, and monitors for the first time. Today's *fourth-generation* computers use *microprocessors* and have a variety of input, output, and storage devices. They are frequently connected to the *Internet* and other *networks*. Some people believe that we are at the beginning of a *fifth generation* of computers, likely based on *artificial intelligence*.

A computer is made up of **hardware** (the actual physical equipment that makes up the computer system) and **software** (the computer's programs). Common hardware components include the *keyboard* and *mouse* (*input devices*); the *CPU* and *memory* (*processing devices*); *monitors* and *printers* (*output devices*); and *drives*, as well as *disks*, *flash memory cards*, and other *storage media* (*storage*). Most computers today also include a *modem*, *network adapter*, or other type of *communications* hardware.

All computers need **system software**, such as an *operating system* like *Windows* or *Mac OS*, to function and **application software** to perform word processing, Web browsing, photo touch-up, and most other computer tasks. Software programs are written using a *programming language*, such as *BASIC*, *Visual Basic*, *Pascal*, *COBOL*, *C++*, and *Java*.

Data is the raw, unorganized facts that are input into the computer to be processed. Data that the computer has processed into a useful form is called **information**. Data can exist in many forms, representing *text*, *graphics*, *audio*, and *video*.

Computer users are the people who use the computer system. Within a computing environment, many types of computer professionals help users meet their computing needs; for example, **programmers** are responsible for writing computer programs.

COMPUTER NETWORKS AND THE INTERNET

Computer networks are used to connect individual computers and related devices so that users can share hardware, software, and data as well as communicate with one another. Many networks use a *network server* to host common files and programs and to manage the traffic on the network.

Chapter Objective 6: Describe the purpose of a network and what the Internet is.

The **Internet** is the largest and most well-known computer network in the world. People typically access the Internet through *Internet service providers* (*ISPs*). There is a vast amount of information available through the Internet, typically located on *Web pages. E-mail* is another widely used Internet activity.

To access a computer network, you need some type of *modem* or *network adapter* and appropriate software. Typically *user IDs* and passwords are used to grant access to the network. A resource that is available through a network is said to be *online*; resources that are not currently available through the network are *offline*.

COMPUTERS TO FIT EVERY NEED

Small computers used by individuals at home or work are called **microcomputers** or **personal computers** (**PCs**). Most PCs today are either **desktop computers** (with a *desktop, tower,* or *all-in-one case*) or **portable PCs** (**notebook, tablet,** or **handheld computers**) and typically conform to either the *PC-compatible* or *Macintosh* standard. Tablet PCs come in both *slate* and *convertible tablet PC* formats. **Thin clients** (also called **network computers** or **NCs**) are designed solely to access a network and usually use the network for storage, programs, and processing, instead of using local hardware. A type of network computer called an **Internet appliance** is designed specifically for accessing the Internet and e-mail.

Chapter Objective 7: List the five basic types of computers, giving at least one example of each type of computer and stating what that computer might be used for.

Mobile devices are usually based on a wireless phone or pager and are commonly used for accessing Web page data and e-mail, in addition to their regular phone or pager functions. Wireless phones with computing capabilities built in are sometimes referred to as *smart phones.* Mobile devices are used by individuals to maintain communications with the office while on the road, as well as for quick checks of weather forecasts, stock prices, flight information, and other Internet resources available for that particular device.

Medium-sized computers, or **midrange servers**, are used in small- to medium-sized businesses to host data and programs that can be accessed by the company network. The powerful computers used by most large businesses and organizations to perform the information processing necessary for day-to-day operations are called **mainframe computers**. The very largest, most powerful computers, which typically run one application at a time, are classified as **supercomputers**.

While categories of computers based on size can provide helpful distinctions, in practice it is sometimes difficult to classify computers that fall on the borders of these categories, and the computers that fit in each category are continually changing as technology improves.

COMPUTERS AND SOCIETY

Because of the vast amount of information now available through the Internet, this era is sometimes referred to as the *information age.* Computers and devices based on related technology have become indispensable tools for modern life, making ordinary tasks easier and quicker than ever before and helping make today's worker more productive than ever before. However, their growing use and our *networked economy* has also created potential problems, ranging from health concerns to personal security and privacy issues to ethical dilemmas.

Chapter Objective 8: Discuss the societal impact of computers, including some benefits and risks related to their prominence in our society.

KEY TERMS

Instructions: Match each key term on the left with the definition on the right that best describes it.

a. application software

b. computer

c. computer network

d. hardware

e. input

f. Internet

g. mainframe computer

h. microcomputer

i. midrange server

j. mobile device

k. network computer (NC)

l. notebook computer

m. output

n. portable PC

o. processing

p. software

q. storage

r. supercomputer

s. system software

t. tablet PC

1. _____ A collection of computers and devices that are connected together to share hardware, software, and data, as well as to communicate electronically with one another.

2. _____ A computer system based on a microprocessor, designed to be used by one person at a time; also called a personal computer or PC.

3. _____ A computer used in large organizations (such as hospitals, large businesses, and colleges) that need to manage large amounts of centralized data and run multiple programs simultaneously.

4. _____ A fully functioning portable PC that opens to reveal a screen and keyboard.

5. _____ A medium-sized computer used to host programs and data for a small network.

6. _____ A PC designed to access a network for processing and data storage, instead of performing those tasks locally.

7. _____ A portable PC about the size of a notebook that is designed to be used with an electronic pen.

8. _____ A programmable, electronic device that accepts data input, performs operations on that data, and presents and stores the results.

9. _____ A small personal computer, such as notebook, tablet, or handheld PC, designed to be carried around easily.

10. _____ A very small device, usually based on a wireless phone or pager, that has some type of computing or Internet capability built in.

11. _____ Performing operations on data that has been input into a computer to convert that input to output.

12. _____ The process of presenting the results of processing; can also refer to the results themselves.

13. _____ Programs that enable users to perform specific tasks on a computer, such as writing a letter or playing a game.

14. _____ Programs, such as the operating system, that control the operation of a computer and its devices, as well as enable application software to run on the PC.

15. _____ The operation of saving data, programs, or output for future use.

16. _____ The fastest, most expensive, and most powerful type of computer.

17. _____ The instructions, also called computer programs, that are used to tell a computer what it should do.

18. _____ The largest and most well-known computer network, linking millions of computers all over the world.

19. _____ The physical parts of a computer system, such as the keyboard, monitor, printer, and so forth.

20. _____ The process of entering data into a computer; can also refer to the data itself.

REVIEW ACTIVITIES

Answers for the self-quiz appear at the end of the book in the References and Resources Guide.

True/False

Instructions: Circle **T** if the statement is true or **F** if the statement is false.

T   F   **1.** Software includes all the physical equipment in a computer system.

T   F   **2.** The mouse is a common input device.

T   F   **3.** A computer can run without an operating system if it has good application software.

T   F   **4.** To access Web pages located on the World Wide Web, you need to be connected to the Internet.

T   F   **5.** One of the most common types of home computers is the midrange server.

Completion

Instructions: Supply the missing words to complete the following statements.

6. _____ is the operation in which data is entered into the computer.

7. Devices such as a floppy disk drive or DVD drive would be classified as _____ devices.

8. With desktop PCs that have a(n) _____ case, the system unit is typically located on the floor.

9. Another name for microcomputer is _____.

10. A device designed only for viewing Web pages and/or exchanging e-mail is called a(n) _____.

1. For the following list of computer hardware devices, write the principal function of each device in the space provided. Choices include input device (I), output device (O), storage device (S), processing device (P), and communications device (C).

a. CPU   _____   f. Hard drive _____

b. Mouse   _____   g. Modem   _____

c. Monitor   _____   h. Speakers   _____

d. CD drive _____   i. DVD drive   _____

e. Keyboard _____   j. Microphone _____

2. Select the term from the numbered list below that best matches each of the following descriptions and write the corresponding number in the blank to the left of each description.

a. _____ Allows access to resources located on the Internet.

b. _____ Supervises the running of all other programs on the computer.

c. _____ Helps prepare written documents, such as letters and reports.

d. _____ Used to create application programs.

1. Word processing program
2. Operating system
3. Programming language
4. Web browser

3. Supply the missing words to complete the following statements.

   a. Devices such as a printer or monitor would be classified as _____ devices.
   b. First-generation computers were powered by _____.
   c. The most powerful computers in the world are referred to as _____.
   d. Data organized into a meaningful form is called _____.
   e. The instructions used to tell a computer's hardware what to do are called _____.

4. Order the following types of computers by size by writing the numbers 1 (least powerful) to 5 (most powerful) in the blank to the left of each computer type.

   _____ Notebook computer
   _____ Mainframe computer
   _____ Supercomputer
   _____ Mobile device
   _____ Midrange server

5. Would text data or video data require more processing power and storage space? Explain.

6. List two reasons why a business may choose to network its employees' computers.

7. What is the difference between a tablet PC and a notebook PC?

8. Explain what is incorrect about the statement "Supercomputers are always built as a single, extraordinarily fast computer."

I N T

PROJECTS

1. **SPOT and Smart Objects** A step beyond personal computers and smart appliances are *smart objects*—everyday personal objects, such as wristwatches and alarm clocks, that are designed to be smarter, more personalized, and more useful than before. Microsoft Corporation is at the forefront of the smart object trend with their *SPOT (Smart Personal Objects Technology)* program intended to redesign objects to become smarter and better at their core functions in order to improve people's lives. One of the first products available using SPOT technology is a smart wristwatch which receives and displays convenient, timely, personalized Web content from a variety of sources using Microsoft's new *DirectBand* wireless service.

    For this project, investigate the current status of SPOT, SPOT-enabled products, and the DirectBand service. Which products work with the DirectBand service? How much does the service cost? What types of information are you able to receive for that price? Look for other smart objects besides those being promoted by Microsoft. Do you think these devices are useful and the trend will continue to grow? Or do you view it as a short-term movement that will eventually lose its popularity? At the conclusion of your research, prepare a one-page summary of your findings and submit it to your instructor.

2. **E-Clothing** As computing and communications devices continue to grow smaller and be carried with many individuals at all times, clothing manufacturers have begun to adapt by creating shorts, pants, jackets, vests, and more with pockets and compartments for cell phones, handheld PCs, portable digital music players, ear buds, and so forth.

    For this project, research e-clothing and identify at least two products that are commercially available. Summarize each product, listing all of the capabilities of the garment, what devices the garment is designed for, and what market the product is designed for. Be sure to include where the product can be purchased and the suggested retail price. Would you buy either of these garments? Why or why not? Do you think the e-clothing trend will continue to grow or is it a passing fad? Submit your findings and opinion to your instructor in the format of a one-page paper.

3. **24 Hours** Computers have a tremendous impact on our daily lives. They can be used to generate information or facilitate transactions, as well as be embedded in devices or appliances. On a daily basis, many computers are used by consumers or on behalf of consumers to carry out everyday tasks.

    For this project, take notice of and record all encounters you have with computing devices for the next 24 hours. Be sure to include both the computers that you use and ones that are used on your behalf. You should note both positive and negative impacts of these devices, and what your daily routine might be like without them. At the conclusion of the 24 hours, prepare a one-page summary of your observations and submit it to your instructor.

4. **Buying a New PC** New PCs are widely available directly from manufacturers, as well as in retail, computer, electronic, and warehouse stores. Some stores carry only standard configurations as set up by the manufacturers; others allow you to customize a system.

   For this project, assume that you are in the market for a PC for your personal use. Make a list of your hardware and software requirements (refer to the "Guide for Buying a PC" in the References and Resources Guide at the end of this textbook, if needed), being as specific as possible. Find a current advertisement for PCs from a computer or electronics store (such as Circuit City, BestBuy, or CompUSA) in your local paper or online at the company's Web site. Use the advertised specifications to select the two best PCs for under $1,000 and the two best PCs for $1,500 or less. Be sure all of the computers meet your stated basic needs. Prepare a one-page comparison chart contrasting each of the two computers in each price category, listing each requirement and how each PC meets or exceeds it, plus any additional features each computer includes. Also include information regarding the brand, price, delivery time, shipping, sales tax, and warranty terms for each PC. On your comparison sheet, mark the PC in each category that you think is the best value and then indicate which of the four computers you would prefer to buy and write one paragraph explaining why. Turn in your comparison sheet and summary to your instructor, stapled to copies of the printed ads, specifications printed from Web sites, and any other written documentation that you collected during this project.

5. **The Internet** The Internet and World Wide Web are handy tools that can help you research topics covered in this textbook and complete many of the projects. Chapter 2 explains the functions of the Internet and the World Wide Web, but you may wish to learn how to use these tools now. To accomplish this, you will need to find an Internet-enabled computer on your campus, at home, or at your public library, and then log on and type in an address for a specific Web site.

   For this project, follow the directions provided by your instructor or lab aide to access the Understanding Computers Web site located at www.course.com/uc10. Once you are at the site, note the types of information and activities that are available to you as a student and select a few of them by using your mouse to click on the hyperlinks—usually underlined or otherwise highlighted text or graphical buttons—corresponding to the options you want to explore. At the conclusion of this task, prepare a one-page summary describing the resources available through this textbook's Web site and submit it to your instructor.

6. **Online Education** The amount of distance learning available through the Internet and World Wide Web has exploded in the last couple of years, from being able to take an occasional course online a few years ago to being able to complete an entire college degree online today.

   For this project, look into the online education options available at your college or university and at least two other institutions of higher learning. Compare and contrast the programs in general, including such information as whether or not the institution is accredited, the type of courses available online, whether or not an entire certificate or degree can be earned online, and the required fees. After you have completed your general research, select one online course that interests you and research it more closely. Find out how the course works in an online format, including whether or not any face-to-face class time is required, whether assignments and exams are submitted online, which programs or plug-ins (programs that give extra capabilities to a Web browser) are required, and other class requirements. Summarize your findings in a two- to three-page paper. Be sure to include your opinion as to whether or not you would be interested in taking an online course and why.

7. **The Purpose of Software** Software can be defined as a set of instructions that make a computer work. It is generally categorized as *system software* (if its purpose is to run the computer system), and *application software* (if its purpose is to enable the user to perform some type of task).

   For this project, form a group to discuss software. The group should identify three of the leading microcomputer operating systems, and five categories of application software with two example programs for each category. For each program, find out the manufacturer, version, system or hardware requirements, function or purpose, and current cost, and then draw some conclusions about the dominance of one or more manufacturers in either or both of these software categories. Your group should submit the results of your research and discussions to your instructor in the form of short paper, not more than three pages in length.

8. **Super Supercomputers** Supercomputers today are being used for amazing things. From controlling satellites and missiles, to oil exploration, to mapping weather and environmental changes, to pulling information out of large consumer databases, supercomputer use is growing.

For this project, research one specific application for which a supercomputer is being used. Which computer is it? How large and powerful is the computer? How much did it cost? Is it a cluster or just a single supercomputer unit? What is it being used for? Could the application be done with a less powerful computer? Share your findings with the class in the form of a short presentation. The presentation should not exceed 10 minutes and should make use of one or more presentation aids such as the chalkboard, handouts, overhead transparencies, or a computer-based slide presentation (your instructor may provide additional requirements). You may also be asked to submit a summary of the presentation to your instructor.

9. **Computer Use on the Job** Most jobs today—from an administrative assistant, to the CEO of a multinational corporation, to the check-out clerk at the grocery store—require some level of computer skills.

For this project, form a group to explore the computing requirements for one job that the typical student in your group should be qualified for after graduating from college. Research that position to determine the minimum computer skills needed at the entry level, plus any additional skills that would give an applicant an advantage. If there is a management or other position of advancement that an individual in this position would eventually want to attain, find out if there are any other computer skills that would be needed for advancement. Share your findings with the class in the form of a short presentation. The presentation should not exceed 10 minutes and should make use of one or more presentation aids such as the chalkboard, handouts, overhead transparencies, or a computer-based slide presentation (your instructor may provide additional requirements). Your group may also be asked to submit a summary of the presentation to your instructor.

10. **Computer Literacy** It has been suggested that computer literacy should be one of the basic requirements of a high school or college education. The definition of computer literacy varies but is generally used to refer to a basic knowledge and understanding of computers and their uses. Many schools believe that computer literacy is an essential skill, but are reluctant to adopt a formal computer literacy requirement since students already have so many requirements to complete before graduation.

Select one of the following positions or create your own and express your point of view on the subject. Your instructor will indicate whether your response is to be posted to a class bulletin board, discussed in a class chat room, or discussed as an in-class activity. You may also be asked to submit a summary of your position and point of view to your instructor.
   a. Computer literacy is important, but not as important as reading, writing, or arithmetic, and should not be a basic requirement for graduation from high school or college.
   b. Computer literacy is an essential skill and should be required for graduation at either the high school or college level.

11. **High Tech Sports** Pervasive computing has found its way into the world of sports via the increased number of technological devices and gadgets available for sportspeople. For instance, professional mountain climber Ed Viesturs brings a variety of high-tech gear (such as a notebook computer, digital video camera, satellite phone, solar panels to recharge the equipment, and an all-in-one digital barometer, thermometer, altimeter, and wind gauge) on his climbs. While some benefits of improved sporting technology are obvious—for instance, Viesturs' ability to get updated weather reports on his satellite phone as he is climbing unarguably keeps him safer—is there a chance that this high-tech technology may endanger other, less experienced, sports enthusiasts? Could high-tech gadgets lead individuals into participating in potentially dangerous activities—such as mountain climbing and long-distance sailing and kayaking—that require expert knowledge, physical strength, and special skills to perform successfully and for which they might not otherwise participate? Could high-tech gadgets give individuals who are not properly prepared for an activity enough of a false sense of security that they participate in the activity anyway, assuming that their technological devices will protect them? What about the societal impact—does society have a responsibility to rescue those individuals if something goes wrong? Will even experienced sportspeople rely too much on technology and ignore their good sense? Viesturs says he's not counting on his phone or digital altimeter to get him up or off the mountain; instead he wants to rely on his own experience and instincts. But do others feel the same way? Think of an outdoor sporting activity that you enjoy. Do you think bringing high-tech gear along would enhance or detract from the experience?

    For this project, form an opinion of the use of high-tech sporting gadgets on professional and personal sports. Be sure to use the questions mentioned in the previous paragraph when forming your position. Your instructor will indicate whether your response is to be posted to a class bulletin board, discussed in a class chat room, or discussed as an in-class activity. You may also be asked to submit a summary of your position and point of view to your instructor.

STUDENT EDITION LABS

12. **Student Edition Labs** Reinforce the concepts you have learned in this chapter by working through the "Using Windows" interactive Student Edition Lab, available online. To access this lab, go to www.course.com/uc10/ch01

    If you have a SAM user profile, you have access to even more interactive content. Log in to your SAM account and go to your assignments page to see what your instructor has assigned for this chapter.

CHAPTER 2

OUTLINE

Overview
Starting Your Computer: The Boot Process
Using the Windows Operating System
 The Windows Interface
 Opening Windows and Starting Programs
 Manipulating Windows
 Shutting Down the Computer
Using the Internet and World Wide Web
 What are the Internet and World
  Wide Web?
 What Is a Browser?
 Accessing the Internet
 Internet Addresses
 Surfing the Web
 Using Bookmarks and the History List
 Searching the Web
E-Mail and Other Types of Online
 Communications
 Sending E-Mail
 Receiving E-Mail
 Managing E-Mail
 Discussion Groups, Chat, Instant
  Messaging, and More
 Netiquette
Societal Implications of Cyberspace
 Security
 Privacy
 Differences in Online Communications
 The Anonymity Factor
 Information Integrity

Using Your PC, Windows, and the Web

LEARNING OBJECTIVES

After completing this chapter, you will be able to:

1. Explain what happens when you start up a computer.

2. Identify common elements of the Windows graphical user interface (GUI), such as the desktop, Start menu, windows, and menus, and explain their functions.

3. Demonstrate how to open a program and manipulate open program windows.

4. Explain what the Internet and World Wide Web are and how computers, people, and Web pages are identified on the Internet.

5. Demonstrate how to access a Web page and explain how to search for Web pages containing specific information.

6. Understand how e-mail can be used to send and receive messages to and from other Internet users.

7. Identify several other types of online communications and discuss when each is used.

8. Discuss some societal implications of the Internet, such as security, privacy, and online communications issues.

In the not too distant past, computers were fairly difficult to use and very intimidating. Programs were text-based and the keyboard had to be used to issue all commands. To run an application program, the user had to type the correct sequence of cryptic text-based commands to get the program started, and then issue additional text-based commands to control the program's actions. Even after the mouse and graphical interfaces emerged, computers could only run one program at a time, which meant users had to close one program before opening another.

This situation has radically changed over the last decade or two. Powerful PCs with easy-to-use graphical interfaces and sophisticated multimedia capabilities have emerged as the standard. Today's PCs have the capability of running multiple programs at a time, faster than computer pioneers likely thought possible. These computers, used in conjunction with the vast amount of useful and exciting software applications available today, enable even novice users to perform exciting and powerful computing tasks.

In order to use application software, however, you first need to know how to start the computer and tell it to run the desired programs. You also should be familiar with the commands and mouse actions needed to tell programs what you want them to do. These skills are the focus of this chapter. This chapter will get you up and running so that you can use a computer to perform any computer-based assignments for this course, such as starting a word processing program to type a paper, using the Internet for research, or completing an activity located on this textbook's Web site.

Chapter 2 begins by introducing the basic features of the *Microsoft Windows* operating system, including how to start a PC and how to launch an application program. It covers the wide variety of *menus*, *windows*, and *icons* you are likely to encounter, and it explains how to open, close, resize, and otherwise manipulate the windows that appear on your screen when programs and documents are open. The chapter also explains how *Internet addresses* work and how to gain access to Web pages. Remember when reading this chapter that it is just an overview—operating systems, application software, the Internet, and the World Wide Web are covered in much more detail in later chapters of this book. In addition, selecting and purchasing a PC is discussed in the References and Resources Guide at the end of this textbook. If you need to buy a computer during this course, be sure to read that section of the References and Resources Guide beforehand. ■

STARTING YOUR COMPUTER: THE BOOT PROCESS

The first thing a new computer user needs to know about using a PC is how to power it up, assuming that the computer is already out of the box and the cables are correctly connected (refer to Figure 3-14 in Chapter 3 for cable illustrations and setup descriptions). To turn on a PC, the power button (usually located on the front of the system unit) is used. Once the power button is activated, an indicator light on the front of the system unit typically lights up. If the power indicator light is on but the computer doesn't appear to be active, the monitor may be turned off or the unit may be *asleep*—a low-power *standby mode* designed to save energy and wear-and-tear on the computer. Sleeping computers can usually be awakened by moving the mouse or pressing any key on the keyboard; the power button located on the front of a monitor can be used to turn it on.

After the power button is pressed, the computer begins to **boot**. During the boot process, part of the computer's **operating system**—the program that controls and manages a computer's activities—is loaded into memory. The computer also does a quick diagnostic on the computer and may run special utilities, such as checking for computer viruses, depending on how the computer is set up. You may hear beeps and whirring noises as these procedures take place and some characteristics of the PC (such as amount of memory, the number of attached drives, and the operating system being used) may be briefly displayed on the screen.

PROBLEM	STEPS TO TRY TO REMEDY THE PROBLEM
Power indicator light on the system unit is not on.	1. Make sure the system unit's power cable is securely connected to both the power supply and system unit. 2. Make sure the power supply is turned on. 3. Press the power button located on the computer to turn it on.
Power indicator light on the system unit is on, but there is no picture on the screen.	1. Move the mouse or press a key on the keyboard to wake up the computer if it is asleep. 2. Make sure the monitor's power cable is securely connected to both the power supply and the monitor. 3. Make sure all the switches on the power supply are turned on. 4. Make sure the cable from the monitor to the system unit is securely connected. 5. Press the power button located on the monitor to turn it on. 6. Check to make sure the monitor's brightness and contrast levels are not turned all the way down.
"Non-system disk" error message is displayed on the screen.	1. Remove the disk from the floppy drive and press any key to continue.
Computer boots up, but the keyboard won't work.	1. Check to make sure the keyboard cable is securely connected to the system unit. 2. If using a wireless keyboard, replace the batteries located inside the keyboard.
Computer boots up, but the mouse won't work.	1. Check to make sure the mouse cable is securely connected to the system unit. 2. Reboot the computer if the mouse was unplugged but still doesn't work now that it is connected. 3. If using a wireless mouse, replace the batteries located inside the mouse.

FIGURE 2-1
Common problems encountered when booting a PC.

Several things can prevent a computer from booting properly. A few of the most common and easy to fix problems that occur when booting up a desktop PC are listed in Figure 2-1 with some suggested remedies.

USING THE WINDOWS OPERATING SYSTEM

When a PC has finished the boot process, it is ready to be used and waits for input from the user. The manner in which an operating system or any other type of program interacts with its users is known as its *user interface*. Older software programs used a *text-based user interface*, which required the user to type precise instructions indicating exactly what the computers should do. Most programs today use a **graphical user interface** or **GUI** (pronounced "goo-ey"), which uses graphical objects (such as *icons* and *buttons*) that can be selected with the mouse to tell the computer what to do.

The Windows Interface

The most common operating system for PCs today is **Microsoft Windows**. Windows has come in a variety of versions over the years, such as *Windows 3.1, Windows 95, Windows 98, Windows NT, Windows 2000, Windows Me,* and *Windows XP*. One of the

---

>**Boot.** To start up a computer. >**Operating system.** The main component of system software that enables the computer to manage its activities and the resources under its control, run application programs, and interface with the user. >**Graphical user interface (GUI).** A graphically based interface that allows a user to communicate instructions to the computer easily. >**Microsoft Windows.** The most common operating system for IBM and IBM-compatible PCs.

advantages of using Windows is that application software written for any version of Windows has a similar appearance and works essentially the same way as Windows does. Therefore, if you are comfortable using the Windows interface and some Windows software, most other Windows software should seem familiar. The next few sections describe what the Windows interface looks like and how to use it. Other graphical operating systems, such as *Mac OS* (used on Macintosh computers) and graphical versions of *Linux* (used on some PC computers) look and act similarly to Windows.

The Desktop

The Windows **desktop** appears on the screen after a computer using the Windows operating system has completed the boot process. The desktop is the user's basic workspace—the place where documents, folders, programs, and other objects are displayed when they are being used, similar to the way documents and file folders are laid on a desk when they are being used. Although the appearance of the Windows desktop can be customized and varies somewhat from version to version, all Windows desktops contain common elements, such as the *taskbar*, *task buttons*, the *Start button*, *windows*, and *icons* (see Figure 2-2).

The Taskbar

FIGURE 2-2
The Windows desktop.

The **taskbar** is located along the bottom of the desktop. It houses the *Start button* at the left edge, *toolbars* and *task buttons* in the center, and a clock and other indicators in the *system tray* at the far right edge. The *Start button* is used to display the **Start menu**, the

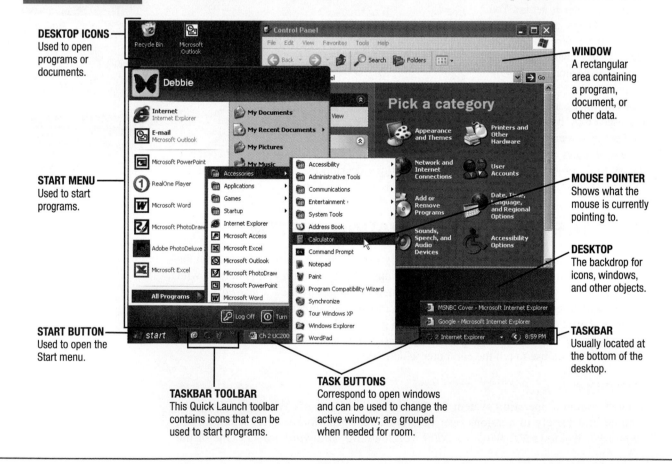

DESKTOP ICONS
Used to open programs or documents.

START MENU
Used to start programs.

START BUTTON
Used to open the Start menu.

TASKBAR TOOLBAR
This Quick Launch toolbar contains icons that can be used to start programs.

TASK BUTTONS
Correspond to open windows and can be used to change the active window; are grouped when needed for room.

WINDOW
A rectangular area containing a program, document, or other data.

MOUSE POINTER
Shows what the mouse is currently pointing to.

DESKTOP
The backdrop for icons, windows, and other objects.

TASKBAR
Usually located at the bottom of the desktop.

>**Desktop.** The background work area displayed on the screen when using Microsoft Windows or another operating system with a graphical user interface. >**Taskbar.** The bar located at the bottom of the Windows desktop that contains the Start button, task buttons, and the system tray. >**Start menu.** The main Windows menu that is used to start programs.

main Windows menu used to start programs. *Taskbar toolbars*, such as the *Quick Launch toolbar* which is shown in Figure 2-2 and is used for launching programs, provide the user with quick access to programs and commands. Toolbars can be added or removed from the taskbar by right-clicking the taskbar and selecting *Toolbars*. Once a toolbar is displayed, users can add and delete icons, as desired.

Task buttons appear on the taskbar for each window that is currently open, although all windows may not be visible on the desktop at all times. As discussed later, these task buttons can be used to hide and display open windows, as well as to change the *active window*; that is, the window with which the user is currently working. As shown in Figure 2-2, multiple windows for the same program (Internet Explorer in Figure 2-2) may be grouped together as one task button in recent versions of Windows; when the grouped task button is clicked, a list of the individual windows belonging to that group is displayed.

Windows

The principal component of the GUI is the **window**—a rectangular area in which programs, documents, and other content is displayed on the desktop. In addition to programs and documents, these windows can contain *icons*, *menus*, *dialog boxes*, and a variety of other elements (see Figure 2-3).

Icons

Icons are small pictures located on the desktop, a taskbar toolbar, or in a window that represent a computer program, document, or other element that can be opened. Icons can be added by the user or created automatically during program installation. When you select an

▶ **FIGURE 2-3**
Common window elements.

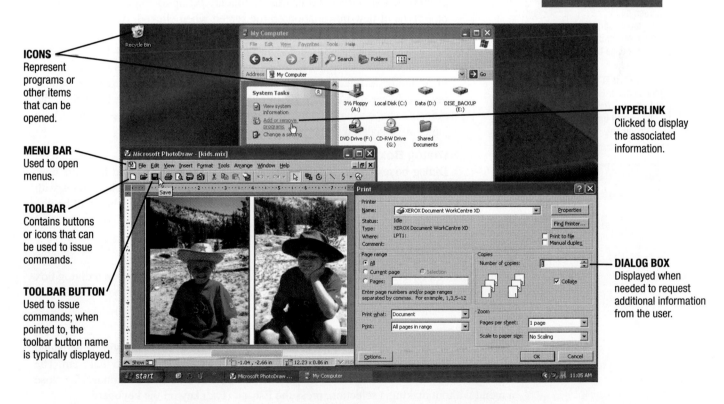

ICONS
Represent programs or other items that can be opened.

MENU BAR
Used to open menus.

TOOLBAR
Contains buttons or icons that can be used to issue commands.

TOOLBAR BUTTON
Used to issue commands; when pointed to, the toolbar button name is typically displayed.

HYPERLINK
Clicked to display the associated information.

DIALOG BOX
Displayed when needed to request additional information from the user.

>**Task button.** A button displayed on the taskbar to represent an open window; using this button, the window can be minimized, restored, or closed. >**Window.** A rectangular area in which programs, documents, and other content are displayed. >**Icon.** A small picture or other type of graphical image that represents a program, command, or document and invokes some action when selected.

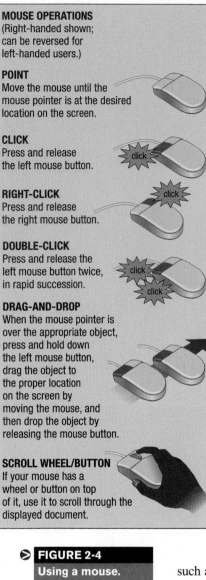

MOUSE OPERATIONS
(Right-handed shown; can be reversed for left-handed users.)

POINT
Move the mouse until the mouse pointer is at the desired location on the screen.

CLICK
Press and release the left mouse button.

RIGHT-CLICK
Press and release the right mouse button.

DOUBLE-CLICK
Press and release the left mouse button twice, in rapid succession.

DRAG-AND-DROP
When the mouse pointer is over the appropriate object, press and hold down the left mouse button, drag the object to the proper location on the screen by moving the mouse, and then drop the object by releasing the mouse button.

SCROLL WHEEL/BUTTON
If your mouse has a wheel or button on top of it, use it to scroll through the displayed document.

FIGURE 2-4
Using a mouse.

icon with the mouse, the software takes the appropriate action for that icon, such as starting or opening a program or document, or displaying the contents stored on a storage medium. To start a program or anything else represented by an icon, the mouse is used. Depending on how Windows is set up, either a single click or a double click of the left mouse button opens the program or document. See Figure 2-4 for a list of common mouse operations.

Menus
Menus are sets of usually text-based items that appear at the top of many windows and can be used to issue commands to that program. Typically a menu has a *menu bar* that shows the main menu categories; when an item on a menu bar is selected, the full menu for that item is displayed.

Toolbars
Toolbars consist of sets of icons or buttons, called **toolbar buttons**, that can be clicked with the mouse to issue commands. Although they can often be moved by the user, toolbars typically stretch horizontally across the top of a window below the menu bar. Each toolbar button has a name, which is displayed if you point to the button with the mouse (see Figure 2-3). Within a *software suite*, such as Microsoft Office or Corel WordPerfect Office, the toolbar buttons that can be used to save a document, print a document, or perform other common tasks have the same appearance in all programs within that suite.

Hyperlinks
Hyperlinks are either text or images that are set up to display a document or other type of new information on the screen when clicked. Although initially found only on Web pages, hyperlinks now appear frequently on other types of Windows applications, such as on the My Computer window in Figure 2-3. Underlined icons on the Windows desktop (see Figure 2-5), as well as underlined and/or different colored text on a Web page or Help screen, generally indicate hyperlinks. When you move the mouse pointer to a hyperlink, the pointer's shape usually changes to a pointing hand. Hyperlinks found on Web pages are discussed in more detail later in this chapter.

Dialog Boxes
Dialog boxes are displayed whenever additional input is needed from the user, such as to specify the desired options when printing or saving a document. Menu items with ellipses (. . .) next to them display dialog boxes. The components of a dialog box will be discussed shortly.

A Closer Look at Menus
Items contained on a menu either display another, more specific, menu; open a dialog box to prompt the user for more information; or execute a command. Some of the elements you may find on a typical menu include the following (see Figure 2-6).

Current Command
A *highlighted item* indicates the *current command*, or the command that will be activated if the Enter key is pressed or the mouse button is clicked while pointing to that item. The highlighted item can be changed by using the keyboard arrow keys or the mouse. To close a menu without making a selection, press the Escape (Esc) key on the keyboard.

Check Marks

A *check mark* next to a menu item indicates that the item is turned on. Clicking a check-marked item *toggles* between checking and unchecking that item. Sometimes only one item in a group of items can be selected. When this is the case, another symbol—a dot or circle called an *option button* or a *radio button*—is used instead to indicate the selected item.

Dimmed Items

A *dimmed* or *grayed-out item* indicates a command that is unavailable in the context of what you're currently doing. For example, as in Figure 2-6, if no footnotes have been created yet in a document, viewing them is impossible. Consequently, that command is dimmed and cannot be selected.

Arrows

An *arrow* next to a menu item indicates that a *submenu* containing more specific options will open when that item is selected. For example, when the *Toolbars* item is selected, as in the rightmost menu in Figure 2-6, the Toolbars submenu opens.

Ellipses

An *ellipsis* next to a menu item indicates that a dialog box requesting more information will open when that item is clicked; once the dialog box has been completed, the appropriate command will be carried out.

Keyboard Shortcuts

A *keyboard shortcut* is a shortcut key combination, such as Ctrl+Z (performed by holding down the Ctrl key while tapping the Z key) for Undo and Ctrl+C for Copy, that can be used to execute a command when the menu is not open.

HYPERLINK
Single-click the mouse to open this icon.

NOT A HYPERLINK
Double-click the mouse to open this icon.

FIGURE 2-5
Desktop icons. Depending on how Windows is set up, desktop icons may be hyperlinks.

FIGURE 2-6
Menu elements.

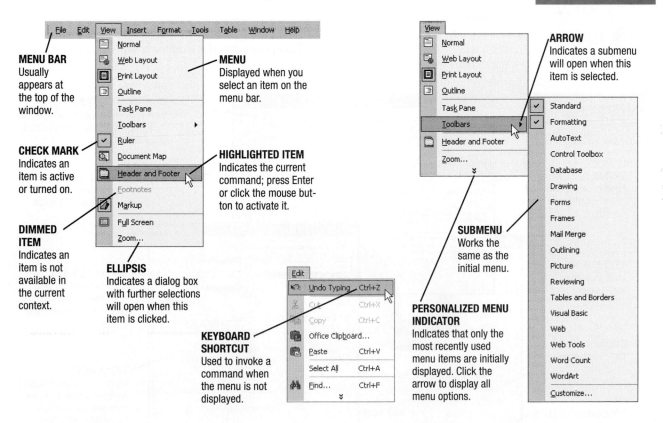

Personalized Menus

A *personalized menu* initially displays only the options on the menu that were most recently used. Waiting a moment or clicking on the double arrow symbol at the bottom of the menu displays all items that belong on that menu. Personalized menus can be turned on or off for a program by the user.

A Closer Look at Dialog Boxes

Dialog boxes contain a variety of elements that allow the user to provide additional information before a command is executed. Some of the most common dialog box elements are illustrated in Figure 2-7 and listed next.

Option Buttons

Option buttons, also known as *radio buttons*, are round buttons that are used when only one item in a group of related items can be selected. When you click an option button, that button becomes filled in to mark it as currently selected; all other option buttons in the group become deselected.

Check boxes

Check boxes are used to indicate if a single option is turned on or off. Clicking a check box toggles the check mark on or off. Check boxes differ from option buttons in that you can select any number of check boxes in a group of related items.

Text Boxes

Text boxes provide spaces for you to enter text-based information, such as a number or the name of a document. A *spin box* consists of a text box into which you can type a number or use the up-arrow and down-arrow buttons to change the value in that box.

Sliders

Sliders can be dragged with the mouse to select a value from a range of values. Sliders are commonly used for adjusting audio volume, changing the monitor resolution, and setting the difficulty level for a computer game.

► FIGURE 2-7
Dialog box elements.

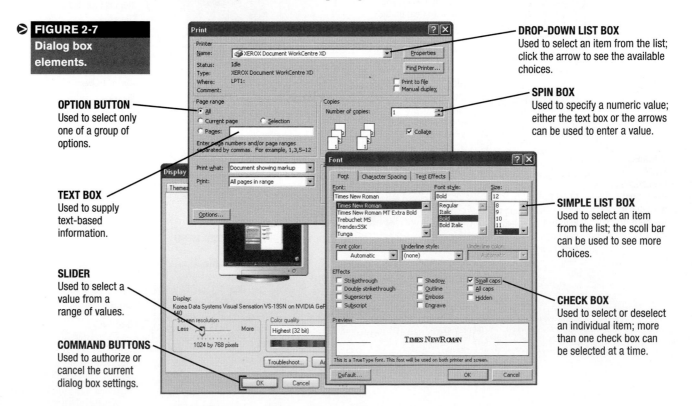

DROP-DOWN LIST BOX
Used to select an item from the list; click the arrow to see the available choices.

SPIN BOX
Used to specify a numeric value; either the text box or the arrows can be used to enter a value.

SIMPLE LIST BOX
Used to select an item from the list; the scoll bar can be used to see more choices.

CHECK BOX
Used to select or deselect an individual item; more than one check box can be selected at a time.

OPTION BUTTON
Used to select only one of a group of options.

TEXT BOX
Used to supply text-based information.

SLIDER
Used to select a value from a range of values.

COMMAND BUTTONS
Used to authorize or cancel the current dialog box settings.

List Boxes

List boxes display a list of choices from which one or more options may be selected. *Simple list boxes* usually display more than one choice initially and a vertical *scroll bar* can be used to see more choices, if the list exceeds the size of the box. A *drop-down list box* displays only one selection initially and the down-arrow button at the edge of the box is used to see the other selections.

Command Buttons

Command buttons are typically used to authorize or cancel the changes made to the dialog box settings. A dimmed command button identifies an action that is unavailable at the present time.

Opening Windows and Starting Programs

To start a program (or open any other type of window) in Windows, a variety of methods are available. The most common procedures for starting a program are listed next and illustrated in Figure 2-8.

▼ Click a taskbar toolbar icon.

▼ Click a desktop icon if it looks like a hyperlink.

▼ Double-click a desktop icon if it doesn't look like a hyperlink.

▼ Click the Start button, and then select the program from the Start menu. The most recent version of Windows puts the most frequently used programs in the left pane of the Start menu; utility items such as the *My Documents* folder, *Help*, and the *Control Panel* are listed in the right pane. For programs not displayed in these two panes, the *All Programs* option is used. As on any other menu, an item on the Start menu with an arrow ▶ to the right of it means that a submenu will open when that item is selected, and an item with an ellipsis (. . .) next to it means that a dialog box will open when that item is clicked. Any item without an arrow or ellipsis starts a program; to start the program, click the item.

▼ In any window that displays documents stored on the PC (such as My Documents or My Computer), double-click a document to open it in its associated program (assuming an appropriate program is installed on the PC).

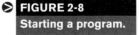

FIGURE 2-8
Starting a program.

DESKTOP ICON
Single-click (if the icon looks like a hyperlink) or double-click (if the icon doesn't look like a hyperlink) to start the associated program.

TASKBAR TOOLBAR
Click a toolbar button to start the associated program.

DOCUMENT
Double-click a document to open it in its associated program.

START MENU
Click any item without an arrow or ellipsis to start that program.

Manipulating Windows

Open windows may occasionally need to be resized or otherwise manipulated in order to work efficiently. Several ways to do this are described next.

The Active Window

When more than one window is open at a time, only one can be the *active window*—the window in which commands will be executed. To identify the active window, look for the window that is on top of the others, has a different colored *title bar* (the top border of the window containing the name of the window), and has a task button with a depressed or different colored appearance (see Figure 2-9).

Only one window can be active at a time. To make any onscreen window active, click the mouse pointer anywhere in the window. Alternately, you can click the window's task button located on the taskbar at the bottom of the Windows desktop to make that window the new active window. If the option to group similar task buttons is turned on, first click on the group taskbar button to display the windows contained in that group, and then click the desired window.

Minimizing, Maximizing, and Closing Windows

Windows can be *minimized* to just a task button on the taskbar or *maximized* to fill the entire screen by clicking the appropriate sizing button with the mouse. The buttons to perform these tasks are located at the top right of most windows (such as those in Figure 2-9) and are described next.

▼ The *Minimize button* ▬ hides a window, leaving only its task button on the taskbar. A program that has been minimized is still running and can be displayed again by clicking its task button.

▼ The *Maximize button* ◻ enlarges the window as much as possible, usually covering the entire desktop.

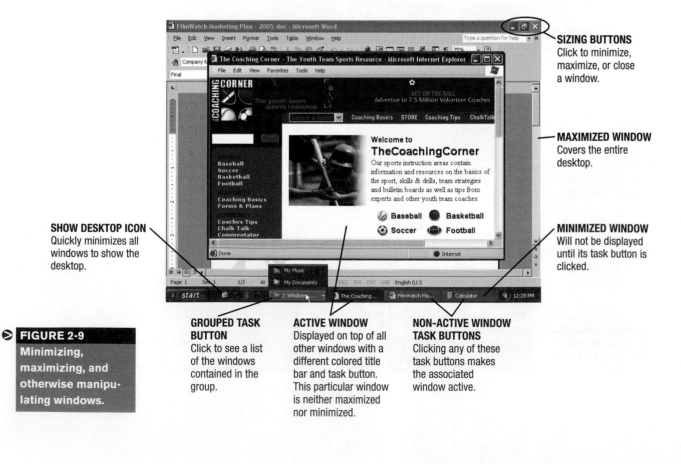

SIZING BUTTONS
Click to minimize, maximize, or close a window.

MAXIMIZED WINDOW
Covers the entire desktop.

MINIMIZED WINDOW
Will not be displayed until its task button is clicked.

SHOW DESKTOP ICON
Quickly minimizes all windows to show the desktop.

GROUPED TASK BUTTON
Click to see a list of the windows contained in the group.

ACTIVE WINDOW
Displayed on top of all other windows with a different colored title bar and task button. This particular window is neither maximized nor minimized.

NON-ACTIVE WINDOW TASK BUTTONS
Clicking any of these task buttons makes the associated window active.

FIGURE 2-9

Minimizing, maximizing, and otherwise manipulating windows.

▼ The *Restore button* ⬒ is displayed instead of the Maximize button when a window is maximized. Clicking the Restore button returns a maximized window to its previous size.

▼ The *Close button* ☒ at the far upper-right corner of virtually all windows closes the window permanently. To reopen the window at a later time, the program or other item must be opened again (such as with a desktop or taskbar toolbar icon, or the Start menu).

When it is necessary to access an icon on the desktop hidden behind open windows, you don't need to minimize each open window. Instead, it is faster to click the *Show Desktop button* ⬚ on the Quick Launch taskbar toolbar (shown in Figure 2-9), if that toolbar is displayed on the screen. Clicking the Show Desktop button again restores the desktop to its previous appearance.

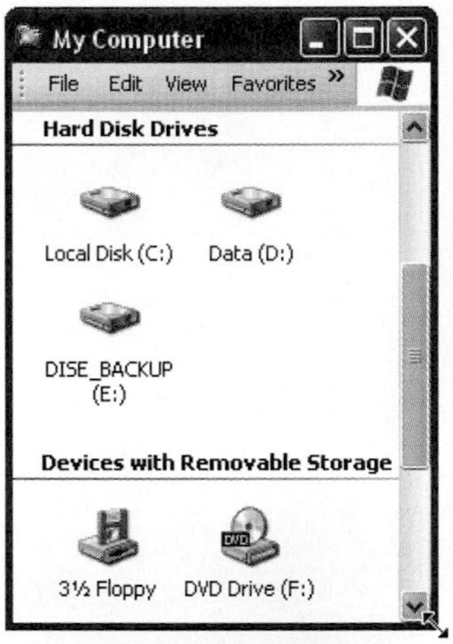

Resizing and Moving Windows

Resizing windows (making them larger or smaller) allows you to view more than one window on the desktop at a time. The active window can be resized using the window's *border* (the edge of the window), as long as the window is not maximized. A window can be resized by following these steps.

1. Point to the desired window border (the left or right border to size the width, the top or bottom border to size the height, or the window corner to adjust a window's width and height simultaneously) to change the mouse pointer to the proper double-headed resizing arrow ↔, ↕, or ⬉, respectively (see Figure 2-10).

2. Hold down the left mouse button.

3. Drag the window border with the mouse until the window is the desired size, and then release the mouse.

When you perform work in individual windows, the mouse pointer often changes its appearance in a *context-sensitive* manner. In other words, the shape of the pointer changes automatically, based on the operation you are performing. For example, when you resize a window, the pointer resembles a double-pointed arrow and when you point to a hyperlink, the pointer changes to a pointing hand. Figure 2-11 identifies some of the mouse pointer shapes that you may see on your screen from time to time.

In addition to resizing windows, you can further customize your desktop by moving a non-maximized window from one place to another. To move a window, point to the window's title bar with the mouse, hold down the left mouse button, drag the window to the desired location, and then release the mouse to complete the move of the window to its new location. This same move procedure can be used to move a desktop icon, or an object or block of text in many application programs.

> **FIGURE 2-10**
> **Resizing a window.** You can change both the width and height of a window at the same time by dragging a corner of the window.

> **FIGURE 2-11**
> **Some common mouse pointer shapes.**

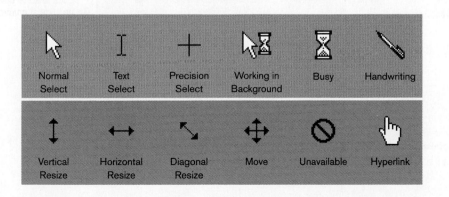

Scroll Bars

Often, a window is not big enough to display all the contents of the window (such as an entire document or an entire group of icons). When this happens, **scroll bars** appear at the bottom and/or right edge of the window (see Figure 2-12). Using a scroll bar, you can *scroll* to see all the information located in the window, one screen at a time. Some common ways to use scroll bars are listed next.

▼ Click one of the two *scroll arrows* at the edge of the scroll bar to move one line at a time in the direction of the arrow.

▼ Click an empty spot on the scroll bar on either side of the *scroll box* (the rectangle located between the two scroll arrows) to move about one screen at a time in that direction.

▼ Drag the scroll box with the mouse to quickly move to a specific location in the document. If you move the scroll box from the top of the scroll bar to the middle, for example, the middle part of the document will be displayed. Many applications display the current page number next to the scroll bar as you scroll in this manner to help you identify the current page as you scroll through the document.

▼ Use the special scroll wheel or button located on the top of your mouse, if one exists, or use the keyboard's directional keys to scroll up or down a document.

The scroll box on a scroll bar typically is sized in proportion to the percentage of information currently being displayed in the window. Therefore, a large scroll box indicates that most of the information in the window is displayed, while a small scroll box indicates that most information is hidden from view. For example, in Figure 2-12 the scroll box is about one-fourth the size of the scroll bar, which indicates that about one-fourth of the document is currently displayed in the window.

> ⊘ **FIGURE 2-12**
> **Scroll bars.** Scroll bars allow you to move through a document that is too large to fit entirely within the window at one time.

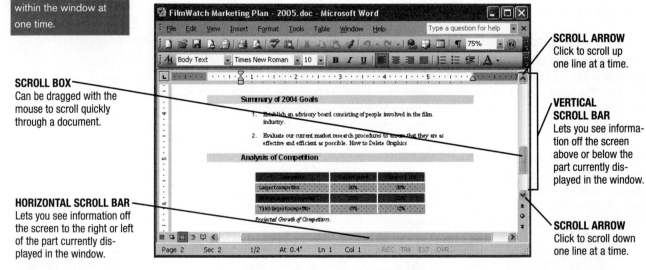

SCROLL BOX
Can be dragged with the mouse to scroll quickly through a document.

HORIZONTAL SCROLL BAR
Lets you see information off the screen to the right or left of the part currently displayed in the window.

SCROLL ARROW
Click to scroll up one line at a time.

VERTICAL SCROLL BAR
Lets you see information off the screen above or below the part currently displayed in the window.

SCROLL ARROW
Click to scroll down one line at a time.

>**Scroll bar.** A horizontal or vertical bar that appears along an edge of a window when the window is not large enough to display its entire content; scroll bars are used to view the rest of the information in the window.

Shutting Down the Computer

At the end of a work session, you will usually leave your PC on if you will be using it again later that day. To reduce power consumption, most computers can be put into standby mode by using the *Standby* option on the *Turn Off Computer* dialog box (discussed next) or a special sleep key on the keyboard. When a computer is in standby mode, the monitor and hard drive are generally turned off to save power and wear-and-tear on the computer. Many PCs can also be set up to automatically go to sleep after a set period of inactivity.

When you are finished working with a computer for the day, you may want to turn it completely off, instead of putting it to sleep. Instead of just pressing the power button, however, it is important to *shut down* the computer. Shutting down a computer properly gives you the opportunity to make sure all the work you have done has been saved and allows Windows to save any information it needs, delete temporary files, and close programs. Turning off a computer without going through the shut down procedure can leave extra data and files on your computer that can eventually take up valuable storage space and potentially cause problems with your computer in the future.

To shut down a computer when necessary, follow these steps.

1. Save and close all open documents, close all open programs, and then click the Start button to display the Start menu.

2. Select the shut down option at the bottom of the Start menu (usually labeled *Shut Down* or *Turn Off Computer*, depending on the version of Windows being used).

3. Choose the appropriate option to shut down the computer.

4. If you see a message stating that it is safe to turn off the computer, press the power button on the computer. If your computer automatically turns the power off for you, like many newer computers do, you don't need to do anything further.

USING THE INTERNET AND WORLD WIDE WEB

What are the Internet and World Wide Web?

As discussed in Chapter 1, the **Internet** is a collection of networks that connects millions of computers all over the world. While the term "Internet" refers to the physical structure of that network, the **World Wide Web** refers to one resource—a collection of documents called **Web pages**—available through the Internet. The Web page files are located on computers (called **Web servers**) that are continually connected to the Internet so they can be accessed at any time by anyone with a computer (or other Web-enabled device) and an Internet connection.

Web pages today can contain text, graphics, animation, sound, video, three-dimensional *virtual reality* (*VR*) objects, and more. Web pages are connected by *hyperlinks*—graphics or text that, when clicked with the mouse, display other Web pages. When a hyperlink is clicked, the appropriate Web page is displayed, regardless of whether the new page is located on the same Web server as the original page, or on a Web server in an entirely different state or country. Hyperlinks can also be used to facilitate file downloads by Web visitors, such as to download images, music, or software programs.

>**Internet.** The largest and most well-known computer network, linking millions of computers all over the world. >**World Wide Web.** The collection of Web pages available through the Internet. >**Web page.** A document, typically containing hyperlinks to other documents, located on a Web server and available through the World Wide Web. >**Web server.** A computer that is continually connected to the Internet and hosts Web pages that are accessible through the Internet.

Today, the vast majority of medium- to large-sized companies in the United States have a **Web site** (a collection of related Web pages), and millions of individuals and small firms have them too. A Web site can contain anywhere from 1 to 1,000 or more pages. Your visit to a Web site often begins at the site's **home page**—the designated starting page for that site, although it may not necessarily be the first page an individual views. A home page typically acts as a table of contents for the site, providing important information that the company would like to convey, as well as containing hyperlinks to the other main pages on the site.

What Is a Browser?

To view Web pages, you need a **Web browser** program. The two most common browsers—*Microsoft Internet Explorer* and *Netscape Navigator*—are illustrated shortly in Figure 2-19; a few alternative browsers are shown in Figure 2-13. Although originally designed to display Web pages, many browsers can also be used for other Internet applications, such as sending and receiving e-mail and downloading files. Instead of using conventional browsers, handheld PCs and mobile devices use browsers—called **microbrowsers**—specifically designed for those devices and their small screen sizes (see Figure 2-13). Many Web sites develop Web pages specifically designed for microbrowsers or use software that automatically alters the Web content on their Web site into formats compatible with handheld PCs and mobile devices. In addition, some microbrowsers and some wireless providers reformat standard Web pages to optimize them for the device being used as the pages are being delivered.

The following sections introduce how to access the Internet and how to use a Web browser to access Web pages, exchange e-mail, and perform the most commonly used Internet tasks.

Accessing the Internet

In order to use the Internet, your computer, Internet appliance, smart phone, or other Internet-access device must be connected to it. Typically, this occurs by connecting your device to a computer—usually belonging to an **Internet service provider** (**ISP**), your school, or your company—that is continually connected to the Internet. Some Internet connections are *direct* or *always-on connections* (in which the computer or other device being used to access the Internet is continually connected to the ISP's computer); others are *dial-up connections* (in which the PC or device must dial up and connect to the ISP's computer when Internet access is needed). ISPs are sometimes also referred to as *online services providers* or *Internet access providers*.

ISPs function as a gateway or onramp to the Internet, providing Internet access to their subscribers. Typically, they are continually connected to a larger network, called a *regional network*, which, in turn, is connected to one of the major high-speed networks within a country called a *backbone network*. Backbone networks within a country are connected to each other and to backbone networks in other countries. Together they form one enormous network of networks—the Internet.

Most ISPs charge a monthly fee for Internet access, although there are some ISPs who offer free access in exchange for onscreen advertising. If you connect to the Internet using a school or company network, the school or company acts as your ISP. If you connect using a smart phone, PDA, or other handheld device, your wireless provider typically is your ISP. Home PC users typically use a national ISP (such as *America Online (AOL)*, *Earthlink*,

FURTHER EXPLORATION

For links to further information about Web browsers, go to www.course.com/uc10/ch02

TIP

The various types of direct and dial-up Internet connections, as well as tips for choosing and getting set up with an ISP, are covered in Chapter 9.

>**Web site.** A collection of related Web pages usually belonging to an organization or individual. >**Home page.** The designated starting page for a Web site. >**Web browser.** A program used to view Web pages. >**Microbrowser.** A special type of Web browser used with handheld PCs and mobile devices. >**Internet service provider (ISP).** A business or other organization that provides Internet access to others, typically for a fee.

AT&T WorldNet, StarBand, or *RoadRunner*) that provides Internet service to a large geographical area, or a local ISP that has a more limited service area. The Web browser you use to access the Internet may be determined by your ISP. For example, users of America Online—one of the largest ISPs in the world—typically use the special AOL browser shown in Figure 2-13 to access both public Internet resources and proprietary AOL content and services only available to AOL subscribers. Most ISPs give you the option of using the browser of your choice, although you may not be able to access proprietary content and services if you don't use the recommended browser.

In addition to accessing the Internet at work, school, or on a device that you own, it is becoming more common for public locations to offer Internet access (see Figure 2-14). For example, many Starbucks coffee houses, Borders bookstores, Internet cafés, airports, and some McDonald's restaurants offer fee-based Internet access, and some taxis and trains offer free Internet service to their riders via a notebook or PDA installed in the cab or train. Free public access is also available at most public libraries.

❯ FIGURE 2-13
Web browsers and microbrowsers.

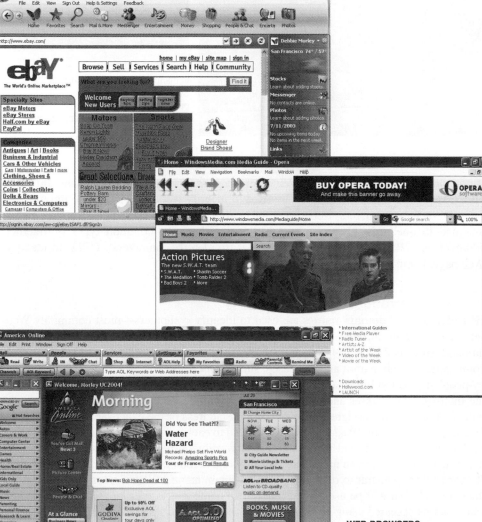

MICROBROWSERS
Display Web-based content on portable PCs and mobile devices, typically in a very efficient format with few images.

WEB BROWSERS
Shown here (top to bottom) are MSN Explorer, Opera, and the browser used with AOL.

INTERNET CAFÉS
This London Internet café offers fee-based public Internet access.

PUBLIC HOT SPOTS
In many public locations (such as the Starbucks coffee house shown here), public wireless access points provide free or fee-based Internet access to the general public.

PUBLIC LIBRARIES
Most public libraries (such as this one in San José, California) offer some free Internet access.

⊘ FIGURE 2-14
Examples of public Internet access.

Internet Addresses

Before looking at how to use a Web browser, it is important to know how **Internet addresses** work. Internet addresses are used to identify resources accessible through the Internet, such as computers, Web pages, and people. Each Internet address is unique and is assigned to one and only one person or thing. The most common types of Internet addresses are *IP addresses* and *domain names* (to identify computers); *URLs* (to identify Web pages); and *e-mail addresses* (to identify people).

IP Addresses and Domain Names

IP addresses and **domain names** are used to identify computers—most commonly Web servers—available through the Internet. IP (short for *Internet Protocol*) addresses are numeric, such as *207.46.134.222*, and are commonly used by computers to refer to other computers. Domain names are text-based, such as *microsoft.com*, and are used most often by people to request information (such as a Web page) from a computer available through the Internet. IP addresses and domain names are unique; that is, there can't be two computers on the Internet assigned the exact same IP address or the exact same domain name. To ensure this, specific IP addresses are allocated to each network to be used with the computers on that network and there is a central worldwide registration system for domain name registration. Domain names are typically registered on an annual basis; the required fee varies from registrar to registrar. When a domain name is registered, the IP address of the computer that will be used with that domain name is also registered, so the computer can either be accessed using its domain name or corresponding IP address.

>**Internet address.** What identifies a computer, person, or Web page on the Internet, such as an IP address, domain name, or e-mail address.
>**IP address.** A numeric Internet address used to uniquely identify a computer on the Internet. >**Domain name.** A text-based Internet address used to uniquely identify a computer on the Internet.

As shown in Figure 2-15, domain names typically identify who owns the computer, followed by a period and then either the computer's location or the type of organization (such as school, commercial business, government, or individual person). The rightmost part of the domain name (beginning with the period and describing the type or location of the organization) is called the *top-level*

DOMAIN NAME	ORGANIZATION	TYPE/LOCATION OF ORGANIZATION
microsoft.com	Microsoft Corporation	Commercial business
stanford.edu	Stanford University	Educational institution
fbi.gov	Federal Bureau of Investigation	Government organization
navy.mil	United States Navy	Military organization
royal.gov.uk	The British Monarchy	Government organization United Kingdom

FIGURE 2-15
Examples of domain names.

domain (TLD). The original TLDs used in the United States include *.com* (for commercial businesses), *.edu* (for educational institutions), *.gov* (for government organizations), *.org* (for noncommercial organizations), *.net* (for network providers and ISPs), and *.mil* (for military organizations). TLDs can also represent a country, such as *.us* (for United States) or *.jp* (for Japan). Because of the high demand for domain names, new top-level domains are periodically proposed to *ICANN* (*Internet Corporation for Assigned Names and Numbers*), the non-profit organization that is charged with such responsibilities as IP address allocation and domain name management. In addition to the original seven TLDs, seven new TLDs have been approved and are in the process of being implemented. Four of the newest TLDs that are currently available are *.biz* (for businesses), *.info* (for general use), *.name* (for individuals), and *.museum* (for museums). Some TLDs are restricted—for instance, only educational institutions can use the *.edu* TLD and only the government can use the *.gov* TLD; others, such as *.info*, are unrestricted, meaning anyone can register domain names using that TLD. However, only the legitimate holder of a trademarked name can use that trademarked name as a domain name.

Although many domain names consist solely of two parts, additional parts can be used to identify an organization more specifically, as in the last example in Figure 2-15. When this occurs, all of the pieces of the domain name are separated by periods.

Uniform Resource Locators (URLs)

Similar to the way an IP address or domain name uniquely identifies a computer on the Internet, a **uniform resource locator** (**URL**) uniquely identifies a Web page. URLs are comprised of a combination of the computer name and domain name of the computer on which the Web page is stored, plus the Web page's filename and the names of any folders in which the file is stored. For example, the Web page shown in Figure 2-16 is called *index.html*, and is stored in a folder called *arthur* on a Web server named *www* in the *pbskids.org* domain.

Some characteristics of the URL shown in Figure 2-16 are common to most URLs. The letters *http* stand for *Hypertext Transfer Protocol*—the protocol typically used to display Web pages. Although Web pages are the most common Internet resource accessed with a Web browser, if a different type of Internet resource is being requested, a different protocol indicator would be used. For example, the protocol *ftp://* can be used to issue requests to download files using *ftp* or *File Transfer Protocol*. The *www* at the beginning of the domain name in Figure 2-16 is the name assigned to that computer by that network's network administrator—*www* (for World Wide Web) is a very common computer name for Web servers. The file extension *.html* stands for *Hypertext Markup Language*—the language usually used to create Web pages—and is the most common file extension for Web pages. Other file extensions are possible, such as *.htm* (Hypertext Markup Language) and *.asp* (*Active Service Pages*).

TIP

URLs for *secure Web pages*—Web pages using *encryption methods* to ensure that any sensitive data (such as your social security number or credit card information) submitted using that page is not intercepted while it travels over the Internet—typically begin with *https* instead of *http*.

>**Uniform resource locator (URL).** An Internet address, usually beginning with http://, that uniquely identifies a Web page.

Web page URLs usually begin with the standard protocol identifier "http://".

This part of the URL identifies the Web server hosting the Web page.

Next comes the folder in which the Web page is stored, if necessary.

This is the filename of the Web page document that is to be retrieved and displayed.

http://www.pbskids.org/arthur/index.html

> **FIGURE 2-16**
> **A Web page URL.**

To request to see a particular Web page, you can enter its URL into the specified area (usually called the *address bar* or *location bar*), typically located toward the top of a Web browser window. Most Web browsers and Web sites allow you to leave off the *http://* and *www* parts of the URL. It is important to type a URL correctly (using the appropriate spelling, capitalization, and punctuation) or the Web browser will not be able to locate the desired Web page. However, you don't always need to type URLs to reach desired Web pages. If the Web page you are viewing contains a hyperlink to a Web page you want to visit, you can simply click the hyperlink to display the page, as illustrated shortly. There are also ways to revisit pages you've been to previously, as discussed later in this chapter.

E-Mail Addresses

To contact people using the Internet, you most often use their **e-mail addresses**. An e-mail address usually consists of a **user name** (an identifying name), followed by the @ symbol, followed by the domain name for the computer that will be handling that person's e-mail (such as a *mail server* belonging to a local ISP, America Online, Hotmail, a company, or a school). For example,

```
jsmith@course.com
maria_s@course.com
sam.peterson@course.com
```

are the e-mail addresses of three hypothetical employees at Course Technology, the publisher of this textbook, respectively assigned to jsmith (John Smith), maria_s (Maria Sanchez), and sam.peterson (Sam Peterson). User names are typically a combination of the person's first and last names and sometimes include periods, underscores, or numbers, but can't include blank spaces. To ensure a unique e-mail address for everyone in the world, user names must be unique within each domain name. So, even though there could be a *jsmith* at Course Technology using the e-mail address *jsmith@course.com* and a *jsmith* at Stanford University using the e-mail address *jsmith@stanford.edu*, the two e-mail addresses are unique. It is up to each organization to ensure that one, and only one, exact same user name is assigned under its domain. Using e-mail addresses to send e-mail messages is discussed later in this chapter. For a look at one unfortunate growing use of e-mail—*e-mail hoaxes*—see the Trend box.

>**E-mail address.** An Internet address consisting of a user name and computer domain name that uniquely identifies a person on the Internet.
>**User name.** A name that uniquely identifies a user on a particular network.

TREND

E-Mail Hoaxes

Computer hoaxes—inaccurate statements or stories—are commonly spread through e-mail today. Common *e-mail hoax* subjects include non-existent computer viruses, serious health risks of a particular product, impending terrorist attacks, chain letters, and free prizes or giveaways. Some hoaxes, like the $250 Neiman Marcus cookie recipe and free trips given away by Disney for forwarding an e-mail to a certain number of people, have been around for years and are still in circulation. Others, like the Applebee's giveaway hoax (see the accompanying illustration), are relatively new.

E-mail hoaxes are written with the purpose of being circulated to as many people as possible. Some are started as experiments to see how fast and widespread information can travel via the Internet; others originate from a joke or the desire to frighten people. Because hoaxes are so common, regardless of how realistic or frightening the information appears to be, it is a good idea to double-check any warning you receive by e-mail before forwarding it to another person. One reliable source to use is the government's Hoaxbusters site found at hoaxbusters.ciac.org. You can also use common sense to identify some hoaxes. For example, for the e-mail messages that state you will receive some sort of free prize or other reward from a known company (such as Disney or Applebee's) for forwarding the e-mail message on to others, ask yourself: how could the company possibly know who you are and if you forwarded the message? The company would need that information in order to send you your reward, so common sense would tell you that the message must

be a hoax. Some hoaxes try to get around this potential problem by stating that the companies are testing some sort of e-mail tracking program that can tell who you forwarded the message to, but that's false—there is no such type of program.

In addition to being annoying and wasting people's time reading and checking into these false stories, e-mail hoaxes bog down e-mail systems and clog up users' mailboxes. An additional problem is the embarrassment factor; that is, when all those people to whom you forwarded an e-mail hoax find out it actually is a hoax. A good rule of thumb is "better safe than sorry"—check out potential hoaxes before hitting the Forward button.

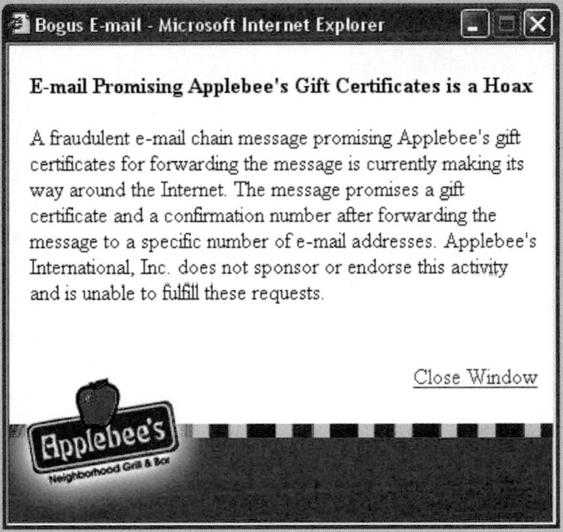

Bogus E-mail - Microsoft Internet Explorer

E-mail Promising Applebee's Gift Certificates is a Hoax

A fraudulent e-mail chain message promising Applebee's gift certificates for forwarding the message is currently making its way around the Internet. The message promises a gift certificate and a confirmation number after forwarding the message to a specific number of e-mail addresses. Applebee's International, Inc. does not sponsor or endorse this activity and is unable to fulfill these requests.

Close Window

Pronouncing Internet Addresses

Because Internet addresses are frequently given verbally, it is important to know how to pronounce them. A few guidelines are listed next, and Figure 2-17 shows some examples of Internet addresses and their proper pronunciations.

▼ If a portion of the address forms a recognizable word or name, it is spoken; otherwise it is spelled out.

▼ The @ sign is pronounced *at*.

▼ The period (.) is pronounced *dot*.

▼ The forward slash (/) is pronounced *slash*.

FIGURE 2-17
Pronouncing Internet addresses.

TYPE OF ADDRESS	SAMPLE ADDRESS	PRONUNCIATION
Domain name	berkeley.edu	berkeley dot e d u
URL	microsoft.com/windows/ie/default.asp	microsoft dot com slash windows slash i e slash default dot a s p
E-mail address	president@whitehouse.gov	president at whitehouse dot gov

Surfing the Web

Assuming you have an ISP and your PC is set up according to your ISP's directions, you are ready to start using the Internet. For most individuals, this would mean *surfing the Web*; that is, using a Web browser to view various Web sites available on the World Wide Web. In addition to being used to display Web pages, most Web browsers today can be used to perform other Internet tasks, such as downloading files, exchanging e-mail, accessing *discussion groups*, and participating in *chat sessions*. The ability to perform a variety of Internet tasks, either as part of the browser program itself or using a separate companion program that is opened automatically when needed, has made the Web browser a universal tool for exploring and using the Internet.

To start surfing the Web with a direct connection, you need to open your browser using either its desktop icon or Start menu item or a special icon or menu item placed there by your ISP (see Figure 2-18). For dial-up connections, most large ISPs include a desktop icon or Start menu item that opens your browser, dials your telephone, and establishes the Internet connection all in one step; smaller, local dial-up ISPs may require you to open your browser and start your dialing program as two separate steps. You may also be asked to enter your user name and password before being connected to the Internet; these will have been assigned or chosen during your ISP setup procedure.

Once your Web browser is open and you are connected to the Internet, the Web page currently designated as your browser's starting page or *home page* will be displayed in the browser window. Often this is the home page for the Web site belonging to your browser, school, or ISP, but you can usually change it to any page—such as a *search site* (a Web site that helps you find Web pages containing the information that you are seeking, as discussed shortly) or any other page that you plan to visit regularly—using your browser's *Options* or *Preferences* dialog box. From your browser's home page, you can move to any Web page you desire.

Two of the most widely used Web browsers, *Microsoft Internet Explorer* and *Netscape Navigator*, are illustrated in Figure 2-19. As shown in the figure, Web browsers have navigational tools to help you move forward or backward through the pages viewed in your current session, as well as buttons or menu options to print Web pages or perform other tasks. Internet Explorer and Netscape Navigator are used in the examples in this book. If you are using a different version of these browsers or a different browser altogether, the screens and steps shown in this text may look a little different than yours, but should be close enough for you to understand how to perform these actions using your browser.

TIP

The *home page* for a Web site is the starting page of that particular site; the *home page* for your browser is the Web page designated as the first page you see each time the browser is opened.

**◆ FIGURE 2-18
Connecting to the Internet.**

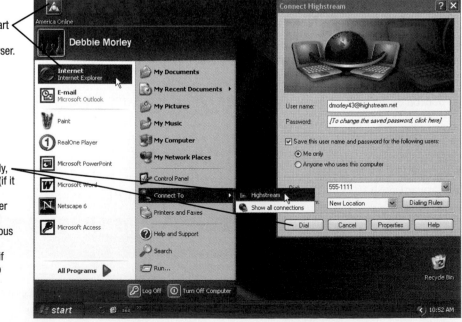

1. Use the desktop icon or Start menu item for your ISP or browser to open your browser.

2. For dial-up connections only, start your dialing program (if it doesn't start automatically when you start your browser program or if your browser was still open from a previous session), then supply your user name and password, if necessary, and click *Dial* to connect to the Internet.

MICROSOFT INTERNET EXPLORER

Title bar

Menu bar

Navigation buttons

Explorer bar

Hyperlinks

Status bar

Internet Explorer logo

Address bar

Scroll bar

NETSCAPE NAVIGATOR

Title bar

Menu bar

Navigation buttons

Browser window tab bar

My Sidebar

Hyperlinks

Status bar

Netscape logo

Location bar

Personal toolbar

Scroll bar

INTERNET EXPLORER	NETSCAPE	DESCRIPTION
		Back is used to move back to a page that has already been displayed during the current Internet session.
		Forward is used to move forward again after using the Back button to move to a previous page.
		Print allows you to print the page that is currently displayed.
		Stop stops the transfer of a page while it is being loaded (useful when a page is taking a long time to display).
		Refresh or *Reload* redisplays the current page (useful if an error prevented the page from loading properly or you want to reload a page that changes frequently, such as one containing stock quotes).

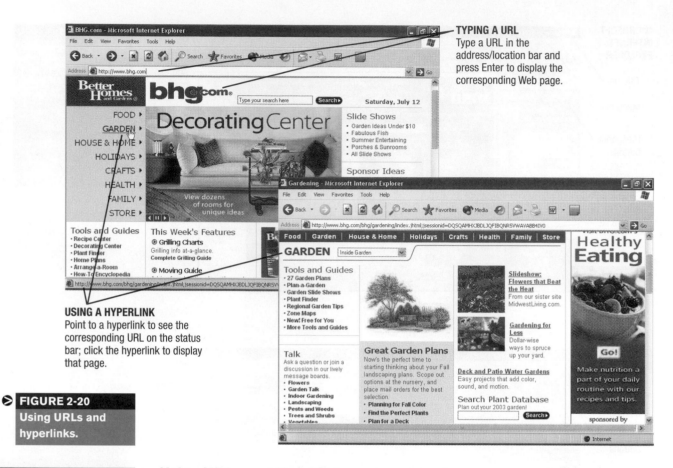

TYPING A URL
Type a URL in the address/location bar and press Enter to display the corresponding Web page.

USING A HYPERLINK
Point to a hyperlink to see the corresponding URL on the status bar; click the hyperlink to display that page.

➤ **FIGURE 2-20**
Using URLs and hyperlinks.

TIP

If you get an error message when trying to load a Web page, first check the spelling of the URL (if you entered it into the address/location bar) and correct it if needed. Next, press Enter to try to load the page again, in case the server was busy. As a last resort, edit the URL to remove any folder or filenames and press Enter to try to load the home page of that site.

Using URLs and Hyperlinks

To change from your browser's starting Web page to a new Web page for which you know the URL, type that URL in the browser's address bar or location bar and press Enter (see Figure 2-20). You can either edit the existing URL or delete it and type a new one, but be sure to match the spelling, capitalization, and punctuation exactly. If you don't know the appropriate URL to type, you can type the URL for a search site and then use that search site to search for an appropriate page, as discussed a little later in this chapter.

If there is a hyperlink displayed for a page you want to visit, you can click the hyperlink to display the page associated with that link. Remember, hyperlinks can be either text- or image-based, and, though text-based hyperlinks are often underlined, they may instead be displayed in a different color or underlined only when pointed to (as in Figure 2-20). If you are not sure if text or a graphic on a page is a hyperlink, rest the mouse pointer on it for a moment. If the item you are pointing to is a hyperlink, the pointer should change to a pointing hand. The URL of the page that will be displayed if the hyperlink is clicked is also listed on the status bar, as shown in the first screen in Figure 2-20. Once you click a hyperlink, that Web page is displayed. To return to a previous page, click the Back button on your browser's toolbar. To print the current Web page, use the browser's Print button or select *Print* from the browser's File menu.

Things You May Encounter on a Web Page

You will encounter a variety of objects on Web pages as you explore the World Wide Web. Although we can't go into an in-depth discussion of the various possible Web-page components here, it is good to be a familiar with the most common ones so you'll know how to use them as you encounter them. Some common things you may run into are listed next and illustrated in Figure 2-21.

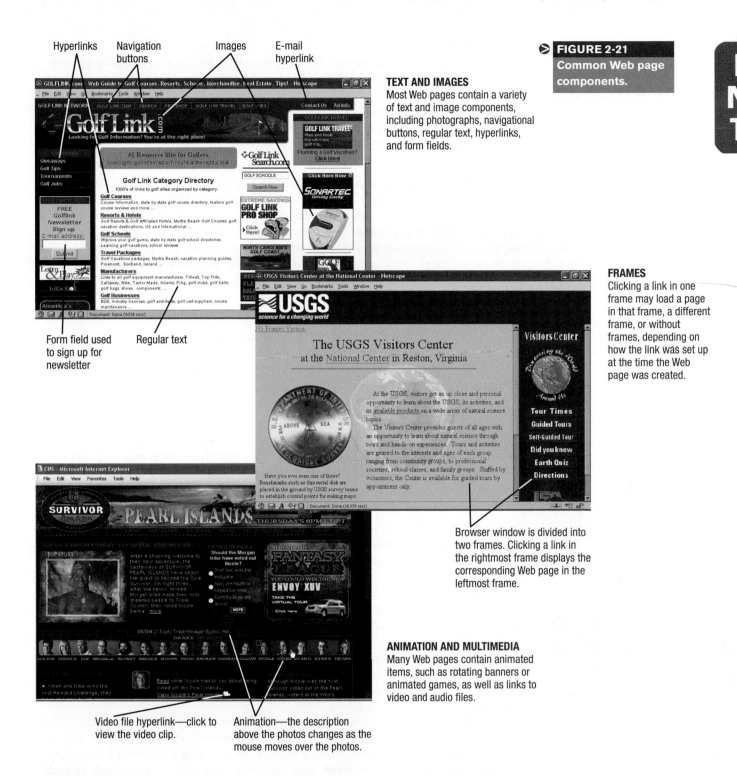

Hyperlinks   Navigation buttons   Images   E-mail hyperlink

> **FIGURE 2-21**
> **Common Web page components.**

INT

TEXT AND IMAGES
Most Web pages contain a variety of text and image components, including photographs, navigational buttons, regular text, hyperlinks, and form fields.

Form field used to sign up for newsletter

Regular text

FRAMES
Clicking a link in one frame may load a page in that frame, a different frame, or without frames, depending on how the link was set up at the time the Web page was created.

Browser window is divided into two frames. Clicking a link in the rightmost frame displays the corresponding Web page in the leftmost frame.

ANIMATION AND MULTIMEDIA
Many Web pages contain animated items, such as rotating banners or animated games, as well as links to video and audio files.

Video file hyperlink—click to view the video clip.

Animation—the description above the photos changes as the mouse moves over the photos.

Text and Images
Most Web pages contain regular text and text-based hyperlinks. Images can include photographs, logos, navigational buttons and icons, and images to be downloaded. A single image that has specific areas individually linked to different Web pages is called an *image map*.

E-Mail Hyperlinks
Hyperlinks to an e-mail address start an e-mail message to the person specified in the link, using your default e-mail program. E-mail hyperlinks start with *mailto:*instead of *http://*.

Form Fields

Many Web pages contain forms used to submit questions, feedback, registration information, or order information. To complete a form, fill in the form fields and then click the Submit button that is usually located at the bottom of the form. Some Web pages contain a single form field for searching or navigational purposes—choose the desired topic from the supplied list or type the desired search term in the designated box and then click the Go button or other navigation button next to the field.

Frames

Frames divide the browser window into separate areas, each containing a different Web page that scrolls individually. Frames are often used to keep a Web page's navigation bar always visible in one frame while the contents of the other frames change as you click on hyperlinks in the navigation frame. The frame in which a new page will load when a hyperlink is clicked is determined by the Web page author when the Web page is created. You can resize the frames by dragging the frame borders with the mouse, unless this capability has been turned off by the Web page author.

Animation

The most common types of animation on a Web page are *animated GIFs* (series of small images displayed one after another to simulate movement), *Java applets* (small programs executed by your browser, such as a scrolling marquee or stock ticker), and *Shockwave* or *Flash* applications (commonly used for games, interactive items, and other types of animation). Animation is discussed in more detail in Chapter 10.

Multimedia

Web pages can automatically play audio or video when the page is loaded; alternately, a page may contain links to play or download audio and video files. Some Web pages contain links to download images, as well. Downloading files from a Web page and multimedia in general are discussed in later chapters of this book.

Using Bookmarks and the History List

Virtually all browsers have a *bookmarks* or *favorites* feature that will save the Web page addresses you specify so that you can return to them easily without typing their URLs. It is common practice to create bookmarks for any page you want to visit on a regular basis. To create a bookmark for a page you are currently viewing, select the appropriate *Add* option from your browser's Bookmarks or Favorites menu. Once a page is bookmarked, selecting that bookmark from the bookmarks or favorites list will redisplay that page. Because bookmark lists can get large and unwieldy, browsers typically have an option on their Bookmarks or Favorites menu that allows you to delete outdated bookmarks or move bookmarks into folders to keep them organized. Some browsers, such as Internet Explorer, can also display the bookmarks or favorites list in a separate pane on the screen so they are always available (click the Favorites toolbar button to turn this feature on or off in Internet Explorer).

In addition to a bookmark or favorites list, browsers usually maintain a *History list*, which is a record of all Web pages visited in the last few weeks (how long a page stays in the History list depends on your browser settings). If you want to revisit a page you've been to recently that isn't bookmarked, click the History button (if one is available on your browser) or select the *History* option from the menu (sometimes located under the Tools menu) to display the History list, and then select the desired page. Figure 2-22 illustrates how to use bookmarks and the History list.

TIP

To open a second browser window to work with two Web pages at one time, select the *New Window* option from your browser's File menu. In recent versions of Netscape Navigator, open windows can be overlapped and the browser window *Tab bar* used to switch between them.

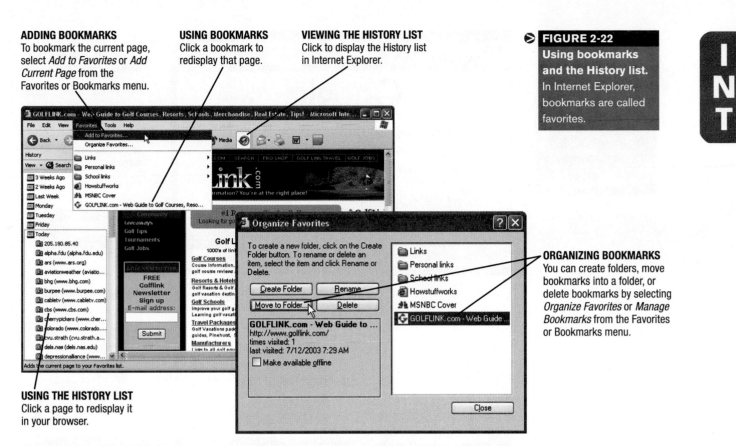

ADDING BOOKMARKS
To bookmark the current page, select *Add to Favorites* or *Add Current Page* from the Favorites or Bookmarks menu.

USING BOOKMARKS
Click a bookmark to redisplay that page.

VIEWING THE HISTORY LIST
Click to display the History list in Internet Explorer.

FIGURE 2-22
Using bookmarks and the History list. In Internet Explorer, bookmarks are called favorites.

ORGANIZING BOOKMARKS
You can create folders, move bookmarks into a folder, or delete bookmarks by selecting *Organize Favorites* or *Manage Bookmarks* from the Favorites or Bookmarks menu.

USING THE HISTORY LIST
Click a page to redisplay it in your browser.

Searching the Web

While casual surfing is a popular Web pastime, people often turn to the Internet to find specific types of information. When you know generally what you want but don't know where to find it, one of your best options is to perform an *Internet search*. There are a number of special Web pages, called *search sites*, available to help you locate what you are looking for on the Internet; numerous *reference sites* are also available to look up addresses, telephone numbers, ZIP codes, maps, and other information. Many recent browsers also contain built-in search and reference capabilities.

Search Sites

Search sites are Web sites designed specifically to help you find Web pages. Most search sites use a *search engine*—a special software program—in conjunction with a huge database of information about Web pages to help visitors find Web pages that contain the information that they are seeking. These databases are usually updated automatically on a regular basis, although some use human editors to manually classify the Web pages according to content.

To begin a search using a search site, type the URL for the desired search site in the address/location bar; most search sites—such as *Yahoo!*, *Excite*, *Ask Jeeves*, and *Google*—are available for use free of charge. These sites are also often classified as *portal pages*, which are Web pages that people visit often for information and may want to use as their browser's home page. Search sites usually allow two types of search operations: (1) typing in keywords or (2) selecting categories (see Figure 2-23).

FURTHER EXPLORATION

For links to further information about search and reference Web sites, go to www.course.com/uc10/ch02

>**Search site.** A Web site designed to help users search for Web pages that match specified keywords or selected categories.

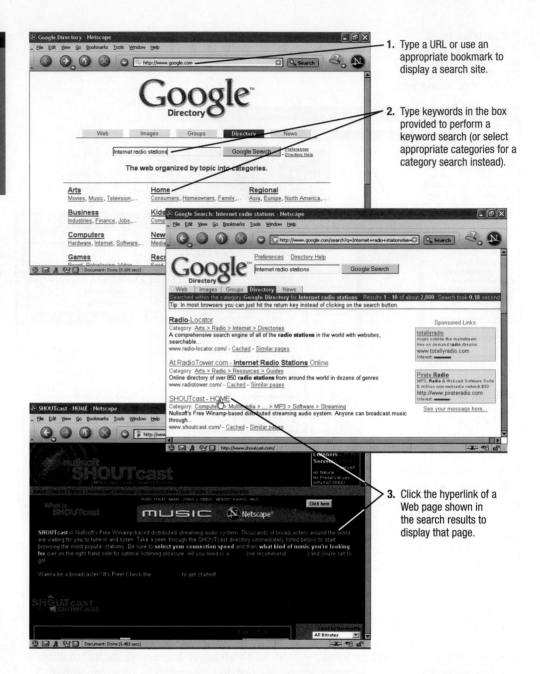

FIGURE 2-23

Web searching.
Many search sites—such as Google shown here—allow you to search by entering keywords, selecting categories, or using a combination of both search methods.

1. Type a URL or use an appropriate bookmark to display a search site.

2. Type keywords in the box provided to perform a keyword search (or select appropriate categories for a category search instead).

3. Click the hyperlink of a Web page shown in the search results to display that page.

TIP

Many browsers allow you to perform a simple keyword search by entering keywords in the address/location bar and pressing Enter.

To use the first type of search operation—using keywords—the search site must contain a search box. To perform a keyword search, enter appropriate keywords describing what you are looking for in the search box and press Enter; the site's search engine then returns a list of matching pages that can be viewed by clicking the desired page's hyperlink. With a keyword search you can usually enter more than one keyword—most sites put the pages containing all of the words that you type at the top of the search results. You can also use special operators, such as the plus key (+), minus key (–), and quotation marks (" "), for a more specific search. For example, you may want to see only pages containing all of your specified keywords or see pages containing one keyword but not another. Usually search tips are available on each search site to explain the various search options for that site; look for a search help or search tips hyperlink on the site's home page.

With the second type of search—selecting categories—a list of categories is displayed on the screen. After clicking a category hyperlink, you are presented with a list of more specific subcategories for the main category that you selected, plus often a list of matching Web pages. To reach more specific subcategories and matching Web pages, keep selecting categories. Whenever the name of an appropriate Web page appears in the list of matching Web pages, clicking its hyperlink displays that page. A search site that utilizes category searching is sometimes called a *directory*.

As illustrated in Figure 2-23, many search sites allow you to use a combination of keywords and categories. Often, starting with keywords and then selecting categories if appropriate Web pages are not immediately listed is an efficient way to utilize a search site.

Reference Sites

Many search sites include some reference functions to help you easily locate maps, addresses, and other reference information. There are also many specialty sites for these purposes, including online telephone directories, atlases, dictionaries, thesauruses, encyclopedias, mapping services, and so forth. To find such sites, check out the "Web Guide" section in the References and Resources Guide located at the end of this book or type the category of the information you are looking for (such as "ZIP code lookup" or "topographical maps") in a search site's search box.

TIP

For more searching tips, see Chapter 9 and the "Web Searching Tips" section of the References and Resources Guide located at the end of this book.

E-MAIL AND OTHER TYPES OF ONLINE COMMUNICATIONS

Electronic mail (more commonly called **e-mail**) refers to electronic messages exchanged between computers over a network—usually the Internet. It is one of the most widely used Internet applications—Americans alone send billions of e-mail messages daily. If you are connected to the Internet, you can send an e-mail message to anyone who has an Internet e-mail address. As illustrated in Figure 2-24, e-mail messages travel from the sender's PC to his or her ISP, and then through the Internet to the recipient's ISP. When the recipient logs on to the Internet and requests his or her e-mail, it is sent to that PC. Because e-mail is stored for an individual until he or she requests it, the sender and the receiver do not have to be online at the same time to exchange e-mail. In addition to text, e-mail messages can include photos and other graphics, as well as attached files.

In order to send or receive e-mail, you typically use an *e-mail program* (such as *Netscape Mail*, *Microsoft Outlook Express*, *Microsoft Outlook*, or a proprietary mail program used by your ISP) that is set up with your name, e-mail address, incoming mail server, and outgoing mail server information. Once your e-mail program has been successfully set up, you don't need to specify this information again, unless you want to check mail from a different e-mail account, change ISPs, or check your e-mail from a different PC. Some browsers allow multiple e-mail accounts (such as both a personal and school account) to be set up at one time. Others support only one e-mail account at a time, so the settings must be changed to check a different e-mail account.

Web-based e-mail—such as *Hotmail* and *Yahoo! Mail*—works a little differently. Instead of downloading messages from your ISP's mail server to your PC and then viewing them with your e-mail program, Web-based e-mail messages are displayed on a Web page

>**Electronic mail (e-mail).** Electronic messages sent from one user to another over the Internet or other network.

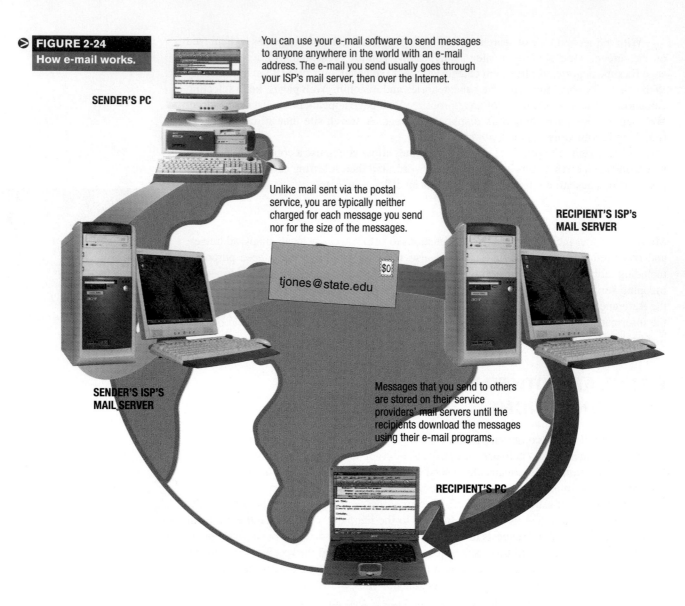

> **FIGURE 2-24**
> **How e-mail works.**

SENDER'S PC

You can use your e-mail software to send messages to anyone anywhere in the world with an e-mail address. The e-mail you send usually goes through your ISP's mail server, then over the Internet.

Unlike mail sent via the postal service, you are typically neither charged for each message you send nor for the size of the messages.

tjones@state.edu

$0

RECIPIENT'S ISP's MAIL SERVER

SENDER'S ISP'S MAIL SERVER

Messages that you send to others are stored on their service providers' mail servers until the recipients download the messages using their e-mail programs.

RECIPIENT'S PC

set up by the Web-based e-mail provider. To view a Web page containing your mail, you just type your user name and password in the designated location on the mail service's Web page. Web-based e-mail is more flexible, since a user's e-mail can be accessed from any computer without changing the e-mail settings. In addition, Web-based e-mail is typically stored on the Web-based e-mail provider's server, which means that all e-mail that has been sent to a user's e-mail address is available to the user regardless of which computers were used to retrieve each message. Consequently, Web-based e-mail is a popular option for travelers, students, and other users who switch between computers frequently. One disadvantage of Web-based e-mail is that it tends to work more slowly than an e-mail program installed on a PC. Some ISPs have Web-based e-mail service and give their subscribers the choice of using either an e-mail program, Web-based e-mail, or both, as the need arises.

Most ISPs used with desktop and portable PCs include e-mail service in their monthly fee and do not charge additional fees for sending or receiving e-mail messages. However, some wireless providers (such as those used with handheld PCs and smart phones) charge an additional fee for e-mail exchanges, if the total number or size of the e-mail messages sent and received during a billing period exceeds a specified limit. Web-based e-mail is typically available as a free service.

For an explanation of how *video e-mail* works, see the How it Works box.

HOW IT WORKS

Video E-Mail

Although off to a slow start, primarily due to slow Internet connections and the large file size video recordings typically require, *video e-mail* is currently available and expected to grow in popularity in the near future. Some e-mail providers, such as Yahoo! Mail and AT&T WorldNet, offer free video e-mail as part of their service, although there is often a limit on the number of total recording and viewing minutes utilized per person, per month, and usually minutes are deducted from your allotment when the video is sent, as well as each time it is played by the recipient. There are also third-party services that can be used to attach video e-mail messages to any regular e-mail message; normally these services charge a monthly fee for a set number of total recording and viewing minutes. Today's video e-mails are typically stored and delivered from the provider's server, which frees up storage space on both the sender's and recipient's PCs, and speeds up delivery time, although some services allow recipients to download the videos to their PC, if desired. Videos are usually played using a standard media player program, such as Windows Media Player, installed on the recipient's PC; some services use a Java applet or proprietary player program instead.

An example of sending and receiving a video e-mail is shown in the accompanying figure. To send a video e-mail, the sender usually completes the send to and subject information, the same as with a regular e-mail message. Next, a record button is clicked and the sender's PC microphone and video camera are used to capture the message. Some services allow the sender to import prerecorded video—such as video taken with a digital camcorder, from a hard drive, or from another storage medium—to be sent instead of a video recorded using the video e-mail program. In either case, the video message can usually be previewed and rerecorded, if needed, before it is sent. Some services also allow the sender to select an appropriate viewing size for the video to match the speed of the recipient's Internet connection. When the Send button is clicked, the message is sent to the video e-mail provider, who delivers it to the recipient. Usually either the video starts to play automatically when the e-mail message is opened by the recipient (as long as the recipient is connected to the Internet so that the video on the video e-mail server can be accessed), or the e-mail contains a hyperlink to play the message from the video e-mail server.

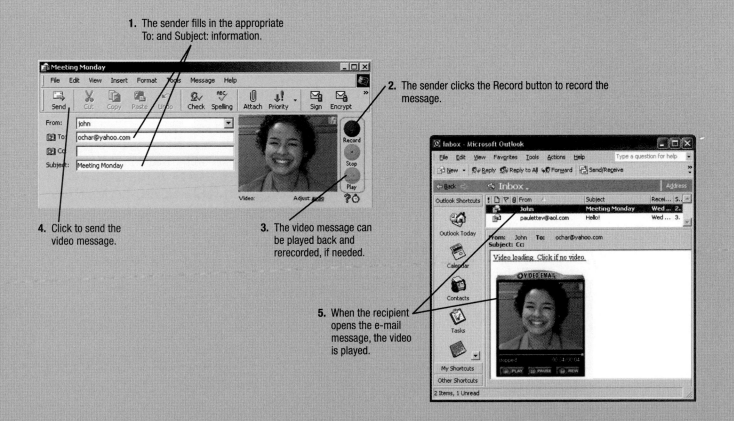

1. The sender fills in the appropriate To: and Subject: information.

2. The sender clicks the Record button to record the message.

4. Click to send the video message.

3. The video message can be played back and rerecorded, if needed.

5. When the recipient opens the e-mail message, the video is played.

TIP

To add someone who sent you an e-mail message to your address book, right-click on the sender's e-mail address and choose an option such as *Add Sender to Address Book*.

TIP

If you have an always-on Internet connection, you can leave your e-mail program open and instruct it to automatically download new messages so you will see your e-mail messages as soon as they arrive.

Sending E-Mail

To send an e-mail message, first open your e-mail program and select the appropriate option to start a new message. Type one or more e-mail addresses in the To: box, enter an appropriate subject line, and then type the message in the appropriate area (see Figure 2-25). Send the message using the Send toolbar button. To start an e-mail message using an e-mail hyperlink (such as sales@abc.com, customer.service@123.com, or johnb@xyz.edu) located on a Web page, simply click that link.

To make it easier to send e-mails to people you contact frequently, you can add their names, nicknames, and their e-mail addresses to your e-mail program's *address book*. When you begin to type a name or nickname in a To: box, the e-mail program will then fill in the appropriate e-mail address automatically.

Receiving E-Mail

In order to receive a new e-mail message, it must be retrieved from your ISP. To retrieve new e-mail messages waiting for you at your ISP's mail server, open your e-mail program. If your new messages are not retrieved automatically, click the appropriate toolbar button, such as Get Msg or Send/Recv (refer to the bottom screens in Figure 2-25). To read a specific e-mail message, click it; double-clicking an e-mail message typically opens the message in a new window for easier reading.

All new e-mail messages are usually placed in your *Inbox* folder. Once an e-mail message is displayed, it can be printed, replied to, forwarded to someone else, filed into a different folder, or deleted using your e-mail program's toolbar buttons.

Managing E-Mail

When you send e-mail, copies of the messages that you send are typically stored in a folder named Sent, Sent Items, Sent Messages, or something similar so that you can read them or resend them, if necessary. These messages remain there, and your retrieved e-mail messages remain in your Inbox folder, until you delete them or move them into a different folder (you can create new folders in most e-mail programs, as needed). Once an e-mail message is deleted, it is usually moved into a special folder for deleted items (called Trash, Deleted Items, Trash Can, or something similar). Messages in a deleted items folder typically remain there until you permanently delete them by selecting the appropriate option (such as *Empty Trash* from Netscape Mail's File menu or *Empty 'Deleted Items' Folder* from Outlook Express' Edit menu). Some Web-based e-mail services empty trash folders for you on a regular basis.

As already mentioned, Web-based e-mail messages are usually stored on the e-mail service's mail server. Typically each user is allotted a specific amount of space for messages; when that limit is reached, the user needs to either delete some messages to make room or purchase additional storage space. With non-Web-based e-mail, your messages may be kept solely on your ISP's mail server, on both your PC and the mail server, or only on your PC, depending on your ISP and how your e-mail program is set up on your PC. While you will likely have a limit on the amount of e-mail that can be stored for you at your ISP's mail server, the only limit on mail downloaded to your PC is your hard drive capacity. Deleting unneeded messages frees up space on your hard drive (for setups that download messages to the user's PC) or on your mail service's server (for Web-based e-mail and setups that store e-mail on the mail server).

SENDING E-MAIL
This example uses Netscape Mail.

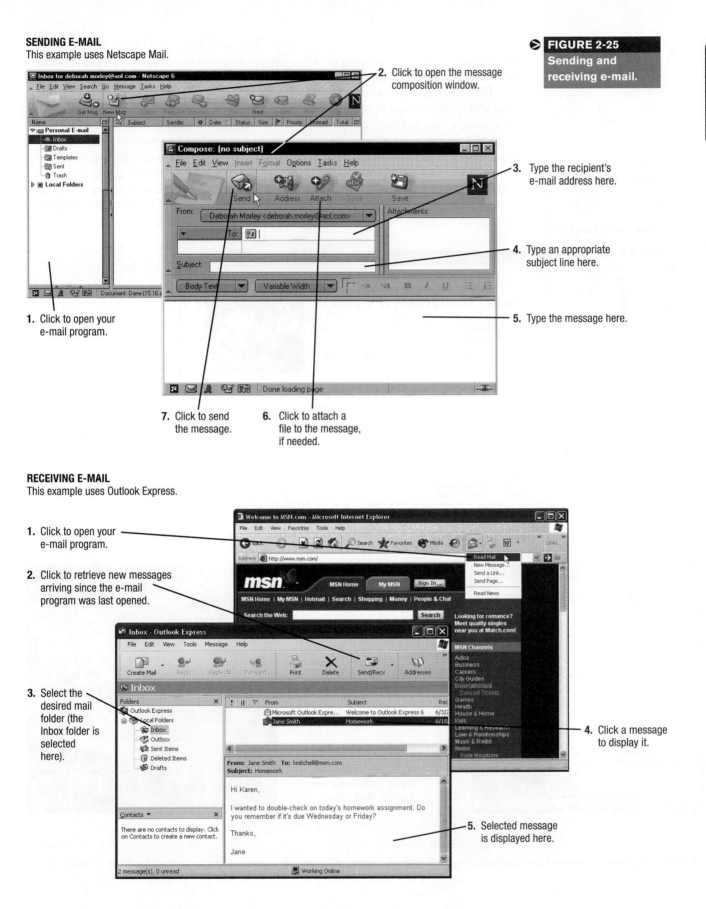

FIGURE 2-25
Sending and receiving e-mail.

2. Click to open the message composition window.

3. Type the recipient's e-mail address here.

4. Type an appropriate subject line here.

5. Type the message here.

1. Click to open your e-mail program.

7. Click to send the message.

6. Click to attach a file to the message, if needed.

RECEIVING E-MAIL
This example uses Outlook Express.

1. Click to open your e-mail program.

2. Click to retrieve new messages arriving since the e-mail program was last opened.

3. Select the desired mail folder (the Inbox folder is selected here).

4. Click a message to display it.

5. Selected message is displayed here.

INT

Discussion Groups, Chat, Instant Messaging, and More

In addition to e-mail, other types of online communications exist. A few of these applications are discussed next and illustrated in Figure 2-26.

Discussion groups (also called *message boards*, *newsgroups*, or *online forums*) facilitate written discussions between people on specific subjects, such as computers, movies, gardening, music, hobbies, and political views. When a participant posts a message, it is displayed for anyone accessing the message board to read and respond to. Messages are organized by topics (called *threads*). Participants can post new messages in response to an existing message and stay within that thread, or they can post discussion group messages that start brand new threads. Many discussion groups can be accessed with just a Web browser, as in Figure 2-26; others require a *newsreader* (a special program for handling newsgroup messages that is often incorporated into e-mail programs).

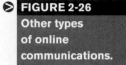

FIGURE 2-26
Other types of online communications.

DISCUSSION GROUPS
Allow individuals to carry on written discussions with a variety of people on a specific topic; since messages remain on the site once they are posted, users don't need to be online at the same time to participate.

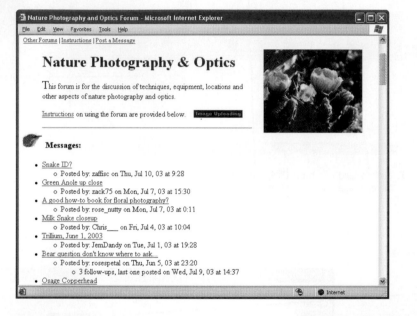

INSTANT MESSAGING
Enables real-time written conversations with friends and other "buddies" who are online at the same time.

VIDEOCONFERENCING
Allows multiple individuals to talk with and see each other during a real-time online meeting. Used both by individuals and businesses.

>**Discussion group.** An Internet communications medium that enables individuals to post messages on a particular topic for others to read and respond to.

A **chat room** is an Internet service that allows multiple users to *chat* or exchange *real-time* typed messages. Unlike e-mail and discussion groups, chat participants are online at the same time and carry on interactive typed conversations. Like discussion groups, chat rooms are typically set up for specific topics. While most chat sessions are open to anyone, an individual can set up a private chat room that is reserved only for users (typically family, friends, or coworkers) who know the proper password.

Instant messaging (**IM**) is a form of private chat that is set up to exchange real-time messages easily with people on your *buddy list*—a list of individuals (such as family, friends, and business associates) that you specify. Popular instant messaging services include *AOL Instant Messenger*, *MSN Messenger*, *Windows Messenger*, and *Yahoo! Messenger*. Because there is no single IM standard at the present time, you and your buddies must use the same (or compatible) instant messaging systems in order to exchange instant messages. Whenever one of your buddies is online (the IM program typically indicates who is available and who is not), you can send a short message to that person and it immediately appears on his or her computer. Typically both the messages that you type and that you receive are displayed within the instant messaging window. In addition to just sending typed messages, IM programs typically include other options, such as sending a photo or file, starting a voice or video conversation, using a shared whiteboard, and more. Still a popular communications method between friends (over 29 million people used AOL Instant Messenger in one month in 2003), IM has also become a valuable business tool. Instant messaging also frequently takes place on mobile phones.

Videoconferencing (also called *teleconferencing* or *Web conferencing*) refers to the use of computers, video cameras, microphones, and other communications technologies to conduct face-to-face meetings via the Internet among people in different locations. Small videoconferences can take place using the participants' PCs; large group conferences may require a more sophisticated setup, such as a dedicated teleconferencing room containing video cameras, large monitors, microphones, and other hardware. Most videoconferences are two-way, with both users sending and receiving video. Some uses for one-way Internet videoconferencing include PC cameras located in childcare centers to allow parents to watch live video of their children throughout the day, and surveillance PC cameras set up in homes and offices to check for intruders and other problems when the location is unoccupied.

Internet telephony is the process of placing telephone calls over the Internet, usually either from your PC to the recipient's PC or from your PC to the recipient's telephone, depending on the setup. Although some free Internet telephony is available for PC-to-PC phone calls—such as those supported by some IM programs—usually there is a charge involved; however, the fee is typically less than for traditional long-distance phone service. Many believe that placing telephone calls through the Internet—also referred to as *voice over IP* (*VoIP*)—will soon be the norm.

Netiquette

A special etiquette—referred to as **netiquette**—has evolved to guide online behavior. Most netiquette has to do with written online communications, such as e-mail, discussion groups, and chat. A good rule of thumb is always to be polite and considerate of others, and to refrain from offensive remarks. This holds true whether you are asking a question via a company's e-mail address, posting a discussion group message, or chatting with a friend. Many users are much more casual with e-mail than with more formal communications, but you should be careful, especially when the communications involve business—check your grammar and spelling to avoid embarrassing yourself. Some specific netiquette guidelines are listed in Figure 2-27.

TIP

Another online communications possibility is the *blog* or *Weblog*— a Web page that serves as a publicly-accessible personal journal for an individual.

TIP

Most e-mail programs have an option—usually in the form of a toolbar button or menu option—to check the spelling of a message before sending it. It is a good idea to use this spell-check option on all business or otherwise important e-mail messages before sending them.

>**Chat room.** An Internet service that allows multiple users to exchange written messages in real time. >**Instant messaging (IM).** A form of private chat set up to allow users to easily and quickly exchange real-time typed messages with the individuals they specify. >**Videoconferencing.** The use of computers, video cameras, microphones, and other communications technologies to conduct face-to-face meetings over the Internet. >**Internet telephony.** The process of placing telephone calls over the Internet. >**Netiquette.** An etiquette for guiding online behavior.

FIGURE 2-27

Netiquette. Use these netiquette guidelines and common sense when communicating online.

Use descriptive subject lines	Use short, descriptive titles for e-mail messages and newsgroup posts. For example, "Question regarding MP3 downloads" is much better than a vague title, such as "Question."
Don't shout	SHOUTING REFERS TO TYPING YOUR ENTIRE E-MAIL MESSAGE USING CAPITAL LETTERS. Use capital letters only when it is grammatically correct to do so or for emphasizing a few words.
Watch what you say	Things that you say or write online can be interpreted as being sexist, racist, ethnocentric, xenophobic, or in just general bad taste. Also check spelling and grammar—nobody likes wading through poorly written materials.
Use emoticons and abbreviations	Use *emoticons* to add emotion to your messages, and use abbreviations and acronyms to save time and make your messages shorter (see the Inside the Industry box for some examples).
Avoid e-mail overload	Don't send *spam mail*—unsolicated bulk e-mails—the Internet equivalent of junk mail. Same goes for forwarding e-mail chain letters or every joke you run across to everyone in your address book.
Read the FAQs	*FAQs* are *frequently asked questions* with the corresponding answers. Reading an FAQ list will help you to avoid common mistakes in protocol that could disrupt a newsgroup or waste a company contact's time answering a question already covered in the FAQs.
Lurk before you leap	*Lurking* refers to observing a newsgroup's activities for a period of time to get the particular spin of the group, before actively participating.
Avoid flame mail	Avoid *flame mail*—caustic or inflammatory remarks directed toward specific individuals. That includes taking part in flame wars, in which several people participate in sending inappropriate messages.

SOCIETAL IMPLICATIONS OF CYBERSPACE

Many people today cannot imagine life without the Internet. The vast amount of useful information and entertainment available through the World Wide Web and other Internet resources has made going online a normal everyday activity for many of us. For countless individuals, exchanging e-mail is as common a means of communication as the telephone. And many of us won't think about making a major purchase (such as a DVD player, computer, or refrigerator) without first researching it online. In fact, it is surprising how fast the Internet and its resources have become an integral part of our society. But despite all its benefits, cyberspace has some risks. How many of us really think about how our online activities might adversely affect us? Some of the most important societal implications of cyberspace surround our security and privacy.

Security

One of the most common online security risks today is your PC becoming infected with a *computer virus*—a software program designed to change the way a computer operates, without the permission or knowledge of the user. Computer viruses often cause damage to the infected PC, such as erasing data or bogging down the computer so it doesn't function well. Viruses can be attached to a program (such as one downloaded from the Internet), as well as to an e-mail message. To help protect your computer from viruses, never open attachments from someone you don't know or that have an executable *file extension* (the last three letters in the filename preceded by a period), such as *.exe*, *.com*, or *.vbs*, without first checking with the sender to make sure the attachment is legitimate. It is also a good idea to install an *antivirus program* on your PC and set it up to scan all e-mail messages, attachments, and files before they are downloaded to make sure they are virus-free, as well as to scan your entire PC periodically for viruses. If a virus is found in a file attached to an e-mail message, the antivirus program will delete the infected file before the message appears in your Inbox; if a virus is found on your PC, the antivirus program will try to remove it. Protecting your PC from viruses, as well as other increasingly common security concerns—such as *identity theft* and data loss due to user error, hardware failure, computer viruses, or other problems—will be discussed in more detail in later chapters.

Privacy

Some individuals view the potential risk to personal privacy as one of the most important issues regarding our networked society. As more and more data about our everyday activities is collected and stored in databases, our privacy is at risk because the potential for privacy violations increases. Today, data is collected about practically anything we buy online or offline, although offline purchases may not be associated with our identity unless we use a credit card or make the purchase at a store using a membership or loyalty card. At issue is not that data is collected—with virtually all organizations using computers for record-keeping that's just going to happen—but how the data is used. Privacy concerns and precautions are discussed in more detail in Chapter 15.

Differences in Online Communications

As you spend more and more time communicating online, you will probably notice some differences between online communications methods (e-mail, chat, and discussion groups, for example) and traditional communications methods (such as telephone calls and written letters). In general, online communications tend to be much less formal. This may be because people usually compose e-mail messages fairly quickly and just send them off, often not taking the time to reread and consider their message content or check their spelling or grammar. There is no doubt that e-mail has helped speed up both personal and business communications and has made them more efficient (no more telephone tag, for instance). However, we all need to be careful not to get so casual in our communications—particularly business communications—that our communications become too personal with people we don't know or appear unprofessional.

For a look at another trend in online communications—the use of acronyms (abbreviations) and *emoticons*—see the Inside the Industry box.

The Anonymity Factor

By their very nature, online communications lend themselves to *anonymity*. Since recipients usually don't hear senders' voices or even see their handwriting, it is difficult to know for sure who the sender is. Particularly in discussion groups and chat rooms, where individuals traditionally use made-up user names instead of real names, there is an anonymous feel to being online.

Being anonymous gives many individuals a sense of freedom, which makes them feel able to say or do anything online. This sense of true freedom of speech can be beneficial. For example, a reserved individual who might never complain about a poor product or service in person may feel comfortable lodging a complaint by e-mail. In political newsgroups or chat discussions, many people feel they can be completely honest about what they think and can introduce new ideas and points of view without inhibition. Anonymous e-mail is also a safe way for an employee to blow the whistle on a questionable business practice, or for an individual to tip off police to a crime or potential terrorist attack.

But, like all good things, online anonymity can be abused. Using the Internet as their shield, some people use rude comments, ridicule, profanity, and even slander to attack people, places, and things they don't like or agree with. Others may use multiple online identities (such as assuming two or more different user names in a discussion group) to give the appearance of increased support for their point of view. Still others, feeling that their identities are protected, may use multiple identities to try to manipulate stock prices (such as by posting multiple negative messages or false information about a company to drive the price

INSIDE THE INDUSTRY

Emoticons and Acronyms: Expressing Yourself Online

One disadvantage of written communications as compared to spoken or in-person conversations is that the emotions of the individuals are not easily conveyed. Since you can't see the individual's face, it is sometimes difficult to tell if a comment is serious or if the person is joking or being facetious. When someone writes a sarcastic or joking comment in an e-mail or discussion group message that was meant to be funny, it will likely be taken seriously unless the person somehow can express the emotional context in which the comment should be read. For this purpose, *emoticons*–short for *emotional icons*

and also called "smileys"–were developed. Emoticons are illustrations of faces showing smiles, frowns, and other expressions, such as the popular :-) smile emoticon (tilt your head to the left to view it), that are created with the keyboard symbols to add emotions to written online communications. With some programs, the symbols you type are changed into actual faces, such as ☺. *Acronyms* are abbreviations for commonly used phrases, such as BTW for "by the way" (see the accompanying table), that are used instead of the full phrase to save time. Acronyms are also commonly used in text messaging and e-mail messages sent with wireless phones and handheld PCs, because text entry is fairly slow.

ACRONYMS		EMOTICONS	
Acronym	Stands for	Symbol	Meaning
ROTFL	"Rolling on the floor laughing"	:-)	Smile
LOL	"Laughing out loud"	:-(	Frown
BTW	"By the way"	;-)	Wink
IMHO	"In my humble opinion"	:-D	Laugh
TTFN	"Ta ta for now"	:-P	Sticking out tongue
BTDT	"Been there, done that"	:->	Sarcastic
BRB	"Be right back"	>:-<	Angry
SAT	"Sorry about that"	<:-)	Dumb
GG	"Gotta go"	:-S	Kind of like it
YGTBK	"You've got to be kidding"	:-O	Surprise
CW2CU	"Can't wait to see you"	(@@)	You're kidding!
JAS	"Just a second"	((H))	Big hug

down), get buyers to trust an online auction seller (by posting fake untrue positive feedback comments about themselves), and other illegal or unethical acts. Over the past few years, there has been a growing number of lawsuits demanding that ISPs reveal the true identities of people posting controversial or potentially libelous discussion group messages online. Typically ISPs will comply with subpoenas for such information, but free speech advocates fear the use of such lawsuits to silence anonymous critics or punish whistle-blowing employees.

It is possible to hide your true identity while browsing or sending e-mail by removing personal information from your browser and e-mail program, or by using a *cloaking service*, such as the Anonymizer service available for about $30 per year. Most individuals who use anonymous Web surfing and e-mail do not intend to communicate with terrorists, defraud people, issue online ransom notes, or perform other types of illegal actions. Instead, they usually just want to protect their identity from advertising agencies and other individuals who may want to track their online shopping habits or send them unsolicited e-mail (called *spam*). But, in fact, even when personal information is removed, ISPs and the government may still be able to trace communications back to a particular computer when a crime has occurred, so it's difficult—perhaps impossible—to be completely anonymous online.

Information Integrity

As stated time and time again, the World Wide Web contains a vast amount of information on a wide variety of topics. While some of the information is factual, other information may be misleading, biased, or just plain wrong. As more and more people turn to the Web for information, it is crucial that they take the time to determine if the information they obtain and pass on to others is accurate. There have been numerous cases of information intended as a joke being restated on a Web site as fact, as well as statements being quoted out of context, which changed the meaning from the original intent. Consequently, it is wise to evaluate carefully the source of information obtained online, and verify important data from multiple sources, if possible.

One of the most direct ways of evaluating online content is by considering the source. If you obtain information from a news source that you trust (such as Web sites belonging to CNN, MSNBC, Fox News, The New York Times, or The Wall Street Journal), you should feel confident that the accuracy of their online information is close to their offline counterparts. For information about a particular product or technology, the originating company is a good source for correct information. For government information, government Web sites are typically better sources for objective information than Web sites belonging to individuals or political organizations that may have a bias.

TIP

Remember: Just because information is published on the Web or is sent in an e-mail, it does not mean it is necessarily true. Use common sense when evaluating what you read and double-check information before passing it on to others.

SUMMARY

STARTING YOUR COMPUTER: THE BOOT PROCESS

Chapter Objective 1:
Explain what happens when
you start up a computer.

The **boot** process occurs when a computer is powered up. During the boot process, quick diagnostics and other utilities may run, and then the computer's **operating system** is loaded into memory. The operating system is a collection of programs that manages a computer's activities.

USING THE WINDOWS OPERATING SYSTEM

Chapter Objective 2:
Identify common elements of
the Windows graphical user
interface (GUI), such as the
desktop, Start menu, windows,
and menus, and explain their
functions.

Microsoft Windows is the most common operating system for IBM and compatible PCs at the present time. As with most programs today, it uses a **graphical user interface (GUI)**. GUIs typically display information in **windows** and more than one window can be displayed on the **desktop** at a time. The Windows **taskbar** contains the *Start button*, **task buttons**, and the *system tray*. Common features found on windows include **menus** and **toolbars** containing **toolbar buttons**, which are used to execute commands; **icons** or small pictures that represent programs or documents; **dialog boxes**, which are used to supply necessary information before a command is executed; and **scroll bars**, which are used to move through the information available in a window. Items located on a menu typically display another menu, start a program, or open a dialog box when they are selected. Both menus and dialog boxes can contain a variety of elements.

Chapter Objective 3:
Demonstrate how to open a
program and manipulate open
program windows.

The **Start menu** is the main menu for the Windows operating system and can be used to start programs. Other possible methods for launching a program include using a taskbar toolbar button or desktop icon, or opening a saved document. Once a window has been opened, it can be resized using the window's *border* or the *Minimize, Maximize,* and *Restore* buttons; moved using the window's *title bar*; and closed using the Windows *Close* button, as necessary. The window which is currently selected is called the *active window*; only one window can be active at a time and the task buttons on the toolbars are typically used to change the active window.

After a short period of inactivity, many PCs automatically go into a standby mode. Computers can be shut down when necessary using the *Shut Down* or *Turn Off Computer* option on the Start menu.

USING THE INTERNET AND WORLD WIDE WEB

Chapter Objective 4:
Explain what the Internet and
World Wide Web are and how
computers, people, and Web
pages are identified on the
Internet.

The **Internet** is a worldwide collection of networks. One resource available through the Internet is the **World Wide Web**—an enormous collection of **Web pages** located on **Web servers**. The starting page for a **Web site** (a related group of Web pages) is called the **home page** for that site. Web pages are viewed with a **Web browser**, such as *Microsoft Internet Explorer* or *Netscape Navigator*. Web pages are connected with **hyperlinks**—text or images linked to Web pages; they can also contain text, graphics, animation, sounds, video, and 3D *virtual reality* (VR) objects. Web browsers used by handheld PCs and mobile devices are called **microbrowsers**.

To access the Internet, an **Internet service provider (ISP)** is used. ISPs serve as onramps to the Internet for individuals and businesses, typically for a fee. After signing up with an ISP, you are assigned a **user name**. This name, used in conjunction with the ISP's **domain name**, determines your **e-mail address**—the address that others use to send you e-mail messages. Most computers available through the Internet have a unique domain name; all computers available through the Internet have a unique numerical **IP address**. One other type of **Internet address** is the **URL** (**uniform resource locator**) used to identify Web pages. Most Web page URLs begin with *http://* and end with a top-level domain such as *.com*, *.edu*, or *.gov*.

The two most widely used browsers are Microsoft Internet Explorer and Netscape Navigator. Once you are connected to the Internet and have opened your browser, Web pages can be displayed by clicking hyperlinks or by typing the appropriate URLs in the browser's address/location bar. You can also use *bookmarks* (*favorites*) or the *History list* to return to favorite Web pages more easily. Browsers typically have toolbar buttons to enable you to print and redisplay Web pages, as well as move back and forward through the pages visited in the current session.

Chapter Objective 5:
Demonstrate how to access a Web page and explain how to search for Web pages containing specific information.

To locate specific information on the Internet, an *Internet search* can be performed using either your browser's built-in search capabilities or a **search site**. Search sites typically employ *search engines* to help you find appropriate Web pages, primarily by supplying Web pages matching the keywords you supplied or the directory categories you selected. Search sites also frequently contain handy reference tools, as well.

E-MAIL AND OTHER TYPES OF ONLINE COMMUNICATIONS

Electronic mail (e-mail) refers to electronic messages exchanged with other users over a company network or the Internet. Messages are sent and received using an *e-mail program*, such as *Netscape Mail*, *Microsoft Outlook*, or *Microsoft Outlook Express*. Once e-mail messages are received, they can be printed, forwarded to another user, filed into an appropriate folder, or deleted. Most e-mail programs allow messages to include attached files, and store received, sent, and deleted e-mail messages in folders on your computer. With *Web-based e-mail*, e-mail is sent and received using the Web-based e-mail service's Web page.

Chapter Objective 6:
Understand how e-mail can be used to send and receive messages to and from other Internet users.

Other types of online communications tools include **discussion groups** (where people post messages on a particular topic for others to read and respond to), **chat rooms** (online locations where multiple users can carry on real-time typed conversations), **instant messaging** (**IM**) (a form of private chat where messages are sent in real time to online "buddies"), **videoconferencing** (real-time meetings taking place online using video cameras and microphones for participants to see and hear each other), and **Internet telephony** (making telephone calls over the Internet). Special etiquette rules for online behavior are referred to as **netiquette**.

Chapter Objective 7:
Identify several other types of online communications and discuss when each is used.

SOCIETAL IMPLICATIONS OF CYBERSPACE

Chapter Objective 8:
Discuss some societal implications of the Internet, such as security, privacy, and online communications issues.

There are many societal implications related to our heavy use of the Internet and the vast amount of information available through the Internet. Issues include privacy and security risks and concerns, the differences in online and offline communications, the anonymity factor, and the amount of unreliable information that can be found on the Internet.

KEY TERMS

Instructions: Match each key term on the left with the definition on the right that best describes it

a. boot

b. chat room

c. desktop

d. dialog box

e. discussion group

f. domain name

g. electronic mail (e-mail)

h. e-mail address

i. hyperlink

j. instant messaging (IM)

k. Internet service provider (ISP)

l. IP address

m. operating system

n. scroll bar

o. search site

p. toolbar

q. uniform resource locator (URL)

r. Web browser

s. Web site

t. World Wide Web

1. ———— A collection of related Web pages usually belonging to an organization or individual.

2. ———— A business or other organization that provides Internet access to others, typically for a fee.

3. ———— A form of private chat set up to allow users to easily and quickly exchange real-time typed messages with the individuals they specify.

4. ———— A horizontal or vertical bar that appears along an edge of a window when the window is not large enough to display its entire content; scroll bars are used to view the rest of the information in the window.

5. ———— A numeric Internet address used to uniquely identify a computer on the Internet.

6. ———— A program used to view Web pages.

7. ———— A set of icons or buttons displayed horizontally or vertically on the screen that can be used to issue commands to the computer.

8. ———— A text-based Internet address used to uniquely identify a computer on the Internet.

9. ———— A type of system software that enables a computer to operate and manage its resources and activities.

10. ———— A Web site designed to help users search for Web pages that match specified keywords or selected categories.

11. ———— A window that requires the user to supply information to the computer about the task being requested.

12. ———— An Internet address consisting of a user name and computer domain name that uniquely identifies a person on the Internet.

13. ———— An Internet address, usually beginning with http://, that uniquely identifies a Web page.

14. ———— An Internet communications medium that enables individuals to post messages on a particular topic for others to read and respond to.

15. ———— An Internet service that allows multiple users to exchange written messages in real time.

16. ———— Electronic messages sent from one user to another over the Internet or other network.

17. ———— Text or an image located on a Web page or other document that is linked to a Web page or other type of document.

18. ———— The background work area displayed on the screen when using Microsoft Windows or another operating systems with a graphical user interface.

19. ———— The collection of Web pages available through the Internet.

20. ———— To start up a computer.

REVIEW ACTIVITIES

Answers for the self-quiz appear at the end of the book in the References and Resources Guide.

True/False

SELF-QUIZ

Instructions: Circle **T** if the statement is true or **F** if the statement is false.

T   F   1. A menu is a set of usually text-based options from which commands may be selected.

T   F   2. When the mouse pointer changes to a double-headed arrow such as ↘, you are ready to resize a window.

T   F   3. With instant messaging, both the sender and the recipient must be online at the same time.

T   F   4. An example of an IP address would be *microsoft.com*.

T   F   5. It isn't possible to tell if a word or image on a Web page is a hyperlink until you click it.

Completion

Instructions: Supply the missing words to complete the following statements.

6. In Windows, programs are normally opened using the _____ menu.

7. When the mouse pointer turns into 🖑, you are pointing to a(n) _____.

8. Web pages are stored on a Web _____.

9. To save the URL for a page you might like to revisit, you can create a(n) _____ for that page.

10. Placing telephone calls through the Internet is called Internet _____.

---

1. Select the icon from the numbered list below that matches each of the following names and write the corresponding number in the blank to the left of each name.

EXERCISES

a. _____ Toolbar button.   **d.** _____ Command button.
b. _____ Option button.   **e.** _____ Maximize button.
c. _____ Close button.   **f.** _____ Minimize button.

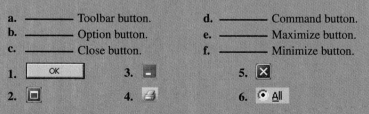

1. [OK]   **3.** [▬]   **5.** [✕]

2. [▢]   **4.** [▤]   **6.** [◉ All]

2. Supply the missing words to complete the following statements.

a. For most Windows programs, the keyboard shortcut Ctrl+C would _____ the selected content.

b. For the e-mail address *jsmith@course.com*, *jsmith* is the _____ name and *course.com* is the _____ name.

c. The e-mail address pronounced *bill gee at microsoft dot com* is written _____.

d. One of the most common online security risks today is your computer becoming infected with a(n) _____, a software program designed to change the way a computer operates, without the permission or knowledge of the user, and that often causes damage to the PC.

3. Explain the difference, if any, between a set of option buttons and a set of check boxes on a dialog box.

4. When you are finished using a computer for the day, is it OK to just turn it off by pressing the power button? Why or why not?

5. Assume that you need to find information about the history of the New York Stock Exchange for a research paper. List the keywords you might use on a search site to find Web pages containing this information. Assuming your first search didn't work, list keywords you could try for a second search.

6. If a computer manufacturer called Apex created a home page for the Web, what would its URL likely be? Also, supply an appropriate e-mail address for yourself, assuming that you are employed by that company.

7. Label the following screen illustration.

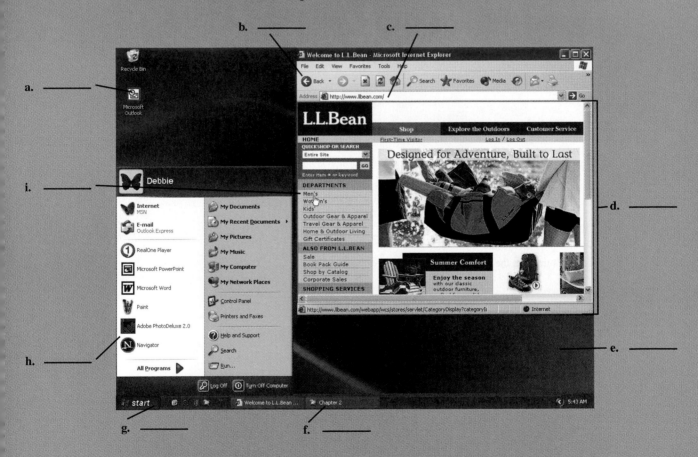

PROJECTS

1. Blogs Short for *Web log*, a *blog* is a Web page that serves as a publicly accessible personal journal for an individual. Blogs have been around for several years but couldn't be implemented on a wide scale because creating and publishing Web pages was fairly complicated; today's *blog tools* make it much simpler to update a blog on a regular basis (many blogs are updated daily). Consequently, there has been a tremendous increase in the use of blogs, for personal expression, as well as for work-related collaborations and in writing classes.

HOT TOPICS

For this project, investigate blogs. By searching a news site (such as MSNBC.com or CNN.com) or by using a search site (such as Google.com), find at least two blogs and review them. What types of information is the user sharing? Why do you think he or she prefers to put this information on the Web, instead of in a private written journal? Would you want to have your own blog? Why or why not? At the conclusion of your research, prepare a one-page summary of your findings and submit it to your instructor.

2. Your ISP As discussed in the chapter, ISPs are used to connect to the Internet. You may have a limited number of options for an ISP, depending on where you live and how much you're willing to spend on Internet service.

**SHORT ANSWER/
RESEARCH**

For this project, research what options you have to connect to the Internet from where you live. For conventional dial-up Internet service, either call a local service provider listed in your telephone book or go to the Web site for America Online, Earthlink, Juno, or another large ISP and determine which ones have a local telephone access number for your area. For faster Internet service, your telephone company should be able to tell you if they offer any types of Internet service (such as *DSL* or *ISDN*) in your area and what the costs are. If you have access to cable, check with your local cable provider for information on cable Internet. If DSL, ISDN, and cable are not available to you, check into satellite service (such as from Star-Band or DirecPC). After you have completed your research, summarize your findings in a one-page paper including the cost and estimated speed for each service, any limitations on e-mail (such as number of e-mail addresses, mailbox size, or size of attachments), and whether or not each service ties up your telephone line. Be sure to include your opinion as to which service you would choose to use and why.

3. Web Lingo There are a number of Web-related terms that you may run into, once you begin surfing the Web.

For this project, research the following terms, using this textbook, computer journals, or an online technical encyclopedia, such as Webopedia.com or Whatis.com: *banner ad*, *cookie*, *spider*, *firewall*, *lurker*, and *avatar*. At the conclusion of your research, prepare a one-page summary of your findings and submit it to your instructor. Be sure to cite the source (book and page number, Web page URL, etc.) of each definition in your summary.

4. Using Windows As discussed in the chapter, there are a number of common procedures and actions that you need to be able to perform in order to use a Windows-based PC efficiently.

HANDS ON

For this project, locate a Windows-based PC (such as one at home, in a campus computer lab, or at your public library) that you are allowed to use. Once the PC has been booted up and is ready to go, perform the following tasks, answering the questions or supplying the requested information as you go.

a. Using the Start menu, open either Paint, WordPad, Notepad, Solitaire, or FreeCell. Determine the purpose of the program you selected, and then make sure the window is not maximized. Size it to fill up about half of the desktop. Using the title bar, drag the window to a new location on the screen. Minimize the window, then use its task button to display it again. On your summary, record the program you selected, its purpose, and what options on the Start menu you needed to select to launch it.

b. Leaving open your window from the previous step, launch another window using either the Start menu, the taskbar toolbar, or a desktop icon. Maximize the window, then use the task button for the window you opened in the first step to switch to that window. On one of your two open windows, use the menu to locate a Save, Exit, or Copy command. On your summary sheet, list the name of the program you opened, how you launched it, which command you found, and on which menu the command was located. Was there a keyboard shortcut listed for your selected command?

c. Close one of your windows by pressing the Alt+F4 keyboard shortcut; close the other by using the Close button located on the window's title bar.

At the conclusion of these tasks, submit your summary sheet to your instructor.

5. **Web Scavenger Hunt** As illustrated in the chapter, search sites (such as Yahoo.com, Google.com, and AltaVista.com) can be used to find Web pages containing specific information.

For this project, go to a search site and search for Web pages that you could use to find the following information. Once you find each of the items specified below, print the page containing the information using your browser's Print button. After you have found all five items, circle or highlight the appropriate information on each printout, staple your printouts together, and turn them in to your instructor. (Note: Some of the printouts will vary from student to student.)

a. A toll-free telephone number for Dell Computer.

b. The current stock price of IBM Corporation (NYSE symbol IBM).

c. A map of where your house, apartment, or dorm is located.

d. The ZIP code for 200 N. Elm Street, Hinsdale, IL.

e. A recipe for Spicy Chicken Wings, Buffalo Chicken Wings, or something similar.

WRITING ABOUT COMPUTERS

6. **E-Voting** *Online voting* or *e-voting* is beginning to become an alternative to the punch cards and optical mark ballots presently used in most areas in the United States. In fact, some binding online votes have already been cast, such as in the March 2000 Arizona Democratic Party primary. Online voting is also being tested in England with hopes of having binding online elections as early as 2006. Online voting has the advantage of convenience, particularly for elderly individuals, people with limited mobility, and voters who live in remote areas. There are some privacy and security concerns, however, including the following: How will the system prevent someone voting as another individual? What will prevent a person's vote from being stored in a database so it can be used against him or her at a later time? Could individuals sell their votes to the highest bidder? Possible precautions including using PINs (Personal Identification Numbers) that are mailed to the registered voter plus personal questions to which only he or she would know the answers to authenticate a voter before casting his or her ballot, *smart cards* that only the registered voter should possess, or *fingerprint readers*.

For this project, write a short essay expressing your opinion about online voting in general, and if you believe it will become widely used in the near future. Would you be comfortable casting your vote online? Would you want some type of authentication method in place to verify your identify before being allowed to submit an online ballot? If so, would you feel comfortable having the necessary data (answers to personal questions or your fingerprint image, for instance) being stored in a national database? At some point, do you think online voting will become the norm? If so, how would you suggest handling individuals who have no Internet access available to them on Election Day? Submit your opinion on this issue to your instructor in the form of a short paper, not more than two pages in length.

7. **Browser Plug-Ins** A *browser plug-in* is a program that adds the ability to experience additional Internet content with your browser, such as to view documents created in certain formats or multimedia elements of a Web page. Common plug-in programs are *Adobe Acrobat Reader*, *Macromedia Flash Player*, *RealNetworks RealOne Player*, *Apple QuickTime Player*, and *Cosmo Software Cosmo Player*.

   For this project, form a group to research the five plug-ins listed above. For each plug-in, determine the types of files or applications the plug-in is used for, the URL of at least one Web site where you can download the plug-in, the cost (if any), what operating systems and browsers the plug-in will work with, and if there are any alternative plug-ins that can be used to view the types of documents or applications associated with the plug-in you are researching. Your group should submit the results of your research to your instructor in the form of a short paper, not more than two pages in length.

PRESENTATION/ DEMONSTRATION

8. **Your Domain** As mentioned in the chapter, domain names are used to identify computers— most commonly Web servers—available through the Internet, and a central registration system is used to ensure that domain names are unique.

   For this project, investigate how a domain name is registered. First, select a domain name you would like to use for your personal Web site or for a fictitious organization. Next, visit at least two registrar Web sites (such as NetworkSolutions.com or Register.com) to determine what information you would need to provide to register your domain name and how much it would cost. Also, investigate the top-level domains *.com*, *.net*, *.org*, *.info*, *.name*, *.biz*, and *.us* to determine who they are designed for. Are there any other possible top-level domains, in addition to the ones listed here? Which top-level domains are available for the domain name you are researching? Determine any requirements—such as length and allowable characters— for domain names using those top-level domains. Using a lookup feature available on a registration site, see if the domain name you would like to use is available. If not, keep trying variations of that name until you find an appropriate available domain name. Finally, find out what *cybersquatting* is and how that may affect your selection of a domain name.

   Share your findings with the class in the form of a short presentation. The presentation should not exceed 10 minutes and should make use of one or more presentation aids such as the chalkboard, handouts, overhead transparencies, or a computer-based slide presentation (your instructor may provide additional requirements). You may also be asked to submit a summary of the presentation to your instructor.

9. **E-Mail Options** If you have access to the Internet, you can exchange electronic messages— including digital photos and other types of files—with any other person who has an e-mail address. This exchange can be accomplished using your computer or a PC available through your school, public library, cybercafé, or other public location. For an e-mail account, you may have the option of using your home or school e-mail account, or a Web-based e-mail service such as Hotmail or Yahoo! Mail.

   For this project, form a group to research what e-mail options are available for the students at your school and surrounding community. Your group should prepare a short presentation of your findings, including a brief summary of how to apply for a student e-mail account at your school and any free Web-based e-mail services that are available. In addition, your group should identify any potential benefits or limitations of using a free Web-based e-mail service, as well as any differences in terms of mailbox size, limitations on attachments, and other features for the e-mail services your group evaluated. The presentation should not exceed 10 minutes and should make use of one or more presentation aids such as the chalkboard, handouts, overhead transparencies, or a computer-based slide presentation (your instructor may provide additional requirements). Your group may be asked to submit a summary of the presentation to your instructor.

INTERACTIVE DISCUSSION

10. **Digital-Only Materials** Traditional print media, such as newspapers, magazines, and books, are costly to produce and distribute. In addition, by the time they are printed and distributed, the information they contain is hours, days, weeks, months, even years old. Publishers that publish in a digital-only format are starting to capture some of the traditional market share because the information they provide is more up-to-date. In order to deal with this issue, most publishers have started to produce and distribute some, or all, of their content in both traditional and electronic format. It is certainly possible that these publishers may decide to discontinue publishing content in the traditional format altogether and opt for the digital-only format.

    Select one of the following positions or create one of your own and express your point of view on the subject. Your instructor will indicate whether your response is to be posted to a class bulletin board, discussed in a class chat room, or discussed as an in-class activity. You may also be asked to submit a summary of your position and point of view to your instructor.

    a. Traditional forms of printed communications will never be discontinued. We may have to pay more in order to read traditional newspapers, but they will always be available.

    b. Traditional forms of printed communications will eventually complete the transition to a digital-only format. We will all have some sort of portable digital display or audio device that will replace traditional newspapers, books, and magazines.

11. **Telesurgery** The Internet, telecommunications technology, and robotics have advanced enough in recent years to allow for a new type of Internet application: *telesurgery* or operating on patients via a PC. For instance, Dr. Louis Kavoussi of Johns Hopkins Bayview Medical Center performs surgery on patients all over the world from his home office instead of in the actual operating room. He uses his PC to control robotic surgical tools and cameras located in the operating room, as well as to give surgeons written and verbal instructions. There are some obvious benefits to using telesurgery in military and space exploration applications, as well as in remote locations where other types of surgical care are unavailable, but will the average citizen go along with having surgery via communications technology? What types of precautions will need to be taken to overcome concerns about software and hardware malfunctions, as well as privacy and security breaches? Is having the best surgeon perform an operation via telesurgery always better than an average surgeon performing the operation via traditional methods? How might an increase in telesurgery impact the medical profession and future physicians? Would you be willing to have telesurgery?

    For this project, form an opinion of the use of telesurgery and its potential impact on personal health and safety, as well as on the medical profession in general. Be sure to use the questions mentioned in the previous paragraph when forming your position. Your instructor will indicate whether your response is to be posted to a class bulletin board, discussed in a class chat room, or discussed as an in-class activity. You may also be asked to submit a summary of your position and point of view to your instructor.

STUDENT EDITION LABS

12. **Student Edition Labs** Reinforce the concepts you have learned in this chapter by working through the "Getting the Most Out of the Internet" and "E-Mail" interactive Student Edition Labs, available online. To access these labs, go to www.course.com/uc10/ch02

    If you have a SAM user profile, you have access to even more interactive content. Log in to your SAM account and go to your assignments page to see what your instructor has assigned for this chapter.

HARDWARE

When most people think of computer systems, usually images of hardware fill their minds. Hardware includes the keyboard, monitor, and all of the other interesting pieces of equipment that you unpack from boxes when you buy a computer system. This module explores the rich variety of computer hardware available today. But as you already know, hardware needs guidance from software to perform any useful function. Hardware without software is like a car without a driver or a canvas and paintbrush without an artist.

This module divides coverage of hardware into three subject areas. Chapter 3 describes the hardware located inside the main box of the computer called the *system unit*—the location where most of the work of a computer is performed. Chapter 4 discusses the types of hardware that provide an indispensable library of resources for the computer—storage devices. Chapter 5 covers the wide variety of hardware that can be used for input and output.

HARDWARE

Chapter 3 The System Unit: Processing and Memory 85

Overview 88

Data and Program Representation 88

Inside the System Unit 95

How the CPU Works 111

Making Computers Faster Now and in the Future 115

Chapter 4 Storage 133

Overview 134

Properties of Storage Systems 134

Magnetic Disk Systems 137

Optical Disc Systems 150

Other Types of Storage Systems 154

Comparing Storage Alternatives 162

Chapter 5 Input and Output 173

Overview 174

Input and Output 174

Keyboards 174

Pointing Devices 176

Scanners and Related Devices 181

Biometric Input Devices 189

Multimedia Input Devices 191

Display Devices 195

Printers 200

Multimedia Output Devices 208

OUTLINE

Overview

Data and Program Representation

Digital Data Representation

Representing Numerical Data: The Binary
Numbering System

Coding Systems for Text-Based Data

Coding Systems for Other Types of Data

Representing Programs: Machine
Language

Inside the System Unit

The Motherboard

CPU

Memory

Buses

Expansion Slots and Cards

Ports

How the CPU Works

Typical CPU Components

The System Clock and the Machine Cycle

Making Computers Faster Now and in the
Future

Speeding Up Your System Today

Strategies for Making Faster Computers

Future Trends

The System Unit: Processing and Memory

LEARNING OBJECTIVES

After completing this chapter, you will be able to:

1. Understand how data and programs are represented to a computer and be able to identify a few of the coding systems used to accomplish this.

2. Explain the functions of the hardware components commonly found inside the system unit, such as the CPU, memory, buses, and expansion cards.

3. Describe how new peripheral devices or other hardware can be added to a PC.

4. Understand how the computer system's CPU and memory components process program instructions and data.

5. Name and evaluate several strategies that can be used today for speeding up the operations of a computer.

6. List some technologies that may be used in future PCs.

The *system unit* of a computer is sometimes thought of as a mysterious "black box" that makes the computer work, and often the user doesn't have much understanding of what happens inside it. In this chapter, we demystify the system unit by looking inside the box and closely examining the functions of the parts inside. In doing so, the chapter gives you a feel for how the *CPU*, *memory*, and other devices commonly found within the system unit work together to process data into meaningful information.

To start, we discuss how a computer system represents data and program instructions. Here we talk about the codes that computers use to translate data back and forth from symbols that the computer can manipulate to symbols that people are accustomed to using. These topics lead into a discussion of how the CPU and memory are arranged with other processing and storage components inside the system unit, and then how a CPU is organized and how it interacts with memory to carry out processing tasks. Finally, we look at strategies that are used today to speed up a computer, plus some strategies that may be used to create faster computers in the future.

While most of you reading this chapter will apply its contents to conventional personal computer systems—such as desktop and notebook PCs—keep in mind that the principles and procedures discussed in this chapter cover a broad range of computer products. These products include microprocessors embedded in toys, household appliances and other devices, as well as powerful servers, mainframes, and supercomputers. ■

DATA AND PROGRAM REPRESENTATION

In order to be understood by a computer, data and programs need to be represented appropriately. There are *coding systems* (also called *coding schemes*) that are used to represent numeric, text, and multimedia data, as well as to represent programs themselves. These concepts are discussed in the next few sections.

Digital Data Representation

Most computers today are *digital computers*; that is, computers that understand only two states—off and on (typically represented by the digits 0 and 1). The mobile devices, microcomputers, midrange servers, mainframes, and supercomputers discussed in Chapter 1 are all digital computers. Digital computers do their processing by converting data and programs into strings of 0s and 1s, which they manipulate at almost unimaginable speed, and then converting the processed results back to a form we can understand. Converting data to digital form so that a digital computer can use it is called *digital data representation*.

The two possible states recognized by a digital computer can be represented in a variety of ways. For example, electronic current is either present or absent, a circuit is either open or closed, a magnetic spot or depression on a storage medium is either present or absent, and so on. This two-state, or *binary*, nature of electronic devices is illustrated in Figure 3-1. Regardless of the form they take, for convenience it is common to think of these binary states in terms of 0s and 1s. In binary representation, these 0s and 1s are called *bits*, which is short for *binary digits*. A bit is the smallest unit of data that a digital computer can recognize. Because computers do all processing and communications by representing programs and data in bit form—in other words, by using just 0s and 1s—binary can be thought of as the computer's "native language."

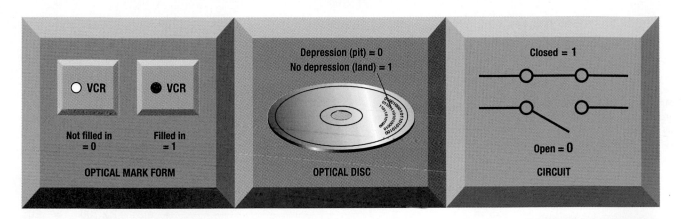

Depression (pit) = 0
No depression (land) = 1

Closed = 1

VCR   VCR

Not filled in   Filled in
= 0   = 1

Open = 0

OPTICAL MARK FORM   OPTICAL DISC   CIRCUIT

People, of course, don't speak binary language. You're not likely to go up to a friend and say,

0100100001001001

which translates into the word "HI" using one binary coding system. People communicate with one another in their *natural languages*, such as English, Chinese, Spanish, and French. For example, this book is written in English, which uses a 26-character alphabet. In addition, most countries use a numbering system with 10 possible symbols—0 through 9. As already mentioned, however, computers understand only two symbols—0 and 1. For us to interact with a computer, a translation process from our natural languages to 0s and 1s and then back again is required. When we enter data into a computer system, the computer translates the natural-language symbols we provide into binary 0s and 1s. After it completes processing, the computer system translates the 0s and 1s that represent the processed results back into the appropriate natural language.

Computers represent programs and data through a variety of binary-based coding schemes. The coding system used depends primarily on the type of data needing to be represented. Coding systems for numerical, text-based, and a few other types of data are discussed in the next few sections.

> **FIGURE 3-1**
> **Ways of representing 0 and 1.** Digital computers recognize only two states—off and on—usually represented by 0 and 1.

Representing Numerical Data: The Binary Numbering System

A *numbering system* is a way of representing numbers. The system we most commonly use is called the *decimal* (or *base 10*) *numbering system* because it uses 10 symbols—the digits 0, 1, 2, 3, 4, 5, 6, 7, 8, and 9—to represent all possible numbers. Numbers greater than nine, such as 21 and 683, are represented by combinations of these 10 symbols.

Because we are so familiar with the decimal numbering system, it may never have occurred to us that we could represent numbers any other way. However, nothing says that a numbering system has to have 10 possible symbols. The **binary numbering system** (sometimes called the *base 2 numbering system* or the *true binary numbering system*), for example, uses just two symbols (0 and 1) instead of 10 symbols. Because this matches the binary nature of computers, the binary numbering system is used extensively with computers to represent and process numbers.

Here's a quick look at how these numbering systems work. In both the decimal numbering system and the binary system, the position of each digit determines the power, or exponent, to which the *base number* (10 for decimal or 2 for binary) is raised. In the decimal numbering system, going from right to left, the first position or column (ones column)

TIP

For a more in-depth look at numbering systems, including arithmetic and conversions, see the "A Look at Numbering Systems" section in the References and Resources Guide at the end of this text.

>**Binary numbering system.** The numbering system that represents all numbers using just two symbols (0 and 1).

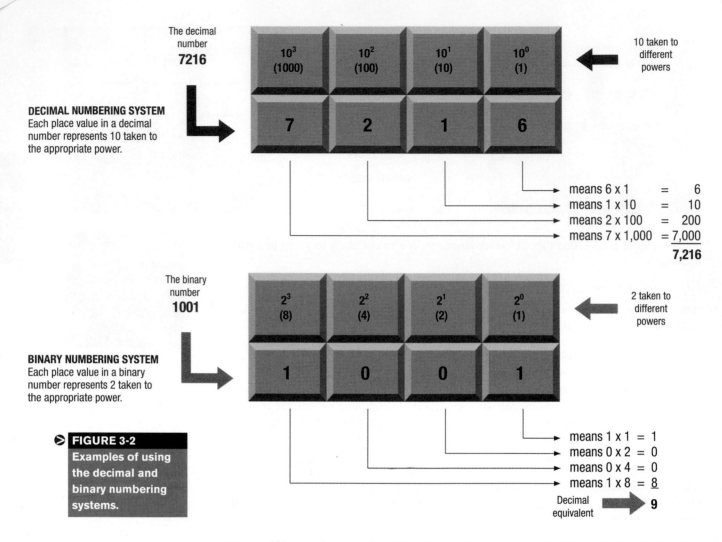

The decimal number **7216**

DECIMAL NUMBERING SYSTEM
Each place value in a decimal number represents 10 taken to the appropriate power.

10 taken to different powers

means 6 x 1   =   6
means 1 x 10   =   10
means 2 x 100 = 200
means 7 x 1,000 = 7,000
7,216

The binary number **1001**

BINARY NUMBERING SYSTEM
Each place value in a binary number represents 2 taken to the appropriate power.

2 taken to different powers

means 1 x 1 = 1
means 0 x 2 = 0
means 0 x 4 = 0
means 1 x 8 = 8
Decimal equivalent   **9**

◆ FIGURE 3-2
Examples of using the decimal and binary numbering systems.

FURTHER EXPLORATION

For links to further information about data representation, go to www.course.com/uc10/ch03

represents 10^0 or 1; the second position (tens column) represents 10^1, or 10; the third position (hundreds column) represents 10^2, or 100; and so forth. Therefore, as Figure 3-2 shows, the decimal number 7,216 is understood as $7 \times 10^3 + 2 \times 10^2 + 1 \times 10^1 + 6 \times 10^0$ or 7,000 + 200 + 10 + 6 or 7,216. In binary, the concept is the same but the columns have different place values. For example, the first column is the ones column (for 2^0), the second column is the twos column (2^1), the third column is the fours column (2^2), and so on. Therefore, as illustrated in the bottom half of Figure 3-2, although 1001 represents "one thousand one" in decimal notation, in the binary numbering system 1001 equals "nine" ($1 \times 2^3 + 0 \times 2^2 + 0 \times 2^1 + 1 \times 2^0$ or 8 + 1 or 9).

Coding Systems for Text-Based Data

While numeric data is represented by the binary numbering system, text-based data is represented by fixed-length binary coding systems specifically developed for text-based data—namely, *ASCII*, *EBCDIC*, and *Unicode*. Such codes represent all characters on the keyboard that can appear in text data, such as numeric characters, alphabetic characters, and special characters such as the dollar sign ($) and period (.).

ASCII and EBCDIC

Among the most widely used coding systems for text-based data are **ASCII** (*American Standard Code for Information Interchange*) and **EBCDIC** (*Extended Binary-Coded Decimal Interchange Code*). Virtually all PCs use ASCII, developed largely through the efforts of the *American National Standards Institute* (*ANSI*). ASCII is also widely adopted as the standard for communications systems. EBCDIC, developed by IBM, is used primarily on IBM mainframes.

Both ASCII and EBCDIC represent each character as a unique combination of 8 bits (see Figure 3-3), although the original version of ASCII was a 7-digit code. A group of 8 bits allows 256 (2^8) different combinations, so an 8-bit code can represent up to 256 characters. This coding scheme leaves more than enough combinations to account for the 26 uppercase and 26 lowercase characters used in the English alphabet, the 10 decimal digits, and the other characters usually found on a keyboard. Because of this, additional special characters not included on a keyboard—such as some mathematical symbols, drawing characters, punctuation marks, and *dingbats* (small graphical symbols)—were also included in these codes. Many computer systems can accept data in either ASCII or EBCDIC.

The 8 bits that represent a character in ASCII or EBCDIC are collectively referred to as a **byte**. It is important to be familiar with this concept because "byte" terminology is frequently used in a variety of computer contexts. For example, document size and storage capacity are measured in bytes, based on the amount of data that is contained in the document or that can be stored on the storage medium. Since one byte holds only a very small amount of data (just one character), prefixes are commonly used with the term *byte*. A **kilobyte** (**KB**) is equal to 1,024 bytes, but is usually thought of as approximately 1,000 bytes. A **megabyte** (**MB**) is about 1 million bytes; a **gigabyte** (**GB**) is about 1 billion bytes; a **terabyte** (**TB**) is about 1 trillion bytes; a *petabyte* (*PB*) is about 1,000 terabytes (2^{50} bytes); an *exabyte* (*EB*) is about 1,000 petabytes (2^{60} bytes); a *zettabyte* (*ZB*) is about 1,000 exabytes (2^{70} bytes); and a *yottabyte* (*YB*) is about 1,000 zettabytes (2^{80} bytes). Therefore, 5 KB is about 5,000 bytes, 10 MB is approximately 10 million bytes, and 2 TB is about 2 trillion bytes.

CHARACTER	ASCII	EBCDIC
0	00110000	11110000
1	00110001	11110001
2	00110010	11110010
3	00110011	11110011
4	00110100	11110100
5	00110101	11110101
A	01000001	11000001
B	01000010	11000010
C	01000011	11000011
D	01000100	11000100
E	01000101	11000101
F	01000110	11000110
+	00101011	01001110
!	00100001	01011010
#	00100011	01111011

> **FIGURE 3-3**
> **Examples from the ASCII and EBCDIC codes.** These common fixed-length binary codes represent all characters as unique strings of 8 bits.

Unicode

A newer code for text-based data that is gaining prominence is **Unicode**. Unlike ASCII, which is limited to just the alphabet used with the English language, Unicode is a universal coding standard designed to represent text-based data written in any language, including those with different alphabets, such as Chinese, Greek, and Russian. It is a longer code (32 bits per character is common, compared to the 8 bits per character used in the ASCII and EBCDIC codes) and can represent over one million characters—more than enough unique combinations to represent the standard characters in all the world's current written languages, as well as thousands of mathematical and technical symbols, punctuation marks, and dingbats. The biggest advantage of using Unicode is that it can be used worldwide with consistent and unambiguous results. Unicode is used widely for Web pages and in recent software programs, such as Windows XP, Mac OS X, Netscape Navigator, and Internet Explorer.

TIP

For more examples of ASCII, EBCDIC, and Unicode, see the "Coding Charts" section in the References and Resources Guide at the end of this book.

>**ASCII.** A fixed-length, binary coding system widely used to represent text-based data for computer processing on many types of computers. >**EBCDIC.** A fixed-length, binary coding system widely used to represent text-based data on IBM mainframe computers. >**Byte.** A group of 8 bits; in ASCII and EBCDIC, it holds a single character of data. >**Kilobyte (KB).** 1,024 bytes. >**Megabyte (MB).** Approximately 1 million bytes. >**Gigabyte (GB).** Approximately 1 billion bytes. >**Terabyte (TB).** Approximately 1 trillion bytes. >**Unicode.** A coding system for text-based data using any written language.

Coding Systems for Other Types of Data

So far, our discussion of data coding schemes has focused on numeric and text-based data, which consist of alphanumeric symbols and special symbols, such as the comma and semicolon. Graphics, audio, and video data must also be represented in binary form in order to be used with a computer. Some common coding schemes used with these types of data are discussed next.

Graphics Data

Graphics data consists of still images, such as photographs or drawings. One of the most common methods for storing graphics data is in the form of a *bitmap*—a grid of hundreds of thousands of dots, called *pixels* (short for *picture elements*), arranged to represent an image. The color to be displayed at each pixel is represented by some combination of 0s and 1s.

A *monochrome* graphic, which is the simplest type of bitmapped image, has only two possible colors. Suppose that these colors are black and white and that the color white is represented by a 1, while a 0 represents black. Using this scheme, the graphic would be represented to the PC as a black-and-white bitmap, such as the one shown in the top part of Figure 3-4, and the binary representation of that image would require one bit per pixel of storage space.

More realism can be achieved using a *grayscale* image. In grayscale images, each pixel can be not only pure black or pure white but also any of the 254 shades of gray in between. Thus, each dot or pixel could appear in any of 256 possible states. Since it takes a single byte (8 bits) to represent 256 (2^8) states, grayscale images require one byte of storage per pixel. So, 11111111 could represent a pure white pixel, 00000000 a pure black one, and any byte pattern in between—such as 11001000 and 00001010—could represent a particular shade of gray (see the middle part of Figure 3-4).

Data representation of *color* images works similarly to grayscale images, in that the color of each pixel is represented by a specific pattern of bits. Computers often represent color graphics with 16 colors, 256 colors, or 16,777,216 colors. In a 16-color image, one-half byte (4 bits, such as 0000, 1111, or some combination in between) is assigned to each pixel to represent the color to be displayed in that pixel. In a 256-color image, 1 byte (8 bits) is assigned to each pixel to represent its color. Finally, in a 16.8-million-color (called photographic quality or *true color*) image, 3 bytes (24 bits) are used to store the color data for each pixel in the image (see the bottom part of Figure 3-4).

Theoretically, the higher number of bits used in color coding, the higher the image quality. In practice, however, it is sometimes difficult for the human eye to tell much of a quality difference between low-end and high-end color images, unless the images have been enlarged. Sixteen-color images, such as those you often see on Web pages, can actually be quite respectable looking. Because using fewer colors results in a smaller file size and a faster download time, Web developers often reduce both true-color images and 256-color images to 16-color images for use on Web pages. This is typically accomplished by a process called *dithering*. Dithering produces colors not available on a limited color palette by coloring neighboring pixels with two available colors that appear to blend together to make a different color. For example, your eye will see a lime green color on the screen when several yellow and green pixels are placed adjacent to one another.

When images need to be resized, however, bitmapped images are not the best choice. When a bitmapped image is resized, the existing pixels are just made larger or smaller (no new pixels are added), so the image usually looks distorted or blurry. A better choice in this situation is *vector-based* images, which use mathematical formulas to represent images instead of a map of pixels; vector-based images can be resized without losing quality.

Audio Data

Audio data—such as the sound of someone speaking or a song on a CD—must be in a digital format in order to be stored on a storage medium or processed by a PC. One common audio format is *waveform audio*. Waveform audio captures several thousand digital snapshots, called *samples*, of the sound sequence every second. When the samples are played in order, they recreate the sound of the voice or music.

MONOCHROME GRAPHICS
With monochrome graphics, the color of each pixel is represented by a single bit, either 0 or 1.

ORIGINAL IMAGE

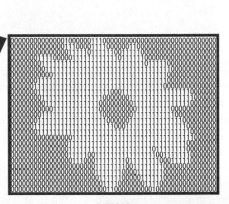

BITMAP

One sample pixel: 1

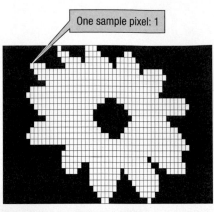

DISPLAYED IMAGE

H
W

GRAYSCALE GRAPHICS
With 256-shade grayscale graphics, the color of each pixel is represented by one byte, such as 01101110. Different byte values represent black, white, and different shades of gray.

One sample pixel:
01101110

One sample pixel:
1110

16-COLOR IMAGE
The color of each pixel is represented using a half byte.

COLOR GRAPHICS
Color images can be 16-color, 256-color, or photographic quality. The more colors used, the better the image quality.

One sample pixel:
01110110

256-COLOR IMAGE
The color of each pixel is represented using one byte.

One sample pixel:
101001100100110111001011

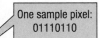

PHOTOGRAPHIC-QUALITY (TRUE COLOR) IMAGE
(16.8 million colors)
The color of each pixel is represented using three bytes.

> **FIGURE 3-4**
> **Representing graphics data.** With bitmapped images, each pixel is assigned some combination of 0s and 1s to represent its shade or color. In color images, the more colors used, the better the image quality.

HOW IT WORKS

MP3 Compression

The *MP3 format* is a compression system for music. It is used to reduce the number of bytes in a song without sacrificing the musical quality. MP3 is officially *MPEG Audio Layer 3*, an *MPEG* (*Moving Pictures Experts Group*) compression standard. Each MPEG layer uses a different sampling rate to obtain different compression results. MP3 (Layer 3)–the norm for digital music today–typically compresses a CD-quality song to about one-tenth of its original size. For example, the 32 MB Norah Jones song shown in the accompanying illustration compresses to less than 3 MB after it is converted to an MP3 file. Because of its efficiency, the MP3 format is widely used for music downloaded from the Internet, as well as when music is copied from a CD to a PC or digital music player. Because of their smaller file size, MP3 files can be downloaded in minutes rather than hours, and hundreds of MP3 files can be stored on a single storage medium.

MP3 utilizes two compression techniques. The first technique uses the principle of *perceptual coding*; that is, removing the parts of the song that the human ear wouldn't hear anyway, such as sounds that occur in frequencies too high or too low to be perceived by the human ear or soft sounds that are played at the same time as louder sounds. Although data is lost by this compression technique, the lost data is considered superfluous, so the size of the song is reduced without significantly altering the quality of the song. The second compression technique, called *Huffman coding*, substitutes shorter strings of bits for frequently used larger strings. Since the bits are reconstructed when the song is played, no information is lost during this process. The resulting MP3 file–saved with the file extension *.mp3*–can then be played on a PC using media player software, burned onto a CD, or copied to a digital music player.

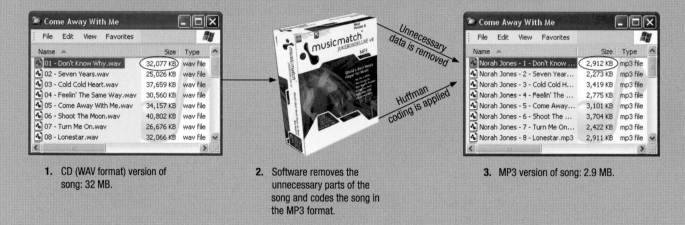

1. CD (WAV format) version of song: 32 MB.

2. Software removes the unnecessary parts of the song and codes the song in the MP3 format.

3. MP3 version of song: 2.9 MB.

For example, audio CDs record sound using 2-byte samples sampled at a rate of 44,100 times per second. As you can imagine, when these sampled sounds are played back at a rate of 44,100 samples per second, the human ear cannot distinguish them, and they collectively sound like continuous voice or music. With so many samples per second, however, you can also understand why sound files take up a great deal of storage space—about 32 MB for a 3-minute song (44,100 times × 16 bits × 180 seconds × 2 channels ÷ 8 bits per byte).

Because of its potentially huge storage size, when audio data is transmitted over the Internet it is often compressed to shorten the download time. For example, files that are *MP3-encoded*—that is, compressed with the MP3 compression algorithm—are about 10 times smaller than their waveform counterparts, so they download 10 times faster and take up much less storage space. Technology used to encode and decode audio or video data into binary form is referred to as a *codec*. For a look at how MP3 compression works, see the How It Works box.

Video Data

Video data—such as home movies, feature films, and television shows—is displayed using a collection of frames; each frame contains a still graphical image. When the frames are projected one after the other—typically at a rate of 30 frames per second—the illusion of movement is created. With so many frames, the amount of data involved in showing a two-hour feature film can be quite substantial. For instance, just a single 256-color image shown on a 640-by-480-pixel display requires 307,200 bytes. When you multiply that figure by 30 times per second, 60 seconds per minute, and 120 minutes you get more than 66 gigabytes of information for a typical two-hour movie. Fortunately, like audio data, video data can be compressed to reduce it to a manageable size. For example, a two-hour movie can be compressed to fit on a 4.7-gigabyte DVD disc.

Representing Programs: Machine Language

Just like data, which must be represented by 0s and 1s, programs also need to be represented and processed in binary form. Before a computer can execute any program instruction, such as requesting input from the user, moving a block of data from one place to another, or opening a new window on the screen, it must convert the instruction into a binary code known as **machine language**. An example of a typical machine-language instruction is as follows:

01011000011100000000000100000010

A machine-language instruction may look like a meaningless string of 0s and 1s, but it actually represents specific operations and storage locations. The 32-bit instruction shown here, for instance, moves data between two specific memory locations on one type of computer system. Similar instructions transfer data from memory to other locations, add or subtract values in memory, and so on. The basic set of machine-language instructions that a CPU can understand is known as that CPU's *instruction set*. Because the instruction sets used with PC-compatible CPUs are different than the ones used with Macintosh CPUs, software programs are typically designated as either for Windows PCs or for Macs (see Figure 3-5).

Early computers required programs to be written in machine language. Today, however, hardly anyone writes machine-language code. Instead, programmers rely on *language translators*—programs that automatically convert instructions written in a more natural-language-like programming language into machine language. The translation is so transparent that most people aren't even aware that it is taking place. Programming languages and language translators are discussed in more detail in Chapter 13.

PC VERSION

MAC VERSION

▶ **FIGURE 3-5**
Software is usually written for a specific type of PC, such as a PC-compatible or a Mac.

INSIDE THE SYSTEM UNIT

The **system unit** is the main case of a computer that houses the processing hardware for that computer, as well as a few other devices, such as disk drives used for storage, memory, the power supply, and cooling fans. The system unit for a desktop PC often looks like a rectangular box, although other shapes and sizes are available, such as in the all-in-one PC illustrated in Figure 1-12 and the modified PCs shown in the Inside the Industry box in Chapter 1. The inside of a system unit for a typical desktop PC system is shown in Figure 3-6 and the various components are discussed in the next few sections. Portable PCs have similar components, but many of the components are smaller and the system unit is typically combined with the computer screen to form a single piece of hardware.

>**Machine language.** A binary-based language for representing computer programs that the computer can execute directly. >**System unit.** The main box of a computer that houses the CPU, motherboard, memory, and other devices.

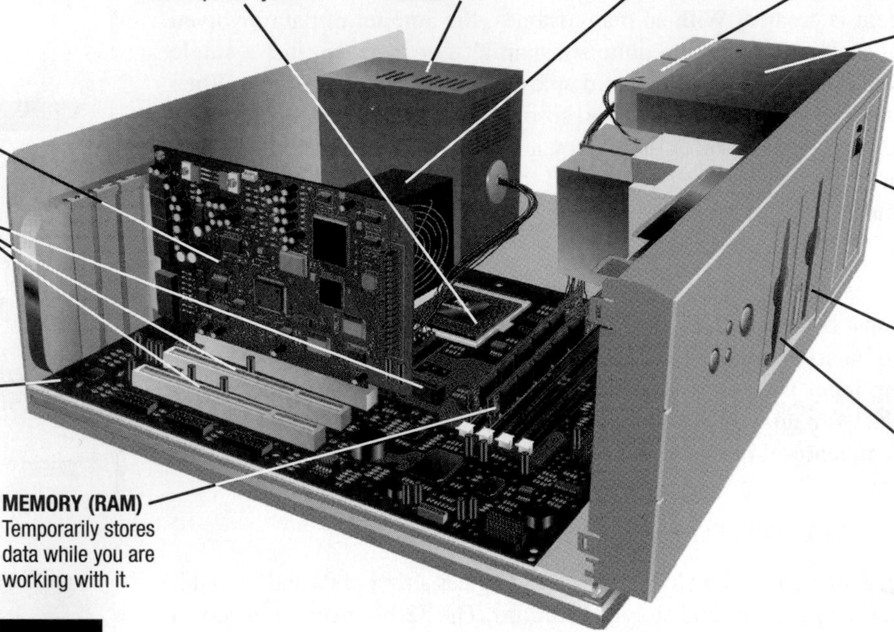

CPU
Performs calculations, does comparisons, and controls the other parts of the computer system.

POWER SUPPLY
Converts standard electrical power into a form the computer can use.

FAN
Cools the CPU and other important components.

HARD DRIVE
Principal storage device for most PCs.

EXPANSION CARD
Adds new peripheral devices or capabilities to a computer system.

EXPANSION SLOTS
Where expansion cards can be inserted.

MOTHERBOARD
The PC's main circuit board; all components of the computer system connect to it.

MEMORY (RAM)
Temporarily stores data while you are working with it.

STORAGE BAYS
Hold storage devices, such as the floppy, CD/DVD, Zip, and hard drives shown here.

CD/DVD DRIVE
Storage device that accesses CDs or DVDs.

FLOPPY DRIVE
Storage device that accesses floppy disks.

ZIP DRIVE
Storage device that accesses Zip disks.

> **FIGURE 3-6**
> **Inside a typical system unit.** The system unit houses the CPU, memory, and other important pieces of hardware.

TIP

Although most desktop PCs have a single motherboard containing a CPU, memory, and other components located inside its system unit, it is becoming increasingly common for servers to use a special chassis containing many individual boards called *blades;* each blade contains a complete server, including processors, memory, and more. These types of servers are called *blade servers.*

The Motherboard

A *circuit board* is a thin board containing *chips*—very small pieces of silicon or other semi-conducting material onto which *integrated circuits* are embedded—and other electronic components. The main circuit board inside the system unit is called the **motherboard** or **system board**. As shown in Figure 3-6, the motherboard has a variety of chips and boards attached to it; in fact, all devices used with a computer need to be connected in one way or another to the motherboard. Typically, *external* devices (such as monitors and printers) connect to the motherboard by plugging into a special connector (called a *port*) exposed through the exterior of the system unit case. The port is either connected directly to the motherboard, or is connected through an *expansion card* plugged into an *expansion slot* on the motherboard. Ports and system expansion are discussed in more detail later in this chapter.

CPU

The **central processing unit** (CPU), also sometimes called the **processor**, consists of a variety of circuitry and components packaged together and plugged directly into the motherboard. The CPU—often referred to as a **microprocessor** when talking about PCs—does the vast majority of the processing for a computer.

Most PCs today use CPUs manufactured by Intel or Advanced Micro Devices (AMD); some examples of their processors are shown in Figure 3-7. CPUs commonly used with desktop PCs include the Intel *Pentium 4* and the AMD *Athlon XP*, although lower-end home PCs may use a *Celeron* CPU instead. A new Athlon CPU named the *Athlon 64* and targeted at the high-end desktop market was released in late 2003. Typically, portable

---

>**Motherboard.** The main circuit board of a computer, located inside the system unit, to which all computer system components connect.
>**System board.** Another name for motherboard. >**Central processing unit (CPU).** The chip located inside the system unit of a computer that performs the processing for a computer. >**Processor.** Another name for CPU. >**Microprocessor.** A CPU for a microcomputer.

INTEL PENTIUM 4   **AMD ATHLON 64**

INTEL PENTIUM M

> **FIGURE 3-7**
> **CPUs.** Shown here are the Pentium 4 and Athlon 64 (for desktop PCs) and the Pentium M (for portable PCs).

computers use either desktop PC CPUs or similar processors designed for portable PC use, such as the Intel *Pentium M* and low-power Transmeta *Crusoe*; powerful *workstations* (powerful PCs designed for users running engineering and other applications requiring extra processing capabilities) and servers use more powerful processors, such as Intel's *Xeon* and *Itanium 2*, AMD's *Opteron* and *Athlon MP*, and Sun's *UltraSPARC* processors. Apple Macintosh computers use *PowerPC* processors—CPUs that were originally developed through a cooperative effort by Apple, Motorola, and IBM. The most recent PowerPC CPU is the *G5*. For a look at other uses for computer chips besides CPUs, see the Trend box.

The type of CPU chip in a computer's system unit greatly affects what can be done with that PC. Software is sometimes designed to work with a specific chip or chip family, and a program that works with one chip may not function on a PC using a different chip. For instance, a program designed for a speedy Intel Pentium 4 chip may not work well, or even at all, on the earlier and far less-capable 80486 chip. Selected CPUs introduced since 2000 are summarized in Figure 3-8; the characteristics listed in Figure 3-8 are discussed next.

Processing (Clock) Speed

Virtually all CPUs come in a variety of *processing speeds*, also known as *clock speeds*. **Clock speed** indicates how many ticks of the *system clock*—the internal clock for a computer that synchronizes all its operations—occur per second. Clock speed is rated in *megahertz (MHz)* or *gigahertz (GHz)*, which is millions or billions of ticks per second, respectively. A higher clock speed means that more instructions can be processed per second than the same CPU with a lower clock speed. For instance, a Pentium 4 microprocessor running at 3.06 GHz would be faster than a Pentium 4 running at 2.8 GHz, if all other components remained the same. CPUs for the earliest PCs ran at less than 5 MHz; today's fastest CPUs run at more than 3 GHz. Although processing speed is an important factor in computer performance, other factors (such as the amount of memory, the speed of peripheral devices, *bus width*, and *bus speed*) greatly affect performance, as well.

Word Size

A computer *word* is the amount of data (measured in bits or bytes) that a CPU can manipulate at one time. Different CPUs may have different *word sizes*. Some newer CPUs are designed for 64-bit words, which means that data moves around within the CPU and from the CPU to memory in 64-bit (8 byte) chunks. Usually, a larger word size allows faster processing in a computer system.

FURTHER EXPLORATION

For links to further information about CPUs, go to
www.course.com/uc10/ch03

>**Clock speed.** The number of ticks of the system clock that occurs per second.

Type of Processor	Year Introduced	CPU Name	Manufacturer	Clock Speed*	Word Size	Cache Memory			System Bus Width	System Bus Speed
						Level 1	Level 2	Level 3		
D E S K T O P	2003	Athlon 64	AMD	2–2.2 GHz	64 bit	128 KB	1 MB	n/a	64 bit	400 MHz
	2003	PowerPC G5	Apple/IBM	1.6–2 GHz	64 bit	64 KB	512 KB	n/a	64 bit	1 GHz
	2003	Pentium M	Intel	900 MHz–1.7 GHz	32 bit	64 KB	1 MB	n/a	64 bit	400 MHz
	2002	Celeron (Pentium 4-based)	Intel	1.7–2.8 GHz	32 bit	20 KB	128 KB	n/a	64 bit	400 MHz
	2001	Athlon XP	AMD	1.33–2.25 GHz	32 bit	128 KB	256–512 KB	n/a	64 bit	266–400 MHz
	2000	Pentium 4	Intel	1.3–3.2 MHz	32 bit	20 KB	256–512 KB	n/a	64 bit	400–800 MHz
S E R V E R	2003	Opteron	AMD	1.4–2.2 GHz	64 bit	128 KB	1 MB	n/a	64 bit	667 MHz
	2002	Itanium 2	Intel	900 MHz–1.5 GHz	64 bit	32 KB	256 KB	1.5–6 MB	128 bit	400 MHz
	2001	Athlon MP	AMD	1–2.13 GHz	32 bit	128 KB	256–512 KB	n/a	64 bit	266 MHz
	2001	Xeon (Pentium 4-based)	Intel	1.4–3.2 GHz	32 bit	20 KB	256–512 KB	0–2 MB	64 bit	400–533 MHz
	2001	Itanium	Intel	733–800 MHz	64 bit	32 KB	96 KB	2–4 MB	64 bit	266 MHz

* Higher speeds expected in the future

▶ FIGURE 3-8
Characteristics of recent CPUs.

TIP

For information about earlier CPUs, see the "CPU Characteristics" section in the References and Resources Guide at the end of this book.

Cache Memory

Cache memory is a special group of fast memory chips located on or close to the CPU chip. It is used to speed up processing by storing the most frequently and recently used data and instructions in handy locations. It works, in theory, the same way you might work at a desk with file folders or documents that you need most often placed within an arm's length. Other useful materials might be placed somewhat farther away, but still within easy reach.

The computer works in a similar manner. Although it can access materials in its main memory (*RAM*) relatively quickly, it can work much faster if it places the most urgently needed materials into areas that allow even faster access. These areas—cache memory—contain the most frequently and recently used data and instructions. To make cache memory more effective, when the cache is full and the CPU calls for a new instruction, the system overwrites the data in cache memory that hasn't been used for the longest period of time. This way, the high-priority information that's used continuously stays in cache, while the less frequently used information is overwritten.

>**Cache memory.** A group of fast memory chips located on or near the CPU to help speed up processing.

TREND

Unusual Uses for Computer Chips: Smart Bullets, Smart Tennis Shoes, and High-Tech Pets

We all know that small computer chips (*microchips*) can be used to build tiny computers and make household appliances work, but did you know they can also be used to steer bullets in combat, track runners in a race, and keep your pet safe? These are just a few of the more innovative uses for microchips.

In the first major update to the Army's M-16 rifle since 1967, a new infantry rifle system—called the XM29—is currently in development. According to the rifle's manufacturer, ATK, the XM29 is five times more effective at over twice the range than existing rifle systems. Instead of relying on a soldier's perfect aim, this new gun uses a laser and smart bullets to hit its mark. Once the soldier marks the desired target with a red dot in his or her laser sights, microprocessors located inside the bullet determine how many times the bullet must revolve in flight to reach the marked destination. In addition to increased accuracy, the gun has the advantage of being able to be fired from up to 1,000 meters away.

A less lethal, but no less interesting, chip application is the smart tennis shoe. Used now for several years in races such as the Boston Marathon, New York Marathon, and Ironman competitions, the heart of the smart tennis shoe is the ChampionChip. This chip, typically attached to the runner's shoe, contains a transponder chip and energizing coil. When the chip passes a special antenna located at the start line, finish line, and selected locations in between, the athlete's ID number is transmitted to the timing computer. At any time during the race, the runner's status can be displayed on the race's Web site. Family and friends can also enter in a runner's ID number to immediately receive an update on the athlete's progress.

To keep tabs on your pet, pet identification systems, such as PETtrac, can be used. These systems register dogs, cats, and other pets with identifying microchips implanted just under

ChampionChips provide a fast, accurate timing system for a variety of athletic events. Whenever an athlete passes over a mat containing a send antenna (as shown here), his or her ID number is broadcast to a receive antenna. The system allows start, split, and ending times to be instantaneously, electronically recorded.

the skin. Similar to tracking systems used by animal researchers, the pet ID chip and an antenna are encased in a tiny glass tube and injected under the skin. When the animal is scanned with a special scanner, its unique ID number is revealed. On implantation, this ID number is entered into a database along with the information about the pet, owner, and veterinarian. When lost pets are scanned at animal shelters, animal hospitals, and other locations with scanners that can read these chips, their owners are quickly identified. Unlike physical tags, which can fall off or become unreadable, or bar-code tattoos, which can wear off, chip identification lasts the entire life of the animal.

Cache memory can be internal or external. *Internal cache* is built right into the CPU chip; *external cache* is located close to, but not inside, the CPU. Level numbers indicate the distance between a particular cache and the CPU: *Level 1* is closest (virtually always internal cache), *Level 2* (usually internal cache) is the next closest, and *Level 3* (appearing now in newer computers as external cache) would be further away. The cache closest to the CPU is always faster but generally costs more and holds less data than other levels of cache. Typically all levels of cache memory are faster than the PC's RAM. As you might guess, the computer looks for data in the closest locations first—first in Level 1 cache, then in Level 2 cache, then in Level 3 cache (if it exists), and then in RAM. Typically a larger cache memory results in faster processing.

Bus Width and Speed

A **bus** is an electronic path within a computer over which data can travel. You can picture a bus as a highway with several lanes; each wire in the bus acts as a separate lane, transmitting one bit at a time. The number of bits being transmitted is dependent on the *bus width*—the number of wires in the bus over which data can travel. Just as in a highway, the wider (or more lanes) a bus has, the more data that can be transferred at one time.

The bus that moves data around within the CPU is usually referred to as the PC's *internal bus*; the bus that moves data back and forth between the CPU and memory is called the *system bus*. Today's computers typically have a specific system bus to connect the CPU to RAM called the *frontside bus* (*FSB*). The *backside bus* (*BSB*) transfers data between the CPU and external cache. Many CPUs today have 64-bit internal and system buses, although the speed of the system bus varies, as indicated in Figure 3-8. Generally a faster system bus indicates a faster PC, and a faster frontside bus creates less of a bottleneck in the overall performance of the system.

Memory

When someone uses the term *memory* in reference to computers, they are usually referring to the computer's main memory—*random access memory* or *RAM*. As discussed in Chapter 1, RAM is volatile and is the location where data and programs are temporarily stored until they are no longer needed. RAM is comprised of a group of chips attached to the motherboard and is used primarily by the computer. This is in contrast to *storage media* (discussed in Chapter 4), which are typically disk-based and are used more actively by the user. It's important to use the terms *memory* and *storage* properly. In general, "memory" refers to chip-based storage—usually the amount of RAM located inside the computer. In contrast, "storage" refers to the amount of long-term storage available to a PC—usually in the form of the PC's hard drive or removable storage media such as floppy disks and CDs, all discussed in the next chapter. While the distinction between memory and storage is important today, it may not necessarily be so in the future because of advances being made in *non-volatile memory*, as discussed in the Inside the Industry box.

In addition to RAM, there are four other types of memory of which computer users should be aware. Two of these—*cache memory* and *registers*—are volatile, similar to RAM; *read-only memory* (*ROM*) and *flash memory* are non-volatile. Cache memory has already been discussed; the other types of memory are explained next.

RAM

RAM (random access memory)—the computer system's main memory—is used to store the essential parts of the operating system while the computer is running, as well as programs and data with which the computer is currently working. Since RAM is volatile, its content is erased when the computer is shut off. Data is also erased when it is no longer needed, such as when the program in which the data was created is closed. To save a document before closing the program and erasing the document from RAM, a storage device needs to be used. The document can then be retrieved from the appropriate storage medium at a later time.

Like the CPU, RAM consists of circuits etched onto chips. These chips are arranged onto circuit boards called *memory modules*; more specifically, they are referred to as *single in-line memory modules* (*SIMMs*), *dual in-line memory modules* (*DIMMs*), or *Rambus in-line memory modules* (*RIMMs*), depending on the type of memory and type of circuit board used. DIMMs are currently the most common format. Memory modules plug into the system board, as shown in Figure 3-6. Most—but not all—desktop PCs sold today come with empty memory slots so the user can add additional memory modules, if needed.

>**Bus.** An electronic path on the motherboard or within the CPU or other computer component along which data is transferred. >**RAM (random access memory).** Chips located on the motherboard that provide a temporary location for the computer to hold data and program instructions while they are needed.

INSIDE THE INDUSTRY

Non-Volatile Memory

Non-volatile memory–memory chips that don't lose their data when the power goes off–are used in a variety of devices today from PCs (in the form of ROM and flash memory chips), to TV set-top boxes, to cell phones, digital cameras, and other portable devices. Flash memory chips are one type of non-volatile chip, but they are not as fast as other types of memory, may wear out sooner, and are approaching their limit on how small they can be manufactured. In response, technology companies are looking to other types of non-volatile memory as eventual replacements for flash memory, as well as potential replacements for the various other types of memory used in a computer–possibly even for the hard drive.

Several new types of memory currently being researched include *magnetic RAM (MRAM)*, *Ovonyx unified memory (OUM)*, *four-bit memory*, *nanocrystals*, *ferroelectric RAM (FeRAM)*, and *polymer memory (polymeric ferroelectric RAM)*. Two of the closest to becoming viable products are magnetic RAM and polymer memory.

As the name suggests, *magnetic RAM* uses magnetic rather than electrical technologies to store data. Unlike volatile memory that requires a constant stream of electricity to retain data, MRAM chips are non-volatile. They store data using magnetic orientation to represent 0s and 1s, similar to a hard drive. MRAM chips are physically smaller than conventional memory chips, but can store more data and can access it faster. They are also less expensive to make than flash memory chips. Because of these characteristics, MRAM chips could conceivably replace all of the conventional RAM and flash memory in a PC; they are also expected to be used with handheld PCs, cell phones, and other mobile devices. As an added bonus, MRAM chips will allow PCs to become instant-on devices, similar to a light switch or television, according to one of the leaders in this area, IBM (see the accompanying photo). MRAM chips are expected to be on the market as early as 2005.

Polymer memory–also called *polymeric ferroelectric RAM (PFRAM)*–uses a layer of polymer (plastic) sandwiched between a grid of intersecting wires. Data is stored where the wires intersect by changing the *electrical resistance* (the ability to conduct electricity) of the polymer. Advantages of polymer memory include the ability to stack layers to form three-dimensional chips, low manufacturing costs, and non-volatility. They also are expected to eventually become faster than today's memory chips. According to one of the companies in the forefront of polymer memory research–Coatue–polymer memory is initially intended to replace flash memory and RAM. Coatue's long-term goal is to eventually combine all of the memory and storage inside a PC, such as ROM, RAM, and the hard drive, into a single 3-D memory stack that sits on top of the microprocessor. Products based on polymer memory technology are expected to be on the market by the end of 2004.

Magnetic RAM. Here, an IBM researcher uses a machine to create magnetic tunnel junctions for magnetic RAM experiments.

For example, in the motherboard shown in Figure 3-6, there are two memory modules already installed and room to add an additional two modules, if necessary.

RAM capacity is measured in bytes. Because the cost of RAM has been decreasing, most PCs today come with significantly more memory than just a year ago. Very low-end PCs may come with 128 MB of RAM, but 256 or 512 MB is much more common in desktop PCs. Servers and workstations typically have between 1 and 4 GB of RAM. Today's 32-bit CPUs can only address up to 4 GB of RAM, so higher amounts of RAM are expected once 64-bit processors (which can address a virtually unlimited amount of RAM) become more widely available. It is important for a PC to have enough RAM to run the needed applications (minimum RAM requirements are almost always stated on a software program's packaging), as well as to work efficiently (more RAM allows more programs to be opened at one time).

Types of RAM

Ordinary RAM is often referred to as *DRAM* (*dynamic RAM*) in technical literature. This name refers to its need for regular recharging as processing takes place. During recharge, DRAM cannot be accessed by the CPU. A faster type of RAM—called *SRAM* (*static RAM*)—does not need recharging. Since SRAM chips are more expensive than DRAM, computer makers use them sparingly. A newer type of DRAM is *SDRAM* (*synchronous DRAM*). SDRAM is much faster than DRAM because it is synchronized to the system clock; *RDRAM* (*Rambus DRAM*) is even faster. *Double-data rate* (*DDR*) *SDRAM* sends data twice per clock tick so it is twice as fast as the same speed SDRAM. DDR SDRAM was the standard for desktop PCs at the time this book was published; *double-data rate-II* (*DDR-II*) *SDRAM*, which sends about four times as much data per clock tick as SDRAM with half the power consumption, is expected to be released shortly.

Memory Speed

Memory speed is typically measured in megahertz (MHz) like CPU speed, although some memory manufacturers measure speed in *nanoseconds* (billionths of a second) instead. Common speeds in megahertz are 133 MHz for SDRAM, 133 MHz for SRAM, 400 MHz for DDR SDRAM, 667 MHz for DDR-II SDRAM, and 1,066 MHz (1.066 GHz) for RDRAM. Memory manufacturers are continually working on ways to make memory faster. Having components, such as RAM or buses, operate at a slower speed than the CPU has caused processing bottlenecks in the past, where the CPU sits idle while it waits for the appropriate component to finish what it needs to do first. Increasing the speed of slower components helps to avoid this problem.

Some memory today is *dual-channel memory*, which can transfer twice as much data at one time as *single-channel memory* of the same speed. It is expected that some memory in the near future will be *four-channel*. Because of these newer types of memory, as well as double-data rate RAM, it is becoming more common and more accurate to express memory speed in terms of its *bandwidth*; that is, the actual amount of data transferred (in GB) per second. For example, single-channel DDR SDRAM running at 400 MHz transfers 3.2 *GBps* (*gigabytes per second*), while dual-channel DDR SDRAM running at 400 MHz transfers data at a rate of 6.4 GBps.

Memory Addressing

Once the CPU stores something in RAM, it must be able to find it again when needed. To accomplish this, each location in memory has an *address*. Whenever a block of data, instruction, program, or result of a calculation is stored in memory, it is stored into one or more consecutive addresses, depending on its size (see Figure 3-9). Computer systems automatically set up and maintain directory tables that provide the addresses of the first character of all data stored in memory, along with the number of addresses used, to facilitate the retrieval of data.

When the computer has finished processing a program or set of data, it frees up that memory space to hold other programs and data. Thus, the content of each memory location constantly changes. This process can be roughly compared with the handling of the mailboxes in your local post office: the number on each P.O. box (memory location) remains the same, but the mail (data) stored inside changes as patrons remove their mail and as new mail arrives.

Registers

Registers are another type of high-speed memory built into the CPU. They are used by the CPU to temporarily store each program instruction and piece of data just before it is processed. Registers are the fastest type of memory used by the CPU, even faster than

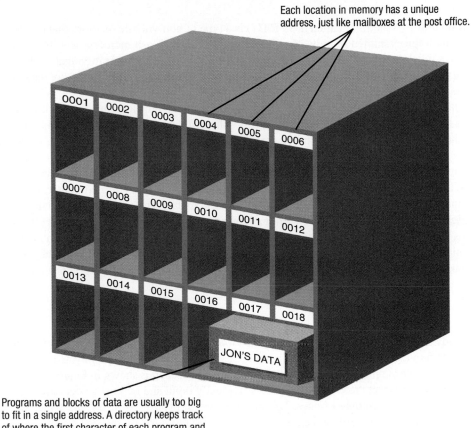

Each location in memory has a unique address, just like mailboxes at the post office.

FIGURE 3-9
Memory addressing.

H
W

Programs and blocks of data are usually too big to fit in a single address. A directory keeps track of where the first character of each program and data block can be found and the number of addresses it spans.

Level 1 cache. Generally, the more data a register can contain at one time, the faster the CPU performs. Register size usually matches word and internal bus size and so is usually 32 bits, although the newer 64-bit chips such as the Itanium 2, Opteron, and Athlon 64 use 64-bit registers and word sizes (refer again to Figure 3-8). Most CPUs contain several registers; registers are discussed in more detail later in this chapter.

ROM

ROM (read-only memory) consists of non-volatile chips into which data or programs have been permanently stored; the data or programs are retrieved by the computer when they are needed. Like RAM, these chips are attached to the motherboard inside the system unit. An important difference, however, is that you can neither write over the data or programs in ROM chips (which is the reason ROM chips are called *read-only*), nor destroy their contents when you shut off the computer's power.

Important pieces of system software are often stored in ROM chips. For instance, one of the computer's first activities when you turn on the power is to perform a power-on self-test or *POST*. Traditionally, the instructions for the POST have been stored in ROM. POST takes an inventory of system components, checks each component for proper functioning, and initializes system settings, which produces the beeps you hear as your PC boots up.

>ROM (read-only memory). Non-erasable chips located on the motherboard into which data or programs have been permanently stored.

Flash Memory

Flash memory (sometimes called *flash RAM*) is a type of non-volatile memory that can be erased and reprogrammed in units of memory called *blocks*. Flash memory gets its name because a block is erased in a single action or *flash*. This type of organization makes flash memory faster than RAM, although it is more expensive than RAM and has to store data in block-size, not byte-size, pieces.

Flash memory chips have begun to replace ROM for system information, such as to hold a PC's *BIOS* or *basic input/output system*—the sequence of instructions the PC follows during the boot process, including the POST discussed earlier. By storing this information in flash memory instead of ROM, the BIOS information can be updated as needed. Flash memory chips are also used to store programs in portable PCs and mobile devices.

While some flash memory chips within a PC are used only by the computer, other flash memory chips are used by the user. Because flash memory chips are small and hold a significant amount of data, they are commonly used as storage media for portable PCs, as well as for cell phones, digital cameras, MP3 players, and other small devices. Flash memory chips used for user storage can be built directly into the PC or other device; they are also built into a variety of removable *flash memory media*, such as flash memory cards, sticks, and drives. Flash memory media is discussed in more detail in Chapter 4.

FURTHER EXPLORATION

For links to further information about memory, go to www.course.com/uc10/ch03

Buses

As already discussed, a bus is an electronic path within a computer over which data travels. In addition to moving data within the CPU, buses are used to tie the CPU to memory and peripheral devices. An example of how the buses in a PC might be set up is shown in Figure 3-10.

Buses that connect the CPU to peripheral (typically input and output) devices are usually referred to as **expansion buses**. Expansion buses, typically 16 to 64 bits wide, are etched onto the motherboard, and either connect the CPU to *ports* on the system unit case or to *expansion slots* on the motherboard. There are a variety of expansion bus standards. As illustrated in Figure 3-10, most CPUs today use a *chipset* of one or more chips that help bridge or connect the various buses to the CPU. Some of the most common types of expansion buses are discussed next; expansion slots and ports are discussed shortly.

ISA Bus

The *ISA (Industry Standard Architecture)* bus has been around since 1984. Although it is still included on some new PCs (typically connected to the PCI bus, as shown in Figure 3-10), it is beginning to be phased out and replaced by the newer bus standards discussed next. The ISA bus is slow, transmitting 8 or 16 bits at one time. Consequently, when an ISA bus is used, it is for slower devices—such as the system's mouse or sound card.

PCI Bus

The *PCI (Peripheral Component Interconnect)* bus is one of the most common types of expansion buses. It can transmit up to 64 bits at a time (although 32 bits is more common) and is significantly faster than the ISA bus, delivering a bandwidth of more than 100 *MBps* (*megabytes per second*). A newer, faster version of PCI introduced in 2000 is called *PCI-X*. PCI-X supports a 64-bit bus width and a bandwidth of more than 1,000 MBps (1 *GBps*). In addition to connecting the CPU to the PCI expansion slots, the PCI bus is used to connect other buses to the CPU, such as the ISA and USB buses, as shown in

---

>**Flash memory.** A type of non-volatile memory that can be erased and reprogrammed; commonly implemented in the form of sticks or cards.
>**Expansion bus.** A bus that connects the CPU to peripheral devices.

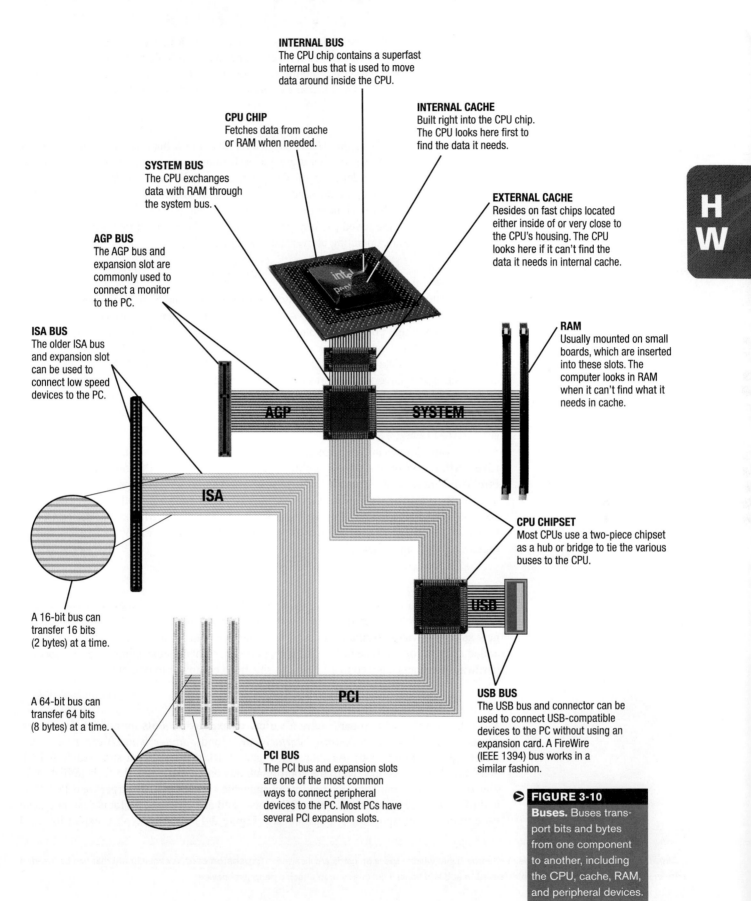

INTERNAL BUS
The CPU chip contains a superfast internal bus that is used to move data around inside the CPU.

INTERNAL CACHE
Built right into the CPU chip. The CPU looks here first to find the data it needs.

CPU CHIP
Fetches data from cache or RAM when needed.

SYSTEM BUS
The CPU exchanges data with RAM through the system bus.

EXTERNAL CACHE
Resides on fast chips located either inside of or very close to the CPU's housing. The CPU looks here if it can't find the data it needs in internal cache.

AGP BUS
The AGP bus and expansion slot are commonly used to connect a monitor to the PC.

ISA BUS
The older ISA bus and expansion slot can be used to connect low speed devices to the PC.

RAM
Usually mounted on small boards, which are inserted into these slots. The computer looks in RAM when it can't find what it needs in cache.

A 16-bit bus can transfer 16 bits (2 bytes) at a time.

CPU CHIPSET
Most CPUs use a two-piece chipset as a hub or bridge to tie the various buses to the CPU.

A 64-bit bus can transfer 64 bits (8 bytes) at a time.

PCI BUS
The PCI bus and expansion slots are one of the most common ways to connect peripheral devices to the PC. Most PCs have several PCI expansion slots.

USB BUS
The USB bus and connector can be used to connect USB-compatible devices to the PC without using an expansion card. A FireWire (IEEE 1394) bus works in a similar fashion.

H
W

AGP

SYSTEM

ISA

USB

PCI

▶ **FIGURE 3-10**
Buses. Buses transport bits and bytes from one component to another, including the CPU, cache, RAM, and peripheral devices.

Figure 3-10. Eventually, the PCI bus may be replaced by a faster architecture, such as a newer version of PCI called *PCI Express*, expected to be available by the end of 2004 with an initial bandwidth of 16 GBps, and the emerging *InfiniBand* architecture, expected to be used primarily with servers and support a bandwidth exceeding 2.5 GBps.

AGP Bus

The *AGP* (*Accelerated Graphics Port*) bus is a relatively new bus standard that was developed in response to the trend toward greater performance requirements for graphics display. With the increasing demands of 3D graphics and full-motion video playback, both the processor and the video card need to process more information much more quickly than before. Although the standard PCI bus has been adequate for video displays in the past, AGP provides improved performance with a fast, 32-bit, direct interface between the video card and RAM, operating at over 2,000 MBps (2 GBps).

USB Bus

One of the more versatile new bus architectures in recent years is the *Universal Serial Bus* (*USB*). The USB standard enables up to 127 devices to be connected to a computer's PCI bus through a single port on the computer's system unit. At 1.5 MBps, the original USB standard transmitted data at a much slower rate than both PCI and AGP. The newer *USB 2* standard supports data transfer rates of 60 MBps—still slower than PCI and AGP, but the convenience and universal support of USB have made it one of the most widely used standards for peripherals today.

FireWire/IEEE 1394 Bus

FireWire (also known as *IEEE 1394*) is a newer external bus standard developed by Apple. Like USB, FireWire can connect multiple external devices to the PCI bus via a single port. FireWire is fairly fast, supporting data transfer rates of up to 40 MBps, and is commonly used with video cameras and other multimedia peripherals for both Apple and IBM-compatible computers. The even newer *FireWire 2* (*IEEE 1394b*) standard supports data transfer rates up to 100 MBps. It is expected that USB and/or FireWire will eventually replace the ISA and other types of older buses.

Expansion Slots and Cards

Most PCs have a way to add additional capabilities to the PC when new needs arrive. For instance, a user may need to add a *modem* for Internet connectivity, a better sound card, a new storage device or printer, or a *network interface*. The overall ways these devices are added depends on the type of PC (desktop, portable, or handheld) being used; the specific hardware that can be added to a PC also varies from computer to computer.

Expansion for Desktop PCs

Most desktop PC motherboards have a variety of **expansion slots** into which **expansion cards** (also called *add-in boards*, *interface cards*, and *adapter boards*) can be inserted (refer again to Figure 3-6). As shown in Figure 3-10, the expansion slots (such as PCI, AGP, and ISP) are connected to the appropriate bus on the motherboard. It is important to realize that expansion slots are not interchangeable—ISA slots are larger than PCI slots and AGP slots are a little smaller than PCI slots—and each expansion slot is designed to be used with its corresponding expansion card. Figure 3-11 shows a typical expansion card

---

>**Expansion slot.** A location on the motherboard into which expansion cards are inserted. >**Expansion card.** A circuit board that can be inserted into an expansion slot on a PC's motherboard to add additional functionality or to attach a peripheral device.

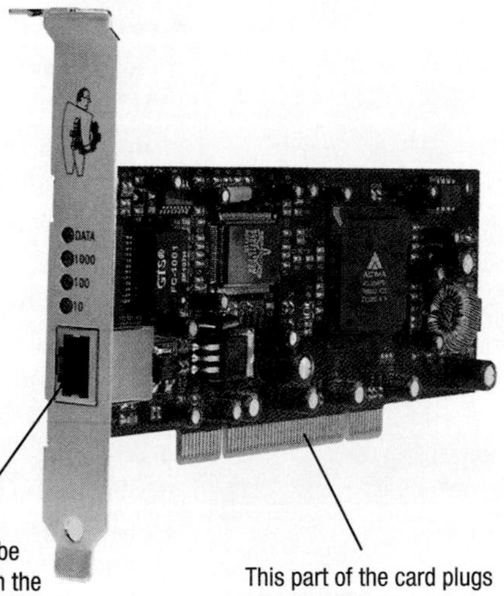

The port on this network card will be accessible through the exterior of the system unit's case.

This part of the card plugs into an empty PCI slot on the motherboard.

COMMON EXPANSION CARDS	
Card Type	Purpose
Accelerator board	Uses specialized processor chips that speed up overall processing.
Disk controller card	Enables a particular type of disk drive to interface with the PC.
Modem card	Provides communications capabilities to connect to a company network or the Internet.
Network interface card	Enables a PC to connect to a network.
Sound card	Enables users to attach speakers to a PC and provides specific sound capabilities.
TV tuner card	Allows a PC to pick up television signals.
Video capture board	Allows video images to be input into the computer from a video camera.
Video graphics board	Enables the connection of a monitor; may provide additional graphics capabilities.

and lists a variety of common types of expansion cards. As shown in this figure, most expansion cards have a port that is exposed through the case of the system unit; this port is used to connect the external device (such as a monitor, printer, scanner, or networking cable) being added to the system. Ports are discussed in more detail shortly.

Instead of using expansion boards and tying up valuable expansion slots inside the system unit, some PCs integrate sound, video, or other capabilities into chips that are attached directly to the motherboard. When an integrated feature is used, a special bus connects that chip to the appropriate port on the outside of the system unit so the appropriate device can be attached to the PC.

> **FIGURE 3-11**
> **Expansion cards for desktop PCs.**

TIP

When buying a desktop PC, check to see how many available (non-used) expansion slots the PC has and what types they are. You should also have at least two USB ports to add additional hardware available in USB format.

PC Cards: Expansion for Notebook and Tablet PCs

Because space is so limited inside portable PCs, usually expansion cards and devices are not installed inside the system unit. Instead, most notebook and tablet PCs come with a **PC card slot** (sometimes called a *PCMCIA card* slot) that conforms to the standards developed by the *Personal Computer Memory Card International Association*. PC card slots are typically located on the side of a notebook or tablet computer's case (see Figure 3-12); these slots connect to the *PC card bus* inside the PC. **PC cards** can be typically plugged in or unplugged while the computer is turned on and they come in three different thicknesses, from *Type I* (the thinnest) to *Type III* (the thickest). Some notebook PCs may have a slot that can hold more than one of the thinner PC cards—it is a good idea to double-check the number and sizes of PC cards your computer can use before buying a new PC card. In addition to PC card slots, notebook computers often have a universal *drive bay* which can be used to alternate between a second hard drive, CD or DVD drive, and floppy drive, as needed.

>**PC card slot.** A slot on the exterior of a computer into which a PC card is inserted. >**PC card.** A small card that fits into a slot located on the exterior of a computer to provide new functionality or to attach a peripheral device.

COMMON PC CARDS	
Card Type	**Purpose**
Bluetooth card	Provides communication with other Bluetooth-compatible devices.
Flash media adapter	Creates ports for one or more types of flash memory cards.
Flash memory card	Provides additional storage.
Hard drive card	Provides an additional hard drive.
Modem card	Provides communications capabilities.
Networking card	Enables a PC to connect to a network.
Serial card	Creates a serial port to be used with serial printers, mice, and other hardware.
USB or FireWire card	Creates a USB or FireWire port to connect USB or FireWire devices.
Video output card	Enables the connection of a second video device (monitor, computer data projector, etc.).

Ports, if they exist, are exposed here; this card doesn't have any ports since it's a wireless networking card.

PC card plugs into slot on side of notebook.

FIGURE 3-12
PC cards for notebook and tablet PCs.

FIGURE 3-13
Portable PC expansion. Most handheld PCs have at least one expansion slot.

SD slot   SD card

Expansion for Handheld PCs and Mobile Devices

Most handheld PCs and mobile devices have a limited amount of expandability, but most come with at least one built-in expansion slot designed for special expansion cards used to attach peripheral devices or add additional capabilities. Increasingly, the slot is designed for postage-stamp-size *SD cards*—flash memory cards and hardware adhering to the *Secure Digital Input/Output* (*SDIO*) standard (see Figure 3-13). Although SD slots are often used with flash memory storage cards (as discussed in Chapter 4), SD slots will also accept *Secure Digital Input/Output* (*SDIO*) *devices*—small devices, such as a digital camera or networking adapter—that are attached to an SD card. A limited number of SDIO devices are currently available, but more are expected to become available in the near future. Some handheld PCs support additional types of flash memory cards; a few include a PC card slot.

Ports

Most system units feature exterior connectors or sockets called **ports** that enable you to plug in external hardware devices. Each port is attached to the appropriate bus on the motherboard so that the devices plugged into each port can communicate with the CPU. Typical ports for a desktop PC are shown in Figure 3-14. As shown in this figure, there are unique connectors for each type of port on a computer system. When connecting cables to the system unit, it is important to pay attention to the *gender* of the port, in addition to the shape, pin count, and pin configuration. *Male* connectors have the pins extended and connect to *female* connectors with matching holes. If a port is of the proper type (such as serial), but is the wrong gender or has the wrong number of pins, adapters or special cables can sometimes be used to convert the connector to the desired configuration.

To add a new device to your PC, if there is an available port for the device you want to add you just need to plug it in (shut down the computer first, unless the device uses a USB

>Port. A connector on the exterior of a PC's system unit to which a device may be attached.

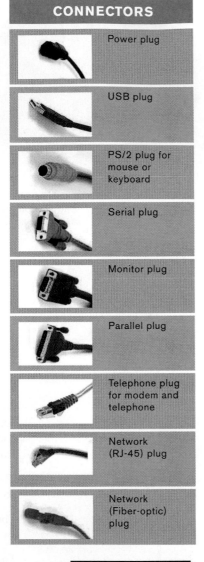

CONNECTORS

Power plug

USB plug

PS/2 plug for mouse or keyboard

Serial plug

Monitor plug

Parallel plug

Telephone plug for modem and telephone

Network (RJ-45) plug

Network (Fiber-optic) plug

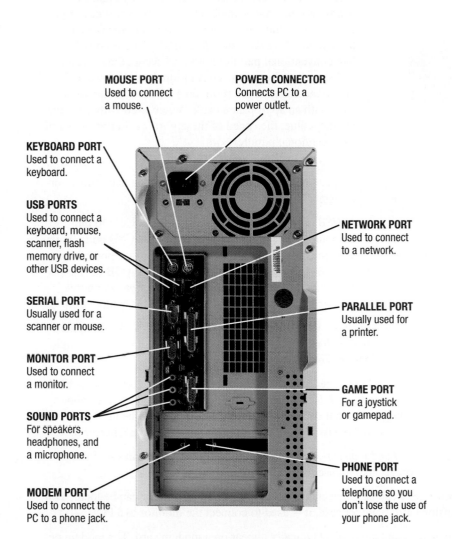

MOUSE PORT
Used to connect a mouse.

POWER CONNECTOR
Connects PC to a power outlet.

KEYBOARD PORT
Used to connect a keyboard.

USB PORTS
Used to connect a keyboard, mouse, scanner, flash memory drive, or other USB devices.

SERIAL PORT
Usually used for a scanner or mouse.

MONITOR PORT
Used to connect a monitor.

SOUND PORTS
For speakers, headphones, and a microphone.

MODEM PORT
Used to connect the PC to a phone jack.

NETWORK PORT
Used to connect to a network.

PARALLEL PORT
Usually used for a printer.

GAME PORT
For a joystick or gamepad.

PHONE PORT
Used to connect a telephone so you don't lose the use of your phone jack.

H W

FIGURE 3-14
Typical ports and connectors for a desktop PC.

or FireWire port). If there isn't an available port, you need to either insert the appropriate expansion card to create one or use a USB or FireWire version of the device, if you have one of those two ports available on your PC. Because a wide variety of hardware is available in USB format today, most recent PCs come with at least two USB ports. In fact, it is becoming common to see USB ports located on the front of a system unit for easier access, such as to connect a digital camera or USB *flash memory drive* on a regular basis. Some of the most common ports are discussed next.

▼ *Serial ports* can transmit data only a single bit at a time. However, they use very inexpensive cables and they can reliably send data over long distances. Serial ports can be used for such devices as keyboards, mice, and modems, although most systems today come with dedicated ports to attach the mouse and keyboard, as shown in Figure 3-14. *Serial connectors* typically have 9 or 25 pins and are referred to as *DB-9* or *DB-25 connectors*.

▼ *Parallel ports* can transmit data one byte (8 bits) at a time—making data transfers several times faster than those through serial ports—but they require more expensive

TIP

Some of the older ports, such as *serial* and *parallel*, are beginning to be referred to as *legacy ports* and are being eliminated on some new PCs.

Up to four USB devices can connect here.

Connection from PC goes here.

> **FIGURE 3-15**
A USB hub can be used to connect multiple USB devices to a single USB port.

cables and cannot reliably send data across distances greater than 50 feet. Parallel ports typically connect nearby printers and scanners to a PC. Newer types of parallel ports include the *Enhanced Parallel Port* (*EPP*) and the *Extended Capabilities Port* (*ECP*). These ports look like conventional parallel ports and accept the same size and shape of plug as the conventional parallel port (a 25-pin connector), but are more than 10 times faster when used with an appropriate cable. When used with a regular parallel cable, the speed of these ports is similar to that of a conventional parallel port.

▼ *SCSI* (*Small Computer System Interface*) *ports* are high-speed parallel ports generally used to attach printers or scanners.

▼ *USB ports* are used to connect USB devices to the computer. Most new PCs come with two USB ports, but a *USB hub*—a device that plugs into your PC's USB port to convert one port into several USB ports (see Figure 3-15)—can be used to connect multiple USB devices to a single USB port, when necessary. In addition, USB devices are *hot-swappable*, meaning that they can be attached and removed while the computer is turned on.

▼ *FireWire* (*IEEE 1394*) *ports* are used to connect FireWire devices to the computer. Similar to USB, a *FireWire hub* can be used to connect multiple devices to a single port and FireWire devices are hot-swappable.

▼ *Network ports* are used to connect a PC to a local area network. Most network cards contain a port that accepts an *RJ-45 connector*, which looks similar to a telephone connector but is larger. Coaxial cable or fiber optic connectors can be used for network connections, as well. Networks are discussed in more detail in Chapter 8.

▼ The *keyboard port* and *mouse port* typically use a *PS/2 connector* and are used to connect the keyboard and mouse to the system unit.

▼ The *monitor port* can be connected directly to the motherboard or can be located on an expansion card. In either case, it is used to connect the monitor to a PC.

▼ The *modem port* and *phone port* typically appear on a modem card. The modem port is used to connect the modem card to your phone outlet. The phone port can be used to connect a telephone, if desired, so you can still have a telephone connected to the phone jack being used.

▼ A *MIDI port* is used to connect a *MIDI* (*musical instrument digital interface*) device to the computer. MIDI devices include musical keyboards and other instruments that can be connected to the computer to compose music to be stored electronically. A MIDI port usually looks similar to a keyboard port.

▼ An *IrDA* (*Infrared Data Association*) *port* receives infrared transmissions from such devices as wireless keyboards, wireless mice, and portable devices. Since the transmission is wireless, the port doesn't use a plug. With infrared transmission, there cannot be anything blocking the infrared light waves, so newer wireless mice and keyboards tend to use radio wave transmission instead. However, IrDA ports are commonly used to "beam" data from a handheld PC or other portable device to another PC.

▼ A *game port* is used to connect a joystick, gamepad, steering wheel, or other device commonly used with computer game programs.

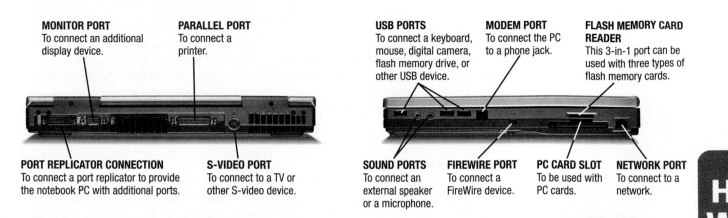

MONITOR PORT
To connect an additional display device.

PARALLEL PORT
To connect a printer.

USB PORTS
To connect a keyboard, mouse, digital camera, flash memory drive, or other USB device.

MODEM PORT
To connect the PC to a phone jack.

FLASH MEMORY CARD READER
This 3-in-1 port can be used with three types of flash memory cards.

PORT REPLICATOR CONNECTION
To connect a port replicator to provide the notebook PC with additional ports.

S-VIDEO PORT
To connect to a TV or other S-video device.

SOUND PORTS
To connect an external speaker or a microphone.

FIREWIRE PORT
To connect a FireWire device.

PC CARD SLOT
To be used with PC cards.

NETWORK PORT
To connect to a network.

H W

> **FIGURE 3-16**
Notebook ports.
Shown here are ports on the back (left) and side (right) of a typical notebook computer.

Notebook computers have ports similar to desktop PCs, but sometimes don't have as many. One type of port not often found on desktop PCs is one used to connect a *port replicator*—a hardware device containing additional ports (such as serial, parallel, PS/2, USB, and networking ports) that can be used with the notebook whenever the port replicator is connected (some port replicators connect via a USB or PC card slot instead). Some typical notebook ports are illustrated in Figure 3-16. Additional ports not shown in this figure that are commonly found on notebook computers include IrDA ports for infrared transmission and those used to connect the notebook to a *docking station*—a device with peripheral devices (such as a monitor, keyboard, mouse, and printer) always attached; these devices can be used whenever the PC is attached to the docking station.

As already discussed, most handheld PCs and some smart phones have an external port that accepts flash memory cards; some also have proprietary ports for additional devices. For instance, many Palm PCs have a *Universal Connector* to which a variety of hardware devices can be attached (see Figure 3-17). Some portable PCs made by Handspring (which was recently acquired by Palm) use proprietary *Springboard modules* to add additional devices, such as a digital camera or GPS receiver. Many portable PCs and some smart phones also have a port to connect a special portable keyboard designed for the device. Common add-on devices for portable PCs include modems, networking adapters, keyboards, and MP3 players.

> **FIGURE 3-17**
Handheld PC ports.
Most handheld PCs and smart phones have some type of connector for attaching peripheral devices.

The Universal Connector on the bottom of this Palm PC can be used with a variety of accessories, such as a GPS receiver, wireless modem, battery charger, keyboard, and more.

HOW THE CPU WORKS

Regardless of size, every computer's CPU is basically a collection of electronic circuits and components. Electronic impulses from an input device pass through RAM and enter the CPU through a system bus. Within the CPU, these impulses move through the circuits and various components (as directed by the program) to create a series of new impulses. Eventually, a set of electronic impulses leaves the CPU headed for an output device.

The key element of the microprocessor is the *transistor*—a device made of semiconductor material that acts like a switch controlling the flow of electrons inside a chip. Today's CPUs contain tens of millions of transistors. A recent breakthrough reduced the size of the transistor by 30%, which will enable future microprocessors to contain a billion transistors. These microscopic transistors can turn on and off more than a trillion times per second and microprocessors created with these transistors could complete close to a billion calculations in the blink of an eye—a significant speed increase over current CPUs. The primary components of a CPU are discussed next.

Typical CPU Components

To begin to understand how a CPU works, you need to know how the CPU is organized and what components it includes. This information will help you understand how electronic impulses move from one part of the CPU to another to process data. The architecture and components included in a CPU (referred to as *microarchitecture*) vary from microprocessor to microprocessor. A simplified example of the principal components that may be included in a typical CPU is shown in Figure 3-18 and discussed next.

Arithmetic/Logic Unit (ALU)

The **arithmetic/logic unit** (**ALU**) is the section of the CPU that performs arithmetic (addition, subtraction, multiplication, and division) and logical operations (such as comparing two pieces of data to see if they are equal or determining if a specific condition is true or false). In other words, it's the part of the CPU that computes. The fact that the CPU can perform only basic arithmetic and logical operations might not seem very impressive, but when combined in various ways at tremendous speeds, these operations enable the computer to perform immensely complex and data-intensive tasks, in a very short period of time—a remarkable feat. For example, editing a digital photograph in an image-editing program, running the spelling checker in a word processing program, and burning a music CD are all performed by the ALU using only arithmetic and logical operations.

FIGURE 3-18
Inside a CPU.

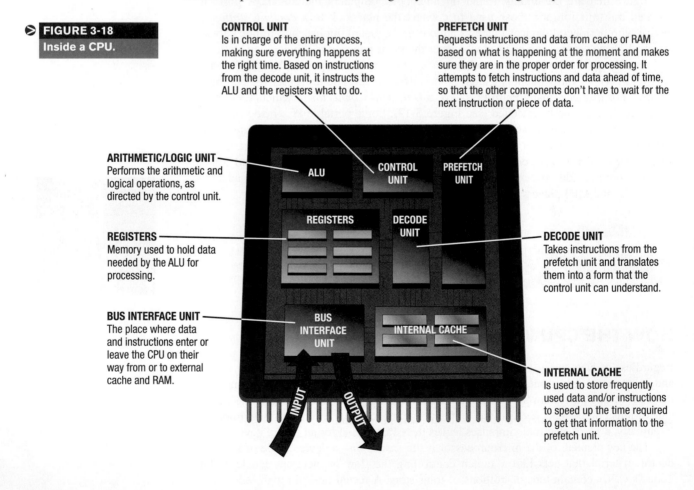

CONTROL UNIT
Is in charge of the entire process, making sure everything happens at the right time. Based on instructions from the decode unit, it instructs the ALU and the registers what to do.

PREFETCH UNIT
Requests instructions and data from cache or RAM based on what is happening at the moment and makes sure they are in the proper order for processing. It attempts to fetch instructions and data ahead of time, so that the other components don't have to wait for the next instruction or piece of data.

ARITHMETIC/LOGIC UNIT
Performs the arithmetic and logical operations, as directed by the control unit.

REGISTERS
Memory used to hold data needed by the ALU for processing.

BUS INTERFACE UNIT
The place where data and instructions enter or leave the CPU on their way from or to external cache and RAM.

DECODE UNIT
Takes instructions from the prefetch unit and translates them into a form that the control unit can understand.

INTERNAL CACHE
Is used to store frequently used data and/or instructions to speed up the time required to get that information to the prefetch unit.

ALU   CONTROL UNIT   PREFETCH UNIT

REGISTERS   DECODE UNIT

BUS INTERFACE UNIT   INTERNAL CACHE

INPUT   OUTPUT

>**Arithmetic/logic unit (ALU).** The part of the CPU that performs arithmetic and logical operations.

Control Unit

The **control unit** coordinates and controls the computer's operations, such as retrieving instructions and passing them on to the ALU for execution. In other words, it directs the flow of electronic traffic within the CPU, much like a traffic cop controls the flow of vehicles on a roadway. Essentially, the control unit tells the ALU what to do and makes sure that everything happens at the right time in order for the appropriate processing to take place.

Registers

As discussed earlier in this chapter, **registers** are groups of high-speed memory located within the CPU into which data is transferred just before processing. The ALU uses registers to temporarily store data, intermediary calculations, and the final results of processing. A CPU may have a variety of registers for different purposes, such as an *instruction register* to hold instructions, and an *accumulator register* to hold intermediary processing results. One of Intel's most recent chips—the Itanium 2—has a total of 328 different registers.

Prefetch Unit

The **prefetch unit**, present in many recent microprocessors, orders data and instructions from cache or RAM based on the task at hand. By attempting to retrieve the necessary instructions and data ahead of time, the prefetch unit helps to avoid delays in processing. It also ensures that all instructions are lined up correctly to send off to the *decode unit*.

Decode Unit

The **decode unit** translates instructions into a form that can be processed by the ALU and stored in the registers. After decoding, the instructions go to the control unit for processing.

Internal Cache

As mentioned earlier, internal cache (such as Level 1 and Level 2 cache) is used to store frequently used instructions and data. If the necessary items are not in internal cache, they must be retrieved from external cache or RAM.

Bus Interface Unit

The **bus interface unit** is the place where instructions and data flow in and out of the CPU. It connects the CPU to the system bus to connect the CPU to external cache and RAM.

The System Clock and the Machine Cycle

As mentioned at the beginning of this chapter, every instruction that you issue to a computer—either by typing a command or clicking something with the mouse—is converted into machine language. In turn, each machine-language instruction in a CPU's *instruction set* (the collection of basic machine-language commands that the CPU can understand) is broken down into several smaller, machine-level instructions called *microcode*. Microcoded instructions, such as moving a single piece of data from one part of the computer system to another or adding the numbers located in two specific registers, are built into the CPU to provide its basic instructions.

As previously discussed, a PC's **system clock** synchronizes the computer's operations. This clock typically resides on the motherboard and sends out a signal on a regular basis to all other computer components, similar to a musician's metronome or a person's

---

heartbeat. Each signal is referred to as a *cycle*; the number of cycles per second is measured in hertz (Hz). One megahertz (MHz) and one gigahertz (GHz) are equal to one million and one billion ticks of the system clock, respectively.

During each tick or clock cycle, the CPU executes a certain number of pieces of microcode. Consequently, a PC with a higher system clock speed processes more instructions per second than the same PC using a lower system clock speed. Older computers may take more than one clock tick for each instruction; today's faster *superscaler* computers are able to perform multiple instructions per clock tick. Different computers can process a different number of instructions per clock tick. Consequently, for a more universal measurement, processing speed can be measured in the number of instructions the CPU can process per second instead of the number of cycles per second. In this case, the terms *mips* (millions of instructions per second), *megaflops*, *gigaflops*, and *teraflops* (millions, billions, and trillions of floating-point operations per second, respectively) are used. Although originally used only with mainframe and supercomputers, today's microcomputers have become so fast that their speeds are now sometimes being quoted using this terminology. For example, Apple rates the speed of its PowerPC G4 CPU at over one gigaflop.

Despite the number or fraction of clock ticks required per instruction, when the CPU processes a single piece of microcode, it is referred to as a **machine cycle**. Each machine cycle consists of the four operations that follow (see Figure 3-19):

1. *Fetch*—the program instruction or information about a needed piece of data is fetched.

2. *Decode*—the instructions are decoded so the control unit and ALU can understand them.

3. *Execute*—the ALU executes the appropriate instruction, if any arithmetic computation or logical comparisons are required.

4. *Store*—the original data or the result from the ALU's execution is stored either in a register or memory, depending on the instruction.

FIGURE 3-19

A machine cycle. A machine cycle is typically accomplished in four steps, although some newer computers divide executing the instruction into two steps, resulting in a five-step machine cycle.

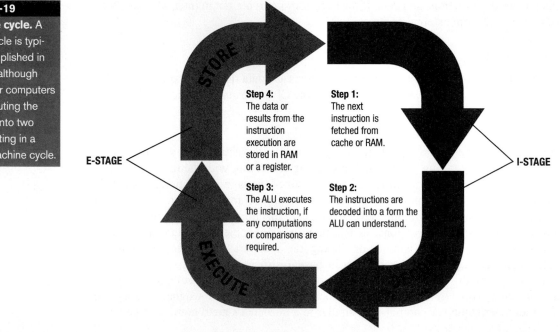

STORE

E-STAGE

I-STAGE

EXECUTE

Step 4:
The data or results from the instruction execution are stored in RAM or a register.

Step 1:
The next instruction is fetched from cache or RAM.

Step 3:
The ALU executes the instruction, if any computations or comparisons are required.

Step 2:
The instructions are decoded into a form the ALU can understand.

>**Machine cycle.** The series of operations involved in the execution of a single machine-level instruction.

Because a machine cycle only processes a single instruction, many seemingly simple commands (such as adding two numbers) may require more than one machine cycle, and a computer may need to go through thousands, millions, or even billions of machine cycles to complete a single program's processing. Consequently, the machine cycle is repeated as many times as necessary to complete a user command or program instruction. A simplified example of how a CPU might process the command *2 + 3 =* is illustrated in Figure 3-20. In this example, four machine cycles are used, as follows:

1. The number 2 is fetched and temporarily stored in internal cache, then sent to the decode unit where it is determined that the number needs to be stored, and then sent with the proper command to the control unit, which stores the number in a register.

2. The number 3 is fetched and temporarily stored in internal cache, then sent to the decode unit where it is determined that the number needs to be stored, and then sent with the proper command to the control unit, which stores the number in a register.

3. The addition symbol is fetched and temporarily stored in internal cache as an addition instruction, which is then sent to the decode unit where it is determined that the two numbers held in the registers need to be added. That instruction is then sent to the control unit, which instructs the ALU to add the two numbers and store the result in another register.

4. The equal sign is fetched and temporarily stored in internal cache as an output instruction, which is then sent to the decode unit where it is determined that the sum located in a register needs to be output. That instruction is then sent to the control unit, which outputs the sum located in a register.

MAKING COMPUTERS FASTER NOW AND IN THE FUTURE

Over the years, computer designers have developed a number of strategies to achieve faster performance in their machines. Researchers are also constantly working on ways to speed up the computers of the future. This section discusses several of these methods. There are also some things that you can do to speed up your computer today, as discussed next.

Speeding Up Your System Today

Several strategies that may speed up your current computer are listed next.

Add More Memory

With today's graphic-intensive interfaces and applications, much more memory is required than was necessary even a couple of years ago. If you seem to have to wait too long when opening programs or saving documents and your CPU is relatively fast (over 1 GHz), you should consider adding more memory to your system to bring it up to a minimum of 512 MB. Be sure to check inside your PC first to determine if there is room for more memory modules, and then check with your PC manufacturer to determine the appropriate type and speed of RAM that your PC uses. If all your RAM slots are full, you can usually remove some of the old modules and replace them with newer, higher capacity ones.

Perform System Maintenance

As you work and use your hard drive to store and retrieve data, and as you install and uninstall programs, most PCs tend to become less efficient. Part of the reason for this is as large documents are stored, retrieved, and then stored again, they often become *fragmented*—that is, not stored in contiguous (adjacent) storage areas. Because the different pieces of the document are physically located in different places, it takes longer for the computer to retrieve or store it. Another reason a computer may become inefficient is that when programs are

H
W

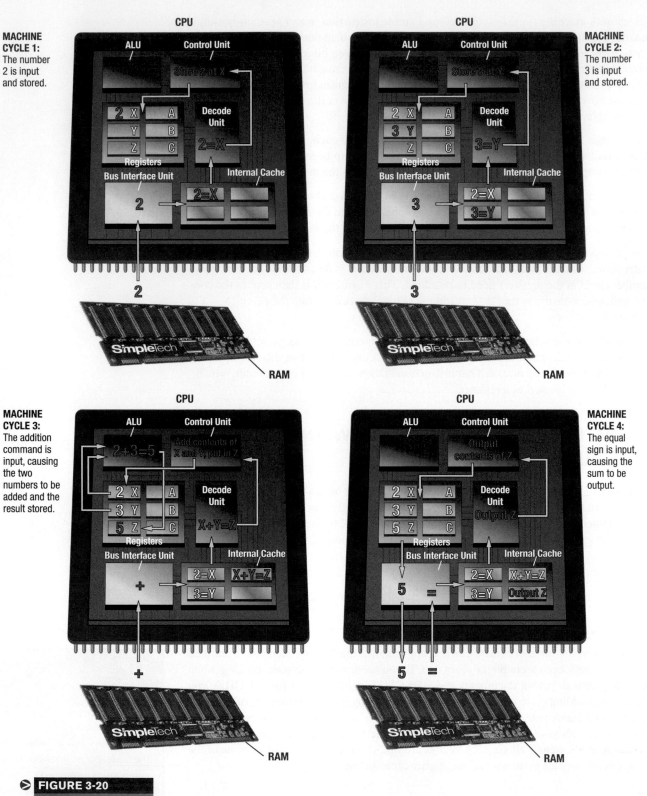

MACHINE CYCLE 1: The number 2 is input and stored.

MACHINE CYCLE 2: The number 3 is input and stored.

MACHINE CYCLE 3: The addition command is input, causing the two numbers to be added and the result stored.

MACHINE CYCLE 4: The equal sign is input, causing the sum to be output.

> **FIGURE 3-20**
> **Machine cycle examples.** This command, to add two numbers, requires 4 machine cycles.

uninstalled, pieces of the program are sometimes left behind or references to these programs are left in operating system files. Yet another reason is that as a hard drive begins to get full, it takes longer to locate and manipulate the data stored there. All of these factors can result in a system performing more slowly than it should.

To alleviate some of these problems, regular *system maintenance* should be performed. Here are some ideas.

▼ Uninstall any programs that you no longer want on your computer to free up space on your hard drive. Be sure to use the designated removal procedure for your operating system such as the Add/Remove Programs option in the Windows Control Panel or an "Uninstall" option for that program located on the Start menu to remove the program for Windows PCs.

▼ If you have large files (such as digital photos or other graphical images) stored on your computer that you don't need on a regular basis, consider moving them to a removable storage medium, such as a *Zip disk, CD-R disc, or DVD-R disc*. Once copied onto the new medium, the files can be deleted from your hard drive to free up space. If the files are important, you may want to make two copies, just to be safe. Be sure to open the files from the storage medium to confirm that the transfer was successful before deleting the files from your hard drive and store multiple disks containing the same files in different locations. Copying files, deleting files, and storage media will be discussed in more detail in later chapters.

▼ Delete the temporary files stored by your browser (choose *Internet Options* from the Tools menu, if you are using Internet Explorer; select *Preferences* from the Edit menu, and then choose *Advanced* and *Cache* in Netscape Navigator). Browsers tend to store a huge amount of data—it's not unusual to have over 1,000 temporary Internet files—including your browsing history and copies of Web pages you've recently visited. If you no longer need this information, delete the files to make room on your hard drive. Deleting temporary Internet files can also speed up your Internet browsing.

▼ Open the Recycle Bin (or similar location holding deleted files on your PC) and empty it. As long as you are sure that none of the files in the Recycle Bin needs to be restored, those files are taking up room on your hard drive needlessly.

▼ Use a *utility program*, such as Windows' Disk Cleanup, to delete unnecessary files left over from installing programs, uninstalling programs, and browsing the Internet. There are also a variety of utility programs that can be purchased to clean up your hard drive (see Figure 3-21).

▼ Use a utility program, such as Windows' Disk Defragmenter, to arrange the files on your hard drive more efficiently. On large hard drives, this may need to be done during the night because of the length of time required. Defragmentation, utility programs, and other system maintenance activities are discussed more in Chapter 6.

FIGURE 3-21
Utility programs. This particular program contains a variety of utilities to protect your PC from virus threats, optimize performance, fix and prevent problems, recover from system failures, clean out Internet clutter, and more.

Buy a Larger or Second Hard Drive

As already mentioned, hard drives get less efficient as they fill up. If your hard drive is almost full and you don't have any data or programs that you can remove, you should consider buying and installing a second hard drive, assuming that you have an empty storage bay inside your computer. Some users can comfortably install a second hard drive themselves; others prefer to have the new drive installed for them. In either case, once the drive is installed, you can either transfer your data to the new drive and use it solely as a data drive, or uninstall a few of the larger programs on your first drive and install them again on the new drive. Alternatively, you can replace your existing hard drive with a larger one, although the data transfer process will be a little more complicated. Before purchasing a second hard drive, be sure to check if there is room inside your PC for an additional drive; if not, you can buy a USB hard drive, assuming you have a free USB port.

Upgrade Your Internet Connection

If your system seems slow primarily when you are on the Internet, the culprit might be your Internet connection. If you are using standard dial-up access, you can sometimes upgrade your service to a premium faster service for a little more money per month. If you use the Internet a great deal for work or multimedia purposes, consider switching to cable, satellite, DSL, or other type of *broadband* Internet service. Although they are more expensive, they are significantly faster. The differences between these and other types of Internet connections are described in Chapters 8 and 9.

Upgrade Your Video Card

If you're a gamer, computer artist, graphical engineer, or otherwise use 3D-graphic-intensive applications, consider upgrading your video card to one that better supports 3D graphics. If you don't use 3D applications, upgrading your video card won't usually improve your speed.

Upgrade Your CPU

Upgrading your CPU used to be a popular choice, since the price difference between a new system and a new CPU was relatively large. With today's low computer prices and fast basic processor speeds, however, this upgrade is becoming less common. If you have a fairly slow Pentium chip (less than 600 MHz), you might want to look into whether your motherboard would support a faster chip and the cost involved, but most of the time it would be better to put that money into a new system.

Strategies for Making Faster Computers

There are several strategies that researchers and manufacturers are working on to build faster PCs. Some are described next.

Moving Circuits Close Together

As complex as computers seem, all must follow one intuitive natural law: Circuits that are physically located closer together require less time to move bits between them. During the past several decades, computer-chip makers have packed circuitry closer and closer together. Today, they fit several million circuits on a single, fingernail-size chip. This remarkable achievement doesn't mean that chip makers can continue to shrink circuitry without constraint, however. When the circuits are in use, they generate heat, and circuits placed too close together can become hot enough to melt the chip. For this reason, virtually all CPUs today employ fans, *heat sinks* (small components typically made out of aluminum with fins that help to dissipate heat), or some combination of the two to cool the CPU. Low-power CPUs that run cooler than traditional CPUs are being introduced and new cooling technologies are continually being tested, such as liquid-filled tubes that act as radiators to draw heat away from processors and misters that spray a fine mist of liquid onto chips when they become too hot. At the time of this writing, computer manufacturer NEC had recently released what they call the world's first water-cooled PC. This PC, called the Valuestar, uses water to cool the CPU. An added bonus is that operating noise is cut in half, because a CPU fan is not required.

Faster and Wider Buses and Faster Memory

As discussed earlier, wider buses lead to faster processing. Buses also vary in speed; faster buses tend to result in faster processing. Buses today run as fast as 1,000 MHz. Faster memory also helps speed up processing. Memory today typically runs at over 100 MHz. One of the faster types of RAM available—Rambus RDRAM—runs at over 1 GHz in hopes of more closely matching memory speed with CPU speed to reduce or eliminate bottlenecks.

Improved Materials

Traditionally, CPU chips used aluminum circuitry etched onto a silicon backing. As the limit of the number of aluminum circuits that can be packed onto a silicon chip without heat damage or interference approached, chip makers began to look for alternate materials. Copper was one of the next choices, since it is a far better electrical conductor and it can produce chips containing more circuitry at a lower price. A more recent development is *SOI (silicon on insulator)*. SOI chips use a thin layer of insulating material over the silicon to reduce heat and power consumption. This results in being able to place the circuits closer together than is possible without the insulating material.

One possibility for the future is the use of *superconductive materials*. Superconductive materials resist heat buildup and can be used to pack a chip's circuitry closer together, resulting in chips with faster speeds. Two technologies being researched are *ceramic superconductors* and a new form of carbon consisting of 60 carbon atoms surrounding a hollow cluster. When one or more alkali metals are inserted into the empty space between the carbon atoms, the resulting compound—called a *fulleride*—often becomes a superconductor.

An even more radical idea currently in the testing stages is replacing the CPU entirely with *field-programmable gate arrays* (*FPGAs*). An FPGA is a type of chip that can be programmed and reprogrammed as needed. To replace a CPU, such as in the system developed by Wincom Systems that does the work of 50 or more $5,000 servers but costs only $25,000, groups of these chips work together to process several tasks at the same time. In addition to being a possible replacement for CPUs in future PCs, FPGAs are currently being used in storage devices, networking hardware, cell phones, and digital cameras.

Pipelining

In older PC systems, the CPU had to completely finish processing one instruction before starting another. More recent PCs, however, can process multiple instructions at one time. One way this is accomplished is through **pipelining**. With pipelining, a new instruction begins executing as soon as the previous one reaches the next stage of the machine cycle. Figure 3-22 illustrates this process with a 4-stage pipeline. Notice that while the pipelined CPU is executing one instruction, it is simultaneously fetching and getting the next instruction ready for execution. Without a pipeline, the arithmetic part of the processor would be idle while an instruction is being fetched and decoded. CPUs today are commonly built with multiple pipelines, which increases the number of instructions performed per machine cycle.

Multiprocessing and Parallel Processing

Despite the astounding evolution of computer technology over the past half century, the vast majority of desktop PCs are still driven by single CPUs. In the race to develop tomorrow's ever-faster computer systems, scientists have developed *multiprocessing* and *parallel processing*. In contrast to techniques that enable multiple operations to be performed simultaneously within a single CPU, multiprocessing and parallel processing use two or more coordinated CPUs to perform operations simultaneously.

With **multiprocessing**, each CPU typically works on a different job. Because multiple jobs are being processed simultaneously, they are completed faster than with a single processor. With **parallel processing**, multiple processors work together to make one job finish sooner (see Figure 3-23). Two of the most common designs are *symmetric multiprocessing* (*SMP*) and *massively parallel processing* (*MPP*). With SMP, a single copy of the operating system is in charge of all the processors and the processors share memory. Typically, SMP systems do not exceed

---

>**Pipelining.** A CPU feature designed to begin processing a new instruction as soon as the previous instruction completes the first stage of the machine cycle. >**Multiprocessing.** The capability of an operating system to use multiple processors in a single computer, usually to process multiple jobs at one time faster than could be performed with a single processor. >**Parallel processing.** A processing technique that uses multiple processors simultaneously in a single computer, usually to process a single job as fast as possible.

Stages

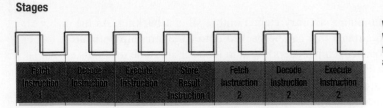

WITHOUT PIPELINING
Without pipelining, an instruction finishes an entire machine cycle before another instruction is started.

Stages

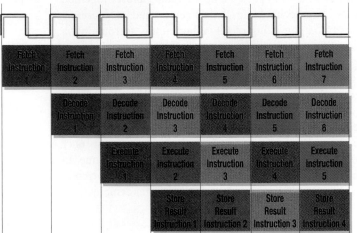

WITH PIPELINING
With pipelining, a new instruction is begun when the preceding instruction moves to the next stage of the machine cycle.

FIGURE 3-22

Pipelining. Pipelining streamlines the machine cycle by executing different stages of multiple instructions at the same time, so the different parts of the CPU are idle less often. In today's CPUs, 10- to 20-stage pipelines are typical.

64 processors. MPP systems, in contrast, can use hundreds or thousands of microprocessors and each processor has its own copy of the operating system and its own memory. MPP systems are typically more difficult to program than SMP systems.

Multiprocessing can increase astronomically the number of calculations performed in any given time period. For example, NEC's Earth Simulator (shown in Figure 1-17 in Chapter 1) operates at approximately 40 teraflops. In other words, it can process about 40 trillion operations per second (most desktop PCs today operate slightly faster than 1 gigaflop). When tremendous amounts of processing are required but access to a supercomputer is not feasible, one recent trend called *grid computing* uses the computing capabilities of a large collection of PCs to work together to process the necessary data. For instance, large businesses can use their employees' desktop workstations to process data overnight while the office is closed. These *distributed processing* systems can be as powerful as a supercomputer. For example, one business that uses 5,000 engineering workstations after their employees go home at night has reached a combined computing speed of 6 teraflops. Grid computing can also be performed over the Internet with home PCs. Usually a small program is downloaded and then, when the system is idle, the software puts the PC to work on a small piece of the current project. Often the projects to which individuals donate their PC's processing time involve scientific or medical research.

Hyperthreading

A technique being used with some CPUs today that is related to multiprocessing and parallel processing is **hyperthreading**. Hyperthreading, developed by Intel, enables software

---

>**Hyperthreading.** A technique used in some Intel CPUs to enable software to treat the CPU as two processors to complete processing more quickly.

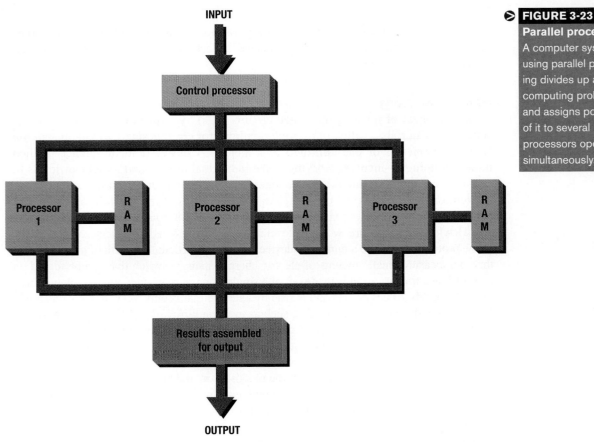

INPUT

Control processor

Processor 1 — R A M

Processor 2 — R A M

Processor 3 — R A M

Results assembled for output

OUTPUT

> **FIGURE 3-23**
> **Parallel processing.**
> A computer system using parallel processing divides up a computing problem and assigns portions of it to several processors operating simultaneously.

H W

to treat a single processor as two processors. Since it utilizes processing power in the chip that would otherwise go unused, this technology lets the chip operate far more efficiently, resulting in faster processing, provided the software being used supports hyperthreading.

Improved Instruction Set Design

An earlier discussion in this chapter mentioned that each computer has its own *instruction set*. Traditionally, computers have been built under a design principle called *complex instruction set computing (CISC)*. A computer chip with CISC design contains a relatively large instruction set. Starting in the mid-1970s, processors with instruction sets limited to only the most frequently used instructions became available. These devices follow a principle called *reduced instruction set computing (RISC)*. Experience has shown that computers using the RISC design work faster, unless the instruction is extraordinarily complex.

With the introduction of 64-bit CPUs, such as Intel's Itanium chip and AMD's Opteron, a new design option—*explicitly parallel instruction computing (EPIC)* emerged. The primary philosophy behind EPIC is *instruction-level parallelism (ILP)*. With ILP, individual operations are executed in parallel, significantly speeding up processing. ILP is made possible by increasing the number of transistors on a chip to enable multiple operations to be performed at one time.

Related technologies that help to expand the instruction set design for Intel CPUs are *MMX (Multimedia Extensions)*, *streaming SIMD extensions (SSEs)*, and the newer *streaming SIMD extensions 2 (SSE2)*. MMX is a set of 57 multimedia instructions for handling many common multimedia operations. SSE and SSE2 help CPUs perform floating-point-intensive applications like video and audio handling, 3-D modeling, and physical simulations much more quickly than before, provided the software being used supports the extensions being used.

Future Trends

While some of the strategies discussed in the prior sections are currently being used, some new ideas are further from being implemented. Selected trends we may see in the near future are discussed next.

Nanotechnology

Today's process of forming integrated circuits (ICs) by imprinting patterns on semiconductor materials—called *lithography*—allows for circuits smaller than one *micron* (1,000 *nanometers* or one-millionth of a meter). A newer field of science—called **nanotechnology**—involves working at the individual atomic and molecular levels to create computer chips and other components that are thousands of times smaller than conventional technologies permit (one nanometer is one-billionth of a meter). Researchers at several organizations—such as IBM, Motorola, Dow Chemical, Xerox, and Hewlett-Packard—are working to create nanometer-sized products and materials. Some prototypes include a miniscule device (about one-fiftieth the width of a human hair) that can measure small amounts of electric charge; a single switch that can be turned on and off like a transistor but is made out of a single organic molecule; and a miniature hard drive that holds 20 GB of data and is read by a device that is only a few nanometers thick. Using newly developed technologies, such as *extreme ultraviolet* (*EUV*) *light*, transistors as small as 15 nanometers have been created in lab settings. Current nanotechnology consumer applications include stain-resistant fabrics and long-life tennis balls. Possible future applications include improved military uniforms that protect against bullets and germ warfare, microscopic robots that can enter the bloodstream and perform tests or irradiate cancerous tumors, molecular circuits that can function similar to today's silicon-based circuits but that are much, much smaller and much more efficient, and memory and storage media significantly smaller and denser than is currently possible. Nanotechnology is also expected to eventually lead to computers that are small enough to be woven into the fibers of clothing or embedded into paint and other materials. In addition, nanotechnology may eventually solve much of the toxic waste problem associated with *e-trash* (electronic waste, such as old computer equipment) by being able to rearrange dangerous components at the atomic level to become inert substances. The federal government has had increased interest in nanotechnology recently, holding Senate hearings, forming a *National Nanotechnology Research Program*, and introducing legislation to increase funding for nanotechnology research and development.

Organic Computers

Biotechnology is the term commonly used to describe combining biology with technology. Biotechnology is involved with creating *organic computers*—computers containing organic matter. Biotechnology enables circuits to be grown and shaped as tiny molecules. Although some researchers estimate that it may be 10 years before a molecular computer is available to consumers, they feel it will be worth the wait. With estimates of ultra-tiny processors 100 billion times faster than the most powerful processors available today, and the possibility of microscopic organic sensors that can be embedded in paint, clothing, or medical diagnostic machines that are as small as the bacteria they analyze, organic computers hold great promise for the future.

>**Nanotechnology.** The science of creating tiny computers and components by working at the individual atomic and molecular levels.

Quantum Computing

The idea of **quantum computing** emerged in the 1970s, but has received renewed interest lately along with nanotechnology. Quantum computing applies the principles of quantum physics and quantum mechanics to computers, going beyond traditional physics to work at the subatomic level. Quantum computers differ from conventional computers in that they utilize atoms or nuclei working together as quantum bits or *qubits*; qubits function simultaneously as both the computer's processor and memory. Each qubit can represent much more than just the two states (0 and 1) available to today's electronic bits; a qubit can even represent many states at one time. Because of this, quantum computers theoretically can perform calculations exponentially faster than conventional computers. Quantum computers in the future may consist of a thimbleful of liquid whose atoms are used to perform calculations as instructed by an external device.

While quantum computers are still in the pioneering stage, working quantum computers do exist. For instance, in 2001 the researchers at IBM's Almaden Research Center in San Jose, California created a seven-qubit quantum computer (comprised of the nuclei of seven atoms, which can interact with each other and be programmed by radio frequency pulses) that can successfully factor the number 15 (see Figure 3-24). Although this is not a complicated computation for a conventional computer, the fact that it was possible for a person to supply a quantum computer with the problem and have it compute the correct answer is viewed as a highly significant event in the area of quantum computer research. A primary application area for quantum computers is expected to be encryption and code breaking.

> **FIGURE 3-24**
> **Quantum computers.** The vial of liquid shown here contains the seven-qubit computer used by IBM researchers in 2001 to perform the most complicated quantum computation to date—factoring the number 15.

Optical Computing

Optical chips, which use light waves to transmit data, are currently in development. A possibility for the future is the *optical computer*—a computer that uses light, such as from laser beams or infrared beams—to perform digital computations. Because light beams don't interfere with each other, optical computers can be much smaller and faster than electronic PCs. For instance, according to one NASA senior research scientist, an optical computer could solve a problem in one hour that would take an electronic computer 11 years to solve. While some researchers are working on developing an all-optical computer, others believe that a mix of optical and electronic components—or an *optoelectronic computer*—may be the best bet for the future. In fact, the first chips that have both optical and electrical functions combined on a single silicon chip—a feat that was thought to be impossible until recently—have started to become available.

3-D Chips

Three-dimensional (3-D) chips are another technique for solving the problem of trying to pack an increasing number of components onto small chips. With 3-D chips, either multiple layers of circuitry are used or the circuitry stands vertically, rather than horizontally. In either case, a successful 3-D chip design is predicted to increase capacity and speed by a factor of 10 at no additional cost. One company—Matrix Semiconductors—has announced it should have a 3-D memory chip on the market soon.

>**Quantum computing.** A technology that applies the principles of quantum physics and quantum mechanics to computers to direct atoms or nuclei to work together as quantum bits (qubits), which function simultaneously as the computer's processor and memory.

SUMMARY

DATA AND PROGRAM REPRESENTATION

Chapter Objective 1:
Understand how data and programs are represented to a computer and be able to identify a few of the coding systems used to accomplish this.

The electronic components of a digital computer work in a two-state, or *binary*, fashion. It is convenient to think of these binary states in terms of 0s and 1s. Computer people refer to such 0s and 1s as *bits*. Converting data to these 0s and 1s is called *digital data representation*.

Computers use the **binary numbering system** to represent numbers and perform numeric computations. Text-based data can be represented with one of several fixed-length binary codes. Two popular coding schemes are **ASCII** and **EBCDIC**. These systems represent single characters of data—a numeric digit, alphabetic character, or special symbol—as strings of eight bits. Each string of bits is called a **byte**. **Unicode** is another binary code used with text-based data that can represent text in all written languages, including those that use alphabets different than English, such as Chinese, Greek, and Russian.

The storage capacity of computers often is expressed in **kilobytes** (**KB**), or thousands of bytes; **megabytes** (**MB**), millions of bytes; **gigabytes** (**GB**), billions of bytes; and **terabytes** (**TB**), trillions of bytes. Other possibilities are the *petabyte* (*PB*), about 1,000 terabytes; the *exabyte* (*EB*), about 1,000 petabytes; the *zettabyte* (*ZB*), about 1,000 exabytes; and the *yottabyte* (*YB*), about 1,000 zettabytes.

The binary system can represent not only text but graphics, audio, and video data, as well. **Machine language** is the binary-based code through which computers represent program instructions. A program must be translated into machine language before the computer can execute it.

INSIDE THE SYSTEM UNIT

Chapter Objective 2:
Explain the functions of the hardware components commonly found inside the system unit, such as the CPU, memory, buses, and expansion cards.

PCs typically contain a variety of hardware components located inside the **system unit**. For instance, *chips* are mounted onto *circuit boards*, and those boards are positioned in slots on the **motherboard** or **system board**—the main circuit board for a PC.

Every PC has a **central processing unit** (**CPU**) chip—also called a **processor** or **microprocessor**, when referring to PCs—attached to its motherboard that performs the processing for the computer. CPU chips differ in many respects, such as what type of PCs the CPU is designed for, its **clock speed**, and *word size*. Another difference is the amount of **cache memory**—memory located on or very close to the CPU chip to help speed up processing. Other important differences are the general architecture of the CPU and the bus speed and width being used.

The main memory chips for a PC are commonly referred to as **RAM**, for **random access memory**. RAM is volatile and used to temporarily hold programs and data while they are needed. RAM is available in different types and speeds. Memory chips that store non-erasable programs comprise the computer's **ROM**, for **read-only memory**. Non-volatile memory that can be erased and reprogrammed in blocks is called **flash memory**. Flash memory chips can be found in PCs and mobile devices; flash memory chips mounted on small cards can be used for storage with portable PCs, digital cameras, and other smaller devices. Memory built into the CPU chip to hold instructions and data before or during processing are called **registers**.

A computer **bus** is an electronic path along which bits are transmitted. Common buses include *internal buses*, which move data around within the CPU; *system buses*, which move data between the CPU and RAM; and **expansion buses**, which connect the CPU to peripheral devices. Common buses include *PCI*, *AGP*, *USB* (*Universal Serial Bus*), and *FireWire*.

Many system units have external **ports** through which peripheral devices connect to the computer. Common types of ports include *serial, parallel, USB, FireWire, network, keyboard, mouse, monitor,* and *modem ports.* Also, many desktop PCs contain limited numbers of internal **expansion slots**, into which users can insert an **expansion card** to give the computer added functionality. Owners of notebook and tablet PCs normally expand their systems by adding **PC cards**, which are inserted into the PC's **PC card slot**. Handheld PC and mobile device users often add new capabilities with *SD cards* or other types of flash memory cards; some include a PC card slot or proprietary expansion system.

Chapter Objective 3:
Describe how new peripheral devices or other hardware can be added to a PC.

HOW THE CPU WORKS

A PC's CPU has two major sections. The **arithmetic/logic unit** (**ALU**) performs arithmetic and logical operations on data. The **control unit** directs the flow of electronic traffic between memory and the ALU and also between the CPU and input and output devices. **Registers**—high-speed temporary holding places within the CPU that hold program instructions and data immediately before and during processing—are used to enhance the computer's performance. The **prefetch unit** requests data and instructions before or as they are needed, the **decode unit** decodes the instructions input into the CPU; internal cache stores frequently used instructions and data; the **bus interface unit** inputs data and instructions from RAM.

Chapter Objective 4:
Understand how the computer system's CPU and memory components process program instructions and data.

The CPU processes instructions in a sequence called a **machine cycle**. Each machine-language instruction is broken down into several smaller instructions called *microcode,* and each piece of microcode corresponds to an operation (such as adding two numbers located in the CPU's registers) that can be performed in the CPU's circuits. The computer system has a built-in **system clock** that synchronizes all of the PC's activities. A machine cycle consists of four steps.

In addition to measuring a PC's speed by its CPU's clock speed (the number of machine cycles per second stated in *megahertz, MHz,* or *gigahertz, GHz*), the more universal measurement of number of instructions processed per second can be used. The terms *mips* (millions of instructions per second), *megaflops* (millions of floating-point operations per second), *gigaflops* (billions of operations per second), and *teraflops* (trillions of operations per second) are commonly used.

MAKING COMPUTERS FASTER NOW AND IN THE FUTURE

There are several possible remedies for a computer that is performing too slowly, including adding more memory, performing system maintenance to clean up the PC's hard drive, buying a larger or additional hard drive, and upgrading the computer's Internet connection, video card, or CPU, depending on the primary role of the computer and where the processing bottleneck appears to be.

Chapter Objective 5:
Name and evaluate several strategies that can be used today for speeding up the operations of a computer.

To make computers work faster over all, computer designers have developed a number of strategies over the years, and researchers are continually working on new strategies. Some of the strategies already being implemented include moving circuits closer together; using faster buses and memory; building components out of better materials; using **pipelining**, **multiprocessing**, **parallel processing**, and **hyperthreading**; and improving the instruction set design.

One possibility for future computers is **nanotechnology** research, which focuses on building computer components at the individual atomic and molecular levels. There has been some progress in this field and the federal government has become actively involved in its development. *Organic computers* containing organic matter is another possibility being researched, along with **quantum computing** and *optical computers. Three-dimensional (3-D) chips* are an alternative to nanotechnology to pack more components on a smaller sized chip.

Chapter Objective 6:
List some technologies that may be used in future PCs.

H W

KEY TERMS

Instructions: Match each key term on the left with the definition on the right that best describes it.

a. arithmetic/logic unit (ALU)

b. ASCII

c. binary numbering system

d. bus

e. byte

f. cache memory

g. central processing unit (CPU)

h. control unit

i. expansion slot

j. machine language

k. motherboard

l. nanotechnology

m. parallel processing

n. PC card

o. port

p. random access memory (RAM)

q. register

r. system clock

s. system unit

t. Unicode

1. _____ A binary-based language for representing computer programs that the computer can execute directly.

2. _____ A coding system for text-based data using any written language.

3. _____ A processing technique that uses multiple processors simultaneously in a single computer, usually to process a single job as fast as possible.

4. _____ A connector on the exterior of a PC's system unit to which a device may be attached.

5. _____ A fixed-length, binary coding system widely used to represent text-based data for computer processing on many types of computers.

6. _____ A group of 8 bits; in ASCII and EBCDIC, it holds a single character of data.

7. _____ A group of fast memory chips located on or near the CPU to help speed up processing.

8. _____ A location on the motherboard into which expansion cards are inserted.

9. _____ A small card that fits into a slot located on the exterior of a portable computer to provide new functionality or to attach a peripheral device.

10. _____ An electronic path on the motherboard or within the CPU or other computer component along which data is transferred.

11. _____ Chips located on the motherboard that provide a temporary location for the computer to hold data and program instructions while they are needed.

12. _____ High-speed memory built into the CPU that temporarily stores data during processing.

13. _____ The chip located inside the system unit of a computer that performs the processing for a computer.

14. _____ The main box of a computer that houses the CPU, motherboard, memory, and other devices.

15. _____ The main circuit board of a computer, located inside the system unit, to which all computer system components connect.

16. _____ The numbering system that represents all numbers using just two symbols (0 and 1).

17. _____ The part of the CPU that coordinates its operations.

18. _____ The part of the CPU that performs arithmetic and logical operations.

19. _____ The science of creating tiny computers and components by working at the individual atomic and molecular levels.

20. _____ The timing mechanism within the computer system that synchronizes the computer's operations.

REVIEW ACTIVITIES

Answers for the self-quiz appear at the end of the book in the References and Resources Guide.

True/False

SELF-QUIZ

Instructions: Circle **T** if the statement is true or **F** if the statement is false.

T   F   **1.** A hard disk that can hold 5 GB can hold about 5 billion characters.

T   F   **2.** ASCII is the coding system used by a computer to perform mathematical computations.

T   F   **3.** The logical operations a CPU may perform could include such things as addition, subtraction, multiplication, and division.

T   F   **4.** A bus is a pathway, such as on the motherboard or inside the CPU, along which bits can be transferred.

T   F   **5.** Computers that process data with light are referred to as quantum computers.

Completion

Instructions: Supply the missing words to complete the following statements.

6. The binary number 1101 is equivalent to the decimal number _____.

7. Level _____ cache memory would be further from the CPU than Level 2 cache.

8. The main board for the computer to which all hardware needs to be connected is referred to as the _____.

9. A(n) _____ is a connector on the exterior of a computer's system unit into which a peripheral device may be plugged.

10. With _____, the CPU is able to begin executing a new instruction as soon as the previous instruction finishes the first stage of the machine cycle.

1. What does each of the following acronyms stand for?

EXERCISES

  a. RAM _____

  b. ROM _____

  c. USB _____

  d. AGP _____

  e. CPU _____

2. Number the following terms from 1 to 10 to indicate their size from smallest to largest.

  a. _____ Petabyte   **f.** _____ Byte

  b. _____ Kilobyte   **g.** _____ Zettabyte

  c. _____ Gigabyte   **h.** _____ Terabyte

  d. _____ Yottabyte   **i.** _____ Bit

  e. _____ Exabyte   **j.** _____ Megabyte

3. Using the ASCII code chart in this chapter or in the References and Resources Guide at the end of the book, decode the following word. What does it say?

01000011   01000001   01000110   01000101

_____   _____   _____   _____

4. Assume you have a USB mouse, USB keyboard, and USB printer to connect to a PC, but you have only two USB ports. Explain one solution to this problem that doesn't involve buying a new mouse, keyboard, or printer.

5. Select the picture from the numbered list below that matches each of the following names and write the corresponding number in the blank to the left of each name.

   a. _____ memory module   d. _____ CPU
   b. _____ expansion card   e. _____ keyboard port
   c. _____ parallel port   f. _____ PC card

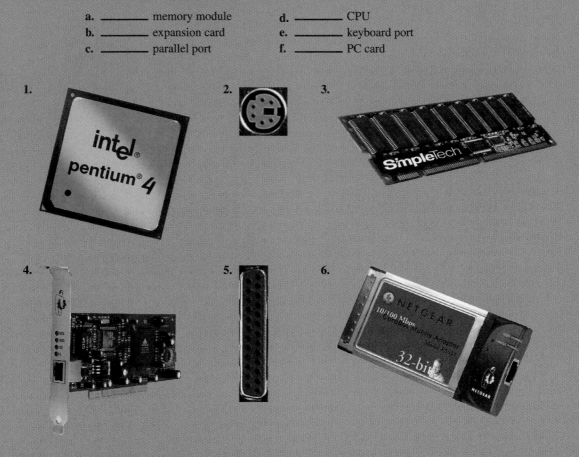

6. If your PC seems sluggish, list two things you could do to try to speed it up without resorting to purchasing an entirely new system.

7. What is nanotechnology? List at least one current nanotechnology application and one possible application for the future.

PROJECTS

1. **Non-Volatile RAM** Non-volatile RAM—memory chips that don't lose their data when the power goes off—are used in a variety of devices today, from PCs (in the form of ROM and flash memory chips), to TV set-top boxes, to cell phones, digital cameras, and other portable devices. While flash memory chips have the advantage of non-volatility over conventional DRAM and SRAM chips, they are not as fast and may wear out sooner. The memory industry has been in search of the perfect type of memory for decades—one that is fast, high density, low cost, non-volatile, and rewritable. As newer types of memory are developed that get closer to this ideal, flash, DRAM, and SRAM memory, as well as possibly even hard drives, might be replaced, as discussed in the Inside the Industry box. Some emerging types of memory currently being researched and developed are *magnetic RAM (MRAM), Ovonyx unified memory (OUM), four-bit memory, nanocrystals, ferroelectric RAM (FeRAM),* and *polymer memory (polymeric ferroelectric RAM or PFRAM).*

   For this project, select two of the above types of new memory possibilities and research them to determine what they are, how they work, and the current state of research. Are either of your choices expected to be available in a commercial product any time soon? In addition, research the current state of flash memory. Have there been any recent developments to improve flash memory? Any new flash memory applications? At the conclusion of your research, prepare a one- to two-page summary of your findings and submit it to your instructor.

   HOT TOPICS

2. **Adding Memory** Adding additional RAM to a PC is one of the most common computer upgrades. Before purchasing additional memory, however, a little research is in order to make sure that the purchased memory is compatible with the PC.

   For this project, select a computer that you can assume you want to add additional memory to. It doesn't matter if you own the computer or not, but it needs to be one you can find out information about, such as your own PC, a school PC if there is someone there to whom you can ask questions about it, or a computer for sale at a local store. For your selected PC, determine the following: manufacturer and model number, CPU, current amount of memory, total memory slots, and the number of available memory slots. (If you look inside your own PC, be sure to unplug the power cord first and do not touch any components inside the system unit.) For a school PC, you may be able to find some of the information on the front of the PC; you'll have to ask someone in charge of that PC for the rest of the information. For a PC at a local store, determine what you can from an advertisement or by looking at the PC in a store, then ask a salesperson in person or over the telephone questions to determine any missing information. Once you have the necessary information, call a local store or use your information and a memory supplier's Web site to determine the appropriate type of memory needed for your selected PC. What choices do you have in terms of capacity and configuration? Can you add just one memory board or do you have to add memory in pairs? Can you keep the old memory boards or do they have to be removed? At the conclusion of your research, prepare a one-page summary of your findings and submit it to your instructor.

   SHORT ANSWER/ RESEARCH

3. **In Review** It is a good idea to start the process of expanding or upgrading your computer by reading hardware reviews in offline or online computer journals, such as Computerworld, PC World, or MacWorld or on tech news sites such as CNET.com or ZDNet.com. Reviews available online are often organized by category, providing you with the latest information about compatibility, performance, cost, reliability, and overall value.

For this project, select a piece of hardware that you would like to upgrade on your PC or add to your computer system (if you don't have a PC, just assume that you do). Some possible options include adding a new video board, modem, sound card, scanner, digital camera, printer, DVD drive, CD-R drive, network interface, or flash memory reader. Research specific brands and models of your selected product and select the one that would best suit your needs, noting why you selected the model you did over its competitors. In your findings, be sure to identify how the device will be connected to your PC. If an expansion card is required, identify which slot the card would need to be inserted into and make certain that there is an empty slot of that type on your PC. If there isn't an available slot, check whether the product is available in a format compatible with your PC, such as in a USB format. At the conclusion of your research, prepare a one-page summary of your findings and submit it to your instructor.

HANDS ON

4. **Ports** As mentioned in the chapter, external hardware connects to the computer via ports located on the exterior of the system unit. Conventional ports include parallel, serial, joystick, PS/2 (keyboard/mouse), monitor, and game ports. Newer ports include USB, USB 2, and FireWire (IEEE 1394). Many PCs today also have a modem and/or networking port. Some of the older ports—particularly parallel and serial—are beginning to be referred to as "legacy ports." They are being omitted from some new computers today, and many people predict that they will eventually be replaced by newer types of ports.

    For this project, find one computer (such as at home, your school, public library, or a computer store) that you can look at the exterior of the entire system unit. Draw a sketch of all four sides of the PC case, including all of its ports. On your sketch, label each port with a note about what that port is being used for (for the ports in use) or might be used for (for the available ports) on that particular PC. Does the PC you selected use legacy ports? If you wanted to add a flash memory drive or reader that plugs into a USB port, would you be able to use it with your selected PC? Why or why not? Turn in your labeled sketch along with the answers to these questions to your instructor.

5. **Intel Museum Tour** Intel Corporation has a great deal of interesting information about microprocessors and related technology on their Web site, including information available through their online museum.

    For this project, go to the Intel Museum at www.intel.com/intel/intelis/museum (if this URL no longer works at the time you do this project, go to the Intel home page at www.intel.com and search for "Intel Museum" using the site's search feature). Once you are at the Intel Museum home page, select an Online Exhibit related to microprocessors, such as *How the Transistor Works*, *How the Microprocessor Works*, *How Chips Are Made*, or *What is a Clean Room?* and tour the exhibit. As you tour, make a note of at least three interesting facts you learned. At the conclusion of this task, prepare a short summary listing the tour you took and the interesting facts you recorded and submit it to your instructor.

WRITING ABOUT COMPUTERS

6. **Wearable PCs** The Chapter 1 Trend box took a look at wearable computers—computers small enough to be worn on a belt or wrist, like a portable MP3 player or Walkman. Although they have been available in some form for commercial applications for several years, their entry into the consumer market is just beginning. Some current features of wearable PCs, such as corded components and using an eye-piece display device that some individuals view as unattractive, may make today's wearable PCs less desirable than those that are expected to become available in the future.

    For this project, write a short essay expressing your opinion about wearable computers. Take another look at the wearable computer shown in the Chapter 1 Trend box. Would you be willing to wear one in public today? Why or why not? If not, how (if at all) would wearable computers need to be changed in order for you to be willing to wear one? As they become smaller, wireless, and controllable by our voices, do you think their use by consumers will increase? Will their use be looked at any differently than wearing a Walkman or MP3 player in public? Think about your chosen profession—is wearable or portable computer use needed or useful today? What advantages and disadvantages do you see regarding wearable computer use in that profession? Submit your opinion on this issue to your instructor in the form of a short paper, not more than two pages in length.

7. **The IC Story** The transistor is the basic building block of modern day integrated chips (ICs), and is often referred to as the most important invention of the 20th century. The story behind the invention of transistors and their eventual application to the development of microprocessors is filled with luck, mistakes, chances, the Apollo space mission, and pioneering engineers.

    For this project, form a group to investigate and summarize the major historical events leading to the development of microprocessors, as we know them today. Does your group think we would have CPUs today if the U.S. government had not been in a race to put the first man on the moon? Your group should submit your findings and opinions to your instructor in the form of a short paper, not more than two pages in length.

8. **True Binary** As discussed in the chapter, all numbers processed by the CPU must be represented in a binary format. The conversion from decimal (base 10) to and from true binary (base 2) format is a fairly straightforward process and can be accomplished with basic arithmetic. The conversion from true binary format to hexadecimal (base 16) format is also a fairly straightforward process, and is generally used to conserve memory whenever possible.

    For this project, form a group to demonstrate how to convert a three-digit decimal number to both binary and hexadecimal and back again, without the use of a calculator (your group may wish to read the "A Look at Numbering Systems" section of the References and Resources Guide located at the end of this book first). Next, use your knowledge of binary and decimal numbering systems to determine how to represent the decimal number 10 in both base 3 and base 4 and include these examples in your presentation. The presentation should not exceed 10 minutes and should make use of one or more presentation aids such as the chalkboard, handouts, overhead transparencies, or a computer-based slide presentation (your instructor may provide additional requirements). Your group may be asked to submit a summary of the presentation to your instructor.

9. **Today's Processors** As mentioned in the chapter, most processor chips used in PC-compatible desktop computers today are made by Intel or Advanced Micro Devices (AMD).

    For this project, research the CPUs currently available from these two companies. Which chips are available at the present time? What are the clock speed options for each chip? Are there any new chips expected to come out in the next six months? Do any of the chips have any significant advantages over the others? You should also check recent newspaper ads or search computer stores online to determine which CPUs appear to be the most common today and how much Level 1 and Level 2 cache memory is typically available. Share your findings with the class in the form of a short presentation. The presentation should not exceed 10 minutes and should make use of one or more presentation aids such as the chalkboard, handouts, overhead transparencies, or a computer-based slide presentation (your instructor may provide additional requirements). You may also be asked to submit a summary of the presentation to your instructor.

10. **Latest and Greatest** It seems as though no matter what computer you purchase, it will be out of date in a year or two. This assertion is based on the hardware, operating system, and memory requirements specified on the packaging of the latest and greatest programs that you may need in order to remain productive at your job.

H
W

PRESENTATION/
DEMONSTRATION

INTERACTIVE
DISCUSSION

Select one of the following positions or create one of your own and express your point of view on the subject. Your instructor will indicate whether your response is to be posted to a class bulletin board, discussed in a class chat room, or discussed as an in-class activity. You may also be asked to submit a summary of your position and point of view.

a. You don't need to purchase a new system every two years, because the hardware is upgradeable and allows for the replacement of the CPU and the insertion of additional memory. Besides, the idea that someone would have to continually purchase the latest and greatest version of a program is absurd. In most cases, the increase in the marginal utility of these programs does not even justify the software purchase price, let alone the cost of the required hardware upgrades.

b. You will need to purchase new hardware approximately every two years since the processing ability of the CPU tends to double every 18 to 24 months, and the hardware is not as upgradeable as the vendors lead you to believe. It is not simply a matter of just plugging in a few expansion boards. You will need to purchase a completely new motherboard, which will likely require a different type of memory and other components, so you won't be able to reuse many of your old parts. When you add up the cost involved in the upgrade process, it becomes less expensive just to purchase a new system. From a software point of view, you must use the latest versions, or risk not being compatible with others.

11. **People Chips** One additional use for chips not covered in the chapter Trend box is implanting them in humans. One such implantable chip is the *VeriChip*, a tiny chip about the size of a grain of rice that is designed to be implanted under a person's skin, such as on the forearm. Each VeriChip contains a unique verification number that can be read when a proprietary scanner is passed over the implanted chip. Although the VeriChip doesn't contain any personal data at the present time, it can be used in conjunction with a database to access needed data, such as to provide hospital emergency room personnel with health information about an unconscious patient. According to the company that invented VeriChip, future applications could include access control for secure facilities, personal computers, cars, and homes, as well as to authenticate users for ATM and credit card transactions. Versions of the VeriChip with GPS capabilities could also be used to find missing individuals, such as kidnap victims and lost Alzheimer's patients, similar to the clip-on and wristwatch monitoring systems available today that allow for continuous location information to be broadcast to a proprietary receiver. After months of heated debate and prior to FDA approval, a Florida family became the first humans implanted with the VeriChip in 2002. Although privacy-rights advocates worry that a chip like this could someday be used by the government to track citizens, others view the chip no differently than a medical ID bracelet and aren't concerned because it is available on a purely voluntary basis. What do you think? Would you be willing to have a VeriChip implanted under your skin if it made some tasks (such as unlocking your home or car) easier or some types of transactions (such as withdrawing money from your bank account or shopping online) more secure? Do you think it would make these tasks easier or more secure?

For this project, form an opinion of the use of human-implantable chips. Be sure to use the questions mentioned in the previous paragraph when forming your position. Your instructor will indicate whether your response is to be posted to a class bulletin board, discussed in a class chat room, or discussed as an in-class activity. You may also be asked to submit a summary of your position and point of view to your instructor.

STUDENT EDITION LABS

12. **Student Edition Labs** Reinforce the concepts you have learned in this chapter by working through the "Binary Numbers" and "Understanding the Motherboard" interactive Student Edition Labs, available online. To access these labs, go to www.course.com/uc10/ch03

If you have a SAM user profile, you have access to even more interactive content. Log in to your SAM account and go to your assignments page to see what your instructor has assigned for this chapter.

CHAPTER 4

OUTLINE

Overview

Properties of Storage Systems

Storage Devices and Media

Non-Volatility

Removable vs. Fixed Media

Random vs. Sequential Access

Logical vs. Physical Representation

Magnetic Disk Systems

Floppy Disks and Drives

High-Capacity Removable Magnetic Disks
and Drives

Hard Disk Drives

Optical Disc Systems

Read-Only Discs: CD-ROM and
DVD-ROM Discs

Recordable Discs: CD-R, DVD-R, and
DVD+R Discs

Rewritable Discs: CD-RW, DVD-RW,
DVD+RW, DVD-RAM, and Blue
Laser Discs

Other Types of Storage Systems

Magneto-Optical Discs

Flash Memory Media

Magnetic Tape Systems

Remote Storage Systems

Smart Cards

Holographic Storage

Comparing Storage Alternatives

Storage

LEARNING OBJECTIVES

After completing this chapter, you will be able to:

1. Explain the difference between storage systems and memory.

2. Name several general properties of storage systems.

3. Identify the two primary types of magnetic disk systems and describe how they work.

4. Discuss the various types of optical disc systems available and how they differ from each other and from magnetic systems.

5. List at least three other types of storage systems.

6. Summarize the storage alternatives for a PC, including which storage systems should be included on a typical PC and for what applications other systems would be appropriate.

In Chapter 3, we discussed the role of RAM, the computer's main memory. RAM *temporarily* holds program instructions, data, and output until they are no longer needed by the computer. As soon as the computer finishes with any given program and its data, those items are erased from RAM. Consequently, if programs, data, and processing results are to be preserved for future use, a computer system needs more permanent storage. **Storage** systems fill this role.

We begin this chapter with a discussion of characteristics common among storage systems. Then we cover one of the most important kinds of storage systems in use today—those based on *magnetic disks*. While this part of the chapter is primarily about *floppy disk drives* and *hard disk drives*, we also look at other common magnetic storage devices, such as *Zip®* drives. From there, we study *optical discs*, namely *CDs* and *DVDs*, and then turn to other types of storage systems, such as *magnetic tape*, *flash memory*, *online storage*, and *smart cards*. The chapter concludes with a summary and comparison of the storage devices covered in the chapter. ■

PROPERTIES OF STORAGE SYSTEMS

Several important properties characterize storage systems. In this section, we consider some of the most significant, including the two physical parts of a storage system, the non-volatility property of storage media, the ability to remove storage media from many storage devices, and the methods used to access and represent data.

Storage Devices and Media

There are two parts to any storage system: a **storage device** and a **storage medium**. The storage medium is where the data is actually stored (such as a *floppy disk* or *CD*); a storage medium needs to be inside the appropriate storage device (such as a *floppy drive* or *CD drive*) to be read from or written to. Often the storage device and medium are two separate pieces of hardware, though with some systems—such as a *hard drive*—the two parts are permanently sealed together to form one single piece of hardware.

Storage devices can be *internal* (located inside the system unit), *external* (plugged into an external port on the system unit), or *remote* (located on another computer, such as a network server). Internal devices have the advantage of requiring no additional desk space and are often faster than their external counterparts. External devices can be more easily used with multiple computers, or added to a PC that has no room left inside its system unit. Remote devices are accessed over a network, such as a home network, a company network, or the Internet. Regardless of how they are connected to the computer, letters of the alphabet and/or names are assigned to each storage device, so the devices can be identified when they need to be used (see Figure 4-1).

>**Storage.** Saving data, results, or programs for future use. >**Storage device.** A piece of hardware, such as a floppy drive or CD drive, into which a storage medium is inserted to be read from or written to. >**Storage medium.** The part of a storage system where data is stored, such as a floppy disk or CD disc.

Non-Volatility

Storage media are **non-volatile**. This means that when you shut off power to a storage device, the data stored on that device's storage medium will still be there when you turn the device back on. This feature contrasts with RAM, which is **volatile**. As discussed previously, data held in RAM is erased once it is no longer needed or the power to the computer is turned off.

Removable vs. Fixed Media

In many storage systems, although the storage device is always connected to the computer, the storage medium used with that device can be inserted and removed. These are called *removable-media* storage systems. Floppy disks, CDs, and DVDs are examples of removable media. On the other hand, *fixed-media* storage systems, such as most hard drive systems, seal the storage medium (such as the hard disk) inside the storage device (such as the hard drive) and users cannot remove it.

Fixed-media devices generally provide higher speed and better reliability at a lower cost than removable-media alternatives. Removable-media devices have other advantages, however, including the following.

- ▼ *Unlimited storage capacity*—You can insert a new medium into the storage device to replace one that has become full.

- ▼ *Transportability*—You can easily share media between computers and people.

- ▼ *Backup*—You can make a duplicate copy of valuable data on a removable medium and store the copy away from the computer, for use if the original copy is destroyed.

- ▼ *Security*—Sensitive programs or data can be saved on removable media and stored in a secured area.

Virtually all desktop, notebook, and tablet PCs include both removable-media and fixed-media storage systems.

Random vs. Sequential Access

When the computer system receives an instruction that requires data or programs located in storage, it must go to the designated location on the appropriate medium and retrieve the requested data or programs. This procedure is referred to as *access*. Two basic access methods are available: random and sequential.

Random access, also called *direct access*, means that data can be retrieved directly from any location on the medium, in any order. With *sequential access*, however, the data

The letter C is usually assigned to the first hard drive.

The letters A and B are usually reserved for floppy disk drives.

The letter D is often assigned to a CD or DVD drive, if there isn't a second hard drive.

Other letters, beginning with E in this example, would be used for any other drives attached to the PC, such as a second hard drive, Zip drive, or shared network drive.

H W

> **FIGURE 4-1**
Storage device identifiers. To keep track of storage devices in an unambiguous way, the computer system assigns letters of the alphabet or names to each of them.

FURTHER EXPLORATION

For links to further information about removable storage devices and media, go to www.course.com/uc10/ch04

>**Non-volatile.** Describes a storage medium that retains its contents when the power is shut off. >**Volatile.** Describes a medium whose contents are erased when the power is shut off.

can only be retrieved in the order in which it is physically stored on the medium. Most of a PC's storage devices—including hard disk drives, floppy disk drives, and CD/DVD drives—are random access devices. They work like audio CDs or movie DVDs—the user can jump directly to a particular selection or location, as needed. One type of PC storage device that uses sequential access is a *tape drive*. Computer tapes work like audio cassette tapes or videotapes—to get to a specific location on the tape, you must play or fast-forward through all of the tape before it. Media that allow random access are sometimes referred to as *addressable* media. This means that the storage system can locate each piece of stored data or each program at a unique *address*, which is determined by the computer system.

Logical vs. Physical Representation

Anything (such as a program, letter, digital photograph, or song) stored on a storage medium is referred to as a **file**. Data files are also sometimes called *documents*. When a document that was just created (such as a memo or letter in a word processing program) is saved, it is stored in a new file on the storage medium that the user designates. During the storage process, the user is required to give the file a name, called a **filename**; that name is used when the user requests to see the document at a later time.

To keep files organized, related documents are often stored inside **folders** located on the storage medium. For example, one folder might contain memos to business associates while another might hold a set of budgets for a specific project (see Figure 4-2). To further organize files, you can create *subfolders* within a folder. For instance, you might create a "Letters" folder that contains one subfolder for letters sent to friends and a second sub-folder for letters sent to potential employers. In Figure 4-2, both *Budgets* and *Memos* are subfolders inside the *My Documents* folder.

Although both the user and the computer use drive letters, folder names, and filenames to save and retrieve documents, the way a user perceives this process differs from the way a computer implements this process. Typically, a user views how data is stored (what we have discussed so far in this section and what appears in the Windows Explorer screen in Figure 4-2) using *logical file representation*. That is, we view a document stored as one complete unit in a particular folder on a particular drive. In contrast, the physical way data

● **FIGURE 4-2**
Organizing data.
Folders can be used to organize related items on a storage medium.

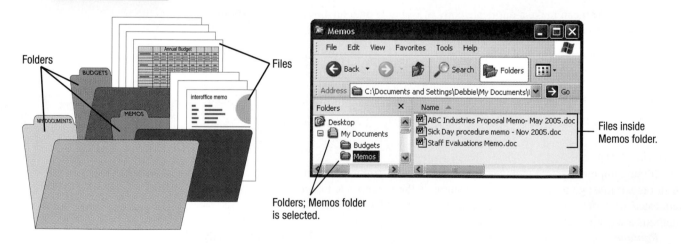

Folders

Files

interoffice memo

Annual Budget

Files inside Memos folder.

Folders; Memos folder is selected.

>**File.** Something stored on a storage medium, such as a program, document, or image. >**Filename.** A name given to a file by the user that is used to retrieve the file at a later time. >**Folder.** A named place on a storage medium into which files can be stored to keep the medium organized.

is stored and organized on the storage media (as viewed by the computer) is called *physical file representation*. For example, the ABC Industries Proposal Memo file shown in Figure 4-2 is *logically* located within the Memos folders inside the My Documents folder on the hard drive C, but the data in these folders could be *physically* stored in many different pieces scattered across that hard drive. When this occurs, the computer keeps track of the various locations used and the logical representation (filename, folder names, and drive letter) that is being used to identify that file. Fortunately, we don't have to be concerned with how files are physically stored on a disk, because the computer keeps track of that and retrieves files for us whenever we request them.

MAGNETIC DISK SYSTEMS

Speedy access to data, relatively low cost, and the ability to erase and rewrite data make **magnetic disks** the most widely used storage media on today's computers. With magnetic storage systems, data is written by *read/write heads* magnetizing particles a certain way on a medium's surface. The particles retain their magnetic orientation until the orientation is changed again, so files can be stored, rewritten to the disk, and erased, as needed. Storing data on a magnetic disk is illustrated in Figure 4-3. The most common type of magnetic disk is the *hard disk*; another common type of magnetic disk is the *floppy disk*.

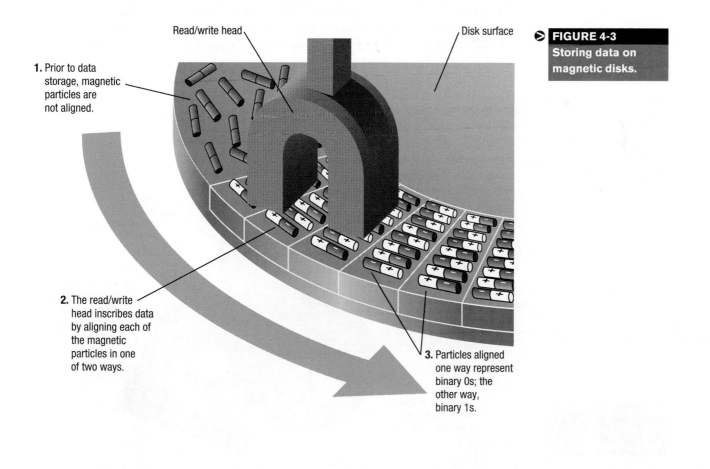

Read/write head

Disk surface

1. Prior to data storage, magnetic particles are not aligned.

2. The read/write head inscribes data by aligning each of the magnetic particles in one of two ways.

3. Particles aligned one way represent binary 0s; the other way, binary 1s.

> **FIGURE 4-3**
> **Storing data on magnetic disks.**

>**Magnetic disk.** A storage medium that records data using magnetic spots on disks made of flexible plastic or rigid metal.

Floppy Disks and Drives

Over the years, most PCs have been set up to use a **floppy disk**—sometimes called a *diskette* or *disk*—to accommodate removable storage needs. Floppy disks are a removable medium and very inexpensive, so they are handy for such tasks as backing up small amounts of data, sending small files to others, and sharing data between two computers—such as a computer at home and one at school. Floppy disks are written to and read by **floppy disk drives** (commonly called just *floppy drives*). Because floppy drives are relatively slow and their capacity is relatively small compared to newer removable storage options, some manufacturers refer to the floppy drive as a *legacy drive* and are no longer automatically including one as part of their computer systems. Instead of having an internal floppy drive, some PC buyers are opting for an external portable floppy drive that they can move from PC to PC, as needed.

Floppy Disk Characteristics

A floppy disk consists of a round piece of flexible plastic coated with a magnetizable substance. The disk is protected by a square, rugged plastic cover lined with a soft material that wipes the disk clean as it spins (see Figure 4-4). The surface of a floppy disk is organized into circular rings called **tracks**, and pie-shaped **sectors**. On most PC systems, the smallest storage area on a disk is a **cluster**—the part of a track that crosses a specific number (always two or more) of adjacent sectors (see Figure 4-5). Data is stored along the tracks of the disk; tracks, sectors, and clusters are numbered so that the computer can record where data is stored and can retrieve it at a later time. To accomplish this, the PC keeps a directory—called the *file directory* or *file allocation table (FAT)*—of where each

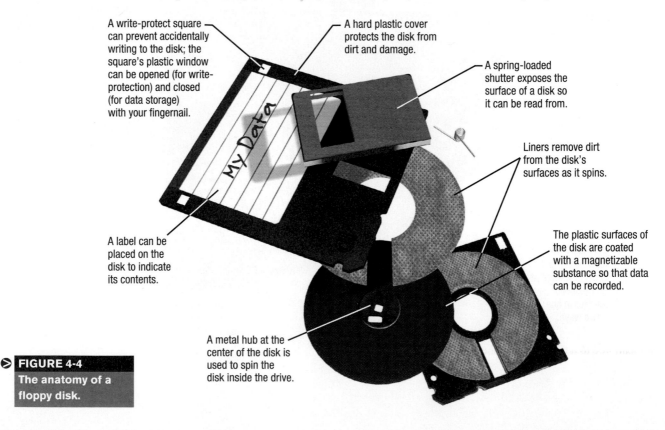

A write-protect square can prevent accidentally writing to the disk; the square's plastic window can be opened (for write-protection) and closed (for data storage) with your fingernail.

A hard plastic cover protects the disk from dirt and damage.

A spring-loaded shutter exposes the surface of a disk so it can be read from.

Liners remove dirt from the disk's surfaces as it spins.

A label can be placed on the disk to indicate its contents.

The plastic surfaces of the disk are coated with a magnetizable substance so that data can be recorded.

A metal hub at the center of the disk is used to spin the disk inside the drive.

FIGURE 4-4
The anatomy of a floppy disk.

>**Floppy disk.** A low-capacity, removable magnetic disk made of flexible plastic permanently sealed inside a hard plastic cover.
>**Floppy disk drive.** A storage device that reads from and writes to floppy disks. >**Track.** A concentric path on a disk where data is recorded.
>**Sector.** A pie-shaped area on a disk surface. >**Cluster.** The part of a track on a disk that crosses a fixed number of adjacent sectors; it is the smallest addressable area of a disk.

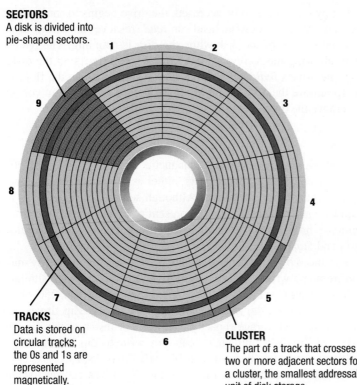

SECTORS
A disk is divided into pie-shaped sectors.

TRACKS
Data is stored on circular tracks; the 0s and 1s are represented magnetically.

CLUSTER
The part of a track that crosses two or more adjacent sectors forms a cluster, the smallest addressable unit of disk storage.

> **FIGURE 4-5**
> **Magnetic disks (such as floppy disks) are organized into tracks, sectors, and clusters**.

H
W

file is physically stored, its size, and what filename the user has assigned to it. When the user requests a document (always by filename), the computer uses the FAT to retrieve it. A cluster is the smallest addressable area on a disk; consequently, everything stored on a disk always takes up at least one cluster of space on the disk. When a file takes up more than one cluster of space, each cluster contains directions pointing to the next cluster used, so the computer can retrieve all pieces of the file in the proper order when it is needed.

Most floppy disks in use today measure 3½ inches in diameter (small enough to fit into a shirt pocket) and can store 1.44 MB of data, which is sufficient to store about 500 or so pages of double-spaced text created using a common word processing program. Digital photographs, music files, or documents containing a lot of images usually require a higher capacity removable storage media—such as a CD, DVD, or high-capacity magnetic disk—which are discussed shortly.

Using Floppy Disks

To use a floppy disk, it must first be inserted into a floppy drive (with the label area facing up and closest to the user, as illustrated in Figure 4-6). When it is completely inserted, the disk clicks into place, the metal shutter is moved aside to expose the surface of the disk, and the *eject button* on the front of the drive pops out. Because the drive openings for some other types of removable disks (such as *Zip disks*, discussed shortly) are similar in size and appearance to a floppy drive opening, be careful when inserting a floppy disk to ensure that you are using the proper drive. If the disk does not fit into or doesn't "click" into place inside the drive opening, you are likely inserting it into the wrong drive.

Before a floppy disk can be used, it must be *formatted* to prepare it for use. Most floppy disks sold today are already formatted for either IBM or Macintosh computers and, therefore, are ready to use. Formatting a disk that already contains data erases everything on the disk. Although in the past users would reformat floppy disks if they became unreliable, today users typically discard floppy disks when they become unreliable because of their very low cost. The formatting process is sometimes used, however, to quickly erase a floppy disk for reuse.

> **FIGURE 4-6**
> **Inserting a floppy disk into a floppy drive.** Disks go into a drive only one way–label side up, with the disk shutter facing the drive door.

When the floppy disk needs to be accessed, the drive begins to rotate the disk within its plastic cover. The drive's read/write head can *read* (retrieve) data from or *write* (store) data onto the actual surface of the disk while the disk is spinning. The read/write heads move in and out, allowing the read/write head access to all tracks on the disk. While the disk is spinning, the drive's *indicator light* goes on—don't remove the floppy disk while this light is on. To remove the disk, wait until the light goes off, and then you can press the eject button to remove the disk.

High-Capacity Removable Magnetic Disks and Drives

A number of higher-capacity removable magnetic storage media—sometimes called *superdiskettes*—have emerged in recent years, either as replacements for standard floppy disks or as supplemental storage solutions. Although some of these systems have a large installed base and are still widely used at the present time, that may not be the case in the future as *recordable optical disc* technology improves. High-capacity removable disks include *Zip disks* and *SuperDisks*.

Zip disks, introduced by Iomega Corporation in 1995, are high-capacity magnetic disks that can be read from and written to only with *Zip drives*. Zip disks are similar in size and appearance to floppy disks (see Figure 4-7) but have a capacity of 100, 250, or 750 MB. Zip drives are *downward compatible*, meaning the higher-capacity Zip drives can read any Zip disks at their designated storage capacity or lower. For instance, the Zip 750 drive can read all three sizes of Zip disks (although it can only write to Zip 250 and Zip 750 disks), while the Zip 100 drive can only be used with 100 MB Zip disks. Zip disks cannot be used in a conventional floppy disk drive, and none of the Zip drives can read standard floppy disks. Zip drives are most appropriate for users who need to back up large files or transfer large files between PCs or other users that have a Zip drive. Because Zip drives were one of the first high-capacity removable storage solutions, they enjoy widespread use.

SuperDisk drives, originally made by Imation and more technically called *laser servo (LS) drives*, are similar to Zip drives in that they accept disks—called *SuperDisks* or *LS-120* or *LS-240 disks*, depending on their capacity—with larger capacities (120 or 240 MB) than standard floppy disks. While SuperDisk drives are slower than Zip drives, they have the advantage of being able to read from and write to standard floppy disks, in addition to SuperDisks. A regular floppy drive, however, cannot read a SuperDisk.

SuperDisk drives are no longer being manufactured by Imation, although other LS drives are available.

It is expected that other types of high-capacity media—such as optical discs and flash memory media—will eventually replace both the conventional floppy disk and high-capacity magnetic disks.

Hard Disk Drives

With the exception of computers designed to use only network storage devices (such as network computers and some Internet appliances), virtually all PCs come with a **hard disk drive** (commonly referred to as *hard drive*) that is used to store most programs and data used with that PC. Hard drives are typically located inside the system unit and are not designed to be removed, unless they

❯ FIGURE 4-7

Zip disks. Zip disks are read by Zip drives; the newest Zip disks hold 750 MB.

>**Hard disk drive.** A storage system consisting of one or more metal magnetic disks permanently sealed with an access mechanism inside its drive.

need to be repaired or replaced. In common practice, the terms *hard disk*, *hard disk drive*, *hard disk system*, and *hard drive* are used interchangeably.

Hard Drive Characteristics

Similar to floppy drives, hard drives store data magnetically; their disks are organized into tracks, sectors, and clusters; and they use read/write heads to store and retrieve data. However, the *hard disks* used with a hard drive are made out of metal and are permanently sealed (along with the read/write heads and access mechanisms) inside the hard drive. One drive may contain a stack of several hard disks, as shown in Figure 4-8. Hard drives are typically fixed-media systems in which the storage media (the hard disks) are not removable from the storage device (the hard drive); one exception is a hard drive that uses a removable *hard disk cartridge*, as discussed later in this chapter.

Hard drives are faster than removable-media systems and can store a great deal more data. The capacity of a typical internal hard drive for today's desktop PCs ranges from 40 to 300 GB. Internal hard drives for notebook computers are also getting larger—up to 80 GB. Most hard drives for desktop PCs use 3½-inch hard drives, although a switch to 2½-inch hard drives is expected in the near future; most notebook computers use a 2½-inch hard drive. Even smaller hard disk systems are becoming available for systems requiring tiny drives, such as the 1-inch *Microdrive* developed by IBM, who is now partnered with Hitachi for their hard drive systems. Hitachi recently announced that a 4 GB version of the Microdrive will be available by the end of 2003. The increased capacity is due to a new storage technology developed by IBM called *Pixie Dust*, which sandwiches three atoms of the precious metal ruthenium between two magnetic layers. This technology enables data to be stored at much higher densities on magnetic media than previously possible.

Like floppy disks, hard disk surfaces are divided into tracks, sectors, and clusters when formatted, but include many more of each. A new hard drive is typically formatted for use at the factory before it is sold, so it is ready for software and data as soon as it is installed. Because reformatting a disk erases everything on the disk, hard drives are rarely reformatted. This task is only performed if errors are preventing the hard drive from operating properly and there is no other option.

FURTHER EXPLORATION

For links to further information about hard drives, go to www.course.com/uc10/ch04

H W

> **FIGURE 4-8**
Inside a hard drive.
The metal magnetic disks of a hard drive typically are sealed permanently inside the drive.

ACCESS MECHANISM
The access mechanism moves the read/write heads in and out together between the hard disk surfaces to access required data.

MOUNTING SHAFT
The mounting shaft spins the disks at a speed of several thousand revolutions per minute while the computer is turned on.

READ/WRITE HEADS
There is a read/write head for each disk surface. On most systems, the heads move in and out together and will be positioned on the same track and sector on each disk.

SEALED DRIVE
The hard disks and the drive mechanism are hermetically sealed inside a case to keep them free from contamination.

HARD DISKS
There are usually several hard disk surfaces on which to store data. Most hard drives store data on both sides of each disk.

In addition to tracks, sectors, and clusters, hard drives use the concept of a **cylinder**. A cylinder is the collection of one particular track on each disk surface, such as the first track or the tenth track on each disk surface. In other words, it's the area on all of the hard disks inside the hard drive that can be accessed without moving the read/write access mechanism, once it has been moved to the proper position. For example, the four-disk system in Figure 4-9 contains eight possible recording surfaces (using both sides of each disk), so a cylinder on that system would consist of eight tracks, such as track 13 on all eight surfaces. Hard drives are commonly organized into anywhere from a few hundred to a few thousand cylinders. The number of tracks on a single disk is equal to the number of cylinders in the disk system.

Most hard drives are hermetically sealed units. This precaution keeps the disk surfaces completely free of contamination, enables the disks to spin faster, and limits causes of operational problems. Hard disks typically spin between 5,400 and 15,000 revolutions per minute (rpm), depending on the type and size of the drive. In addition to spinning faster than most other types of storage systems, the hard disk constantly rotates when your computer is turned on instead of only rotating when it needs to be accessed. This feature eliminates the delay of waiting for the drive to come up to the correct speed. (Most PCs can be set up to go to sleep and turn off the hard drive after a specified period of inactivity to save power; in this case, touching the keyboard or mouse starts the hard disks spinning again.)

To retrieve or store data, most hard drives have at least one read/write head for each recording surface. These heads are mounted on an *access mechanism*; similar to a floppy disk, this mechanism moves the heads in and out among the tracks together. It positions all the heads on the cylinder containing the track from which data is to be read or to which data is to be written. It is important to realize that a hard drive's read/write heads never touch the surface of the hard disk at any time, even during reading and writing. If the read/write heads do touch the surface—such as if the PC is bumped while the hard drive is spinning or a foreign object gets onto the surface of the disk, a *head crash* occurs, which may do permanent damage to the hard drive. Because the heads are located extremely close to the surface of the disk—usually less than a millionth of an inch above

> **FIGURE 4-9**
>
> **A disk cylinder.** Hard drives use cylinders, in addition to tracks, sectors, and clusters, to keep track of where data is stored.

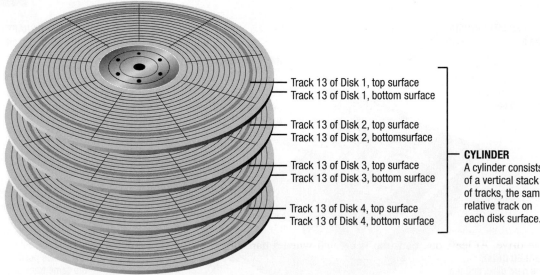

Track 13 of Disk 1, top surface
Track 13 of Disk 1, bottom surface

Track 13 of Disk 2, top surface
Track 13 of Disk 2, bottomsurface

Track 13 of Disk 3, top surface
Track 13 of Disk 3, bottom surface

Track 13 of Disk 4, top surface
Track 13 of Disk 4, bottom surface

CYLINDER
A cylinder consists of a vertical stack of tracks, the same relative track on each disk surface.

>**Cylinder.** The collection of tracks located in the same location on a set of hard disk surfaces.

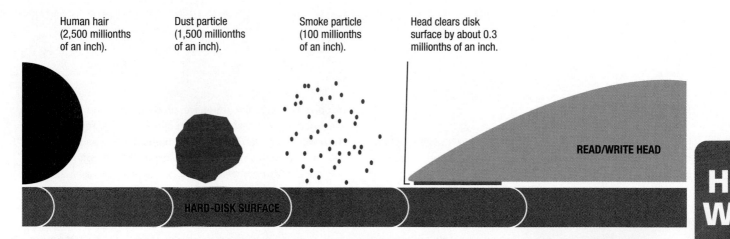

Human hair (2,500 millionths of an inch).

Dust particle (1,500 millionths of an inch).

Smoke particle (100 millionths of an inch).

Head clears disk surface by about 0.3 millionths of an inch.

READ/WRITE HEAD

HARD-DISK SURFACE

H W

the surface—the presence of a foreign object the width of a human hair or even a smoke particle (about 2,500 and 100 millionths of an inch, respectively) on a hard disk's surface is like placing a huge boulder on a road and then trying to drive over it with your car (see Figure 4-10). One never knows when a hard drive will crash—there may be no warning whatsoever—and this is a good reason for keeping the drive backed up regularly. Backing up a computer system is discussed in more detail in Chapter 6. When hard drives containing critical data become damaged, *data recovery firms* may be able to help out, as discussed in the Inside the Industry box.

In order for a hard drive to read or write data, the following three events must be carried out, all of which may add time to the total **disk access time**.

1. Move the read/write heads to the cylinder that contains (or will store) the desired data—called *seek time*.

2. Rotate the disks into the proper position so that the read/write heads are located over the part of the cylinder to be used—called *rotational delay*.

3. Read the data from the disk and transfer it to memory or transfer the data to be written to the disk from memory and then store it on the disk—called *data movement time*.

Typical hard disk access times are from 10 to 20 milliseconds. To minimize disk access time, drives usually store related data on the same cylinder. This strategy sharply reduces the seek-time component and improves the overall access time.

In addition to being used with computers, hard drives are increasingly being incorporated into consumer products, such as *digital video recorders* (*DVRs*) like TiVo and *game boxes* like Xbox and PlayStation. Although growth in the computer storage industry has been slowing, demand for storage products for consumer applications is on the rise.

Partitioning and File Systems

Partitioning a hard drive enables you to logically divide the physical capacity of a single drive into separate areas called *partitions*. You can then treat each of the partitions as an independent disk drive, such as a C drive and a D drive, although they are physically still one drive. At least one partition is created when a hard drive is first formatted; you can change the number and sizes of the partitions at a later time, although this action usually

> **FIGURE 4-10**
> **Obstacles on a hard-disk surface.** A human hair or even a smoke particle on a fast-spinning hard-disk surface can damage both the surface and the read/write head.

>Disk access time. The time it takes to locate and read data from (or position and write data to) a storage medium.

INSIDE THE INDUSTRY

Data Recovery Experts

It happens far more often than most people imagine. A hard drive quits working the day before a big report is due, a laptop is dropped in the parking lot and then run over by a car, or a business burns down taking the PC containing the only copy of the company records with it. If the data on the drive was recently backed up, it can be installed on a new drive with just a little expense and a short delay. When critical data wasn't backed up and is located on a potentially destroyed hard drive, that's when it's time to seek out a professional data recovery expert.

Data recovery firms, such as DriveSavers in California, specialize in recovering data from severely damaged storage media (see the accompanying photos). The damaged drives are taken apart in a clean room (an airtight room similar to the ones in which computer chips are manufactured), cleaned, put back together, and the data copied onto a server. Then, if the file directory is not recovered, engineers try to match the jumbled data to file types in order to reconstruct the original files. DriveSavers clients have included Barbara Mandrell, whose musical director's hard drive containing several months of work and more than 1,200 orchestra charts needed for a concert nine days away

stopped working; the executive producer of "The Simpsons," whose computer crashed taking scripts for 12 episodes of the show with it; an individual whose notebook PC was trapped for two days beneath a sunken cruise ship in the Amazon River; and a Fortune 500 company, which lost all its financial data and stockholder information when its Unix server went down. In all four cases, DriveSavers was able to recover all of the lost data.

Data recovery firms stress the importance of backing up data. According to Scott Gaidano, president of DriveSavers, "The first thing we tell people is back up, back up, back up. It's amazing how many people don't back up." It is also important to make sure the backup procedure is working. For instance, the Fortune 500 company mentioned previously performed regular backups and kept the backup media in a fire-resistant safe, but when they went to use the backup after their server crashed, they discovered that the backup media were all blank.

Because potentially losing all the data on a drive can be so stressful and traumatic, DriveSavers has its own data-crisis counselor, a former suicide hotline worker. Fortunately for their clients, DriveSavers has a 90% recovery rate. At an average of $900 per recovery, the services of data recovery experts aren't cheap, but when the lost data is irreplaceable, it's a bargain.

Data recovery. All the data located on the hard drive of this computer (left) that was virtually destroyed in a fire was recovered by data recovery experts in less than 24 hours. Recovery takes place in a clean room (right).

destroys any data in the partitions being changed. Consequently, you should back up your data located on that drive to another storage medium before you repartition a hard drive, and then copy the data back onto the repartitioned hard drive. Some operating systems have a limit to the number of partitions that can be used.

Because older operating systems could only address hard drives up to 512 MB, hard drives larger than that limit had to use multiple partitions. Most newer operating systems allow larger drives, but partitioning a large drive can make it function more efficiently. This is because operating systems typically use a larger cluster size with a larger hard drive. When a large cluster size is used, disk space is often wasted because even tiny files have to use up one entire cluster of storage space. When a hard drive is partitioned, each logical drive uses a smaller cluster size, since each logical drive is smaller than the original drive. Windows computers using the *FAT32 file system* are much more efficient than those using the original FAT system since FAT32 systems allow cluster sizes to be as small as 4 KB each, which cuts down on wasted storage space. Windows NT and Windows XP computers have the option of using the *NTFS* file system, which can address much larger drives than either FAT or FAT32.

Another reason for partitioning a hard drive is to be able to use two different operating systems on the same hard drive—such as Windows and Linux. You can then decide which operating system you will run each time you turn on your computer. Creating the appearance of having separate hard drives for file management, multiple users, or other purposes is another common reason for partitioning a hard drive. Some users choose to install their programs on one hard drive (usually C) and store their data on a second drive (such as D). This system of using separate logical drives for data and programs makes locating data files easier, as well as enables users to back up all data files simply by backing up the entire data drive (program files aren't typically backed up as frequently as data files, if at all). Operating systems and backing up data are discussed in more detail in Chapter 6.

Disk Cache

A *cache* (pronounced *cash*) is a place to store something temporarily. For instance, in Chapter 3 we learned that *cache memory* is a group of very fast memory chips located on or near the CPU that are used to store the most frequently and recently used data and instructions. Because transferring that data and instructions from cache memory to the CPU is much faster than transferring them from RAM or the hard drive, cache memory typically results in faster processing. *Disk caching* is similar in concept—it is a strategy for speeding up system performance by storing data or programs that might be needed soon in a designated area of RAM to avoid having to retrieve them from the hard drive when they are requested. Since retrieving data from RAM is much faster than from the hard drive, disk caching can speed up performance.

The location in RAM where disk caching takes place is called the **disk cache**. When a hard drive uses disk caching (as most do today), any time the hard drive is accessed the computer copies the requested program and data, as well as extra programs or data located in neighboring areas of the hard drive (such as the entire track or cylinder), to the disk cache. The theory behind disk caching assumes that neighboring data will likely have to be read soon anyway (research indicates that there is an 80 to 90% chance the next request will be for data located adjacent to the data last read), so the computer can reduce the number of times the hard drive is accessed by copying that data into RAM early. When the next data is requested, the computer system checks the disk-cache area first, to see if the data it needs is already there. If it is, the data is retrieved for processing; if not, the computer retrieves the requested data from the disk (see Figure 4-11). Disk caching saves not only time but also wear and tear on the hard drive. In portable computers, it can also extend battery life.

>**Disk cache.** A dedicated part of RAM used to store additional data adjacent to data retrieved during a disk fetch to improve system performance.

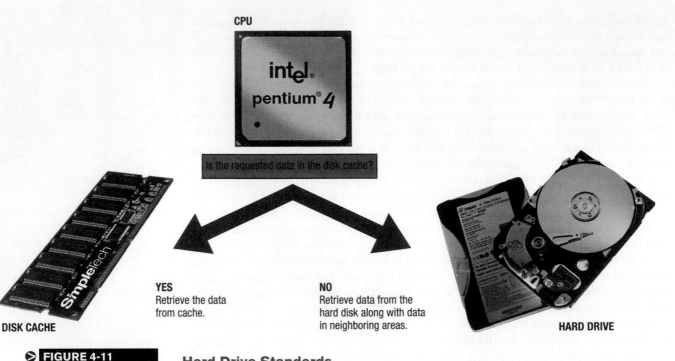

CPU

Is the requested data in the disk cache?

YES
Retrieve the data
from cache.

NO
Retrieve data from the
hard disk along with data
in neighboring areas.

DISK CACHE

HARD DRIVE

> **FIGURE 4-11**
> **Disk cache.** Disk
> cache is a special area
> of RAM used to store
> small amounts of disk
> data. Such data can later
> be accessed thousands
> of times faster than it
> could be from a disk.

Hard Drive Standards

Hard drives connect, or interface, with a computer using one of several different standards. These standards determine performance characteristics, such as the density with which data can be packed onto the disk, the speed of disk access, how large the disk can be, and the way the disk drive interfaces with other hardware. Some of the most common interfaces are discussed next.

With *EIDE*, for *enhanced integrated drive electronics*, the *hard drive controller*—the chip that controls the flow of data to and from the hard drive—is built into the drive. *SCSI*, for *small computer system interface* and pronounced "skuzzy," hard drive controller chips are either attached directly to the motherboard or are located on a *SCSI interface card* to which the drive is connected. Both EIDI and SCSI are very fast and can support multiple hard drives. EIDE has a variety of different specifications, such as *ATA*, *Fast ATA*, *Fast IDE*, or *ATA-2*, *ATA/100*, and *serial ATA*. EIDE drives are typically less expensive than SCSI drives; consequently, EIDI drives are found more often in desktop PCs. SCSI is usually faster for server operations with multiple users. In addition to being used with hard disk drives, SCSI interfaces can also be used to connect some scanners, CD drives, and DVD drives.

Fibre Channel is a newer storage standard that is expected to become widely used with network storage systems, as well as in other high-capacity business storage applications. Fibre Channel storage devices connect to the host computer using a special *Fibre Channel interface card* and have the advantage of reliability, flexibility, and very fast data delivery—up to two gigabits per second. Because it is more expensive than other standards and is geared for long-distance, high-bandwidth applications, Fibre Channel is not expected to be widely used with PCs and low-end servers, at least not in the near future. It is, however, expected to eventually replace SCSI for high-end storage systems.

Some *external hard drives* today follow none of these standards; instead they connect to the PC using USB or FireWire standards through a USB or FireWire port.

Portable Hard Drive Systems

While most hard drive systems are designed to be internal devices permanently located inside the system unit, *portable hard drives* are available. Portable hard drives fall into two basic categories: those in which the entire drive is transported from one location to another, and those in which a cartridge containing the hard disk is removed from the hard drive and transported. When the entire drive is portable—essentially an external hard drive—the drive is typically attached to the PC through a USB, FireWire, or PC card port (see Figure 4-12).

PC CARD DRIVES
Notebook PCs often use portable hard drives that are inserted into, or have a connector to plug into, the PC card slot.

USB AND FIREWIRE DRIVES
Both desktop and notebook PCs can use external hard drives that connect via a USB or FireWire port.

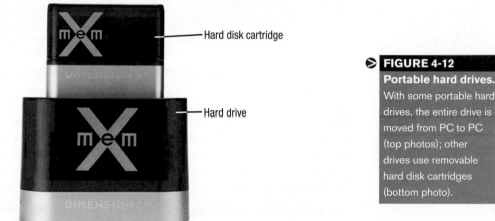

Hard disk cartridge

Hard drive

HARD DRIVES WITH REMOVABLE CARTRIDGES
With these drives, only the cartridges are moved from PC to PC.

> **FIGURE 4-12**
> **Portable hard drives.**
> With some portable hard drives, the entire drive is moved from PC to PC (top photos); other drives use removable hard disk cartridges (bottom photo).

Common capacities for external hard drives are 20 to 160 GB. Portable hard drive systems using removable *hard disk cartridges* use a hard drive that remains attached to the PC in conjunction with hard disk cartridges that can be inserted into and removed from the drive, similar to a floppy disk system. Also similar to a floppy drive, the hard drives used with hard disk cartridges can be internal or external, but external devices are more widely used. Hard disk cartridges can usually store about 20 GB, although larger storage capacities are expected in the near future. Most removable hard disk cartridges are proprietary, so they can only be used with their respective drives.

Both types of portable hard drive systems are useful for storing and backing up very large files, transporting large files from one PC to another, and for exceptionally secure facilities—such as government and research labs—that require all hard drives to be locked up when not in use. They are also commonly used for complete system backups. Although their portability has its advantages, portable hard drives generally perform more slowly than conventional fixed internal hard drives.

Storage Systems for Large Computer Systems and Networks

Hard drive systems for large computer systems (such as those containing mainframe computers and midrange servers) implement many of the same standards and principles as PC-based hard drives, but on a much larger scale. Instead of finding a single hard drive

> **FIGURE 4-13**
> **Storage for larger computer systems.** Storage systems for larger computers often consist of a collection of hard drives.

This IBM storage system can hold several racks of hard drives for a total storage capacity from 36 GB to over 32 TB.

Each rack typically holds multiple hard drives. Capacities for the hard drives range from approximately 18 GB to nearly 150 GB each.

installed within the system unit, you are most likely to find a **storage server**—a separate piece of hardware containing multiple high-speed hard drives—connected to the computer system. Large storage servers, such as the one shown in Figure 4-13, contain racks of hard drives capable of storing a total of 30 TB or more. These types of storage systems—also referred to as *enterprise storage systems*—usually use fast Fibre Channel connections. In addition to being used as stand-alone storage for large computer systems, storage servers may also be used in *network attached storage (NAS)*, *storage area network (SAN)*, and *RAID* storage systems.

Network Attached Storage (NAS) and Storage Area Networks (SANs)

Storage servers are increasingly being used to provide storage for computer networks. With the huge amounts of data that many companies need to manage and store today—for instance, Yahoo! needs to store on an on-going basis more than a petabyte of data generated by Yahoo! e-mail users—network-based storage has become increasingly important.

One possibility is the **network attached storage** (**NAS**) device. NAS devices are high-performance storage servers that are individually connected to a network to provide storage for the computers on that network. **Storage area networks** (**SANs**) also provide storage for a network, but consist of a separate network of hard drives or other storage devices. That storage area network is, in turn, attached to the main network. The primary difference between NAS and SANs is whether the storage devices act as individual network nodes, just like PCs, printers, and other devices on the network (NAS), or whether they are located in a completely separate network of storage devices that is accessible by the main network (SAN). However, in terms of functionality, the distinction between NAS and SANs is blurring, since they both provide storage services to the network. Both NAS and SAN systems are scalable, so new devices can be added as more storage is needed and devices can be added or removed without disrupting the network.

>**Storage server.** A hardware device containing multiple high-speed hard drives. >**Network attached storage (NAS).** A high-performance storage server individually connected to a network to provide storage for computers on that network. >**Storage area network (SAN).** A network of hard drives or other storage devices that provide storage for another network of computers.

RAID

RAID (*redundant arrays of independent disks*) is a method of storing data on two or more hard drives that work in combination to do the job of a larger drive. Although RAID can be used to increase performance, it is most often used to protect critical data on a storage server. Because RAID usually involves recording redundant (duplicate) copies of stored data, the copies can be used, when necessary, to reconstruct lost data. This helps to increase the *fault tolerance*—the ability to recover from an unexpected hardware or software failure, such as a system crash—of a storage system.

There are six different RAID designs or levels (0 to 5) that use different combinations of RAID techniques. For example RAID level 0 uses *disk striping*, which spreads files over several disk drives (see the leftmost part of Figure 4-14). Although striping improves performance, since multiple drives can be accessed at one time to store or retrieve data, it doesn't provide fault tolerance.

Another common RAID technique is *disk mirroring*, in which data is written to two duplicate drives simultaneously (see the rightmost part of Figure 4-14). The objective of disk mirroring is to increase fault tolerance—if one of the disk drives fails, the system can instantly switch to the other drive without any loss of data or service. RAID level 1 uses disk mirroring. Levels beyond level 1 use some combination of disk striping and disk mirroring, with different types of error correction provisions.

Because using RAID is significantly more expensive than just using a traditional hard drive storage system, it has been reserved for use with network and Internet servers. However, recently RAID has become more popular with PC users looking for increased performance. One recent test by *PC World* magazine showed that two RAID-connected drives completed some tasks in 40% less time than one drive of the same type. To implement RAID on a desktop PC, a RAID expansion card must be used.

H W

> **FIGURE 4-14**
RAID. Disk striping is used to increase performance; disk mirroring is used to increase fault tolerance.

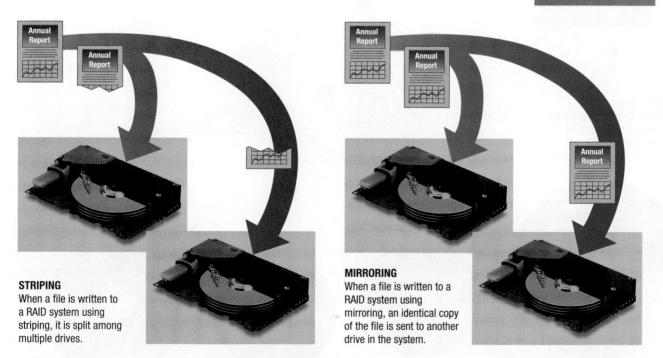

STRIPING
When a file is written to a RAID system using striping, it is split among multiple drives.

MIRRORING
When a file is written to a RAID system using mirroring, an identical copy of the file is sent to another drive in the system.

>**RAID.** A storage method that uses several small hard disks in parallel to do the job of a larger disk.

OPTICAL DISC SYSTEMS

Optical discs (such as *CDs* and *DVDs*) store data *optically*—using laser beams—instead of magnetically, like floppy and hard disks. Lasers can write and read data at densities much higher than magnetic technology, so the storage capacity of optical discs is much higher than magnetic disks of the same physical size—usually from 650 MB on up.

Optical discs are made out of plastic with a reflective metallic or otherwise light-sensitive coating. Data can be stored on one or both sides of an optical disc, depending on the disc. Most optical discs are 4½ inches in diameter, although smaller discs are sometimes used. To keep data organized, optical discs are divided into tracks and sectors like magnetic disks, but use a single grooved spiral track beginning at the center of the disc (see Figure 4-15), instead of a series of concentric tracks. Because lasers can be very precise, the track can be quite narrow and the spiral can be very tight—when measured from end to end, the total length of the track on a typical CD is over 3 miles. The number of sectors used varies depending on the size and type of disc, but a standard 650 MB CD has over 330,000 sectors. Because the track starts at the center of the disc, optical discs can be made into a variety of sizes and shapes—such as a heart, triangle, custom shape, or the hockey-rink shape commonly used with business card CDs—the track just stops when it reaches the outer edge of the disc. Standard shapes are molded and less expensive; custom shapes—such as those that match a key product or service being sold (such as a soda can, musical instrument, saw blade, candy bar, or house)—are custom cut and are more costly. The practice of using optical discs to replace ordinary objects, such as the business card discs shown in Figure 4-15, is becoming more common. For a closer look at business card CDs, see the How it Works box.

> FIGURE 4-15
Optical discs.

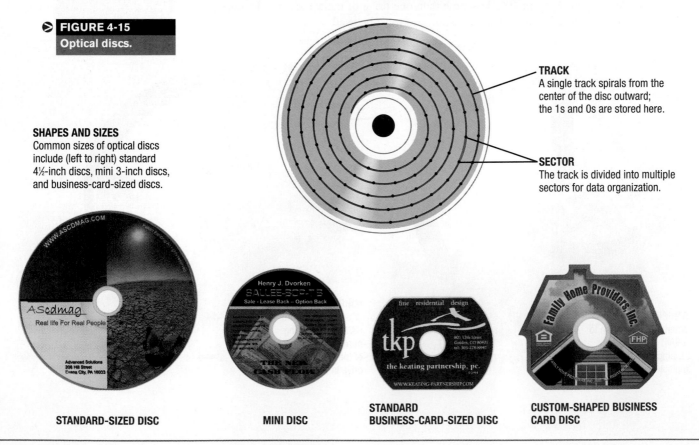

TRACK
A single track spirals from the center of the disc outward; the 1s and 0s are stored here.

SECTOR
The track is divided into multiple sectors for data organization.

SHAPES AND SIZES
Common sizes of optical discs include (left to right) standard 4½-inch discs, mini 3-inch discs, and business-card-sized discs.

STANDARD-SIZED DISC

MINI DISC

STANDARD BUSINESS-CARD-SIZED DISC

CUSTOM-SHAPED BUSINESS CARD DISC

>**Optical disc.** A type of storage medium read from and written to using a laser beam.

HOW IT WORKS

Business Card CDs

With computers being used at most businesses and many homes today, use of business card CDs is on the rise. Business card CDs are similar to conventional CDs, but they are physically smaller, come in different shapes, and hold less data. They can, however, be played using CD and DVD drives, just like any other CD. Business card CD-R discs can also be recorded using a standard recordable CD drive, but are more commonly mass-produced once a master CD has been developed.

Business card CDs today can contain a wide variety of content, such as résumés in Word or PDF format, multimedia presentations, portfolio material (such as copies of ad campaigns created by advertising executives, digital images created by graphic artists, Web sites created by Web site designers, or photographs of an artist's or architect's work), catalogs, and copies of the company Web site. The accompanying figure takes a closer look at one business card CD; as in

this example, it is becoming common for business card CD content to be developed using a multimedia authoring program so that the content, along with animated effects to catch the user's interest, can be incorporated into a professional-looking presentation that is automatically played after the CD is inserted into a PC's CD or DVD drive.

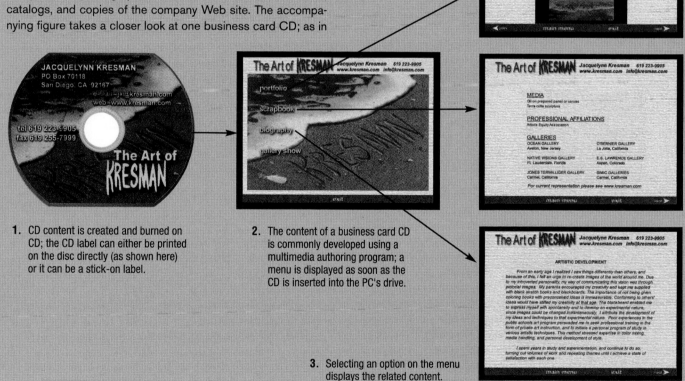

1. CD content is created and burned on CD; the CD label can either be printed on the disc directly (as shown here) or it can be a stick-on label.

2. The content of a business card CD is commonly developed using a multimedia authoring program; a menu is displayed as soon as the CD is inserted into the PC's drive.

3. Selecting an option on the menu displays the related content.

CD and DVD discs are read by *CD* and *DVD drives*. The speed of a CD or DVD drive is rated as a number followed by the "×" symbol to indicate how fast the drive is compared to the first version of that drive. For instance, a 52× CD drive is 52 times faster than the original CD drive, and a 4× DVD drive is four times faster than the original DVD drive. Most optical discs have a title and other text printed only on one side and are inserted into the drive with the printed side facing up (the data is stored on the bottom, non-printed side of the disc). When inserting a CD or DVD, be careful not to get dirt, fingerprints, scratches, or anything else that might hinder light reflectivity on the disc's reflective recording surface. The advantages of CDs and DVDs include their large capacity—typically 650 or 700 MB per CD and 4.7 GB per DVD, although double-sided DVDs currently hold 9.4 GB and are expected eventually to reach 17 GB—and their small size. (Because DVD technology uses smaller pits and the tracks are closer together, DVDs hold more data than CDs.) Another advantage is that optical discs last longer and are more durable than magnetic media, although the discs should be handled carefully and stored in a protective *jewel case* when not in use to prevent scratches and fingerprints from getting on the disc. Optical discs are the standard today for software delivery; they are also commonly used for storing and transporting high-capacity music and video files.

There are a variety of types of CDs and DVDs. Some of the most important types and characteristics of CDs and DVDs are discussed next.

Read-Only Discs: CD-ROM and DVD-ROM Discs

CD-ROM (*compact disc read-only memory*) **discs** were the first optical discs of wide acceptance. Because they are *read-only*, the data on CD-ROM discs cannot be erased, changed, or added to. Data on a CD-ROM is stored by burning tiny depressions (called *pits*) into the disc's surface with a high-intensity laser beam; the parts of the disc that aren't changed are called *lands*. The disc is read by a lower-intensity laser beam inside the *CD-ROM drive*; based on the reflection of light from the disc as it hits the pits and lands, the 1s and 0s can be determined (see Figure 4-16). Because the storage process permanently alters the surface of the CD-ROM, the data cannot be erased and no data can be added to the disc.

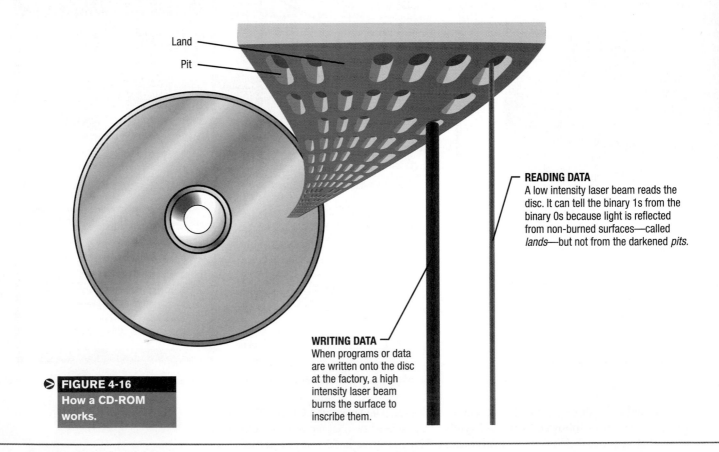

Land

Pit

READING DATA
A low intensity laser beam reads the disc. It can tell the binary 1s from the binary 0s because light is reflected from non-burned surfaces—called *lands*—but not from the darkened *pits*.

WRITING DATA
When programs or data are written onto the disc at the factory, a high intensity laser beam burns the surface to inscribe them.

FIGURE 4-16
How a CD-ROM works.

>**CD-ROM disc.** An optical disc, usually holding about 650 MB, that can be read, but not written to, by the user.

DVD-ROM (*digital versatile disc read-only memory*) **discs** are similar to CD-ROM discs, but they are newer and have a higher storage capacity. While CD-ROM discs typically hold 650 MB, DVD-ROMs can contain from 4.7 GB to 17 GB, depending on the number of recording layers and disc sides being used. The DVD was initially developed to store the full contents of a standard two-hour movie, but is now also used for prerecorded music, videos, and software. DVD-ROM discs are designed to be read by a *DVD-ROM drive*.

CD-ROM drives can usually play audio CDs, in addition to data CDs. DVD-ROM drives can typically play data and audio CDs, data CDs, DVD-ROM discs, and DVD movies.

For a look at an emerging issue—*copy protection* for CDs and other digital media— see the Trend box.

Recordable Discs: CD-R, DVD-R, and DVD+R Discs

Recordable discs can be written to, but the discs cannot be erased and reused. Recordable CDs are referred to as **CD-R discs**; recordable DVDs are called **DVD-R** or **DVD+R discs**, depending on the standard being used (different optical disc and drive manufacturers support different standards). CD-R, DVD-R, and DVD+R discs are recorded in *CD-R*, *DVD-R*, and *DVD+R drives*, respectively; CD-R discs can be read by most types of CD and DVD drives, and DVD-R or DVD+R discs can be read by most DVD drives. Recordable CDs are com-

➤ **FIGURE 4-17**
Recordable and rewritable CDs and DVDs.

monly used for backing up files, sending large files to others, and creating custom music CDs from MP3 files legally downloaded from the Internet or from songs on CDs the user owns. DVD-Rs can be used for similar purposes when more storage space than is available on a CD-R disc is needed, as well as for storing home movies and other video applications since video requires a tremendous amount of storage space. As shown in Figure 4-17, recordable CDs and DVDs look very similar to their read-only counterparts. Standard-sized 4½-inch CD-R discs hold 700 MB, 3-inch mini CD-R discs hold about 200 MB, business-card-sized CD-R discs hold 50 MB, and DVD-R or DVD+R discs can store 4.7 GB per side.

Storing data on a recordable disc is similar to the concept illustrated in Figure 4-16, but the discs contain a light-sensitive dye or chemical embedded beneath layers of protective plastic instead of a reflective metallic layer. The recording laser inside the CD-R or DVD-R drive is less powerful than the one used to create read-only discs, but still makes permanent marks on the disc to represent 0s and 1s. The process of recording data onto an optical disc is called *burning*. To burn a CD-R or DVD-R disc, special software is needed. Many commercial programs are available, and burning capabilities are also included in many recent operating systems, such as Windows XP.

RECORDABLE CD-R DISC
Holds 700 MB.

REWRITABLE DVD+RW DISC
Holds 4.7 GB.

REWRITABLE DVD-RAM DISC
Holds 9.4 GB.

REWRITABLE BLUE LASER DISC
Holds 23.3 GB.

>**DVD-ROM disc.** An optical disc, usually holding 4.7 GB, that can be read, but not written to, by the user. >**CD-R disc.** A recordable CD.
>**DVD-R/DVD+R discs.** Recordable DVDs.

TIP

Recordable and rewritable CD and DVD drives are also referred to as *CD burners* and *DVD burners,* respectively.

Rewritable Discs: CD-RW, DVD-RW, DVD+RW, DVD-RAM, and Blue Laser Discs

The newer rewritable discs can be recorded on, erased, and overwritten just like a magnetic disk. The most common types of rewritable optical media are **CD-RW**, **DVD-RW**, and **DVD+RW** discs. CD-RW discs are written to using a CD-RW drive and can be read by most CD and DVD drives. DVD-RW discs and DVD+RW discs are recorded using a DVD-RW drive or DVD+RW drive, respectively, and can be read by most DVD drives. An additional rewritable DVD format is **DVD-RAM**, which requires the DVD disc to be located inside a cartridge (see Figure 4-17) in order for the disc to be used. The newest recordable and rewritable technologies use blue lasers instead of infrared (CDs) or red (DVDs) lasers to store data more compactly on the disc. *Blue laser* discs based on this technology—developed by Sony and called *Blu-ray*—can hold 23.3 GB per disc. A similar, but competing, format developed by Toshiba and NEC is called the *Advanced Optical Disc* format and is capable of storing up to 36 GB of data on a dual-layer disc. In contrast, CD-RW discs hold 700 MB, DVD+RW and DVD-RW discs hold 4.7 GB per side, and DVD-RAM discs typically hold between 2.6 and 9.4 GB, depending on the speed of the disc and the number of sides used.

To record and erase rewritable optical discs, *phase-change* technology is most often used. With this technology, the recordable CD or DVD disc is coated with a special metal alloy compound that has two different appearances once it's been heated and then cooled, depending on the temperature reached during the heating process. With one temperature, the surface is reflective; with a higher temperature, it's not. Before any data is written to a disc, the disc is completely reflective. To record onto the disc, pits are burned into the surface by creating non-reflective areas; unburned areas (lands) remain reflective. Just as with other CDs and DVDs, these pits and lands are interpreted as 1s and 0s when the disc is read. To erase the disc, the appropriate temperature is used to change the areas to be erased back to their original reflective state.

It is important to realize that the DVD industry has not yet reached a single standard, so there are competing formats that are not necessarily compatible with each other. Luckily, many DVD drive manufacturers are introducing new drives that support more than one standard, such as one drive from Sony that is compatible with DVD+RW, DVD+R, DVD-RW, DVD-R, CD-RW, and CD-R discs. Because of the format controversy, recordable and rewritable DVD technology has taken off more slowly than originally anticipated. However, just as CD-R and CD-RW drives have virtually replaced CD-ROM drives, it is expected that, eventually, rewritable DVD drives will replace CD drives. About 4 million recordable DVD drives were in use in 2002; that number is expected to exceed 37 million by 2005.

FURTHER EXPLORATION

For links to further information about DVD technology, go to www.course.com/uc10/ch04

OTHER TYPES OF STORAGE SYSTEMS

Other types of storage systems include *magneto-optical discs*, *flash memory media*, *magnetic tape*, *remote storage*, and *smart cards*. A possibility for the future is *holographic storage*.

Magneto-Optical Discs

There are a few types of storage systems that use a combination of magnetic and optical technology—the *magneto-optical (M-O) disc* is one of the most common. *Magneto-optical drives* read special M-O discs, which are usually optical discs inside a rectangular cartridge, similar in appearance to the DVD-RAM disc shown in Figure 4-17. M-O discs are available in both 3½-inch and 5¼-inch sizes and can store up to 9.1 GB per disk.

TIP

One new type of DVD—such as the *EZ-D* currently in the testing stages—is the *disposable DVD.* Designed for non-returnable movie rentals, the discs work for only 48 hours once they are unwrapped. Receiving strong objections from environmentalists about the *e-waste* factor, time will tell if the disposable DVD becomes a viable option for content delivery.

>**CD-RW.** A rewritable CD. >**DVD-RW/DVD+RW/DVD-RAM discs.** Rewritable DVDs.

TREND

Digital Copy Protection

Citing billions of dollars of estimated losses due in large part to copies of songs being illegally shared via the Internet, the music industry is looking toward two possible methods to help stop these types of copyright violations. The first, which is backed by the movie industry, is legislation or a Federal Communications Commission (FCC) regulation to require copy protection systems to be built into all devices (such as TV sets, PCs, digital video recorders, and CD, DVD, and MP3 players) that accept digital input to prevent the transfer of digital content (such as songs and movies) over the Internet. The second possibility is copy protection built into CDs themselves. While copy-protected CDs may sound like a good thing for the music industry, consumer advocacy groups are protesting their use. The primary objection is that copy-protected CDs—which can't be duplicated and, sometimes, not even played in a PC's CD drive—prevent consumers from exercising their "fair use" rights to use the media they buy on any device of their choosing for personal use, such as copying a song from a purchased CD to a PC in order to listen to it through the PC speakers or make a custom CD for personal enjoyment. In fact, the act of copying the contents of a purchased copy-protected CD would be ille-

gal because the *Digital Millennium Copyright Act* (*DMCA*) passed in 2000 forbids the circumvention of any copyright protection method built into a product.

Digitally-locked CDs have been available for several years in Europe and Japan, but have not been widely used in the United States. That is expected to change, however, in late 2003 as more copy-protected CDs are due to hit music-store shelves in the U.S. In fact, the first lawsuit regarding copy-protected CDs in the U.S. has already been filed and settled. The lawsuit, filed in 2001 by a California woman, claimed that the copy-protected CD she purchased illegally violated consumer expectations by not offering a disclaimer that it will not operate on computer CD players and required the purchaser to register personal information before being allowed to download digital versions of the songs on the CD from the Internet. The suit was settled in 2002 when the companies involved agreed to stop collecting personally identifiable information from consumers, to purge their files of such information, and to include labels that warn consumers the CD doesn't work in DVD players, MP3 players, or CD-ROM players.

Proponents of mandatory copy protection believe that it will reduce the potential for piracy, which, in turn, will reduce the reluctance of media companies to make entertainment content available through the Internet. Opponents counter that while professional pirates will likely figure out a way to bypass any security measures adopted, copy-protection schemes will only prevent innocent consumers from exerting their "fair use" rights to use the music CDs and other digital content that they acquire legally. The outcome of the push for mandatory copy protection is as yet uncertain, but it will likely have an important impact on the future direction of digital media in general, as well as computer hardware, digital entertainment equipment, and Internet technologies.

Flash Memory Media

Unlike magnetic and optical storage systems whose drives have moving parts, **flash memory media** consists of chips and other circuitry that don't move within the drive as it's being accessed—called a *solid-state* storage system. Because flash memory devices and media are very small, use much less power than conventional drives, and are resistant to shock and vibration since they have no moving parts, they are especially appropriate for use with digital cameras, digital music players, handheld PCs, notebook computers, smart phones, and other types of portable devices (see Figure 4-18).

>**Flash memory media.** Memory-chip-based storage media commonly implemented in the form of sticks or cards.

Today, flash memory is found in the form of rewritable sticks, cards, or drives. Some computers and many mobile devices contain at least one *flash memory port*; when an appropriate port is not built into the device, a *flash memory card reader* or adapter can be used. Typically, flash memory media is purchased blank, but some flash-memory-card-based software is available, such as games, encyclopedias, language translators and more. Although flash memory media is relatively expensive per gigabyte, its convenience and universal acceptance makes it an appealing storage option for many purposes.

Flash Memory Sticks

Flash memory sticks were introduced by Sony initially for use with their digital music players. Since then, however, flash memory use has expanded to digital cameras, PCs, printers, and other applications. Some newer computers come with a *memory stick port* built in; if not, an external reader can be used. Flash memory sticks are about the size of a stick of gum (see Figure 4-18) and hold from 32 MB to 1 GB each; a 128 MB card cost about $50.

Flash Memory Cards

Flash memory cards are the primary removable storage media for handheld PCs, digital cameras, portable entertainment products, and mobile devices. Flash memory cards come in a variety of formats and are typically inserted into a *flash memory port* located on the PC

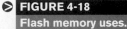

> FIGURE 4-18

Flash memory uses.
Flash memory sticks and cards are used by a variety of devices, such as digital cameras, digital music players, PCs, smart phones, and more.

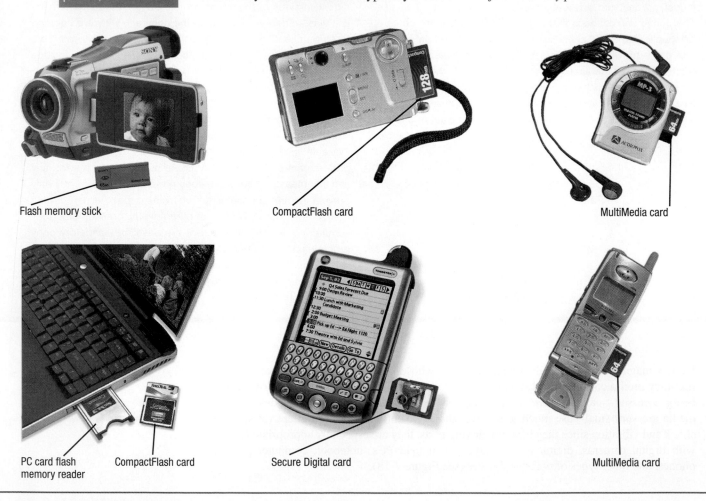

Flash memory stick   CompactFlash card   MultiMedia card

PC card flash   CompactFlash card   Secure Digital card   MultiMedia card
memory reader

>Flash memory stick. A type of flash memory media about the size of a stick of gum. **>Flash memory card.** A small, rectangular type of flash memory media, such as a CompactFlash or Secure Digital card.

or device. Some flash memory ports accept only one type of memory media; others can read from and write to several types. Just as with flash memory sticks, external card readers are available that read one or more memory media formats. Typically, these readers plug into a PC card slot or USB port. The main types of flash memory cards are listed next; some are illustrated in Figures 4-18 and 4-19. Of the following flash media formats, *CompactFlash* and *Secure Digital (SD)* are the most widely used at the present time.

▼ *CompactFlash cards* are widely used with digital cameras, handheld and portable PCs, digital music players, printers, and other portable devices. CompactFlash card capacity ranges from 32 MB to 4 GB.

▼ *Secure Digital (SD) cards* are one of the most commonly used cards for handheld PC and smart phone storage. Also used with digital cameras, digital music players, and digital camcorders, the capacity of the stamp-sized SD card ranges from 32 MB to 1 GB.

▼ *MiniSD cards* are a smaller version of Secure Digital cards that became available in 2003. Geared primarily for use with mobile and smart phones, capacity currently ranges from 16 MB to 256 MB.

▼ *MultiMedia cards (MMC)* are most commonly used with digital music players and digital camcorders. Because they are the same size as SD cards, some devices can use these two types of cards interchangeably. Capacity ranges from 16 MB to 128 MB.

▼ *SmartMedia cards* are frequently used with digital cameras, although other devices may accept them as well. Larger in physical size than the other types of flash media, SmartMedia cards can hold from 8 MB to 128 MB of data.

▼ *xD cards* (sometimes called *xD Picture cards*) are one of the newest formats and are designed primarily for digital camera use; capacity of these cards range from 32 MB to 512 MB.

COMPACTFLASH CARD

SECURE DIGITAL (SD) CARD

XD PICTURE CARD

FLASH MEMORY CARD READER
This reader connects to a USB port and can be used with CompactFlash, SmartMedia, Memory Stick, MultiMedia, Secure Digital (SD), and xD cards.

FIGURE 4-19
Flash memory cards.
Shown here are three of the most widely used types of flash memory cards and a multi-card reader.

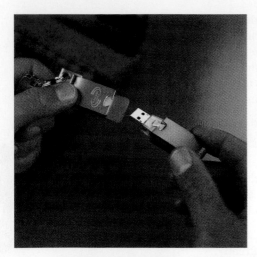

⊘ **FIGURE 4-20**

Flash memory drives. Small USB flash drives are becoming increasingly popular for portable personal storage.

⊘ **FIGURE 4-21**

Magnetic tape. Most magnetic tape media today is in the form of cartridge tapes. Since it is a sequential media, magnetic tape is used primarily for backup.

Flash Memory Drives

Flash memory drives (sometimes also called *USB mini-drives*, *removable flash drives*, or *key drives*), are self-contained storage systems that consist of flash memory media and the drive hardware necessary to write to and read from that media. Because they have no moving parts, flash memory drives are much more resistant to shock and vibration than conventional drives and are therefore appropriate for harsh environments, as well as for transporting data from one place to another in a briefcase or pocket. They also have a longer expected life than removable magnetic media. Although larger flash memory drives exist to replace conventional hard drives in situations where the PC will be subjected to jarring movements, strong vibrations, or other unstable conditions that might harm a conventional hard drive, most flash memory drives are designed to be very portable and so are small enough to fit in a pocket or be carried on a keychain (see Figure 4-20). To read from or write to a flash memory drive, it is plugged into a PC's USB port and then it is automatically assigned a drive letter by the computer, like any other type of drive attached to a PC. Files can be read from or written to the drive until it is unplugged from the USB port. Some flash memory drives have their flash memory media permanently sealed inside; others use standard flash memory cards and can be opened to replace the drive with a new memory card when the original is full or if it becomes damaged. Flash memory drives today are available in capacities from 32 MB to 2 GB.

Magnetic Tape Systems

Magnetic tape consists of plastic tape coated with a magnetizable substance that is polarized to represent the bits and bytes of digital data, similar to magnetic disks. Tape was once a prominent storage medium for computer systems, but because of its sequential-access property it has since been replaced by magnetic disks, optical discs, and flash memory media for day-to-day use. It is still used today for backup and archival purposes because it is a very inexpensive medium.

Most computer tapes today are in the form of *cartridge tapes* (similar to a video or audio tape), instead of the older reel-to-reel format. Tapes are read by *tape drives*, which can be either an internal or external piece of hardware (an internal tape drive is shown in Figure 4-21). Tape drives contain one or more read/write heads over which the tape passes to allow the drive to read or write data. Just as with other magnetic storage technologies, the 1s and 0s stored on magnetic tape are represented magnetically.

There are a variety of sizes and formats of cartridge tapes, such as *digital audio tape* (*DAT*), *quarter-inch-cassette* (*QIC*), *Travan*, *digital linear tape* (*DLT*), *advanced intelligent tape* (*AIT*), *Super advanced intelligent tape* (*S-AIT*), and *linear tape-open* (*LTO*). Sizes and formats of tapes are not generally interchangeable, but since magnetic tapes are most often used for backup with a specific tape drive, this incompatibility is usually not a problem. A typical tape cartridge holds between 4 GB to 240 GB, although some can hold up to 1 TB. When a larger capacity is needed, some tape drives are designed to be used with multiple tape cartridges, increasing the potential storage capacity to well over 2 TB.

Remote Storage Systems

Remote storage refers to using a storage device that is not connected directly to your PC system; instead, the device is accessed through a local network or the Internet. Using remote storage devices and media works similarly to using *local storage* (the storage devices and media that are directly attached to your PC); you just need to select the appropriate remote storage device (typically a hard drive attached to a network server), and then you can store data on or retrieve data from it. When the remote device is accessed through a local network, it is sometimes referred to as *network storage*; the term *online storage* most commonly refers to storage accessed via the Internet. Individuals and businesses can use online storage Web sites to transfer files between two computers, to share files with others, and for backup in case of a fire or other disaster. For some Internet appliances, network computers, and mobile communications devices with little or no local storage capabilities, online storage is especially important.

It is becoming increasingly common for individuals to want to share files—particular digital photographs—through the Internet. Some Web sites dedicated to online storage offer the service for free to individuals; others charge a small fee, such as $5 per month for up to 75 MB of storage space (business accounts typically cost more). Although some sites allow access to anyone, most online storage sites are set up to have file access only by password to limit access to just yourself and anyone else you give your password to. Some sites allow you to e-mail links to others to download specific files in your online collection without having to supply a password. Other online storage sites contain an automatic back up option in which the files in designated folders on your PC are uploaded to your online account at regular specified intervals. Two examples of online storage sites are shown in Figure 4-22.

Smart Cards

A **smart card** is a credit-card-sized piece of plastic that contains some computer circuitry, typically a processor, memory, and storage (see Figure 4-23). Although the storage capacity of a smart card is fairly small—usually from a few kilobytes to a few megabytes—it can be used to hold specific pieces of information that may need to be updated periodically. Typically, smart cards are used for payment or identification purposes. For example, a smart card can store a prepaid amount of digital cash for purchases using a smart card-enabled vending machine or PC; loyalty system information (frequent flyer points, for example); identification data for accessing facilities or computer networks; or an individual's medical history and insurance information for fast treatment and hospital admission in an emergency. Smart cards are also increasingly being used for national ID cards and student ID cards (see the Campus Close-Up box). Although these applications have used conventional *magnetic stripe* technology in the past, the microprocessor in a smart card protects the integrity of the data on the card (in contrast with the straight data storage capabilities of a flash memory card or CD, for example), and data stored in the card's memory can be added or modified as needed. For an even higher level of security, some smart cards today contain *biometric data*—such as a fingerprint—to ensure the authenticity of the user (biometrics is discussed in more detail in Chapter 8). Many debit and credit cards today are also smart cards.

>**Remote storage.** A storage device that is not directly a part of the PC being used, such as network storage or online storage.
>**Smart card.** A credit-card-sized piece of plastic containing a chip and other circuitry into which data can be stored.

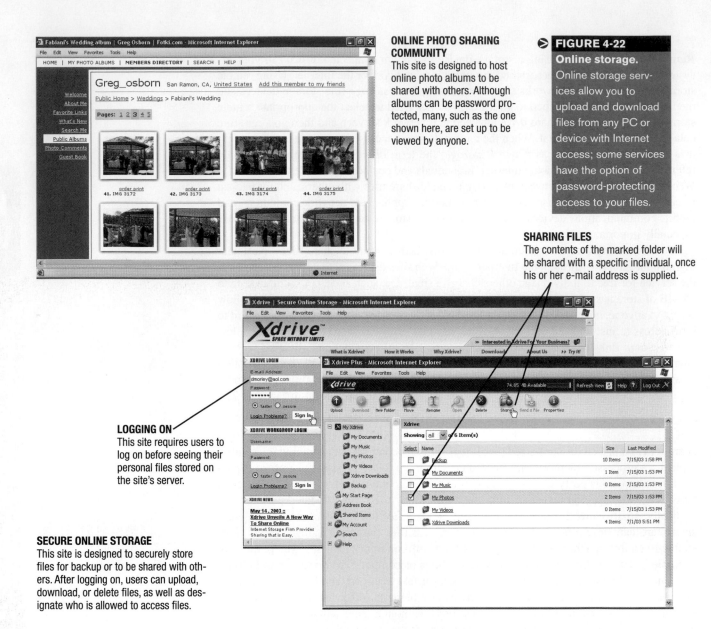

ONLINE PHOTO SHARING COMMUNITY
This site is designed to host online photo albums to be shared with others. Although albums can be password protected, many, such as the one shown here, are set up to be viewed by anyone.

FIGURE 4-22
Online storage.
Online storage services allow you to upload and download files from any PC or device with Internet access; some services have the option of password-protecting access to your files.

SHARING FILES
The contents of the marked folder will be shared with a specific individual, once his or her e-mail address is supplied.

LOGGING ON
This site requires users to log on before seeing their personal files stored on the site's server.

SECURE ONLINE STORAGE
This site is designed to securely store files for backup or to be shared with others. After logging on, users can upload, download, or delete files, as well as designate who is allowed to access files.

To use a smart card, it must be inserted into a card reader built into or attached to a PC, vending machine, or other item. Some keyboards now have a built-in smart card reader to facilitate secure *e-commerce* applications, such as online shopping. Once a smart card has been accepted, the transaction—such as making a purchase or unlocking a door—can be completed. While many smart card readers require direct contact between the smart card and the reader, *contactless* smart card systems using wireless technology allow the card to be read when it is within a particular distance of the reader without physical contact. E-commerce is covered in more detail in Chapter 11.

One new smart card application is a combination smart card/magnetic disk. This emerging product, such as the *StorCard*, has a flexible magnetic disk housed inside a tiny cavity created between the top and bottom layers of the smart card. A proprietary reader is able to access the disk via a shutter, similar to a floppy disk, to read from and write to the card. Current capacity is about 100 MB. The smart card capabilities of this product enable the data on the card to be *encrypted* or otherwise protected using smart card technology.

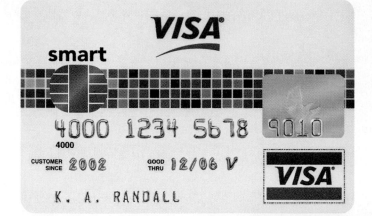

WHAT IS A SMART CARD?
A smart card looks like an ordinary credit or debit card, but typically contains a wafer-thin chip and circuitry for processing and storage. When inserted into a reader, the information stored on the card can be accessed and updated. Some readers use biometric data stored on the cards to authenticate the user.

Fingerprint reader can be used when needed to authenticate the smart card user.

Smart card reader

Smart card

Smart card circuitry

WHAT ARE SMART CARDS USED FOR?
Smart card applications abound, such as a replacement for cash in vending machines, for identifying individuals for access or medical treatment, and for securely paying for goods and services online.

FIGURE 4-23
Smart cards.

Holographic Storage

Storing information in three dimensions is far from a new idea. DVDs use multiple layers to store more data on the same size disc as a CD, and 3D memory chips are in the works. One very promising technology for 3D storage systems being researched by such companies as IBM, Lucent Technologies, and Imation is **holographic storage**. Holographic storage systems use multiple laser beams to store data in three dimensions, in order to store more data on the disc. Data is stored in a "page" format, in which all data on each page is stored and retrieved together. Because a million or more bits can be located on each page and thousands of pages can be stored in material no larger than a small coin, holographic systems offer the possibility of compact storage media holding many terabytes of information. The additional advantages of no moving parts and simultaneous access of all information stored in a page give this technology the potential for very rapid access. Some predictions include a data-throughput rate of at least 1 billion bps (bits per second).

Potential applications for holographic data storage systems include high-speed digital libraries and image processing for medical, video, and military purposes—applications for which data needs to be stored or retrieved quickly in large quantities, but rarely changed. Rewritable holographic storage is an expected improvement in the future.

>**Holographic storage.** An emerging type of storage technology that uses multiple laser beams to store data in three dimensions.

CAMPUS CLOSE-UP

Penn State ID+ Smart Cards

At Pennsylvania State University, the traditional school ID card has become much more than just an ID card. In addition to a traditional magnetic stripe, the ID card has a built-in chip, making it a smart card. The chip can hold "LionCash"—digital cash values loaded onto the card. The smart card can then be used in designated laundry, vending, and copy machines, as well as a variety of retail stores and restaurants located both on and off campus. When the cash stored in the card is used up, the card can be reloaded at a card value center using cash or a credit card. Other uses for the Penn State ID+ card are identifying

The Penn State University ID+ Card can be used for a wide variety of on- and off-campus activities.

students for exams and meal service, and providing access to secure areas, such as labs and residence halls. It even can be used as a long-distance phone card and ATM card.

Smart card ID systems like this are not unique on college campuses today. Many colleges and universities across the country have either replaced or augmented their magnetic stripe cards with smart card technology. The convenience of smart ID cards is a good fit with college students. They need to carry their student ID around anyway and can buy lunch, a soda, do laundry, or make copies without having to worry about how much cash they have on hand.

And the storage capability of the chip on the typical smart card—up to 500 times more than traditional magnetic stripe cards and growing all the time—will lead to new applications being created for college smart cards. Possibilities include using the card to access school records, check test scores, register for classes, tally customer loyalty points at stores and restaurants, store medical information, and make travel arrangements—not to mention online shopping. And using any computer with Internet access and a smart-card reader, students could even access their school information or securely participate in online class activities from anywhere in the world.

The biggest drawback of smart cards is that losing a preloaded card is the same as losing cash. However, colleges report that card loss is generally fairly low. Because of the variety of uses for the card, students tend to take them with them everywhere they go and keep good track of them. When a lost card is turned in, remarkably it usually has the cash value still on it.

COMPARING STORAGE ALTERNATIVES

Storage alternatives are often compared by weighing a number of product characteristics and cost factors. Some of these product characteristics include speed, compatibility, storage capacity, convenience, and the portability of the media. Keep in mind that each storage alternative normally involves trade-offs. For instance, most systems with removable media are slower than those with fixed media, and external drives are typically slower than internal ones. Although cost is a factor when comparing similar devices, it is often not the most compelling reason to choose a particular technology. For instance, although the flash memory drives are very expensive per GB, many users find them essential for transferring files between work and home or for taking presentations on the road. For drives that use a USB interface, the type of USB port is also significant. For instance, a typical flash memory drive designed for the original USB 1.1 port transfers data at up to 1.5 MB per second; USB 2.0 flash memory drives are about 40 times faster.

With so many different storage alternatives available, it's a good idea to research which devices and media are most appropriate for your personal situation. In general, most users today need a hard drive (for storing programs and data), some type of CD or DVD drive (for installing programs, backing up files, and sharing files with others), and a floppy drive (for sharing small files with others). Some users may choose to include an additional drive for a particular type of high-capacity removable media, such as Zip disks, if they only need to use the disks in their PC or a PC they know has a drive compatible with that medium. Users who plan to transfer music, digital photos, and other multimedia data on a regular basis between several different devices—such as a PC, digital camera, handheld PC, and printer—will want to select and use the flash memory media that is most compatible with the devices they are using and obtain the necessary adapter for their PC. Some of the most common types of portable storage media are compared in Figure 4-24.

> **FIGURE 4-24**
> **Portable storage alternatives.** When comparing removable storage mediums, look at storage capacity, speed, cost, and device compatibility.

H W

Medium	Capacity	Relative Speed	Approximate Cost (per GB)*	Can Be Read By	Best For
Conventional 3½-inch floppy disk	1.44 MB	Slow	$175.00	Conventional floppy drive, SuperDisk drive	Transferring small files between users
Zip 750 disk	750 MB	Medium	$15.00	Zip 750 drive	Archiving files or transferring large files between Zip users
SuperDisk (LS-240)	240 MB	Medium	$30.00	SuperDisk (LS-240 drive)	Transferring files between SuperDisk users
CD-R disc	700 MB	Medium	$0.10	Most CD and DVD drives	Transferring large files between users; archiving large files; making music CDs
CD-RW disc	700 MB	Medium	$0.50	CD-RW drives, some other CD drives, most DVD drives	Transferring large files between users; archiving large files
DVD-R disc	4.7 GB	Medium	$0.20	Most DVD drives	Transferring large files between users; archiving large files; backup; making home movie DVDs
DVD+RW	4.7 GB	Medium	$0.15	Most DVD drives	Transferring large files between users; archiving large files; backup; making home movie DVDs
DVD-RAM	9.4 GB	Medium	$0.85	DVD-RAM drives	Transferring large files between DVD-RAM users; archiving large files; backup
Flash memory drive (USB)	2 GB	Medium	$250.00	Any device with a USB port	Transferring small to medium-sized files between users or PCs
Removable hard disk cartridge	80 GB	Fast	$5.00	Proprietary drive to which that cartridge belongs	Archiving large files; securing sensitive data; backup
Portable hard drive (USB or PC card)	250 GB	Fast	$1.00	Any device with a USB port or PC card slot, respectively	Extending PC storage; securing sensitive data; backup
Flash memory sticks and cards	4 GB	Fast	$200.00	Compatible flash memory reader	Transferring small- to medium-sized files between users, PCs, or multimedia devices (digital cameras, MP3 players, etc.)

*Cost as of 2003

SUMMARY

PROPERTIES OF STORAGE SYSTEMS

Chapter Objective 1:
Explain the difference between storage systems and memory.

Storage systems make it possible to save programs, data, and processing results for later use. They provide **non-volatile** storage, so when the power is shut off, the data stored on the storage medium remains intact. This differs from *memory*, which is **volatile**. The most common types of storage media are magnetic disks and optical discs, which are read by the appropriate type of drive. Drives can be *internal* or *external*.

Chapter Objective 2:
Name several general properties of storage systems.

All storage systems involve two physical parts: A **storage device** and a **storage medium**. In addition to being non-volatile, storage devices can record data either on *removable media*, which provide access only when inserted into the appropriate storage device, or *fixed media*, in which the media is permanently located inside the storage device. Removable media provide the advantages of unlimited storage capacity, transportability, safer backup capability, and security. Fixed media have the advantages of higher speed, lower cost, and greater reliability.

Two basic access methods characterize secondary storage systems: Sequential and random access. *Sequential access* allows a computer system to retrieve the records in a file only in the same order in which they are physically stored. *Random access* (or *direct access*) allows the system to retrieve records in any order.

Files (sometimes called *documents*) stored on a storage medium are given a **filename** and can be organized into **folders**. This is referred to as *logical file representation*. *Physical file representation* refers to how the files are physically stored on the storage medium by the computer.

MAGNETIC DISK SYSTEMS

Chapter Objective 3:
Identify the two primary types of magnetic disk systems and describe how they work.

Magnetic disk storage is most widely available in the form of hard disks and floppy disks. Computer systems commonly include **floppy disk** storage because it provides a uniform removable storage system at a low cost. Each side of a floppy disk holds data and programs in concentric **tracks** encoded with magnetized spots representing 0s and 1s. **Sector** boundaries divide a floppy disk surface into pie-shaped pieces. The part of a track crossed by a fixed number of contiguous sectors forms a **cluster**. The disk's *file directory* or *file allocation table* (*FAT*), which the computer system maintains automatically, records where files stored on the disk are physically located. To use a floppy disk, you insert it into a **floppy disk drive**. Today, floppy disks are facing challenges from other removable media with much higher storage capacities, such as *Zip disks*, *SuperDisks*, CDs, DVDs, and flash memory media.

Hard disk drives are the main storage medium for most PCs. They offer faster access than floppy disks and much greater storage capacity. A hard drive contains one or more *hard disks* permanently sealed inside along with an *access mechanism*. A separate read/write head corresponds to each disk surface, and the access mechanism moves the heads in and out among the tracks to read and write data. All tracks in the same position on all surfaces of all disks in a hard drive form a disk **cylinder**. Hard drives can be divided into multiple *partitions* (logical drives) to reduce cluster size or to facilitate multiple users or operating systems.

Three events determine the time needed to read from or write to most disks: *seek time*, *rotational delay*, and *data movement time*. The sum of these three time components is called **disk access time**. A **disk cache** strategy, in which the computer fetches program or data contents in neighboring disk areas and transports them to RAM whenever disk content is retrieved, can speed up access time.

Three disk standards—*EIDE*, *SCSI*, and *Fibre Channel*—dominate the hard drive market, although some external drives can connect via a USB port. If portability is required, portable hard drives, in which either the entire drive or a removable hard drive cartridge can be moved to another PC, are available. Hard drives for notebook PCs can be internal, external, or in a PC card format.

Disk drives on larger computers implement many of the same standards as PC-based hard drives. Instead of finding a single set of hard disks inside a hard drive permanently installed within a system unit, however, a **storage system** separate from the system unit often encloses several removable racks of hard disk drives, sometimes called an *enterprise storage system*. **Network attached storage (NAS)** and **storage area networks (SANs)** are commonly used to provide storage for a business network. **RAID** technology can be used on larger systems to increase *fault tolerance* and performance.

OPTICAL DISC SYSTEMS

Optical discs store data *optically* using laser beams much more densely than magnetic disks. They are divided into tracks and sectors like magnetic disks, but use a single grooved spiral track instead of concentric tracks. Optical discs are available in a wide variety of *CD* and *DVD* formats and are read by *CD* or *DVD drives*. **CD-ROM discs** come with data already stored on the disc. Data is represented by *pits* and *lands* permanently burned into the surface of the disk. CD-ROM discs cannot be erased or overwritten—they are *read-only*. **DVD-ROM discs** are similar to CD-ROM discs, but they hold much more data (4.7 GB instead of 700 MB). *Recordable discs* (**CD-R, DVD-R**, and **DVD+R discs**) and *rewritable disks* (**CD-RW, DVD-RW, DVD+RW, DVD-RAM**, and *blue laser discs*) can all be written to, but only recordable discs can be erased and rewritten to, similar to a floppy disk or hard drive. Recordable CDs and DVDs store data by burning permanent marks onto the disc, similar to CD-ROM and DVD-ROM discs; rewritable discs typically use *phase-change* technology to change the reflectivity of the disc to represent 1s and 0s. It is expected that, eventually, some form of DVD disc will eventually replace CDs as the optical disc standard.

Chapter Objective 4:
Discuss the various types of optical disc systems available and how they differ from each other and from magnetic systems.

OTHER TYPES OF STORAGE SYSTEMS

Other types of storage systems include *magneto-optical (MO) discs*, which use a combination of magnetic and optical technology and **magnetic tape**, which stores data on plastic tape coated with a magnetizable substance. Magnetic tapes are usually enclosed in cartridges and are inserted into a *tape drive* to be used.

Flash memory media are a rapidly growing new storage alternative. They are used with digital cameras, portable PCs, and other portable devices, as well as with desktop PCs. Flash memory can be in the form of **flash memory sticks, flash memory cards**, or **flash memory drives. Remote storage**—using a storage device that is not directly a part of your PC system—typically involves using a *network storage* device or an *online storage* service. Online storage services enable users to share files with others over the Internet, access files while on the road, and backup documents. **Smart cards** are credit-card-sized pieces of plastic that contain a chip or other circuitry usually used to store data or a monetary value. **Holographic storage**, which uses multiple laser beams to store data in three dimensions, is a possibility for the future.

Chapter Objective 5:
List at least three other types of storage systems.

COMPARING STORAGE ALTERNATIVES

Most PCs today include a hard drive, floppy disk drive, and some type of CD or DVD drive. The type of optical drive and any additional storage devices are often determined by weighing a number of product characteristics and cost factors. These characteristics include speed, compatibility, capacity, removability, and convenience.

Chapter Objective 6:
Summarize the storage alternatives for a PC, including which storage systems should be included on a typical PC and for what applications other systems would be appropriate.

H
W

KEY TERMS

Instructions: Match each key term on the left with the definition on the right that best describes it.

a. CD-R disc

b. disk cache

c. DVD-ROM disc

d. file

e. flash memory drive

f. flash memory media

g. floppy disk

h. folder

i. hard disk drive

j. magnetic tape

k. non-volatile

l. optical disc

m. RAID

n. remote storage

o. sector

p. smart card

q. storage device

r. storage medium

s. track

t. volatile

1. _____ A concentric path on a disk where data is recorded.

2. _____ A credit-card-sized piece of plastic containing a chip and other circuitry into which data can be stored.

3. _____ A dedicated part of RAM used to store additional data adjacent to data retrieved during a disk fetch to improve system performance.

4. _____ A type of storage medium read from and written to using a laser beam.

5. _____ A named place on a storage medium into which files can be stored to keep the medium organized.

6. _____ A low-capacity, removable magnetic disk made of flexible plastic permanently sealed inside a hard plastic cover.

7. _____ An optical disc, usually holding 4.7 GB, that can be read, but not written to, by the user.

8. _____ A piece of hardware, such as a floppy drive or CD drive, into which a storage medium is inserted to be read from or written to.

9. _____ A pie-shaped area on a disk surface.

10. _____ A plastic tape with a magnetizable surface that stores data as a series of magnetic spots; typically comes in a cartridge.

11. _____ A recordable CD.

12. _____ A small drive that usually plugs into a PC's USB port and contains flash memory media.

13. _____ A storage device that is not directly a part of the PC being used, such as network storage or online storage.

14. _____ A storage method that uses several small hard disks in parallel to do the job of a larger disk.

15. _____ A storage system consisting of one or more metal magnetic disks permanently sealed with an access mechanism inside its drive.

16. _____ Describes a medium whose contents are erased when the power is shut off.

17. _____ Describes a storage medium that retains its contents when the power is shut off.

18. _____ Memory-chip-based storage media commonly implemented in the form of sticks or cards.

19. _____ Something stored on a storage medium, such as a program, document, or image.

20. _____ The part of a storage system where data is stored, such as a floppy disk or CD disc.

REVIEW ACTIVITIES

Answers for the self-quiz appear at the end of the book in the References and Resources Guide.

True/False

Instructions: Circle **T** if the statement is true or **F** if the statement is false.

T F **1.** A CD-R disc typically holds 4.7 GB.

T F **2.** The smallest amount of space a file on a disk can take up is one cluster.

T F **3.** A computer system with a C and D drive must have two physical hard drives.

T F **4.** Iomega's Zip disks can be read by a Zip drive or a conventional floppy drive.

T F **5.** Most PCs today include a hard disk drive.

Completion

Instructions: Supply the missing words to complete the following statements.

6. A storage medium is _____ if it loses its contents when the power is shut off.

7. A recordable compact disc is typically called a(n) _____.

8. DAT, QIC-80, and DLT are types of _____ storage.

9. A(n) _____ looks similar to a credit card, but contains a chip and other circuitry into which data can be stored.

10. Secure Digital cards are a type of _____ media.

1. Assume, for simplicity's sake, that a kilobyte is 1,000 bytes, a megabyte is 1,000,000 bytes, and a gigabyte is 1,000,000,000 bytes. You have a 20-gigabyte hard drive with the following content:

ITEM	STORAGE SPACE USED
Operating system	65 MB
Other systems software	1.5 GB
Office suite	85 MB
Other software	250 MB
Documents	6.7 MB

Approximately how much room is left on the drive? _____

2. On PC-compatible storage systems, what type of storage device would normally be assigned the following drive letters?

a. A: _____

b. C: _____

c. D: _____

3. Which storage media would be appropriate for someone who needed to exchange large (5 MB to 75 MB) files with another person? List at least three different types, stating why each might be the most appropriate under specific conditions.

4. Select the image from the numbered list below that matches each of the following names, and write the corresponding number in the blank to the left of each name.

a. _____ Hard drive
b. _____ Floppy disk
c. _____ Optical disc
d. _____ Smart card
e. _____ Flash memory drive
f. _____ Flash memory card

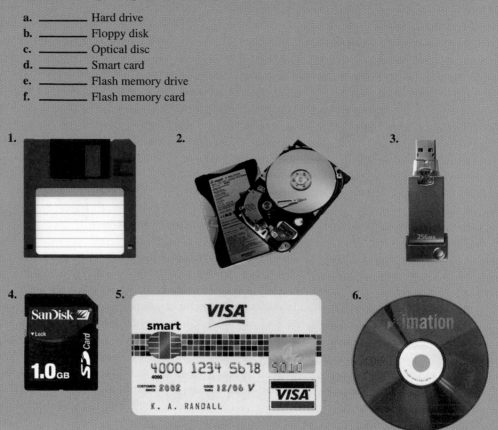

5. For each of the following terms, indicate the type of storage medium to which they are related (such as hard drive, floppy disk, optical disc, flash memory, or smart card).

a. cylinder   _____
b. pit   _____
c. CompactFlash   _____
d. CD-R   _____

6. Explain why CD-ROM discs are not erasable, but CD+RW discs are.

7. What does the term "solid-state drive" mean? List one storage device to which this term applies.

PROJECTS

HOT TOPICS

**H
W**

1. **Blue Laser Discs** As mentioned in the chapter, an emerging technology that uses blue lasers can increase the capacity of a standard-sized DVD disc significantly. At the time of this writing, Sony Blu-ray DVD drives were only available in Japan and were extremely expensive. In addition, two competing consortiums were developing two different, and incompatible, blue-laser standards (Blu-ray and Advanced Optical Disc).

    For this project, research the current state of blue laser DVDs. Are there any products available in the United States? Have the standard wars been settled or is there still more than one competing standard? What is the current capacity of discs using blue laser technology? At the conclusion of your research, prepare a one- to two-page summary of your findings and submit it to your instructor.

**SHORT ANSWER/
RESEARCH**

2. **Smart IDs** The chapter Campus Close-Up box discusses the growing use of smart cards as campus ID cards. Some credit cards are now being issued as smart cards, and smart cards have been proposed to replace conventional drivers' licenses, medical insurance cards, and other important documents—some countries have already implemented smart-card-based national ID cards. The ability of a smart card to hold a larger amount of personal data than a conventional magnetic stripe card is viewed as a benefit by some, as is the ability to confirm online credit card orders via a smart card reader attached to your PC. The additional information potentially available through a card (such as an individual's medical history or purchasing record), however, is viewed as a privacy risk to others.

    For this project, consider the points raised above and write a short essay expressing your opinion about using smart cards to replace conventional magnetic stripe cards. If it isn't already, would you want your campus ID card to become a smart card? Why or why not? Do you think smart cards will be used any differently by consumers than conventional magnetic stripe cards? List any pros and cons of replacing magnetic stripe cards with smart cards and provide a concluding paragraph stating other possible uses for smart cards that would be beneficial and/or accepted by the general public. Submit your opinion on this issue to your instructor in the form of a one-page paper.

3. **Auto Backup** For those of us who forget to back up our files on a regular basis, there is an alternative—using an automatic backup utility that performs this task for you on a regular basis. Several companies sell this type of software and it is not very expensive. In addition, many companies that sell storage devices with removable media include this software for free with the purchase of the device. Another option is using an online storage service that offers an automatic backup option.

    For this project, research a few of the options that are available for performing automatic backups, and summarize the alternatives that you find. At the conclusion of your research, prepare a one-page summary of your findings and submit it to your instructor.

HANDS ON

4. **Storage Evaluation**   Most PCs have multiple storage devices, such as a hard drive, floppy drive, CD or DVD drive, and so on.

   For this project, find one computer (such as at home, your school, or a public library) that you are allowed to use, preferably the one you will use most often for this course. By looking at the outside of the PC, as well as by using a file management program such as Windows Explorer, identify each storage device on your selected PC. For each device, list the type of storage device (such as floppy disk drive, CD drive, or hard drive) and its assigned drive letter. In Windows Explorer, right-click each hard drive icon and select Properties to determine the size of the drive and how much room is left. At the conclusion of this task, prepare a one-page summary of your observations and submit it to your instructor.

5. **Online Storage**   There are a number of online storage services (such as Xdrive, Yahoo! Briefcase, and IBackup) designed to allow users to backup and share files with others; specialty online storage services designed for digital photo sharing include Fotki and Yahoo! Photos.

   For this project, visit at least one online storage site designed for backup and file exchange, and at least one designed for digital photo sharing. You can try the sites listed above or use a search site to find alternative sites. Tour the sites you select to determine what features each service offers, what it costs, the amount of storage space available, and your options for sending your uploaded files to others. Do the sites you selected password-protect your files or are they available for anyone with an Internet connection to see? What are the benefits for using these types of online storage services? Can you think of any drawbacks? Would you want to use any of the online storage sites you visited? Why or why not? At the conclusion of this task, prepare a short summary containing the information and answering the questions listed above and submit it to your instructor.

WRITING ABOUT COMPUTERS

6. **MP3 Downloads**   There is a great deal of music available through the Web, including songs you can download to your PC, usually as MP3 files. Although there are some free downloads available on some sites (such as songs designated as free downloads by the artist for publicity purposes), to adhere to copyright laws sites that facilitate music downloads must pay the artist and record label their arranged royalties and, consequently, typically charge for downloads. The required fees vary from site to site—most charge per download, although some charge a flat rate per month for an unlimited number of downloads.

   For this project, first research the copyright controversy between the music industry and the *Napster* peer-to-peer file-sharing service that resulted in legitimate download sites charging fees for music downloads. What was the music industry's position? What was Napster's response? Do you agree with the decision to stop file-sharing via the original Napster service? (Note: The new Napster 2.0 service that became available in late 2003 is completely different from the original.) Next, visit at least one site offering music downloads and determine the cost and procedure for downloading an MP3 file. Can you download songs one at a time to your PC or do you need to burn a CD during the download process? What is the advantage, if any, for using these services instead of purchasing a music CD at a retail store? Submit your findings and opinion on this issue to your instructor in the form of a short paper, not more than two pages in length.

7. **Storage Solutions**   The selection of an appropriate storage solution is usually based on the computer being used and the individual's storage requirements.

   For this project, form a group to discuss and define the storage requirements for each of the following three scenarios, and determine an appropriate storage solution for each one. The first system is for a home computer where several family members will be using the computer for homework, shopping, taxes, downloading and playing music, playing multimedia games, and surfing the Web. The second system is for a small accounting company that has only one computer and is using it to support all the administrative and information needs of the company. The third system is for a two-person video editing and multimedia production company that has two computers and specializes in recording and producing videos of weddings and other special occasions. Feel free to modify or clarify the three scenarios defined above in order to make your storage solutions match more closely with the diverse number of possibilities and storage options available today. Your group should submit this project to your instructor in the form of a short paper, not more than three pages in length.

---

8. **CD/DVD Burners** The cost of recordable and rewritable CD and DVD drives and discs have dropped significantly in the past few years and they are commonly used to store and distribute large files (such as photographs, video, or audio files). Before buying a CD or DVD burner, however, you should take a few issues into consideration, such as compatibility, interface, speed, capacity, and cost. In addition, you should decide whether you want to have an internal or external drive.

     For this project, suppose that you are in the market for an optical drive. Make a list of the tasks you will want to use it for (such as for burning custom audio CDs, storing home movies, or archiving your digital photographs) and then research and select three different drives that might meet your needs. Compare and contrast them to determine which drive would be the best option for your situation. Prepare a short presentation that explains your assumptions, the type of drive you selected and why, the three drives you evaluated, and your final conclusion. The presentation should not exceed 10 minutes and should make use of one or more presentation aids such as the chalkboard, handouts, overhead transparencies, or a computer-based slide presentation (your instructor may provide additional requirements). You may be asked to submit a summary of the presentation to your instructor.

9. **Flash Cards** The number of uses for flash memory cards has been growing at a tremendous rate. Primarily developed for use with digital cameras, today's possibilities include storage for portable and desktop PCs and a variety of other devices, as well as providing programs and peripheral devices for some PCs.

     For this project, form a group to research the various uses for flash memory cards. Find at least two examples of flash memory products in each of the following three categories: user storage, software, and an interface for a peripheral device. Prepare a short presentation on the products you found and their specifications, as well as your group's opinion regarding the flash card market in the future. Be sure to include any current or potential application you find in your research in addition to the three categories listed here. The presentation should not exceed 10 minutes and should make use of one or more presentation aids such as the chalkboard, handouts, overhead transparencies, or a computer-based slide presentation (your instructor may provide additional requirements). Your group may be asked to submit a summary of the presentation to your instructor.

**PRESENTATION/
DEMONSTRATION**

---

10. **Information Overload** As the ability of the computer to process data and generate information continues to improve, and the number of systems that generate information continues to grow, we are increasingly becoming overwhelmed by information. Much of the time, it seems as though we are already generating more information than we can use to make a decision, and that additional information only tends to confuse and slow down the decision-making process. An analogy is a restaurant that produces a menu with too many selections. The more time customers spend looking at the menu trying to decide what they would like to eat, the less money the restaurant makes because they end up with less time to serve additional customers. It could be argued that additional information leads to a better decision, but at what point is the additional information counterproductive?

**INTERACTIVE
DISCUSSION**

Select one of the following positions or create one of your own and express your point of view on the subject. Your instructor will indicate whether your response is to be posted to a class bulletin board, discussed in a class chat room, or discussed as an in-class activity. You may also be asked to submit a summary of your position and point of view to your instructor.

a. You can never have too much information. The human information processing system is capable of discerning the relevant from the non-relevant information that a computer system generates and thus it is important to gather as much information as possible. If you limit the amount of information collected, you run the risk of being misinformed and this could lead to bad decisions.

b. Too much information can be as bad as no information at all. We as humans will need to limit the amount and type of information that we consider in the decision-making process. As with the restaurant example, if we choose to consider too much information, we run the risk of failing to meet our objectives because we spent so much time analyzing and making the decision.

11. **Big Brother?** Some of the storage technology used today, such as smart cards, can help facilitate faster and more secure access to locked facilities, protect against the use of stolen credit card numbers, and, when used in conjunction with a biometric characteristic, unequivocally identify a user to a computer system. They can also be used for employee monitoring, informing a business where each employee carrying or wearing his or her smart card is at all times. While some people find benefits to the applications just discussed, others worry that smart cards and other devices will be used to track our movements. Is the convenience of smart card technology worth the possibility that information about you and your actions will be recorded in a database somewhere? Do you think employers or the government have the right to track individuals' movements? If so, under what conditions do they have this right? What are some advantages and disadvantages for the government and your employer always knowing where you are? Have you ever used a smart card or been identified with a biometric system? If so, how do you rate the experience?

For this project, form an opinion of the use of smart cards and similar technology to identify individuals for various applications. Be sure to use the questions mentioned in the previous paragraph when forming your position. Your instructor will indicate whether your response is to be posted to a class bulletin board, discussed in a class chat room, or discussed as an in-class activity. You may also be asked to submit a summary of your position and point of view to your instructor.

STUDENT EDITION LABS

SAM

12. **Student Edition Labs** Reinforce the concepts you have learned in this chapter by working through the "Managing Files and Folders" interactive Student Edition Lab, available online. To access this lab, go to www.course.com/uc10/ch04

If you have a SAM user profile, you have access to even more interactive content. Log in to your SAM account and go to your assignments page to see what your instructor has assigned for this chapter.

CHAPTER 5

OUTLINE

Overview
Input and Output
Keyboards
Pointing Devices
   Mice
   Electronic Pens
   Touch Screens
   Other Pointing Devices
Scanners and Related Devices
   Scanners
   Optical Mark Readers (OMRs)
   Bar-Code Readers
   Optical Character Recognition (OCR)
     Devices
   Magnetic Ink Character Recognition
     (MICR) Readers
Biometric Input Devices
Multimedia Input Devices
   Digital Cameras
   Audio Input Devices
Display Devices
   Display Device Characteristics
   CRT Monitors
   Flat-Panel Displays
   Smart Displays
   HDTV Monitors
   Data and Multimedia Projectors
   Emerging Display Technologies and
     Applications
Printers
   Printer Characteristics
   Laser Printers
   Ink-Jet Printers
   Special-Purpose Printers
   Fax Machines and Multifunction Devices
Multimedia Output Devices
   Speakers
   Voice-Output Systems

Input and Output

LEARNING OBJECTIVES

After completing this chapter, you will be able to:

1. Identify several types of input and output devices and explain their functions.

2. Describe the characteristics of the input equipment that most users encounter regularly—namely, keyboards and pointing devices.

3. Explain what source data automation is and discuss how scanners and other related devices can be used to accomplish it.

4. Understand what the term "biometrics" means and the purpose of biometric input devices.

5. List several types of multimedia input devices and discuss their purposes.

6. Describe the characteristics of the output equipment that most users encounter regularly—namely, display devices and printers.

7. Understand what hardware devices are used for multimedia output.

In Chapter 4, we covered storage devices. Although some of those devices can also perform input and output functions, storage is their main function. In this chapter, the focus is on equipment designed primarily for inputting data into the computer and outputting results to the user.

We begin the chapter with a look at input. First we discuss *keyboards* and then *pointing devices*, such as the *mouse*. Most home and office PCs use these types of devices to enter commands or data into the PC. Next, we cover hardware designed for scanning images, text, and bar codes, as well as other devices used for fast, relatively error-free input in some applications. We also discuss *biometric* and *multimedia input devices*.

Next, we explore output, starting with *display devices*. Here, we highlight some of the qualities that distinguish one type of display device from another and look at some of the most common types of display devices available today and in the near future. Then, we turn to *printers*. In this section, you will learn about the wide variety of devices that place computer output on paper. We also discuss *multifunction devices* and *multimedia output devices*.

Keep in mind that this chapter describes only a sample of the input and output equipment available today. In fact, there are thousands of input and output products, and they can be combined together in many ways to create a computer system to fit almost any conceivable need. ■

INPUT AND OUTPUT

Input and output equipment enables people to communicate with computers. An **input device** takes data—such as the letters, numbers, and other natural-language symbols that humans conventionally use in reading and writing—from the user and submits that data to the computer so that it can be processed. Input devices can also be used to convey instructions to the computer, as well as to input data in a variety of formats other than text, such as images, audio, and video.

Output devices convert the processed 0s and 1s back into a form understandable to humans and present the results to the user. Typically, output occurs on the screen or paper. *Hard copy* output refers to output permanently recorded onto a physical medium, such as paper. The term *soft copy* refers to output that appears temporarily, such as on a computer screen.

KEYBOARDS

Desktop and notebook computers usually use a **keyboard** for most text-based input. A typical PC keyboard is shown in Figure 5-1 with a description of the purposes of most of the

---

>**Input device.** A piece of hardware that supplies input to a computer. >**Output device.** A piece of hardware that accepts output from the computer and presents it in a form the user can understand. >**Keyboard.** An input device containing numerous keys, arranged in a configuration similar to that of a typewriter, that can be used to input letters, numbers, and other symbols.

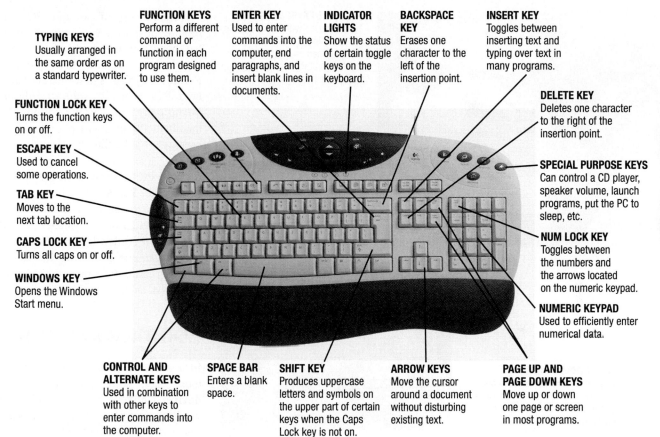

TYPING KEYS
Usually arranged in the same order as on a standard typewriter.

FUNCTION LOCK KEY
Turns the function keys on or off.

ESCAPE KEY
Used to cancel some operations.

TAB KEY
Moves to the next tab location.

CAPS LOCK KEY
Turns all caps on or off.

WINDOWS KEY
Opens the Windows Start menu.

FUNCTION KEYS
Perform a different command or function in each program designed to use them.

ENTER KEY
Used to enter commands into the computer, end paragraphs, and insert blank lines in documents.

INDICATOR LIGHTS
Show the status of certain toggle keys on the keyboard.

BACKSPACE KEY
Erases one character to the left of the insertion point.

INSERT KEY
Toggles between inserting text and typing over text in many programs.

DELETE KEY
Deletes one character to the right of the insertion point.

SPECIAL PURPOSE KEYS
Can control a CD player, speaker volume, launch programs, put the PC to sleep, etc.

NUM LOCK KEY
Toggles between the numbers and the arrows located on the numeric keypad.

NUMERIC KEYPAD
Used to efficiently enter numerical data.

CONTROL AND ALTERNATE KEYS
Used in combination with other keys to enter commands into the computer.

SPACE BAR
Enters a blank space.

SHIFT KEY
Produces uppercase letters and symbols on the upper part of certain keys when the Caps Lock key is not on.

ARROW KEYS
Move the cursor around a document without disturbing existing text.

PAGE UP AND PAGE DOWN KEYS
Move up or down one page or screen in most programs.

keys on the keyboard. For example, the user can press the *Delete* and *Backspace* keys to delete characters from the screen. The *Enter* key is used to enter commands into the computer, as well as to begin a new paragraph while using a word processing program. Keyboards also feature several *function keys*, which are labeled F1, F2, F3, and so on. When the user presses one of these keys, the keystroke initiates a specific command, dependent on the program being used. For example, pressing the F2 key in your word processing program may indent the current paragraph, but the same keystroke in your spreadsheet program may let you edit what you've typed in a cell. Some keyboards today (as in the one shown in Figure 5-1) have two purposes for each function key. Pressing the *function lock* (*F lock*) key on the keyboard switches (or *toggles*) the function keys between two sets of uses. Similarly, the *Caps Lock* key toggles between typing uppercase and lowercase letters. Keys like these that are used to both turn on and turn off a function are called *toggle keys*.

Most keyboards also have a *numeric keypad* to allow you to easily and quickly enter numbers, as well as directional keys—such as *arrows*, *Page Up* (*PgUp*), and *Page Down* (*PgDn*)—to allow you to use the keyboard to scroll through a document. In addition, many keyboards today contain a variety of special keys to perform common tasks, such as to access favorite Web sites, open an e-mail program, control the volume of the CD/DVD player, and put the computer into standby mode. Special-purpose keyboards also contain additional keys for a specific purpose or software program, such as an Internet keyboard with additional keys designed for convenient Internet use or an Office keyboard containing additional keys to perform specific tasks in Microsoft Office software programs. When buying a PC, look carefully at the keyboard to be sure it fits your needs.

Notebook PCs usually have a keyboard that is smaller and contains fewer keys, and the keys are typically placed closer together than on a conventional keyboard. Because of this, notebook buyers should try out the keyboard before buying, whenever possible. Notebook users can connect and use a conventional keyboard, when needed, if the notebook contains a keyboard or USB port.

> **FIGURE 5-1**
> **A typical desktop keyboard.**

TIP

The key layout of most keyboards is the *QWERTY* layout, named for the first six letter keys in the top left row of letters on the keyboard. An alternative layout, *Dvorak,* is purported to allow faster input, but is rarely used.

H W

FOLDABLE KEYBOARDS
Typically used with handheld PCs; are either in a hard format that can be folded once or twice or in a soft format that can be rolled up to become pocket-sized.

SLIP-ON THUMB PADS
Designed for both portable PC and smart phone use; the keys on these keyboards are pressed with the thumbs instead of the fingers.

⊗ FIGURE 5-2

Portable keyboards.
Portable keyboards can be used with handheld PCs, smart phones, and other mobile devices for easier data entry.

As the use of portable PCs and mobile devices has increased, there has been a proliferation of new keyboards designed for these devices. Portable keyboards designed for handheld PCs typically fold or roll up; *thumb pads* slip over the bottom of a handheld PC or smart phone and are pressed with the thumbs instead of the fingers (see Figure 5-2). Some portable PCs now come with a built-in thumb pad. *Wireless keyboards* can be used when the user would like to sit a little farther from the system unit than a keyboard cord will allow. There are also *ergonomic keyboards* that can be used to lessen the strain on the hands and wrist, as discussed in Chapter 16.

POINTING DEVICES

In addition to a keyboard, most PCs today have some type of **pointing device**. Unlike keyboards, which are used to enter characters at the *insertion point* (sometimes called the *cursor*) location, pointing devices are used to move an onscreen *mouse pointer*—usually an arrow. Once that pointer is pointing to the desired object on the screen, the object can be selected (usually by pressing a button on the device) or otherwise manipulated. Some common types of pointing devices are the *mouse, electronic pen, touch screen, joystick,* and *trackball*.

Mice

A **mouse** (the most commonly used pointing device for desktop PCs) rests on the desk or other flat surface close to the user's PC and is moved with the user's hand in the appropriate direction. As the mouse is moved, the mouse pointer on the screen moves in a corresponding manner. When the mouse pointer is pointing to the desired object on the screen, the user presses one of the buttons on top of the mouse to select that object. Older *mechanical mice* have a ball exposed on the bottom surface of the mouse to control the pointer movement; newer *optical mice* (such as the one in Figure 5-3) are completely sealed and track movements with light instead of ball movement. While mechanical mice are usually used in conjunction with a protective *mouse pad* and require regular cleanings to operate properly, optical mice typically don't. Mice are commonly used to start programs; open, move around, and edit documents; draw or edit images; and more. Some of the most common mouse operations are summarized next.

▼ To activate a desktop icon or toolbar button, point to it on the screen and press—or *click*—the left mouse button once or twice, depending on how your PC is set up.

▼ To move an object from one part of the screen to another, point to the object, hold down the left mouse button, move the mouse to *drag* the object to its new position, and then release the mouse button to *drop* the object in its new location. This operation is commonly known as *dragging and dropping* and can be used to move paragraphs of text, images, or other objects to a new location.

▼ To quickly scroll through an open document, roll the *scroll wheel* or press the *scroll button* located on the top of the mouse, if one exists.

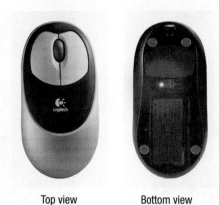

Top view   Bottom view

AN OPTICAL MOUSE

**MOVING THE
MOUSE POINTER**

**H
W**

❯ **FIGURE 5-3**
A typical mouse.

While most mice sold with PCs connect via a serial, USB, or PS/2 port on the computer's system unit, *wireless mice* are also available. These mice, powered by batteries, send wireless signals to a receiver usually plugged into the computer's serial or USB port. Although earlier wireless mice used infrared signals and needed to be within *line-of-sight* of their receivers, newer models use *radio waves* and, therefore, don't use line-of-sight transmission, although there is a limit on the allowable distance between the mouse and the receiver. Even newer are mice that are *Bluetooth-compliant*, meaning they communicate with the PC via a Bluetooth wireless networking connection. (Bluetooth and wireless networking are covered in more detail in Chapter 8.) Conventional, wireless, and small travel mice can all be used with desktop, notebook, and tablet PCs, as desired, as long as the appropriate port is available.

Electronic Pens

An **electronic pen** is a pointing device that is used as an alternative to a mouse to select objects, draw, or write electronically on the screen. There are two main types of electronic pens. A *light pen* is usually connected to the computer with a cable and senses marks or other indicators through a light-sensitive cell in its tip (see Figure 5-4). A **stylus** is a cordless electronic pen that looks similar to a ballpoint pen and is commonly used with handheld PCs, tablet PCs, and other devices that accept pen input.

Although their capabilities vary with the type of computer and software being used, electronic pens are typically used to issue commands to the PC, such as selecting options from a menu or checking check boxes on the screen. In addition, some pen-based devices can accept handwritten text and sketches as graphical images; PCs with *handwriting recognition* capabilities can accept handwritten input (commands, notes, e-mail messages, and so forth) as text input. Some specific pen-based devices, as well as handwriting recognition, are discussed in more detail next.

Graphics Tablets

A **graphics tablet**—also called a *digitizing tablet*—is a flat, touch-sensitive tablet usually used in conjunction with a stylus (see Figure 5-4). Anything drawn or written on the graphics tablet is automatically transferred to the connected PC in graphic form.

>**Electronic pen.** An input device that resembles an ordinary pen. >**Stylus.** A cordless electronic pen often used with pen-based PCs.
>**Graphics tablet.** A flat, rectangular input device that is used in conjunction with a stylus to transfer drawings, sketches, and anything written on the device to a PC in graphic form.

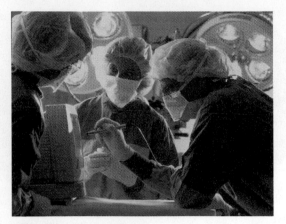

LIGHT PEN
Allows precise onscreen selection down to a single pixel, enabling users in some applications to work much more efficiently.

GRAPHICS TABLET
Drawn on with a stylus; the resulting image is transferred to the computer.

DIGITAL WRITING TOOL
Transfers everything written with the included electronic pen to the attached PC in real time.

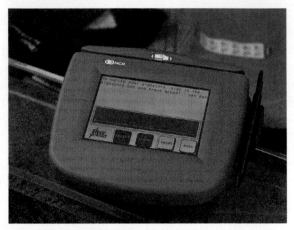

SIGNATURE CAPTURE DEVICE
Used to input signatures, such as to authorize credit card purchases (as shown here), or to record the delivery of merchandise.

PEN-BASED PCS
Includes handheld (left) and tablet (right) PCs.

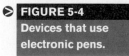

FIGURE 5-4
Devices that use electronic pens.

Digital Portfolios and Digital Pens

Similar to a graphics tablet, a *digital portfolio* includes a writing surface that is used to input drawings or other handwritten data into the computer. There are digital portfolios available for a variety of types of PCs, such as notebook and pocket computers. Some portfolios are sold separately from the PC; others come with a handheld PC built in. Typically, a digital portfolio opens to reveal a notepad on one side and the PC on the other. Using either a special electronic pen or a special notepad surface, everything written on the notepad is transmitted simultaneously and wirelessly to the PC. Instead of a complete portfolio, other products consist primarily of a special *digital pen* that electronically captures anything written with that pen. Some digital pens require a special type of paper; others may be used on any surface. Typically, whatever is written with the digital pen is either transferred wirelessly to the PC in real time (as in the example shown in Figure 5-4) or stored inside the pen and transferred to the PC when the pen is inserted in a special docking station attached to the PC. Typically, all input from these types of *digital writing tools* is captured as an image, not as text that can be edited.

Signature Capture Devices

Another type of pen-based input device is the *signature capture device* (see Figure 5-4). These devices are commonly attached to point-of-sale equipment to electronically record signatures used to authorize credit card purchases. Delivery companies and other service businesses may use a special signature capture device to record delivery signatures. Signature capture may also be performed using a handheld or tablet PC with appropriate software.

Pen-Based Computers

Pen-based computers—typically handheld or tablet PCs—are one of the fastest-growing types of computers sold today. These devices usually use a stylus instead of a mouse or other pointing device to make selections from the screen and to input handwritten information. With some pen-based PCs, the pen is the only source of input; others use the pen to supplement keyboard input.

Portable pen-based PCs are appropriate for and currently used by inspectors, factory workers, sales representatives, real-estate agents, police officers, doctors, nurses, insurance adjusters, store clerks, business people, and truck drivers—in other words, anyone who would otherwise regularly carry around a clipboard or notebook to record information or fill out forms.

Handwriting Recognition

If a pen-based PC needs to recognize pen input as actual text instead of just a graphical image, **handwriting recognition** technology is required (see Figure 5-5). Depending on the device and technology used, the PC may be capable of accepting handwritten input, such as handwritten commands, notes, text to be sent via e-mail, and so forth, but have special requirements for the way the text is written, such as the *Palm Graffiti* alphabet used with Palm handheld PCs. The newest types of systems can understand handwriting written in the users' personal style. Although this type of handwriting recognition typically requires some training for the PC to adjust to the particular style of the user and the input is not always interpreted correctly, it is expected to continue to improve and become even more widely used in the near future.

>**Handwriting recognition.** The ability of a device to identify handwritten characters.

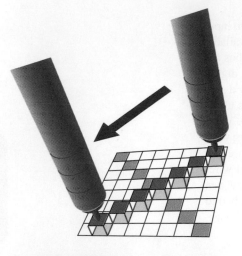

1. READING PEN INPUT
As the pen moves, the computer continually calculates its position, instructing the pixels it passes over to turn on.

2. PATTERN RECOGNITION
At the end of a pen stroke, the computer compares the pattern that was input to other patterns it has stored. It makes allowances within certain limits for imprecision.

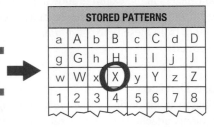

STORED PATTERNS							
a	A	b	B	c	C	d	D
g	G	h	H	i	I	j	J
w	W	x	X	y	Y	z	Z
1	2	3	4	5	6	7	8

3. CONTEXT RECOGNITION
After a pattern is recognized, the computer looks at the context in which the pattern was made before it decides what to do. For instance, an "X" in a check box means selecting a certain action whereas an "X" over filled-in text implies a deletion operation.

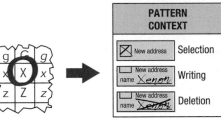

PATTERN CONTEXT	
☒ New address	Selection
New address name *Xenon*	Writing
New address name ~~Xenon~~	Deletion

> **FIGURE 5-5**
> **How handwriting recognition works.**

Handwriting recognition differs from *optical character recognition* (*OCR*), discussed shortly, in that handwriting recognition interprets writing performed directly on the screen of the device, while OCR involves recognizing data input into the computer from a physical form, such as text printed on paper.

Touch Screens

As PCs have become more and more integrated into the life of the consumer, **touch screens** have become increasingly prominent. With a touch screen, the user touches the screen with his or her finger to select commands or options (see Figure 5-6). People with little computer experience are generally more comfortable using a touch screen than a keyboard or a mouse—a definite advantage for touch-screen consumer applications. Touch screens are widely employed today in kiosks found in stores and other public locations for accessing bridal registry information, creating greeting cards, withdrawing cash, looking up products, and other applications. Touch screens are also useful for factory applications and other on-the-job applications where users wear gloves or using a keyboard or mouse may otherwise be impractical.

>**Touch screen.** A display device that is touched with the finger to issue commands or otherwise generate input to the connected PC.

Other Pointing Devices

A few other common pointing devices are described next and shown in Figure 5-7. There are also pointing devices specifically designed for users with limited mobility. These pointing devices—along with *ergonomic keyboards*, *Braille keyboards*, and other types of input devices designed for users with special needs—are discussed in Chapter 16.

Joysticks and Other Gaming Devices

A **joystick**, which looks similar to a car's gearshift, is most often used with computer games. The direction the joystick moves controls an onscreen object, such as a player or vehicle in a game. Buttons on the joystick are usually assigned functions by the program being used, such as jumping or firing a weapon. Today, some games can be used with gloves containing built-in sensors, enabling the computer to detect hand movements directly. Other related possibilities are *gamepads* that are held in the hand and contain buttons similar to those on a joystick and *steering wheels* for driving games.

Trackballs

Similar to an upside-down mechanical mouse, a **trackball** has the ball mechanism on top, instead of on the bottom. The ball is rotated with the thumb, hand, or finger to move the onscreen pointer. Because the device itself doesn't need to be moved, trackballs take up less space on the desktop than mice; they also are easier to use for individuals with limited hand or finger mobility.

FIGURE 5-6
Touch screens.

Pointing Sticks

A **pointing stick**, which appears in the middle of the keyboard of some notebook computers, is a device shaped like a pencil eraser that works similarly to a trackball. Instead of moving a ball, however, the thumb or finger pushes the stick in the appropriate direction, and the stick is pushed down to perform mouse clicks. Many notebooks have a *touch pad* instead of a pointing stick.

Touch Pads

A **touch pad** is a rectangular pad across which a fingertip or thumb slides to move the onscreen pointer. The buttons that appear next to the touch pad surface are used to perform clicks and other mouse actions; often the pad can be tapped to make selections, as well. Although usually found on notebook computers, external touch pads and keyboards with built-in touch pads are available for use with desktop computers.

SCANNERS AND RELATED DEVICES

In many applications, the necessary input already exists in physical form. These documents—such as order forms, timecards, photographs, or the *bar code* on a product—are referred to as *source documents*. Transferring source documents manually into digital form to be used with a computer can sometimes result in thousands of hours of wasteful, duplicated effort, as well as mistakes and delays. Capturing input directly from the original

TIP

A cross between touch pads and mice are devices that support *gesture recognition*—a new input method in which gestures are made with the fingers and hand to perform mouse operations and commands such as opening a file, copying and pasting text, and so forth. Gesture recognition is currently built into mouse-pad-sized pads and some keyboards and is designed to replace the use of a mouse.

>Joystick. An input device that resembles a car's gear shift and is often used for gaming. **>Trackball.** An input device, similar to an upside-down mouse, that can be used to control an onscreen pointer and make selections. **>Pointing stick.** An input device shaped like a pencil eraser that appears in the middle of some notebook computer keyboards and is used as a pointing device. **>Touch pad.** A small rectangular-shaped input device, often found on notebook computers, that is touched with the finger or thumb to control an onscreen pointer and make selections.

FIGURE 5-7
Other common pointing devices.

JOYSTICK
Used most often in computer games.

TRACKBALL
Mouse alternative; takes up less desk space and is easier for some users to manipulate.

POINTING STICK
Mouse alternative found on some notebook PCs. The stick is pushed in different directions to move the onscreen pointer.

TOUCH PAD
Mouse alternative commonly found on notebook PCs, keyboards, or as a stand-alone device.

source document or initially collecting data in digital form is referred to as *source data automation* and can eliminate much of this wasted time and potential for error.

Source data automation has transformed a number of information-handling tasks. For example, workers who take orders over the phone today usually enter the order data directly into the computer, so they don't have to record the same data twice. Source data automation also speeds up checkout lines and streamlines inventory procedures at supermarkets, improves quality control operations in factories, and helps with check processing at banks. In addition, source data automation allows the people who know the most about the events that the data represent to be the ones who collect the data, which helps ensure accuracy during the data-entry process. For instance, an insurance adjuster or auto mechanic entering data directly into a computer about the condition of a car involved in an accident will likely have less input errors than if he or she recorded that data on paper and then it was later keyed into a PC by an assistant; and a pharmacist electronically verifying the identity of a prescription medicine against a customer's record and prescription before giving it to the customer can help reduce prescription errors (see Figure 5-8).

Many of the most common devices used in source data automation are *scanning* or *reading devices*; that is, devices that read printed text, codes, or graphics, and translate the results into digital form that can be used by a computer. The next few sections discuss several different types of scanning and reading devices.

RECORDING DATA DIRECTLY INTO A PC

CAPTURING DATA FROM ITS SOURCE DOCUMENT

Scanners

A **scanner**, more officially called an *optical scanner*, captures the image of a usually flat object (a printed document, photograph, or drawing, for instance) in digital form and transfers that data to a PC. Typically, the entire document (including text and graphics) is input as a single graphical image that can be resized, inserted into other documents, posted onto a Web page, e-mailed, or printed, just like any other graphical image, but any text in the image cannot be edited. If **optical character recognition** (**OCR**) software is used in conjunction with the scanner, scanned text can be recognized by the computer as text, which means that the text can be edited using word processing or similar software. OCR is an immense time-saver for users who have traditionally had to retype printed documents in order to enter them into their computer system, such as office workers in the business and legal fields.

Scanners exist in a variety of configurations (see Figure 5-9). A **flatbed scanner** is designed to scan flat objects one page at a time. Flatbed scanners work in much the same way that photocopiers do—whatever is being scanned remains stationary while the scanning mechanism moves underneath it to capture the image. Most models can scan in color, and some even have attachments for scanning slides and film negatives. A *sheetfed scanner* works similarly to a flatbed scanner, but documents are inserted into the top of the scanner instead, similar to a fax machine. This design reduces the scanner's cost and the amount of desk space required. However, the feature also prevents the device from scanning bound-book pages or other items thicker or larger than a sheet of paper.

Handheld scanners are useful for capturing short newspaper or magazine articles, as well as Web addresses, names, and telephone numbers. The handheld scanner shown in Figure 5-9 uses flash memory to store up to 2,000 pages of text and can transfer stored data to a handheld or desktop PC via a serial or infrared (IrDA) connection.

> **FIGURE 5-8**
> **Source data automation.** Recording data initially in digital form or capturing data directly from a source document can both help reduce data input errors and save time.

H W

FLATBED SCANNER
Used to input photos, sketches, slides, bound books, and other relatively flat documents into the computer.

HANDHELD SCANNER
Useful for capturing small amounts of text.

SHEETFED SCANNER
Can scan one flat document at a time.

RESOLUTION
Most scanners let you specify the resolution (in dpi) at which you wish to scan. High-resolution images look sharper but result in larger file size.

96 dpi
(833 KB)

300 dpi
(1,818 KB)

600 dpi
(5,374 KB)

▶ FIGURE 5-9
Optical scanners.

Applications requiring the most professional results may require the use of a *drum scanner*. A drum scanner is much more expensive and more difficult to operate than the other types of scanners discussed here. When a drum scanner is used, the documents to be scanned are mounted on a glass cylinder, which is then rotated at high speeds around a sensor located inside the scanner. Multimedia and medical applications may require the use of a *three-dimensional (3-D) scanner*, which can scan an image or person in 3D. For example, when making the movie *Hollow Man*, in which the main character played by Kevin Bacon becomes invisible by losing layer-by-layer of skin, bones, and muscles, Kevin Bacon's body was scanned using a 3D scanner. This gave the animators the images they needed to generate a digital model of Kevin Bacon, which they used to create the necessary digital effects and illusions.

The quality of scanned images is indicated by *resolution*, measured in the number of *dots per inch (dpi)*. Scanners today usually scan at between 600 and 4,800 dpi and *48-bit color*—using 48 bits (or 6 bytes) to store the color for each **pixel** for a possible 281 trillion colors—is common. Higher resolution and a larger number of colors results in better images, but also results in a larger file size, as illustrated in the bottom right image in Figure 5-9. Higher resolution is needed, however, if the image is to be enlarged significantly or if only a part of the image is to be extracted and enlarged. The file size of a scanned image is also determined in part by the physical size of the image. When saving an image, it is important to keep in mind the resolution of the output device to be used. Typically 96 dpi is used for images to be displayed on a monitor (such as on a Web page), and 300 dpi or higher is used for images to be printed. Once an image has been scanned, it can usually be resized and then saved in the appropriate file format and resolution for the application with which the image is to be used.

A final caution when evaluating different scanners is to watch for optical resolution measurements versus interpolated resolution. While *optical resolution* measures how many actual dots an image contains, *interpolated* or *enhanced resolution* is software-enhanced resolution that is often at least twice as high as the scanner's optical resolution. Interpolated resolution includes the actual dots, plus additional dots that are inserted between the actual dots—the scanner estimates the colors of the new pixels. When evaluating scanner quality, compare optical resolution. Scanners can cost anywhere from less than one hundred dollars to one thousand dollars or more.

FURTHER EXPLORATION

For links to further information about scanning documents and photographs, go to www.course.com/uc10/ch05

Optical Mark Readers (OMRs)

One of the oldest reading device applications is processing tests and questionnaires completed on special forms using *optical marks*—marks made by individuals in certain locations on paper that can be read by an *optical mark reader* (*OMR*). For example, most students have taken true-false or multiple-choice tests by bubbling the correct answers with a number 2 pencil on a Scantron or similar form. You may have also filled out a survey, Census form, voting ballot, lottery form, or other document using optical marks.

To tally the responses made on an optical mark form, the OMR scans the form being used (see Figure 5-10). Filled-in responses reflect the light and those responses are recorded by the OMR. If it is an exam or some other type of objective instrument, a form containing the correct responses is input first, and then the OMR can indicate any wrong answers and print the total correct on each exam form; surveys and other subjective forms are usually just tallied and the results printed on a tally sheet instead. In either case, the results can be input to a computer system or the data can be stored on a disk or other storage medium, if the optical mark reader is connected to a computer.

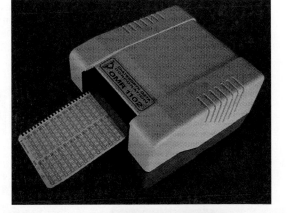

FIGURE 5-10
Optical mark readers. OMRs are commonly used to score tests and tally questionnaires.

Bar-Code Readers

A **bar code** is an *optical code* consisting of several bars of varying widths that form a unique, identifiable code. Bar codes are typically read either with *fixed* **bar-code readers** (often used in retail stores for identifying goods being purchased) or *portable* bar-code readers (used by workers who need to scan bar codes while on the go, such as while walking through a warehouse or at a variety of different retail locations). To read the identifying data encoded in the bar code, the light from the laser in the bar-code reader is reflected by the light spaces on the code (the dark bars absorb the light). By reading the patterns of the white space in the bar code, the bar-code reader identifies the numbers and/or letters represented by the bar code. Bar-code

>**Pixel.** The smallest colorable area in an electronic image, such as a scanned document, digital photograph, or image displayed on a display screen. >**Bar code.** A machine-readable code that represents data as a set of bars. >**Bar-code reader.** An input device that reads bar codes.

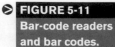

FIGURE 5-11
Bar-code readers and bar codes.

FIXED BAR-CODE READERS
Can be handheld (right) or stationary (below) and are most often used in consumer checkout applications.

BAR CODES
Uniquely identify a product or other item.

PORTABLE BAR-CODE READERS
Are self-contained units (right) or handheld PCs with bar-code reader capabilities built in and can be used when portability is needed.

0 12345 67890 5

**UPC (UNIVERSAL
PRODUCT CODE)**

123ABC

CODE 39

Ι.ΙΙ..ΙΙ....ι.Ι....Ι...ΙΙΙ

POSTNET CODE

TIP

The length of the PostNet bar code varies depending on the amount of information represented (the one in Figure 5-11 represents the ZIP code 60521). Numbers are coded in binary (a short bar represents 0 and a long bar represents 1) and the code begins and ends with a long bar. It takes five bars to represent one digit, such as 01100 for the digit 6.

readers are frequently used in *point-of-sale (POS) systems*—systems that record sales transaction data at the point where the product or service is purchased, such as a checkout or sales counter (see Figure 5-11).

The most familiar bar code is the *UPC (Universal Product Code) code* commonly found on packaged goods in supermarkets. When a shopper checks out, the clerk uses a bar-code reader to identify each item so that the necessary information about the item can be retrieved and recorded, such as the description of the product and its current price. Businesses and organizations can also create and use custom bar codes to fulfill their unique needs. For instance, shippers such as FedEx, UPS, and the U.S. Postal Service use their own bar codes to mark and track packages; hospitals use custom bar codes to match patients with their charts and medicines; libraries and video stores use bar codes for checking out books and movies; researchers use bar codes to tag and track animals; and law enforcement agencies use bar codes to mark evidence. In fact, any business with a bar-code printer and appropriate software can create custom bar codes for use with its products or to

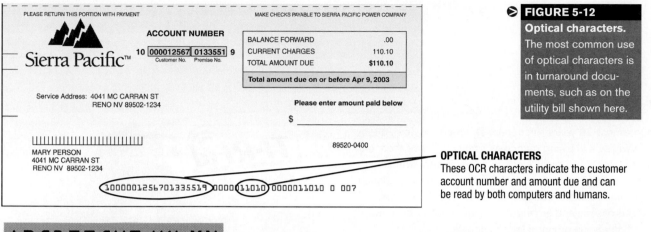

OPTICAL CHARACTERS
These OCR characters indicate the customer account number and amount due and can be read by both computers and humans.

OPTICAL FONTS
This is a common OCR font named *OCR-A.*

classify items used within its organization, such as client or employee files, computers, office equipment, sales receipts, and more. The most popular bar code for non-food use is *Code 39*, which was developed to encode the alphabet as well as numbers into a bar code. Examples of a UPC code, Code 39 bar code, and *POSTNET* code (used by the U.S. Postal Service to represent a ZIP or postal code) are shown in Figure 5-11. The chapter Inside the Industry box discusses a new type of bar code—the *smart bar code*.

Optical Character Recognition (OCR) Devices

Optical characters are characters specifically designed to be identifiable by humans as well as by some type of *optical character recognition* (*OCR*) device. Optical characters conform to a certain font design, such as the one shown in Figure 5-12. The optical reader shines light on the characters and converts the reflections into electronic patterns that the machine can recognize. The OCR device can identify a character only if it is familiar with the font standard used. Today, most machines are designed to read several standard OCR fonts, even when these fonts are mixed in a single document.

Optical characters are widely used in processing *turnaround documents*, such as the monthly bills for credit card, utility, and cable-TV companies (see Figure 5-12 for a sample utility bill using OCR fonts). These documents contain optical characters in certain places on the bill to aid processing when consumers send it back with payment—or "turn it around." Sometimes it's easy to spot the optical characters on a document. Today, however, many OCR fonts look so much like normal text that it's hard for an ordinary person to tell what parts the computer system can read and what parts it can't.

Magnetic Ink Character Recognition (MICR) Readers

Magnetic ink character recognition (*MICR*) is a technology confined primarily to the banking industry, where it is used to facilitate high-volume processing of checks. Figure 5-13 illustrates a check encoded with MICR characters and a reader/sorter that processes such checks. The standard font adopted by the banking industry contains only 14 characters—the 10 decimal digits (0 through 9) and four special symbols. MICR characters are inscribed on checks with magnetic ink by a special machine. As people write and cash checks, the recipients deposit them in the banking system. At banks, reader/sorter machines magnetically read and identify the MICR-encoded bank and account information on the check, magnetically-encode the amount of the check onto the check, and sort the checks so that they can be routed to the proper banks for payment.

INSIDE THE INDUSTRY

RFID: The Smart Bar Code

It's been almost 30 years since the first bar-coded item—a ten-pack of Wrigley's chewing gum—was scanned. Since then, bar codes have appeared on all kinds of items, from products and shipped packages, to office file folders and police evidence bags, to retail receipts and airline tickets. Bar codes help all kinds of businesses and organizations keep track of their inventories and otherwise organize important data.

Now the bar code is getting smart. New advances in radio communications have led to the development of *radio frequency identification*, or *RFID*. RFID relies on tiny chips and radio antennas that can store and transmit data located in an *RFID tag*. These tags can be attached permanently to products, product packaging, product labels, badges, wristbands, and key ring tags (see the accompanying photo)—printed antennas make them thin enough to be glued onto items. Data can be stored into the tag before it is attached, and that data can be updated as needed even after the tag is attached to its designated item.

RFID applications used in recent years include tracking inventory pallets in warehouses or huge shipping containers in transit. Consumer applications include special key fobs or wands that allow customers to pay for gas or fast food by waving the wand close to a special reader (the purchase amount is automatically deducted from a checking account or charged to a credit card, depending on which option each customer selected when registering for the system). An increasing number of highways in the United States use RFID tags on cars for automatic toll collection. Singapore has gone a step further by using them to charge different toll prices at different times of the day to encourage drivers to stay off busy roads during busy times.

RFID tags are also beginning to be used on product labels in conjunction with a unique identifying product code referred to as an *electronic product code* or *ePC* and are expected to eventually replace UPC bar codes. Advantages of RFID tags over conventional bar codes include the ability to hold more data and the ability to update that data throughout the life of the product. The use of ePC codes in conjunction with the Internet also enables consumers to obtain product data, menu suggestions, and other useful information pertaining to a purchased product; manufacturers and retailers can use RFID tags to streamline the supply chain, as well as identify recalled or expired products, and products that need reordering. RFID tags also have the advantage of being read by radio waves that do not require line of site, can be read from a distance of up to 15 feet, and can pass through materials such as cardboard and plastic.

RFID tags are starting to be used on a wider scale by a number of manufacturers and retailers. For instance, Gillette recently ordered one-half billion low-cost RFID tags expected to

A key ring RFID tag.

be used with end products; Visa and Philips Electronics have announced a partnership to develop RFID credit cards; Wal-Mart has ordered its suppliers to begin using RFID tags on shipping pallets and product cases beginning in January 2005; and Delta Airlines announced it would begin testing RFID luggage tags. In addition to logistical and inventory applications, RFID tags can also be used for other purposes. For example, when an ePC-marked product is brought into a dressing room at a Prada (Italian luxury goods designer) store, the RFID chip causes a video to play showing models wearing the item and the designer suggesting the appropriate accessories needed to complete the ensemble, in hopes of increasing sales. To help reduce errors and save money (drug-related errors cost about $75 billion in 2002), Johns Hopkins Hospital, the Red Cross, and several drug manufacturers are beginning to use RFID tags on medicine, blood packets, drug syringes, IV bags, and other medical products. Although RFID tags are beginning to be used on expensive products, at about 5 cents each they are still too costly to put on a soda can, pack of gum, or other low-price item. Many experts predict that once the cost reaches 1 cent or less apiece, RFID tags will be a viable replacement for all product bar codes.

Despite all its advantages, privacy advocates are concerned about a global use of RFID technology, because it can allow stores (and anyone else with an appropriate scanner) to know where you bought your clothes and any other items you have with you that contain a permanent RFID tag. And with the need to minimize the cost of such tags, many are skeptical about the inclusion of any form of privacy protection. Possible solutions for consumer RFID tag objections include allowing consumers to deactivate a tag after purchase (similar to the concept used to deactivate the anti-theft device in a borrowed library book or rented video during the check-out procedure), or developing ways to allow end users to delete information from their tags after purchase.

MICR READER
This device that reads and sorts checks and other MICR-encoded documents can process around 500 documents per minute (dpm); faster units can process up to 2,000 dpm.

> **FIGURE 5-13**
> **Magnetic ink character recognition (MICR).**

H W

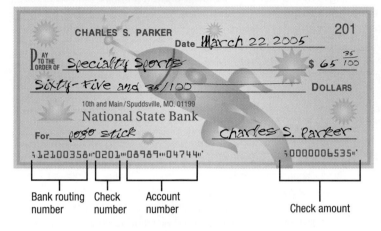

CHARLES S. PARKER   201

Date *March 22, 2005*

PAY TO THE ORDER OF *Specialty Sports* $ 65 35/100

Sixty-Five and 35/100   DOLLARS

10th and Main / Spuddsville, MO. 01199
National State Bank

For *pogo stick*   *Charles S. Parker*

⑆121003581⑆0201⑈08989⑈04744⑈   ⑆0000006535⑈

Bank routing number   Check number   Account number   Check amount

MICR-ENCODED CHECK
MICR characters on the bottom of the check respectively identify the bank, check number, account number, and check amount. The characters on the left are put on when checks are preprinted; the numbers representing the check amount are added when the check is cashed.

BIOMETRIC INPUT DEVICES

Biometrics is the study of identifying individuals based on measurable biological characteristics. *Biometric input devices* are used to input biometric data about a person into a computer system so that the individual can be identified based on a particular unique physiological characteristic (such as a fingerprint, hand geometry, face, or iris of the eye) or personal trait (such as a voice or signature). As shown in Figure 5-14, biometric input devices can be stand-alone or built into another piece of hardware, such as a keyboard or mouse. Some handheld and notebook PCs today have built-in fingerprint scanners or touchpads capable of inputting fingerprint images to allow only authorized users access to the PC. Biometric input devices are increasingly being used to restrict access to facilities or computer systems, authorize electronic payments, log on to secure Web sites, and more, as discussed in greater detail in subsequent chapters of this text. For a look at how one type of biometric identification—*face recognition*—works, see the How it Works box. Biometrics is covered in more detail in Chapter 8.

> **FIGURE 5-14**
> **Biometric input devices can be either stand-alone (left) or built into another piece of hardware (right).**

STAND-ALONE HAND GEOMETRY READER
Often used for access control, such as to authenticate NHL Mighty Ducks players at the Anaheim Pond arena shown here.

BUILT-IN FINGERPRINT READER
Often used for access control or to authorize electronic financial transactions.

HOW IT WORKS

Face Recognition

A variety of biometric techniques exist to identify individuals. Fingerprint identification has been used for several years and has the advantage of being very affordable and accurate. Hand scanning is a similar possibility. Iris scanning (scanning the eye) is very accurate but is significantly more expensive. Voice identification has great potential for the future. One biometric technique that is being used with increasing frequency is *face recognition*.

With face recognition, one or more video cameras scan the individual's face (the camera can be attached to an individual PC or to a computer controlling a locked door for access applications, or can be mounted in a public place and connected to a monitoring computer for surveillance applications). Face recognition is especially suited for surveillance applications, since it requires no direct contact with the reading device and can be used from a distance. Regardless of how the video data is taken, it is then digitized and compared with a database of photos, such as a database of known criminals (for law-enforcement applications) or a database of employees (for granting access to secure facilities). Because face recognition can perform one-to-many matching (which locates one specific individual from a database of many photographs), instead of just one-to-one authentication (where the system needs to know the person's identity first and then can authenticate that the person is truly the stated individual), face recognition can be used in a broad range of applications. For example, face recognition is currently being used to verify the identity of ATM

users, to admit individuals to secure areas, and to look for fugitives or terrorists at airports, the Super Bowl, parks, and other public locations. Future possibilities for face recognition include validating e-commerce transactions and distance learning testing. When a match is found for a photographed individual, the system operator is notified (for surveillance situations) or the appropriate access is granted (for computer or facility access applications). An example of how face recognition might work is shown in the accompanying illustration.

Because of its "Big Brother" connotations, use of face recognition technology in public locations has been very controversial. Law enforcement agencies contend that face recognition systems are no different than the many video surveillance systems in place today in a wide variety of public locations. They view it as just one more tool to be used to protect the public, similar to scanning luggage at the airport. Privacy advocates fear being under perpetual police surveillance and the eventual expansion of these security surveillance systems, such as using them to look for "deadbeat Dads" or other applications not vital to national security. The level of public acceptance regarding digital lineups of consumers purchasing groceries at the grocery store or pumping gas at a service station remains to be seen, but a recent study by Saflink Corporation found that over 80% of Americans supported the use of biometric devices to enhance airline security and approximately 60% were accepting of their use at public events. Public support of public video surveillance is likely to grow in the wake of continued terrorist attacks, random snipers, and other frightening acts of public violence.

2. The software creates a digital faceprint of the captured photograph, based on the distance between the eyes, the width of the nose, and other measurable characteristics.

1. A camera (located in a public location or controlling access to a secure facility or computer system, for instance) scans the user's face.

3. This faceprint is compared to the ones located in a database, at a rate of about one million comparisons per second, to look for a match.

4. Once a match is made, the captured image and database image are displayed on the screen and the appropriate action is taken (sounding an alarm, granting computer access, or unlocking the door, for instance).

Captured image   Database image

Match and alarm information

MULTIMEDIA INPUT DEVICES

As multimedia becomes increasingly integrated into computer and Web-based applications, the use of *multimedia input devices*—hardware such as *digital cameras*, *microphones*, and more—continues to grow in variety and importance. Two of the most common types of multimedia input devices—digital cameras and audio input devices—are discussed next.

Digital Cameras

Digital cameras are much like conventional cameras, but instead of recording images on film or videotape they record them on some type of digital storage medium. Typically, the storage medium is removable, such as a flash memory card (see Figure 5-15) or a recordable CD or DVD disc. Digital cameras can either be *still* cameras (which take still photos) or *video* cameras (which capture moving video images), or a combination of the two.

Digital Still Cameras

Digital still cameras are available in a wide variety of sizes and capabilities. For instance, you can get an inexpensive (less than $100) consumer stand-alone, point-and-shoot model; a professional digital camera with removable lenses; a *digital camera watch*; or a digital camera attachment for your handheld PC or phone (see Figure 5-15). Regardless of the

**H
W**

> **FIGURE 5-15**
> **Digital cameras.**
> Digital cameras, which record images on digital media instead of on film, are available in many shapes and sizes.

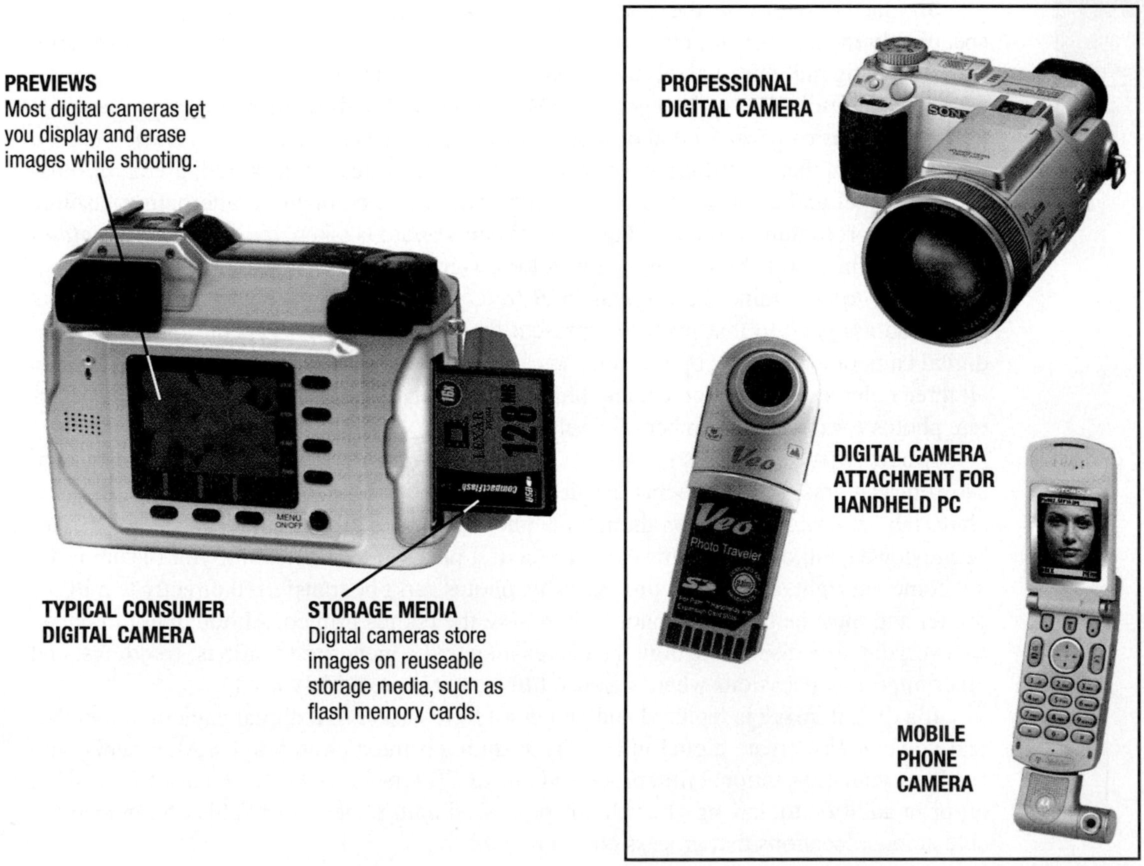

PREVIEWS
Most digital cameras let you display and erase images while shooting.

PROFESSIONAL DIGITAL CAMERA

DIGITAL CAMERA ATTACHMENT FOR HANDHELD PC

TYPICAL CONSUMER DIGITAL CAMERA

STORAGE MEDIA
Digital cameras store images on reuseable storage media, such as flash memory cards.

MOBILE PHONE CAMERA

>**Digital camera.** An input device that takes pictures and records them as digital data (instead of film or videotaped) images.

format, all digital cameras store the photos captured in digital form, usually on flash memory media. Digital cameras are useful for many types of business and recreational applications. For instance, an insurance adjuster may need a quick picture of a damaged car, a business owner may require a simple snapshot for a newsletter or a Web page, a parent may wish to e-mail a quick photo of a child to the child's grandparents, or a news photographer may need to capture an image immediately to e-mail to an anxious editor.

One of the most compelling advantages of digital cameras is that you can immediately preview and use the photographs as you take them, without having to shoot an entire roll of film and wait to get it developed first. Because you can preview the image immediately after it is taken, a new photo can be shot if the image is not acceptable. The number of photos that can be stored in the camera at one time depends on the capacity of the flash memory media being used and the resolution of the photos being taken (many cameras let you choose the resolution to be used). At any time, the photos can be transferred to a PC or printer (usually by removing the flash memory card and inserting it into the PC or printer, although some cameras are designed to transfer images via a USB, FireWire, or serial cable instead, or have a special camera docking station attached to the printer or PC). Once the photos have been transferred to a PC, the storage medium can be erased to make room for more photos and the photos can be retouched with image-enhancement software, if desired, adjusting contrast, brightness, color, and focus, adding special effects, or removing red eye. The digital photos can be saved, printed, or used just as any other image; they can also be burned onto a CD or DVD disc.

Similar to scanners, the quality of digital cameras is measured by resolution—specifically the number of pixels used to capture an image. Today's cameras are *megapixel* cameras, using millions of pixels to store the data for each image. Consumer digital cameras usually have resolutions of 2 megapixels (MP) or higher for about $150 on up; professional 14 MP cameras can cost $5,000 or more. Most digital cameras use *CCD* (*charge-coupled device*) sensors that record information about just one of three colors (red, green, or blue) for each pixel and each pixel is permanently assigned a color in an alternating fashion, forming a sort of three-color checkerboard. When a photo is taken, the camera *interpolates* (estimates) the results by looking at the color assigned to one pixel and at least three adjacent pixels to determine the original *RGB* (red, green, and blue) color combination that should be assigned to that pixel to represent the original color. A recent improvement in digital camera technology by Foveon uses a new *X3* three-layer sensor to initially capture all three color values (red, green, and blue) for each pixel, resulting in sharper, more accurate photos for the same number of pixels.

A new twist on digital still cameras is the *disposable digital camera*. Similar to one-use film cameras, these cameras are designed to be used once and then submitted to a photo lab for processing. Even though the photos are taken in digital form, photos cannot be previewed, although on some cameras the last photo can be deleted if you're sure it did not come out right, and, at this time anyway, photos can't be transferred directly to a PC or printer and must be taken to a photo lab to have the photos printed. Although not intended for everyday use, disposable digital cameras may find a niche for vacations, weddings, and other important occasions where one-use film cameras are widely used.

If a digital image is required and you don't have access to a digital camera, remember that you can also create digital images by scanning printed photographs. Alternately, you can have your conventional film processed onto a CD (such as a *Kodak PictureCD*) instead of, or in addition to, having your photos processed onto photo paper. This option is available at most locations that process conventional film.

Digital Video Cameras

Digital video cameras include *digital camcorders* and small *PC video cameras* (see Figure 5-16). Digital camcorders are similar to conventional *analog* camcorders, but they store images on digital media instead of film, the same as digital still cameras. Because of the large amount of storage space needed for video, either high-capacity flash memory cards

FURTHER EXPLORATION

For links to further information about digital cameras and digital photography, go to www.course.com/uc10/ch05

or rewritable DVDs are often used. Once the video is recorded in digital form, it can be transferred to a PC, edited with software as needed, and stored on a DVD or other medium.

PC video cameras—commonly called *PC cams*—are usually designed to transmit video images over the Internet, such as during a *videoconference* or *video phone call*. Although video phone calls can be one-sided (with only one person sending video and the other person only receiving it), usually during a videoconference each person has a PC video camera attached to his or her PC to transmit images to the other person, as in Figure 5-16. Some one-way applications include PC cameras located in child-care centers that allow

DIGITAL CAMCORDER
Typically allows you to view video during and after it is recorded; digital media, such as the DVD shown here, are used for storage instead of videotape.

Video camera

PC VIDEO CAMERA
Commonly used to deliver video over the Internet, such as in the family videoconference shown here.

parents to watch live video of their children during the day, and surveillance cameras set up in homes and offices that broadcast images to the owner's PC so he or she can check for intruders and monitor the location remotely. PC cameras can also be used to broadcast images continually to a Web page, such as the cameras frequently found in zoo animal exhibits, on top of mountains, or other locations of interest to the general public. In this type of application, the video camera is referred to as a *Web cam*.

Images transmitted from a PC video camera can either be displayed on the screen continuously, or can be static images taken at regular intervals, depending on the application and hardware being used. PC video cameras can also be used to capture video and store it in the computer for later use, although this application requires special software and a great deal of storage space. Stored video can be played again when needed, or inserted into a multimedia presentation. Short video clips can also be e-mailed to others. Many PC video cameras can take still images, as well.

Digital video cameras can also be used for identification purposes, such as with face recognition technology to authorize access to a secure facility or computer resource. These and other types of security applications are discussed in more detail in Chapters 8 and 15.

Audio Input Devices

Audio input is the process of entering audio data into the computer. Such input can include both voice and music.

Voice-Input Systems

A hardware-and-software combination used to input spoken words and convert them to digital form is known as a **voice-input system**. All voice-input systems consist of a *microphone* or *headset* (a set of *headphones* with a microphone built in) and appropriate software, such as *IBM ViaVoice* or *Dragon NaturallySpeaking*. Voice-input capabilities are also increasingly being incorporated into both desktop and portable PC operating systems.

FIGURE 5-16
Digital video cameras. Common types include digital camcorders and PC video cameras.

TIP

Video data can also be transferred from a conventional analog camcorder to a PC—the camcorder typically connects to a port on a *video capture card* installed inside the PC.

>**Voice-input system.** A system that enables a computer to recognize the human voice.

1. The user speaks into a microphone that cancels out background noise and inputs the speech into the computer.

The big black dog...

4. The spoken words appear on the screen in the application program (word processor, e-mail program, etc.) being used.

The big black dog...

2. An analog-to-digital converter on the sound card located inside the PC converts the spoken words to phonemes, the fundamental sounds in the language being used, and digitizes them.

3. Voice-recognition software matches up the phoneme combinations to determine the words spoken. Sentence structure rules are used to select one word if it is a questionable match or a word with a homonym.

> **FIGURE 5-17**
> How voice recognition works.

Voice input can be recorded to be sent via e-mail or used in a multimedia presentation, or it can be used in *telephony* applications—making telephone calls or other telephone-oriented tasks using the computer. Voice input can also be used to dictate text or commands the computer will recognize, as an alternative to mouse or keyboard input. This latter type of voice-input system is more specifically called a *voice-recognition system.*

For example, with voice recognition you can dictate documents to your word processing program and dictate e-mail messages to your e-mail program. You may also be able to issue commands to your computer, such as to open a particular program or save a document. Specialty voice-recognition systems are even becoming available to assist in surgical procedures, such as to control robots, microscopes, and other electronic equipment.

Here's a quick look at how a voice-recognition system might work (refer to Figure 5-17). First, a microphone is used to input the spoken words into the PC, and then the sounds are broken into digital representations of *phonemes*—the basic elements of speech, such as *duh*, *aw*, and *guh* for the word "dog." (The English language contains about 50 phonemes.) Next, the voice-recognition software analyzes the content of the speech to convert the phonemes to words. Once words are identified, they are displayed on the screen. If a match is questionable or a homonym is encountered (such as the choice between "their," "there," and "they're,") the program analyzes the context in which the word is used in an attempt to identify the correct word. If the program inserts an inappropriate word while converting the user's voice input to text, the user can usually override it. To increase accuracy, most voice-recognition software can be trained by individual users to allow the program to become accustom to the user's speech patterns, voice, accent, and pronunciation.

> **FIGURE 5-18**
> A combination PC/MIDI keyboard.

Music-Input Systems

Musical input can be recorded for use in musical arrangements, to accompany a multimedia presentation, or to create a custom music CD. Music can be input into a PC via a CD or DVD player. For original compositions, a *MIDI* (*musical instrument digital interface*) device, such as a MIDI musical keyboard with piano-type keys instead of, or in addition to, alphanumeric keys (see Figure 5-18), can be used. Once the music is input into the computer, it can be saved, modified, played, or inserted into other programs, as necessary.

DISPLAY DEVICES

A **display device**—the most common form of output device—presents output visually, typically on some type of computer screen. With desktop PCs, the computer screen is more formally called a **monitor**. With all-in-one PCs, notebook computers, handheld PCs, and other devices for which the screen is built into the unit, the term *display screen* may be used instead. Display screens are also built into *e-books* (small book-sized devices used to display electronic versions of books), digital picture frames, portable DVD players, and other consumer products. A *data projector* is a display device that projects computer output onto a wall or projection screen for a large group presentation.

Display devices are used to view output while working on the computer. To read a document away from the computer, another output device—the *printer*, discussed later in this chapter—is used.

Display Device Characteristics

There are several characteristics and features that differentiate one type of display device from another. The following sections discuss a few of the most significant characteristics.

Color vs. Monochrome Displays

Display devices form text characters, graphical images, and video images by lighting up the proper configurations of pixels. *Monochrome displays* use only two colors (usually black and white or black and green) and are not commonly used today. *Color displays* are the norm and form all colors available on the screen by mixing combinations of only three colors—red, green, and blue (see Figure 5-19). Three colors may not sound like much of a base, but when a display device blends red, green, and blue light of varying intensities—for each of the hundreds of thousands of pixels on the screen—it can produce an enormous spectrum of colors.

Size

The display size of a display device is measured in inches diagonally from corner to corner, similar to the way TV screens are measured. It is important to realize, however, that the actual viewing area of many display devices is smaller than the stated size. For

> **FIGURE 5-19**
> **A color CRT monitor.**

COLOR PIXELS
Each pixel on the screen is made up of some combination of red, green, and blue light. When red, green, and blue light of varying intensities are blended, a very wide range of colors is possible.

REFRESH RATE
Pixels on a typical desktop display screen are refreshed—that is, recharged with built-in electron guns so they will remain bright—at a rate of about 60 times each second.

>**Display device.** An output device that contains a viewing screen. >**Monitor.** A display device for a desktop PC.

> **FIGURE 5-20**
Screen resolution. A higher screen resolution (measured in pixels) displays everything smaller than a lower screen resolution.

One pixel

800 × 600 SCREEN RESOLUTION   **1,024 × 768 SCREEN RESOLUTION**

example, one 17-inch monitor might have a *viewable image size* (*VIS*) of 16 inches, while another 17-inch monitor might have a viewable image size of 15.7 inches. Although 0.3 inches may not sound like much of a difference in size, small size variations can be noticeable and are important to keep in mind when comparing the quality and price of two display devices. Common display sizes today are 17 and 19 inches for desktop PCs, 15 and 17 inches for notebooks, and 10 inches for tablet PCs.

Screen Resolution

The number of pixels used on a display screen determines the *screen resolution*, which affects the size of the elements displayed on the screen. When a high resolution is selected, such as 1,024 pixels horizontally by 768 pixels vertically (written as 1,024 × 768 and read as 1,024 by 768), more data can fit on the screen, but everything will be displayed smaller than with a lower resolution, such as 640 × 480 or 800 × 600 (see Figure 5-20). Most PCs and video cards allow the user to select the resolution that they prefer, depending on what software they will be using and the size of their monitor (on Windows PCs, display options are changed using the Control Panel). Very high-resolution monitors are available for special applications, such as viewing digital X-rays.

Graphics Standards

On a desktop PC, a video card or integrated video component built directly into the motherboard is used to connect a display device to the computer. The type of video card used helps to determine such display characteristics as the screen resolutions available, the number of bits used to store color information about each pixel (called the *bit depth*), and the total number of colors that can be used to display images. Video cards also contain memory chips (frequently called *video RAM* or *VRAM*) to support graphics display, although some systems use some of the PC's regular RAM as video RAM instead. Over the years, there have been several *graphics standards* to which video cards adhered. For example, the older *VGA* (*video graphics array*) standard dictates a resolution of 640 by 480 pixels and allows a screen to display at most 256 colors. Most monitors and display screens today use the *SVGA* (*super VGA*) standard, which allows for higher resolutions and true color (16.7 million colors). To support higher resolutions, bit depths, and number of colors, a sufficient amount of video RAM is required. A typical amount of video RAM today is about 64 MB.

FURTHER EXPLORATION

For links to further information about display devices, go to www.course.com/uc10/ch05

CRT Monitors

The traditional type of monitor for a desktop PC is the **CRT (cathode-ray tube) monitor**, like the ones shown in Figures 5-19 and 5-20. With a CRT, an electron gun sealed inside a large glass tube fires at a phosphor-coated screen to light up the appropriate pixels in the appropriate color to display the images, similar to a conventional television. Because the phosphors only glow for a limited amount of time, the monitor image must be redrawn (*refreshed*) on a continual basis, relighting each pixel in the appropriate color—typically this occurs about 60 times per second or faster.

As with conventional TVs, CRT monitors are large, bulky, and heavy (refer again to Figure 5-19). However, many CRT monitors provide a clear, sharp picture and the image on the screen can be seen from a fairly wide viewing angle. One important image quality measurement for CRT monitors is *dot pitch*, which indicates how tightly the pixels are packed together. A smaller dot pitch results in a better, sharper image; common dot pitch for monitors today ranges from .24 to .27 millimeters. Unlike screen resolution, the dot pitch for a monitor cannot be changed by the user.

H W

Flat-Panel Displays

Thinner and lighter **flat-panel displays** (see Figure 5-21) form images by manipulating electronically-charged chemicals or gases sandwiched between thin panes of glass

TIP

Unlike CRT monitors, the stated size of a flat-panel display (such as 15 inches or 17 inches) almost always corresponds to its actual viewable image size.

DESKTOP PCS
Many desktop users are selecting flat-panel displays because of their small footprints.

CONSUMER PRODUCTS
Many consumer products, such as this digital photo frame that can receive and display digital photographs, have an integrated flat-panel display.

PORTABLE PCS AND MOBILE DEVICES
Virtually all portable PCs, smart phones, and other mobile devices use flat-panel technology.

❯ **FIGURE 5-21**
Flat-panel displays.
These compact, light-weight, low-power-consumption displays suit a wide range of applications.

>**CRT (cathode-ray tube) monitor.** A display device that projects images onto a display screen using a technology similar to the one used with conventional TVs. >**Flat-panel display.** A slim type of display device.

instead of firing a bulky electron gun. Common flat-panel technologies include *liquid crystal display* (*LCD*) and *gas plasma*. LCD displays light up charged liquid crystals located between two sheets of material (usually glass), and special color filters manipulate this light to draw the appropriate images on the screen. Gas plasma displays work similarly (but uses a layer of gas instead of liquid crystals) and are used primarily with larger displays.

Flat-panel displays take up little space, are lightweight, and require less power than CRT monitors. Because of these features, they are commonly found on portable computers, mobile devices, and a variety of consumer products, such as handheld video games, TVs, and DVD players; car navigation systems; and digital photo frames, as shown in Figure 5-21. Flat-panel technology is also used in eyepiece displays, commonly found on wearable PCs. Important image quality characteristics for flat-panel displays include sharpness, brightness, contrast ratios, and viewing angle (many flat-panel displays can only be read when directly in front of the display, not from the side).

> **FIGURE 5-22**

Smart displays.

When docked, a smart display acts like a flat-panel desktop PC display; when lifted out of its docking station, it can be used like a portable PC, as long as it stays within range of its host PC.

> **FIGURE 5-23**

Living room PCs.

This living room PC has a gas plasma screen and uses Microsoft Windows XP Media Center to control computer, as well as television, tasks.

Smart Displays

Smart displays (sometimes called *wireless monitors*) are portable monitors that are wirelessly connected to a desktop PC so they can remotely access that PC from anywhere within a home or office. Although similar in appearance to a tablet PC (see Figure 5-22), an important difference is the location of the computing hardware. Unlike a tablet PC, which contains all processing hardware inside the tablet and is independent of any other device, a smart display is designed to always be used in conjunction with its associated PC. Smart displays use a wireless *Wi-Fi* networking connection (discussed in more detail in Chapter 8) to connect the display to the system unit, provided the distance between the two items is about 100 feet or less. Typically, the mouse and keyboard attached to the docking station are used when the smart display is connected to its docking station, and touch or pen input is used when the smart display is being carried around the home.

HDTV Monitors

HDTV (*high-definition television*) is a new type of television technology that supports high-resolution, digital broadcast signals. *HDTV monitors* are capable of receiving HDTV broadcasts, as well as displaying computer images. Because HDTV monitors have up to three times more pixels than analog TVs, they have very crisp, clear pictures. One advantage of high-definition broadcasting for the computer industry is that it is more compatible with interactive data services that the industry wants to deliver via television broadcast technology. In fact, the trend of using a large high-definition television as a living room PC monitor for computer and Internet tasks, in addition to TV viewing, is growing (see Figure 5-23). Other digital-television-related recreational activities, such as *video-on-demand* (renting movies online that are downloaded to your PC or digital DVR recorder instead of physically picking them up at a movie rental store) and *interactive TV* (television with some interactive activities that you can perform while watching the show) are expected to grow once HDTV technology and fast Internet access become more commonplace. These topics are discussed in more detail in Chapter 9.

>**Smart display.** A portable display device that connects wirelessly to its associated system unit.

Data and Multimedia Projectors

A **data projector** connects to a computer and projects any output sent to the computer monitor through the projector onto a wall or projection screen (see Figure 5-24). Most data projectors today (sometimes referred to as *data/video projectors*, *multimedia projectors*, or *digital projectors*) can project video, in addition to computer output. In classrooms, conference rooms, and similar locations, projectors are often permanently mounted onto the ceiling. They are also an important component of a new trend in classrooms—the *smart classroom*, discussed in the Campus Close-Up box. Portable projectors are also available, either as freestanding units or small panels used in conjunction with a standard overhead projector. Portable projectors are commonly used for business presentations that occur out of the office.

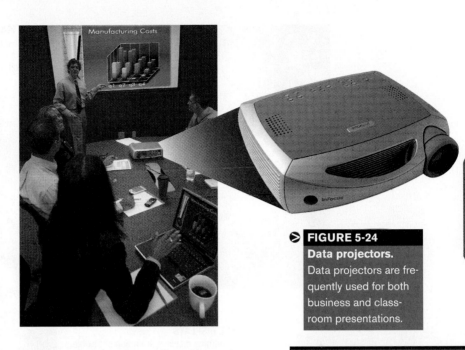

H W

> **FIGURE 5-24**
> **Data projectors.**
> Data projectors are frequently used for both business and classroom presentations.

Emerging Display Technologies and Applications

As new applications for computerized services arise or as new ways to interact with PCs are created, often new types of displays are developed. For instance, Figure 5-25 shows three new or emerging displays.

Using technology to target advertising to consumers when they are waiting in a checkout line, riding in an elevator or taxi, in the restroom, or some other location where they are captive for a few minutes is a new trend called *captive marketing*. Using displays built into the appropriate location (such as the elevator wall in Figure 5-25), advertisers can now target ads to consumers at locations that were previously untapped. Many captive marketing users also include continually updated additional information—such as stock quotes, news headlines, and weather reports—to catch consumers' attention.

Flexible displays—displays that can roll up when not in use—are being developed by several companies. Instead of using layers of glass around the liquid crystals, as in conventional flat-panel displays, flexible displays are made out of flexible plastic. Several prototypes are available (such as the one-half-millimeter thick screen shown in Figure 5-25), but no products have yet been released. Possible uses for flexible screens include making lighter desktop and portable PC monitors, enabling pullout displays to be built into smart phones, integrating displays on military uniform jackets and sleeves, and allowing retractable wall-mounted big screen televisions and monitors. One technology for making flexible displays involves using *FOLEDs* (*flexible organic light-emitting diodes*); related *OLED* (*organic light-emitting diode*) displays are beginning to replace LCD screens in some portable PCs and devices since they, like FOLEDs, are thinner, brighter, and more energy efficient than LCDs. A related application—*e-paper*—is discussed in the Trend box. Integrated PCs—computer hardware built into other objects (such as desks, refrigerators, countertops, and more) is another recent trend. The kitchen countertop display shown in Figure 5-25 is one example.

TIP

According to government timetables, analog broadcasting is scheduled to cease at the end of 2006 and be replaced entirely with digital HDTV broadcasting, although that date may be extended in particular areas until at least 85% of the homes in that area have access to digital television broadcasts.

TIP

Display devices and printers designed for visually-impaired PC users and other users with special needs are discussed in Chapter 16.

>**Data projector.** A display device that projects all computer output to a wall or projection screen.

CAPTIVE MARKETING
These flat-panel displays installed in elevators and other public locations continually flash news headlines and other timely information along with ads for a variety of companies.

FLEXIBLE DISPLAYS
These emerging displays are made of flexible plastic and can be rolled up when not in use.

INTEGRATED DISPLAYS
Computers and displays are beginning to become integrated into everyday appliances and furniture, such as the display built into the kitchen countertop shown here.

▶ FIGURE 5-25
New and emerging display applications.

PRINTERS

Instead of the temporary, ever-changing soft-copy output that a monitor produces, **printers** produce hard copy; that is, a permanent copy of the output on paper. Most desktop PCs are connected to a printer; portable PCs can use printers as well.

Printer Characteristics

Printers differ in a number of important respects. One involves the technology through which they output images. Another is size; you can hold some computer printers in your hand, while others are large, stand-alone pieces of equipment. Some general printer characteristics are touched on next, followed by a discussion of the most common types of printers.

CAMPUS CLOSE-UP

Smart Classrooms

Across the nation, classrooms are getting smart. The idea behind the *smart classroom* is to provide instructors immediate access to all the multimedia resources they might need for effective class meetings. At a basic level, a smart classroom may contain an instructor station with a PC connected to the school network and an overhead projector so that software can be demonstrated, Internet resources can be accessed, and PowerPoint presentations can be displayed. An even smarter classroom might also include a videotape and DVD player, a document camera (for projecting images from physical objects to a wall-mounted projection screen), and a sound system. High-end smart classrooms can include two-way audio and video conferencing capabilities; network connections at all student desks, enabling students to plug in their portable PCs for immediate access to the campus intranet, class Web content, and Internet resources; and the ability for the instructor to send images (for instance, the image on his or her monitor or an image on a student's monitor) to all student PCs.

Typically, smart classrooms have an instructor's station containing a PC and controls for room lighting and multimedia equipment. The University of Pittsburg engineering classroom shown in the accompanying photo features a touch-screen plasma monitor for this purpose. Some smart classrooms are sized for traditional classroom meetings; others, such as Flint, Michigan's Mott Community College teleconferencing auditorium shown in the accompanying photo, are designed for large audiences. These larger facilities can be used for teleconferences, large lecture classes, and more.

Smart classrooms can range from small classrooms with individual PCs and a projection system (left) to large teleconferencing auditoriums (right).

ENGINEERING CLASSROOM AT THE UNIVERSITY OF PITTSBURG

TELECONFERENCING AUDITORIUM AT MOTT COMMUNITY COLLEGE

Print Resolution

Most printing technologies today form images with dots, similar to the way monitors display images with pixels. In contrast, if you look at the printing mechanism of an old typewriter, you'll notice that each character on the typewriter is embossed as a single solid image on a print head attached to a metal spoke. Many of the earliest computer printers used similar print heads to stamp output onto paper. However, virtually all of today's printers form images with dots instead, making their output much more versatile—they can print text in virtually any size, as well as print photos and other graphical images. The dots are most often formed with liquid ink or flecks of ink toner powder.

Regardless of how the dots are formed on the printed paper, printer quality (called *print resolution*) is typically measured in *dots per inch* (*dpi*); the higher the dpi, the better the quality of the printout. Although most printers today output at least good quality images, a printer with a higher resolution will print sharper, smoother, less grainy text and images than a lower resolution printer.

TREND

Electronic Paper

Electronic paper (*e-paper*) consists of a display device onto which written content is displayed in electronic form, but that is thinner and more paper-like than other types of display devices. Still in the early stages of development at a number of companies, such as Gyricon Media, Xerox, and E Ink, electronic paper is expected eventually to become a viable replacement for some traditional paper and ink applications. Practical applications from an environmental standpoint include any documents that only need to be kept for a short time, such as newspapers, retail display signs, and some e-mail messages. Instead of being discarded when their useful life has ended, using e-paper these documents could be erased and then reused.

So how does e-paper work? One product (currently in the testing stage) consists of two sheets of very thin transparent plastic with millions of very small beads—each smaller than a grain of sand and sealed inside a tiny pocket surrounded by liquid (these beads and their liquid are sometimes referred to as *electronic ink* or *e-ink*). Each bead (see the accompanying photo) has two colors—such as half white and half black—and can rotate within its pocket only when an electrical signal is received. To change the text or images displayed on the "paper," electronic signals—usually sent to the paper through a wireless transmission—instruct the beads to rotate appropriately to display either their black sides or white sides to form the proper text and images, similar to the way pixels are used to display images on a monitor. The content remains displayed until another transmission changes the pattern, such as changing all the beads to display their white sides to "erase" the paper. Current e-paper products can be written to and erased electronically thousands of times, but in the near future that number is expected to increase to several million times.

One of the first areas in which e-paper has been applied is retail signs, such as those found in department stores and other retail establishments (large stores often spend thousands of dollars on printed paper signs each week). These *e-signs* look like ordinary paper signs, but their text can be changed wirelessly (see the Macy's sign in the accompanying photo). Consequently, instead of continually having to print new paper signs, e-signs can be changed electronically to be reused, which saves the time and expense of printing, delivering, and setting up new signs, as well as disposing of the old ones. Other retail applications currently in development include e-paper shelf price tags that always match the price in the store's database and newspaper dispenser boxes that are updated periodically during the day to reflect the latest headlines or a featured section of the newspaper.

As e-paper technology improves, it is expected that the paper will more easily support the smaller text needed for personal printouts. Types of e-paper expected in the future include regular-sized e-paper that can be inserted into a special computer printer to be printed electronically and then reused over and over again; regular and newspaper-sized e-papers that can wirelessly download new content from the Internet; and *e-books* that look and feel like real paper books, but whose content can be rewritten to display the content of a different book when directed by the user.

Improvements that need to be made before e-paper and other e-ink applications become more commonplace include color capabilities, lower cost, increased life span, and thinner and more flexible paper. Future possibilities for e-ink include its use on billboards, T-shirts, and even paint for easy redecorating. *Conductive e-ink* currently in development can carry electricity after it is printed; conductive e-ink will potentially enable keyboards to be printed onto military uniform sleeves, light switches to be printed onto wallpaper, and radio circuitry and controls to be printed onto clothing and other everyday objects.

E-paper products, such as the e-sign shown here (right) are written electronically using tiny beads (left) and can be erased and rewritten over and over again.

The extended pins
print dots on the paper.

The least-expensive dot-matrix printers have a print head containing 9 vertical pins. As the print head moves from left to right, specific pins are extended to form the text and images.

More expensive dot-matrix printers have a 24-pin head that produces crisp-looking text.

**H
W**

Impact vs. Non-Impact Printing

Printers produce images through either impact or non-impact technologies. *Impact printers* have a print mechanism that actually strikes the paper to form the image, similar to old ribbon typewriters. On such a typewriter, pressing a key makes the metal spoke containing an embossed character strike an inked ribbon to transfer that character's image onto the paper. An impact computer *dot-matrix printer* works in a similar fashion, only the print head is comprised of pins—instead of fully formed characters—that strike the ribbon. As illustrated in Figure 5-26, the appropriate pins are extended to form the appropriate words or images. When the pins press into the ribbon, dots of ink are transferred onto the paper. Impact printers are primarily used today for producing multipart forms, such as invoices and credit-card receipts.

Most printers today are *non-impact printers*; that is, they form images without the print mechanism actually touching the paper. Non-impact printers (such as the *laser* and *ink-jet printers* discussed shortly) usually produce higher-quality images and are much quieter than impact printers. In addition to paper, both impact and non-impact printers can print on transparencies, envelopes, mailing labels, and more.

Color vs. Black and White

Color printers are widely available today. Essentially, color printers work the same as black and white printers, except they use four different colors of ink—cyan (blue), magenta (red), yellow, and black—instead of just black ink. Color printers either apply all four colors in one pass, or they go through the entire printing process four times, applying one color during each pass. By combining these four colors in the appropriate proportions, color printers can output a vast number of colors and shades.

Personal vs. Network Printers

Most printers found in homes and many found in small businesses today are commonly referred to as *personal printers*—that is, printers connected to one computer and not shared with others. *Network printers*, in contrast, are printers shared by multiple users. Although multiple users can share a personal printer through a home or office network, network printers are designed for high-volume, high-speed printing.

> **FIGURE 5-26**
> **Dot-matrix printers.**
> Dot-matrix printers are impact printers; today they are typically high-speed printers used in manufacturing, shipping, or similar applications.

> **FIGURE 5-27**
> Personal and network printers.

PERSONAL PRINTER
Typically connected to a single PC and
not shared with others.

NETWORK PRINTER
Connected to a network to provide
high-speed printing for multiple users.

Network printers are usually larger than personal printers (see Figure 5-27), work up to about 10 times faster than personal printers, and cost anywhere from $500 to $10,000 or more. Some network printers are *line printers* (which print one line of text at a time), but most are *page printers*, which print a full page of output at a time.

Speed

The speed of some printers is measured in *characters per second* (*cps*), but a more typical measurement is *pages per minute* (*ppm*). How long it takes a document to print depends on the actual printer being used, as well as the content being printed. For instance, pages containing photos or other graphics typically take longer to print than pages containing only text, and full-color pages take longer to print than black and white pages. Common speeds for personal printers today range from about 6 to 25 ppm; network printers typically print from 45 to 100 ppm. Some high-end models can also collate and staple.

Laser Printers

Laser printers are the standard for business documents and come in both personal and network styles (both printers shown in Figure 5-27 are laser printers). To print a document, the laser printer first uses a laser beam to charge the appropriate locations on a drum to form the page's image, and then *toner powder* (powdered ink) is released from a *toner cartridge* and sticks to the drum. The toner is then transferred to a piece of paper when the paper is rolled over the drum, and a heating unit fuses the toner powder to the paper to permanently form the image (see Figure 5-28). As you might guess from this description, laser printers print an entire page at one time.

Most laser printers use only black toner powder, similar to photocopying machines, although color laser printers are available. Laser printers typically print faster and have better quality output than *ink-jet printers* (discussed next). Common print resolution for laser printers is between 600 and 2,400 dpi; speeds for personal laser printers range from about 6 to 20 ppm. Laser printers start at about $200.

TIP

When a toner cartridge runs out of toner powder, it is removed and replaced with a full one. Toner cartridges can be purchased new or *recharged* (refilled); recharged cartridges typically cost about one-third less than new cartridges and last at least as long.

>**Laser printer.** An output device that uses toner powder and technology similar to that of a photocopier to produce images on paper.

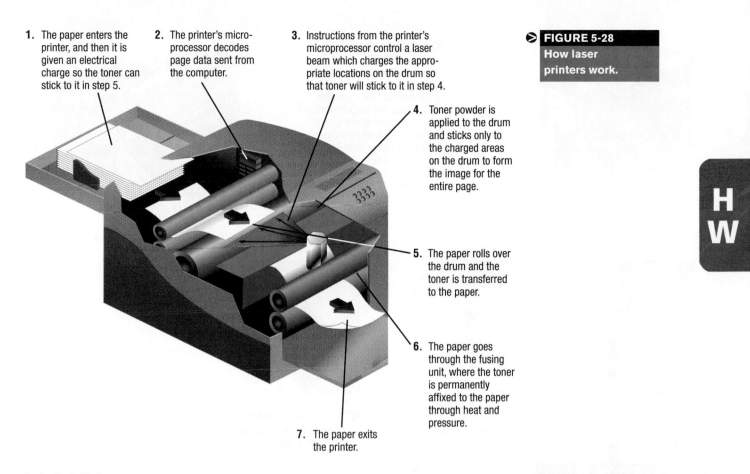

1. The paper enters the printer, and then it is given an electrical charge so the toner can stick to it in step 5.

2. The printer's microprocessor decodes page data sent from the computer.

3. Instructions from the printer's microprocessor control a laser beam which charges the appropriate locations on the drum so that toner will stick to it in step 4.

4. Toner powder is applied to the drum and sticks only to the charged areas on the drum to form the image for the entire page.

5. The paper rolls over the drum and the toner is transferred to the paper.

6. The paper goes through the fusing unit, where the toner is permanently affixed to the paper through heat and pressure.

7. The paper exits the printer.

> **FIGURE 5-28**
> **How laser printers work.**

H W

Ink-Jet Printers

Ink-jet printers form images by spraying tiny drops of liquid ink onto the page. The most widely used type of ink-jet printer uses *bubble-jet* technology to squeeze the ink out of the cartridge onto the paper (see Figure 5-29). Some printers print with a single size of ink droplet; others use multiple nozzles or varying electrical charges to print different sizes of ink droplets for more precise printing.

Because they are relatively inexpensive, have reasonable-quality output, and can print in color, ink-jet printers are often the printer of choice for home use. With the use of special photo paper, many ink-jet printers can also print respectable-looking photographs. At less than $100 for a simple home printer, ink-jet printers are affordable, although the cost of the supplies (such as the *ink cartridges* that are replaced when they are emptied and special photo paper) can add up, especially if you do a lot of color printing. Ink-jet printers print one line at a time and typically print more slowly than laser printers.

There are a wide variety of materials available to use with ink-jet and other color printers for creating specialty items, such as note cards and themed stationary for announcements and invitations, magnetic sheets for creating custom refrigerator magnets, iron-on decals for decorating clothing and mouse pads, and more. Some printers are capable of printing directly on to CDs and DVDs that have a printable surface, instead of printing stick-on labels (a special tray inserts the disc to be printed on).

> **TIP**
>
> Ink-jet technology is also being used in the development of a number of emerging applications unrelated to current ink-jet printers, such as dispensing liquid metals, aromas, computer chips and other circuitry, and even "printing" human tissue and other organic materials for medical purposes.

>**Ink-jet printer.** An output device that sprays droplets of ink to produce images on paper.

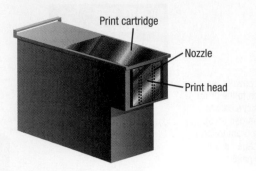

Print cartridge

Nozzle

Print head

HOW BUBBLE-JET INK-JET PRINTERS WORK

Color ink-jet printers create colors by mixing different combinations of four colors of ink—magenta, cyan, yellow, and black. The different colors can be in one or multiple cartridges. Each cartridge is made up of 300 or more tiny ink-filled firing chambers, each attached to a nozzle smaller than a human hair. To print images, the appropriate color ink is ejected through the appropriate nozzles.

PERSONAL INK-JET PRINTER

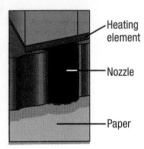

Heating element

Nozzle

Paper

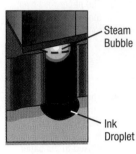

Steam Bubble

Ink Droplet

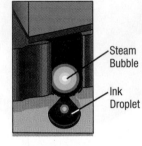

Steam Bubble

Ink Droplet

1. A heating element makes the ink boil and a steam bubble forms.

2. As the bubble expands, it pushes ink through the nozzle.

3. The pressure of the bubble forces an ink droplet to be ejected onto the paper. When the steam bubble collapses, more ink is pulled into the print head.

> **FIGURE 5-29**
> How bubble-jet ink-jet printers work.

Special-Purpose Printers

Some printers are specifically designed for a particular purpose. Some of the most common *special-purpose printers* are discussed next and illustrated in Figure 5-30.

Photo Printers

Photo printers (also sometimes called *snapshot printers*) are color printers designed to print photographs. Photo printers have become increasingly popular as digital cameras have become more prominent. Many photo printers use ink-jet technology and some can accept the flash memory media used with digital cameras so that photos can be printed without transferring them first to a computer; other printers have a special docking station connected to the printer into which the camera is inserted to print photos. For more professional photo printing applications, *thermal-transfer* or *dye-sublimation printers* can be used. These technologies use either heated wax or dye on special paper, which produces a better image than an ink-jet printer, but at a greater expense. Consequently, these types of printers are typically used only when professional-quality output is required.

Bar-Code and Label Printers

Bar-code printers enable businesses and other organizations to print custom bar codes on price tags, shipping labels, and other documents for identification or pricing purposes.

>**Photo printer.** An output device designed for printing digital photographs. >**Bar-code printer.** An output device that prints bar-coded documents.

Photos can be previewed and edited here.

Flash memory media can be inserted here.

PHOTO PRINTERS
Photo printers are used to print photos taken with a digital camera or scanned into the computer.

BAR-CODE PRINTERS
Bar-code printers can print a variety of bar codes, such as for price tags or stickers, document tracking, inventory control, and so forth.

H W

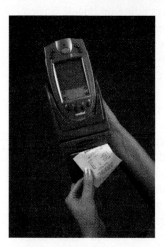

WIDE-FORMAT PRINTERS
Wide-format ink-jet printers are useful for printouts that are too big for a standard-sized ink-jet printer.

PORTABLE PRINTERS
Portable printers allow users to print from a notebook or handheld computer.

> **FIGURE 5-30**
> **Special-purpose printers.**

Most bar-code printers can print labels in a variety of bar-code standards. For other types of labels, such as for envelopes, packages, and file folders, regular *label printers* may come in handy. Some label printers can print *electronic postage* (sometimes called *e-stamps* or *PC postage*)—valid postage stamps that can be printed once a postage allotment has been purchased via the Internet and an e-stamp vendor; postage values are deducted from your allotment as you print the e-stamps. Some e-stamp services allow stamps to be printed on labels and envelopes using laser or ink-jet printers, as well.

Portable Printers

Portable printers are small, lightweight printers that can be used with a notebook, handheld, or other portable computer. Some portable printers need to be physically connected to the computer; others can receive documents to be printed using wireless transmission. The portable printer featured in Figure 5-30 is designed for printing receipts, bar codes, and other small items; many portable printers can print on regular-sized (8½-by-11-inch) paper.

Plotters and Wide-Format Ink-Jet Printers

A *plotter* is an output device that is designed primarily to produce charts, drawings, maps, blueprints, three-dimensional illustrations, and other forms of large documents. Although plotters are available using a variety of technologies, *electrostatic plotters* are the most common. These devices create images using toner in a manner similar to a photocopying machine or laser printer, but instead of drawing the image with a laser, they use a matrix of tiny wires to charge the paper with electricity. When the charged paper passes over the toner bed, the toner adheres to it and produces an image.

When a very large color image is needed for posters, signs, advertising banners, and other similar applications, an *ink-jet plotter*—more commonly called a *wide-format ink-jet printer* (see Figure 5-30)—would likely be used. Although typically used to print on paper, some recent wide-format ink-jet printers can print directly on fabric and other types of materials.

Fax Machines and Multifunction Devices

While many people wouldn't automatically think of a *fax machine* as an output device for a computer, it indeed can be. In fact, you can fax from a PC to a fax machine, as well as from PC to PC, fax machine to fax machine, or fax machine to PC. Therefore, a fax machine can act as both an input and output device to a PC, depending on how it is used. When a document is faxed from a fax machine, it is scanned and the image of that document is transmitted over telephone lines to the receiving fax machine or PC (when a document is faxed directly from a PC, it is sent in its already electronic form). The fax machine then prints the document. If the fax is received by a PC, it can be viewed, saved, or printed, just as any other image-based file.

A *multifunction device* (sometimes called a *multifunction printer*) is a device that offers some combination of printing, copying, scanning, and faxing capabilities. Most commonly, these types of devices are based on color ink-jet printer technology, although laser devices are also available. The advantage of using a multifunction device is that it takes up less space and is less expensive than multiple machines. The disadvantages include possibly not being able to find a multifunction device that has exactly the components you would get if you bought them separately, and the risk that when the device breaks down, you will lose all of its functions if the device needs to be repaired off site. Although multifunction devices have traditionally been desktop units used in small offices and home offices, larger workgroup multifunction devices are now available that are designed for multiple users, either as stand-alone stations or as networked units.

MULTIMEDIA OUTPUT DEVICES

Whereas PCs include some multimedia input devices, multimedia output devices are also very common. Most PCs today come with *speakers*, which can be used to output sound from programs and CDs, as well as for *voice output*.

Speakers

Most computer systems sold today come with a set of **speakers** (see Figure 5-31). Speakers provide audio output for such consumer-oriented multimedia applications as playing computer games, listening to audio or video clips on the Internet, listening to background music from a CD, and watching television or a DVD movie in an onscreen window. Common business applications include video and multimedia presentations, as well as videoconferencing and telephony.

>**Speakers.** Output devices that produce sound.

Computer speaker systems resemble their stereo-system counterparts and are available in a wide range of prices. Some speaker systems consist of only a pair of speakers, others include a subwoofer for better bass tones, and still others are capable of surround sound effects. Many speakers have a *headphone jack*, which allows a headphone or headset to be used so the sound won't disturb others (such as in a school computer lab or public library); if not, there is almost always a headphone port on the outside of the system unit (coming from the sound card or integrated sound component). Instead of being stand-alone units, the speakers for some desktop PCs are built directly into, or permanently attached to, the monitor. Portable PCs almost always have their speakers integrated into the device.

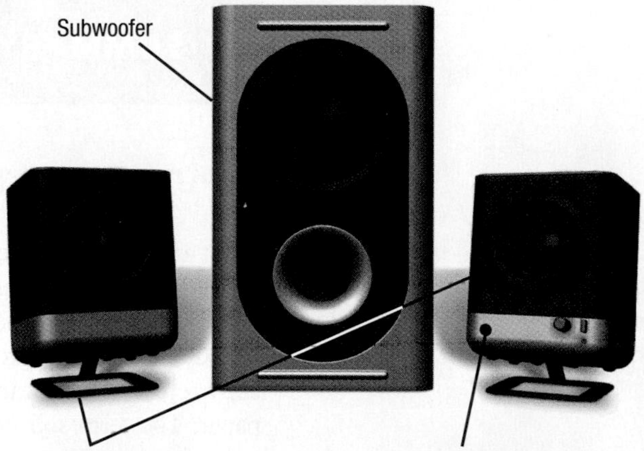

**H
W**

> **FIGURE 5-31**
> **Typical PC speakers.**
> Many speaker systems today come with a subwoofer and a headphone jack.

Voice-Output Systems

For a number of years, computers have been able to communicate with users by imitating human speech. How often have you dialed a phone number only to hear, "We're sorry, the number you are trying to reach, 555-0202, is no longer in service," or "To place an order, press 1," or "Your current balance is $150.59?" **Voice-output systems**, the hardware and software responsible for such automated personalized messages, convert digital data into spoken output. These systems are used extensively by businesses to automate such customer-service functions as relaying information about airline flight departures and arrivals, quoting the current price of stocks, routing telephone calls to the appropriate departments, and conveying current account balances and credit limits.

There are two types of voice-output systems. The first type digitizes voice messages, stores them electronically, and then converts them back to voice messages when the user triggers a playback command, such as with digital answering machines and the *voice mail* systems that answer telephone calls at many businesses. The second type of system produces synthetic speech by storing digital patterns of word sounds and then creating sentences extemporaneously, such as quoting a particular customer's account balance. Many of the systems that rely on synthetic speech have vocabularies of several hundred words and limited abilities to combine words dynamically to form intelligible sentences. As a result, these devices perform best in creating short messages.

>**Voice-output system.** A system that enables a computer to play back or imitate the human voice.

SUMMARY

INPUT AND OUTPUT

Input and output devices enable people and computers to communicate. **Input devices** convert data and program instructions into a form the CPU can process. **Output devices** convert computer-processed information into a form that people can comprehend.

Output devices produce results in either hard-copy or soft-copy form. The term *hard copy* refers to output that has been recorded in a permanent form onto a medium such as paper. The term *soft copy*, in contrast, generally refers to display output, which appears only temporarily. Hard-copy output is the more portable of the two, but it costs more to produce and creates waste.

KEYBOARDS

Most people use a **keyboard** as one of the two main sources of computer input. Keyboards typically include *function keys* and a *numeric keypad*; they may include special multimedia buttons, as well. For users with special needs, there are *ergonomic*, *wireless*, and portable keyboards, among others.

POINTING DEVICES

Pointing devices are hardware devices that move an onscreen *mouse pointer* or similar indicator. The most widely used pointing device is the **mouse**. Some other common pointing devices are the **electronic pen** and the **stylus** (used with special monitors, portable PCs, mobiles devices, and **graphics tablets**), **touch screen**, **joystick**, **trackball**, **pointing stick**, and **touch pad**. Some pen-based computers use **handwriting recognition** technology to recognize handwritten characters.

SCANNERS AND RELATED DEVICES

Source data automation involves collecting data in digital form at its point of origin. Many different input devices can be used for this purpose. A **scanner** allows users to input printed data, such as photographs, drawings, and printed documents, into a computer system. Most scanners are of the **flatbed**, *sheetfed*, *drum*, or **handheld** type. Scanners are often accompanied by **optical character recognition (OCR)** software that enables a computer system to recognize scanned text characters and store them in a form that they can be manipulated. If not, the data is input as an image.

Optical mark readers read specific types of marks on certain forms, such as on testing forms and voter ballots. **Bar-code readers** read **bar codes**, such as the *UPC codes* used to identify products in many retail stores. *Optical character recognition* (*OCR*) *devices* read special printed *optical characters*; *magnetic ink character recognition* (*MICR*) is used by the banking industry to rapidly sort, process, and route checks to the proper banks.

BIOMETRIC INPUT DEVICES

Biometrics is the study of identifying individuals based on a measurable biological characteristic. *Biometric input devices* are used to authenticate people, such as for access control, logging onto secure Web sites, or financial transactions, based on biometric data.

Chapter Objective 4:
Understand what the term "biometrics" means and the purpose of biometric input devices.

MULTIMEDIA INPUT DEVICES

There are several different devices that can be used for multimedia input. **Digital cameras** work much like regular cameras, but record digital images on some type of digital storage medium, instead of on conventional film or videotape. The images can later be transferred to a PC for manipulation or printing, as desired. *Digital still cameras* take still photos; *digital video cameras* consist of *digital camcorders* and *PC cams* are used to capture video images for videoconferencing, video phone calls, or to broadcast via a Web site.

Systems that can be used to capture audio input include **voice-input systems**, which enable computer systems to recognize spoken words. Voice-input technologies offer tremendous work-saving potential, but they are only slowly reaching market acceptance. Musical input can be created on a PC using a *MIDI* device.

Chapter Objective 5:
List several types of multimedia input devices and discuss their purposes.

DISPLAY DEVICES

Display devices or **monitors**—hardware with a television-like viewing screen—are the most common type of output device. Monitors are available in a wide variety of sizes and are generally either **CRT monitors** or **flat-panel displays**. Flat-panel displays generally use *liquid crystal display* (*LCD*) or *gas plasma* technology. The quality of a monitor can be measured by the *dot pitch* or distance between the **pixels** on the screen; the number of pixels on a screen is referred to as the *resolution*.

Smart displays are portable monitors for a desktop PC that wirelessly connect the user to the PC within a distance of about 100 feet. *HDTV* is a new television standard that uses high-resolution, digital broadcasts. HDTV should replace analog TV in the near future. *HDTV monitors* provide a much sharper and clearer image than an analog TV. **Data projectors** connect to a PC and project any output sent to the PC's monitor through the projector onto a wall or projection screen.

Chapter Objective 6:
Describe the characteristics of the output equipment that most users encounter regularly—namely, display devices and printers.

PRINTERS

Printers produce hard-copy output through either *impact* or *non-impact* printing technology. Most printers today form images as matrices of dots, although with many technologies, the dots are too small to be visible. Quality of printers is usually measured in *dots per inch* (*dpi*); speed is typically measured in *pages per minute* (*ppm*).

The most popular printers today for personal use are **laser printers** and **ink-jet printers**. Most laser printers do not print in color, though most ink-jet printers do. *Network printers* today are commonly used in schools and larger businesses. Special purpose printers include **photo** and **bar-code printers**, as well as *portable printers, plotters*, and *wide-format ink-jet printers*.

MULTIMEDIA OUTPUT DEVICES

Output devices used for multimedia applications include **speakers**, to output music or spoken voice, and **voice-output systems**, which enable computer systems to play back or compose spoken messages from digitally stored words, phrases, and sounds.

Chapter Objective 7:
Understand what hardware devices are used for multimedia output.

KEY TERMS

Instructions: Match each key term on the left with the definition on the right that best describes it.

a. code

b. CRT monitor

c. digital camera

d. electronic pen

e. flat-panel display

f. handwriting recognition

g. ink-jet printer

h. input device

i. keyboard

j. laser printer

k. mouse

l. photo printer

m. pixel

n. pointing stick

o. printer

p. scanner

q. smart display

r. speakers

s. touch screen

t. voice-input system

1. _____ A common pointing device that the user slides along a flat surface to move a pointer around the screen and clicks its buttons to make selections.

2. _____ A display device that is touched with the finger to issue commands or otherwise generate input to the connected PC.

3. _____ A display device that projects images onto a display screen using a technology similar to the one used with conventional TVs.

4. _____ An input device containing numerous keys, arranged in a configuration similar to that of a typewriter, that can be used to input letters, numbers, and other symbols.

5. _____ An input device shaped like a pencil eraser that appears in the middle of some notebook computer keyboards and is used as a pointing device.

6. _____ An input device that reads printed text and graphics and transfers them to a computer in digital form.

7. _____ An input device that resembles an ordinary pen.

8. _____ An input device that takes pictures and records them as digital data (instead of film or videotaped) images.

9. _____ A machine-readable code that represents data as a set of bars.

10. _____ An output device designed for printing digital photographs.

11. _____ An output device that produces output on paper.

12. _____ An output device that sprays droplets of ink to produce images on paper.

13. _____ An output device that uses toner powder and technology similar to that of a photocopier to produce images on paper.

14. _____ A piece of hardware that supplies input to a computer.

15. _____ A portable display device that connects wirelessly to its associated system unit.

16. _____ A slim type of display device.

17. _____ A system that enables a computer to recognize the human voice.

18. _____ Output devices that produce sound.

19. _____ The ability of a scanning device to recognize handwritten or typed characters and convert them to electronic form as text, not images.

20. _____ The smallest colorable area in an electronic image, such as a scanned document, digital photograph, or image displayed on a display screen.

REVIEW ACTIVITIES

Answers for the self-quiz appear at the end of the book in the References and Resources Guide.

True/False

SELF-QUIZ

Instructions: Circle **T** if the statement is true or **F** if the statement is false.

T   F   **1.** A keyboard is an example of a pointing device.

T   F   **2.** The function keys on a keyboard are used to more easily input numerical data.

T   F   **3.** UPC is a type of bar code.

T   F   **4.** Consumer kiosks located in retail stores commonly use touch screens for input.

T   F   **5.** An ink-jet printer normally produces a better image than a laser printer.

Completion

Instructions: Supply the missing words to complete the following statements.

6. The term _____ copy generally refers to output that has been recorded on a permanent medium such as paper.

7. The small dots that comprise a screen image or digital photograph are called _____.

8. A(n) _____ can be used to convert flat printed documents, such as a drawing or photograph, into digital form.

9. Handheld and pocket PCs typically use a(n) _____ for input.

10. Portable PCs most always use _____ displays, while many desktop PCs still use the larger, more bulky _____ monitors.

---

1. Select the input device from the numbered list below that best matches each of the following input applications and write the corresponding number in the blank to the left of each application. Note that all input devices will not be used.

EXERCISES

a.   _____ Gaming

b.   _____ Pen-based computing

c.   _____ Consumer kiosk

d.   _____ Dictation

e.   _____ Text-based data entry

f.   _____ Identification via face recognition

1. Digital camera   **5.** Mouse

2. Keyboard   **6.** Microphone

3. Joystick   **7.** Ink-jet printer

4. Stylus   **8.** Touch screen

2. For the following list of computer input and output devices, write the appropriate abbreviation (I or O) to indicate whether each device is used for input (I) or output (O).

   a. Light pen   _____
   b. Graphics tablet   _____
   c. Speaker   _____
   d. Photo printer   _____
   e. Flat-panel display _____

   f. Digital camera _____
   g. Pointing stick _____
   h. Microphone   _____
   i. HDTV monitor _____
   j. Joystick   _____

3. Select the type of printer from the numbered list below that best matches each of the following printing applications and write the corresponding number in the blank to the left of each application. Note that all types of printers will not be used.

   a. _____ To get inexpensive color printouts for a wide variety of documents.
   b. _____ To print a large map.
   c. _____ To print all output for an entire office.
   d. _____ To print receipts for jet-ski rentals at the beach.
   e. _____ To print business letters and reports at home.

   1. Personal laser printer
   2. Network laser printer
   3. Color laser printer
   4. Photo printer

   5. Bar-code printer
   6. Plotter
   7. Ink-jet printer
   8. Portable printer

4. Select the hardware device from the numbered list below that best matches each of the following terms and write the corresponding number in the blank to the left of each term. Note that all devices may not be used and devices may be used more than once.

   a. _____ Dots per inch (dpi)
   b. _____ Megapixel
   c. _____ 800 × 600 resolution
   d. _____ Pages per minute (ppm)

   e. _____ Dot pitch
   f. _____ Flatbed
   g. _____ Drag and drop
   h. _____ Function key

   1. Digital camera
   2. Printer
   3. Monitor
   4. Scanner

   5. Speaker
   6. Mouse
   7. Keyboard
   8. Microphone

5. Why is voice recognition a difficult technology to perfect?

6. If you could select only one type of input device to be used with an Internet appliance (a device to browse the Web and exchange electronic mail) you were marketing to senior citizens, which one would you choose? Why?

7. List one personal or business application that you believe is more appropriate for a dot-matrix printer, instead of another type of printer, and explain why.

PROJECTS

1. **E-Paper** The chapter Trend box discusses electronic paper (e-paper)—an erasable, reusable alternative to traditional paper and ink for computer output. Although currently in its early stages, some experts predict that it will become a viable product for many personal applications in the very near future. Some of the first widespread applications for e-paper include retail signs, shelf labels, and newspapers. The obvious benefit of e-paper is reducing the use of traditional paper and ink and the resources needed to create and dispose of paper and ink. Two disadvantages at the current time are longevity (the medium is not designed to display an image for long periods of time) and expense.

    For this project, research the current state of e-paper. Are there any products available in the U.S.? What products are expected in the near future? When more products become available, do you think businesses or individuals will choose to use these types of products if the only incentive is a cleaner environment? Or will there need to be an economic incentive, such as savings on the cost of paper and ink surpassing the cost of using e-paper? What applications do you think are the most appropriate and exciting for the use of e-paper technology? At the conclusion of your research, prepare a one- to two-page summary of your findings and submit it to your instructor.

2. **New Keyboards** The design and capability of keyboards continue to evolve to meet new user needs. Newer keyboards offer special features such as ergonomic design, Internet buttons, wireless connection, multimedia control buttons, and built-in fingerprint and smart card readers.

    For this project, research the various types of keyboards that are currently for sale. Select at least three different models and identify the special features and cost of each. At the conclusion of your research, prepare a one-page summary of your findings and submit it to your instructor.

3. **Printer Shopping** Printers today have many more features than a few years ago. These features may include improved quality, more memory, photo printing capabilities, digital camera connectivity, built-in flash memory card readers, and faster speed.

    For this project, suppose you are in the market for a new printer, primarily for personal and school applications. Make a list of the most important features needed to meet your needs, and then research printers currently on the market to identify which ones you feel would be the best printer for your needs. Be sure to take into consideration both the price of the printer and the price of consumables (paper, ink cartridge, toner, etc.) in your evaluation process. At the conclusion of your research, prepare a one-page summary of your findings and submit it to your instructor.

4. **Will it Fit?** Many new PCs today come with very large—such as 17-inch or 19-inch—monitors. Although they make output much easier to see, sometimes it may be difficult to get the monitor to fit on your desk.

    For this project, suppose you are in the market for a new PC and you'd like to have at least a 17-inch monitor. By researching ads in the newspaper, manufacturer Web sites, or systems for sale at your local stores, find two 17-inch and two 19-inch CRT monitors made by different manufacturers and determine their physical size (most manufacturers have size and other specifications listed by model on their Web sites). Next, select the desk or table at home that you would use for the PC and measure it. Draw a sketch to scale of the top surface of the desk (bird's-eye view), and then add each monitor to your sketch (drawn to scale) to illustrate how well each one would fit. Are there any significant size differences between the manufacturers you selected? Would you need to eliminate any of these models due to lack of space? Next, find two 17-inch and two 19-inch flat-panel monitors made by different manufacturers and determine their physical size. How much difference is there between these models and the CRT models you tried to fit earlier? Compute the average price of the two 17-inch CRTs and the average price of the two 17-inch flat-panel monitors you selected. Do you think the price difference justifies the convenience of a smaller *footprint* (the amount of room it takes up on the desk)? Prepare a summary of your findings to turn in to your instructor along with your sketches.

5. **Keyboarding Speed Test**   Although voice input and other alternative means of input are emerging, most of the time input is a matter of entering large amounts of data via the keyboard. Proper keyboarding technique and practice can help increase both your speed and accuracy. Keyboarding tests are available online to evaluate your keyboarding ability; keyboarding tutorials are available both online and in software form.

   For this project, find a site (such as Typingtest.com) that offers a free online typing test (often the test requires your browser to have Java compatibility). Take the available typing test to test your keyboarding speed and accuracy. At the conclusion of the test, rate your keyboarding ability and determine whether a keyboarding course or tutor program, or just keyboarding experience, will help bring you up to speed if you do not already keyboard at least 20 correct words per minute (cwpm). Take the test one more time to see if your speed improves now that you are familiar with how the test works. If your speed is fast, but your accuracy is low, take the test one more time, concentrating on accuracy. If you test less than 20 correct words per minute on all tests, use a search site to locate a site with a free typing tutor and evaluate it to see if it would be helpful to increase your speed and accuracy. At the conclusion of this task, prepare a short summary of your experience, including the typing test site used and your best score.

WRITING ABOUT COMPUTERS

6. **Fast and Accurate**   As described in the text, source data automation is the collection of data in digital format, directly from the original source document. The use of special devices for this purpose has resulted in significant cost savings to many organizations.

   For this project, form a group to identify three different organizations or businesses located in your area that use some type of source data automation and research them. For each organization, determine the purpose and devices used and what benefits your group thinks the organization realizes by using this technology. Do the members of your group think that source data automation in general is beneficial to society or is it seen as a threat to future employment? Your group should submit this project to your instructor in the form of a short paper, not more than two pages in length.

7. **All-in-One**   Some printers today are marketed as multifunction devices because they contain capabilities beyond only printing.

   For this project, research current types of multifunction devices available today and what options a buyer has for the type of technology used and the included capabilities. Identify three specific models and contrast them in terms of their cost, capability, functionality, and maintainability. In addition, you should draw some conclusions about the advantages and disadvantages to purchasing a multifunction device for corporate, small business, and personal use. Submit this project to your instructor in the form of a short paper, not more than two pages in length.

8. **Instant Photos** There are a wide variety of digital cameras today—from inexpensive consumer models, to serious replacements for consumer film cameras, to professional-quality cameras.

    For this project, research digital cameras to determine the types, qualities, and price ranges currently available. Select one inexpensive consumer camera, one medium-priced consumer camera, and one professional-quality camera and review their specifications. In addition to quality differences, determine the types of storage available for use with the cameras you select, as well as the options for transferring digital photos from the camera to a PC or printer. Share your findings with the class in the form of a short presentation. The presentation should not exceed 10 minutes and should make use of one or more presentation aids such as the chalkboard, handouts, overhead transparencies, or a computer-based slide presentation (your instructor may provide additional requirements). You may also be asked to submit a summary of the presentation to your instructor.

9. **Assistive Computing** As mentioned in the chapter, there are a variety of *assistive* input and output devices that physically challenged individuals can use to make computing easier and more efficient.

    For this project, form a group to research assistive technology. As a group, select one type of disability, such as being blind, deaf, paraplegic, quadriplegic, or having the use of only one arm or hand. Research the hardware and software options that could be used with a new PC for someone with the selected disability. Make a list of potential limitations of any standard PC hardware and the assistive hardware and software that would be appropriate for this individual to use to overcome the limitation of that hardware. Research each possibility, comparing such factors as ease of use, cost, and availability. As a group, determine the best computer system for your selected hypothetical situation. Share your findings with the class in the form of a short presentation. The presentation should not exceed 10 minutes and should make use of one or more presentation aids such as the chalkboard, handouts, overhead transparencies, or a computer-based slide presentation (your intructor may provide additional requirements). Your group may also be asked to submit a summary of the presentation to your instructor.

10. **The Written Word** The use of computer input and output devices to facilitate written communication has had both positive and negative effects on our ability as humans to perform basic reading and writing tasks. On the positive side, computers can allow us to focus on the content of our communication independent of the final formatting of a document and spelling and grammatical errors, as these tasks can be performed after the document content has been completed. In addition, most computers now have powerful tools for proofreading and formatting that will perform these tasks for you automatically. On the negative side, we as humans may not develop some abilities, or potentially lose our ability to perform some tasks, if we become too dependent on computers for one of our basic forms of communication.

    Select one of the following positions or create one of your own and express your point of view on the subject. Your instructor will indicate whether your response is to be posted to a class bulletin board, discussed in a class chat room, or discussed as an in-class activity. You may also be asked to submit a summary of your position and point of view to your instructor.

    a. These skills are developed and maintained independent of computers and we have nothing to be concerned about. In addition, when voice activation becomes the standard way of communicating with the computer, we will still have nothing to worry about.

    b. We should each take positive steps to maintain our basic writing skills and be careful not to become too dependent on computers for our written communications. It has been long understood that if we do not use a skill, that skill will atrophy.

11. **Biometrics and Personal Privacy** Biometric input devices, such as the use of fingerprint readers, hand geometry readers, or iris scanners, are increasingly being used for security purposes. Common activities that some employees are required to use at work include using a biometric reader to clock in and out of work or to obtain access to locked facilities, a computer, or a computer network. Other uses of biometric technology are more voluntary, such as expedited airport-screening programs used by some frequent travelers. After a background check and entering personal data and a biometric characteristic into a computer database, these programs allow the travelers to speed past the identity checks required of other passengers. While viewed as a time-saving tool by some, other individuals may object to their biometric characteristics being stored in a database for this purpose. Is convenience worth compromising some personal privacy? What about national security? Would you be willing to sign up for a voluntary program, such as the airport-screening system described above or a fingerprint payment system that enabled you to purchase goods and services (automatically charged to your credit card or deducted from your bank account) at retail stores and restaurants using only your fingerprint? Would you work at a job that required you to use a biometric input device on a regular basis? Do you think a national ID card (such as a standard hard-to-forge national driver's license containing a thumbprint or other biometric data) could help prevent terrorist attacks, such as the September 11, 2001 attacks? If so, do you think most Americans would support their use?

For this project, form an opinion of the use of biometric input devices and any potential impact their use may have on personal privacy. Be sure to use the questions mentioned in the previous paragraph when forming your position. Your instructor will indicate whether your response is to be posted to a class bulletin board, discussed in a class chat room, or discussed as an in-class activity. You may also be asked to submit a summary of your position and point of view to your instructor.

STUDENT EDITION LABS

SAM

12. **Student Edition Labs** Reinforce the concepts you have learned in this chapter by working through the "Using Input Devices" and "Peripheral Devices" interactive Student Edition Labs, available online. To access these labs, go to www.course.com/uc10/ch05

If you have a SAM user profile, you have access to even more interactive content. Log in to your SAM account and go to your assignments page to see what your instructor has assigned for this chapter.

MODULE

SOFTWARE

In Chapter 2, we looked at the basic software concepts needed to get a computer system up and running. We continue that focus in this module, discussing in more depth both *system software*—the software used to run a computer—and *application software*—the software that performs the specific tasks that users want to accomplish using a computer.

System software, the subject of Chapter 6, consists of the programs that enable the hardware of a computer system to operate and run application software. Chapter 7 offers a brief introduction to some of the most common types of application software, such as word processing, spreadsheet, database, presentation graphics, and multimedia software.

SOFTWARE

Chapter 6 System Software: Operating Systems and Utilities 219

Overview 222

System Software vs. Application Software 222

The Operating System 223

Operating Systems for Desktop PCs and Servers 232

Operating Systems for Handheld PCs and Mobile Devices 240

Operating Systems for Larger Computers 242

Utility Programs 243

The Future of Operating Systems 251

Chapter 7 Application Software 261

Overview 262

The Basics of Application Software 262

Word Processing Concepts 271

Spreadsheet Concepts 276

Database Concepts 281

Presentation Graphics Concepts 285

Graphics and Multimedia Concepts 288

Other Types of Application Software 297

OUTLINE

Overview
System Software vs. Application Software
The Operating System
  Functions of an Operating System
  Processing Techniques for Increased
   Efficiency
  Differences Among Operating Systems
Operating Systems for Desktop PCs and
  Servers
  DOS
  Windows
  Mac OS
  UNIX
  Linux
  NetWare
  OS/2 and OS/2 Warp
  Solaris
Operating Systems for Handheld PCs and
  Mobile Devices
  Embedded and Mobile Versions of
   Windows
  Palm OS
  Symbian OS
Operating Systems for Larger Computers
Utility Programs
  File Management Programs
  Antivirus Programs
  Diagnostic and Disk Management Programs
  Uninstall Utilities
  File Compression Programs
  Backup and Recovery Utilities
  Encryption Programs
  Network and Internet Utilities
The Future of Operating Systems

System Software: Operating Systems and Utilities

LEARNING OBJECTIVES

After completing this chapter, you will be able to:

1. Understand the difference between system software and application software.

2. Explain the different functions of an operating system and discuss some ways that operating systems can differ from one another.

3. List several ways in which operating systems can enhance processing efficiency.

4. Name today's most widely used operating systems for desktop PCs and servers.

5. State several devices other than desktop PCs and servers that require an operating system and list one possible operating system for each type of device.

6. Describe the role of utility programs and outline several duties that these programs can perform.

7. Speculate about what the operating systems of the future may be like.

System software consists of the programs that control the various parts of a computer system and coordinate them to make the parts work together and run efficiently. These programs perform such tasks as translating your commands into a form the computer can understand, opening and closing application software programs at your request, managing your program and data files, helping to keep your computer running smoothly and efficiently, and getting your application software and hardware to work together, among other things.

Most users aren't aware of all the tasks that system software performs. For example, issuing a command for your PC to store a document on your hard drive requires your PC's system software to first make sure that such a drive exists, then look for adequate space on the disk, then write the document onto this space, and finally update the disk's directory with the filename and disk location so that the document can be retrieved again when needed. Clicking an icon to start an application software program requires your PC's system software to determine which program that icon is associated with and where the program is stored on the hard drive, to verify that the program file exists in that location, and then to launch that program. In addition to managing your local computer, if you are connected to a network then system software may perform such additional tasks as checking the validity of your user ID or password before granting you access to network resources and ensuring that you have permission to access the data or programs you are requesting.

System software is usually divided into two categories: *operating system software* and *utility programs*. After taking a look at the difference between system software and application software, this chapter examines the operating system, the primary component of system software. Here we discuss what operating systems do and explore the most widely used operating systems today. Then we cover utility programs, or *utilities*. Utilities typically perform support functions for the operating system, such as allowing you to manage your files, perform maintenance on your computer, check your PC for viruses, or recover inadvertently erased files. The chapter closes with a look at what the future of operating systems may hold. ■

SYSTEM SOFTWARE VS. APPLICATION SOFTWARE

Computers run two general types of software: system software and application software.

▼ **System software** consists of the "background" programs that allow you to use your computer. These programs enable the computer to start up and run application software, as well as facilitate important jobs such as transferring files from one storage medium to another, configuring your computer system to work with a specific brand of printer or monitor, managing files on your hard drive, and protecting your computer system from unauthorized use.

>**System software.** Programs, such as the operating system, that control the operation of a computer and its devices, as well as enable application software to run on the PC.

▼ **Application software** includes all the programs that allow a user to perform certain specific tasks on a computer, such as writing a letter, preparing an invoice, viewing a Web page, listening to an MP3 file, checking the inventory of a particular product, playing a game, preparing financial statements, and so forth. Application software is discussed in detail in Chapter 7.

In practice, the difference between system and application software is not always clear cut, primarily because system software often contains application software components. For example, the *Microsoft Windows* operating system contains several application software programs, including a Web browser, calculator, painting program, and text editor. A program's classification as system or application software usually depends on the principal function of the program.

THE OPERATING SYSTEM

A computer's **operating system** is a collection of programs that manage and coordinate the activities taking place within the computer system. The operating system boots the computer, launches application software programs, and ensures that all actions requested by a user are valid and processed in an orderly fashion. It also manages the computer system's resources to perform those operations with efficiency and consistency. For example, when you want to finish the letter or research paper you started yesterday, your operating system must perform several different tasks, such as booting up your PC when you turn it on, starting your word processing program when you click that icon, and then working with your word processing program to find and load the document when you issue that command. As you work with the document and the word processor carries out its processing tasks, the operating system acts as a supervisor—monitoring every action to make sure the program doesn't perform an operation, often referred to as an *illegal operation*, that would corrupt other computer-system resources. If that happens, the operating system tries to close the offending application with the least amount of impact on the rest of the system. The operating system is also needed to print the finished document or save it back onto your hard drive, when you issue those commands.

In general, the operating system serves as an intermediary between the user and the computer (see Figure 6-1). The operating system plays a central

> **FIGURE 6-1**
> **The intermediary role of the operating system.** The operating system acts as a middleman between the user and the computer, as well as between application software programs and the computer system's hardware.

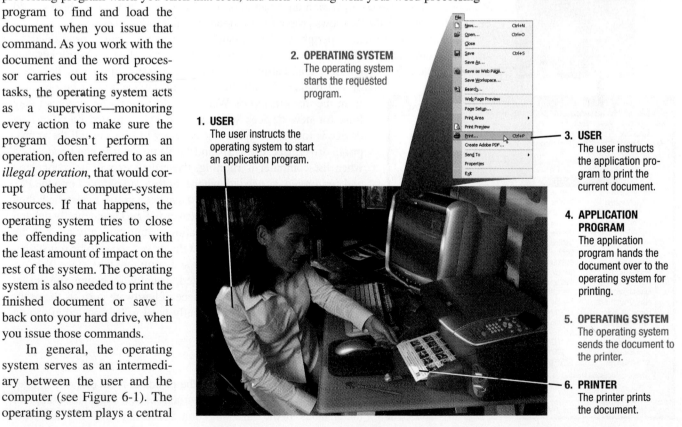

1. USER
The user instructs the operating system to start an application program.

2. OPERATING SYSTEM
The operating system starts the requested program.

3. USER
The user instructs the application program to print the current document.

4. APPLICATION PROGRAM
The application program hands the document over to the operating system for printing.

5. OPERATING SYSTEM
The operating system sends the document to the printer.

6. PRINTER
The printer prints the document.

>**Application software.** Programs that enable users to perform specific tasks on a computer, such as writing a letter or playing a game.
>**Operating system.** The main component of system software that enables the computer to manage its activities and the resources under its control, run application programs, and interface with the user.

role in coordinating all of the computer's work and is the most critical piece of software in the computer. Without an operating system, no other program can run and the computer cannot function. Many of the operating system's actions, however, may go unnoticed by the user because the operating system works in the background much of the time.

Functions of an Operating System

Operating systems have a wide range of functions—some of the most important are discussed next. As we examine these functions and properties, keep in mind that not all of them may apply to the operating system on your PC.

Booting the Computer and Configuring Devices

As discussed in Chapter 2, the first task your operating system performs when your PC is initially turned on is to assist in *booting* the PC. During the boot process, certain parts of the operating system (called the *kernel*) are loaded into memory. The kernel remains in memory the entire time the PC is on so that it is always available; other parts of the operating system are retrieved from the hard drive when they are needed. Before the boot process ends, the operating system determines which hardware devices are connected and properly configured, and it reads an opening batch of instructions. These instructions—which the user can customize to some extent when necessary—assign tasks for the operating system to carry out before the current session begins; for instance, checking for computer viruses or starting up a few programs to continually run in the background. Typically, many tasks are running in the background at any one time, even without application software running (see Figure 6-2). In Windows, the system configuration information is stored in the *registry* files, which should be modified only by the Windows program itself or advanced Windows users.

To communicate with a peripheral device (such as a monitor, printer, or scanner), a small program called a **device driver** (*driver* for short) is used. Most operating systems today include drivers for widely used hardware. In addition, drivers often come on a disk or CD packaged with the peripheral device or can be obtained from the manufacturer's Web site. Most operating systems today look for new devices whenever the PC is turned on. If a new device is found, the operating system will try to install the appropriate driver. Because USB and FireWire devices can be attached when the computer is running, those devices will be recognized and configured, as needed, whenever they are plugged into the PC.

Once a device and its driver have been properly installed, they usually work fine. If the device driver file gets accidentally deleted or becomes corrupted, the operating system typically notifies the user during the boot process that the driver needs to be reinstalled and attempts to install the driver and configure the device. When a device driver becomes corrupted, usually repeating the initial installation procedure for that piece of hardware corrects the problem. Device drivers also frequently need to be updated after you upgrade your operating system.

Interfacing with Users

As Figure 6-1 suggests, one of the principal roles of every operating system is to translate user instructions into a form the computer understands. In the other direction, it translates any feedback from

FIGURE 6-2
Windows Task Manager. Even with no application programs open, many programs and tasks—launched by the operating system or during the boot process—run in the background and continually tie up part of a PC's memory.

Image Name	User Name	CPU	Mem Usage
csrss.exe	SYSTEM	00	3,064 K
ctfmon.exe	Debbie	00	2,508 K
CTNotify.exe	Debbie	00	5,076 K
CTSVCCDA.EXE	SYSTEM	00	1,492 K
devldr32.exe	Debbie	00	4,404 K
DSSAGENT.EXE	Debbie	00	3,020 K
explorer.exe	Debbie	00	17,232 K
LMSXXD.EXE	Debbie	00	1,524 K
lsass.exe	SYSTEM	00	5,532 K
Mediadet.exe	Debbie	00	4,480 K
MsPMSPSv.exe	SYSTEM	00	1,632 K
NAVAPSVC.EXE	SYSTEM	00	2,136 K
NAVAPW32.EXE	Debbie	00	6,028 K
nvsvc32.exe	SYSTEM	00	2,156 K
realsched.exe	Debbie	00	140 K
services.exe	SYSTEM	00	3,320 K
smss.exe	SYSTEM	00	464 K
spoolsv.exe	SYSTEM	00	4,188 K
svchost.exe	SYSTEM	00	2,992 K

Show processes from all users   End Process

Processes: 28   CPU Usage: 0%   Commit Charge: 97M / 1250M

>**Device driver.** A program that enables an operating system to communicate with a specific hardware device.

the hardware—such as a signal that the printer has run out of paper or the scanner is turned off—into a form that the user understands.

Managing and Monitoring Resources and Jobs

As a session begins and you start to request programs and data, the operating system retrieves them from disk and loads them into RAM. Once the operating system opens an application software program, it relinquishes some control to that program. While a program such as a word processor or spreadsheet might accept keystrokes from users or conduct a spelling check on its own, it generally uses the operating system to monitor proper use of storage and availability of hardware. Therefore, the operating system is in charge of managing *system resources* and making them available to devices and programs when they are needed. If a problem occurs—perhaps a program stops functioning or there are too many programs open for the amount of memory available—it will typically notify the user and suggest a solution, such as to close some programs.

Along with assigning system resources, the operating system performs a closely related process: scheduling user jobs to be performed using those resources. *Scheduling routines* in the operating system determine the order in which jobs are processed on the computer system hardware, such as hard drives and printers, as well as which commands get executed first if the user is working with more than one program at a time. An operating system serving multiple users does not necessarily assign jobs on a first-come, first-served basis. For example, some users may have higher priority than others or the devices needed to process the next job in line may not be available—these factors affect how system resources are allocated.

The operating system also schedules operations throughout the computer system so that different parts of the system can work on different portions of the same job at the same time. Because input and output devices work much more slowly than the CPU itself, the CPU may complete billions of calculations for several different programs while a single document is being printed. Using a number of techniques, the operating system juggles the computer's work in order to employ system devices as efficiently as possible. The methods that allow a computer to process a number of jobs at more or less the same time—such as *multitasking* and *multiprocessing*—are discussed in a later section.

File Management

One of the more important tasks of the operating system is *file management*—keeping track of the files stored on a PC so that they can be retrieved when needed. As discussed in Chapter 4, to simplify file management, operating systems organize the files on a disk or hard drive hierarchically into *folders*. Usually the operating system files are stored in one folder and each application software program is stored in its own separate folder. Some folders are created by the operating system during program installation; other folders may be created by the user for storing and organizing files.

Files and folders are usually viewed in a hierarchical format, with the top of the hierarchy for any storage medium being the *root directory* (such as C:\ for the root directory of the hard drive C shown in Figure 6-3). The root directory usually contains both files and folders. To access a file, you generally navigate to the folder where the file you want to work with is stored by opening the appropriate drive, folder, and subfolders. Alternatively, you can type the *path* to a file's exact location. For example, as Figure 6-3 shows, the path

C:\My Documents\Letters\Mary

leads through the root directory of the C drive and the *My Documents* and *Letters* folders to a file named *Mary*. A similar path can also be used to access the files *John* and *Bill*. As discussed in a previous chapter, users specify a filename for each file when they initially save the file on a storage medium; there can be only one file with the exact same filename in any particular folder on a storage medium.

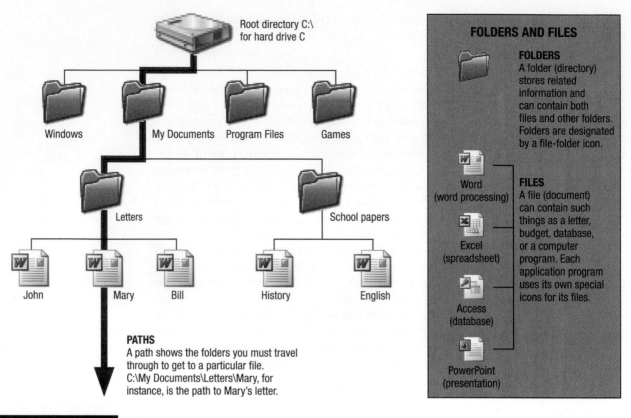

FOLDERS
A folder (directory) stores related information and can contain both files and other folders. Folders are designated by a file-folder icon.

FILES
A file (document) can contain such things as a letter, budget, database, or a computer program. Each application program uses its own special icons for its files.

Word (word processing)

Excel (spreadsheet)

Access (database)

PowerPoint (presentation)

PATHS
A path shows the folders you must travel through to get to a particular file. C:\My Documents\Letters\Mary, for instance, is the path to Mary's letter.

> **FIGURE 6-3**
> **A sample hard drive organization.**

> **FIGURE 6-4**
> **File extensions.**

WIDELY USED FILE EXTENSIONS

DOCUMENTS

.doc .txt .htm .html .xml .mht .mhtml .xls .mdb .ppt .rtf .pdf

PROGRAMS

.com .exe

GRAPHICS

.bmp .tif .jpg .eps .gif .png .pcx .svg

AUDIO

.wav .au .mp3 .snd .aiff .midi .aac .wma

VIDEO

.mpg .mov .avi .mpeg .rm .wmv

COMPRESSED FILES

.zip .sit .sitx .tar

The rules for how files can be named vary with each operating system. For instance, all current versions of Windows support *long filenames*; that is, filenames that are from 1 to 255 characters long and may include numbers, letters, spaces, and any special characters except \ / : * ? " < > and |. Filenames almost always contain a *file extension* at the end of the filename. File extensions are generally three characters preceded by a period and are automatically added to a filename by the program in which that file was created, although sometimes the user may have a choice of file extensions supported by a program. Some common file extensions are listed in Figure 6-4. Using a *file management program*, such as *Windows Explorer*, users can open, move, copy, rename, or delete files, as well as create new folders. However, file extensions shouldn't be changed by the user because the operating system uses them to identify the program with which the document should be opened. For instance, if you give the command in Windows Explorer to open a file named *Letter to Mom.doc*, the document will open it using the Microsoft Word program because *.doc* is the Microsoft Word file extension. Depending on how your PC and file management program are set up, you may or may not be able to see file extensions; they are typically hidden by default, although that setting can be changed by the user. If the file to be opened doesn't have a file extension that your operating system recognizes, the operating system asks you which program should be used to open the file. Using the operating system's file management program and other included utilities are discussed near the end of this chapter.

Security

A computer's operating system can protect against unauthorized access by using *passwords* or other security procedures to prevent outsiders from accessing system resources that they are not authorized to access. Although passwords can be used on individual PCs to prevent unauthorized use or to preserve customized settings (desktop colors, toolbars, menus, organization, and so forth) for multiple users (see Figure 6-5), many home PCs are not password protected. Many office PCs and virtually all networks, however, have restricted access. Network security is a very important topic today and will be discussed in much more detail in later chapters of this book.

Processing Techniques for Increased Efficiency

Operating systems often utilize various processing techniques to operate more efficiently. These techniques usually involve either processing multiple programs at the same time or almost at the same time, or processing one program more quickly. Consequently, these techniques—sometimes referred to as *interleaved processing techniques*—increase system efficiency and the amount of processing the computer system can perform in any given period of time. Some of the techniques most commonly used by operating systems to increase efficiency are discussed in the next few sections.

Multitasking

Multitasking refers to the ability of an operating system to work with more than one program (called a *task*) at one time. For example, this feature would allow a user to edit a spreadsheet file in one program while loading a Web page in a Web browser in another window, or retrieve new e-mail messages while editing a word processing document. Without multitasking ability, an operating system would require the user to close one program before opening another, as is the case with the older *DOS* operating system.

Although multitasking enables multiple programs to be open and used at one time, the CPU can technically only do one thing at a time. Consequently, it rotates between programs, spending a small fraction of time on one program's processing before moving to the next task. Since today's CPUs work very fast, even though the operating system is rotating between processing tasks—executing part of one program, then part of another, and so on—to the user it appears as though all programs are executing at the same time. Virtually all operating systems today are multitasking.

The term *multitasking* is most commonly used in reference to single-user operating systems. Multitasking with a multiuser operating system is usually referred to as *multi-programming*.

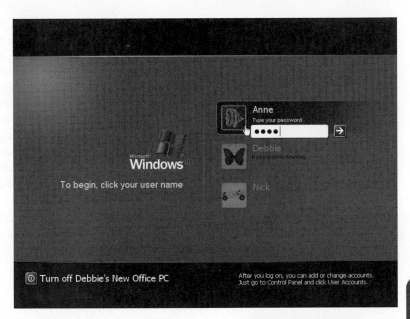

Multithreading

A *thread* is a sequence of instructions within a program that is independent of other threads. Examples might include spell checking, printing, and opening documents in a word processing program. *Multithreading* operating systems have the ability to process multiple threads within a program at one time, without opening multiple occurrences of the program, as long as the program was written to use multiple threads. This type of scheduling is more efficient, and helps speed up processing. Most current operating systems have multithreading capability, in addition to multitasking capability.

Time-Sharing

Time-sharing is a technique that enables multiple programs to share processing on a rotating basis, similar to multitasking. The two techniques differ in the way they allocate processing time, however. A time-sharing computer spends a fixed amount of time on each

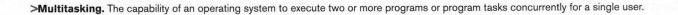

>**Multitasking.** The capability of an operating system to execute two or more programs or program tasks concurrently for a single user.

program and then goes on to another. A multitasking computer works on a program until it encounters a logical stopping point, such as a need to read more data or get other input from the user, before going on to the next program.

Time-sharing techniques are commonly used to allow a single computer system—usually a mainframe—to support numerous users at separate workstations. The operating system cycles through all the active programs in the system that need processing and gives each one a small time slice during each cycle. For example, suppose that users are currently working with 20 programs and the system allocates a time slice of 1 second for each one. In this example, the computer would work on program 1 for 1 second, then on program 2 for 1 second, and so forth. When it finishes working on program 20 for 1 second, it returns to program 1 for another second, program 2 for another second, and so on. Therefore, if 20 programs run concurrently on this system, each program will get 1 second of processing time every 20 seconds for a total of 3 seconds of processing per minute. However, time-sharing systems usually slice processing time in pieces much smaller than this, and the time allocated to each program is not necessarily the same. From a user's perspective, the processing for any one task with a time-sharing system usually appears to be continuous.

Multiprocessing, Parallel Processing, and Coprocessing

As discussed in Chapter 3, **multiprocessing** and **parallel processing** both involve using two or more CPUs in a computer system to perform work more efficiently. The primary difference between these two techniques is that, with multiprocessing, each CPU typically works on a different job; with parallel processing, the processors usually work together to make one job finish sooner. In either case, all CPUs perform tasks *simultaneously* (at precisely the same instant), in contrast with multitasking and multithreading, which use a single CPU processing several programs or tasks *concurrently* (taking turns). Figure 6-6 illustrates the difference between concurrent and simultaneous processing. Multiprocessing and parallel processing are typically not used in personal computer systems; however, they are commonly used with servers and in some high-end desktops, such as the new Apple *Power Mac G5* desktop PC, which utilizes dual G5 processors.

Closely related to multiprocessing is *coprocessing*. Coprocessing utilizes special-purpose processors (called *coprocessors*) to assist the CPU with specialized chores. For example, a *math coprocessor* performs mathematical computations and a *graphics coprocessor* performs high-speed calculations for fast screen graphics display. The number of coprocessors used, whether or not they share memory, and other characteristics vary with the design of the PC.

Memory Management

Another key function of the operating system is optimizing the use of RAM—often referred to as *memory management*. The operating system allocates RAM to programs as needed and then reclaims that memory when the program is closed. With today's memory-intensive programs (Windows XP requires a minimum of 64 MB of RAM, although 128 MB is recommended, and most programs require at least 15 MB additional RAM per program), good memory management can help speed up processing.

One memory-management technique used by some operating systems—**virtual memory**—allows the use of more RAM than is physically installed in the PC. With virtual memory, a portion of the hard drive is treated by the computer system as additional RAM. Programs and data ready for processing are stored in the virtual memory area of the hard drive (sometimes called the *swap file*). There, the contents of virtual memory are divided into either

---

>**Multiprocessing.** The capability of an operating system to use multiple processors simultaneously in a single computer, usually to process multiple jobs at one time faster than could be performed with a single processor. >**Parallel processing.** A processing technique that uses multiple processors simultaneously in a single computer, usually to process a single job as fast as possible. >**Virtual memory.** A memory-management technique that uses hard drive space as an extension to a PC's RAM.

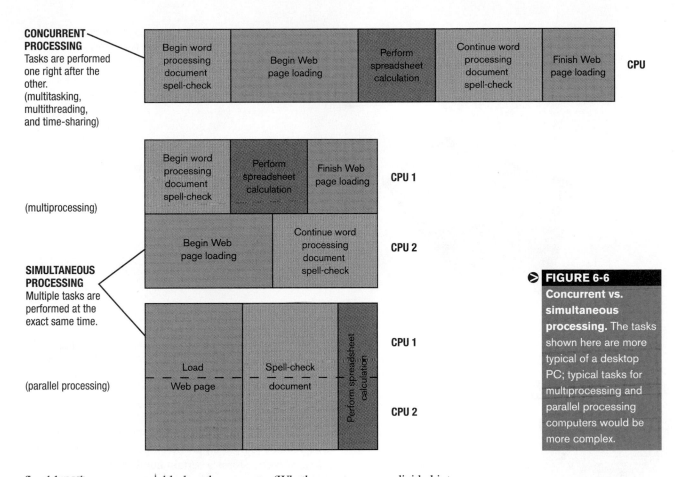

CONCURRENT PROCESSING
Tasks are performed one right after the other. (multitasking, multithreading, and time-sharing)

(multiprocessing)

SIMULTANEOUS PROCESSING
Multiple tasks are performed at the exact same time.

(parallel processing)

> **FIGURE 6-6**
> **Concurrent vs. simultaneous processing.** The tasks shown here are more typical of a desktop PC; typical tasks for multiprocessing and parallel processing computers would be more complex.

fixed-length *pages* or variable-length *segments*. (Whether programs are divided into pages or segments depends on the operating system.) For example, a virtual memory system might break a program requiring 20 MB of storage space into 10 pages of 2 MB each. As the computer executes the program, it stores only some of the pages in actual RAM and the rest in virtual memory. As it requires other pages during program execution, it retrieves them from virtual memory and writes over the pages in RAM that are no longer needed (pages in RAM containing data not yet in virtual memory are copied to virtual memory before they are overwritten in RAM). All pages remain intact in virtual memory as the computer processes the program so, if the computer needs a page that was overwritten in RAM, it can be readily fetched from virtual memory again. This process—sometimes called *swapping* or *paging*—continues until the program finishes executing (see Figure 6-7).

Not all operating systems utilize virtual memory. Although this technique permits a computer system to use more memory than the system would otherwise allow, it can waste a lot of processing time swapping pages or segments in and out of RAM, which might reduce the overall processing efficiency of the computer since data is accessed more slowly from the hard drive than from RAM. Most operating systems that support virtual memory—such as Windows XP—allow the user to specify the total amount of hard drive space to be used for virtual memory.

Buffering and Spooling

Some input and output devices are exceedingly slow, compared to today's CPUs. If the CPU had to wait for these slower devices to finish their work, the computer system would face a horrendous bottleneck. For example, suppose a user just sent a 50-page document to the printer. Assuming the printer can output 10 pages per minute, it would take 5 minutes for the document to finish printing. If the CPU had to wait for the print job to be completed before performing other tasks, the PC would be tied up for 5 minutes.

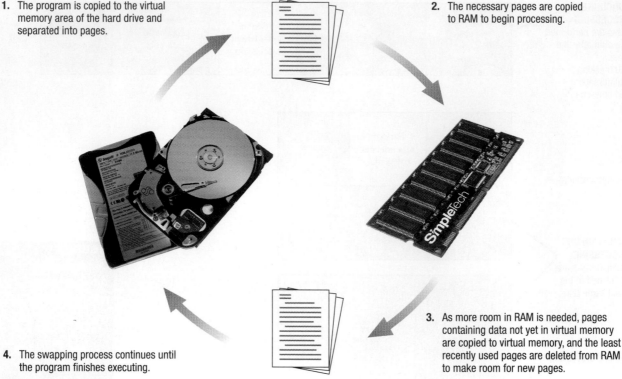

1. The program is copied to the virtual memory area of the hard drive and separated into pages.

2. The necessary pages are copied to RAM to begin processing.

3. As more room in RAM is needed, pages containing data not yet in virtual memory are copied to virtual memory, and the least recently used pages are deleted from RAM to make room for new pages.

4. The swapping process continues until the program finishes executing.

> **FIGURE 6-7**
Virtual memory. With virtual memory, the operating system uses a portion of the hard drive as additional RAM.

> **FIGURE 6-8**
A print queue. Spooling print jobs to a buffer frees up the PC to do other tasks while the documents are being printed.

To avoid this problem, most operating systems use buffering and spooling. A **buffer** is an area in RAM or on the hard drive designated to hold input and output on their way in or out of the system. For instance, a *keyboard buffer* stores a certain number of characters as they are entered on the keyboard, and a *print buffer* stores documents that are waiting to be printed. The process of placing items in a buffer so they can be retrieved by the appropriate device when needed is called **spooling**. The most common use of spooling and buffering is for print jobs. It allows multiple documents to be sent to the printer at one time and they will print, one after the other, in the background while the computer and user are performing other tasks. The documents waiting to be printed are said to be in a *print queue*, which designates the order the documents will be printed. While in the queue, some operating systems allow the order of the documents to be rearranged, as well as the cancellation of a print job (see Figure 6-8).

Differences Among Operating Systems

Because people's needs and preferences vary, there is a wide selection of operating systems available and there are often significant differences among them. Some of the major distinctions between operating systems include the type of user interface utilized, whether the operating system is targeted for personal or network use, and what type of processing and CPU the operating system is designed for.

XEROX Document WorkCentre XD					
Printer Document View Help					
Document Name	Status	Owner	Pages	Size	Submitted
Microsoft Word - Fax Cover Sheet...	Printing ...	Debbie	1	248 KB	10:30:25 AM
Expenses for First Quarter.xls		Debbie	1	68.2 KB	10:32:23 AM
Microsoft Word - FilmW		Debbie	4	347 KB	10:32:25 AM
http://www.microsoft.		Debbie	2	244 KB	10:33:19 AM

Pause
Restart
Cancel
Properties

Cancels the selected docum

>**Buffer.** An area in RAM or on the hard drive designated to hold input and output on their way in or out of the system. >**Spooling.** The process of placing items in a buffer so they can be retrieved by the appropriate device (such as a printer) when needed.

Command Line vs. Graphical User Interface

Most PC operating systems today use a *graphical user interface (GUI)*. The older *DOS* operating systems and some versions of *UNIX* and *Linux*—alternative operating systems to Windows that are discussed shortly—use a *command line interface*, although graphical versions of UNIX and Linux are available. With a command line interface, commands are typed on the keyboard to give instructions to the computer; as explained in Chapter 2, graphical user interfaces allow the user to issue commands by selecting icons, buttons, menu items, and other graphical objects with a mouse or other pointing device (see Figure 6-9). Operating systems for larger computers, such mainframes, tend to use command line interfaces.

COMMAND LINE INTERFACE
Commands are entered using the keyboard.

Personal vs. Network Operating Systems

About 10 or 15 years ago, when PCs were far less powerful than today's machines, most operating systems accommodated either single users or multiple users, but not both. Single-user products (such as DOS) served people working alone on their home or office PCs. Multiple-user products (such as UNIX) served those working on larger computer systems and networks. Today, there are still single-user **personal** (*desktop*) **operating systems** and multiuser **network** (*server*) **operating systems**, but the distinction between these two categories is blurring. Some personal operating systems, such as recent versions of Windows, can be used for home networking and other small networks. In addition, many operating systems—such as Windows, UNIX, Linux, and *Mac OS*—can be purchased in either a personal or server version. These operating systems are discussed in more detail shortly.

GRAPHICAL INTERFACE
Icons, buttons, menus, and other objects can be selected with the mouse to issue commands to the PC.

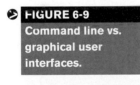

FIGURE 6-9
Command line vs. graphical user interfaces.

Personal operating systems are installed on user PCs; network or server operating systems are installed on network servers. When a network operating system is used, each PC attached to the network still has its own personal operating system installed, just as with a stand-alone PC; it may also need special *client* software to access the network and issue requests to the server. The network operating system—*Novell NetWare*, for example—resides on the server and controls access to network resources, while the personal operating system controls the activity on the local PC. An overview of a typical NetWare scenario is described next and illustrated in Figure 6-10; many other network operating systems work in a manner similar to this example.

When you boot a PC connected to the network, the network typically displays a log-on dialog box. To log on to the network, you must supply an appropriate user name and password. After the operating system accepts and verifies your input, it gives you access rights to the network and you are free to do any network operation within those assigned access rights. Possible operations include reading or writing to files, executing programs, printing documents, and creating or deleting files. With most of these network activities, you are working with a *shared hard drive* (such as on the file server shown in Figure 6-10). Shared hard drives generally act just like another disk drive (such as F or G) on your own computer system. Similarly, network printers are included on your list of available printers whenever you are connected to a network and you open a Print dialog box.

If you ever choose to not work on the network or if the network is down and you have to work locally, you simply do not log on to the network. Assuming you are using a PC, not a network computer without a local hard drive, you can then work just as you would on a stand-alone PC. Keep in mind, however, that you can gain access to a program on the network server, save a document to a network hard drive, or print using a shared printer only after you are able to establish a network connection.

>**Personal operating system.** A type of operating system designed for single users. >**Network operating system.** A type of operating system designed to support multiple users over a network.

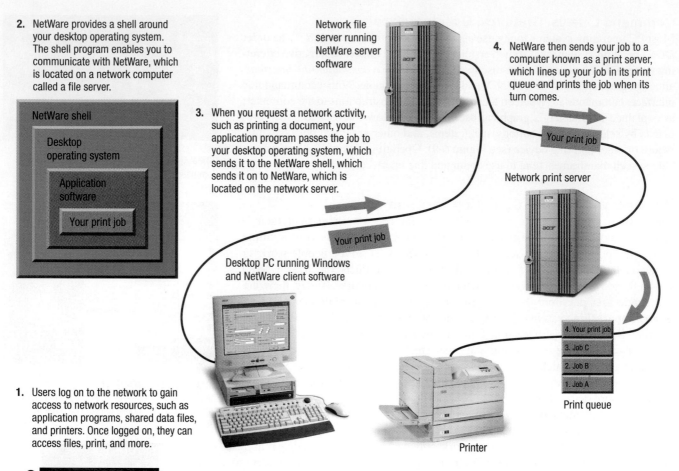

2. NetWare provides a shell around your desktop operating system. The shell program enables you to communicate with NetWare, which is located on a network computer called a file server.

NetWare shell

Desktop operating system

Application software

Your print job

Network file server running NetWare server software

3. When you request a network activity, such as printing a document, your application program passes the job to your desktop operating system, which sends it to the NetWare shell, which sends it on to NetWare, which is located on the network server.

4. NetWare then sends your job to a computer known as a print server, which lines up your job in its print queue and prints the job when its turn comes.

Your print job

Network print server

Your print job

Desktop PC running Windows and NetWare client software

1. Users log on to the network to gain access to network resources, such as application programs, shared data files, and printers. Once logged on, they can access files, print, and more.

4. Your print job
3. Job C
2. Job B
1. Job A

Print queue

Printer

> **FIGURE 6-10**
A network operating system in action. This example uses NetWare; other network operating systems work in a similar manner.

The Types and Numbers of Processors Supported

Most operating systems today are designed to be used with a specific type of processor, such as Intel or AMD CPUs for IBM-compatible PCs; or PowerPC processors for Apple computers. Instead of only supporting one CPU, some operating systems today—particularly those used with servers and some high-end desktop PCs—support two (called *dual-processors*) or more processors. Operating systems are also usually designed for either 32-bit or 64-bit CPUs. As discussed in Chapter 3, the typical desktop PC microprocessor—such as the Intel Pentium 4—is a 32-bit processor; some newer CPUs—such as the Intel Itanium 2 and AMD Opteron—are 64-bit processors.

Because their word size is twice as large, 64-bit processors can process twice as much data per clock cycle as a 32-bit processor and they can address more than 4 GB of RAM. Both of these factors help to speed up processing in some applications, if a 64-bit operating system is being used. Operating systems that support 64-bit chips—such as some versions of Windows, *Solaris*, UNIX, Mac OS, and Linux—often include other architectural improvements that together may result in a more efficient operating system and, consequently, faster operations.

OPERATING SYSTEMS FOR DESKTOP PCS AND SERVERS

As discussed in the previous section, PC operating systems today are usually designed either for desktop PCs (personal operating systems) or network servers (network operating systems) and many new PC operating systems are available in both personal and server versions. Two older operating systems are *DOS* and *UNIX*; more recent operating systems include *Windows*, *Linux*, *Mac OS*, and *NetWare*. The following sections describe these operating systems in greater detail.

DOS

During the 1980s and early 1990s, **DOS (Disk Operating System)** was the dominant operating system for microcomputers. DOS traditionally uses a command line interface, although newer versions of DOS support a menu-driven interface. DOS is not widely used today because it doesn't utilize a graphical user interface and doesn't support modern processors and processing techniques. A sampling of DOS commands is provided in Figure 6-11.

There were two primary forms of DOS: *PC-DOS* and *MS-DOS*. Both were originally developed by Microsoft Corporation, but PC-DOS was created originally for IBM microcomputers, whereas MS-DOS was used with IBM-compatible PCs. PC-DOS is now owned by IBM—the latest version, PC-DOS 2000, works on both IBM PCs and PCs made by other manufacturers. Microsoft still owns MS-DOS, but no longer updates the program; Version 6 was the last Microsoft update. A newer version of DOS, called *DR-DOS* and recently acquired by DeviceLogics, is currently being marketed for use with thin clients and devices that use embedded operating systems.

FIGURE 6-11

DOS. Even though DOS has become technologically obsolete, some PCs still use it. This table lists some of the most commonly used DOS commands, and the screen shows DOS in action.

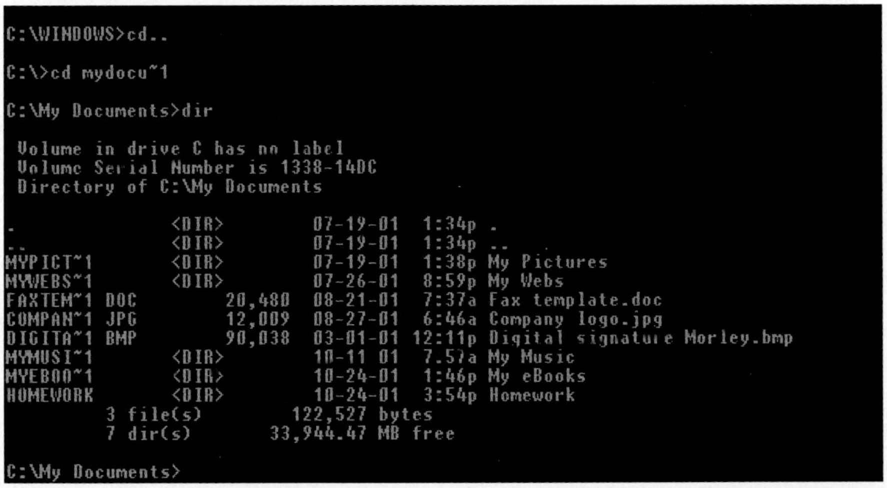

```
C:\WINDOWS>cd..

C:\>cd mydocu~1

C:\My Documents>dir

 Volume in drive C has no label
 Volume Serial Number is 1338-14DC
 Directory of C:\My Documents

.              <DIR>         07-19-01  1:34p .
..             <DIR>         07-19-01  1:34p ..
MYPICT~1       <DIR>         07-19-01  1:38p My Pictures
MYWEBS~1       <DIR>         07-26-01  8:59p My Webs
FAXTEM~1 DOC      20,480     08-21-01  7:37a Fax template.doc
COMPAN~1 JPG      12,009     08-27-01  6:46a Company logo.jpg
DIGITA~1 BMP      90,038     03-01-01 12:11p Digital signature Morley.bmp
MYMUSI~1       <DIR>         10-11-01  7:57a My Music
MYEBOO~1       <DIR>         10-24-01  1:46p My eBooks
HOMEWORK       <DIR>         10-24-01  3:54p Homework
         3 file(s)        122,527 bytes
         7 dir(s)      33,944.47 MB free

C:\My Documents>
```

COMMAND	DESCRIPTION	EXAMPLE	EXPLANATION
COPY	Copies individual files	**COPY BOSS A:WORKER**	Makes a copy of the file BOSS located in the current directory on the current disk and stores it on the disk in the A drive using the filename WORKER.
DIR	Displays the names of files on a disk	**DIR A:**	Displays names of files stored on the disk in the A drive.
DEL	Deletes individual files	**DEL A:DOLLAR**	Deletes the file DOLLAR from the disk in the A drive.
REN	Renames individual files	**REN SAM BILL**	Renames the file SAM located in the current directory on the current disk to BILL.
CD	Changes to a new directory	**CD HOMEWORK**	Changes the current directory to HOMEWORK, located one level down from the current location on the current disk.
FORMAT	Prepares a disk for use, erasing what was there before	**FORMAT A:**	Formats the disk in the A drive.

>**DOS (Disk Operating System).** The operating system designed for and widely used on early IBM and IBM-compatible PCs.

Windows

There have been many different versions of Microsoft's **Windows** operating systems over the last several years. The next few sections chronicle the main developments of the Windows operating system.

Windows 3.x

Microsoft created *Windows 3.x* in an effort to meet the needs of users frustrated by having to learn and use DOS commands. Windows 3.x—the *x* stands for the version number of the software, such as Windows 3.0, 3.1, or 3.11—is an interconnected series of programs that provide a graphical user interface for DOS computers. By replacing the DOS command line with a system of menus, windows, and icons, Windows 3.x was much more user friendly.

Windows 3.x, however, was not a full-fledged operating system. It was instead an *operating environment*—a graphical shell that operated around the DOS operating system—designed to make DOS easier to use. Windows 3.x also allowed DOS to address more than 1 MB of RAM, perform multitasking, and run several built-in utility applications—such as a card file, calendar, and paint program. Still, the shortcomings of DOS limited the effectiveness of Windows 3.x and it is no longer widely used.

Windows 95 and Windows 98

In 1994, Microsoft announced that all versions of Windows after 3.11 would be full-fledged operating systems, not just operating environments. It also announced a new numbering system. Instead of calling the next upgrade Windows 4.0, as many had anticipated, it would number new versions of Windows based on the year of release. So, for instance, *Windows 95* refers to the 1995 version of Windows and *Windows 98* refers to the 1998 version.

Both Windows 95 and 98 used a similar but easier to use GUI than the one in Windows 3.x. Along with an improved interface and performance, Windows 95 and 98 permitted multitasking and long filenames. Improvements in Windows 98 over Windows 95 included a higher degree of Internet integration, more options for customizing the desktop user interface, improved support for large hard drives, and support for both DVD and USB devices. New PCs come with newer versions of Windows, but many older PCs still run Windows 98 (and to a lesser extent, Windows 95).

Windows Me

Windows Me (*Millennium Edition*) replaced Windows 98 as the Windows personal operating system designed for home PCs. Although it supported improved home networking and a shared Internet connection, it was a personal operating system, not a network operating system. In addition to easier home networking, Windows Me featured improved multimedia capabilities, better system protection, a faster boot process, and more Internet-ready activities and games. Windows Me was replaced by *Windows XP*, introduced in 2002.

Windows NT

Windows NT (*New Technology*) was Microsoft's standard network operating system for many years. Windows NT is a multitasking operating system that uses a GUI similar to Windows 95 and Windows 98. The *Workstation* version was geared toward high-end single users, while the *Server* version was designed to run small networks. Windows NT was replaced by *Windows 2000*.

>**Windows.** The primary PC operating system developed by Microsoft Corporation; the most recent version is Windows XP.

>**Windows NT.** An earlier version of the Windows network operating system designed for both high-end single-user and network applications that was replaced by Windows 2000.

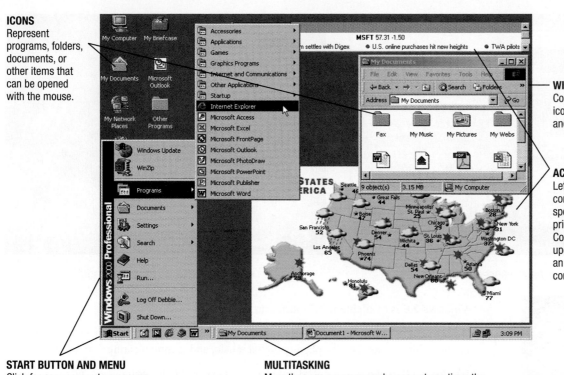

ICONS
Represent programs, folders, documents, or other items that can be opened with the mouse.

WINDOW
Contains programs, icons, documents, and so forth.

ACTIVE DESKTOP
Lets you add active Web content–such as weather, sports news, and stock prices–to your desktop. Content is continually updated when there is an active Internet connection.

START BUTTON AND MENU
Click for easy access to programs.

MULTITASKING
More than one program can be open at one time; the taskbar buttons can be used to switch the active window.

> **FIGURE 6-12**
> **Windows 2000.** The interface used with Microsoft Windows 2000 is similar to the interface used in Windows 95, 98, Me, and NT.

Windows 2000

Windows 2000—the upgrade to Windows NT—was released in 2000. Although primarily a network operating system geared toward business use and server computers, Microsoft did release a *Professional* edition targeted to users working on powerful desktop computers, in addition to its *Server* family of products. Windows 2000 was built using Windows NT technology, instead of the Windows 9x kernel like Windows 95, Windows 98, and Windows Me, making it a more powerful and more stable operating system. Despite the differences in underlying technology, Windows 95, 98, Me, NT, and 2000 all used a similar interface; the Windows 2000 interface is illustrated in Figure 6-12. Although still available at the time of this writing, Windows 2000 was replaced by *Windows XP* and *Windows Server 2003*.

Windows XP

Windows XP is the latest version of Windows and replaces both Windows 2000 (for business use) and Windows Me (for home use). It is based on Windows NT technology and is more stable and powerful than earlier versions of Windows built on the Windows 9x kernel. Windows XP has a new user interface (see Figure 6-13), but the basic elements of Windows (Start menu, taskbar, menu bars, and so forth) are still present. In addition, users have the option of using the classic Windows interface—the one used in Windows 2000, Me, and 98—instead of the new interface, if they prefer. Some of the newest features of Windows XP are related to multimedia and communications, such as improved photo, video, and music editing and sharing; the ability to switch between user accounts without closing open windows; the ability to access a PC remotely via a network; improved networking capabilities; and the use of real-time voice communications and application sharing.

>**Windows 2000.** The upgrade to Windows NT. >**Windows XP.** The latest version of Windows; designed to replace both Windows Me and Windows 2000.

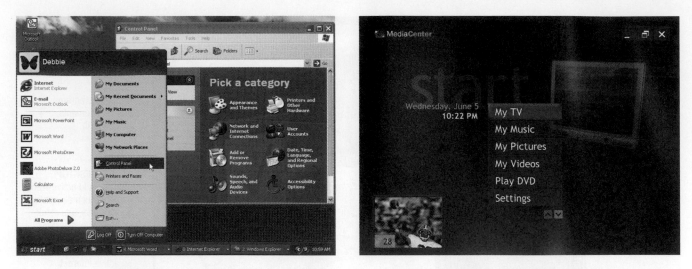

WINDOWS XP PROFESSIONAL   **WINDOWS XP MEDIA CENTER EDITION**

> ⊛ **FIGURE 6-13**
> **Windows XP.**
> Most versions of
> Windows XP look like
> the Professional edi-
> tion (left); Windows XP
> Media Center (right),
> however, has a differ-
> ent appearance.

Windows XP is available in five different versions.

▼ *Windows XP Home Edition*—designed for home PCs. Includes improvements for working with digital photographs, playing digital music, and communicating with others.

▼ *Windows XP Professional*—designed for business users and home users needing
additional capabilities. In addition to the features included in the Home Edition,
Professional has additional premier security and privacy features, advanced recovery
options, improved ability to connect to large networks, the ability to remotely access
one PC from another, and more.

▼ *Windows XP Tablet PC Edition*—designed for use with tablet PCs. Includes
extended pen and speech input capabilities, as well as improved wireless connectivity. This version of Windows is only available already installed on a tablet PC.

▼ *Windows XP Media Center Edition*—designed for living room PCs and other PCs
designated as Windows Media Center PCs. Combines computing, television, and
multimedia capabilities; incorporates additional features for watching live TV,
recording TV shows, watching DVDs, and managing music, video, and photo collections on a PC or TV display. This version of Windows is only available already
installed on a Windows Media Center PC.

▼ *Windows XP 64-Bit Edition*—designed specifically for high-end business PCs using
the 64-bit Itanium 2 processor.

Windows Server 2003

Windows Server 2003 is the most recent version of Windows designed for server use. It
builds on Windows 2000 Server, but strives to make it easier to deploy, manage, and use. It
also incorporates Microsoft .NET applications for connecting information, people, systems, and devices. Windows Server 2003 comes in four versions: *Standard Edition* for
small to medium networks with standard workloads; *Enterprise Edition* for larger, more
mission-critical servers; *Datacenter Edition* for high-level servers requiring the highest
levels of scalability and reliability; and *Web Edition* for dedicated Web servers. Both the
Enterprise and Datacenter editions support 64-bit Itanium-based servers.

>**Windows Server 2003.** The most recent version of Windows designed for server use.

MENU BAR
Allows you to select options from pull-down menus.

WINDOWS
Contain programs, icons, documents, and so forth.

ICONS
Represent programs, folders, documents, or other items that can be opened with the mouse.

> **FIGURE 6-14**
> **Mac OS X Panther.**

USER LIST
Lets you change users without closing your work.

I CHAT AV PROGRAM
Built-in videoconferencing capabilities.

DOCK
Contains commonly used icons.

Mac OS

Mac OS—previously called *Macintosh Operating System*—is the proprietary operating system for computers made by Apple Corporation. The Apple Macintosh, introduced in 1984, set the standard for graphical user interfaces. Many of today's new operating systems follow the trend that the Mac started and, in fact, highly resemble Apple's operating system.

Mac OS has grown with the times, keeping pace with increases in power brought by each new CPU chip and Apple computer model. The latest version of the operating system is **Mac OS X** version 10.3, also known as *Panther* (see Figure 6-14). Like earlier versions of Mac OS X, Panther allows multithreading and multitasking; it also supports dual 64-bit processors, such as in the new Power Mac G5 PC. Mac OS X works almost exclusively on Apple computers and is available in both personal and server versions. The heart of Mac OS is a UNIX-based core operating system, called *Darwin*. UNIX is discussed next.

UNIX

UNIX was originally developed in the late 1960s at AT&T Bell Laboratories as an operating system for midrange servers. UNIX is a multiuser, multitasking operating system. Unlike other operating systems—such as Windows, which is designed for Intel-type chips, or Mac OS, which is designed for PowerPC chips—UNIX is not built around a single family of processors. Computer systems ranging from microcomputers to mainframes can run UNIX, and it can support a variety of devices from different manufacturers. This flexibility gives UNIX an advantage over competing operating systems for many types of applications. But the same features that give UNIX its flexibility make it run more slowly than operating systems tailored around a particular family of microprocessors, which limits the benefits of running UNIX in an environment dominated by one type of PC, such as Windows-based machines. UNIX also requires a higher level of PC knowledge and tends to be harder to install, maintain, and upgrade than most other commonly used operating systems.

Both UNIX itself and licenses to develop and then sub-license new versions of UNIX have been sold many times over the years. Consequently, there are many different operating systems based on UNIX. These operating systems—such as Mac OS and *Linux*, discussed next—are sometimes referred to as *UNIX flavors*. In fact, the term "UNIX," which initially referred to the original operating system, has evolved to be used today to refer to a

---

>**Mac OS.** The operating system for Apple's Macintosh line of computers. >**Mac OS X.** The most recent version of Mac OS. >**UNIX.** A multiuser, multitasking operating system developed in the 1970s for midrange servers and mainframes.

TIP

At the time of this writing, Sun Microsystems had just negotiated deals with Wal-Mart and Office Depot to include Sun's Linux-based *Java Desktop System* on some low-priced desktop and notebook PCs. The system was also being widely received in China and the U.K.

group of similar operating systems based on UNIX. Many UNIX flavors are not compatible with each other, which creates some problems when a program is moved from one system to another running a different flavor of UNIX. A new universal UNIX specification is expected to be used with upcoming versions of UNIX-based operating systems to alleviate this incompatibility problem. Both personal and server versions of UNIX-based operating systems are available.

Linux

Linux is a version of UNIX that has achieved a loyal band of followers since its introduction in 1991. Originally developed by Linus Torvalds when he was a student at the University of Helsinki in Finland, the operating system was released to the public domain as *open source software*. As an open source program, the program's *source code* is available to the public and can be modified to improve it or to customize it to a particular application. Over the years, volunteer programmers from all over the world have collaborated to improve Linux, sharing their modified code with others over the Internet. Some versions of Linux are available as free downloads from the Internet; companies are also permitted to customize Linux and sell it as a retail product. Some of the most widely known commercial versions of Linux are from Red Hat, SCO, and SUSE (recently acquired by Novell).

Although Linux originally used a command line interface, most recent versions of Linux programs use a graphical interface (see Figure 6-15). These interfaces are generally built around either the *KDE* or *GNOME* desktop environments, products of the KDE Internet project and the GNOME project and foundation, respectively. Both organizations are committed to developing free, easy-to-use desktop environments and powerful application frameworks for Linux and other UNIX-like operating systems. Purchased Linux operating systems usually come with more support materials than the versions downloaded for free.

Linux has grown from an operating system used primarily by computer techies who disliked Microsoft to a widely accepted operating system in recent years. There is also an increasing amount of support from mainstream companies, such as Sun, IBM, HP, and Novell. This, combined with the introduction of graphical user interfaces to make it more user-friendly, is expected to increase the acceptance and use of Linux. It has been speculated that the biggest growth of Linux may be at the lower-end desktop, Internet appliance, and point-of-sale terminal use. With the continued improvement and growth of Linux software such as *OpenOffice.org*—a free desktop software suite that is compatible with Microsoft Office documents—some predict Linux will give Windows a run for its money in the desktop market, as well. As discussed in the Inside the Industry box,

> **FIGURE 6-15**
>
> **Linux.** Linux is a rapidly growing alternative to Windows and Mac OS that is available free of charge over the Internet. Purchased versions are also available, such as the one shown here.

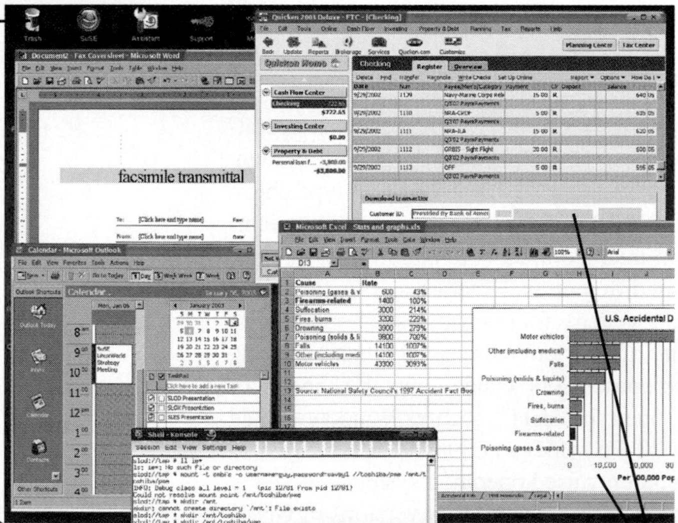

ICONS
Represent programs, folders, documents, or other items that can be opened with the mouse.

MENU BUTTON
Opens the main menu used to start programs.

TOOLBAR
Contains icons that can be used to start programs.

MULTITASKING
Buttons can be used to switch between open windows.

WINDOWS
Contain programs, icons, documents, and so forth.

>**Linux.** A version of UNIX that is available without charge over the Internet and is increasingly being used with PCs, servers, mainframes, and supercomputers.

INSIDE THE INDUSTRY

Linux Desktops: The Wave of the Future?

Although Linux has been around for many years and is now commonly used for business servers and mainframes, it has only recently spread to mainstream desktop PC use. The primary reason companies are switching over to Linux and other open source software is cost. For example, Burlington Coat Factory reported a savings of one-half million dollars due to its recent switch to Linux desktops for its stores.

The move to Linux for desktop PC use is occurring in a wide range of companies, from small retail outfits that need only a limited number of applications to companies employing programmers, engineers, and other technical workers who are already familiar with Linux or UNIX servers. Linux supporters assert that Linux desktops crash less often, are less prone to viruses and other security hazards, and are easy to run on older equipment. One reason for the increased use of Linux for desktop PCs is the recent availability of adequate application software. Using free or low-cost office suites compatible with Microsoft Office documents paired with a Linux-compatible Web browser and e-mail program can enable a business to work competitively while at the same time saving several hundreds of dollars per machine (see the accompanying chart). Although most of these programs do not incorporate as many features as Microsoft Office, many users find them adequate for their needs. Most experts predict that the use of Linux and other open source software will continue to grow.

One possible stumbling block is the intellectual property rights lawsuit filed in March, 2003 against IBM by the SCO Group, the company claiming to own the copyright to UNIX. (At the time of this writing, the rights to UNIX were in dispute since

Novell maintains that they hold the copyright to UNIX.) SCO's lawsuit contends that IBM improperly inserted proprietary UNIX code in the Linux kernel and then donated it to the Linux open source project. The $1 billion suit demands a royalty fee for all copies of Linux distributed by IBM and other vendors. The outcome of the suit is uncertain and complicated by royalty fees being prohibited by the *GNU General Public License* (*GPL*) that governs Linux, so some speculate that the uncertainty may cause some consumers to shy away from Linux for the time being. To prevent this, several countermeasures have been taken by Linux distributors, such as IBM countersuing SCO, Hewlett-Packard offering full indemnity to customers against any SCO-related action by promising to take over the customer's defense and assume liability on their behalf, and Red Hat establishing an Open Source Now Fund to cover legal expenses associated with infringement claims brought against companies developing software under the GPL license.

TYPE OF SOFTWARE	PROGRAM	APPROXIMATE COST
Operating system	Microsoft Windows XP	$200–300
	Linux	Free–$60
Office suite	Microsoft Office 2003	$400–500 ($130–200, Academic edition)
	OpenOffice.org 1.0	Free
	Sun StarOffice 7.0	$75 (Free, Education users)

Cost of Microsoft vs. alternative software.

the growth of new free or low-cost application software programs for Linux PCs has helped make Linux a viable option for business desktop PCs.

NetWare

NetWare—developed by Novell during the mid-1980s—is one of the most widely used operating systems today on PC-based networks. It is a direct competitor with the server versions of Windows. As discussed earlier and illustrated in Figure 6-10, NetWare provides a shell around your personal desktop operating system through which you can interact with network resources, such as a shared hard drive or printer. The latest version of NetWare is *NetWare 6.5*; *NetWare 7.0* is expected to be available sometime in 2004.

>**NetWare.** A widely used operating system for PC-based networks.

FURTHER EXPLORATION

For links to further information about operating systems, go to www.course.com/uc10/ch06

OS/2 and OS/2 Warp

OS/2 is an operating system designed by IBM for high-end PCs. The newest version of OS/2 is called *OS/2 Warp*. OS/2 Warp supports multitasking and multithreading and is capable of running programs written for DOS and Windows, in addition to programs written for OS/2. The *OS/2 Warp Server* version is geared primarily toward server use; a *Client* version can be used with client PCs that will access the OS/2 server. The latest version is *OS/2 Warp 4.0*.

Solaris

Solaris is a UNIX-based operating system developed by Sun Microsystems for Sun computers. The Solaris operating system can run on desktop systems and servers, as well as on some supercomputers. There is also a Solaris operating environment that can be used to bring enhanced stability and functionality to UNIX machines. The latest version of Solaris—*Solaris 9*—is designed for multiprocessing and 64-bit computing, and it can support clustered servers with hundreds of CPUs.

OPERATING SYSTEMS FOR HANDHELD PCS AND MOBILE DEVICES

Handheld PCs, as well as smart phones, pagers, and other mobile devices, usually require a different operating system than a desktop PC requires. Typically the operating system used is one designed for mobile devices in general or is a proprietary operating system designed solely for that specific device. For handheld PCs, the most commonly used operating systems are mobile versions of Windows and the *Palm OS* operating system. Smart phones, pagers, and similar devices may use one of these operating systems or a proprietary operating system designed solely for that device. In many smaller devices, the operating system is embedded into the device using flash RAM chips or similar hardware.

Embedded and Mobile Versions of Windows

There are both embedded and mobile versions of Windows targeted for handheld PCs, smart phones, and other mobile devices. These versions of Windows have some of the look and feel of the larger desktop versions of Windows (see Figure 6-16), and typically support handwriting recognition and Internet activities such as e-mail and Web browsing. Versions of Windows designed for handheld PCs are categorized as either *Windows Embedded* or *Windows Mobile*. In addition to PCs and mobile devices, operating systems are beginning to be embedded in a large variety of objects containing computers or computer components, such as toys, robots, refrigerators, telephones, game boxes, watches, and cars. For a look at some of the features computers built into some *smart cars* can now provide, see the Trend box.

Windows Embedded

Windows Embedded is a family of operating systems based on Windows that is designed for non-personal computer-based devices such as cash registers, ATM machines, thin clients, and consumer electronic devices, as well as some handheld PCs. Two of the most widely used Windows-based embedded operating system are *Windows CE .NET* and *Windows XP Embedded*.

> **FIGURE 6-16**
> **Windows Mobile.**
> Both mobile and embedded versions of Windows resemble desktop versions of Windows, but on a smaller scale. For example, the Windows Mobile screen shown here includes a Start menu and taskbar.

START BUTTON
Opens the Start menu, which contains programs that can be launched, similar to other versions of Windows.

TASKBAR
Contains a system tray, similar to other versions of Windows.

>**Windows Embedded.** A family of operating systems based on Windows and designed for non-personal computer devices, such as cash registers and consumer electronic devices.

TREND

Smart Cars

Computers have been integrated into cars for years to perform such tasks as regulating fuel consumption, controlling emissions, assisting with gear shifting and braking, and more. Lately, however, we are beginning to see and use our cars' onboard computers more than in the past. Essentially, cars are getting smart.

One of the first and still one of the most popular smart features in a car is the navigation system. Some car navigation systems utilize maps and route information on CD or obtained through a call center; newer systems obtain their information via GPS (global positioning system) and the Internet. Internet integration can add tremendous capabilities, such as pairing up travel route data with information about restaurants, hotels, and attractions along the way; it also allows for e-mail exchange, Web browsing, and other online activities.

In addition to navigation systems and Internet access, the newest smart cars offer safety systems such as adaptive cruise control systems that adjust the speed of your vehicle based on the speed of the car in front of you; lane-departure warning systems that use a camera to monitor the car's position in relation to the lane marker and warn the driver if the car begins to drift out of its lane, as well as help drivers adjust speed for negotiating curves (see the accompanying photo); and bumper-based collision warning systems that use sensors to warn you if you get too close to another car or other object. Other computer-based safety systems can also control smart air bags that determine the weight of the occupant and deploy the air bag with the minimum force necessary during a collision, night vision systems that use infrared sensors to project images on the windshield, and rearview cameras that display images of what is behind the car when the car is put into reverse. Another possibility is the use of fingerprint readers to enable keyless ignition and automatic adjustment of the seat position to the driver's specifications. In the future, onboard computers could also be used to automate such tasks as merging and lane changes, as well as to work in conjunction with smart intersections to notify drivers with flashing text or images displayed inside the car, at the intersection, or

Lane departure systems help drivers stay in the proper lane and negotiate upcoming curves.

both that they are approaching a red light or that it is not yet safe to make a turn.

One of the biggest challenges for smart car technologies is the safe use of all the smart gadgets being incorporated into cars. The concern stems from studies consistently showing that distracted drivers are the cause of a huge number of crashes—up to a third of them, according to one study. Voice controlled digital dashboards, cell phones, and other devices help because they are hands-free. Some of the most recent systems allow drivers to activate vehicle features—such as to adjust and use the car's sound system, air conditioning, phone, interior lighting, door locks, windows, and more—via voice commands. For instance, the 2004 Acura TL uses *Bluetooth* wireless networking technology to automatically recognize compatible cell phones; once a phone is recognized, an icon appears on the dashboard and calls can be placed by just speaking a name or number. The navigation system is also voice-operated and recognizes nearly 300 different commands.

Windows Mobile
Windows Mobile is a new name introduced by Microsoft in 2003 for versions of the Windows operating system designed for handheld PCs, smart phones, and other mobile devices.

>**Windows Mobile.** A family of operating systems based on Windows and designed for handheld PCs, smart phones, and other mobile devices.

Windows Mobile designed for Pocket PC handhelds is now referred to as *Windows Mobile software for Pocket PCs*. Windows Mobile designed for smart phones based on Microsoft's Smartphone platform is called *Windows Mobile software for Smartphones*.

Palm OS

Palm OS is the operating system designed for Palm handheld devices. The philosophy behind the Palm OS was to design an operating system specifically for mobile devices, instead of trying to convert an entire desktop operating system into a smaller package. Consequently, Palm OS was designed to use memory and battery power very efficiently. Palm OS is developed by PalmSource, a subsidiary of Palm, Inc. The latest version is *Palm OS 5*.

In addition to being used on Palm handheld PCs, Palm OS has been increasingly used by other manufacturers of handheld PCs, smart phones, and mobile devices, such as Acer, Garmin, Kyocera, Symbol, and Sony (see Figure 6-17). Palm recently acquired one of its biggest rivals—Handspring—and has announced that they will continue to sell Handspring's Visor product. Palm also recently acquired Be, Inc.—the maker of the *BeOS* alternative operating system—and plans to integrate Be's technology into its Palm OS platform.

A SONY CLIÉ HANDHELD PC RUNNING PALM OS

Symbian OS

Symbian OS is one of the leading operating systems for smart phones and it is based on the *EPOC* operating system developed by UK technology company Psion. Symbian OS was initially released in 1998 by the private company Symbian, which was established by Psion and several wireless industry leaders, including Nokia, Ericsson, and Motorola. Symbian OS is an advanced, multithreaded, multitasking operating system that includes support for Web browsing, e-mail, handwriting recognition, synchronization, and a range of other applications designed for mobile communications and computing. Symbian OS has a flexible user interface framework that enables mobile phone manufacturers to develop and customize user interfaces to meet the needs of their customers. A smart phone using Symbian OS Version 6.1 and one possible user interface is shown in Figure 6-17.

OPERATING SYSTEMS FOR LARGER COMPUTERS

Larger computer systems—such as high-end servers, mainframes, and supercomputers—sometimes use operating systems designed solely for that type of system. For instance, IBM's *Z/OS*, *Z/VM*, and *VSE/ESA* operating systems are designed for their various mainframes and many larger Sun computers are powered by the Solaris operating system. Conventional operating systems, such as Windows, UNIX, and Linux, are also used with both mainframes and supercomputers. Linux is increasingly being used with both mainframes and supercomputers; often a group of Linux PCs are linked together to form what is referred to as a *Linux supercluster* supercomputer. Larger computer systems may also use a customized operating system based on a conventional operating system. For example the world's fastest supercomputer—Earth Simulator—uses a UNIX-based operating system called *SUPER-UX* that was developed for NEC supercomputers and many IBM mainframes use *AIX*, a version of UNIX developed by IBM.

A SIEMENS MOBILE PHONE RUNNING SYMBIAN OS

> **FIGURE 6-17**
> Palm OS and
> Symbian OS.

>**Palm OS.** The operating system designed for Palm handheld PCs. >**Symbian OS.** A leading operating system for smart phones.

UTILITY PROGRAMS

A **utility program** is a type of software that performs a specific task, usually related to managing or maintaining the computer system. Utility programs are often built into an operating system. For instance, utility programs for finding files, diagnosing and repairing system problems, cleaning up your hard drive, and backing up files accompany virtually all operating systems. Utilities are also available as stand-alone programs. Stand-alone utilities can be purchased to add new functions not included in your operating system, as well as to replace operating system utilities that don't fully meet your needs. Some of the most commonly used utility programs are discussed next. For a look at how to download and install a utility or any other type of program, see the How it Works box.

File Management Programs

File management programs allow you to perform such file management tasks as formatting a disk; looking at the contents of a storage medium; and copying, moving, deleting, and renaming folders and files. A related task sometimes incorporated into a file management program and sometimes kept as a separate utility is a *search* tool. Searching is used to find files located somewhere on the specified storage medium that meet a particular pattern, such as being in a certain folder, including certain characters in the filename, and/or having a particular modification date. The search functions of some operating systems also include locating people or devices on a network, or finding resources on the Internet.

The primary file management program included with Windows XP is *Windows Explorer*. Common file management tasks using this program are illustrated in Figure 6-18 and summarized next.

Looking at the Contents of a PC

Once a file management program is open, you can look at the files and folders stored on your PC.

▼ To see the files and folders stored on your floppy disk, hard drive, or any other storage medium, click the appropriate letter or name for that medium (some programs or setups may require you to double-click instead of single-click).

▼ To look inside a folder, double-click the folder. To close that folder and go back up one level in the structure, click the Up 🔼 toolbar button.

▼ To open a file in its associated program, double-click it.

▼ To create a new folder in the current location, select *New* and then *Folder* from the File menu, and then enter the name for the new folder while the default name *New Folder* is highlighted.

Copying, Moving, Renaming, and Deleting Files and Folders

To copy or move a file, follow the steps listed next. (To copy or move an entire folder, use the same procedure, but select the folder instead of a file.)

1. Open the drive and folder where the file is located.

2. Select the desired file.

>**Utility program.** A type of software that performs a specific task, usually related to managing or maintaining the computer system.
>**File management program.** A utility program that enables the user to perform file management tasks, such as copying and deleting files.

FIGURE 6-18
Using Windows Explorer.

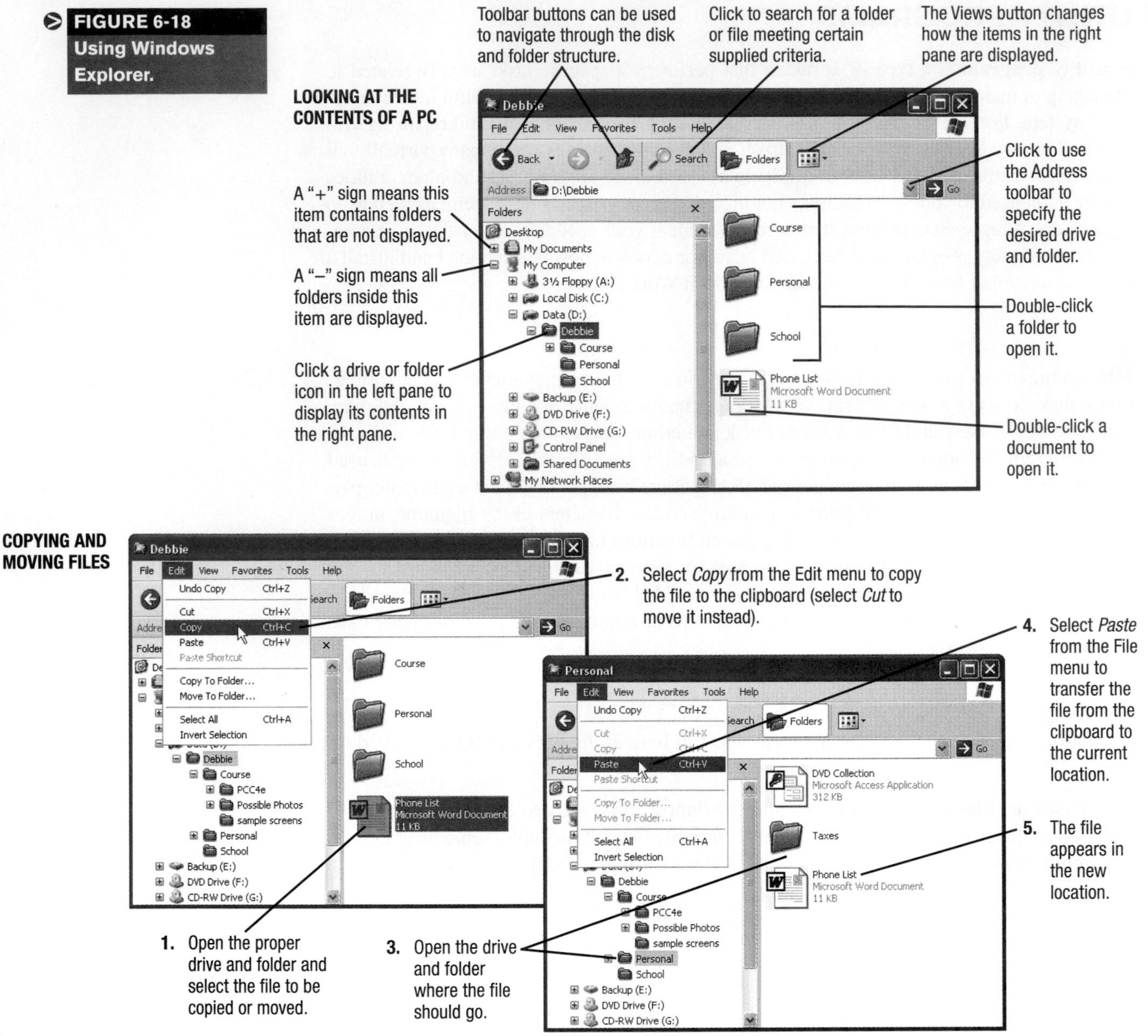

LOOKING AT THE CONTENTS OF A PC

Toolbar buttons can be used to navigate through the disk and folder structure.

Click to search for a folder or file meeting certain supplied criteria.

The Views button changes how the items in the right pane are displayed.

A "+" sign means this item contains folders that are not displayed.

A "−" sign means all folders inside this item are displayed.

Click a drive or folder icon in the left pane to display its contents in the right pane.

Click to use the Address toolbar to specify the desired drive and folder.

Double-click a folder to open it.

Double-click a document to open it.

COPYING AND MOVING FILES

2. Select *Copy* from the Edit menu to copy the file to the clipboard (select *Cut* to move it instead).

4. Select *Paste* from the File menu to transfer the file from the clipboard to the current location.

5. The file appears in the new location.

1. Open the proper drive and folder and select the file to be copied or moved.

3. Open the drive and folder where the file should go.

3. Select *Copy* from the Edit menu (see Figure 6-18) to copy the file to a temporary storage area called the *clipboard*. (If you want to move the file instead of copying it, select *Cut* instead of *Copy*).

4. Open the drive and folder where you want the file to go, and then select *Paste* from the Edit menu to transfer the item from the clipboard to the new location.

To change the name of a file or folder:

1. Open the drive and folder where the item to be renamed is located.

2. Select the item you want to rename.

3. Choose *Rename* from the Edit menu, or click a second time on the filename or folder name.

4. When the name is highlighted, either type the new file or folder name or click the highlighted name to display an insertion point, and then edit the name.

TIP

To retrieve a file or folder accidentally deleted from your PC's hard drive, open your PC's *Recycle Bin* and *restore* the file to its original location. (Files and folders deleted from a removable disk cannot be restored in this manner.)

HOW IT WORKS

Downloading and Installing Programs

Many software programs are available to download via the Web. To download a program, generally a hyperlink is clicked and then the file is downloaded to your PC in the location that you specified (see Step 1 of the accompanying illustration). To install a downloaded file, locate the file on your hard drive and open it; to install a program from a CD instead, insert the CD and the installation process usually starts automatically. With some installations, you can specify the location in which the program will be installed on your PC. Many installations require that you accept the terms of a license agreement before the program will be installed; some also require you to type in the *CD key code* printed on the CD jewel case or product documentation. Once the installation process has been completed, the program can be launched.

STEP 1: DOWNLOADING THE PROGRAM

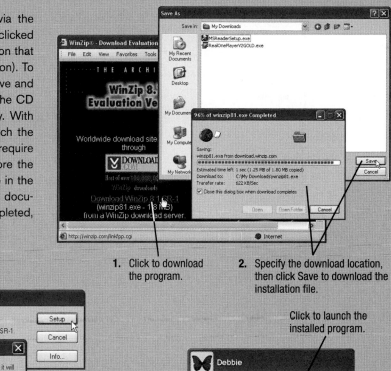

1. Click to download the program.

2. Specify the download location, then click Save to download the installation file.

STEP 2: INSTALLING THE PROGRAM

1. Double-click to launch the installation program.

2. Specify the desired installation location, then click OK.

3. You will often have to agree to the terms on a license agreement before installation will take place.

Click to launch the installed program.

STEP 3: USING THE INSTALLED PROGRAM

To delete a file or folder:

1. Open the drive and folder where the item to be deleted is located.

2. Select the item you want to delete, and then press the Delete key on the keyboard.

3. At the Confirm File/Folder Delete dialog box, select *Yes* to delete the file or folder. (Deleting a folder will delete all the files and folders contained within the folder being deleted. To cancel the deletion of a file or folder, select *No* at the Confirm File/Folder Delete dialog box.)

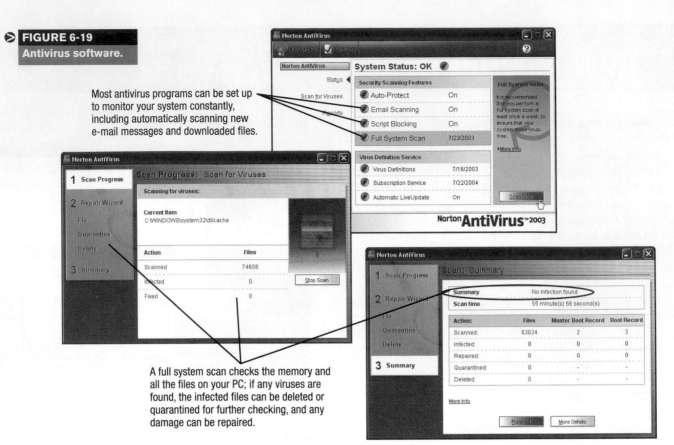

FIGURE 6-19
Antivirus software.

Most antivirus programs can be set up to monitor your system constantly, including automatically scanning new e-mail messages and downloaded files.

A full system scan checks the memory and all the files on your PC; if any viruses are found, the infected files can be deleted or quarantined for further checking, and any damage can be repaired.

Antivirus Programs

A **computer virus** is a software program that is designed to cause damage to the computer system or perform some other malicious act. At best, a computer virus is annoying; at worst, it destroys your data or harms your PC. As will be discussed in more detail in Chapter 8, today's computer viruses are most often spread via the Internet. Protecting your PC against computer viruses is the role of **antivirus programs.** To be effective, antivirus programs should be set up to run continuously whenever your computer is on and to periodically run a complete scan of your PC. Antivirus software can protect against getting a virus in the first place (by checking files and e-mail messages being downloaded to your PC before they are stored on your PC), as well as detect and remove any viruses that may find their way onto your PC (see Figure 6-19). If a known virus is found, the program can remove it and try to repair any files that the virus damaged. Because new viruses are introduced all the time, virtually all antivirus programs have regular updates available through the software company's Web site. Many programs come with a year of free updates; additional years can be purchased after that.

Diagnostic and Disk Management Programs

Diagnostic programs evaluate your system, looking for problems and making recommendations for fixing any errors that are discovered. *Disk management programs* diagnose and repair programs related to your hard drive. Diagnostic and disk management utilities can perform such tasks as checking the Windows registry for errors, cleaning out extra system files that are no longer needed, checking your hard drive for errors, recovering damaged or

---

>Computer virus. A software program, installed without the user's knowledge, designed to alter the way a computer operates or to cause harm to the system. **>Antivirus program.** Software used to detect and eliminate computer viruses.

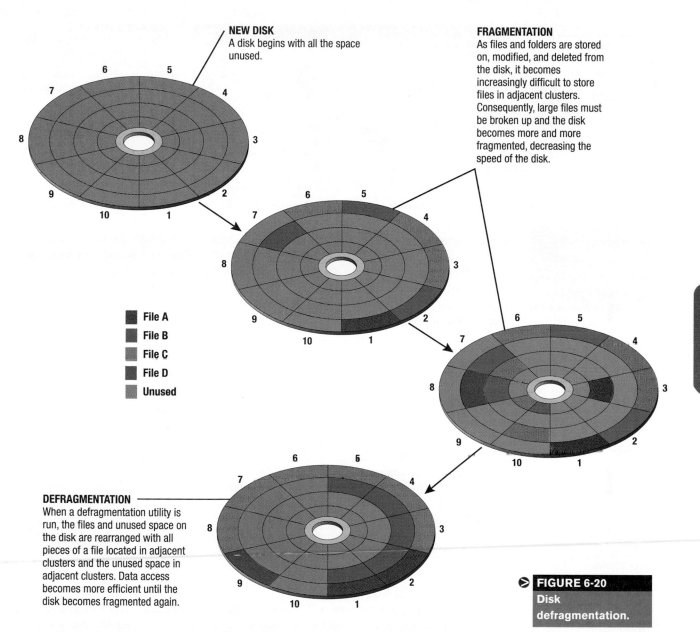

NEW DISK
A disk begins with all the space unused.

FRAGMENTATION
As files and folders are stored on, modified, and deleted from the disk, it becomes increasingly difficult to store files in adjacent clusters. Consequently, large files must be broken up and the disk becomes more and more fragmented, decreasing the speed of the disk.

- ■ File A
- ■ File B
- ■ File C
- ■ File D
- ■ Unused

DEFRAGMENTATION
When a defragmentation utility is run, the files and unused space on the disk are rearranged with all pieces of a file located in adjacent clusters and the unused space in adjacent clusters. Data access becomes more efficient until the disk becomes fragmented again.

> **FIGURE 6-20**
Disk defragmentation.

erased files, and optimizing your hard drive so it works more efficiently. Some examples of these types of programs included in Windows XP are *Disk Cleanup* and *Disk Defragmentor*.

Disk Defragmentor is a special type of disk management utility called a *disk defragmentation* or *disk optimizer* program—a program that rearranges the data on a hard drive so that it can be accessed faster. As files are retrieved from a hard drive, modified, and resaved, they often become *fragmented*; that is, stored in non-contiguous (non-adjacent) clusters on the hard drive. When this happens, it takes longer to retrieve and save the file; when a hard drive becomes highly fragmented, overall performance can suffer. A disk defragmentation utility rearranges the files and free space on the hard drive so that all files are stored in contiguous locations and free space is consolidated into a single block (see Figure 6-20).

Uninstall Utilities

When programs are *uninstalled* (removed from the hard drive), small pieces of the programs can be left behind on the hard drive or in system files. If programs are removed by deleting the program's folder without using an *uninstall utility* (not the recommended method for removing programs), a huge amount of extraneous data can accumulate on the hard drive over time. Uninstall utilities remove the programs themselves, along with all references to

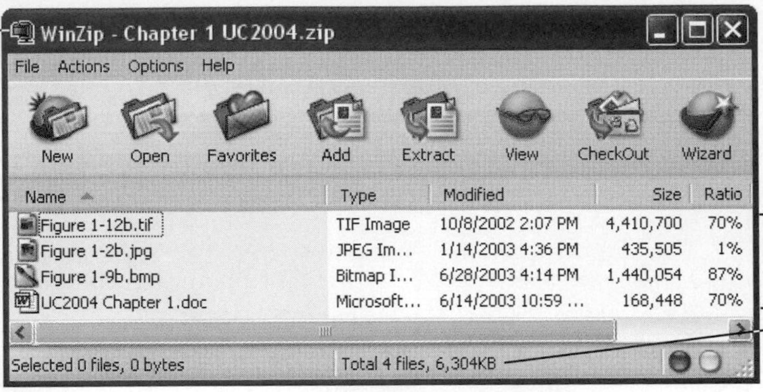

ZIP FILE
This single *.zip* file, called "Chapter 1 UC2004.zip," will be stored at the location specified when the files were zipped.

COMPRESSION RATIOS
Certain file formats (such as *.bmp*) compress more than others (such as *.jpg*, which is already in a compressed format). Text files (such as *.doc*) fall somewhere in between.

FILE SIZE
The 4 files, totaling over 6 MB, are zipped into a single 2 MB *.zip* file.

> **FIGURE 6-21**
> **File compression.**
> File compression can be used with both image and text files.

those programs in your system files. Some uninstall capabilities are built into most operating systems, uninstall utility programs are available as stand-alone programs, and sometimes an uninstall option is included in a program's folder when that program is originally installed.

Occasionally, uninstall utilities can remove files that are also used by other programs remaining on your system. Be cautious when uninstalling programs; if an uninstall utility asks you whether to keep or delete a system file (such as a *.dll* file), it is always safer to keep it.

File Compression Programs

File compression programs make files smaller so they can be stored in a smaller amount of storage space. This helps to free up disk space when archiving files, as well as to speed up transmission when the file is sent over the Internet. The most common format for user-compressed files in the Windows environment is the *.zip* format, created by file compression programs such as the *WinZip* program shown in Figure 6-21. (Mac users typically use *StuffIt* or a similar program instead.) A file compression program is required to both compress (*zip*) and decompress (*unzip*) files, unless the zipped file is made *executable*. Executable zipped files have the extension *.exe* and decompress automatically when they are opened, even if the appropriate file compression program isn't installed on the recipient's PC. Typically, file compression programs can compress either single or multiple files into a single compressed file. When multiple files are compressed, they are separated back into individual files when the file is decompressed.

Backup and Recovery Utilities

Virtually every computer veteran will warn you that, sooner or later, you will lose some critical files. Maybe a storm will knock down power lines, causing your electricity to go out and shutting off your PC—erasing the document that you haven't saved yet. Perhaps your PC will stop working in the middle of finishing that term paper that's due tomorrow. Or, more likely, you'll accidentally delete or overwrite an important file or the file just won't open properly anymore. And don't forget major disasters—a fire or flood can completely destroy your PC and everything that is stored on it.

Creating a **backup** means making a duplicate copy of important files so that when a problem occurs, you can restore those files using the backup copy. Theoretically, you can back up any file on your computer system, but generally users are most concerned about backing up data files. Depending on their size, backup data can be placed on a floppy disk, recordable or rewritable CD or DVD disc, second hard drive, or virtually any other storage medium. Good backup procedures can help protect against data loss.

>**Backup.** A duplicate copy of data or other computer contents in case the original version is destroyed.

It is essential for all businesses to have backup procedures in place to back up either all data files or all data files that have changed since the last backup. Backups for businesses should occur on a frequent, regular basis—such as every night—and a rotating collection of backup media should be used so it is possible to go back beyond the previous day's backup, if needed. Individuals, however, tend to back up in a less formal manner. Personal backups can be as simple as copying an important document to a floppy disk or e-mailing that document to a second PC you have access to, or as comprehensive as backing up the entire contents of your PC. You can perform backups by manually copying files using your file management program, but there are *backup utility* programs that make the backup process easier. Stand-alone backup programs are available; most operating systems have some sort of backup capabilities, as well, such as the Windows Backup program shown in Figure 6-22. Using the Internet for backup is becoming another viable option, especially for storing duplicates of important selected files.

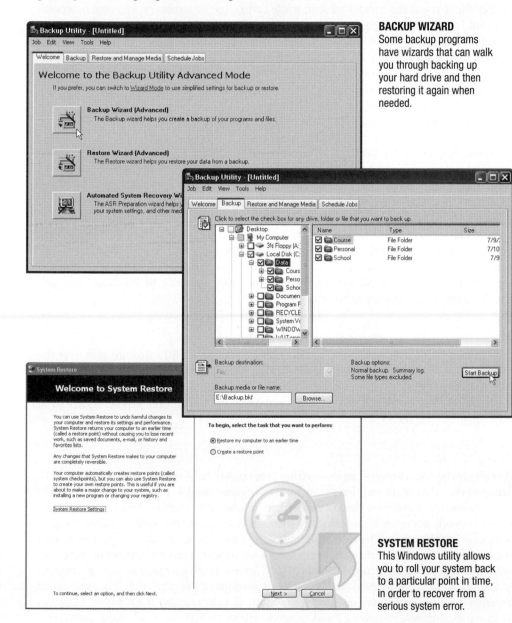

BACKUP WIZARD
Some backup programs have wizards that can walk you through backing up your hard drive and then restoring it again when needed.

MANUAL BACKUP
Many backup programs allow you to select just the files you want backed up. In this example, just the checked folders will be backed up to a CD+RW disc in the E drive.

SYSTEM RESTORE
This Windows utility allows you to roll your system back to a particular point in time, in order to recover from a serious system error.

FIGURE 6-22
Backup and recovery utilities. Most backup utilities, such as the Windows Backup program shown here, allow you to back up an entire hard drive or just specific folders and files; Windows XP also includes a System Restore utility.

S
W

Backup programs can typically back up the files you specify on demand or can be set up to back up specified files on a regular basis (such as every Friday night). Many backup programs can also create a backup of your entire PC once all programs have been installed and the PC is configured correctly. You can use this backup to restore your system to that configuration quickly if something goes wrong with your PC at a later time, which saves you the time and bother of having to reinstall all your programs and settings manually. Once your entire system has been backed up, you can just back up data from that point on, unless you make enough major changes to your system to warrant a new full system backup. To protect against fires and other natural disasters, backup media should be stored in a different physical location than your PC or inside a fire-resistant safe.

For a quick backup before editing a document, you can use the *Save As* option of the program's File menu to make a duplicate copy of the file onto your hard drive. Although this backup won't be any help in case of fire or system failure, it can be used to restore the original file if you make a major mistake while editing the document or for some other reason would prefer to start again with the original document. When editing a document, it is a good idea to save it to your hard drive every few minutes, in case of a power failure or a problem with the program you are using that causes that program to close. Most Windows programs allow you to use the quick Ctrl+S keyboard shortcut to save a document under its current name. Performed using the left hand, users can save documents in just a split second with that key combination. Many application software programs also have an *auto backup* option that can save the current version of an open document at regular intervals, so that the last saved version can be retrieved following a power failure or if the program shuts down unexpectedly. While the auto backup feature is helpful, you should not rely on this feature but rather should save your documents deliberately on a regular basis as you are modifying them.

Recovery utilities are designed to help you recover from a major computer problem—for example, if your operating system stops functioning. One recovery feature included in Windows XP is *System Restore*, which lets you roll back the contents of your hard drive to a particular date and time. Although any programs added to your hard drive since that date would need to be reinstalled, this utility doesn't affect your data files and is helpful if you accidentally delete a critical system file or a program or piece of hardware you just installed causes your system to become unstable.

Encryption Programs

Encryption programs are used to secure e-mail messages and files that are sent over the Internet or other networks so they cannot be read if they are intercepted during transmission. Individual files can also be encrypted before they are stored on a hard drive so they will be unreadable if opened by an unauthorized person. Encryption will be discussed in more detail in Chapter 15.

Network and Internet Utilities

Virtually all business servers use some utility programs to help monitor or increase the efficiency of the network, in addition to any utility programs used to manage the server. There are *performance monitors* to keep track of network activity, such as the amount of room left on network storage media, how much memory is free, and how response time changes as more network users try to access the same resources. There are also *logging programs* that keep track of all attempts of network access for security reasons; reviewing these logs could indicate an attempt from outsiders to gain access to the network, as well as attempts by authorized network users to access restricted portions of the networks. Programs called *directory services* or *identity management programs* help manage the network *identities* (such as user names, passwords, and network access rights) for employees, customers, partners, suppliers, and others who are allowed to access the company network.

TIP

To make backing up your data easier, as well as to protect your data if the hard drive containing your operating system and program crashes, consider using a second hard drive just for data. Your system can be rolled back or your operating system can be reinstalled without jeopardizing your data, and the data hard drive can be moved to a new PC, if a major PC problem occurs.

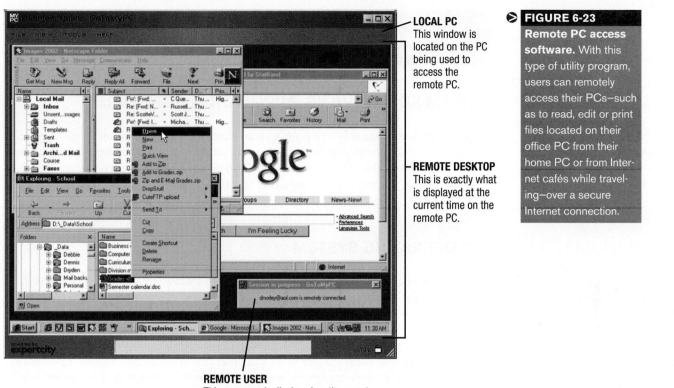

LOCAL PC
This window is located on the PC being used to access the remote PC.

REMOTE DESKTOP
This is exactly what is displayed at the current time on the remote PC.

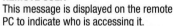
REMOTE USER
This message is displayed on the remote PC to indicate who is accessing it.

> **FIGURE 6-23**
> **Remote PC access software.** With this type of utility program, users can remotely access their PCs—such as to read, edit or print files located on their office PC from their home PC or from Internet cafés while traveling—over a secure Internet connection.

There are also a variety of utilities for assisting with Internet tasks. For instance, *firewall programs* help to protect your PC against unauthorized access while it is connected to the Internet, and *antispam* and *e-mail filtering programs* help to stop and filter out unsolicited e-mail messages. Other Internet utility programs can delete the temporary files generated by Internet activity, suppress annoying pop-up ads, or help you fill out online forms. New programs that allow users—after supplying the proper name and password—to access and use their PCs from remote locations (see Figure 6-23) are also becoming more popular, along with similar programs that allow the files on two or more PCs to be automatically synchronized at all times, using the computers' Internet connections.

> **FURTHER EXPLORATION**
>
> For links to further information about utility programs, go to www.course.com/uc10/ch06

THE FUTURE OF OPERATING SYSTEMS

The future configuration of operating systems is anyone's guess, but it is expected that they will continue to become more user-friendly and, eventually, be driven primarily by a voice interface. Operating systems are also likely to continue to become more stable and self-healing, repairing or restoring system files as needed, and to support multiple processors and other technological improvements.

With the pervasiveness of the Internet, operating systems in the future may be used primarily to access software available through the Internet or other networks, instead of accessing software on the local device. Improvements will almost certainly continue to be made in the areas of synchronizing and coordinating data and activities between a person's various computing and communications devices, such as his or her desktop PC, handheld PC, and smart phone.

SUMMARY

SYSTEM SOFTWARE VS. APPLICATION SOFTWARE

Chapter Objective 1:
Understand the difference between system software and application software.

System software consists of the programs that coordinate the activities of a computer system. The basic role of system software is to act as a mediator between **application software** (programs that allow a user to perform specific tasks on a computer, such as word processing, playing a game, preparing taxes, browsing the Web, etc.) and the computer system's hardware, as well as between the PC and the user.

THE OPERATING SYSTEM

Chapter Objective 2:
Explain the different functions of an operating system and some ways that operating systems can differ from one another.

A computer's **operating system** is the primary system software program that manages the computer system's resources and interfaces with the user. The functions of the operating system include booting the computer, configuring devices and **device drivers**, communicating with the user, managing and monitoring computer resources, file management, and security. To manage the enormous collection of files typically found on a PC's hard drive, file management programs allow the user to organize files hierarchically into folders. To access a file in any directory, the user can specify the *path* to the file; the path depicts the drive and folders in which the file is located.

Some of the differences between operating systems center around the type of interface used, whether it is a **personal operating system** designed for individual users or a **network operating system** designed for multiple users, and the types and numbers of processors supported.

Chapter Objective 3:
List several ways in which operating systems can enhance processing efficiency.

A variety of processing techniques can be built into operating systems to help enhance processing efficiency. **Multitasking** allows concurrent execution of two or more programs for a single user; *time-sharing* is a technique in which the operating system cycles through all active programs (usually belonging to multiple users) that are currently running on the system and need processing, giving a small slice of time on each cycle to each one; and **multiprocessing** and **parallel processing** involve using two or more CPUs to perform work at the same time. Operating systems can use **virtual memory** to extend conventional memory by using a portion of the hard drive, and **spooling** frees up the CPU from time-consuming interaction with I/O devices such as printers by storing input and output on the way in or out of the system in a **buffer**.

OPERATING SYSTEMS FOR DESKTOP PCS AND SERVERS

Chapter Objective 4:
Name today's most widely used operating systems for desktop PCs and servers.

One of the original operating systems for PCs was **DOS (Disk Operating System)**, which is still in existence, but not widely used. Most desktop PCs today run a version of **Windows**. The older *Windows 3.x*, an *operating environment*, added a GUI shell to DOS that replaced its command line interface with a system of menus, icons, and screen boxes called *windows*. *Windows 95*, *Windows 98*, and *Windows Me*—all successors to Windows 3.x—included an increasing number of enhancements, such as multitasking, a better user interface, and more Internet, multimedia, and communications functions. **Windows NT** and its successor **Windows 2000** are primarily network operating systems that can also be used with powerful desktop PCs. The most recent versions of Windows are **Windows XP** and **Windows Server 2003**.

Mac OS X is the most recent version of **Mac OS**, the operating system used on Apple computers. **UNIX** is a flexible, general-purpose network operating system that works on mainframes, midrange computers, PCs that act as network servers, graphics workstations, and even desktop PCs. A version of UNIX called **Linux** has gathered popularity because it is distributed free over the Internet and can be used as an alternative to Windows and Mac OS. Linux has earned support as a mainstream operating system in recent years and is being used in computer systems of all sizes, from desktop PCs to supercomputers. **NetWare** is an operating system specifically designed to manage the activities of server computers on local area networks (LANs), *OS/2 Warp* is an operating system designed by IBM for some high-end PCs, and *Solaris* is used on Sun computers.

OPERATING SYSTEMS FOR HANDHELD PCS AND MOBILE DEVICES

Handheld PCs and mobile devices usually require a different operating system than a desktop PC. For handheld PCs, mobile versions of Windows (such as **Windows Embedded** and **Windows Mobile**) and **Palm OS** (the operating system designed for Palm handheld PCs) are widely used. Smart phones sometimes use the **Symbian OS**, which is designed around the *EPOC* operating system. Other everyday devices—such as cars—that contain a computer use an operating system, as well.

Chapter Objective 5:
State several devices other than desktop PCs and servers that require an operating system and list one possible operating system for each type of device.

OPERATING SYSTEMS FOR LARGER COMPUTERS

High-end servers, mainframes, and supercomputers may use an operating system designed specifically for that type of system, but are increasingly using customized versions of conventional operating systems, such as Windows, UNIX, and Linux.

UTILITY PROGRAMS

A **utility program** is a type of system software program written to perform specific tasks usually related to maintaining or managing the computer system. **File management programs** enable users to perform file management tasks; *diagnostic* and *disk management programs* deal primarily with diagnosing and repairing PC problems, such as hard drive errors, accidentally deleted files, and performing *disk optimization*. *Uninstall utilities* allow programs to be removed from a hard drive without leaving annoying remnants behind, *disk file compression* programs reduce the stored size of files so they can be more easily archived or sent over the Internet, **backup** programs make it easier for users to back up the contents of their hard drive, *recovery utilities* help users recover from a major computer problem, and *encryption programs* are used to secure e-mail messages and files over the Internet. A variety of network and Internet utilities can help monitor network activity and protect against unauthorized access and other security risks. **Antivirus programs** are used to protect against getting infected by a **computer virus**.

Chapter Objective 6:
Describe the role of utility programs and outline several duties that these programs can perform.

THE FUTURE OF OPERATING SYSTEMS

In the future, operating systems will likely become even more user-friendly, voice-driven, and stable, repairing themselves when needed and causing errors and conflicts much less frequently.

Chapter Objective 7:
Speculate about what the operating systems of the future may be like.

KEY TERMS

Instructions: Match each key term on the left with the definition on the right that best describes it.

a. application software

b. backup

c. buffer

d. computer virus

e. device drive

f. Linux

g. Mac OS

h. multiprocessing

i. NetWare

j. network operating system

k. Palm OS

l. personal operating system

m. spooling

n. system software

o. UNIX

p. utility program

q. virtual memory

r. Windows Embedded

s. Windows Mobile

t. Windows XP

1. _____ A duplicate copy of data or other computer contents for use in the event that the original version is destroyed.

2. _____ A family of operating systems based on Windows and designed for handheld PCs, smart phones, and other mobile devices.

3. _____ A family of operating systems based on Windows and designed for non-personal computer devices, such as cash registers and consumer electronic devices.

4. _____ A memory-management technique that uses hard drive space as an extension to a PC's RAM.

5. _____ A multiuser, multitasking operating system developed in the 1970s for midrange servers and mainframes.

6. _____ An area in RAM or on the hard drive designated to hold input and output on their way in or out of the system.

7. _____ A program that enables an operating system to communicate with a specific hardware device.

8. _____ A software program, installed without the user's knowledge, designed to alter the way a computer operates or to cause harm to the system.

9. _____ A type of operating system designed for single users.

10. _____ A type of operating system designed to support multiple users over a network.

11. _____ A type of software that performs a specific task, usually related to managing or maintaining the computer system.

12. _____ A version of UNIX that is available without charge over the Internet and is increasingly being used with PCs, servers, mainframes, and supercomputers.

13. _____ A widely used operating system for PC-based networks.

14. _____ Programs that enable users to perform specific tasks on a computer, such as writing a letter or playing a game.

15. _____ Programs, such as the operating system, that control the operation of a computer and its devices, as well as enable application software to run on the PC.

16. _____ The capability of an operating system to use multiple processors simultaneously in a single computer, usually to process multiple jobs at one time faster than could be performed with a single processor.

17. _____ The latest version of Windows; designed to replace both Windows Me and Windows 2000.

18. _____ The operating system designed for Palm handheld PCs.

19. _____ The operating system for Apple's Macintosh line of computers.

20. _____ The process of placing items in a buffer so they can be retrieved by the appropriate device (such as a printer) when needed.

REVIEW ACTIVITIES

Answers for the self-quiz appear at the end of the book in the References and Resources Guide.

True/False

SELF-QUIZ

Instructions: Circle **T** if the statement is true or **F** if the statement is false.

T   F   1. Microsoft Windows XP is an example of an application software program.

T   F   2. With multiprocessing, an operating system uses more than one CPU simultaneously in a single computer.

T   F   3. The principal reason so many people like UNIX is that it is much easier to use than competing operating systems.

T   F   4. Windows 2000 is commonly used on handheld PCs and mobile devices.

T   F   5. Linux can be used on mainframe and supercomputers, in addition to PCs and servers.

Completion

Instructions: Supply the missing words to complete the following statements.

6. The specific location of where a file is stored, such as C:\My Documents\Resume.doc, is called a(n) _____ .

7. System software is comprised of _____ software and _____ programs.

8. _____ is the version of UNIX available for free over the Internet.

9. When a file is _____ , it is physically located in non-adjacent sections of the storage medium.

10. To decrease the size of a file, a(n) _____ utility program can be used.

---

1. List one operating system that uses a command line interface and one that uses a graphical user interface. Which type of interface would you expect most users to prefer and why?

EXERCISES

2. Select the operating system from the numbered list below that would most likely be used with each of the following devices and write the corresponding number in the blank to the left of each device. Note that all operating systems will not be used.

a. _____ Home office PC   **d.** _____ Large business local area network
b. _____ Mainframe computer   **e.** _____ Handheld PC
c. _____ Apple iMac   **f.** _____ Living room PC

1. Mac OS   **5.** Windows XP Media Center Edition
2. NetWare   **6.** Palm OS
3. Windows 95   **7.** Symbian OS
4. Windows XP Professional   **8.** UNIX

3. For the following path, identify the drive the document is located on, the name of the file, and whether or not the document is stored inside a folder. If the file is stored inside one or more folders, list the folder name(s).

   C:\My Documents\Resume.doc

4. Select the program or processing technique from the numbered list below that best matches each of the following terms and write the corresponding number in the blank to the left of each term. Note that all programs and processing techniques will not be used.

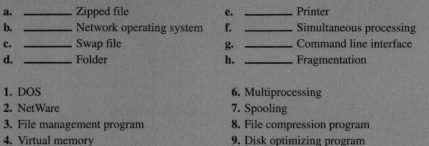

   a. _____ Zipped file   e. _____ Printer
   b. _____ Network operating system f. _____ Simultaneous processing
   c. _____ Swap file   g. _____ Command line interface
   d. _____ Folder   h. _____ Fragmentation

   1. DOS   6. Multiprocessing
   2. NetWare   7. Spooling
   3. File management program 8. File compression program
   4. Virtual memory   9. Disk optimizing program
   5. Encryption program   10. Multitasking

5. Would a person using a notebook PC typically have Windows 3.1, Windows XP, Windows Mobile, or Windows Server as their operating system? Explain your answer.

6. What type of utility program can be used to make a duplicate copy of your hard drive?

7. Identify the purpose of each of the following types of utility program.

   a. Antivirus program   _____
   b. Firewall program   _____
   c. Uninstall utility   _____
   d. Encryption program   _____
   e. File compression program _____

PROJECTS

1. **Autonomic Computing** *Autonomic computing* is a term coined by IBM to refer to computers that can operate on their own with little need of attention from a person. To facilitate this, autonomic computers are expected to have built-in self-diagnostics and other types of utilities, as well as other appropriate software. Autonomic computers will have the ability to recognize, isolate, and recover from problems, with as little human intervention as possible. Some see autonomic computing as a natural progression for computing, similar to the way the telephone system evolved from using a human switchboard operator to a system that automatically routes calls on its own; others are more skeptical.

   For this project, research the current state of autonomic computing. Has the definition of an autonomic computer changed since this project was written? How do the autonomic computing systems being tested today compare in terms of reliability and the ability to recover from errors to conventional computer systems? Are there any autonomic computer systems available in the United States? Do you think all computers in the future will be autonomic? Do you see any disadvantages of autonomic computing? At the conclusion of your research, prepare a one- to two-page summary of your findings and submit it to your instructor.

HOT TOPICS

2. **Suit Happy** Beginning with the lawsuit filed against Microsoft by Apple Corporation in the late 1980s claiming that the Windows interface stole the look and feel of Apple OS, there have been a number of lawsuits involving operating systems. Some more recent legal actions include the antitrust lawsuit filed against Microsoft in 1998 by the Justice Department, the suit filed in 2002 against Microsoft by Sun regarding the inclusion of their Java program in the Windows operating system, and the lawsuit filed in 2003 against IBM by the SCO Group (formerly Caldera Systems) regarding UNIX and Linux.

   For this project, select a lawsuit that involved an operating system product (either one of those mentioned in the previous paragraph or a more recent example) and research it. Be sure to find out what the initial claim was, the defending company's response, and the result of the lawsuit, if it was settled. If it hasn't yet been settled, provide an update of the current status of the suit. If it was settled, do you agree with the ruling? Why or why not? At the conclusion of your research, prepare a one-page summary of your findings and submit it to your instructor.

SHORT ANSWER/ RESEARCH

3. **Compression** As described in the chapter, a compression program can be used to make more efficient use of disk space and speed up the delivery of files over the Internet. They also come in handy for large files—such as digital photographs or other types of graphical images—that you want to archive. The most common compression programs create files with the file extensions *.zip*, *.sit*, *.tar*, and *.exe*. Compression programs usually allow you to create both compressed files and self-extracting compressed files. Self-extracting files automatically decompress when you download them, while compressed files must be decompressed by running a version of the program that compressed them.

   For this project, identify some compression programs associated with each of the file extensions listed above and determine which extensions represent a self-extracting format, and which extensions are associated with the UNIX, Windows, and Mac OS operating systems. For the type of PC you use most often, find at least two compression programs that you might use and compare their costs and capabilities. At the conclusion of your research, prepare a one-page summary of your findings and submit it to your instructor.

4. **File Practice** As discussed in the chapter, all operating systems have at least one program you can use to manage your files; typically, they work similarly to the Windows Explorer program illustrated in Figure 6-18.

For this project, obtain a blank floppy disk for the computer you will be using most often, insert it into the PC, and perform the following tasks.

a. Open the PC's file management program (such as Windows Explorer for Windows PCs). Once the program is open, click or double-click the icon for the floppy drive (usually identified by the letter *A*) to display the contents of your floppy disk (if a message stating the disk needs to be *formatted* appears, select the option to format the disk and then continue with the rest of the steps in this project, provided you know the disk doesn't contain any data since formatting will erase the disk). Are there any files on the disk? By looking at the status bar at the bottom of the file management program's window, or by right-clicking the A drive icon and selecting *Properties*, determine how much room is available on the disk.

b. Open any word processing program available on your PC (such as Word, WordPerfect, or WordPad). Create a new document consisting of just your name. By using the appropriate toolbar button or File menu option, save the document onto your floppy disk (be sure to change the save location to the floppy disk drive and give the document an appropriate name, such as your last name). Return to your file management program and view the contents of your floppy disk. Is your new document stored there? If so, how big is it and how much room is left on your disk now? If it is not there, use your word processor's *Save As* option to save the file again, making sure you are storing it on your floppy disk.

c. Prepare a short summary of your work to submit to your instructor, listing the software programs used, the name of the file you saved on your disk, the size of the file, and the amount of space left on your floppy disk once the file was stored on it.

d. Return to your file management program, display the contents of your floppy disk, and delete the file you stored there.

5. **How Stuff Works: System Software** The How Stuff Works Web site has a number of interesting articles and tutorials explaining how some computer-oriented hardware, software, and technologies work.

For this project, go to the How Stuff Works Web site at www.howstuffworks.com and use either the search option or browse through the computer topics to locate an article related to operating systems or utility programs, such as one explaining how operating systems, file compression, screensavers, or computer viruses work. Read through the article, making note of at least three new things you learned about your chosen topic. At the conclusion of the article, prepare a short summary for your instructor, including the name of the article and the new information you learned from reading it.

6. **Operating System Bugs** Most software, including operating systems, is not error-free when it is first released. Some programs, in fact, contain thousands of problems, called *bugs*. Some are annoying; others leave security holes in your system that can make it vulnerable from attack by a computer virus or unscrupulous individual.

For this project, form a group to identify one recently discovered security hole in a current operating system or a program included with that operating system, such as a utility or Web browser. You may want to review recent computer journals or just search the Internet for the information. Once you have identified your chosen program, find out what the potential problem was, how the problem can be fixed, and where an individual would go to download the appropriate *security patch* or upgrade. Does the security patch fix just that one problem or does it address multiple bugs? Is there a charge for it? If someone bought a PC today with that operating system installed, would it contain the bug? Do the members in your group that own PCs check for operating system updates on a regular basis? What is the easiest way for a Windows user to keep their operating system up-to-date? Your group should submit this project to your instructor in the form of a short paper, not more than two pages in length.

7. **Is Linux for You?** As discussed in the chapter, Linux is a UNIX-type operating system that you can download and install for free. It was originally developed by a student, Linus Torvalds, at the University of Helsinki in Finland, who released it to the public domain as open source freeware. Since that time, the operating system has become very powerful and picked up the support of many large software and hardware companies. This support has allowed Linux to make significant inroads into the mainstream operating system market. Some of the most common reservations about switching to the Linux operating system are that there are few application programs that currently run under this operating system, you may not be able to get support for the operating system if you have problems, and many hardware companies do not currently support this operating system.

    For this project, form a group to research the feasibility of buying a PC running the Linux operating system today. As a group, determine what software and capabilities would be required for an average student buying a PC for your class, and then see if you can find any PCs that you could buy with Linux installed that would meet those needs. If so, what are the advantages of the system? The disadvantages? Be sure to address the common reservations listed above, as well as the various options for obtaining Linux (a free version or a commercial version from a company such as Red Hat or SUSE). Also include any other issues your group feels are appropriate. Your group should submit this project to your instructor in the form of a short paper, not more than three pages in length.

**PRESENTATION/
DEMONSTRATION**

8. **Plug-and-Play?** Newer operating systems are said to be true *plug-and-play*, which means that you should be able to plug in a new piece of hardware and it should play (work) without you having to load any special software or go through any complicated set-up procedure. Since this process does not always work, plug-and-play has been informally dubbed "plug-and-pray" by some. The plug-and-play concept works best when you are adding a common piece of hardware (such as a monitor, printer, or network card) to your system that was widely available prior to the purchase date of your computer. However, if you are trying to add a newer hardware device to an older operating system, or are updating to a newer operating system after you have added several peripheral devices to your existing system, you may be in the situation for which "plug-and-pray" would be the more appropriate phrase.

    For this project, research the current state of plug-and-play and determine whether or not it normally works. Next, assume that you are trying to add a hardware device to your PC and the operating system is not recognizing the hardware. Come up with a list of possible ways you might be able to resolve the problem. Be sure to include the possibility that you no longer have the original installation disks that came with the hardware devices and determine what options are available to you through the Internet. At the conclusion of your research, prepare a short presentation of your findings and recommendations. The presentation should not exceed 10 minutes and should make use of one or more presentation aids such as the chalkboard, handouts, overhead transparencies, or a computer-based slide presentation (your instructor may provide additional requirements). You may be asked to submit a summary of the presentation to your instructor.

9. **OS Support** No matter which operating system you have, it's likely you will eventually need to get some help resolving a system-related hardware or software problem. Support for most popular operating systems includes the following: searchable knowledge bases, technical support phone numbers and e-mail addresses, online support chat, FAQs, and user discussion groups.

    For this project, form a group to select one operating system and research the support options available for that program. Your group should prepare a short presentation that explains what type of help each support option listed in the previous paragraph can be used for and which options are available through the Web site of the manufacturer for your group's chosen operating system. Select one support option and explain in more detail how it would be used and what type of information can be obtained. The presentation should not exceed 10 minutes and should make use of one or more presentation aids such as the chalkboard, handouts, overhead transparencies, or a computer-based slide presentation (your instructor may provide additional requirements). Your group may be asked to submit a summary of the presentation to your instructor.

10. **Bundle, Integrate, or Neither** Microsoft was accused of unfair business practices when it integrated its Web browser into its operating system. Opponents of Microsoft felt it should not be permitted to bundle the browser with its operating systems, give it away for free, or integrate it into the operating system in ways that are unavailable to other firms, as this would lead to an unfair competitive advantage and eliminate the competition in the browser market. Proponents contended that the browser is an integral part of the operating system, not a separate application, and is a natural progression in the evolution of the operating system.

Select one of the following positions or create one of your own and express your point of view on the subject. Your instructor will indicate whether your response is to be posted to a class bulletin board, discussed in a class chat room, or discussed as an in-class activity. You may also be asked to submit a summary of your position and point of view.

a. Companies like Microsoft should not be permitted to bundle software with their operating systems, give it away for free, or integrate it with the operating system in ways that are unavailable to other firms, as this would lead to an unfair competitive advantage and eliminate the competition in the software market. The government was correct in labeling Microsoft a monopoly so that it can keep a closer watch on it in the future.

b. Companies like Microsoft should be allowed to bundle or integrate software with the operating system, as this is a natural progression in the evolution of the operating system and is necessary to remain competitive in a rapidly evolving market. The government had no business interfering and should not have labeled Microsoft a monopoly.

11. **Teaching Computer Viruses** When the University of Calgary announced plans to offer a new course in the Fall 2003 semester that included instruction on writing computer viruses, it unleashed a huge round of criticism and objections from the computer industry. Although the course will delve into the ethics and legalities surrounding viruses, the students will be coding actual viruses, which worries many industry leaders. At Calgary, planned precautions include only allowing fourth year students to take the course, not having a network connection in the classroom, and prohibiting the removal of disks from the classroom. Do you think these precautions are sufficient? Should virus-coding be allowed as part of a computer degree curriculum? The University's premise is that students need to know how viruses work to be able to develop antivirus software, however, the antivirus industry disagrees and most antivirus professionals were never virus writers. Who do you think is right? Will including teaching illegal and unethical acts in college classes help to legitimize the behavior in society? Research whether or not the University of Calvary ever offered the class as planned. Do you agree with their decision?

For this project, form an opinion of the inclusion of virus-writing instruction in college classes and its potential impact on society and the computer industry. Be sure to use the questions mentioned in the previous paragraph when forming your position. Your instructor will indicate whether your response is to be posted to a class bulletin board, discussed in a class chat room, or discussed as an in-class activity. You may also be asked to submit a summary of your position and point of view to your instructor.

12. **Student Edition Labs** Reinforce the concepts you have learned in this chapter by working through the "Backing Up Your Computer" and "Maintaining a Hard Drive" interactive Student Edition Labs, available online. To access these labs, go to www.course.com/uc10/ch06

If you have a SAM user profile, you have access to even more interactive content. Log in to your SAM account and go to your assignments page to see what your instructor has assigned for this chapter.

Application Software

OUTLINE

Overview
The Basics of Application Software
  Types of Application Software
  Ownership Rights and Delivery Methods
  Software Suites
  Object Linking and Embedding (OLE)
  Desktop vs. Handheld PC Software
  Getting Help
Word Processing Concepts
  What Is Word Processing?
  Creating and Editing a Word Processing
    Document
  Formatting a Document
  Graphics, Tables, and Templates
  Word Processing and the Web
Spreadsheet Concepts
  What Is a Spreadsheet?
  Creating and Editing a Worksheet
  Formatting a Worksheet
  Charts and What-If Analysis
  Spreadsheets and the Web
Database Concepts
  What Is a Database?
  Creating a Database
  Modifying a Database
  Queries and Reports
  Databases and the Web
Presentation Graphics Concepts
  What Is a Presentation Graphic?
  Creating a Presentation
  Enhancing and Finishing a Presentation
  Presentation Graphics and the Web
Graphics and Multimedia Concepts
  Multimedia Applications
  Types of Graphics and Multimedia Software
  Graphics, Multimedia, and the Web
Other Types of Application Software
  Desktop and Personal Publishing Software
  Accounting and Personal Finance Software
  Educational, Entertainment, and Reference
    Software
  CAD and Other Types of Design Software
  Project Management Software

LEARNING OBJECTIVES

After completing this chapter, you will be able to:

1. Describe what application software is and the different types, ownership rights, and delivery methods available.

2. Detail some characteristics of a software suite and some ways of getting help with a software program.

3. Discuss word processing and identify the basic operations involved in creating, editing, and formatting documents.

4. Explain the purpose of spreadsheet software and identify the basic operations involved in creating, editing, and formatting worksheets.

5. Identify some of the vocabulary used with database software and discuss the basic operations involved with creating, editing, and retrieving information from a database.

6. Describe what presentation graphics are and how they are created.

7. List some multimedia applications and describe some software programs that can be used to create graphics and other multimedia elements.

8. Name several other types of application software programs and discuss what functions they perform.

As discussed in previous chapters, **application software** (sometimes called *end-user programs*) consists of programs designed to perform specific tasks or applications. Today, a wide variety of application programs are available to meet most users' needs. Individuals and businesses can buy software to be used to write letters, keep track of their finances, participate in videoconferences, learn a foreign language, entertain themselves or their children, create music CDs or home movie DVDs, manage a business's inventory, create greeting cards and flyers, make business presentations, process orders, prepare a payroll and tax returns, touch up digital photos, teach their kids the ABCs, and hundreds of other applications.

This chapter begins with a look at some characteristics of application software in general. Then we take a look at five of the most widely used types of application software programs: *word processing*, *spreadsheet*, *database*, *presentation graphics*, and *multimedia software*. The chapter concludes with a look at a few other types of application software not discussed in this chapter or other chapters in this book. ■

THE BASICS OF APPLICATION SOFTWARE

There are some basic characteristics and concepts regarding application software with which all computer users should be familiar. For instance, the types of application software available, the different possible ownership rights and delivery methods, what a software suite is, how desktop and handheld PC software differ, and how to get help with an application program. These topics are discussed in the next few sections.

Types of Application Software

Application software is typically categorized by function, such as utility programs, multimedia programs, accounting programs, word processors, Web browsers, speech recognition programs, games, and more. Five of the most widely used types of application software are:

▼ *Word processing software*—allows users to efficiently create, edit, and print the type of documents that would have been created with a typewriter in the past.

▼ *Spreadsheet software*—provides users with a convenient means of creating documents containing complex mathematical calculations.

▼ *Database software*—allows users to store and organize vast amounts of data and retrieve specific information when needed.

▼ *Presentation graphics software*—allows users to create visual presentations to more easily convey information to others.

▼ *Multimedia software*—provides users with a means for performing multimedia-oriented tasks, such as creating and modifying multimedia elements (images, audio clips, video clips, animations, and so forth), as well as for burning finished multimedia elements or presentations onto optical discs.

Ownership Rights and Delivery Methods

Ownership rights of a software program specify the allowable use of the program and vary depending on whether the program is *commercial*, *shareware*, *freeware*, or *public domain software*. Software also differs in how it is delivered: *installed software* or *Web-based software*. Although these topics are discussed next in the context of application software, they also apply to any type of software, such as system software, which was discussed in Chapter 6, and programming languages, discussed in Chapter 13.

Commercial, Shareware, Freeware, and Public Domain Software

After a software program is developed, the developer holds the ownership rights for that program. Whether or not the program can be sold, shared with others, or otherwise distributed is decided by that developer, who might be an individual or an organization. When a software program is purchased, the buyer isn't actually buying the software. Instead, the buyer is acquiring a **software license** that permits him or her to use the software. This license specifies the conditions under which a buyer can use the software, such as whether or not it may be shared with others and the number of computers on which it may be installed (many software licenses permit the software to be installed on just one PC). In addition to being included in printed form inside the packaging of most software programs, typically the licensing agreement is displayed and must be agreed to by the end user at the beginning of the software installation process (see Figure 7-1). There are four different ownership right categories that can be associated with software. They are listed in Figure 7-2 and discussed next.

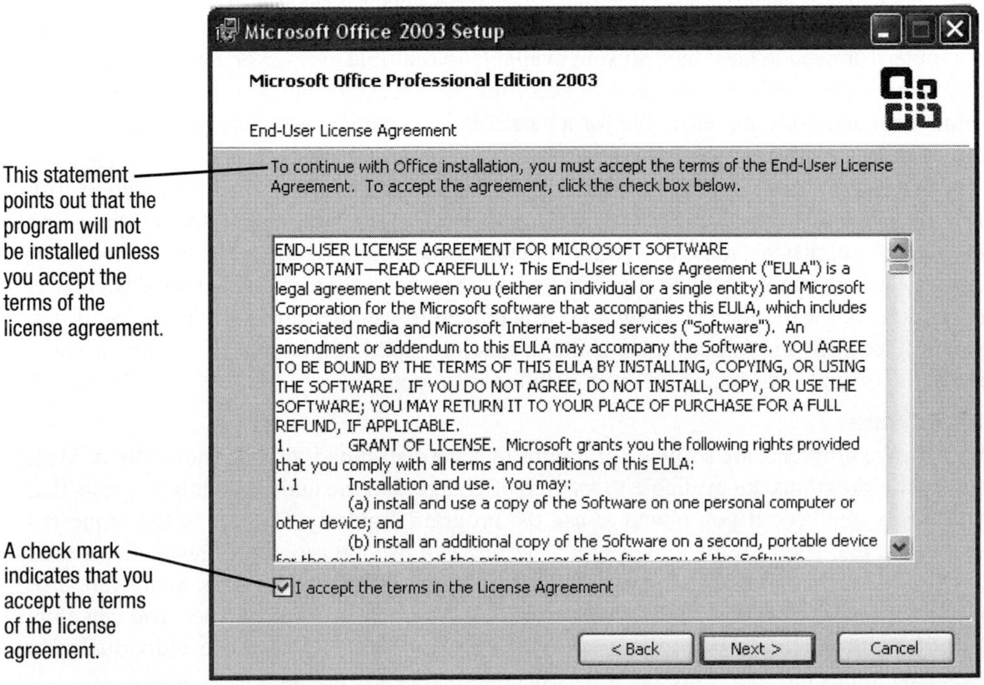

TIP

Ownership rights for original creative works are referred to as *copyrights* and are discussed in more detail in Chapter 16.

This statement points out that the program will not be installed unless you accept the terms of the license agreement.

A check mark indicates that you accept the terms of the license agreement.

FIGURE 7-1
Software licenses. Most software programs display their licensing agreements at the beginning of the installation process, in addition to providing them in paper form.

>**Software license.** An agreement, either included in a software package or displayed on the screen during installation, that specifies the conditions under which a buyer of the program can use it.

TYPE OF SOFTWARE	EXAMPLES	MOST COMMONLY OBTAINED FROM
Commercial software	Microsoft Office (office suite) Norton AntiVirus (antivirus program) Adobe Photoshop (image-editing program) Flight Simulator (game)	Manufacturer's Web site, online stores, and physical stores
Shareware	WinZip (file compression program) Media Jukebox (MP3 player and CD ripper) Paint Shop Pro (image-editing program) Duke Nukem 3D (game)	Manufacturer/author's Web site and download sites, such as CNET's Shareware.com and Tucows.com
Freeware	Netscape Navigator (Web browser) Outlook Express (e-mail program) MusicMatch Jukebox Basic (MP3 player and CD ripper) South Park Space Invaders (game)	Manufacturer/author's Web site and download sites, such as CNET's Shareware.com and Tucows.com
Public-domain software	Linux (operating system) Lynx (text-based Web browser) Pine (e-mail program)	Download, university, and government sites; open source and public-domain organizations

FIGURE 7-2
Software ownership rights.

Commercial Software

Commercial software is software that is developed and sold for a profit. When you buy a commercial software program (such as *Microsoft Office*, *TurboTax*, or *The Sims*), it typically comes with a *single-user license*, which means you cannot legally make copies of the CD to give to your friends, nor can you install the software on their computers using your CD. You usually cannot even install the software on a second PC that you own, unless allowed by the license. For example, some software licenses state that the program can be installed on one desktop PC and one notebook PC; others allow installation on both a home and work PC, as long as the two computers will never be used at the same time. Leasing your copy of a program is also typically forbidden, unless a specific licensing agreement for leasing is obtained. Schools or businesses that need to install the software on multiple computers or need to have the software available to multiple users over a network can usually obtain *site licenses* or *network licenses* for the necessary number of users. To determine what activities are allowable for a particular commercial software program, refer to the licensing agreement for that program.

In addition to a full version, some commercial software is available in a *demo* or *trial version*. Typically these versions can be used free of charge and distributed to others, but often they are missing some key features (such as the ability to save or print a document) or they will not run after the trial period expires. Since these programs are not designed as replacements for the fee-based version, it is ethical to use them only to determine if you would like to buy the full program. If the decision is made against purchasing the product, the demo or trial version should be uninstalled from your PC.

Shareware

Shareware programs are software programs that are distributed on the honor system. Most shareware programs are available to try free of charge, but the author usually requests that you pay a small fee if you intend to use the program regularly. By paying the requested shareware fee, you become a registered user and can use the program forever. Registered users may also be entitled to product support, documentation, and updates. Shareware programs are widely available from a variety of download sites on the Internet. You can copy shareware programs to pass along to friends and colleagues, but those individuals are expected to pay the shareware fee if they decide to keep the product.

>**Commercial software.** Copyrighted software that is developed, usually by a commercial company, for sale to others. >**Shareware.** Copyrighted software that is distributed on the honor system; should be either paid for or uninstalled after the trial period.

Most shareware programs have a specified trial period, such as one month. Although it is not illegal to use shareware past the specified trial period, it is unethical to do so. Ethical use of shareware dictates either paying for the program or uninstalling it from your PC at the end of the trial period. Shareware is typically much less expensive than commercial versions of similar software, because it is often developed by a single programmer and is usually sold directly to consumers with little or no packaging or advertising expenses. Shareware authors stress that the ethical use of shareware helps to cultivate this type of software distribution. Legally, shareware and demo versions of commercial software are similar, but shareware is usually less expensive than comparable commercial programs because it uses the shareware marketing system, and it is typically not missing key features.

Freeware

Freeware programs are software programs that are given away for free by the author. Although freeware is available free of charge and can be shared with others, the author retains the ownership rights to the program so you cannot do anything with it—such as sell it or modify it—that is not expressly allowed by the author. Freeware programs are frequently developed by students, professional programmers, and amateur programmers as a programming exercise or hobby; some commercial software programs are released as freeware as well, such as *Internet Explorer* and *Netscape Navigator*. Like shareware programs, freeware programs are widely available over the Internet.

Public Domain Software

Public domain software is software that is not copyrighted; instead, the ownership rights to the program have been donated to the public domain. Consequently, it is available for free and can be used, copied, and distributed to others without restrictions. Sometimes both the executable program and the program's source code are both available (making it also an open source software program); sometimes only the executable program resides in the public domain.

Installed Software vs. Web-Based Software

Installed software—that is, software that is installed on a PC before it is run—is the most common type of software. Installed software programs are either purchased in physical form (such as in a shrink-wrapped box containing a CD, license agreement, and user's manual) or are downloaded from the Internet (see Figure 7-3). Whether or not downloaded software requires a fee depends on whether the program is a commercial program, a demo program, shareware, freeware, or public domain software. To purchase software in a downloaded format, usually the order is placed and the payment processed in the same manner as if the software was being purchased in a physical format, and then the buyer is provided with a link to download the purchased program. Free downloads usually begin once the appropriate hyperlink is clicked. In either case, sometimes clicking the link downloads and installs the program in one step; other times, an installation program is downloaded that will then need to be run in order to install the application program so it can be used. With a downloaded program, you don't receive a CD containing the program, although some vendors recommend that you back up a downloaded installation program onto a CD as soon as it is downloaded in case the program needs to be reinstalled some time in the future.

Instead of being available in an installed format, some software is run directly from the Internet as *Web-based software*. Web-based software programs can only be accessed via the Internet, and can be free (such as an interactive game available through a Web site) or fee-based (such as software available from an *application service provider* or *ASP*—a company that manages and distributes software over the Internet). There is a wide range of

---

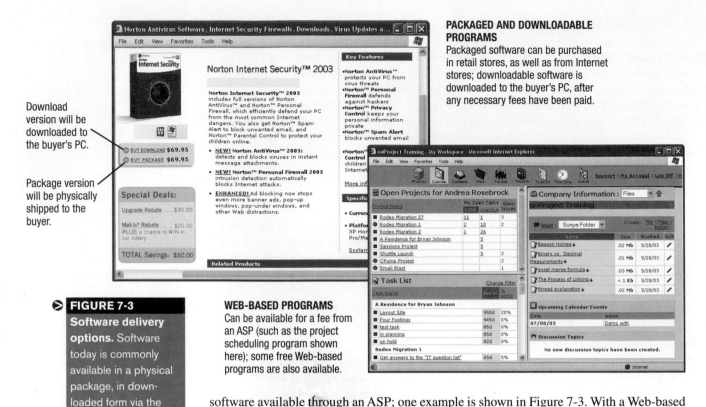

PACKAGED AND DOWNLOADABLE PROGRAMS
Packaged software can be purchased in retail stores, as well as from Internet stores; downloadable software is downloaded to the buyer's PC, after any necessary fees have been paid.

Download version will be downloaded to the buyer's PC.

Package version will be physically shipped to the buyer.

> **FIGURE 7-3**
> **Software delivery options.** Software today is commonly available in a physical package, in downloaded form via the Internet, or as a Web-based application.

WEB-BASED PROGRAMS
Can be available for a fee from an ASP (such as the project scheduling program shown here); some free Web-based programs are also available.

software available through an ASP; one example is shown in Figure 7-3. With a Web-based program, usually a monthly or yearly fee is charged for its use. One advantage of Web-based software over installed software is that the programs and your files can be accessed from any PC with an Internet connection, not just a specific PC on which the program is installed. Another is that the software may be updated on a regular basis for no additional cost to the user. Some potential disadvantages are that the cost may eventually exceed the cost of buying a similar shrink-wrapped package, and you can't access the program and your data when the server on which they reside goes down.

Software Suites

Related software programs are sometimes sold bundled together as a **software suite**. Sometimes a suite may include a collection of graphics or utility programs, but more commonly a software suite consists of a group of office-related software, sometimes called *productivity software* or an *office software suite*. The typical office software suite contains at least a word processing program and a spreadsheet program. One of the predominant software suites is *Microsoft Office*; the latest version is *Microsoft Office 2003*. The Standard Edition of Office 2003 includes *Word 2003* (for word processing), *Excel 2003* (for spreadsheet work), *PowerPoint 2003* (for presentation graphics), and *Outlook 2003* (for managing e-mail, contacts, schedules, etc.). The *Professional Edition* adds *Access 2003* (for database management) and *Publisher 2003* (for creating business publications). Similar suites (see Figure 7-4) are available from Corel (*WordPerfect Office*), IBM (*Lotus SmartSuite*), and Sun (*StarOffice*). A free alternative similar to *StarOffice* is called *OpenOffice.org* and is available as a free download via the Internet from the OpenOffice.org Web site or on CD for a small fee from various distributors. Not all of these suites are available for all operating systems.

>**Software suite.** A collection of software programs bundled together and sold as a single software package.

❯ **FIGURE 7-4**
Common software suites.

The primary advantages of using a software suite are a total cost that is lower than buying the programs individually and a common interface. Although, as mentioned in an earlier chapter, most programs written for the same operating system (such as Windows) use similar interfaces and commands, a software suite goes one step further. Usually the menu and toolbar structure is very similar from program to program in the suite. This similarity isn't just for the basic commands (such as *Save* and *Print*)—all commands (such as adding borders and shading or inserting a row or column) that appear in more than one program in the suite are performed in the same manner. This arrangement makes it easier to learn a new program in a suite, once you have some experience working with any of the other programs in that suite. Some of the most common application software commands are described in Figure 7-5, with examples of the toolbar buttons and keyboard shortcuts used to perform these operations in Microsoft Office. Many of these commands would be performed in the same manner in other Windows programs.

Closely related to software suites are *integrated software programs*—such as *Microsoft Works*—which are similar to full suites, but are less powerful. Instead of including a full-featured word processor or spreadsheet, for instance, an integrated software program typically incorporates versions of each program that have limited functionality,

❯ **FIGURE 7-5**
Common Microsoft Office document-handling commands.

COMMAND	TOOLBAR BUTTON	KEYBOARD SHORTCUT	DESCRIPTION
New document		Ctrl+N	Creates a new blank document.
Open		Ctrl+O	Opens a previously saved document from a storage medium, usually for editing or printing.
Save		Ctrl+S	Saves the current version of the document to a storage medium.
Print		Ctrl+P	Prints the current version of the document onto paper.
Spelling and grammar		F7	Starts the spelling and grammar check for the entire document.
Cut		Ctrl+X	Moves the selected item to the clipboard.
Copy		Ctrl+C	Copies the selected item to the clipboard.
Paste		Ctrl+V	Pastes the contents of the clipboard to the current location.
Undo		Ctrl+Z	Undoes the last change to the document.
Close		Alt+F4	Closes the document. Any changes made to the document are lost if the document wasn't saved first.

providing only the main features of each program in a single package. Users in the home market usually don't miss the omitted capabilities and, since they are usually less expensive and require less hard disk space and memory to run than the full suite, integrated software programs are often a good choice for the home user. It is common for integrated software programs to be preloaded on home PCs, instead of their full-suite counterparts.

Object Linking and Embedding (OLE)

One very useful tool available with many programs and software suites is the ability to share documents or parts of documents created with one program with documents created with the same or another program. For instance, let's say you are writing a letter in your word processing program, and you want to insert some data from a spreadsheet file. You can open the spreadsheet file using your spreadsheet program, and then copy and paste data from your spreadsheet into your letter—all without ever closing the word processing program (see Figure 7-6).

> **FIGURE 7-6**
>
> **OLE.** You can link or embed information developed in one software program into another document created with the same or different software program.

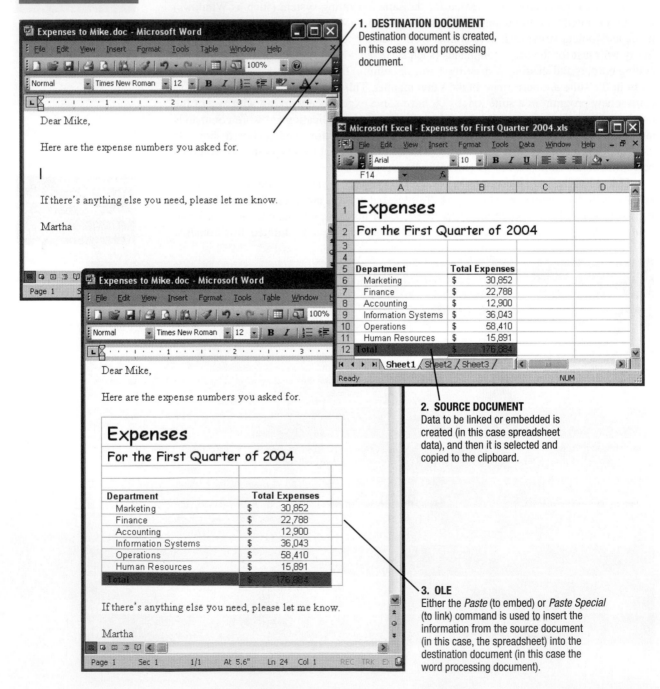

1. DESTINATION DOCUMENT
Destination document is created, in this case a word processing document.

2. SOURCE DOCUMENT
Data to be linked or embedded is created (in this case spreadsheet data), and then it is selected and copied to the clipboard.

3. OLE
Either the *Paste* (to embed) or *Paste Special* (to link) command is used to insert the information from the source document (in this case, the spreadsheet) into the destination document (in this case the word processing document).

The procedure just discussed is sometimes referred to as *embedding* an object created in one program into a document created in another. This procedure can be performed using any pair of programs that support copying and pasting. In addition to embedding objects, many software suites also allow you to *link* objects created in one program into a second document. With both linking and embedding, the two documents can be the same type of program (such as both spreadsheet documents) or can be entirely different types of programs (such as one word processing document and one spreadsheet document). The *source document* contains the data to be embedded or linked; that data can be text, a part of a spreadsheet, a graphic, or any other object. With embedding, the object is physically stored within the *destination document*; if the original source file is changed at a later point, the destination document containing the embedded object will not change. With linking, however, a link is created between the source file and the destination file so that the data to be displayed in the destination file always comes from the most current version of the source file. Consequently, as long as the two files remain linked, whenever the source file (the spreadsheet, in this example) is opened and modified, those changes will automatically display in the document containing the linked object (the letter in this example) whenever that destination document is opened. Double-clicking a linked object opens the corresponding file in the appropriate program (in this case, the spreadsheet program) to be edited. The concept of linking and embedding objects is commonly referred to as *object linking and embedding* (*OLE*).

Desktop vs. Handheld PC Software

Unlike notebook and tablet PCs, which usually run the same application software as desktop PCs, handheld PCs require specially designed application software. As discussed in Chapter 6, the two most popular operating systems for handheld PCs are Palm OS and Windows Mobile. A wide variety of application software is available today for both handheld PC platforms, such as personal information programs (designed to maintain and use a calendar, address book, alarm clock, memo pad, or calculator), language translators, currency converters, games, reference software, multimedia software, Web browsers, utility programs, and portable versions of popular productivity programs like Word, Excel, PowerPoint, and Outlook (see Figure 7-7).

FIGURE 7-7
Handheld PC software. There is a wide variety of handheld PC software available today.

In addition to having a more compact, efficient appearance, many handheld applications include features for easier data input, such as an onscreen keyboard, phrase list, or handwriting recognition capabilities. When exchanging documents between a handheld PC and a desktop PC is necessary, there are many handheld PC programs that are designed to be compatible with popular desktop PC software. For example, both *Documents to Go* (for handheld PCs running Palm OS) and *Pocket Office* (for handheld PCs running Windows Mobile) are compatible with Microsoft Office documents.

Getting Help

Most people run into problems or need some help as they work with a software program. There are various options for getting help when you need it, such as through a help feature built in to a software program, on the Web, printed materials, or in-person assistance.

Application-Based Help

Most application programs have a built-in help feature, typically available through a *Help* option on the menu bar. The type and amount of built-in help available varies from program to program, but some of the most common configurations are illustrated in Figure 7-8 and listed next.

- ▼ *Table of Contents*. A table of contents in a help system works similarly to the table of contents in a book with related help topics organized under main topics. With most help systems, selecting a main topic reveals the help topics related to that subject; selecting a help topic displays that information on the screen.

- ▼ *Index*. An index in a help system works similarly to an index in a book with all help topics organized as an alphabetical list. Typically typing the name of a help topic scrolls the index to that help topic, if it is contained in the index; selecting a help topic displays the related information on the screen.

- ▼ *Search*. Many programs today allow you to search for help topics by typing a keyword or phrase (similar to a search site) and then the help system displays a list of possible matching help topics. For instance, in Microsoft Office, clicking the question-mark icon located on the standard toolbar opens the *Help task pane* shown in Figure 7-8 that can be used to search for topics. Once a list of possible help topics is displayed, clicking a help topic displays that information on the screen. Because a help search feature usually looks for all help screens containing the search term (not just all help topics containing the search term), a help search generally returns more help screens than searching for the same term using a help index feature.

Web-Based Help

There is a vast amount of free information about application software programs available via the Web. Many software manufacturers include online tutorials and lists of tips and tricks for their programs on their Web site. There are also general-purpose software tutorial sites that provide online tutorials for a variety of programs, as well as sites dedicated to a particular application, such as desktop publishing or digital photo touch-up. In addition, many software programs have at least one public discussion group where you can search for answers to your questions or post new questions, as needed.

FURTHER EXPLORATION

For links to further information about application software resources, go to www.course.com/uc10/ch07

Offline Help

There are numerous resources for offline help, including periodicals (such as magazines and journals) that often contain articles about how to most effectively use particular software programs, books (both reference books and textbooks) on how to use any number of software programs, and tutorial videos that demonstrate how to use specific pieces of software. You may also be able to get help in person by taking software classes at your local college or computer training center, attending computer club meetings, or talking with a computer sales professional at a local store that sells the software program in question.

TABLE OF CONTENTS
Organizes help screens into books by topic.

Each book represents a major topic that displays more specific topics when clicked.

Selecting a topic displays the corresponding help screen.

Typing a search phrase displays a list of matching topics.

Selecting this topic displays the same "Print a document" help screen shown above.

SEARCH
Lets you type in search topics or a search phrase to see a list of matching topics.

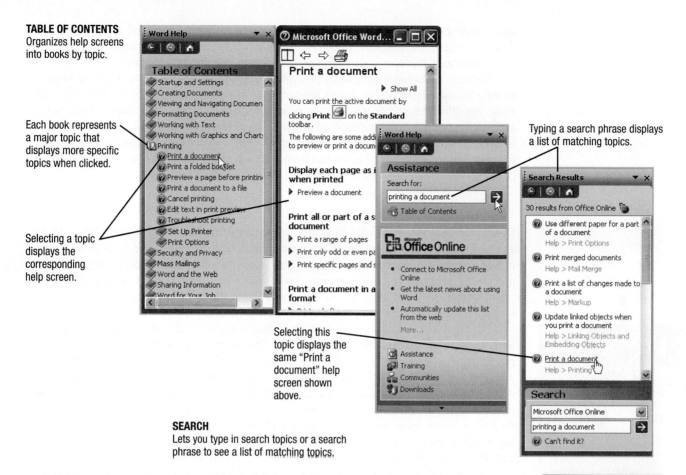

FIGURE 7-8
Help systems. Most application programs have a built-in help system available in one or more formats.

WORD PROCESSING CONCEPTS

Word processing is one of the most widely used application programs today. Although the actual commands and features vary somewhat from program to program, it is important to be familiar with the basic features of word processing and the general concept of what word processing enables you to do. The following sections discuss these features and concepts.

What Is Word Processing?

Word processing refers to using a computer and **word processing software** to create, edit, save, and print written documents such as letters, legal contracts, manuscripts, newsletters, and reports. At its most basic level, word processing is used to do what was done on a typewriter before computers were commonplace. More complex word processing documents include content that was not possible to create using a typewriter, such as photos and other types of graphics, hyperlinks, video clips, and text in a variety of sizes and appearances. One of the greatest advantages of using word processing over a typewriter is that you can make changes without retyping the entire document because the document is created and then saved on a storage medium, instead of it being typed directly

>**Word processing.** Using a computer and word processing software to create, edit, save, and print written documents, such as letters, contracts, and manuscripts. >**Word processing software.** Application software used to create, edit, save, and print written documents.

onto paper. Consequently, the document can be retrieved, modified, and printed as many times as needed. Increasingly, word processing programs are including support for speech and handwritten input, as well as improved collaboration and security tools.

Virtually all formal writing today is performed using a word processing program. Among today's best-selling word processing programs are *Microsoft Word*, *Corel WordPerfect*, and *Lotus WordPro*—all part of the software suites mentioned earlier in this chapter. Most word processing programs offer hundreds of features, but virtually all support a core group of features used to create, *edit*, and *format* documents. Some of these basic features are described in the next few sections, with illustrations from the most recent version of the Microsoft Word program—*Microsoft Office Word 2003*.

Creating and Editing a Word Processing Document

Every word processor contains an assortment of operations for creating and editing documents. Usually these operations allow for both text and graphics to be inserted and then moved, copied, edited, or deleted as needed. To create a new document, open your word processing program and start entering text (most word processing programs display a blank document when they are first opened). To retrieve a document to edit or print instead, use the *Open* command on the File menu or toolbar.

Editing refers to making changes to the actual content of a document, such as inserting or deleting words or correcting a spelling error. The **insertion point** displayed within a word processing document typically looks like a blinking vertical line (see Figure 7-9) and indicates the current location in the document; that is, where the next change will be made to that document. For instance, if you type a new word or character, it will appear at the insertion point location and the insertion point will move to the right as you type. To delete text, press the Delete key to delete one character to the right of the insertion point; press the Backspace key to delete one character to the left. If the insertion point is not in the proper location for the edit, it must first be moved (by pointing and clicking with the mouse or by using the arrow keys on the keyboard) to the appropriate location in the document. As the insertion point moves, the status bar at the bottom of the screen usually changes to reflect the current position of the insertion point.

One important thing to know when entering text in a word processing document is when to press the Enter key. Word processing programs use a feature called **word wrap**, which means the insertion point automatically moves to the beginning of the next line when the end of the screen line is reached. Consequently, the Enter key isn't pressed until it is time to begin a new paragraph. As long as Enter is not pressed until that point, when changes are made to the document—such as adding, modifying, or deleting text or changing the text size or page margins—the program will automatically adjust the amount of text on each screen line, as needed.

Other common types of edits include *copying* and *moving* content to a new location. To copy or move content, either the *Copy* command (to make a duplicate copy of the content at the new location, without removing the original text) or the *Cut* command (to delete the text from the original location and move it to the new location) is used to copy the selected content to the clipboard. The *Paste* command is then used to insert that content at the insertion point location.

Virtually all word processing programs also have a spelling and grammar check feature to help you locate and correct spelling and grammatical errors in your documents, as well as a variety of other useful editing tools.

>**Insertion point.** An onscreen character that indicates the current location in a document, which is where the next change will be made to the document. >**Word wrap.** The feature found in a word processing program that automatically returns the insertion point to the next line when the end of the screen line is reached.

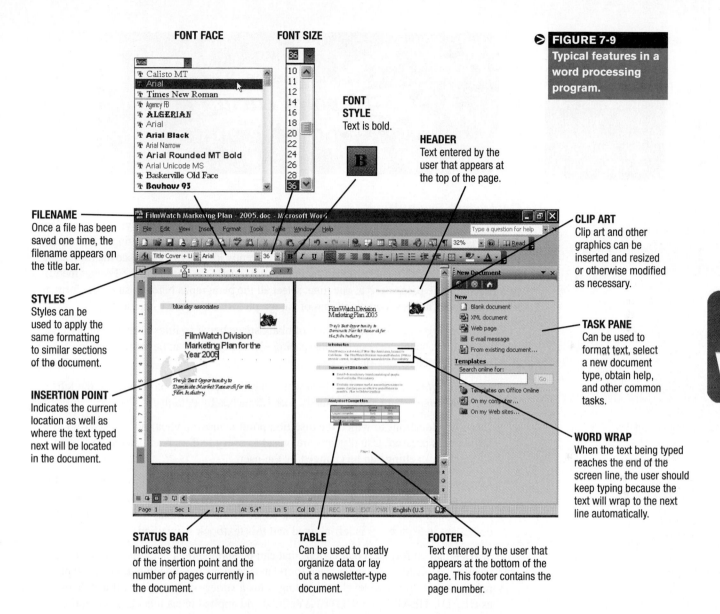

FONT FACE

FONT SIZE

FONT STYLE
Text is bold.

HEADER
Text entered by the user that appears at the top of the page.

> **FIGURE 7-9**
> **Typical features in a word processing program.**

FILENAME
Once a file has been saved one time, the filename appears on the title bar.

STYLES
Styles can be used to apply the same formatting to similar sections of the document.

INSERTION POINT
Indicates the current location as well as where the text typed next will be located in the document.

CLIP ART
Clip art and other graphics can be inserted and resized or otherwise modified as necessary.

TASK PANE
Can be used to format text, select a new document type, obtain help, and other common tasks.

WORD WRAP
When the text being typed reaches the end of the screen line, the user should keep typing because the text will wrap to the next line automatically.

STATUS BAR
Indicates the current location of the insertion point and the number of pages currently in the document.

TABLE
Can be used to neatly organize data or lay out a newsletter-type document.

FOOTER
Text entered by the user that appears at the bottom of the page. This footer contains the page number.

Formatting a Document

While editing changes the actual content of a document, *formatting* changes the appearance of the document. Formatting can usually be applied at the character, paragraph, and document levels.

Character Formatting

Character formatting changes the appearance of individual characters. To format characters, they usually are first selected with the mouse, and then the appropriate format is applied (usually using either toolbar buttons or the *Font* option on the Format menu). Common types of character formatting are *font face*, *font size*, and *font style*.

A *font face* or *typeface* is a named collection of text characters that share a common design, such as Arial or Times New Roman. The characters in a font face are usually available in a wide variety of *font sizes* measured in *points* where 72 points equals one-inch-tall text. All the characters in a particular font face and font size are referred to as a *font*; for example, 12-point Times New Roman is a font. *Font style* refers to formatting that adds additional features to the text, such as bold, italic, underline, or embossed. Figure 7-10 illustrates different fonts; using the toolbar to change the font face, font size, and font style is illustrated in Figure 7-9.

FIGURE 7-10

Fonts. The font face and font size of text can be specified in word processing and many other application programs. In font size, 72 points equals one inch.

This is 10-point Helvetica
This is 12-point Times New Roman
This is 18-point Lucida Italic
This is 24-point Comic Sans

Paragraph Formatting

Paragraph formatting changes an entire paragraph at one time, such as specifying *line spacing*, *left* and *right margins*, *tabs*, *alignment*, and *styles*. To apply paragraph formatting to the current paragraph (the one in which the insertion point is currently located) simply issue the formatting command (usually using either toolbar buttons or the *Paragraph* option on the Format menu); to format multiple paragraphs at one time, select all the paragraphs before issuing the formatting command. The most common types of paragraph formatting are listed next.

- ▼ *Line spacing*—controls the amount of blank space between lines of text. Usually it is set to single spacing (1) or double spacing (2), although it can be set to fractional spacing—such as 1.5—as well.

- ▼ *Left* and *right margins*—indicate how much blank space will be printed on the left and right edges of the paper (usually 1 or 1.5 inches by default).

- ▼ *Tabs*—the locations to which the insertion point is moved when the Tab key on the keyboard is pressed. Usually tabs are preset to every half inch across the document, although this setting can be changed by the user.

- ▼ *Alignment*—determines how the paragraph is aligned in relation to the left and right margins of the document. Usually the options are *align left*, *center*, *align right*, or *justify* (flush with both the left and right edges of the document). For example, the document in Figure 7-9 is left-aligned and this textbook is justified.

- ▼ *Styles*—named format specifications that can be applied on a paragraph-by-paragraph basis to keep a uniform appearance for related sections in a document. For example, a report may include two levels of headings plus a variety of quotations. If a style (such as HEAD1, HEAD2, or QUOTE) is defined and applied to each occurrence of these parts of the report, those sections of the document will have a consistent appearance. In addition, changing the specified format of a particular style (such as font face, font size, font color, or alignment) reformats all text in the document to which that style has been applied.

Page and Document Formatting

Most word processing programs allow users to choose *page formatting* options, such as the *top* and *bottom margins*, the *paper size* being used, and whether you want the page to use the traditional *portrait orientation* (8½ inches wide by 11 inches tall on standard paper) or the wider *landscape orientation* (11 inches wide by 8½ inches tall on standard paper). Most page formatting options are found under *Page Setup* on the File menu. You can also choose whether to include page numbers at the top or bottom of the page, usually as part of a header or footer (as shown in Figure 7-9, a *header* is specified text or images that print automatically at the top of every page; a *footer* is printed at the bottom of every page). Many of these options can be applied to an individual page as page formatting or to the entire document (called *document formatting*). Other types of document formatting include generating footnotes and end notes, a table of contents, or an index, as well as applying a background or theme to the entire document.

Graphics, Tables, and Templates

A word processor's graphics feature enables images (such as a photograph, a drawing from another program, or a *clip art image*, as in Figure 7-9) to be inserted into a document. Many word processors also include a set of drawing tools (such as the Word Drawing toolbar shown in Figure 7-11) to enter shapes, lines, arrows, graphical text, or other objects into a document. After an image is inserted, it can be moved, resized, or otherwise modified. The Word Picture toolbar available through many Microsoft Office programs that can be used to crop, rotate, recolor, adjust the brightness or contrast, or otherwise modify images is also shown in Figure 7-11.

A word processor's *table* feature lets you organize content into a grid of *rows* and *columns*. Once a table has been created, shading, borders, and other formatting can be applied to the table and/or its contents. The widths and heights of the *cells* in a table can also be changed or the table can be set up to automatically adjust its size to fit the contents. Rows and columns of an existing table can be inserted or deleted, as needed.

For common types of memos or reports, many word processors have a set of templates or a wizard available to help you create an attractive document quickly. A *template* is an already created and formatted document that fits a particular purpose, such as a fax cover sheet, resume, memo, business card, newsletter, Web page, and more. Usually placeholder text is included for any text that should be customized, so all the user needs to do is fill in the blanks on the template document. A *wizard* goes beyond a template in that it consists of a series of screens that prompt you for the necessary information or actions to create a particular type of document; after completing all the screens, the appropriate document is generated. Wizards are often available for creating such specialized documents as envelopes, legal pleadings, calendars, agendas, as well as for tasks such as sending a fax or publishing a Web page.

Word Processing and the Web

The most recent versions of word processing programs include features that bring document preparation and the Web closer together. With a single mouse click, a document can be saved as a Web page or, conversely, a Web page can be opened and edited in the word processing program. In most word processing programs, when a Web address is typed, it is automatically created as a hyperlink, and clicking a hyperlink in a word processing document opens that Web page in your Web browser program. Many word processing programs allow you to create and send e-mail from within the word processing program. Some also support *Extensible Markup Language* (*XML*)-based documents—documents using the XML standard for data and formatting that has become increasingly common in Web documents and databases—and the *MHTML* (*MIME Hypertext Markup Language*) format—a new standard for combining all the elements of a Web site (text, images, sound files, animated items, and other elements) into a single file.

> **FIGURE 7-11**
> **Drawing and Picture toolbars.** The Drawing (top) and Picture (bottom) toolbars available in most Office programs allow you to insert, create, and modify graphical images.

S W

FURTHER EXPLORATION

For links to further information about word processing software, go to www.course.com/uc10/ch07

SPREADSHEET CONCEPTS

Another application program that any businessperson should learn—whether he or she is a manager, an analyst, a secretary, or a sales representative—is a *spreadsheet program.* Spreadsheet software is to the current generation of business people what the pocket calculator was to previous generations—a convenient means of performing calculations. But while most pocket calculators can compute and display only one result each time new data is entered, electronic spreadsheets can present hundreds or even thousands of results each time you enter a single new value or command. Spreadsheet programs also typically allow you to create charts of, and do various types of analysis on, the data contained in a spreadsheet. Although the actual commands and features vary slightly from program to program, the basic features and concepts of spreadsheet programs discussed next remain the same.

What Is a Spreadsheet?

A **spreadsheet** is a group of values and other data organized into rows and columns, similar to the ruled paper worksheets traditionally used by bookkeepers and accountants. **Spreadsheet software** is the type of application software used to create computerized spreadsheets. Advantages of using a computerized spreadsheet include the ability to save, modify, retrieve, and print the spreadsheet as often as necessary. Because spreadsheets tend to contain a great deal of numbers and mathematical calculations, however, there is a further benefit—the computer's mathematical ability and tremendous speed. These characteristics allow a spreadsheet to contain numeric formulas that the computer will compute and keep up to date as data in the spreadsheet changes. This tremendously improves accuracy of the spreadsheet and saves the user from manually recomputing and then reentering values into the spreadsheet as data changes.

A spreadsheet document is typically called a **worksheet**. Most spreadsheet programs allow multiple worksheets to be saved together in a single spreadsheet file, called a **workbook**. Today's most widely used spreadsheet programs are *Microsoft Excel, Corel Quattro Pro,* and *Lotus 1-2-3*—again, all part of the software suites mentioned at the beginning of this chapter. Some of the basic features supported by all spreadsheet programs are described in the next few sections. The spreadsheet program used in the illustrations in this section is *Microsoft Office Excel 2003.*

Creating and Editing a Worksheet

To create a new document, first open your spreadsheet program to start an empty workbook containing one or more blank worksheets. To retrieve an existing spreadsheet to edit or print instead, use the *Open* command on the File menu or toolbar. Worksheets are divided into **rows** and **columns**. The intersection of a row and a column is called a **cell**, and each cell is identified by its *cell address* comprised of the column letter followed by the row number, such as B4 or E22. The *cell pointer* places a box around the *current cell* to identify it. The current cell is the one into which typed content will go or to which formatting commands will be applied. If more than one cell is selected, as in Figure 7-12, the box is placed around all of the selected cells (called a *block* or *range*) and the current cell is the cell within the block that is not highlighted (such as cell E8 in Figure 7-12). To type or otherwise input data into a worksheet, move the cell pointer to the appropriate cell and then type or otherwise input the desired content. Cell content is typically a *label*, a *constant value*, or a *formula* or *function*.

>**Spreadsheet.** A group of values and other data organized into rows and columns. >**Spreadsheet software.** Application software used to create spreadsheet documents, which typically contain a great deal of numbers and mathematical computations and are organized into rows and columns. >**Worksheet.** A document in a spreadsheet program. >**Workbook.** A collection of worksheets saved in a single spreadsheet file. >**Row.** In a spreadsheet program, a horizontal group of cells on a worksheet. >**Column.** In a spreadsheet program, a vertical group of cells on a worksheet. >**Cell.** The location at the intersection of a row and column on a worksheet into which data can be typed.

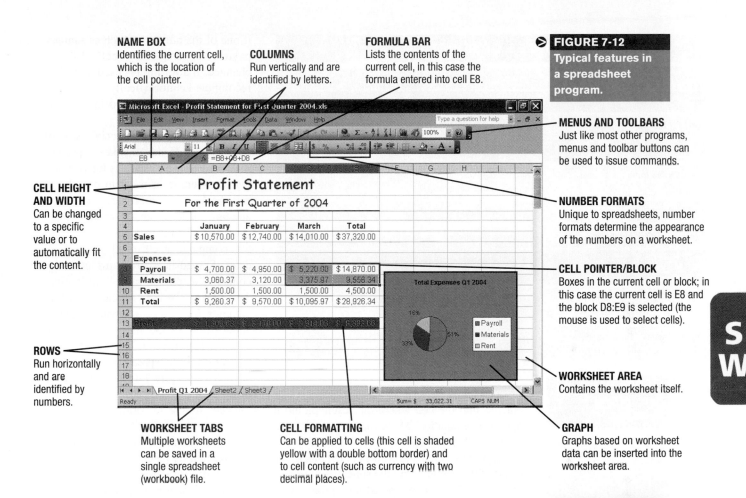

NAME BOX
Identifies the current cell, which is the location of the cell pointer.

COLUMNS
Run vertically and are identified by letters.

FORMULA BAR
Lists the contents of the current cell, in this case the formula entered into cell E8.

FIGURE 7-12
Typical features in a spreadsheet program.

MENUS AND TOOLBARS
Just like most other programs, menus and toolbar buttons can be used to issue commands.

CELL HEIGHT AND WIDTH
Can be changed to a specific value or to automatically fit the content.

NUMBER FORMATS
Unique to spreadsheets, number formats determine the appearance of the numbers on a worksheet.

CELL POINTER/BLOCK
Boxes in the current cell or block; in this case the current cell is E8 and the block D8:E9 is selected (the mouse is used to select cells).

ROWS
Run horizontally and are identified by numbers.

WORKSHEET AREA
Contains the worksheet itself.

WORKSHEET TABS
Multiple worksheets can be saved in a single spreadsheet (workbook) file.

CELL FORMATTING
Can be applied to cells (this cell is shaded yellow with a double bottom border) and to cell content (such as currency with two decimal places).

GRAPH
Graphs based on worksheet data can be inserted into the worksheet area.

Entering Labels and Constant Values

Labels are words, column headings, and other non-mathematical data, such as *Profit Statement* and *January* in Figure 7-12. **Constant values** are numbers, such as *105* or *12740.25*. To enter a label or constant value into a cell, move the cell pointer to that cell, type the appropriate content (without any additional characters, such as a dollar sign or comma), and press the Enter key.

Entering Formulas and Functions

Formulas perform mathematical operations on the contents of other cells—such as adding or multiplying them—and display the results in the cell containing the formula. When entering a formula into a cell, most spreadsheet programs require that you begin with some type of mathematical symbol (usually the equal sign =), and then you enter the cell addresses and mathematical operators (see Figure 7-13) to create the formula. When creating formulas, it is important to always use the cell addresses of *where* the numbers you want to include in the calculation are located (such as = B8 + C8 + D8 for the formula used to calculate the value displayed in cell E8 in Figure 7-12), rather than the numbers themselves (such as = 4700 + 4950 + 5220). If the actual numbers are used in the formula instead, the result of that formula (such as the total in cell E8) will not be correctly updated

FIGURE 7-13
Mathematical operators. These mathematical operators are universal operators used by most application programs that perform calculations, including spreadsheet programs.

Symbol	Operation
+	Addition
−	Subtraction
*	Multiplication
/	Division
^	Exponentiation

>**Label.** A text-based entry in a worksheet cell that identifies data on the worksheet. >**Constant value.** A numerical entry in a worksheet cell.
>**Formula.** An entry in a worksheet cell that performs computations on worksheet data and displays the results.

EXAMPLES OF FUNCTIONS

= SUM (range)	Calculates the sum of all values in a range.
= MAX (range)	Finds the highest value in a range.
= MIN (range)	Finds the lowest value in a range.
= NOW ( )	Inserts the current date and time.
= COUNT (range)	Counts the number of non-empty cells containing numerical values in a range.
= AVERAGE (range)	Calculates the average of values in a range.
= ABS (cell or expression)	Calculates the absolute value of the cell or expression.
= FV (rate, number of payments, payment amount)	Calculates the future value of an annuity at a specified interest rate.
= PMT (rate, number of payments, loan amount)	Calculates the periodic payment for a loan.
= IF (conditional expression, value if true, value if false)	Supplies to a cell a value that depends on whether the conditional expression is true or false.

> **FIGURE 7-14**
> **Spreadsheet functions.**

if one of the numbers (such as January payroll expenses in cell B8) is changed. If a formula is used, it will be recomputed automatically every time any data in the cells used in that formula is changed.

A **function** is a special type of named formula that invokes a preprogrammed formula (such as for computing the average of a group of cells or calculating a mortgage payment amount), or looks up information from other cells in the spreadsheet or from the computer itself (such as today's date). Spreadsheet programs normally contain a hundred or more built-in functions that can be used instead of writing complex formulas for a wide range of applications in the fields of business, science, engineering, and more. Some commonly used spreadsheet functions are listed in Figure 7-14. Like formulas, functions must begin with an equal sign (or other allowable formula symbol). Functions are entered into the cell where the result should be displayed, similar to formulas, using the appropriate notation. Many functions perform operations on a block of cells, such as to add several cells in a single row or column. Blocks are always rectangular and are identified by specifying two opposite corners of the block, such as D8 through E9 (usually typed as *D8:E9* or *D8..E9*, depending on the spreadsheet program being used) for the four cells highlighted in Figure 7-12. Many spreadsheet programs also include a function wizard to walk you through creating a function step by step.

Editing the Contents of a Cell

To edit any type of cell content, first move the cell pointer to the appropriate cell and then either retype the contents or edit the contents using the *formula bar*—the bar between the toolbar and worksheet area that displays the contents of the current cell. Different from the actual cell, the formula bar always displays cell content as it was typed, so you see the actual formula entered, not the result of that formula (refer back to Figure 7-12). To delete the contents of a cell, most spreadsheet programs allow you to move the cell pointer to that cell and press the Delete key.

Inserting and Deleting Rows or Columns

All spreadsheet programs allow you to insert or delete columns or rows in a worksheet. Inserting or deleting involves moving the cell pointer to the appropriate position on the worksheet and issuing the proper command from either the Edit or Insert menu. When a row or column is inserted or deleted, the spreadsheet program moves the remaining rows and columns accordingly.

Moving and Copying Cells

As with most application programs, spreadsheet programs permit users to copy or move the contents of one cell (or block of cells) to another location. Some spreadsheet programs

>**Function.** A named formula that can be entered into a worksheet cell to perform some type of calculation or to extract information from other cells in the worksheet.

COPYING WITH RELATIVE CELL REFERENCES
In most formulas, cell addresses are relative and will be adjusted as the formula is copied.

COPYING WITH ABSOLUTE CELL REFERENCES
The dollar ($) signs mark a cell reference as absolute; it will be copied exactly as it appears in the source cell.

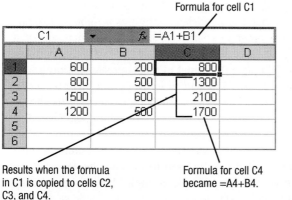

Formula for cell C1

Results when the formula in C1 is copied to cells C2, C3, and C4.

Formula for cell C4 became =A4+B4.

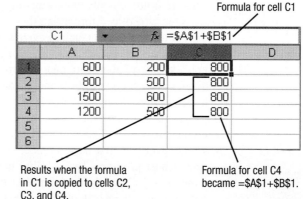

Formula for cell C1

Results when the formula in C1 is copied to cells C2, C3, and C4.

Formula for cell C4 became =$A$1+$B$1.

have a shortcut for quickly copying a cell to adjacent cells, such as dragging the bottom right corner of the original cell in Microsoft Excel. Any type of content—such as a label, value, formula, or function—can be moved or copied. When formulas or functions are copied, however, the resulting formulas or functions depend on the type of *cell referencing* used in the original formula or function, as discussed next.

> **FIGURE 7-15**
> Relative vs. absolute cell referencing.

Relative vs. Absolute Cell Referencing

Relative cell references are used in most spreadsheet programs by default. With relative referencing, the cell addresses in the copied formula are adjusted to perform the same operation as in the original formula, just in the new location (instead of copying the cell addresses in the formula verbatim). In other words, the formula in the new location does the same *relative* operation as in the original location. For example, in the left screen in Figure 7-15, the relative formula from cell C1 (that adds the two cells to the left of the formula cell) is copied to cells C2 through C4. Because the cell references are all relative, when the formula is copied to the new cells, the cell references are adjusted to continue to add the two cells to the left of the formula cell. For instance, the formula in cell C2 became = A2 + B2 and the formula in cell C3 became = A3 + B3.

With *absolute cell references*, in contrast, formulas are copied exactly as they are written (see the right screen in Figure 7-15). It is appropriate to use an absolute cell reference when you always want to add, subtract, multiply, or divide by a specific cell in all copies of the formula. That is, you don't want that cell address to be adjusted when the formula is copied. To make a cell reference in a formula absolute, a special symbol—usually a dollar sign ($)—is placed before each column letter and row number that should not change. For example, both of the cell references in the formula in cell C1 in Figure 7-15 are absolute, resulting in the formula = $A$1 + $B$1 being placed in all three cells (C2 through C4) when the formula is copied.

Formatting a Worksheet

Data in a worksheet is frequently formatted. In most spreadsheet programs, formatting can be applied at the cell, row or column, and worksheet levels.

Cell Formatting

Common types of *cell formatting* include changing the font face, font size, font style, and alignment, similar to formatting characters in a word processing program. A difference is that the formatting is applied on a cell-by-cell basis, instead of character-by-character or paragraph-by-paragraph. For example, changing the font size while in cell A1 would change the size of all text located in cell A1, and clicking the center button while in cell B1 would center the contents of that cell just within the cell, not between the page margins. A block of cells can be selected with the mouse or keyboard before issuing a cell formatting command (such as Bold) to apply that formatting to all of the selected cells at one time.

One type of cell formatting that is unique to spreadsheet programs is *numeric formatting*. Number formats (such as *currency*, *percent*, or *comma*) change the way numbers on a spreadsheet appear, such as how many decimal places are displayed, if the numbers are preceded by a dollar sign, and so forth. The default format in most spreadsheet programs displays no special symbols and as many decimals as will fit in the cell, if there is a decimal portion to the number. Because this results in an inconsistent appearance, users should format most worksheet cells containing numbers to insure a consistent appearance. The number format toolbar buttons are most commonly used for numeric formatting. After selecting the desired basic number format (such as currency, percent, or comma), most spreadsheet programs have toolbar buttons that can be used to increase or decrease the number of decimal places displayed, as needed. For example, a single click of the currency button might change "90000" to "$90,000.00" and then two clicks on the decrease decimal button would change the display to "$90,000".

Other possible cell formatting includes changing the text color, changing the text direction, wrapping text within a cell, and adding borders or shading.

Row or Column Formatting

Row or column formatting generally includes changing the height of a row or the width of a column. Most spreadsheet programs allow you to select a specific cell width or row height, or choose to have the width or height fit the contents of the cells.

Worksheet Formatting

Worksheet formatting includes changing the worksheet margins and adding headers, footers, and page numbers. Some spreadsheet programs also allow you to apply one of several different *autoformatting* styles. With autoformatting, the spreadsheet program analyzes your worksheet and automatically applies the color scheme and format you select based on the position of headings, borders, and data. Another common option is adding a background image.

Charts and What-If Analysis

Charts are often added to worksheets to better illustrate some of the numbers and computations included in the worksheet, as well as to prepare presentation materials; *what-if analysis* is frequently used to help make business decisions.

Charts

Most spreadsheet programs include some type of *charting* or *graphing* capability. Because the data to be included in many business charts is often already located on a spreadsheet, using that program's charting feature eliminates reentering data. Instead, the cells containing the data to be charted are selected, and then the type of chart—as well as titles and other customizations—can be specified. The finished chart can usually be inserted into a block of cells on an existing worksheet or placed in a blank worksheet by itself. Types of charts are discussed in more detail later in this chapter.

What-If Analysis

Because spreadsheet programs automatically recalculate all formulas on a worksheet every time a cell on the worksheet is edited, they are particularly useful for *what-if analysis*—also called *sensitivity analysis*. For example, suppose you wish to know *what* profit would have resulted for January in Figure 7-12 *if* sales had been $15,000 instead of $10,570. You can simply enter the new value, 15000, into Cell B5, and the spreadsheet program automatically recomputes all formulas, allowing you to determine (from looking at the new value in cell B13) that the profit would have been $5,739.63.

In just a fraction of a second, spreadsheets can perform calculations that would require several hours to do manually. This allows businesspeople to run through many more possibilities in a shorter period of time before making decisions than in the past when all such calculations had to be performed by hand. Another type of sensitivity analysis (called *goal seeking* in Microsoft Excel) involves having the spreadsheet compute the amount a constant value would need to be in order for the result of a particular formula to become a specified amount (such as the total sales required to obtain a January profit of $5,000, if all of the expenses stayed the same).

FURTHER EXPLORATION

For links to further information about spreadsheet software, go to www.course.com/uc10/ch07

Spreadsheets and the Web

As with word processors, recent spreadsheet programs also have built-in Web capabilities. Although they are less commonly used to create Web pages, many spreadsheet programs have an option on the File menu to save the current worksheet as a Web page, and hyperlinks can be inserted into worksheet cells. Groups of cells can also be selected and copied to a Web publishing or word processing program to insert spreadsheet data into a Web page as a table.

DATABASE CONCEPTS

People often need to retrieve large amounts of data rapidly. For example, a customer service representative may need to locate a customer's order status quickly while the customer is on the telephone. The registrar of a university may have to look up a student's grade point average or rapidly determine if the student has any outstanding fees before processing his or her class registration. A clerk in a video store may need to determine if a particular movie is available for rental and, if not, when it is due to be returned. The type of software used for such tasks is a *database management system*. Computer-based database management systems are rapidly replacing the paper-based filing systems that people have had to wade through in the past to find the information that their jobs require. The most common type of database used on PCs today is called a *relational database*. The basic features and concepts of PC-based relational database software are discussed next. Other types of database programs are covered in Chapter 14.

What Is a Database?

A **database** is a collection of related data that is stored on a computer and organized in a manner enabling information to be retrieved as needed. A *database management system* (*DBMS*)—also sometimes called just **database software**—is the type of program used to create, maintain, and organize data in a database, as well as to retrieve information from it.

Although not all databases are organized identically, most PC-based databases are organized into fields, records, and files. A **field** (now more commonly called a **column**) is a single type of data to be stored in a database, such as a person's name or a person's telephone number. A **record** (now more commonly called a **row**) is a collection of related fields—for example the ID number, name, address, and major of Phyllis Hoffman (see Figure 7-16). A **table** is a collection of related rows (such as all student address data, all student grade data, or all student schedule data). One or more related tables can be stored in a database file.

>**Database.** A collection of related data that is stored in a manner enabling information to be retrieved as needed; in a relational database, a collection of related tables. >**Database software.** Application software that allows the creation and manipulation of an electronic database. >**Field.** A single category of data to be stored in a database, such as a person's name or telephone number. Also called a column. >**Column.** In a database, a field. >**Record.** A collection of related fields in a database. Also called a row. >**Row.** In a database program, a record. >**Table.** In a relational database, a collection of related records (rows).

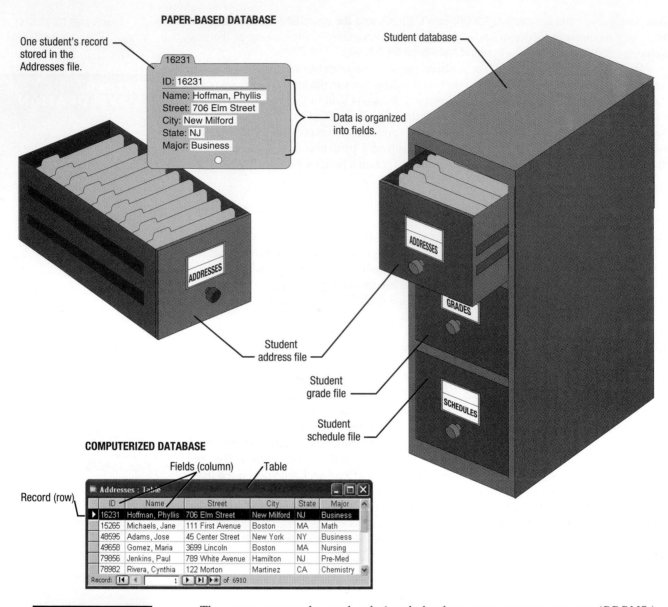

PAPER-BASED DATABASE

One student's record stored in the Addresses file.

16231

ID: 16231
Name: Hoffman, Phyllis
Street: 706 Elm Street
City: New Milford
State: NJ
Major: Business

Data is organized into fields.

Student database

ADDRESSES

GRADES

SCHEDULES

ADDRESSES

Student address file

Student grade file

Student schedule file

COMPUTERIZED DATABASE

Fields (column)   Table

Record (row)

ID	Name	Street	City	State	Major
16231	Hoffman, Phyllis	706 Elm Street	New Milford	NJ	Business
15265	Michaels, Jane	111 First Avenue	Boston	MA	Math
48595	Adams, Jose	45 Center Street	New York	NY	Business
49658	Gomez, Maria	3699 Lincoln	Boston	MA	Nursing
79856	Jenkins, Paul	789 White Avenue	Hamilton	NJ	Pre-Med
78982	Rivera, Cynthia	122 Morton	Martinez	CA	Chemistry

Addresses : Table

Record: 1 of 6910

FIGURE 7-16

Paper-based vs. computerized databases. Data is organized into fields (columns), records (rows), and tables.

The most commonly used *relational database management systems* (*RDBMSs*) include *Microsoft Access*, *Corel Paradox*, and *Lotus Approach*—again, all part of their respective software suites—as well as the stand-alone *Oracle* database product from Oracle Corporation. Some of the basic features supported by database programs in general will be described in the next few sections using *Microsoft Office Access 2003* as the example.

Creating a Database

A database can contain a variety of *objects* (see Figure 7-17). The object created first in a new database is the table, and then other objects (such as *forms*, *queries*, and *reports*, discussed shortly) can be created and used in conjunction with that table.

To begin to create a database table, after opening your database program and choosing the necessary options to create a new table, the *structure* of the table is specified. A table's structure includes a list of fields and their properties (see Figure 7-18). As a minimum all fields need to have a *field name* (an identifying name unique within the table) and *data type* (the type of data to be contained in the field, such as text, numbers, or date) defined. Other possible properties include the *field size* (the maximum number of characters allowed for the contents of that field), *default value* (the initial contents of the field that remains until it is changed), the format with which the field contents should be displayed, and whether or not the field is *required* (must contain some content).

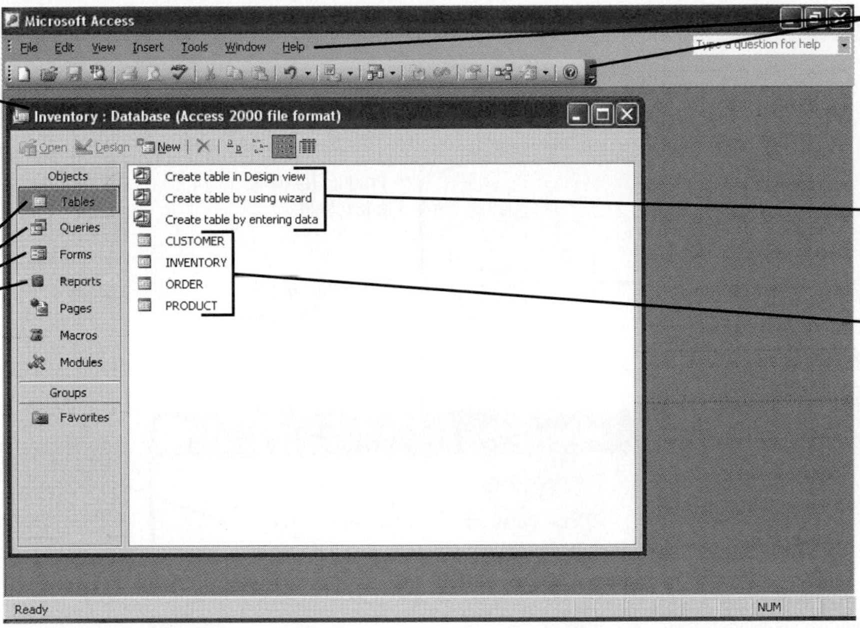

MENUS AND TOOLBARS
Just as with most other programs, menus and toolbar buttons can be used to issue commands.

DATABASE FILE
All of the Inventory database objects are stored within the Inventory database file.

DATABASE OBJECTS
Common database objects are tables (for storing data), forms (for viewing table data), and queries and reports (for retrieving information from a table). Here, the Tables object is selected.

One of these options can be selected to create a new table.

Four tables have been created within the Inventory database file. Double-clicking a table name will open that table in the table Datasheet view.

After the table structure has been created, data may be entered into the table. Data entry can be performed in the regular *Table view*—sometimes called *Datasheet view*, since the table looks similar to a spreadsheet—or a *form* can be created and used to enter the data. A form allows you to view or edit table content in a more formal manner—usually just working with one record at a time, instead of a full page of records, as in Datasheet view. Using a form and Datasheet view are both illustrated in Figure 7-18.

Modifying a Database
Once a database table has been created, it may need to be modified. Changes may be made to the table structure or to the data located in the table as needed.

Modifying the Table Structure
The table structure needs to be modified only when there are changes to the field properties. For example, a field size may need to be increased to accommodate a name that is longer than was anticipated when the table structure was created, the wrong field type may have been initially selected, or a new field may need to be added. To modify a table's structure, the user opens the table in *Design view* using the appropriate toolbar button or menu option, and then makes any necessary changes. Design view shows the table fields and properties and is used only to initially create the table structure (as in Figure 7-18) or to make changes to that structure.

Editing, Adding, and Deleting Records
To make changes to the actual data in a table, the table must first be opened (either using Datasheet view or a form), and then the necessary changes can be made. To move to a particular record to edit its contents, either the keyboard arrows or the record buttons located at the bottom of the window (see Figure 7-18) can be used. There is also usually a *New Record* button in the group of record buttons that automatically moves you to a blank record; new records are typically added to the bottom of a table.

To delete the current record, either the Delete key on the keyboard or some type of *Delete Record* option on the menu bar is used. Since deleting a record by accident can be disastrous in a business database, most programs require the user to confirm the deletion in some manner before it is carried out.

> **FIGURE 7-17**
> **Typical database objects.** Common database objects include tables, forms, queries, and reports. The first object to be created is the table.

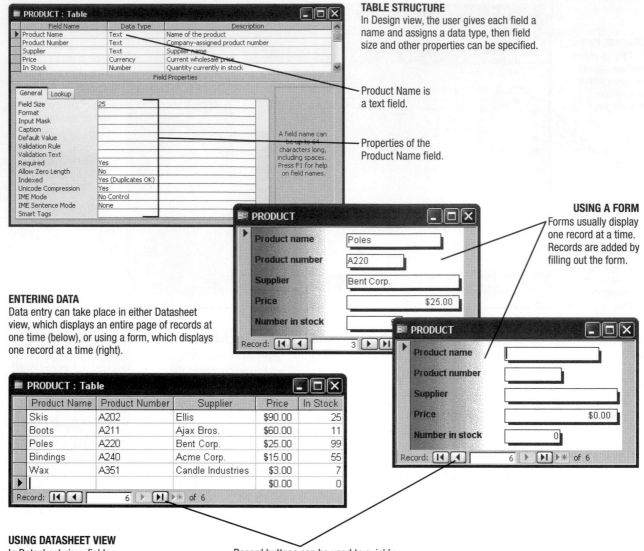

TABLE STRUCTURE
In Design view, the user gives each field a name and assigns a data type, then field size and other properties can be specified.

Product Name is a text field.

Properties of the Product Name field.

USING A FORM
Forms usually display one record at a time. Records are added by filling out the form.

ENTERING DATA
Data entry can take place in either Datasheet view, which displays an entire page of records at one time (below), or using a form, which displays one record at a time (right).

USING DATASHEET VIEW
In Datasheet view, fields appear as columns, and records appear as rows.

Record buttons can be used to quickly move up or down the table, as well as to the end of the table to add a new record.

> **FIGURE 7-18**
> **Creating a database.**

TIP

Databases, queries, and reports are discussed in much more detail in Chapter 14.

Queries and Reports

To retrieve information from a database, *queries* and *reports* are used.

Queries

A *query* is a question, or, in database terms, a request for specific information from the database. A query takes your instructions about what information you want to find and displays only that requested information. When creating a query, you can specify both the records (rows) and fields (columns) that you want to see in the query results. To indicate which records you want to see, you specify search *criteria*—specific conditions that must be met in order for a record to be included in the query results. For instance, criteria could specify all products in the Product table shown in Figure 7-18 that come from the supplier "Ajax Bros." or all products that have less than 10 units in stock. Many database programs include a wizard that helps users create queries quickly and easily. Once a query has been created, it can be saved so that the results can be redisplayed at a later time. Whenever a query is opened and displayed, only the records meeting the specified criteria at the current time are displayed, so the query results always accurately reflect the current data in the database.

Reports

Reports are created when a more formal printout of an entire table or of a query result is required. Like queries, many database programs have a wizard available to assist users in creating a report. There is also usually an editing option available to enable users to create a report from scratch or to modify a report that was initially created using a wizard.

When a report object is created, the instructions for what the report should look like are saved under the report name. Whenever the report is opened, the appropriate table data is displayed in the specified locations on the report. Consequently, just as with queries, reports always display the data contained in a table at the time the report is generated. Many database programs allow reports to be created in a variety of styles, and can incorporate text formatting, clip art, and other enhancements.

Databases and the Web

Databases and the Web are very closely related. Many Web sites use one or more databases to keep track of inventory; allow searching for people, documents, or other information; place real-time orders, and so forth. To try out a Web database yourself, go to a retail Web site that allows you to search for products (such as Amazon.com or Walmart.com). After typing keywords in the search box displayed on the screen, the results of your search (query) are displayed on the screen. How Web databases work is explained in Chapter 14.

PRESENTATION GRAPHICS CONCEPTS

If you try to explain to others what you look like, it may take several minutes. Show them a color photograph, on the other hand, and you can convey the same information within seconds. The saying "a picture is worth a thousand words" is the cornerstone of *presentation graphics*.

What Is a Presentation Graphic?

A **presentation graphic** is an image designed to visually enhance a presentation, typically to more easily convey information to other people. Often, presentation graphics take the form of an *electronic slide show*—a group of electronic **slides** displayed one after the other on a large monitor or on a projection screen. Slides typically consist of text, images, or other elements arranged on a screen-size page. Presentation graphics can also be printed handouts or overhead transparencies, or images inserted into a word processing or other type of document. Some of the elements commonly found in presentation graphics are illustrated in Figure 7-19. To create presentation graphics, **presentation graphics software** is used.

Because it is generally easier and more effective to convey information graphically, instead of presenting text-only or numeric-only output containing the same information, presentation graphics are used widely in both business and educational presentations. Slide-show presentations are used frequently to hold the interest of the audience while conveying information, and studies have found that presentation graphics also make the presenter look more professional in the eyes of others. Often the design, colors, and types of graphics used can determine how well your point will come across.

Some of today's most common presentation graphics programs are *Microsoft PowerPoint*, *Corel Presentations*, and *Lotus Freelance Graphics*. The presentation graphics program illustrated in the figures in the following sections is *Microsoft Office PowerPoint 2003*.

FURTHER EXPLORATION

For links to further information about database software, go to www.course.com/uc10/ch07

S
W

>**Presentation graphic.** An image, such as a graph or text chart, designed to visually enhance a presentation. >**Slide.** A one-page presentation graphic that can be displayed in a group with others to form an online slide show. >**Presentation graphics software.** Application software used to create presentation graphics and online slide shows.

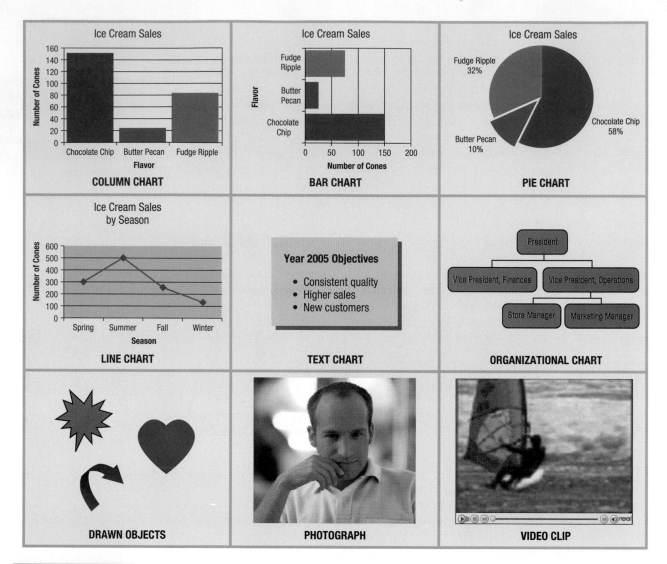

FIGURE 7-19

Sample presentation graphic elements. Presentation graphics can include a variety of charts, text, images, video clips, and more.

Creating a Presentation

To create a new document, first open your presentation graphics program and start a new blank presentation. Some programs initially display a list of slide layouts containing placeholders for the various elements in the slide (such as text, images, or charts) that can be selected to quickly create the basic slide (see Figure 7-20). Once a layout is selected, the placeholders located on the slide are selected and replaced with the proper content. After the first slide has been created, a new slide can be inserted into the presentation and the procedure repeated until the entire presentation is completed.

Just as with the other application programs discussed so far, toolbar buttons can be used to format slide text to use the desired font face, font size, style, and alignment. There are also toolbar buttons and menu options to add other objects to the slide, such as images and charts. Images can be photographs, graphics created in another program, scanned images, or shapes drawn using the Drawing toolbar button. Charts can be copied from a spreadsheet program or created in the presentation graphics program.

OUTLINE AND SLIDES PANES
Slide text can be created and edited using the Outline pane; the Slides pane shows thumbnails of the presentation.

CLIP ART
Clip art or other graphcs can be inserted and resized or otherwise modified.

TEXT
Can be formatted with the toolbar buttons the same as in other Windows programs.

FIGURE 7-20
Typical features in a presentation graphics program.

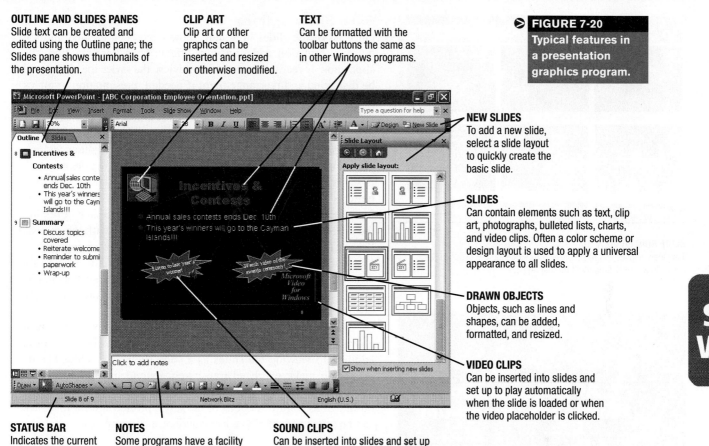

NEW SLIDES
To add a new slide, select a slide layout to quickly create the basic slide.

SLIDES
Can contain elements such as text, clip art, photographs, bulleted lists, charts, and video clips. Often a color scheme or design layout is used to apply a universal appearance to all slides.

DRAWN OBJECTS
Objects, such as lines and shapes, can be added, formatted, and resized.

VIDEO CLIPS
Can be inserted into slides and set up to play automatically when the slide is loaded or when the video placeholder is clicked.

STATUS BAR
Indicates the current slide number and how many slides are in the presentation.

NOTES
Some programs have a facility for adding speaker notes which can be viewed by the presenter during the slide show or printed.

SOUND CLIPS
Can be inserted into slides and set up to play automatically when the slide is loaded or when the sound placeholder is clicked.

Enhancing and Finishing a Presentation

Increasingly, sound, video, and animated effects are being added to presentations to create more exciting and dynamic presentations. Video and audio clips can be inserted into slides using the menu and can be set up to play automatically when the slide is displayed, or, alternatively, to play when their placeholders on the slide are clicked with the mouse. Other enhancements and finishing touches are discussed next.

Animation and Transitions

Animated effects include animating existing text or other objects located on a slide and using *transitions* between slides. When text is animated, a variety of effects can be used to initially display the text when the slide is viewed, such as *flying* the text in from the edge of the screen or *dissolving* the text in from a blank slide. Animation settings can also be specified to indicate the sequence chart objects will be displayed (such as to build a bulleted list one item at a time), whether or not a video will loop continuously, and more.

Transitions determine how one slide in a slide show leaves and how the next slide is displayed. Most presentation programs include a wide variety of transitions that can be assigned to individual slides or to an entire presentation. Sometimes a random transition option is available to apply transitions in random order to each slide in the slide show—a timesaving feature if specific transitions for each slide are not necessary. Sound effects can also be part of a transition in many presentation programs.

FURTHER EXPLORATION

For links to further information about presentation graphics software, go to www.course.com/uc10/ch07

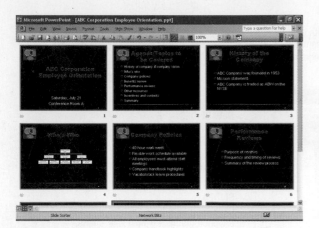

SLIDE SORTER VIEW
This view allows you to preview and rearrange the order that the slides in a presentation will be displayed.

SLIDE SHOW
When a slide show is run, it will usually be displayed full screen. Slides can be advanced at predetermined intervals or by clicking the mouse or pressing the spacebar.

FIGURE 7-21
Slide shows. The slides in a slide show can be rearranged as necessary, then displayed as a full-screen slide show. Slides can also be printed as handouts or overheads, when necessary.

Slide Show Options

Once all of the slides in a slide show have been created and the desired animation and transition effects have been applied, the slide show is ready to be run. To preview the order the slides will be displayed and rearrange them if needed, presentation graphics programs typically have a special view, such as the *slide sorter view* shown in Figure 7-21. Using this view, slides can easily be rearranged by dragging them with the mouse to their new location in the presentation. When the slide show is run, the slides are displayed in the designated order. Depending on how the presentation is set up, the slides either automatically advance after a specified period of time, or the speaker (or person viewing the slide show, for a stand-alone presentation) moves to the next slide by pressing the spacebar or clicking anywhere on the screen with the mouse. Some presentation graphics programs have a pen or highlighter tool that the speaker can use during the presentation to temporarily write on the slides while the slide show is running, such as to circle a particular sentence for emphasis or draw an arrow pointing to one part of the slide.

As mentioned previously, most presentation software programs also include print options, which can be used in lieu of or in addition to viewing the slides as a slide show. The slides can be printed to make overhead transparencies and handouts; speaker notes can be printed for the speaker to use; and the presentation outline or miniature versions of the slides printed several to a page can be printed to distribute as an audience handout.

Presentation Graphics and the Web

As with the other application programs discussed so far, presentation graphics programs can be used to generate Web pages or Web page content, and slides can include hyperlinks. Web-based presentations may include the same type of objects included in non-Web presentations, such as text, images, charts, video clips, and sound clips. When a slide show is saved as a series of Web pages and displayed using a Web browser, generally forward and backward navigational buttons are displayed on the slides to allow the user to control the presentation.

GRAPHICS AND MULTIMEDIA CONCEPTS

As previously discussed, *graphics* are graphical images, such as digital photographs, clip art, scanned drawings, images created with a software program, and so forth. **Multimedia** refers to any type of application or presentation that involves more than one type of media. Although, technically, books such as this fit that definition since they use two types of media (text and graphics), typically applications aren't labeled "multimedia" unless they include sound, video, animation, or *interactivity*—the ability for the user to control the speed, content, direction, or other aspect of the information being delivered.

>Multimedia. The integration of a variety of media, such as text, graphics, video, animation, and sound.

Multimedia Applications

Multimedia applications can be found on the Web as stand-alone programs and as consumer applications. Because multimedia elements and applications require a great deal of storage space, multimedia applications are usually run from a CD or DVD, instead of being completely installed on the hard drive, unless they are Web based. Some of the most common multimedia applications are discussed next.

Business Presentations

Multimedia business presentations often consist of presentation graphics slide shows, as previously discussed. Other business presentation possibilities include animated content on the company Web site, on marketing CDs, or on CD business cards.

Reference Materials

One of the most widely used multimedia-based reference materials is the multimedia encyclopedia (see Figure 7-22). Although the passages include text similar to a conventional encyclopedia, multimedia encyclopedias also feature video clips, sound clips, and animation to more easily convey information.

Computer-Based Training (CBT) and Web-Based Training (WBT)

Computer-based training (**CBT**) is an individualized instruction method used to deliver content via a computer. CBT is also called *computer-aided instruction (CAI)*. Some CBT applications are *mastery-based*, which means that the student is required to complete an exercise or test at a specific success rate or higher before moving on to the next exercise. CBT is commonly used to supplement curriculum for all levels of schooling, as well as for industry training. When CBT takes place over the Internet, it is referred to as **Web-based training** (**WBT**). An example of Web-based training is shown in Figure 7-22.

Virtual Reality

Virtual reality (**VR**) is the use of a computer to create environments that look like they do in the real world. VR can be used in conjunction with objects, people, locations, or simulated situations. Through VR, it is possible to participate in activities such as taking "tours" of buildings, museums, vacation destinations, and homes for sale; viewing products from all angles before purchasing them; and receiving training in and practicing a new sport, skill, or technique. VR applications can be found both on and off the Web, and some require special hardware, such as special goggles (which project computer-generated images directly toward the eye) or gloves (containing built-in sensors that change the visual images accordingly when the gloved hands are moved). VR training applications, such as practicing new surgical techniques, learning how to fly an airplane, or performing repairs on expensive aircraft, may require specialized VR hardware for that particular application—some even require a complete simulator, such as those resembling a driver's seat or cockpit, as in the commercial pilot simulator shown in Figure 7-22.

Entertainment

It is very common for computer games designed for both adults and children to be multimedia oriented (see Figure 7-22). Common multimedia elements found in computer games include background music, sound effects, animated effects, narration, talking characters,

---

>**Computer-based training (CBT).** Individualized instruction delivered via a computer. >**Web-based training (WBT).** Instruction delivered on an individual basis via the World Wide Web. >**Virtual reality (VR).** The use of a computer to create three-dimensional environments that look like they do in the real world.

> **FIGURE 7-22**
> **Multimedia applications.** Multimedia applications are commonly found both on and off the Web.

WEB-BASED TRAINING (WBT)
Often includes video clips and animations; online exercises, tutorials, and exams; e-mail links; and other resources.

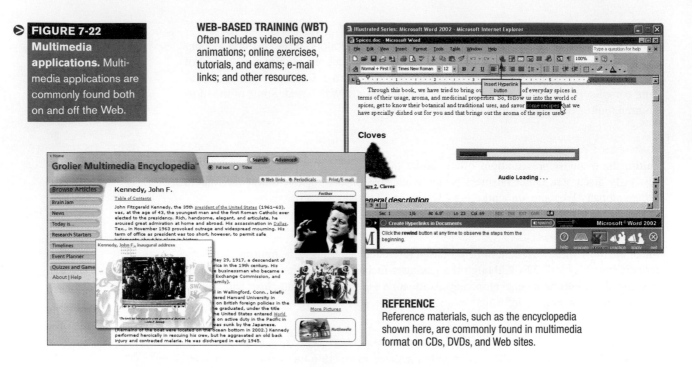

REFERENCE
Reference materials, such as the encyclopedia shown here, are commonly found in multimedia format on CDs, DVDs, and Web sites.

VIRTUAL REALITY (VR)
Used for entertainment and training (as in the commercial pilot simulator, below), as well as to enable 3D views of items featured on a Web site (as in the virtual tour of a home, right).

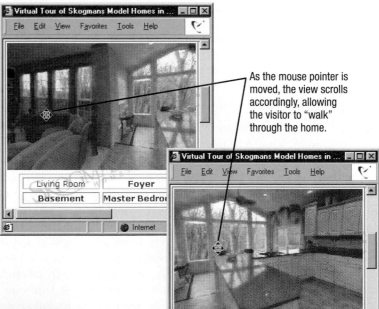

As the mouse pointer is moved, the view scrolls accordingly, allowing the visitor to "walk" through the home.

ENTERTAINMENT
Computer games for both kids and adults alike usually include multimedia elements, such as background music, images, animation, and more.

INSIDE THE INDUSTRY

Jellyvision's Interactive Conversation Interface (iCi)

Beginning with its release in 1995, Jellyvision's *YOU DON'T KNOW JACK* adult trivia game (see the accompanying screen shot) has been a huge success. Key to the program is Jellyvision's concept of "Interactive Conversation" that relies on a user interface called the *Interactive Conversation Interface (iCi)*. The goal of iCi is to create the illusion of conversation between the player (a person) and the game host (a software program). To accomplish this, writers, designers, and actors work together to script and record realistic answers to every possible situation the player will encounter during the game and every response he or she will make to a question, and then develop the program so that the proper responses will be delivered for each possible player action. Crucial to this process is ensuring the dialog is appropriate and doesn't repeat, giving the user only one task to do at a time with a limited number of choices, and keeping the pace steady, including responding appropriately if the user doesn't answer a question. For instance, not answering a question quickly enough in the YOU DON'T KNOW JACK program might cause the host's next assigned line to be "OK, sleepy, let's try that again" or "Excuse me, we've got a game to play!"—in the same manner as a real game show host would prod a contestant who failed to act in a timely manner during a live game show. Adding to the appeal of the YOU DON'T KNOW JACK program is the chatty background atmosphere of a game show

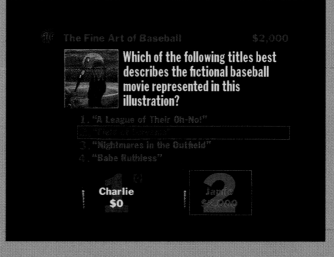

Jellyvision's best-selling YOU DON'T KNOW JACK games use iCi to create realistic conversations between the player and the host.

studio, catchy music and graphics, lots of animation, funny trivia questions, and a host whose casual, but intimate, conversation is funny, as well as sarcastic at times.

In addition to being used with computers games, iCi can be used for a variety of other applications, such as an interactive tour guide who gives you advice via a cell phone as you travel by asking and responding to questions, customized news delivery, interactive customer service support, and more.

and video clips. Multimedia games are widely available on CD and DVD, as well as on Web sites. For a look at the technology behind how one company makes interactive games, including the popular *You Don't Know Jack* program, see the Inside the Industry box.

Information Kiosks

Information kiosks are self-service stations used for accessing information or requesting products or services placed in public locations, such as stores, airports, and hotels. At a minimum, most information kiosks include text, graphics, and interactivity; animation is frequently included, as well.

Types of Graphics and Multimedia Software

There is a tremendous selection of software that can be used to create and edit graphics and other multimedia elements. While some applications—such as drawing a picture or touching up a photo—may only require one program, creating all of the elements needed for a complete multimedia application or Web site typically requires multiple programs. Some of the most common types of graphic and multimedia software are discussed next.

TIP

Creating multimedia elements for Web pages is discussed in more detail in Chapter 10.

Graphics Software

Graphics software is used to create or modify images. Commercial graphics programs are commonly distinguished by whether they are primarily oriented toward painting, drawing, or image editing, although these are general categories, not strict classifications.

Painting programs are typically *raster-based* programs that allow you to create bit-mapped images and color or otherwise modify them pixel by pixel. Usually, the images you create cannot be resized without getting jagged edges or blurred images. However, painting programs are fine for creating and modifying simple images. Common painting programs include *Windows Paint* (shown in Figure 7-23) and *Jasc Paint Shop Pro*.

Drawing programs are typically *vector-based* programs that enable you to create images that can be resized and otherwise manipulated without loss of quality. This is possible because the images are created using mathematical formulas, not by coloring pixels. Drawing programs also usually allow you to *layer* objects, so if you place one object on top of another, you can later separate the two images, if desired. In contrast, because a painting program colors the actual pixels in an image, if you move one object on top of another, the pixels are recolored and the objects can't be separated. Widely used drawing programs include *Adobe® Illustrator®* (see Figure 7-23), *Macromedia Freehand*, and *CorelDRAW*.

Image-editing programs are drawing or painting programs specifically designed for touching up or modifying images. Editing options include correcting brightness or contrast, eliminating red eye, cropping, resizing, and applying filters or other special effects. Most programs also include options for *optimizing* images to reduce the file size. Optimization techniques include reducing the number of colors used in the image and converting the

> FIGURE 7-23
Graphics software.
Both painting and drawing programs can be used to create and modify images.

PAINTING PROGRAMS
Painting programs typically create raster images pixel by pixel so images cannot be layered or resized.

DRAWING PROGRAMS
Drawing programs typically create vector images using mathematical formulas, so images can consist of multiple objects that can be layered and the images can be resized without distortion.

>**Graphics software.** Application software used to create or modify images.

image to a more appropriate file format. One of the most widely used image-editing programs is *Adobe® Photoshop®*. Image-editing programs specifically designed for touching up digital photos are sometimes referred to as *photo editing software*. Some examples are *Adobe® PhotoDeluxe®* and *Microsoft Photo Editor*.

In practice, the distinction between these three types of programs is blurring as a wider range of features (such as layering and photo editing tools) is being included in graphics programs. Some graphics programs today can also work with both raster and vector graphics.

Audio and Video Editing Software

For creating and editing audio and video files, special *audio editing* and *video editing* software is used. To capture sound, a *sound recorder* can be used to capture input from a microphone or MIDI (musical instrument digital interface) device; to capture sound from a CD, *ripping software* is used. Video is either captured using a video-capture card or is input directly in digital form from a digital video camera's storage medium.

Once the audio or video file has been created or imported, it will likely need to be modified. Background noise or pauses may need to be removed, portions of the selection may need to be edited out, multiple segments may need to be spliced together, and special effects such as fade-ins and fade-outs may need to be applied. Remember that sound and video files tend to be extremely large, so editing a selection to be as short as possible is desirable for Web applications to minimize file size. Common audio editing programs include *Windows Sound Recorder*, *Sony Pictures DigitalSound Forge®*, and *Sony Pictures DigitalACID® Pro* (shown in Figure 7-24). Common video editing programs include *Apple Final Cut Express*, *Sony Pictures DigitalVegas®*, and *Adobe® Premiere®*. Finished audio and video clips can be inserted into multimedia applications and Web pages, or incorporated into animations using *animation software*.

> **FIGURE 7-24**
> **Audio and video editing.** Once sound and video have been converted to digital form, they often need to be edited to make the finished product as efficient as possible, as well as to combine clips and add special effects.

AUDIO EDITING SOFTWARE
Allows audio files to be recorded, cropped, mixed with other sound clips, and otherwise edited.

VIDEO EDITING SOFTWARE
Allows video files to be edited. As shown here, often a timeline can be used to assemble various clips into one finished product.

CD and DVD Burning and Authoring Software

As recordable and rewritable CDs and DVDs become more commonplace, a larger assortment of *CD and DVD burning software*—software used to record data on CDs and DVDs—has become available. Often CD or DVD burning software comes with a recordable or rewritable drive; other software can be used if that software is not capable of everything the user wishes to do. Some programs can burn both CDs and DVDs; many include tools for basic audio and video editing, as well. Two widely used programs are *Roxio Easy CD and DVD Creator* and *Nero 6: The Ultimate CD/DVD Burning Suite*. Software that is designed to create DVD presentations is referred to as *DVD authoring software*. Some examples include *Adobe® Encore DVD®* and *Apple DVD Studio Pro* (see Figure 7-25). In addition to being used professionally, CD and DVD burning and authoring software is increasingly being used for personal use, such as to burn custom music CDs and to edit home movies or burn them on DVDs.

> **FIGURE 7-25**
> **DVD authoring software.**

Media Players

Media players are programs designed to play audio and video files. They are used to play media from your PC—such as music CDs or downloaded music or video—as well as online audio and video clips. Some media players, such as the *RealOne Player* shown in Figure 7-26, can also be used to locate and play music from Internet radio stations. Two other widely used media players are *Windows Media Player* and *MusicMatch Jukebox*. Music players can also be used to burn CDs. For a look at how to burn personalized music CDs from songs purchased on CD or in MP3 format, see the How It Works box.

> **FIGURE 7-26**
> **Media players.** Media players can typically play audio and video files, as well as burn music CDs.

Animation Software

Animation software is used to create animation to be used on Web pages or other multimedia applications. At the low end are animation programs used to create *animated GIFs*. An animated GIF is a group of small images stored in a special animated GIF file; when inserted into a Web page or other application, the images contained in the animated GIF file display one after another to simulate movement. *Animated GIF programs* allow you to import the various images to be included in the animated GIF, rearrange them into the correct order, add transitions between them, and specify the display time for each image and the number of times the animation sequence should repeat. Once all settings have been selected, the entire animation is saved in a single animated GIF file. Animated GIFs typically have a small file size and are commonly used on Web pages.

>**Animation software.** Application software used to create animation to be used on Web pages or other multimedia applications.

HOW IT WORKS

Creating a Custom Music CD

At the present time, copying songs from a music CD you have legally obtained to your PC and custom music CDs is a legal activity, provided the CD is not copy-protected or copying to another medium is not otherwise specifically prohibited. Songs located on a CD are stored in *WAV* format; when you transfer them to your PC, they are typically converted to the *MP3* format or a special format for the media player program being used in the quality and format specified in the media

player settings—usually near-CD quality (96 Kbps) or CD quality (128 Kbps) is selected to have good audio quality at a reasonable file size. Songs are typically then listed in the media player's *media library*, where they can be organized into *playlists*. Copying songs from a CD to a PC's hard drive using the *Windows Media Player* program is shown in the accompanying illustration—this process is sometimes referred to as *ripping* a CD. Once all the desired songs have been transferred to the PC's hard drive, the media player program can be used to burn the desired songs onto a CD-R disc.

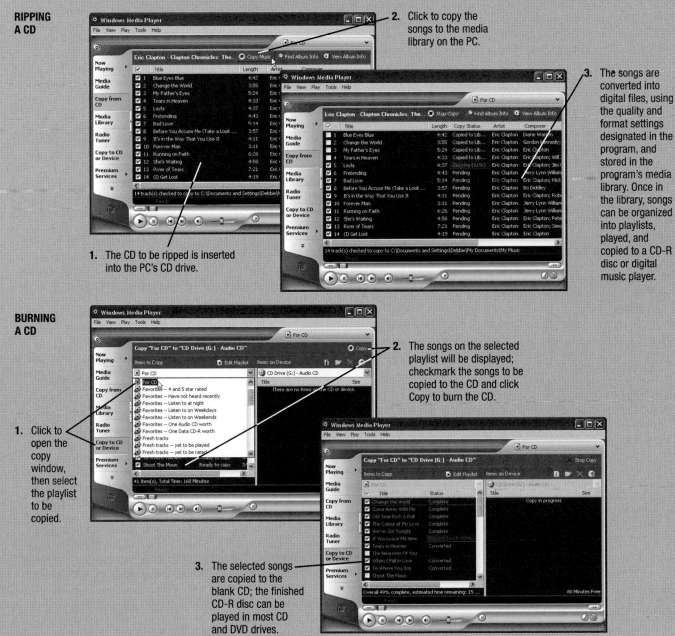

RIPPING A CD

2. Click to copy the songs to the media library on the PC.

3. The songs are converted into digital files, using the quality and format settings designated in the program, and stored in the program's media library. Once in the library, songs can be organized into playlists, played, and copied to a CD-R disc or digital music player.

1. The CD to be ripped is inserted into the PC's CD drive.

BURNING A CD

2. The songs on the selected playlist will be displayed; checkmark the songs to be copied to the CD and click Copy to burn the CD.

1. Click to open the copy window, then select the playlist to be copied.

3. The selected songs are copied to the blank CD; the finished CD-R disc can be played in most CD and DVD drives.

For more complex animations, developers typically turn to a more powerful animation program, such as *Macromedia Fireworks* or *Flash,* or *Adobe® LiveMotion®* or *AfterEffects®.* These programs enable developers to create Web animations complete with interactivity and sound. You can import or create a variety of still and moving objects, combine and layer them, as desired, and then add special effects, movement, and sound.

When choosing an animation program, it is important to make sure it can create images in a format you will need, depending on the program that is going to be used to create the finished application. Some programs, such as AfterEffects and LiveMotion, are designed to be compatible with other specific programs, such as Illustrator and Photoshop. Some programs create finished elements in a standard format, such as *Shockwave,* Flash, or animated GIF, that can be inserted into various types of applications. Remember, however, that some formats— such as Flash and Shockwave files—require a special player to be viewed. For some types of animation, *Dynamic HTML (DHTML), virtual reality modeling language (VRML),* or *JavaScript* may be more appropriate than an animation program. These tools are discussed with *Web site authoring software* in Chapter 10. Programming languages, such as *Java,* may also be used to implement Web page animation. Java is discussed with programming languages in Chapter 13.

Multimedia Authoring Software

Multimedia authoring software consists of programs designed to create stand-alone multimedia applications to be delivered via CD, DVD, or the Web. One of the most prominent companies in this area is Macromedia—both *Director* and *Authorware* are widely used multimedia authoring programs. Director is an *object-based authoring program,* where all objects are viewed as part of a movie production, such as cast members, a stage, and a score (see Figure 7-27). Director is frequently used to create Shockwave content to be incorporated into multimedia Web sites. Authorware is an *icon-based authoring program.* Icons representing the multimedia elements in an application (such as text, graphics, and video) are placed on a *flowline* to indicate the sequence in which the elements should be displayed. Authorware is most often used for multimedia training and educational applications.

Graphics, Multimedia, and the Web

Graphics and multimedia, as just discussed, play important roles on the Web. Many Web pages today contain multimedia content, such as graphics created with graphics software, audio and video clips edited with audio and video editing software, and animated effects created using animation software. In addition, games, tutorials, and demonstrations available on the Web are often created with multimedia authoring software. Multimedia Web sites are the focus of Chapter 10.

> **FIGURE 7-27**

Multimedia authoring software. In the Director program shown here, objects are viewed as cast members on a stage and a score combines and controls all the components of the presentation.

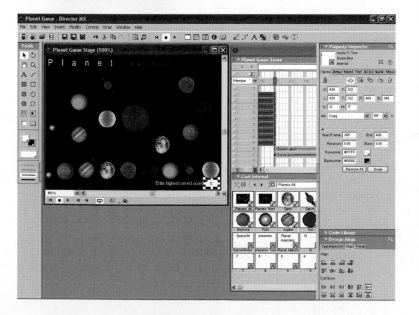

>**Multimedia authoring software.** Application software designed to create stand-alone multimedia applications to be delivered via CD, DVD, or the Web.

OTHER TYPES OF APPLICATION SOFTWARE

There are many other types of application software. Some are geared for business or personal productivity; others are designed for entertainment or educational purposes. Still others are designed specifically for a particular business application, such as a custom application program to generate a business's payroll or inventory reports. A few of the most common types of application software not previously covered are discussed next; some are featured in Figure 7-28. For a look at a relatively new undesirable type of software—*spyware*—see the Trend box.

Desktop and Personal Publishing Software

Desktop publishing refers to using a desktop PC to combine and manipulate text and images to create attractive documents that look as if they came off a professional printer's press (see Figure 7-28). Although many desktop publishing effects can be produced using

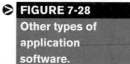

FIGURE 7-28
Other types of application software.

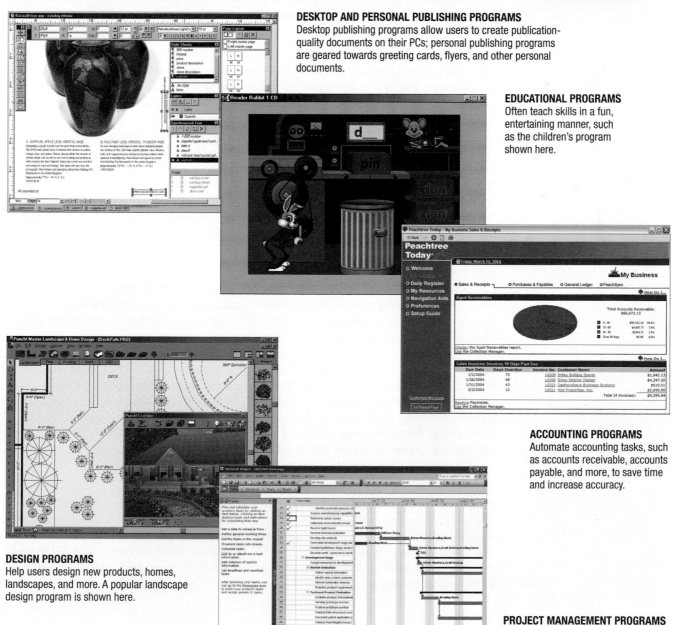

DESKTOP AND PERSONAL PUBLISHING PROGRAMS
Desktop publishing programs allow users to create publication-quality documents on their PCs; personal publishing programs are geared towards greeting cards, flyers, and other personal documents.

EDUCATIONAL PROGRAMS
Often teach skills in a fun, entertaining manner, such as the children's program shown here.

ACCOUNTING PROGRAMS
Automate accounting tasks, such as accounts receivable, accounts payable, and more, to save time and increase accuracy.

DESIGN PROGRAMS
Help users design new products, homes, landscapes, and more. A popular landscape design program is shown here.

PROJECT MANAGEMENT PROGRAMS
Help users plan, track, and manage the various parts of a project; used in a wide range of industries.

a word processing program, users who frequently create publication-style documents would likely find a desktop publishing program a more efficient means of creating those types of documents. *Personal publishing* refers to creating desktop-publishing-type documents for personal use—such as greeting cards, invitations, flyers, calendars, certificates, and so forth. Personal publishing programs are very popular with home users.

Accounting and Personal Finance Software

Accounting software is used to automate some of the accounting activities that need to be performed on a regular basis. Common tasks include writing and printing checks, recording purchases and payments (refer again to Figure 7-28), creating payroll documents and checks, and preparing financial statements. *Personal finance software* is commonly used at home by individuals to write checks and balance checking accounts, track personal expenses, manage stock portfolios, and prepare income taxes. Increasingly, personal finance activities are becoming Web-based, such as the *online banking* and *online portfolio management* services available through many banks and brokerage firms and discussed in more detail in Chapter 9.

Educational, Entertainment, and Reference Software

There are a wide variety of educational and entertainment application programs available. *Educational software* is designed to teach one or more skills, such as reading, math, spelling, a foreign language, world geography, or to help prepare for standardized tests. *Entertainment software* includes games, simulations, and other programs that provide amusement. A hybrid of these two categories is sometimes called *edutainment*—educational software that also entertains—such as the children's program illustrated in Figure 7-28.

Reference software is another common type of application software. Reference software includes encyclopedias, dictionaries, atlases, ZIP code directories, mapping/travel programs, cookbook programs, and any other program designed to provide valuable information (an encyclopedia program was shown in Figure 7-22). In addition to being available as stand-alone software packages, reference information is widely available on the Internet.

CAD and Other Types of Design Software

Computer-aided design (*CAD*) *software* enables designers to dramatically reduce the time they spend developing designs in such areas as manufacturing and architecture. For example, by using electronic pens and powerful PCs, engineers or architects can sketch ideas directly into the computer system and then instruct it to analyze the proposed design in terms of how well it meets a number of design criteria. Because drawings are typically displayed in 3D, CAD is especially helpful in designing automobiles, aircraft, ships, buildings, electrical circuits (including computer chips), and even clothing. Besides playing an important role in the design of durable goods, CAD is useful in fields such as art, advertising, law, architecture, and movie production. In addition to the powerful CAD programs used in business, there are also design programs designed for home and small business use, such as for making new home and remodeling plans, interior designs, and landscape designs (see Figure 7-28).

Project Management Software

Project management software, illustrated in Figure 7-28, is used to plan, schedule, track, and analyze the tasks involved in a project, such as a construction project, installing a new manufacturing system, preparing a large advertising campaign for a client, and so forth. This software shows how project activities are related and when they must start and finish. Once created, schedules prepared by such software can be shared with others and updated as the project progresses.

TREND

Spyware

Spyware is the term used for any software that is installed without the user's knowledge and that secretly gathers information about the user and transmits it through his or her Internet connection to advertisers or other interested parties when the user is connected to the Internet—usually for marketing purposes. The information gathered by spyware is typically not associated with a person's identity; instead it is usually used to provide advertisers with information to be used for marketing purposes, such as to help select advertisements to display on each person's PC. Spyware programs are often installed unknowingly at the same time another program—often a free program, such as file-sharing software—is installed on the user's computer. Some spyware programs—sometimes referred to as *stealthware*—are getting more aggressive, delivering ads regardless of the activity you are doing on your PC, resetting your browser settings, and other annoying actions. Once a spyware program is installed on a PC, it typically does not show up on any list of installed programs, making it difficult for users to realize that the spyware program has been installed and to uninstall it.

Another type of related software spyware is *adware*—free or low-cost software that is supported by onscreen advertising. Many free programs that can be downloaded from the Internet, such as the free version of the NetZero e-mail program and the Gator e-Wallet, include some type of onscreen advertising. The difference between spyware and adware is that adware typically doesn't gather information and relay it to others via the Internet and it isn't installed without the user's consent. It may, however, be installed without the user's direct knowledge if the user doesn't read the licensing agreement before clicking *OK* or checking an "I agree" box to install the software program. This is at least partially blamed on the complexity and difficult wording found in some agreements (one analysis of an agreement for a software program containing spyware found its sentences to be over three times as complex as a standard tax form, and the agreement was judged to be written at a 16th grade reading level).

Both spyware and adware that is unintentionally installed can be annoying and ties up valuable system resources. In addition, privacy advocates object to spyware because it also collects and transmits data about individuals to others, and can bog down a user's Internet connection, all without the user's knowledge.

To prevent adware from being installed on your PC, it is important to read the *end-user licensing agreement* (*EULA*) that is typically displayed on the screen at the beginning of a software installation process. To prevent spyware from being installed on your PC, you can use a Web site such as Spychecker.com to check to see if a program you would like to download and install has been classified as spyware. To locate and remove spyware and adware already installed on your PC, a program such as Ad-Aware (see the accompanying screen shot) can be used.

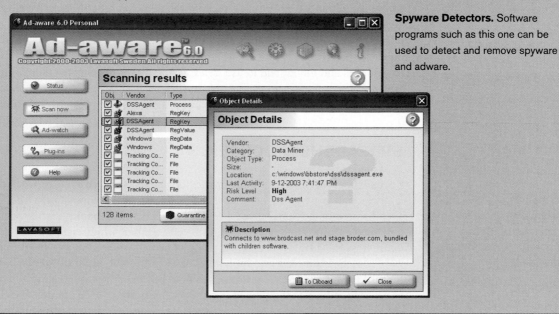

Spyware Detectors. Software programs such as this one can be used to detect and remove spyware and adware.

SUMMARY

THE BASICS OF APPLICATION SOFTWARE

Chapter Objective 1:
Describe what application software is and the different types, ownership rights, and delivery methods available.

Application software is software designed to carry out a specific task. Common types of application software include games, Web browsers, word processing programs, multimedia software, utility programs, and more. Many application software programs on the market today are **commercial software** programs that are developed and sold for a profit. When a software program is purchased, individual users receive a **software license** authorizing them to use the software. Some commercial software is available in a *trial version*. Other software is available as **shareware**. Other classes of software are **freeware** and **public domain software**. Most software is *installed* on a local PC or network server; other software is *Web-based*. Organizations that provide Web-based software are referred to as *application service providers (ASPs)*.

Chapter Objective 2:
Detail some characteristics of a software suite and some ways of getting help with a software program.

Many office-oriented programs are sold bundled together as a **software suite**. A commonly used application software tool, especially between programs in a software suite, is *object linking and embedding (OLE)*. Although different in purpose, most application software programs share some of the same concepts and functions, such as similar document-handling operations and help features. Handheld PCs require specially designed application software.

WORD PROCESSING CONCEPTS

Chapter Objective 3:
Discuss word processing and identify the basic operations involved in creating, editing, and formatting documents.

Word processing refers to using a PC and **word processing software** to create, manipulate, and print written documents, such as letters, contracts, and so forth. The **insertion point** identifies the current position in a document and a **word wrap** feature automatically moves the insertion point to the next line when the end of the screen line is reached.

When *editing* a document, text and graphics can be *selected* and then deleted, *moved*, or *copied*. Common types of *formatting* include changing the *font face*, *font size*, or *font style* of selected text; adjusting *line spacing*, *margins*, *indentation*, *tabs*, *alignment*; and changing the top and bottom margins, paper size, and adding *headers* and *footers*. Other enhancements found in most word processing programs include the ability to include graphical images and *tables*, and to use *styles*, *templates*, or *wizards* for more efficient document creation. Documents can also include hyperlinks and be saved as Web pages in many programs. Most word processors also include a spell-checking feature and other useful tools.

SPREADSHEET CONCEPTS

Chapter Objective 4:
Explain the purpose of spreadsheet software and identify the basic operations involved in creating, editing, and formatting worksheets.

Spreadsheet software is used to create documents (**spreadsheets** or **worksheets**) that typically include a great deal of numbers and mathematical computations; a collection of worksheets stored in the same spreadsheet file is called a **workbook**. A worksheet is divided into **rows** and **columns** that intersect to form **cells**, each of which can be accessed through a *cell address*, such as B3. A rectangular group of cells is referred to as a *block* or *range*.

Content is entered into individual cells and may consist of **labels**, **constant values**, **formulas**, or **functions**. Formulas can be typed using *relative cell* or *absolute cell references*, depending on the type of computation required. Once created, the contents of individual cells may be edited and formatted. *Numeric formats* are used to change the appearance of numbers, such as adding a dollar sign or displaying a specific number of decimal places. Spreadsheet programs commonly include a *charting* or *graphing* feature and the ability to perform *what-if analysis*. Some spreadsheet programs allow worksheets to be saved in the form of a Web page and the inclusion of hyperlinks in cells.

DATABASE CONCEPTS

A *database management system* (*DBMS*) or **database software** program enables the creation of a **database**—a collection of related data stored in a manner so that information can be retrieved as needed. In a relational DBMS (the most common type found on PCs), a **field** or **column** is a collection of characters that comprise a single piece of data, such as a name or phone number; a **record** or **row** is a collection of related fields; and a **table** is a collection of related records. One or more tables can be stored in a database file.

A relational database typically contains a variety of *objects*, such as tables; *forms* to input or view data; *queries* to retrieve specific information; and *reports* to print a formal listing of the data stored in a table or the results of a query. When a table is created, the table fields are specified along with their characteristics, such as *field name*, *field size*, and *data type*. After this *structure* has been created, data can be entered into the table. Both the data in the table and the table structure can be modified. Databases are commonly integrated into the Web, such as to keep track of inventory and to facilitate online ordering.

Chapter Objective 5:
Identify some of the vocabulary used with database software and discuss the basic operations involved with creating, editing, and retrieving information from a database.

PRESENTATION GRAPHICS CONCEPTS

Presentation graphics software is used to create **presentation graphics**—images that visually enhance the impact of information communicated to other people, such as with *online slide shows* consisting of electronic **slides**. Individual slides are created and then they can be edited and formatted, as can the overall appearance of the slides. Multimedia elements, such as images and video clips, can also be included. After all slides have been created for a presentation, the order of the slides can be rearranged and *transitions* between the slides can be specified. It is becoming increasingly common to find slide-based presentations available through the Web. Web-based slide shows can include multimedia elements, as well as hyperlinks and other navigational buttons.

Chapter Objective 6:
Describe what presentation graphics are and how they are created.

GRAPHICS AND MULTIMEDIA CONCEPTS

Graphics are graphical images, such as digital photographs, clip art, and original art. **Multimedia** refers to applications that include more than one type of media, typically text, graphics, animation, and interactivity. Multimedia applications include **computer-based training (CBT)**, **Web-based training (WBT)**, **virtual reality (VR)** applications, entertainment products, and information kiosks. To create graphics, **graphics software**—such as a *painting*, *drawing*, or *image-editing program*—can be used. *Audio editing*, *video editing*, and **animation software** can be used to create additional multimedia elements. To pull all the elements together into a single presentation, **multimedia authoring software** is used. Finished presentations can be burned on a CD or DVD using *CD* or *DVD burning software*; *media players* can be used to play audio and video files.

Chapter Objective 7:
List some multimedia applications and describe some software programs that can be used to create graphics and other multimedia elements.

OTHER TYPES OF APPLICATION SOFTWARE

Other types of application software include *desktop publishing* and *personal publishing* programs, *computer-aided design* (*CAD*) and other types of design *software*, *project management software*, *accounting software*, and *personal finance software*. *Educational*, *entertainment*, and *reference software* are very popular with home users.

Chapter Objective 8:
Name several other types of application software programs and discuss what functions they perform.

S
W

KEY TERMS

Instructions: Match each key term on the left with the definition on the right that best describes it.

a. cell

b. commercial software

c. database

d. field

e. formula

f. graphics software

g. label

h. presentation graphics software

i. public domain software

j. record

k. row

l. shareware

m. software license

n. software suite

o. spreadsheet software

p. table

q. virtual reality (VR)

r. Web-based training (WBT)

s. word processing software

t. workbook

1. _____ A collection of related data that is stored in a manner enabling information to be retrieved as needed; in a relational database, a collection of related tables.

2. _____ A collection of related fields in a database. Also called a row.

3. _____ A collection of software programs bundled together and sold as a single software package.

4. _____ A collection of worksheets saved in a single spreadsheet file.

5. _____ A database record.

6. _____ An agreement, either included in a software package or displayed on the screen during installation, that specifies the conditions under which a buyer of the program can use it.

7. _____ An entry in a worksheet cell that performs computations on worksheet data and displays the results.

8. _____ Application software used to create spreadsheet documents, which typically contain a great deal of numbers and mathematical computations and are organized into rows and columns.

9. _____ Application software used to create, edit, save, and print written documents.

10. _____ Application software used to create or modify images.

11. _____ Application software used to create presentation graphics and online slide shows.

12. _____ A single category of data to be stored in a database, such as a person's name or telephone number. Also called a column.

13. _____ A text-based entry in a worksheet cell that identifies data on the worksheet.

14. _____ Copyrighted software that is developed, usually by a commercial company, for sale to others.

15. _____ Copyrighted software that is distributed on the honor system; should be either paid for or uninstalled after the trial period.

16. _____ In a relational database, a collection of related records (rows).

17. _____ Instruction delivered on an individual basis via the World Wide Web.

18. _____ Software that is not copyrighted and may be used without restriction.

19. _____ The location at the intersection of a row and column on a worksheet into which data can be typed.

20. _____ The use of a computer to create three-dimensional environments that look like they do in the real world.

REVIEW ACTIVITIES

Answers for the self-quiz appear at the end of the book in the References and Resources Guide.

True/False

Instructions: Circle **T** if the statement is true or **F** if the statement is false.

T   F   **1.** Microsoft Office is one example of a software suite.

T   F   **2.** In a word processing document, the Enter key is always pressed at the end of each screen line to move down to the next line.

T   F   **3.** Changing the font size in a document is an example of a formatting operation.

T   F   **4.** The cells referenced in spreadsheet formulas do not usually contain labels.

T   F   **5.a** Multimedia presentations are typically created using a media player program.

Completion

Instructions: Supply the missing words to complete the following statements.

6. With a _____ program, the author allows people to freely duplicate and give the program to others to try it out, but a payment is requested for continued use of the product.

7. Times New Roman is an example of a(n) _____; 12-point Times New Roman is an example of a(n) _____.

8. The location where a row and column in a spreadsheet program meet is called a(n) _____.

9. In a database, all of the fields that belong to one person or thing (displayed as a row in a table) is called a(n) _____.

10. A collection of pages created in a presentation graphics program designed to be displayed one after the other is usually called a(n) _____.

---

1. List four programs in the Microsoft Office 2003 software suite and identify the tasks for which each program is designed.

2. Select the spreadsheet element from the numbered list below that best matches each of the following spreadsheet terms and write the corresponding number in the blank to the left of each term. Note that all spreadsheet elements will not be used.

a. _____ An absolute cell address   **e.** _____ A constant value

b. _____ A formula   **f.** _____ A relative cell address

c. _____ A block   **g.** _____ The multiplication symbol

d. _____ A label   **h.** _____ A function

1. =SUM(A1:A2)   **6.** =B6*C6

2. John Smith   **7.** /

3. $D$4   **8.** =

4. 150   **9.** *

5. B6   **10.** F18:F28

3. Would rearranging the paragraphs in a document using a word processing program use a move operation or a copy operation? Explain your answer.

4. Referring to the database table below, answer the following questions.

CUSTOMER NUMBER	NAME	STREET	CITY	STATE	ZIP	BALANCE $
810	John T. Smith	31 Cedarcrest	Boulder	CO	80302	10.00
775	Sally Jones	725 Agua Fria	Santa Fe	NM	87501	0
690	William Holmes	3269 Fast Lane	Boulder	CO	80302	150.35
840	Artis Smith	2332 Alameda	Lakewood	CO	80215	3.50

   a. How many records are there? _____
   b. How many fields are there? _____
   c. For a query that lists the records in which the State was "CO" and the Customer Balance was less than $10, how many customers would the query results contain? _____

5. Think of one example of a multimedia application you have encountered recently and list the various multimedia elements used in the application. Explain whether or not you think the multimedia elements added to the application's effectiveness.

6. Select the type of presentation element from the numbered list below that is most appropriate for each of the following presentation graphics applications and write the corresponding number in the blank to the left of each application. Note that all graphics types will not be used.
   a. _____ Illustrating the monthly sales for the past six months.
   b. _____ Conveying the new company privacy policy.
   c. _____ Illustrating the percent of sales coming from each sales territory.
   d. _____ Showing what the latest prototype of an upcoming product looks like.

   1. Pie chart
   2. Bar chart
   3. Drawn object
   4. Text chart
   5. Organizational chart
   6. Photograph

7. Select the type of application software program from the numbered list below that best matches each of the following applications and write the corresponding number in the blank to the left of each application. Note that all software types will not be used.
   a. _____ Creating a home movie DVD.
   b. _____ Practicing your multiplication tables.
   c. _____ Creating a child's birthday invitation.
   d. _____ Looking up the capital of Brazil.
   e. _____ Listening to a music CD.

   1. Media player
   2. Reference software
   3. Project management software
   4. Accounting software
   5. Educational software
   6. Personal publishing software
   7. Burning software
   8. CAD software

PROJECTS

1. **Spyware** As discussed in the chapter Trend box, *spyware* is software that is installed on your PC without your knowledge and secretly provides advertisers with information about your Web activities. Spyware programs are usually installed along with another program and it may be difficult for the user to realize a spyware program is installed, unless a special software program is used to detect it, or the person receives a message from their firewall software that the spyware program is trying to access the Internet.

    For this project, research the current state of spyware programs and spyware detection. Has there been an increase or decrease in the use of spyware? Have there been any significant instances reported in the news or any spyware programs involved in any legal action? How does spyware differ from *adware*? Have you used a program that included adware before? Would you be willing to install a program that included an adware or spyware component? Why or why not? What types of programs are available today to identify adware or spyware programs? Do they just identify them or can they remove them from your system? At the conclusion of your research, prepare a one- to two-page summary of your findings and submit it to your instructor.

2. **Software Search** Just as with toys, movies, and music, the price of a software program can vary tremendously, based on where you buy it, sales, rebates, and more. Although most packages claim a manufacturer's suggested retail price, it is almost always possible to beat that price—sometimes by a huge amount—with careful shopping.

    For this project, select one software program that you might be interested in buying and research it. Either by reading the program specifications in a retail store or on a Web page, determine the minimum hardware and software requirements (such as processor type and speed, amount of free hard drive space, amount of memory, and operating system) for your chosen program. By checking in person, over the phone, or via the Internet, locate a minimum of three price quotes for the program. Be sure to check availability and estimated delivery time, and include any sales tax and shipping charges. If any of the online vendors have the option to download the software, instead of sending a physical package, be sure to record that information, as well. At the conclusion of this task, prepare a one-page summary of your research and submit it to your instructor. Be sure to include a recommendation of where you think it would be best to buy your chosen product and why.

3. **CD Cards** CDs the approximate shape and size of a business card are increasingly being used to replace traditional business cards. Advantages include being able to include a complete multimedia presentation or Web site on the CD, as well as photographs, portfolio materials, and other useful content.

    For this project, research CD business cards. How much data can they contain? Can individuals or businesses create their own CD cards or do they have to be purchased from a CD business card development agency? How much do the discs cost? Are they widely available? Locate one CD business card development agency (either a local business or an agency with a Web site) and determine what type of content they can supply for a custom card. What are the advantages and disadvantages of using a CD business card? Would you prefer to hand out a multimedia CD card or a traditional business card when meeting new business acquaintances? At the conclusion of your research, prepare a one-page summary of your findings and submit it to your instructor.

4. **Templates and Wizards** Most word processing, spreadsheet, database, and presentation graphics software programs include a variety of templates, wizards, and other tools to help you create new documents faster and easier.

    For this project, select one office suite program that you have access to (select one you will be using in this course, if applicable) and identify three tools included in the program that can be used to create a new document. For each tool, explain how it is accessed and what type of document is created with the tool. Next, pick one of your selected tools and use it to create a new document to evaluate how easy it is to work with and how useful the tool is. At the conclusion of your research, prepare a one-page summary of your findings and submit it to your instructor.

5. **Online Tours** There are many online tours and tutorials for widely used application programs. Some are available through the software company's Web site; others are located on third-party Web sites.

    For this project, locate an online tour or tutorial for a program you are interested in (go to www.course.com/uc10/ch07 to see the "Application Software Resources" Further Exploration links to tutorials for a variety of application programs) and work your way through the tour or tutorial. Be sure to take some notes about those features that are of most interest to you, and evaluate how helpful you think the tutorial is for someone who is just learning how to use the program in question. At the conclusion of this task, prepare a one-page summary of your efforts and submit it to your instructor.

6. **Multimedia Education** Multimedia is commonly incorporated in all levels of education today. Many college instructors use multimedia presentations to deliver classroom instruction; some courses—particularly those delivered using distance learning—include multimedia content that students access via the Internet. In addition, there is a wide variety of educational software programs on the market today.

    For this project, form a group to identify at least two different types of multimedia applications that are used in conjunction with courses at your college or university. Determine the purpose of the application and the benefits, if any, of using multimedia delivery for that application. Include any potential disadvantages, as well. Next, locate two different types of educational or edutainment software programs that include multimedia and explain the purpose of the multimedia components and whether or not the program would be as effective, or more effective, without multimedia. For each program, also determine the minimum hardware and software requirements (such as processor type and speed, amount of free hard drive space, amount of memory, and operating system) and the approximate retail price. Your group should submit your findings and opinions for this project to your instructor in the form of a short paper, not more than two pages in length.

7. **Reference Tools** As described in the chapter, reference software includes encyclopedias, dictionaries, atlases, ZIP code directories, mapping/travel programs, and more. Many of these programs are available as commercial software that can be purchased; others are available over the Internet for free or with a paid subscription.

    For this project, identify two different types of reference tools that are available via the Internet (use a search site to search for Web sites offering particular reference tools until you find two that interest you). For each of your chosen online reference tools, try out the reference tool (if it is available at no cost) and see how helpful and easy to use it is. If the tool requires a fee or subscription, don't try it out—just make a note of what the service is supposed to consist of and the fee involved. Next, for each of your chosen reference tools, locate a similar offline version of the tool in the form of a hard copy book or an installable software program (visit a local software retailer, local bookstore, or search the Internet to find these non-Web-based alternative reference tools). Evaluate each offline reference tool, noting its capabilities, price, and how this version differs from the online version. At the conclusion of your research, submit this project to your instructor in the form of a short paper, not more than two pages in length. Be sure to include your opinion regarding the availability and usefulness of online versus offline reference tools, which of the tools you evaluated you would prefer to use, and why.

8. **Software FAQs** Companies that sell application programs often offer online support for their customers, usually free of charge. Online support options can include features such as a searchable knowledge base; one or more tutorials; an e-mail link, online form, or chat facility to submit a question to an online support person; and a set of *frequently asked questions* (*FAQs*).

For this project, visit the customer support section of the Web site for the company who makes one of the software applications that you are learning in conjunction with this course (if you are not learning any software in your class, select a widely used program by a large software publisher, such as Microsoft, Corel, or Lotus). Note the types of services available and how useful you think the support features are. In addition, select a few of the FAQs and answers that you found most helpful. Prepare a short presentation of your findings and experiences, including a summary of your selected FAQs. The presentation should not exceed 10 minutes and should make use of one or more presentation aids such as the chalkboard, handouts, overhead transparencies, or a computer-based slide presentation (your instructor may provide additional requirements). You may be asked to submit a summary of the presentation to your instructor.

9. **Compatibility** Files created by an application program are often upward-compatible, but not always downward-compatible. In other words, if you create a file using the most recent version of Microsoft Word and attempt to open the file using Word 95, you may get an error message. However, you would be able to open a Word 95 file in a later version of Word. In addition, you may be able to open a document created in a different program, if the program is of a similar type (such as opening a Word document in WordPerfect). Some application programs feature a "Save As" option to save the file in a format appropriate for an older version of the program, for an entirely different program, or for a more universal file format, such as *.rtf* (*Rich Text Format*) and *.html* (*Hypertext Markup Language*).

For this project, form a group to investigate the compatibility issues discussed above for one popular program and present your findings in the form of a short presentation. For your selected program, your group should determine in which file formats the program can save documents, and which file formats the program can open. If there are older versions of the program, are documents upward-compatible? Downward compatible? If the program can save a document in a plain text (*.txt*) file, is there a downside? In addition, your group should research the *.rtf* and *.html* formats, and determine what their purpose is, in what programs each of these formats can be opened, and in what programs each of these formats can be edited. What about the *Portable Document Format* (*.pdf*)? Does your program support it and when might it be useful? Have any of the members of your group experienced a compatibility problem with a document? If so, how was the problem resolved? The presentation should not exceed 10 minutes and should make use of one or more presentation aids such as the chalkboard, handouts, overhead transparencies, or a computer-based slide presentation (your instructor may provide additional requirements). Your group may be asked to submit a summary of the presentation to your instructor.

10. **The Games We Play** In the past few years, games—both PC games and games played via a gaming device, such as a GameBoy, Nintendo, PlayStation, or Xbox, have become a large part of the entertainment industry. They are now competing with TV, movies, and music as an entertainment medium of choice for today's youth. Many of these games have evolved from what used to be action, adventure, and strategy, into games containing a central theme of violence. It seems like only a few years ago that we had games called Pac-Man, Frogger, and Mario Brothers, and now we have games called Street Fighter, Mortal Combat, Freedom Fighters, Command and Conquer, Tomb Raider, Special Forces, and DOOM. In the future, as these games improve in their ability to surround us with realistic graphics, surround sound, and other types of virtual reality components, we will need to think hard about restricting, controlling, or managing the access our youth have to these games.

Select one of the following positions or create one of your own and express your point of view on the subject. Your instructor will indicate whether your response is to be posted to a class bulletin board, discussed in a class chat room, or discussed as an in-class activity. You may also be asked to submit a summary of your position and point of view to your instructor.

a. Man has been engaging in violent behavior for thousands of years. We have not been induced into engaging in acts of violence because of video games. Besides, we as humans have the ability to control our primal instincts and resolve confrontational situations in a manner that would not involve physical combat. In short, video games don't play a significant role in shaping the minds and actions of our youth and no regulation or control is warranted. Even the voluntary rating system used by game makers is unnecessary.

b. Our youth are very impressionable, and there is direct correlation between the violence enacted in video games and the potential for aggressive behavior in our youth. In the absence of some sort of regulation or control over this medium of entertainment, our youth will be affected by what they see and hear in these video games, which may lead to much heartache and tragedy in the future. The voluntary game rating system used today doesn't go far enough—violence and other inappropriate content should not be incorporated into games that minors are likely to play.

11. **Emotion-Recognition Software** An emerging application is *emotion-recognition software*, which tries to read people's emotions. Similar to face-recognition systems, emotion-recognition systems use a camera and software to analyze individuals' faces, but instead of trying to identify the individual, the system attempts to recognize his or her current emotion. The first expected application of such a system is for ATM machines, which already have the necessary hardware installed. One expected feature is changing the advertising display to more specifically target each individual, based on the customer's emotional response to displayed advertising. Even more helpful applications would include rephrasing instructions if the customer appeared confused or enlarging the screen text if the customer appeared to be squinting. Emotion-recognition applications for the future could include using this type of system to help therapists understand a patient's emotional state. It is not surprising that privacy advocates are concerned about the emotions of citizens being read in public locations without their consent. They also dislike the idea of customer emotions at an ATM machine being connected with their identity. Proponents of the technology argue that it's no different than when human tellers or store clerks interpret customers' emotions and modify their treatment of the customer accordingly. Is this is a worthy new technology or just a potential invasion of privacy? What are the pros and cons of such a system from a business point of view, and then from a customer point of view? Are there any safeguards that could be implemented or specific ways of using an emotion-recognition system that would alleviate many of the disadvantages? What other potential uses for such a system might there be besides the ones mentioned in this project? Would you object to using an ATM machine with emotion-recognition capabilities?

For this project, form an opinion of the use of emotion-recognition systems in public locations, as well as in private situations, such as a therapist's office or in the home. Be sure to use the questions mentioned in the previous paragraph when forming your position. Your instructor will indicate whether your response is to be posted to a class bulletin board, discussed in a class chat room, or discussed as an in-class activity. You may also be asked to submit a summary of your position and point of view to your instructor.

STUDENT EDITION LABS

12. **Student Edition Labs** Reinforce the concepts you have learned in this chapter by working through the "Word Processing," "Spreadsheets," and "Presentation Software" interactive Student Edition Labs, available online. To access these labs, go to www.course.com/uc10/ch07

If you have a SAM user profile, you have access to even more interactive content. Log in to your SAM account and go to your assignments page to see what your instructor has assigned for this chapter.

NETWORKS AND THE INTERNET

Computer networks and the Internet play a critical role in society and business today. This module takes a look at computer networks in general, as well as the world's largest network—the Internet.

Chapter 8 introduces basic networking principles. Here you learn about several networking and communications applications, as well as many of the hardware and software products that are commonly used to create a computer network. You will also become familiar with the various types of possible networks and how networks work.

The Internet and World Wide Web are the topics of Chapter 9. Although they were introduced in Chapter 2, Chapter 9 explains how the Internet and World Wide Web originated, and looks more closely at how to find information on the Web. Useful strategies, such as how to select an ISP and how to perform Internet searches, are some of the topics included in this chapter.

NETWORKS AND
THE INTERNET

Chapter 8 Computer Networks 311

Overview 312

Networking and Communications Applications 312

What is a Network and How Does it Transmit Data? 317

Types of Networks 327

Networking Hardware 331

Communications Protocols 336

Network Security Issues 344

Chapter 9 The Internet and World Wide Web 363

Overview 364

Evolution of the Internet 364

Getting Set Up to Use the Internet 371

Searching the Internet 379

Beyond Browsing and E-Mail 385

Censorship and Privacy Issues 401

The Future of the Internet 407

OUTLINE

Overview
Networking and Communications Applications
  Wireless Phones
  Paging and Messaging
  Global Positioning Systems (GPSs)
  Satellite Radio
  Online Conferencing
  Collaborative Computing
  Telecommuting
  Telemedicine
What is a Network and How Does it
  Transmit Data?
  Data Transmission Characteristics
  Wired vs. Wireless Connections
  Wired Network Transmission Media
  Wireless Network Transmission Media
Types of Networks
  Network Topologies
  Network Architectures
  LANs, WANs, and Other Types of Networks
Networking Hardware
  Network Adapters
  Modems
  Hubs, Switches, and Other Networking
   Hardware
Communications Protocols
  Ethernet
  Token Ring
  TCP/IP
  802.11 (Wi-Fi)
  Bluetooth
  Wireless Application Protocol (WAP)
  Other Networking Protocols
Network Security Issues
  Unauthorized Access and Use
  Computer Sabotage

Computer Networks

LEARNING OBJECTIVES

After completing this chapter, you will be able to:

1. Describe several uses for communications technology.

2. Understand characteristics about data and how it travels over a network.

3. Name specific types of wired and wireless transmission media and explain how they transmit messages from one device to another.

4. Explain the difference between local area, wide area, and other types of networks.

5. List several types of networking hardware and explain the purpose of each.

6. Identify the different protocols that can be used to connect the devices on a network.

7. Discuss some security issues involved with computer network usage and some security precautions that can be taken.

The term **communications**, when used in a computer context, refers to *telecommunications*; that is, data sent from one device to another using communications media, such as phone lines, privately owned cables, and the airwaves. Communications usually take place over a company network, the Internet, or a telephone network.

In business, communications networks are essential. For instance, business people throughout the world regularly use telephone, e-mail, and messaging systems to communicate with fellow employees, business partners, and customers. Documents are commonly sent electronically in mere moments, instead of being physically delivered from person to person. Ordering systems allow ordering to take place in real time via the Internet or telephone, and shipping systems regularly communicate with supplier computers to facilitate timely deliveries. Outside salespeople and traveling executives use portable PCs to keep in constant touch with others, as well as to access real-time data on the company network and Web site. The list of business communications applications is seemingly endless.

The Internet—the world's largest computer network—also has a tremendous impact on our personal lives. It allows us to communicate with faraway friends, work from remote locations, locate useful information, and access services and entertainment. Information on virtually any topic, stored on computers located almost anywhere on the globe, can be retrieved within seconds. With communications companies scrambling to bring faster transmissions into the home and with the Internet evolving to deliver new forms of services and entertainment, many industry experts predict that the best is yet to come.

The purpose of Chapter 8 is to introduce you to the concepts and terminology surrounding a computer network, the hardware and software involved, and the different ways the computers and other devices on a network communicate with each other. First, we look at some common communications and networking applications. From there, we touch on a number of technical issues, including the ways in which computers transmit data and the types of transmission media involved. We then proceed to the major types of networks, including *local area networks* and *wide area networks*, and the hardware involved with these networks, followed by an explanation of how networked devices communicate with one another. The chapter closes with a discussion of some important network security issues. ■

NETWORKING AND COMMUNICATIONS APPLICATIONS

Today, a wide variety of important business and personal networking and communications applications exist. Two of the most important applications are accessing Web pages and exchanging e-mail, both of which were discussed in Chapter 2. Some other significant communications applications are mentioned briefly next.

>**Communications.** The transmission of data from one device to another.

FIGURE 8-1
Wireless phones.
Types of wireless phones include cellular phones (left) and satellite phones (right). Wireless phones can frequently be used to access Internet resources, such as e-mail or Web page content, as well as their regular voice communications function.

Wireless Phones

Wireless phones (sometimes also called *mobile phones*) are phones that use a wireless network for communications instead of being connected to a conventional telephone jack. The most common type of wireless phone is the *cellular (cell) phone*. Another, but less common, type of wireless phone is the *satellite phone* (see Figure 8-1). Although their use is similar, the technology driving each type of phone differs, as discussed later in this chapter. Both types of phones allow people to communicate with other people using wireless phones, as well as with people using conventional *landline* phones. Some wireless phones can also be used for e-mail access, retrieving information from the Web, and instant messaging. Wireless phones are widely used in the United States, as well as other countries. In developing countries and other locations with a poor traditional communications infrastructure, wireless phones and communications networks offer a much easier and cheaper alternative for communications than fixing current facilities or installing new wired systems.

FIGURE 8-2
Messaging devices.
Today's versatile messaging devices can be used to send and receive e-mail messages, participate in chat and instant messaging sessions, and make phone calls.

Paging and Messaging

Two communications applications related to e-mail and wireless phones are *paging* and *messaging*. *Paging* is the term generally used for one-way communications, in which short numeric or text messages are sent to a person's pager from a phone or another pager using the recipient's pager number. The fastest-growing type of pager used today is two-way paging, generally referred to as *messaging*. These newer types of pagers—typically called *messaging devices*—are designed to send and receive text-based messages from other messaging devices, as well as text-based e-mail messages. Some even allow downloading selected information—such as news, sports scores, and stock quotes—from the Internet, and others can be used as a telephone. As shown in Figure 8-2, messaging devices usually have some type of built-in keyboard; traditional pagers don't. Both types of devices communicate over wireless networks, similar to wireless phones. Messaging systems are extremely popular in many countries and their popularity is rapidly growing in the United States.

>**Wireless phone.** A cellular or satellite phone.

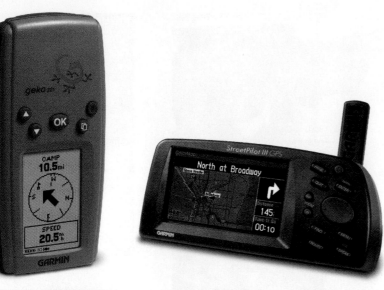

HANDHELD GPS RECEIVER   **CAR-MOUNTED GPS RECEIVER**

⊘ FIGURE 8-3
GPS receivers.
Global positioning systems are used by people who need to know their exact geographical location, usually for safety or navigational purposes.

FURTHER EXPLORATION

For links to further information about GPS, go to www.course.com/uc10/ch08

Global Positioning Systems (GPSs)

A **global positioning system** (**GPS**) is a satellite-based locating and navigating system. It consists of *GPS receivers* (usually handheld or mounted in vehicles or boats) and a group of 24 Department of Defense *GPS satellites*. The receivers receive and interpret the data sent via the satellites to determine the receiver's exact geographic location, including the latitude, longitude, and altitude. Handheld GPS receivers are about the size of a cell phone (see Figure 8-3); some mobile phones and handheld PCs have GPS capabilities built-in or available as an add-on feature. Although originally used solely by the military, GPS receivers are now widely available for business and personal use. GPS is commonly used by hikers and motorists, surveyors, farmers, fishermen, soldiers, and other individuals who want or need to know their precise geographical position at specific times. In the past, the government required consumer GPS receivers to be less accurate than they were technologically able to be for national security reasons. This practice was discontinued in 2000, leading to more accurate GPS receivers. Today's GPS systems are accurate to within 3 meters (less than 10 feet).

Satellite Radio

Another application that employs the use of satellites is *satellite radio*. Originally designed for the car, but now available for the home, satellite radio offers delivery of clear digital music, news, and other radio content across an entire country, instead of just a limited broadcast area like conventional radio stations—and it's often commercial-free. This means that one could drive from coast to coast without ever switching the radio station. Two popular satellite radio providers are SIRIUS and XM Radio. To receive satellite radio broadcasts, you need to have a tuner and antenna compatible with your chosen satellite radio provider and then sign up for service (satellite radio works on a subscription basis; a typical fee is about $10 per month for about 100 radio stations). Since each provider typically has its own set of two or three broadcast satellites, some satellite radio hardware is not interchangeable.

Online Conferencing

There are a number of ways that computers and communications networks can bring two or more individuals together in real time to talk, discuss ideas, collaborate on projects, and have other types of interaction. **Online conferencing** (also referred to as *online meeting*) is a general term for having some type of real-time meeting using computers and communications networks. One type of online conference—*videoconferencing*—allows users to both talk and view images (either periodic photographs or live video) of each other. A videoconference can take place between two individuals using their PCs, if each is

---

>**Global positioning system (GPS).** A system that uses satellites and a receiver to determine the exact geographic location of the receiver.
>**Online conferencing.** A real-time meeting that takes place between people in different locations via computers and communications media.

equipped with a video camera, microphone, speakers, and appropriate software. Videoconferences can also take place on a much larger scale, such as a videoconference broadcast to hundred or thousands of individuals via their PCs or broadcast to designated videoconferencing locations (such as with some corporate, government, and distance learning videoconferences). PC-based videoconferences typically use a messaging or chat program that allows voice and video exchange (such as *Microsoft Messenger, MSN Messenger,* or *Apple iChat AV*) or a special program designed just for PC videoconferences, such as *CUseeMe*. In addition to audio and video, some online conferencing programs include a shared electronic whiteboard or workspace, so documents and suggested modifications can be viewed by all participants.

It is becoming increasingly common for businesses to use an *online conferencing service provider* for their online conferencing needs. With these organizations, such as Infinite Conferencing and WebEx (see Figure 8-4), participants typically log on to the provider's Web site, select the appropriate meeting and supply their designated password, and then dial a telephone number to join the meeting. Once an individual has joined a meeting, he or she can talk and hear all spoken conversations via the telephone, and see all shared activity, use the whiteboard or chat area, and do other online activities via his or her PC. This type of online meeting is frequently called a *Web conference*. Web conferencing companies typically charge a fee based on the number of participants and the total connection time. Web conferences may or may not have video capabilities.

Immediately following the tragic events of September 11, 2001, interest in online conferencing grew rapidly due in part to the initial closure of the airports, followed by increases in travel restrictions and a fear of travel for many individuals. Even now, with the high cost and tighter security measures involved with travel, online conferencing can be a cost-effective and time-saving alternative for some types of business meetings. As the speed, capabilities, and convenience of online conferencing services continue to improve, many believe that it will become an increasingly popular business and personal communications method.

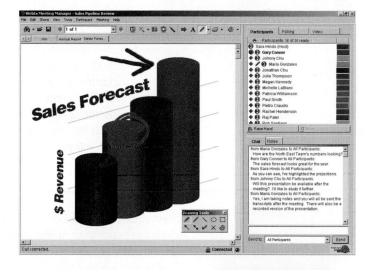

> **FIGURE 8-4**
> **Online conferencing**. This Web conference has 14 participants who can talk with each other, see the shared workspace, and enter written comments in the chat area.

Collaborative Computing

Another way of collaborating with others using a computer is using collaborative software tools to work together on documents and other project components—often called *workgroup computing* or *collaborative computing*. There are many industries in which collaboration is a very important business tool. For example, engineers and architects commonly collaborate on designs, advertising firms and other businesses route proposals and other important documents to several individuals for comments before preparing the final version, and newspaper, magazine, and book editors must read and edit drafts of articles and books before they are published. Instead of these types of collaborations taking place on paper, as in the not-too-distant past, electronic *collaboration tools* are typically used. These tools, such as the revision tools available in Microsoft Office and specialized collaboration software, allow multiple individuals to edit and make comments in a document without destroying the original content. When a document has been routed to all individuals and is returned to the original author, he or she can read the comments and accept or reject changes that others have made. Other collaboration programs may incorporate shared calendars, project scheduling, and other tools in addition to document sharing. Collaborative computing takes place via both private company networks and the Internet.

TIP

Videoconferencing is typically two way, where both individuals can communicate with one another. One-way videoconferences, such as when a corporate officer or industry expert broadcasts a speech that can be viewed live via a Web site or videoconferencing facility, are usually referred to as *videocasts* or *Webcasts*.

N E T

Telecommuting

Telecommuting refers to people working at home, communicating with their place of business and clients via the Internet, fax machines, telephones, pagers, and other communications methods. Using the communications tools that are available today, offsite employees can retrieve company database information, exchange phone calls and e-mails, participate in online conferences, and more—all from the comfort and convenience of home. Telecommuting allows the employee to be flexible, working non-traditional hours or remaining with the company after a relocation, for example. It also enables a company to save on office and parking space and, as an environmental plus, helps cut down on the traffic and pollution caused by traditional work commuting.

Telemedicine

Telemedicine is the use of communications technology to provide medical information and services. It exists today in the form of telephone consultations and videoconferences, remote monitoring, and remote diagnosis of patients. An emerging telemedicine application is *telesurgery*, in which surgeons control robotic surgery hardware remotely, such as over the Internet from a computer at another physical location (see Figure 8-5). Any type of robotic surgery (whether the robotic device is controlled by a surgeon from a control console located in the operating room, by voice command from within the operating room, or remotely via the Internet) has the advantage of working very precisely and with much smaller incisions than are possible by human surgeons. These smaller incisions allow for less invasive surgery (for example, not having to crack through the rib cage to access the heart), resulting in less pain for the patient, a faster recovery time, and fewer potential complications. Telesurgery and other forms of telemedicine have enormous potential for providing quality care to individuals who live in rural or underdeveloped areas without access to sufficient medical care. It will also be necessary for future long-term space exploration—such as a trip to Mars and back that may take three years or more—since astronauts will undoubtedly need medical care while on the journey.

> **FIGURE 8-5**
> **Telemedicine applications.**

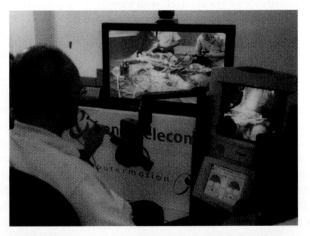

REMOTE DIAGNOSIS
At remote locations, such as the New York child care center shown here, trained employees provide physicians with the real-time data (sent via the Internet) they need for diagnosis.

TELESURGERY
Using voice and computer commands, surgeons can now perform surgery via the Internet; a robotic system actually operates on the patient, according to the surgeon's commands. Shown here is a photo taken during "Project Lindbergh", the world's first transatlantic surgery that took place with surgeons in New York and the patient in France in late 2001.

>**Telecommuting.** The use of computer and electronic devices to enable an individual to work from his or her home. >**Telemedicine.** The use of communications technology to provide medical information and services.

WHAT IS A NETWORK AND HOW DOES IT TRANSMIT DATA?

As discussed in Chapter 1, a **computer network** is of a collection of computers and other hardware devices connected together so that network users can share hardware, software, and data, as well as electronically communicate with each other. Networks are widely used in both homes and businesses today, with the number of home networks increasing at a rapid pace. The research firm Parks Associates estimates that over 7 million U.S. households are networked at the present time and expects that number to increase to over 20 million by 2006. Some common uses for networks are listed in Figure 8-6.

The data transmitted over a network has specific characteristics and it can travel over a network in various ways. Network devices communicate either through a *wired connection*—via physical cables—or by a *wireless connection*—typically through radio signals.

Data Transmission Characteristics

Data that travels over a computer network has a variety of transmission characteristics.

Analog vs. Digital

One of the most fundamental distinctions in data communications is the difference between analog and digital transmissions. The regular phone system, established many years ago to handle voice traffic, carries *analog* signals—that is, *continuous* waves over a certain frequency range (see Figure 8-7). Changes in the continuous wave reflect the variations in the pitch of the human voice. Transmissions via *cable Internet* and *satellite* also typically use analog signals, as do many wireless networks, such as *Wi-Fi* and *Bluetooth*. Virtually all computing equipment, in contrast, transmit *digital* signals, which handle data coded in two *discrete* states: 0s and 1s. Whenever communications require an interface between digital computers and analog networks, a *modem* is needed. For example, a modem is required to transmit digital computer data over conventional telephone lines. Recent developments in telephone (such as *PCS*) and television (such as *HDTV*) have resulted in digital transmissions for some traditionally analog applications.

Bandwidth and Speed

Over an analog medium, data travels at varied frequencies. The difference between the highest and lowest frequencies is known as the medium's *bandwidth*. For example, many telephone transmission media have a bandwidth of 3,000 hertz (Hz), which is the difference between the highest (3,300 MHz) and lowest (300 MHz) frequencies at which these media can send data. Bandwidth corresponds to the amount of data that can be carried at one time. Transmissions of text data require the least amount of bandwidth; video data requires the most. Just as a wide fire hose permits more water to pass through it per unit of time than a narrow garden hose, a medium with a high bandwidth allows more data to pass through it than a medium with a small bandwidth in the same period of time.

Some of the original types of network cabling were low-bandwidth media; most of today's cabling media are high-bandwidth or *broadband* media. Increasingly, broadband media are being installed in homes and businesses to accommodate the growing number of multimedia information-related products entering the

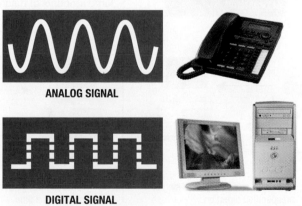

ANALOG SIGNAL

DIGITAL SIGNAL

> **USES FOR NETWORKS**
>
> Sharing a printer or an Internet connection among several users.
>
> Sharing application software so it can be purchased less expensively and only needs to be installed and updated on one computer.
>
> Working collaboratively, such as sharing a company database or using collaboration tools to create or review documents.
>
> Exchanging e-mail and files among network users and over the Internet.

> ❯ **FIGURE 8-6**
> **Uses for computer networks.**

N E T

> ❯ **FIGURE 8-7**
> **Analog vs. digital transmissions.**

>**Computer network.** A collection of computers and other hardware devices that are connected together to share hardware, software, and data, as well as to communicate electronically with one another.

01000001 →

SERIAL TRANSMISSION
All the bits of a byte follow one
another over a single path.

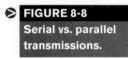

0
1
0
0
0
0
0
1

PARALLEL TRANSMISSION
The bits of a byte are split into
separate paths and are
transmitted at the same time.

FIGURE 8-8
Serial vs. parallel
transmissions.

marketplace. *Transmission speed*—how fast data travels over communications media—is often rated in *bits per second* (*bps*), *Kbps* (thousands of bits per second), or *Mbps* (millions of bits per second). Currently, wired media are typically faster than wireless media, although the actual speed realized depends on the capabilities of the rest of the network hardware. For example, although the type of cabling used with a cable Internet connection can transmit data at speeds of 100 Mbps or higher, speeds for cable Internet service usually top out at 1.5 Mbps, with the speed degrading as more and more people use the network. Improvements in wireless technology are continually increasing data transfer speeds. Speeds up to 2 Mbps are expected in the near future.

Bandwidth and the speed at which data travels over the media determine the *throughput*, or how much data can be transferred over the media in a given period of time. As can be expected, higher bandwidth and higher speed result in a higher throughput.

Serial vs. Parallel Transmission

In most network communications—especially those in which long distances are involved—data travels using *serial transmission*. With **serial transmission**, all of the bits in a message are sent one after another along a single path. On the other hand, **parallel transmission** sends an entire byte at one time with each bit in the byte taking a separate path (see Figure 8-8). As the figure suggests, parallel transmission is much faster than serial transmission. However, because it requires a cable with multiple paths instead of one, its cables are more expensive. Consequently, parallel transmission usually is limited to short distances, such as computer-to-printer communications. Most network traffic uses serial transmission.

Transmission Directions

Another distinction between types of transmissions is the direction in which transmitted data moves (see Figure 8-9).

▼ *Simplex transmission* allows data to travel in a single direction only, such as a doorbell or television broadcast. Simplex transmission is relatively uncommon in computer communications since most devices that are usually one-directional, such as a printer, can still transmit error messages and other data back to the PC.

▼ *Half-duplex transmission* allows messages to move in either direction, but only in one direction at a time, such as a walkie-talkie or two-way radio where only one person can talk at a time. Some network transmissions are half-duplex.

▼ *Full-duplex transmission* works like a standard telephone—data can move in both directions at the same time. Full-duplexing is ideal for hardware devices that need to pass large amounts of data between each other. Most Internet connections are full-duplex.

FIGURE 8-9
Transmission
directions. Transmissions can be simplex
(one direction only),
half-duplex (one direction at a time), or full-duplex (both directions
at one time).

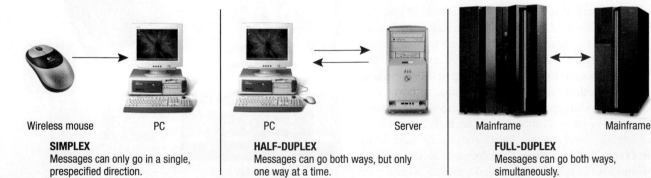

Wireless mouse   PC
SIMPLEX
Messages can only go in a single,
prespecified direction.

PC   Server
HALF-DUPLEX
Messages can go both ways, but only
one way at a time.

Mainframe   Mainframe
FULL-DUPLEX
Messages can go both ways,
simultaneously.

>**Serial transmission.** Data transmission in which every bit in a byte must travel down the same path in succession. >**Parallel transmission.** Data transmission in which an entire byte of data is transmitted at the same time.

Transmission Timing

As previously mentioned, most network data is transmitted using serial transmission. When data is sent serially, a technique must be used to separate the bits into groups so that all the bits in one byte can be identified and retrieved together. Three ways of timing serial transmissions are *synchronous*, *asynchronous*, and *isochronous* (see Figure 8-10). Although with all three methods the bits are sent one at a time, the methods vary with how the bits are organized for transfer.

Synchronous Transmission

In *synchronous* (pronounced "SIN-kre-nuss") *transmission*, data to be transmitted is organized into groups or blocks—each block can consist of thousands of bits. The bits in a block begin transmitting at regular, specified intervals. In other words, the transmissions are synchronized and both devices know when to expect data to be sent and when it should arrive. Synchronous transmission is faster, more efficient, and more accurate than *asynchronous transmission* (discussed next), although it requires more expensive and sophisticated equipment. Most communication within a computer is synchronous, timed by the computer's clock. Network transmissions are also usually synchronous.

Asynchronous Transmission

In *asynchronous* (pronounced "A-sin-kre-nuss") *transmission*, the transmission is not synchronized. Therefore, as soon as the user strikes a key on a keyboard, the byte representation for that character begins transmitting. Striking a second key begins sending the byte for a second character, and so forth. To identify the bits that belong in each byte, a *start bit* and *stop bit* are used at the beginning and end of the byte, respectively. This results in substantial transmission overhead and, because even the fastest typist can generate only a very small amount of data relative to what the line can accept, the line also sits idle a lot of the time, making it a less efficient transmission method. Asynchronous transmission is commonly used for communications between computers and peripheral devices.

Isochronous Transmission

A final alternative is *isochronous* (pronounced "eye-SOCK-ra-nuss") *transmission*. Isochronous—time-dependent—transmission refers to situations in which data must be

> **FIGURE 8-10**
> **Transmission timing.**
> Synchronous (synchronized), asynchronous (not synchronized), and isochronous (time-dependent) transmissions can be used to transmit data. Most network transmissions use synchronous transmission.

**N
E
T**

SYNCHRONOUS TRANSMISSION
Data is sent in blocks and the blocks are timed so that the receiving device knows that it will be getting them at regular intervals.

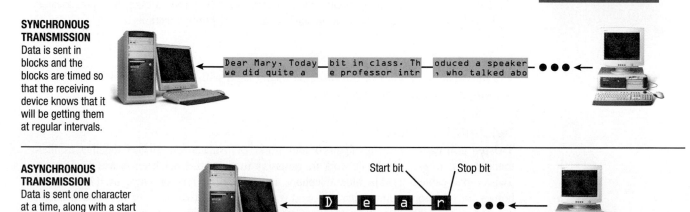

Dear Mary, Today we did quite a   bit in class. The professor intr   oduced a speaker , who talked abo

ASYNCHRONOUS TRANSMISSION
Data is sent one character at a time, along with a start and stop bit.

Start bit   Stop bit

D e a r

ISOCHRONOUS TRANSMISSION
The entire transmission is sent together after requesting and being assigned the bandwidth necessary for all the data to arrive at the correct time.

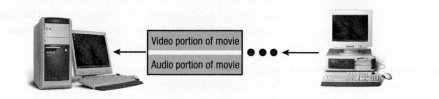

Video portion of movie
Audio portion of movie

delivered within certain time constraints. For example, when sending multimedia data, the audio data must be received in time to be played with the video data. When isochronous transmission is used, the entire necessary bandwidth is reserved for that transmission and no other device can transmit until the transmission is completed, to ensure that the data arrive within the required time period. Because the most common isochronous application is multimedia data, isochronous transfer is supported by FireWire devices.

Wired vs. Wireless Connections

With a **wired network** connection, the PC is physically cabled to the network. Wired networks are very common in schools, business, and government facilities; they are also found in home networks. In general, wired computer networks are less expensive than *wireless networks*, have a longer range (up to 1,800 feet with some types of cabling), and are faster (up to 10 Gbps). They tend to be easier to secure and are the most efficient way of moving large amounts of data, particularly video and other types of multimedia data, at high speeds.

Wireless networks, however, have a number of advantages. For instance, they allow easy connections when physical wiring is impractical or inconvenient (such as inside an existing home or outdoors), as well as give users much more freedom regarding where they can use their PCs. With a wireless network connection, for example, you can surf the Web on your notebook PC from anywhere in your house; access the Internet while traveling just by being close to a public access point in a restaurant, park, or airport; and create a home network without having to run wires between the rooms of your house. Wireless networks are rapidly becoming more popular in both homes and businesses; there is also an increasing number of wireless hot spots available in public locations (coffee houses, businesses, airports, hotels, libraries, and so forth) to allow network access while users are on the road. One recent estimate by IDC forecasts that more than 5 million consumers will access the Internet through U.S. hot spots by 2006.

Some public hot spots can be accessed for free; others charge by the minute or hour. A relatively new alternative for some users is free use of hot spots provided by their Internet providers in public locations, such as the hot spots located at some New York Verizon pay phones for Verizon broadband Internet subscribers. Other Internet providers are looking into similar value-added programs for customers, such as providing free access to hot spots located in phone booths, subway stations, train stations, and other public locations.

Wired Network Transmission Media

The most common types of transmission media used with wired computer networks are *twisted-pair*, *coaxial*, and *fiber-optic cable*.

Twisted-Pair Cable

Twisted-pair cable (made up of pairs of thin strands of insulated wire twisted together, as illustrated in Figure 8-11) is the network transmission medium that has been in use the longest. Twisted-pair cable is used by older telephone networks, is the type of wiring used inside most homes for telephone communications, and is the least expensive type of networking cable. Twisted-pair cable is rated by category. *Category 3* twisted-pair cabling is regular telephone cable; higher speed *Category 5*, *Category 6*, or higher cable is frequently used for home or business networks. Twisted-pair wire is twisted together to reduce interference and improve performance. To further improve performance it can be *shielded* with a metal lining. Twisted-pair cable used for networking has a different connector than those used for telephones. Networking connectors are typically *RJ-45* plugs, which are larger than telephone *RJ-11* connectors.

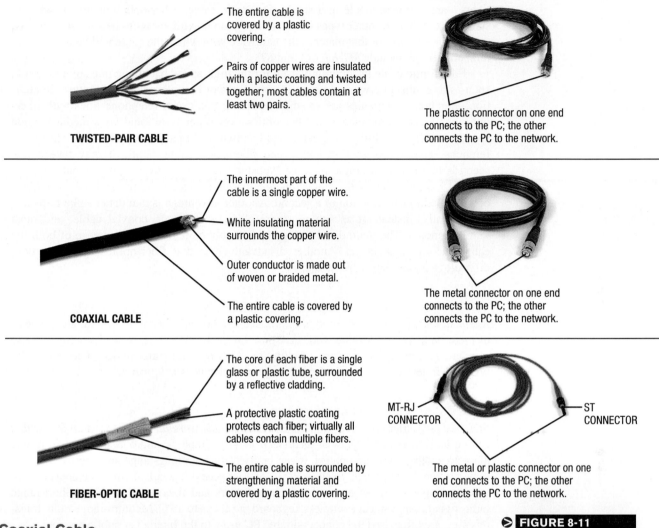

The entire cable is covered by a plastic covering.

Pairs of copper wires are insulated with a plastic coating and twisted together; most cables contain at least two pairs.

TWISTED-PAIR CABLE

The plastic connector on one end connects to the PC; the other connects the PC to the network.

The innermost part of the cable is a single copper wire.

White insulating material surrounds the copper wire.

Outer conductor is made out of woven or braided metal.

The entire cable is covered by a plastic covering.

COAXIAL CABLE

The metal connector on one end connects to the PC; the other connects the PC to the network.

The core of each fiber is a single glass or plastic tube, surrounded by a reflective cladding.

A protective plastic coating protects each fiber; virtually all cables contain multiple fibers.

The entire cable is surrounded by strengthening material and covered by a plastic covering.

FIBER-OPTIC CABLE

MT-RJ CONNECTOR

ST CONNECTOR

The metal or plastic connector on one end connects to the PC; the other connects the PC to the network.

> **FIGURE 8-11**
> Wired network transmission media.

Coaxial Cable

Coaxial cable, the medium pioneered by the cable television industry, was originally developed to carry high-speed, interference-free video transmissions. A coaxial cable (shown in Figure 8-11) consists of a relatively thick center wire surrounded by insulation and then a grounded shield of braided wire (the shield minimizes electrical and radio frequency interference). Coaxial cable is used today in both computer networks and in short-run telephone transmissions outside of the home. Although more expensive than standard telephone cabling, it is much less susceptible to interference and can carry more data more quickly than twisted-pair cables.

Fiber-Optic Cable

Fiber-optic cable is the newest and fastest wired transmission medium. It uses clear glass or plastic fiber strands, each about the thickness of a human hair, to transfer data represented by light pulses (refer again to Figure 8-11). The light pulses are sent through the cable by a laser device at speeds of billions or even trillions of bits per second. Each hairlike fiber has the capacity to carry data for several television stations or thousands of two-way voice conversations. Typically, multiple fibers—sometimes several hundred

---

>**Coaxial cable.** A communications medium consisting of a center wire inside a grounded, cylindrical shield, capable of sending data at high speeds. >**Fiber-optic cable.** A communications medium that utilizes hundreds of hair-thin, transparent fibers over which lasers transmit data as light.

fibers—are wrapped inside in a single fiber-optic cable. Fiber-optic connectors are less standardized than for other types of wired media, so it is important to be sure you obtain a cable with a connector that matches the hardware with which the cable will be used. Common connectors include *MT-RJ*, *SC*, and *ST*.

Fiber-optic cable is commonly used for the high-speed backbone lines of a network, such as to connect networks in separate buildings or for Internet infrastructure. In addition, telephone companies are steadily replacing traditional telephone lines with fiber-optic cables. The advantages of fiber optics over other traditional wire media include speed, security, reliability, longevity, and bandwidth. In particular, enormous speed differences separate conventional wire and fiber-optic cable. While it may take a few seconds to transmit a single page of Webster's dictionary over conventional wire, an entire 15-volume set of the *Encyclopedia Britannica* could be transmitted over fiber-optic cable in just a fraction of a second. Another advantage is that data can be transmitted digitally, instead of as analog signals like twisted-pair, coaxial cable, and most wireless media. The main disadvantage of fiber optics is the initial expense of both the cable and the installation. Another disadvantage is that fiber-optic cables are more difficult to install than wire media.

Wireless Network Transmission Media

Radio signals, similar to those used to broadcast radio and television content, are the heart of most types of wireless network transmission media. Wireless networks today can use standard *broadcast*, *microwave*, *satellite*, or *cellular radio* transmission. One non-radio type of wireless transmission used for very short distances is *infrared*.

Broadcast Radio Transmissions

Standard radio transmissions (sometimes called *broadcast radio* or *RF*, for *radio frequency*) can be used to send all types of data (such as text, graphics, audio, and video) from one place to another. With computers, it can be used for both long-range and short-range data transmission. For instance, *fixed wireless* Internet access is available in some areas to provide high-speed Internet access between end users and fixed wireless ISPs. Short-range radio signals can connect a wireless keyboard or mouse to a PC. Medium-range radio transmissions are often used to connect portable PC users to the Internet at public hot spots.

Broadcast radio signals can penetrate buildings and other objects, enabling devices to only be within the required range to communicate, not within line-of-sight with each other. A *transmitter* is needed to send the radio signals through the air; a *receiver* (usually containing some type of antenna) accepts the data at the other end. Sometimes a single piece of hardware functions as both a receiver and transmitter; if so, it is commonly called a *transmitter-receiver* or *transceiver*. For instance, fixed wireless Internet access requires a transceiver to be mounted on the roof of a business or home utilizing the service. Transceivers are also used with wireless home and office networks and are increasingly being built into notebook PCs and other devices commonly used to access a wireless network.

Microwave and Satellite Transmissions

Microwaves are high-frequency, high-speed radio signals. Microwave signals can be sent using *microwave stations* or via *satellites*. Both methods can transmit data in large quantities and at high speeds, and are ideal for applications such as television and radio broadcasting and Internet transmissions. They are also used for some telephone, paging, and messaging systems.

Microwave stations are earth-based stations that can transmit microwave signals directly to each other over distances of up to about 30 miles. Unlike broadcast radio, microwave transmission is line-of-sight, which means that the microwaves must travel in a straight line from one station to another without encountering any obstacles. To avoid buildings, mountains, and the curvature of the earth obstructing the signal, microwave stations are usually placed on tall buildings, towers, and mountaintops. Microwave stations typically contain both a disc-shaped *microwave antenna* and a transceiver. When one station receives a transmission from another, it amplifies it and passes it on to the next station. Microwave stations can also exchange data transmissions with satellites. Microwave stations designed specifically to communicate with satellites, such as for satellite TV and Internet services, are typically called *satellite dishes*. Satellite dishes are usually installed permanently where they are needed, but can also be mounted on trucks, boats, and other types of transportation devices when portable transmission capabilities are necessary or desirable, such as on military missions or recreational vehicles.

Communications satellites are space-based devices placed into orbit around the earth to receive and transmit microwave signals to and from earth (see Figure 8-12). Originally used primarily to facilitate microwave transmission when microwave stations were either not economically viable (such as over large, sparsely populated areas) or physically impractical (such as over large bodies of water), satellites can now send and receive transmissions to and from a variety of other devices, such as personal satellite dishes used for television and Internet transmissions, GPS receivers, satellite radio receivers, and satellite phones.

Traditional satellites maintain a *geosynchronous* (also called *geostationary*) orbit, 22,300 miles above the earth. Geosynchronous satellites travel at a speed and direction that keeps pace with the earth's rotation, so they appear to remain stationary over a given spot on the globe. Geosynchronous satellites are so far above the surface of the earth that it takes only two of them to blanket the entire planet. Although geosynchronous satellites are

> **FIGURE 8-12**
> **Satellite transmissions.** Communications satellites act as middlemen, relaying data between earth-based satellite dishes.

N
E
T

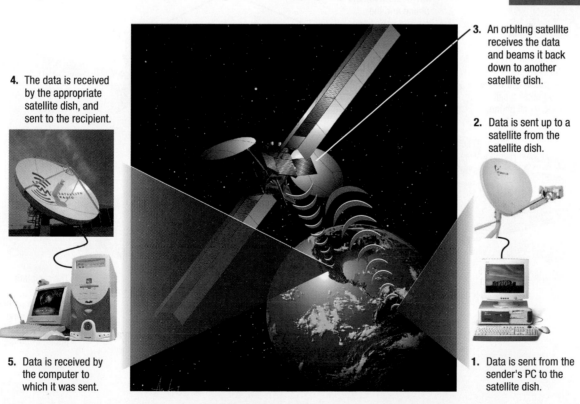

4. The data is received by the appropriate satellite dish, and sent to the recipient.

5. Data is received by the computer to which it was sent.

3. An orbiting satellite receives the data and beams it back down to another satellite dish.

2. Data is sent up to a satellite from the satellite dish.

1. Data is sent from the sender's PC to the satellite dish.

>**Microwave station.** An earth-based device that sends and receives high-frequency, high-speed radio signals. >**Communications satellite.** An earth-orbiting device that relays communications signals over long distances.

excellent for transmitting data, they are so far away that there is a slight delay while the signals travel from the earth, to the satellite, and back to the earth again. This delay—about a half-second—is very small for the distance involved and doesn't really interfere with data communications, but it does makes geosynchronous satellite transmissions less practical for voice, gaming, and other real-time communications.

To avoid this problem with telephone communications, *low earth orbit* (*LEO*) satellite systems were developed. These satellites typically are located about 500 miles above the earth and use between 50 and 60 satellites to cover the earth. LEO satellites are cheaper to build, and, because of their lower orbits, they provide faster message transmission than traditional satellites. *Medium earth orbit* (*MEO*) systems using satellites located about 6,400 miles above the earth are currently being developed for both telephone and Internet service. At about 12,000 miles above the earth, GPS satellites are considered MEO satellites. GPS satellites orbit the earth about every 12 hours.

Cellular Radio Transmissions

Cellular radio is a form of broadcast radio designed for use with cellular telephones. Cellular transmissions take place via *cellular towers*—tall metal poles with antennas on top to receive and transmit cellular radio signals. Cellular service areas are divided into honeycomb-shaped zones called *cells*, each usually measuring between 2 and 10 miles across and containing one cellular tower (see Figure 8-13). When a cell phone user begins to make a call, it is picked up by the cell tower for the cell in which the caller is located.

> **FIGURE 8-13**
> **Cellular transmissions.** Cell phones send and receive calls via cellular radio towers covering a limited geographical area. As the cell phone user moves, the call is transferred from cell tower to cell tower.

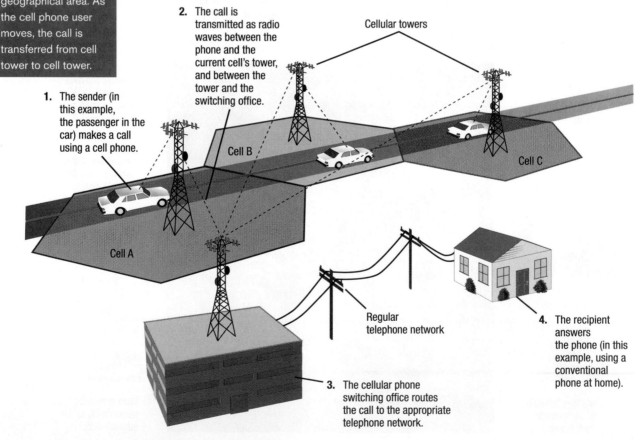

1. The sender (in this example, the passenger in the car) makes a call using a cell phone.

2. The call is transmitted as radio waves between the phone and the current cell's tower, and between the tower and the switching office.

Cellular towers

Cell A

Cell B

Cell C

Regular telephone network

3. The cellular phone switching office routes the call to the appropriate telephone network.

4. The recipient answers the phone (in this example, using a conventional phone at home).

>**Cellular radio.** A form of broadcast radio that broadcasts using antennae located inside honeycomb-shaped cells.

The cell tower then forwards the call to its designated cellular company switching office. From there the call travels to the telephone network belonging to the recipient. Assuming the recipient is using a conventional telephone, as in Figure 8-13, the recipient receives the call via his or her telephone service provider. Calls to a cellular phone work in a similar manner, with the call going through the sender's telephone service provider, to the cellular switching office, to the cell phone tower in the cell in which the cell phone user is currently located, and then to that cell phone. When a cell phone user moves out of the current cell into a new cell, the call is handed off to the appropriate cell tower, usually without the user realizing the call has been transferred. To allow multiple conversations to take place at the same time over a single cellular network, different transmission frequencies are used. To avoid interference, towers in adjacent cells always transmit on different frequencies.

Cellular phone use has become incredibly popular—one estimate is 1.1 billion cell phones worldwide in 2003, expected to reach 2 billion by 2006. Individuals who need to maintain constant contact with the office or clients while on the move—such as a salesperson, truck driver, or real-estate agent—obviously benefit from the ability to carry cell phones. Farmers and others who work outdoors also use cellular technology to stay in contact with others when they cannot afford the time it would take to get to a regular phone. Enormous numbers of individuals also use cell phones to keep in touch with friends and family on a constant basis. In addition to voice transmissions, many cell phones today can be used to access Web pages and exchange e-mail and instant messages.

It is common to think of the cellular evolution in terms of generations (see Figure 8-14). The original *first-generation* phones were analog and used the *Advanced Mobile Phone Service (AMPS)* standard. Newer cell phones, starting with the second generation, are digital and support data in addition to voice transmissions. *Second-generation (2G)* phones can transmit data up to about 14.4 Kbps. *Third generation (3G)* devices are designed to provide enhanced data communications services. Although off to a slow start in the United States, 3G phone service does exist. Designed to transfer 128 Kbps while driving in a car, 384 Kbps in a pedestrian environment, and 2 Gbps in a fixed setup, 3G is significantly faster than earlier types of cell phone services. In addition to being used with cell phones, 3G also works with handheld and notebook PCs. *Fourth-generation (4G)* cellular services, expected to move data at 100 Mbps or more, may arrive as soon as 2006.

There are a number of different cellular standards, such as *GSM (Global System for Mobile Communications)* and *CDMA (Code Division Multiple Access)* for 2G phones, and *GPRS (General Packet Radio Service)*, *UMTS (Universal Mobile Telecommunications System)*, and *WCDMA (Wideband Code Division Multiple Access)* for 3G phones. The United States currently uses two main cell phone standards: GSM and CDMA (roaming agreements between cellular carriers can allow users to communicate with others using a competing standard). Much of the rest of the world has standardized on GSM.

An emerging trend—called *presence technology*—refers to mobile phones and other devices being able to locate and identify each other. For a look at presence technology and a related FCC mandate—*e911*—see the Inside the Industry box.

> **TIP**
>
> Cell phones that fall somewhere between 2G and 3G capabilities are commonly referred to as 2.5G phones.

N E T

> **FIGURE 8-14**
> **Cellular generations.**

GENERATION	ANALOG/ DIGITAL	STANDARDS	DESIGNED FOR	MAXIMUM SPEED
1	Analog	AMPS	Voice	2.4 Kbps
2	Digital	GSM, CDMA	Voice/Data	14.4 Kbps
3	Digital	GPRS, UMTS, WCDMA	Voice/Data (including high-speed Internet and multimedia)	2 Mbps (fixed setting)
4 (not yet available)	Digital	not yet determined	Data (including high-quality full-motion video)	100 Mbps (estimated)

INSIDE THE INDUSTRY

Presence Technology

Presence technology refers to the ability of one computing device (such as a desktop PC, PDA, or smart phone) on a network (such as the Internet) to locate and identify another device on the same network and determine its status. In theory, it can be used to determine when someone on a network is using his or her computer or wireless phone, as well as where that device is physically located at any given time. For example, when an employee at a company using presence technology (sometimes called *presence management* when used in a business context) has a question, he or she can check the directory displayed on his or her PC or cell phone to see which team members are available, regardless of where those team members are physically located (see the accompanying illustration). The employee can then call the team member or send an instant message. Presence technology is also expected to be used on Web pages, so visitors—usually potential or current customers—can see which salespeople, service representatives, or other contacts are currently available. Another possible application is

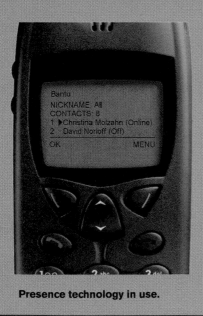

Presence technology in use.

including dynamic presence buttons in e-mail messages—the presence button would display one message (such as "I'm online") if the sender is online at the time the e-mail message is read, and a different message (such as "I'm offline") if the sender is not signed in at that time. The newest version of Microsoft Office, released in 2003, includes support for online presence information.

Although presence technology is currently in the early stages, it has been in the works since 1996 in the form of an FCC *enhanced 911 (e911)* mandate for wireless phones. The e911 mandate was prompted by the tremendous increase in 911 calls made from wireless phones (now estimated to be one wireless call to 911 in the United States every four seconds) paired with the fact that 911 operators are unable to locate the position of wireless callers, unlike callers using land-based telephones. The e911 mandate regulations specify that new cell phones must have built-in GPS capabilities to enable emergency services personnel to pinpoint the location of people calling 911 using a wireless phone. Phase I requires only the location of the nearest cell tower; phase II, which began in October 2001 and is scheduled to be fully implemented by the end of 2005, requires more precise location information. Although designed to assist in emergency services, phone vendors and advertising agencies are expected to develop other uses for these location services. Possibilities include seeing ads targeted specifically at individuals based on where they happen to be physically located at the moment (such as close to a particular restaurant at lunchtime), as well as being able to tell if a family member or friend is available for a telephone call before dialing the number.

Although some aspects of presence technology are intriguing (such as being able to tell that a loved one's flight arrived safely when you notice his or her cell phone is turned on again), privacy advocates are pushing for legislation and standards to ensure that presence technology providers protect users' security and privacy. A bill had been introduced in the House of Representatives requiring informed customer consent for the use of wireless presence information, but the bill was still in committee at the time of this writing.

Infrared Transmissions

Infrared (IR) *transmissions* send data as infrared light rays. Like an infrared television remote control, infrared technology requires line-of-sight transmission. Because of this limitation, many formerly infrared devices (such as wireless mice and keyboards) now use broadcast radio technology instead. Infrared transmissions are still commonly used to beam data between handheld PCs or between a handheld PC and a desktop PC. It is also sometimes used to send documents from a portable PC to a printer, or to connect a portable PC to a company network.

FURTHER EXPLORATION

For links to further information about wired and wireless communications media, go to www.course.com/uc10/ch08

TYPES OF NETWORKS

Networks can be identified by their *topology*, *architecture*, and size. These topics are described in the next few sections.

Network Topologies

Computer networks vary in physical arrangement or *topology*. Three of the most common topologies are *star*, *bus*, and *ring* (see Figure 8-15).

Star Networks

The **star network**—the oldest topology for computer networks—typically consists of a central device (usually a *hub*, *switch*, or *router*, all of which are discussed shortly) to which all the computers and other devices in the network connect, forming a star shape. The central device contains multiple ports that are used to connect the various network devices (such as a server, PCs, and a printer, for instance); all network transmissions are sent through the central device. Star networks are common in traditional mainframe environments, as well as in small office and home networks.

Bus Networks

A **bus network** has no central hub. Instead, it consists of a central cable to which all network devices are attached. For example, the bus network illustrated in Figure 8-15 contains three PCs and a printer attached to a single bus line. In a bus network, all data is transmitted down the bus line from one device to another, and only one device can transmit at a time.

Ring Networks

A less common alternative to the star and bus topologies is the **ring network**. Like a bus network, ring networks don't have a central hub, but the computers and other network devices are connected in a ring formation from one device to the next, without the use of a central cable (see the third illustration in Figure 8-15). In a ring network, data travels from one device to another around the ring in one direction only.

> **FIGURE 8-15**
> **Basic network topologies.** Common topologies are star, bus, and ring.

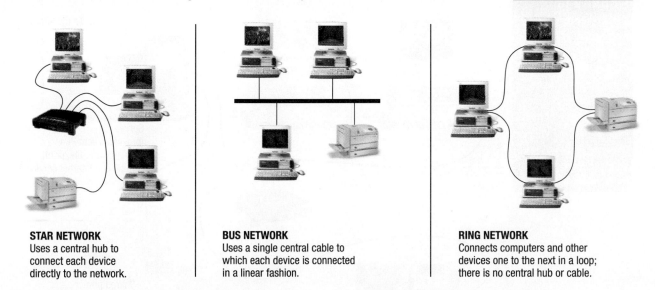

STAR NETWORK
Uses a central hub to connect each device directly to the network.

BUS NETWORK
Uses a single central cable to which each device is connected in a linear fashion.

RING NETWORK
Connects computers and other devices one to the next in a loop; there is no central hub or cable.

>**Star network.** A network that uses a host device connected directly to several other devices. >**Bus network.** A network consisting of a central cable to which all network devices are attached. >**Ring network.** A network that connects devices in a closed loop.

Combination Topologies

Some networks, such as the Internet, don't conform to a standard topology. Networks may combine topologies and connect multiple smaller networks, in effect turning several smaller networks into one larger one. For example, two star networks may be joined together using a bus line.

Network Architectures

In addition to topology, networks vary by their *architecture*; that is, their design. The two most common options are *client-server* and *peer-to-peer*.

Client-Server Networks

Client-server networks include both *clients* (PCs and other devices on the network that request and utilize network resources) and *servers* (computers that are dedicated to processing client requests). There are a number of different tasks that a server can perform. For example, a *network server* manages network traffic, a *file server* manages shared files, a *print server* handles printing-related activities, and a *mail server* and *Web server* are dedicated to managing e-mail and Web page requests, respectively. Not all networks require all of these server functions and a single server can perform more than one function. For instance, there is only one server in the network illustrated in Figure 8-16 to perform all server tasks for that network.

Network servers are typically powerful computers with lots of memory and a very large hard drive. They can be high-end PCs, midrange servers, or mainframe computers. Regardless of the type of server used, retrieving files from a server is called *downloading*; transferring data from a client PC to a server is referred to as *uploading*.

Peer-to-Peer Networks

Networks that don't need a central server may use a *peer-to-peer* architecture instead of a client-server architecture. With a peer-to-peer network, all the computers on the network work at the same level and users have direct access to the other computers and the peripherals

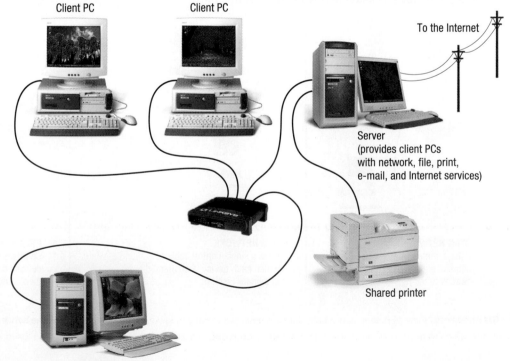

⊗ FIGURE 8-16
Client-server networks. With this type of network, client PCs communicate through one or more servers which handle such requests as print jobs, e-mail and Internet access, programs and files stored on the network, and more.

Client PC

Client PC

To the Internet

Server (provides client PCs with network, file, print, e-mail, and Internet services)

Shared printer

Client PC

attached to the network. For instance, users can access files stored on another peer computer's hard drive and print using the peer computer's printer, provided those devices have been designated as shared devices. Peer-to-peer networks are less expensive and less complicated to implement, since there are no dedicated servers, but they may not have the same performance as client-server networks under heavy use. Peer-to-peer capabilities are built into many personal operating systems for small office or home networks.

Another type of peer-to-peer networking—sometimes called *Internet peer-to-peer computing*—is performed via the Internet. Instead of placing content on a Web server for others to view, content is exchanged directly with the other users of the peer-to-peer network. For instance, one user can copy a file located on another user's hard drive to his or her own PC via their Internet connections. Internet peer-to-peer networking is commonly used for exchanging music files with others over the Internet—an illegal act if the music is copyright-protected. Illegal peer-to-peer music sharing is expected to decline now that the recording industry has begun suing individual peer-to-peer networking users suspected of downloading illegal copies of copyrighted songs; however, some legal applications of Internet peer-to-peer networking do exist. In fact, some peer-to-peer networks are working towards partnerships with the music industry for legal distribution of copyrighted material. The peer-to-peer music sharing controversy is discussed in more detail in Chapter 9; copyright law, ethics, and other topics related to peer-to-peer file exchanges are covered in Chapter 16.

LANs, WANs, and Other Types of Networks

One additional way networks are classified is by their size, which specifies how large of an area the network services and what users the network is designed to service. Some of the most common types of networks are listed next.

Local Area Networks (LANs)

A **local area network** (**LAN**) is a network that covers a relatively small geographical area, such as a home, classroom, or business office. The devices (sometimes called *nodes*) on the network can be connected with either wired or wireless communications media. The network shown in Figure 8-16 is an example of a LAN.

Wide Area Networks (WANs)

A **wide area network** (**WAN**) is a network that covers a large geographical area. Sometimes a WAN is comprised of two or more geographically dispersed LANs. The Internet, by this definition, is the world's largest WAN. WANs may be publicly accessible, like the Internet, or may be privately owned and operated. The wireless networks used for cellular phone service are examples of *wireless WANs*.

Metropolitan Area Networks (MANs)

A *metropolitan area network* (*MAN*) is a network designed for a town or city. MANs usually fall between LANs and WANs in the size continuum and often are used to connect multiple LANs within a single city or town. Most MANs are not owned by a single company or organization. Instead, they are typically owned by either a consortium of users or by a single network provider who sells access to the MAN to others.

>**Local area network (LAN).** A network that connects devices located in a small geographical area, such as within a building. >**Wide area network (WAN).** A network that connects devices located in a large geographical area.

USES FOR INTRANETS

- Facilitating internal electronic mail.
- Providing access to company contact information, procedure manuals, and other frequently updated documents.
- Posting and submitting employee forms.
- Posting internal job listings.
- Providing electronic catalogs for ordering supplies.
- Facilitating collaborative computing.
- Scheduling meetings and appointments.
- Posting financial statements and other types of corporate information.
- Maintaining shared calendars, project timelines, and other project documents.

FIGURE 8-17
Uses for intranets.

Personal Area Networks (PANs)

A *personal area network (PAN)* is a network of personal devices for one individual, such as his or her PC, cell phone, and PDA—the PAN allows the devices to communicate and work together. The feasibility of PANs is growing with the improvement of wireless technology (such as the *Bluetooth* standard discussed in a later section) that enables a collection of devices to communicate automatically and wirelessly with each other when they get within a certain physical distance. For instance, PANs can keep portable devices synchronized with a desktop PC. In a nutshell, PANs are intended to permit an individual's everyday devices to become smart devices that spontaneously network and work together.

Intranets and Extranets

An **intranet** is a private network—usually a LAN or WAN set up by a company for its employees—that implements the infrastructure and standards of the Internet and World Wide Web. Intranets today serve a variety of purposes, such as making company publications available to employees, disseminating forms, and enabling employees to communicate and work together on projects (see Figure 8-17). Since most employees are already familiar with the Internet, having employees use their Web browser to access the company intranet virtually eliminates training requirements. Also, Internet technology (and therefore intranets) can be used with virtually any computer platform, and many companies have diverse mixtures of computers that need to communicate with one another. What's more, development costs are relatively small—no highly unique, proprietary system has to be designed.

An intranet that is at least partially accessible to authorized outsiders is called an **extranet**. Extranets can be used to provide customers and business partners with access to the company data and application they need. Extranets are usually accessed via the Internet. Access to intranets and extranets is typically restricted to employees and other authorized users, similar to company networks.

Virtual Private Networks (VPNs)

A **virtual private network** (**VPN**) is a group of private, secure paths built over a public communications system (usually the Internet) to allow authorized users private, secure access to the company network. For instance, a VPN could allow a traveling employee, business partner, or satellite office to securely connect to the company network. A process called *tunneling* is used to carry the data over the Internet; to secure the data from being intercepted during transit, it is *encrypted*. Other security measures are used to ensure that only authorized users can use the VPN. In essence, VPN is a method of extending a company network to other locations without the cost of extending the physical network.

Storage Area Networks (SANs)

As discussed in Chapter 4, a *storage area network* or *SAN* is a high-speed, dedicated secure network of shared hard drives or other storage devices. It is similar to a dedicated file server, but on a larger scale because multiple storage devices are involved. SANs have become more important in recent years as companies have found their storage requirements increasing dramatically. It has been estimated that the storage needs of traditional businesses double annually—for some companies this amounts to several terabytes per year. An advantage to using a SAN system is that additional storage devices can be added to the SAN as more storage is required, without disrupting the network. In addition to day-to-day data storage, SANs can also be used for backup and disaster recovery purposes.

>Intranet. A private network that is set up similar to the World Wide Web. **>Extranet.** An intranet that is at least partially accessible to authorized outsiders. **>Virtual private network (VPN).** A group of secure paths over the Internet that provide authorized users a secure means of accessing a private network via the Internet.

NETWORKING HARDWARE

To connect to a local network, a PC needs a *network interface card*; to connect to the Internet, a *modem* is required. Appropriate cabling is also needed for wired network connections. There are a number of different network interface cards and modems available to match up with the type of PC being used and the type of network being accessed. In addition, other hardware is typically required to connect all the PCs on a network together, as well as to connect multiple networks. Some of the most common types of networking hardware are discussed next.

Network Adapters

A **network adapter**, also called a **network interface card** (**NIC**) when it is in the form of an expansion card, is used to connect a PC to a network (see Figure 8-18). Its purpose is to connect the PC physically to the network in order to send outgoing data from the PC to the network and retrieve all incoming data sent via the network to the PC. The type of network adapter used depends on the type of network and communications media being used. For instance, most wired networks today are *Ethernet* networks using twisted-pair cabling; PCs connecting to this type of network would need an Ethernet network adapter with an RJ-45 connector. Many wireless networks today are *802.11b* (*Wi-Fi*) networks; PCs connecting to such a network would need an 802.11 network adapter, but no cable since it is a wireless connection. Handheld PCs and wireless phones may need a special network adapter attached to the PC or phone in order to connect to the Internet via their wireless

TIP

Sometimes the term *wireless modem* is used instead of *network adapter* to refer to hardware that connects a handheld PC or wireless phone to the Internet via a wireless phone network.

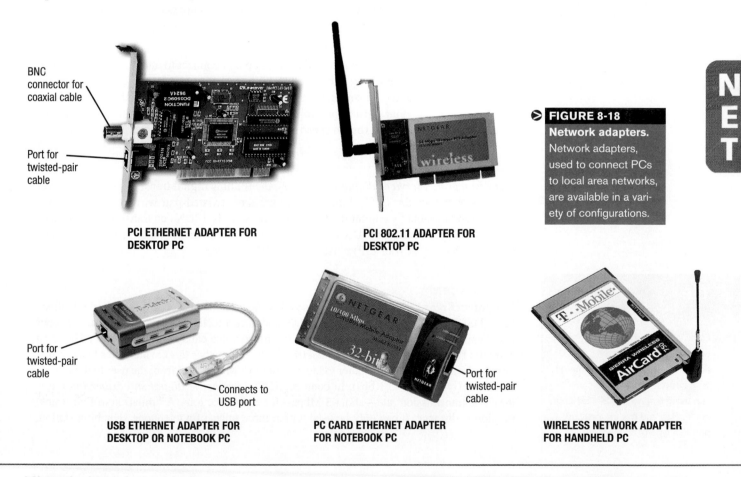

BNC connector for coaxial cable

Port for twisted-pair cable

PCI ETHERNET ADAPTER FOR DESKTOP PC

PCI 802.11 ADAPTER FOR DESKTOP PC

> **FIGURE 8-18**
Network adapters. Network adapters, used to connect PCs to local area networks, are available in a variety of configurations.

Port for twisted-pair cable

Connects to USB port

USB ETHERNET ADAPTER FOR DESKTOP OR NOTEBOOK PC

Port for twisted-pair cable

PC CARD ETHERNET ADAPTER FOR NOTEBOOK PC

WIRELESS NETWORK ADAPTER FOR HANDHELD PC

>**Network adapter.** A network interface, such as an expansion card or external network adapter. >**Network interface card (NIC).** An expansion card through which a computer can connect to a network.

phone provider, although increasingly these capabilities are being integrated directly into the device so an external network adapter isn't required.

Within a specific *networking protocol*, such as Ethernet and 802.11, there are multiple speeds and other differences, so it important to use a networking card that supports the protocol, speed, and communications media being used. The type of network adapter also needs to be the proper configuration for the expansion slot or port to be used, such as a PCI or USB network adapter for a desktop PC, or a PC card or USB network adapter for a notebook PC (refer again to Figure 8-18). Networking protocols are discussed in more detail later in this chapter.

Modems

Modems are devices used to connect computers to the Internet. The name comes from the terms *modulation* and *demodulation*. Modulation refers to converting digital signals (such as those from a PC) to analog form so they can be transmitted over analog media (such as conventional telephone lines). Demodulation refers to the translation from analog form back to digital form. There are a number of different types of modems today, each matching up with a particular type of Internet connection (such as *conventional dial-up*, *cable*, *DSL*, and so forth). Although not all of these types of connections require conversion between analog and digital form, the collection of devices used to connect a PC to the Internet are collectively referred to as "modems." Modems are available in a variety of formats—such as PCI, USB, PC card, and as external devices (see Figure 8-19)—although not all types of modems may be available in all formats. Some common types of modems are discussed next; the types of Internet services that utilize these modems are discussed in more detail in Chapter 9.

Conventional Dial-Up Modems

A *conventional dial-up modem* is needed to dial up and connect to another computer (usually belonging to an ISP for an Internet connection, although this type of modem can also be used to connect to a company network or to send faxes from a PC) using conventional telephone lines. Regular twisted-pair telephone cable is used to connect the modem to a regular phone jack. The maximum speed for a conventional dial-up modem is 56 Kbps.

ISDN Modems

ISDN (integrated services digital network) modems allow digital transmission of data over ordinary telephone lines. ISDN modems use the same twisted-pair wiring as conventional dial-up modems, but by combining (*multiplexing*) signals, ISDN can transmit data faster—up to 128 Kbps. To use an ISDN modem, the computer to which you are connecting (such as the one located at your ISP) must support ISDN service.

DSL Modems

DSL (digital subscriber line) modems also allow faster transmission over standard telephone lines. DSL transmission is faster than ISDN and uses a technology that doesn't tie up your telephone line so you can use the Internet and make voice calls at the same time. The most common type of DSL is *ADSL (asymmetric digital subscriber line)*, which uses faster transmission from the remote computer to the user (up to 8 Mbps) than from the user to the remote computer (typically 640 Kbps). In contrast, *SDSL (symmetric digital subscriber line)* uses the same transmission rate—about 3 Mbps—for both directions. A limitation of DSL transmission is distance: It can only be used within three miles of a telephone switching station,

>**Modem.** A communications device that enables digital computers to communicate over analog media, such as connecting to the Internet via telephone lines.

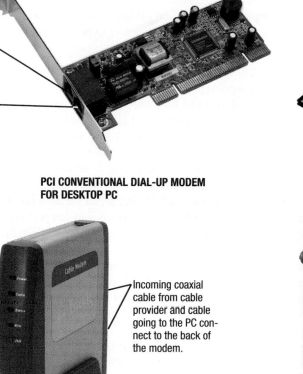

Twisted-pair cable from phone jack connects here.

This port can be used to connect a phone so you don't lose the use of your phone jack.

PCI CONVENTIONAL DIAL-UP MODEM FOR DESKTOP PC

Twisted-pair cable from phone jack connects here.

PC CARD CONVENTIONAL DIAL-UP MODEM FOR NOTEBOOK PC

Incoming coaxial cable from cable provider and cable going to the PC connect to the back of the modem.

CABLE MODEM

Incoming coaxial cable from the satellite dish connects here.

RJ-45 connector to connect PC with twisted-pair cabling (this modem has 4 ports to connect up to 4 PCs).

Outgoing ooaxial cable to the satellite dish connects here.

SATELLITE MODEM

> **FIGURE 8-19**
> Modems.

and the speed degrades as the distance gets closer and closer to the three-mile limit. Consequently, DSL service is not available in all areas. An emerging type of DSL is *VDSL* or *very-high-speed DSL*. VDSL is designed to transmit data very quickly (up to 55 Mbps) over a short distance (no more than 4,500 feet) using standard twisted-pair cabling. It is expected that VDSL will eventually be used to connect a home or other building to the regular telephone network to provide very fast data transmission over regular phone lines, assuming the neighborhood junction box has been upgraded to fiber-optic cabling.

Cable Modems

Cable modems are used to connect a PC to cable Internet service, similar to the way cable boxes are used to obtain cable-TV service. Cable transmissions can be very fast, but transmission speed is reduced as more and more people use it at one time. Because of this, the speed for cable Internet service is less consistent than other types of Internet service with rates around 1.5 Mbps—fairly comparable to ADSL—most of the time.

Satellite Modems

To connect to the Internet using a personal satellite dish, a *satellite modem* is required. At the fairly high transfer rate of about 500 Kbps to 1 Mbps, satellite modems are a little slower than both DSL and cable transmissions, but have the advantage of being able to be used in rural areas. Similar to DSL transmissions, upload speed is generally slower than download speed; some satellite setups can be used to receive satellite television programs, in addition to Internet access.

TIP

On a small network, such as a home network, if one PC has a modem and is set up to access the Internet, all PCs on the network can be set up to share that Internet connection without needing modems—they connect to the Internet via the network.

Hubs, Switches, and Other Networking Hardware

In addition to network adapters, modems, and cabling, other networking hardware is often needed to tie the components of a network together, or to tie multiple networks together.

Hubs, Switches, Routers, and Wireless Access Points

As already mentioned, star topology networks need a central device to connect all the devices on the network. This device can be a *hub*, *switch*, or *router*. All of these devices contain ports to connect the devices together and facilitate communications between the devices, but they differ in how they transfer data. **Hubs** are the least sophisticated and transmit all data received to all network nodes connected to the hub. Consequently, with a hub, the network capacity is shared among the nodes. In contrast, a **switch** identifies the device for which the data is intended and sends the network data to that node only. This allows each node on the network to use the full capacity of the network. **Routers** are even smarter—they pass data on to the intended recipient only, but can plan a path through multiple routers to ensure the data reaches its destination in the most efficient manner possible. Routers are used in LANs, WANs, and the Internet.

A **wireless access point** is a device that functions similarly to a hub, but is used to connect wireless devices to a wired network. Wireless access points can be used in home networks to connect the devices and share an Internet connection; they can also be used at public hot spots to connect wireless users to a wired Internet connection, such as a DSL or cable setup.

Some devices may contain the functions of two or more networking devices. For instance, some cable or satellite modems contain a built-in router to connect multiple PCs to the modem, and some wireless access points have a built-in router to connect a cable or DSL modem plus a built-in switch to connect wired devices to the network.

An example of how all the devices discussed in this section, as well as the other networking hardware discussed in the next few sections, might be used in networks is shown in Figure 8-20.

Gateways and Bridges

When one network needs to connect to another network, a gateway or bridge is used.

▼ A *gateway* is a device that connects two *dissimilar* networks, such as two networks using different networking *communications protocols*.

▼ A *bridge* is a device that connects two networks based on *similar* technology—such as a LAN in one city and a similar LAN in another. Bridges can also be used to partition one large LAN into two smaller ones.

Repeaters

Repeaters are devices that amplify signals along a network. They are necessary whenever signals have to travel farther than would otherwise be possible over the networking medium being used.

Multiplexers and Concentrators

High-speed communications lines are expensive and almost always have far greater capacity than a single device can use. Because of this, signals from multiple devices are often combined and sent together to share a single phone line or other communications medium.

>Hub. A device that is a central location where data arrives and is then transferred in one or more directions. **>Switch.** A device on a network to which data is sent so it can be forwarded on to the appropriate network node. **>Router.** A device on a network that sends data via the most efficient route to travel to a specific location. **>Wireless access point.** A device used to connect wireless devices to a wired network.

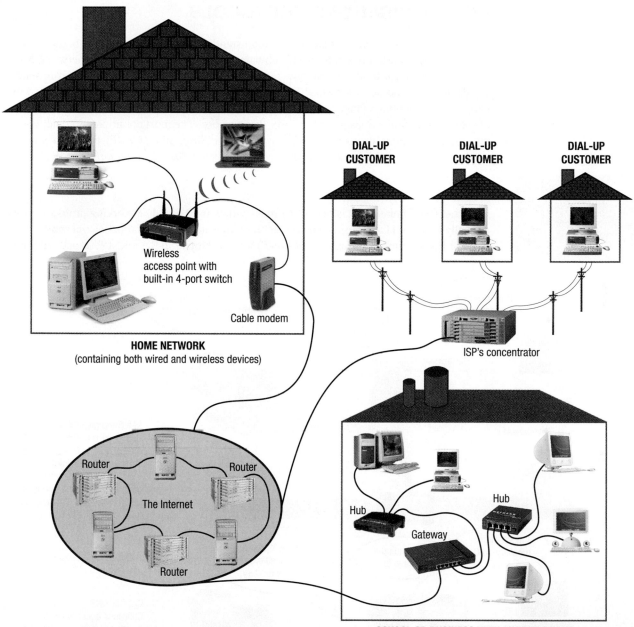

HOME NETWORK
(containing both wired and wireless devices)

SCHOOL OR BUSINESS WITH MULTIPLE LANS

A *multiplexer* combines the transmissions from several different devices and sends them as one message. With *Frequency Division Multiplexing* (*FDM*), each signal is assigned a different frequency over which to travel; with *Wave Division Multiplexing* (*WDM*), each signal is assigned a different wavelength (WDM can be used with fiber-optic cables only). With any type of multiplexing, when the combined signal reaches its destination, the individual messages are separated from one another. Multiplexing is frequently used with fiber-optic cables and other high-capacity media to increase data throughput. For instance, if 8 signals are multiplexed together and sent over each fiber in a fiber-optic cable, the throughput of the cable is increased by a factor of 8. Using even more wavelengths, such as in *Dense WDM* (*DWDM*), even more data can be transmitted at one time.

A *concentrator* is a type of multiplexer that combines multiple messages and sends them via a single transmission medium in such a way that all the individual messages are simultaneously active, instead of being sent as a single combined message. For example, ISPs often use concentrators to combine the signals from their conventional dial-up modem customers to be sent over faster communications connections to their Internet destinations.

> **FIGURE 8-20**
> **Networking hardware.** As shown in this example, many different types of hardware are needed to connect networking devices.

COMMUNICATIONS PROTOCOLS

A *communications protocol* is an agreed-upon standard for transmitting data between two devices on a network. Protocols specify how devices physically connect to a network, how data is packaged for transmission, how receiving devices acknowledge signals from sending devices (a process called *handshaking*), how errors are handled, and so forth. Just as people need a common language to communicate effectively, machines need a common set of rules—communications protocols—for this purpose. The most common wired networking communications protocols are *Ethernet*, *Token Ring*, and *TCP/IP*; the most widely used wireless networking communications protocols are *802.11, Bluetooth*, and *WAP*.

FIGURE 8-21
Ethernet networks.
Ethernet networks use the CSMA/CD access-control method.

Ethernet

Ethernet (see Figure 8-21) is one of the most widely used wired networking protocols. It is typically used with LANs using a bus or star topology and twisted-pair or coaxial cables. The original Ethernet protocol (called *10Base-T*) was developed in the mid-1970s and supports

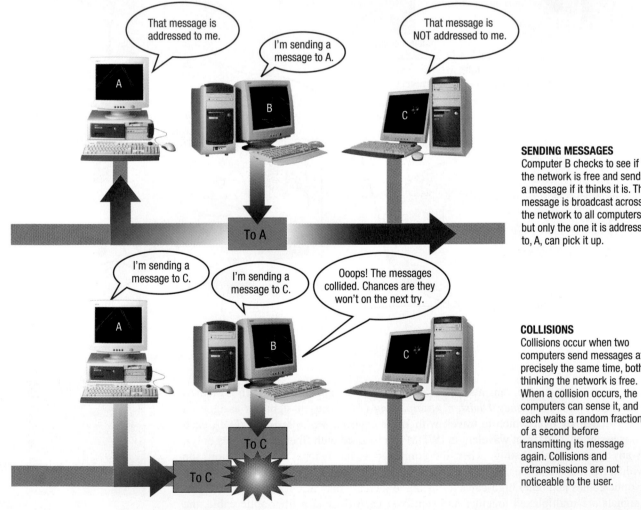

SENDING MESSAGES
Computer B checks to see if the network is free and sends a message if it thinks it is. The message is broadcast across the network to all computers, but only the one it is addressed to, A, can pick it up.

COLLISIONS
Collisions occur when two computers send messages at precisely the same time, both thinking the network is free. When a collision occurs, the computers can sense it, and each waits a random fraction of a second before transmitting its message again. Collisions and retransmissions are not noticeable to the user.

>**Ethernet.** A widely used communications protocol for a LAN.

transmission rates of 10 Mbps. The newer *Fast Ethernet* (*100Base-T*) standard runs at 100 Mbps, and *Gigabit Ethernet* is even faster at 1,000 Mbps (1 Gbps). The emerging *10-Gigabit Ethernet* standard supports data transfer rates of 10 Gbps.

When transmitting data, an Ethernet network uses a set of procedures collectively called *CSMA/CD*, which stands for *Carrier Sense Multiple Access* and *Collision Detection* (refer again to Figure 8-21). *Carrier sense* means that when a computer on the network is ready to send a message, it first "listens" for other messages on the line. If it senses no messages, it sends one. *Multiple access* means that two computers might try to send a message at exactly the same time, so a *collision* may occur. *Collision detection* means that just after a computer transmits a message, it listens to see if the message collided with a message from another computer (collisions are not noticeable to the user). When a collision takes place, the two sending computers wait for very short, random periods of time and send their messages again. The chance of the messages colliding a second time is extremely small.

Token Ring

Token Ring is a LAN protocol developed by IBM. It is usually used with a ring topology and has a different method of controlling access to the network than Ethernet, as shown in Figure 8-22. With a Token Ring network, a small data packet called a *token*—which has room for a message and the appropriate address—is sent around the ring. As the token circulates, the computers on the network check to see if the token is addressed to them; if so, they grab the token to retrieve the message. A token also contains a control area, which specifies whether the token is free or if it carries a message. When a token is free, any computer can take possession of it to attach a message. It does this by changing the status of the token from free to busy, adding the addressed message, and releasing the token. The message then travels around the ring until it reaches the receiving computer. The receiving computer retrieves the message, changes the status of the token back to free, and then releases the token. In general, the Token Ring protocol maintains more order than the Ethernet protocol because it eliminates collisions. However, Token Ring networks are usually slower. Traditionally, Token Ring networks run from about 4 to 16 Mbps. The newer, second-generation Token Ring architecture can operate at 100 Mbps.

TCP/IP

TCP/IP is the protocol used for transferring data over the Internet. It actually consists of two protocols: *Transmission Control Protocol* (*TCP*) and *Internet Protocol* (*IP*). TCP/IP uses a technique called *packet switching* to transmit data over the Internet. With packet switching, messages are separated into small units called *packets*. Packets contain information about the sender and the receiver, the actual data being sent, and information about how to reassemble the packets in order to reconstruct the original message. Packets travel along the network separately, based on their final destination, network traffic, and other network conditions. When the packets reach their destination, they are re-assembled in the proper order (see Figure 8-23).

Support for TCP/IP is built into many operating systems and IP addresses are commonly used in conjunction with other protocols, such as Ethernet, to identify computers on a LAN. In recent years, packet switching has also begun to be used by telephone companies to provide faster, cheaper transmissions over telephone lines. For a look at how IP addresses are used when setting up an Ethernet home network, see the How it Works box.

> **TIP**
>
> Most Ethernet networking hardware is backward compatible, such as 10/100/1000 switches that support devices using any of the 10 Mbps, 100 Mbps, or 1 Gbps Ethernet standards.

> **TIP**
>
> A related protocol, called *Voice over IP* (*VoIP*), involves delivering voice (such as telephone calls) over the Internet using Internet Protocol.

N E T

>**Token ring.** A communications protocol that uses token passing to control the transmission of messages. >**TCP/IP.** The communications protocol that uses packet switching to facilitate the transmission of messages; the protocol used with the Internet.

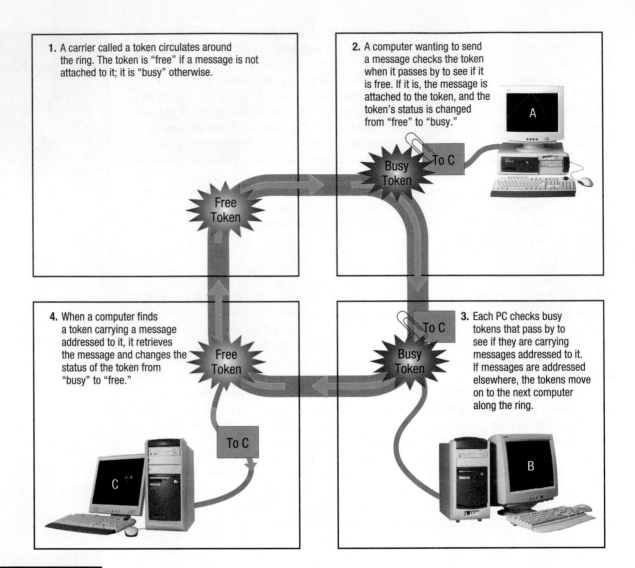

1. A carrier called a token circulates around the ring. The token is "free" if a message is not attached to it; it is "busy" otherwise.

2. A computer wanting to send a message checks the token when it passes by to see if it is free. If it is, the message is attached to the token, and the token's status is changed from "free" to "busy."

4. When a computer finds a token carrying a message addressed to it, it retrieves the message and changes the status of the token from "busy" to "free."

3. Each PC checks busy tokens that pass by to see if they are carrying messages addressed to it. If messages are addressed elsewhere, the tokens move on to the next computer along the ring.

FIGURE 8-22

Token Ring networks. Token Ring networks use token passing to control access.

802.11 (Wi-Fi)

Developed in the late 1990s, **802.11** (sometimes called *wireless Ethernet*) is a family of wireless networking standards. It is also known as **Wi-Fi** (for *wireless fidelity*), although technically the Wi-Fi label can only be used with 802.11 products that are certified by the *Wireless Ethernet Compatibility Alliance* (*WECA*). (Users of Wi-Fi certified products are assured that their hardware will be compatible with all other Wi-Fi certified hardware.) Wi-Fi/802.11 has quickly become the standard for wireless networks at home, in businesses, and at public wireless access points. Wi-Fi devices can be added to existing Ethernet networks by connecting a wireless access point to the network. For instance, a homeowner may wish to add a notebook PC that can be used anywhere in the house or yard to his or her existing wired LAN (as shown in Figure 8-20), or a business may wish to add wireless capabilities to the company network to provide Internet and network access in meeting rooms, lobbies, cafeterias, and other common areas. Public Wi-Fi hot spots are also becoming increasingly common. Although you can't get continuous coverage while on the go (such as with Internet service through a cellular provider), Wi-Fi is a fast alternative for users who need Internet access while close to an

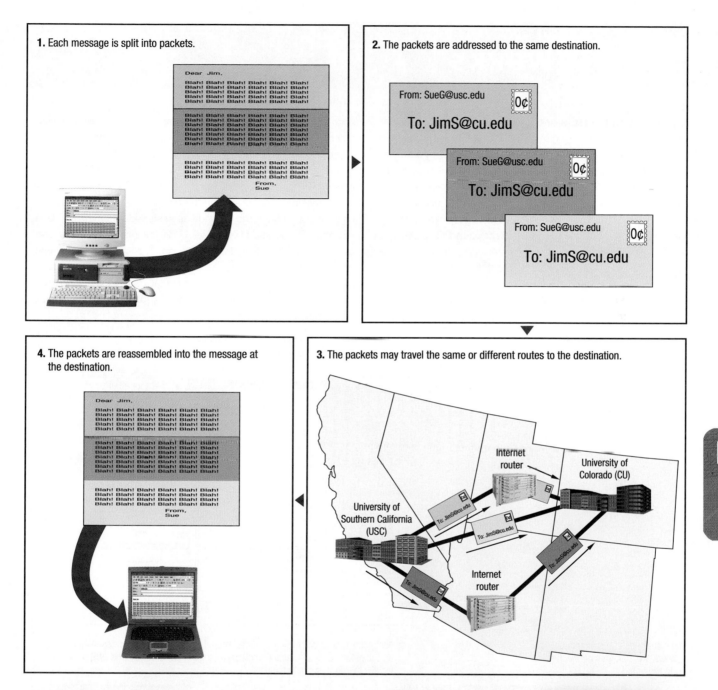

1. Each message is split into packets.

Dear Jim,

Blah! Blah! Blah! Blah! Blah! Blah!
Blah! Blah! Blah! Blah! Blah! Blah!
Blah! Blah! Blah! Blah! Blah! Blah!
Blah! Blah! Blah! Blah! Blah! Blah!
Blah! Blah! Blah! Blah! Blah!

Blah! Blah! Blah! Blah! Blah! Blah!
Blah! Blah! Blah! Blah! Blah! Blah!
Blah! Blah! Blah! Blah! Blah! Blah!
Blah! Blah! Blah! Blah! Blah! Blah!
Blah! Blah! Blah! Blah! Blah! Blah!

Blah! Blah! Blah! Blah! Blah! Blah!
Blah! Blah! Blah! Blah! Blah! Blah!
Blah! Blah! Blah! Blah! Blah! Blah!
From,
Sue

2. The packets are addressed to the same destination.

From: SueG@usc.edu   0¢
To: JimS@cu.edu

From: SueG@usc.edu   0¢
To: JimS@cu.edu

From: SueG@usc.edu   0¢
To: JimS@cu.edu

4. The packets are reassembled into the message at the destination.

Dear Jim,

Blah! Blah! Blah! Blah! Blah! Blah!
Blah! Blah! Blah! Blah! Blah! Blah!
Blah! Blah! Blah! Blah! Blah! Blah!
Blah! Blah! Blah! Blah! Blah! Blah!
Blah! Blah! Blah! Blah! Blah! Blah!

Blah! Blah! Blah! Blah! Blah! Blah!
Blah! Blah! Blah! Blah! Blah! Blah!
Blah! Blah! Blah! Blah! Blah! Blah!
Blah! Blah! Blah! Blah! Blah! Blah!
Blah! Blah! Blah! Blah! Blah! Blah!

Blah! Blah! Blah! Blah! Blah! Blah!
Blah! Blah! Blah! Blah! Blah! Blah!
From,
Sue

3. The packets may travel the same or different routes to the destination.

Internet router

University of Colorado (CU)

University of Southern California (USC)

To: JimS@cu.edu

To: JimS@cu.edu

To: JimS@cu.edu

To: JimS@cu.edu

Internet router

N E T

accessible hot spot. A series of connected hot spots may provide wider, more comprehensive Wi-Fi coverage in the future—such setups are in the experimentation stage.

There are a number of different versions of the 802.11 standard, as listed next in chronological order.

▼ *802.11b*—introduced in 1999, supports data transfer rates of 11 Mbps, and is currently the most prevalent 802.11 standard.

▼ *802.11a* (also called *Wi-Fi5*)—a newer standard that is about five times faster (up to 54 Mbps) than 802.11b, but is more expensive and uses a different radio frequency (5 GHz) than 802.11b (2.4 GHz), making the two standards incompatible.

▼ *802.11g*—an even newer standard that runs at 54 Mbps, but uses the same 2.4 GHz frequency as 802.11b, so their products are compatible. At the time of this writing, most experts were recommending this standard for new consumer purchases.

FIGURE 8-23
TCP/IP networks.
TCP/IP networks (like the Internet) use packet switching.

HOW IT WORKS

Setting Up a Home Network

The first step in setting up a home network is making sure you have the appropriate hardware and that it is installed correctly. For a wired network, you'll need an Ethernet network adapter (usually either an internal card or external USB adapter) for each PC, a hub or switch, and enough Category 5 networking cables with RJ-45 connectors to connect each PC to the hub or switch. (Typically, modems and printers are connected to a single PC the same as they would without the network and then are shared through the network.)

Next, you can run the Windows Networking Wizard or you can change the networking settings manually (as in the accompanying illustration). In either case, you will need to assign a common network name, unique computer name, and unique IP address to each PC. The *host* PC connected to the Internet should use an IP address of 192.168.0.1; the other PCs on the network can use 192.168.0.xxx, with each PC having a different final extension. You can assign the IP addresses manually or you can choose to have the IP address assigned automatically. Use the host IP address (192.168.0.1) as the default *gateway* and *DNS server* for all other PCs on the network and use 255.255.255.0 as the *subnet mask*; also use the host IP address as the *proxy server* for the browsers on all other PCs to share the Internet connection. Finally, share drives, folders, and printers as needed, and you're good to go!

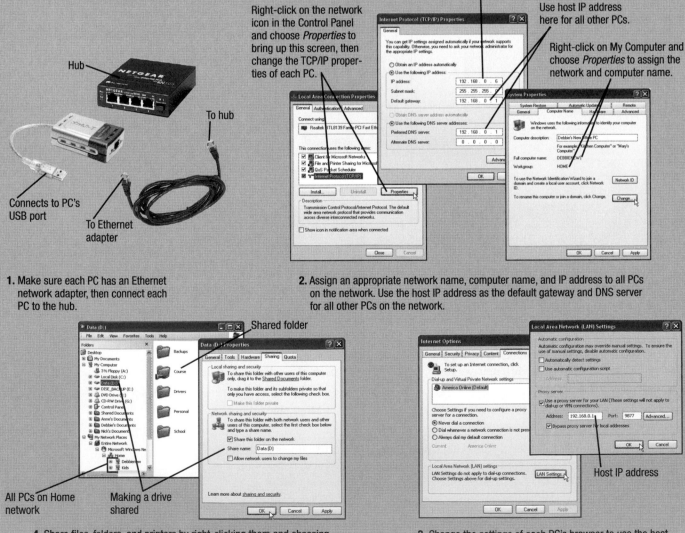

Hub

Connects to PC's USB port

To hub

To Ethernet adapter

Right-click on the network icon in the Control Panel and choose *Properties* to bring up this screen, then change the TCP/IP properties of each PC.

Use an IP address of 192.168.0.1 for the host PC; use a unique IP address for each other PC on the network.

Use host IP address here for all other PCs.

Right-click on My Computer and choose *Properties* to assign the network and computer name.

Shared folder

All PCs on Home network

Making a drive shared

Host IP address

1. Make sure each PC has an Ethernet network adapter, then connect each PC to the hub.

2. Assign an appropriate network name, computer name, and IP address to all PCs on the network. Use the host IP address as the default gateway and DNS server for all other PCs on the network.

4. Share files, folders, and printers by right-clicking them and choosing the *Sharing* option.

3. Change the settings of each PC's browser to use the host IP address as the proxy server.

▼ *802.11e*—an emerging standard expected to have better streaming of data.

▼ *802.11i*—an emerging standard expected to have improved security capabilities.

▼ *802.11h*— an emerging standard expected to have better power management.

Wi-Fi is designed for medium-range data transfers—most versions of 802.11 work up to about 250 or 300 feet away from the access point indoors, and about 1,000 feet away outdoors, although speed degrades as the distance from the access point increases. Other factors, such as the number of solid objects between the access point and the PC, as well as possible interference from cordless phones, baby monitors, and other devices that also operate on the 2.4 GHz frequency, can affect performance. Two emerging standards related to Wi-Fi are *802.16a* (sometimes referred to in its preliminary stages as *Wi-Max* or *Wider-Fi*) and *802.20* (*Mobile-Fi*). Both standards are being developed to widen the range of the wireless access point from 250 feet to several miles. The 802.16a standard is expected to offer speeds somewhere between 10 and 100 Mbps; 802.20 is designed for 16 Mbps access while in cars or while traveling in other vehicles, such as trains, which are moving at up to 120 miles per hour.

TIP

The number *802.11* comes from the official standard number issued by *IEEE (Institute of Electrical and Electronics Engineers)*, a non-profit organization involved with setting standards for computers and communications technology. Although other protocols have IEEE numbers—such as IEEE 802.3 for Ethernet—802.11 is the first standard number that has been widely used by the general public.

Bluetooth

The **Bluetooth** standard uses radio technology similar to Wi-Fi, but is designed for very short-range (less than 10 meters, approximately 33 feet) communications. It is most appropriate for transferring data between a portable PC and a desktop PC, as well as for connecting hardware (such as keyboards, mice, and printers) to desktop PCs, portable PCs, and mobile devices. For example, a Bluetooth earpiece or headset can be used in conjunction with a cell phone left in a pocket or briefcase, a Bluetooth mouse or keyboard can be used with a desktop or portable PC, and a handheld PC can be instantly synchronized with a desktop PC on entering the office. You can also transmit files from a Bluetooth-enabled digital camera or portable PC to a Bluetooth-ready printer. Bluetooth devices automatically recognize each other when they get within transmission range, so handheld PCs, cell phones, and other portable devices can always be networked wirelessly when they are within range. Some industry experts predict that all major household appliances will be Bluetooth-enabled in the future, resulting in an automatic, always connected, smart home.

Bluetooth works using radio waves in the frequency band of 2.4 GHz, the same as Wi-Fi, and supports data transfer rates of up to 1 Mbps, although a newer version of the Bluetooth standard is expected to support speeds of 54 Mbps. Once two Bluetooth-enabled devices come within range of each other, their software identifies each other (using their unique identification numbers) and establishes a link. Because there may be many Bluetooth devices within range, up to 10 individual Bluetooth networks (called *piconets*) can be in place within the same physical area at one time. Each piconet can connect up to eight devices, for a maximum of 80 devices within any 10-meter (approximately 33 feet) radius. To facilitate this, Bluetooth divides its allocated radio spectrum (2,400 to 2,483.5 MHz in the United States and Europe) into 79 channels of 1 MHz each. Each Bluetooth device can use the entire range of frequencies, jumping randomly (in unison with the other devices in that piconet) on a regular basis to minimize interference between piconets, as well as from other devices (such as garage-door openers, Wi-Fi networks, and some cordless phones and baby monitors) that use the same frequencies. Since Bluetooth transmitters change frequencies 1,600 times every second automatically, it is unlikely that any two transmitting devices will be on the same frequencies at the same time.

One device in each piconet acts as the *master* device and continually emits requests for other devices to join the network. Any device wishing to network with the master

---

>**Bluetooth.** A communications standard used to facilitate an automatic connection between devices once they get within the allowable range.

N
E
T

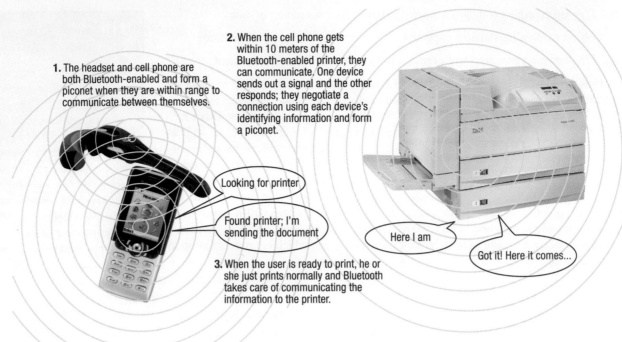

1. The headset and cell phone are both Bluetooth-enabled and form a piconet when they are within range to communicate between themselves.

2. When the cell phone gets within 10 meters of the Bluetooth-enabled printer, they can communicate. One device sends out a signal and the other responds; they negotiate a connection using each device's identifying information and form a piconet.

Looking for printer

Found printer; I'm sending the document

Here I am

Got it! Here it comes...

3. When the user is ready to print, he or she just prints normally and Bluetooth takes care of communicating the information to the printer.

> **FIGURE 8-24**
>
> **How Bluetooth works.** Bluetooth is designed for short-range wireless communications between PCs and other hardware.

device answers with its identification number and becomes a *slave* device in that piconet. Figure 8-24 gives an example of how Bluetooth works.

Wireless Application Protocol (WAP)

Wireless Application Protocol (**WAP**) is a standard for delivering content to mobile devices like smart phones, pagers, and other wireless communications devices, using a cellular telephone network. The content that can be delivered using WAP includes both Web page content and e-mail. To display Web content, a WAP-enabled browser—sometimes called a *microbrowser*—needs to be installed on the device.

Other Networking Protocols

Other networking protocols include *IrDA* and three home-network-oriented protocols designed for a home or small office networks.

IrDA

Similar to Bluetooth, the *infrared* or *IrDA* protocol is used for short-range data transfers between devices (such as cell phones, portable PCs, and printers) that have an IrDA port. Unlike Bluetooth and Wi-Fi, however, IrDA requires line-of-sight transmission, so it can't be used when a wall, piece of furniture, or other obstacle is between the two devices that want to communicate. It also requires the devices to be closer together—typically about 2 feet or less. IrDA is most commonly used to beam data between handheld PCs or between a handheld PC and a desktop PC.

Phoneline Networks

The *Phoneline* (more officially called the *Home Phoneline Networking Association* or *Home PNA*) standard allows computers to be networked through ordinary phone wiring and phone jacks, without interfering with voice telephone calls. Although each PC needs its own Phoneline network adapter, no hub or special cabling is needed since each device is plugged into a standard telephone jack using standard telephone cables. Phoneline adapters can be internal (an expansion card) or USB (as in Figure 8-25). At its current speed of up to 20 Mbps, Phoneline isn't especially fast, but it is geared toward setting up quick and easy home networks, provided that phone jacks already exist at the necessary locations. An emerging new version of this standard—*HomePNA 3.0*—is expected to support speeds up to 128 Mbps.

Powerline Networks

The *Powerline* standard allows PCs to be networked over existing power lines using conventional electrical outlets. Similar to Phoneline networks, no hub is needed, since all devices are connected to standard power outlets. Each PC does require an adapter (called a *Powerline bridge*) to connect the PC to the power outlet. Some adapters connect to a PC's USB port; others require each PC to have an Ethernet card (as in Figure 8-26). At roughly 10 Mbps, Powerline networks are currently slower than Phoneline networks, but have the advantage that houses usually have more power outlets than phone outlets. The Phoneline standard also has great potential for countries where phone jacks are not as prevalent as in the United States. An emerging Powerline standard proposed and named *HomePlug AV* by the HomePlug Powerline Alliance is designed to support distribution of a variety of computing and entertainment communications throughout the home, including computer data, music, and high-definition television (HDTV) signals.

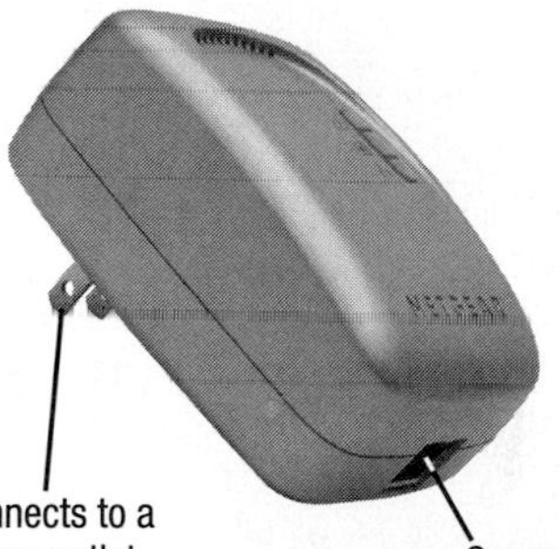

Ultra Wideband (UWB)

Ultra Wideband (*UWB*) *communications* is a wireless technology originally developed for the military in the 1960s; today, it is in the initial stages of experimentation for consumer use. UWB can be used both indoors and outdoors and currently transmits data at speeds up to 40 Mbps, although that is expected to increase eventually to 1 Gbps. UWB transmits data in the wide frequency range of 3.1 GHz to 10.6 GHz by sending out short pulses, as many as 1 billion per second. Higher-frequency signals are best at carrying data; lower-frequency signals are better at penetrating walls. In fact, the main use for UWB for decades has been by the military to look for tanks, enemies, and other objects hidden under foliage, behind walls, or otherwise disguised.

While UWB can be used for general networking, applications currently in development focus on consumer multimedia. For example, BE LABS's *Wireless Multimedia System* (*WMS*) is a within-the-home, Ultra Wideband wireless delivery system for multiple high-quality streaming video, data, and audio sources. Recent tests indicate that an HDTV-quality signal can be transmitted anywhere within a house within a range of about 300 feet. BE LABS is positioning their WMS product as a multimedia gateway to replace wired set-top boxes for cable and satellite TV services, as well as to centralize the delivery of high-speed Internet access, cordless phone services, video-on-demand, and other multimedia services into one comprehensive platform.

To develop standards for networking personal multimedia devices using systems such as UWB, ten leading technology companies recently formed the *WiMedia Alliance*. This non-profit organization will adopt standards and establish a certification program to accelerate widespread consumer adoption of wireless multimedia solutions.

Connects to the
PC's USB port

Connects to
a phone jack

▶ **FIGURE 8-25**
Phoneline adapter.
Connects a desktop or notebook PC to other PCs over standard phone lines inside a home.

Connects to a
power outlet

Connects to the
PC's Ethernet card

▶ **FIGURE 8-26**
Powerline bridge.
Connects a desktop or notebook PC to other PCs over standard power lines inside a home.

NETWORK SECURITY ISSUES

There are numerous security issues related to computer networks. Although Chapter 15 is dedicated to security and privacy issues, network security is so critical today that two security subjects—*unauthorized access and use* and *sabotage*—are discussed next.

Unauthorized Access and Use

Unauthorized access occurs whenever an individual gains access to a computer, network, file, or other resource without permission. **Unauthorized use** involves using a computer resource for unapproved activities and can occur in conjunction with unauthorized access, as well as by someone authorized to access the computer or network being used, but not authorized for that particular activity. Unauthorized access and unauthorized use are criminal offenses in the United States and many other countries and can be committed by strangers, employees, students, and other individuals. For instance, a student looking at faculty payroll files would likely be classified as unauthorized access, and an employee checking personal e-mail at work might be classified as unauthorized use, depending on the policy of the company. Whether or not these types of unauthorized access and unauthorized use are illegal depends on the circumstances, as well as the specific company involved. To explain acceptable computer use to their employees, students, or other users, many organizations and educational institutions publish guidelines for behavior—usually called *codes of conduct*. Codes of conduct typically address prohibited activities, such as installing personal software on the network, violating copyright laws, causing harm to the PC and network, snooping in other peoples files, and so forth. These legal and ethical issues are discussed in more detail in Chapters 15 and 16.

Hacking

Hacking refers to the act of breaking into a remote computer system. The person doing the hacking is called a *hacker*. By definition, hacking involves unauthorized access. Two exceptions are *professional hacking* that takes place at the request of an organization to test the security of its system, and hacking into computers set up (usually by hacker organizations) specifically to enable hackers to practice their skills legally. Unless hacking is authorized, hacking in the United States and many other countries is a crime and is become increasingly more vigorously prosecuted. For example, Kevin Mitnick—one of the world's most famous hackers—was arrested in 1995, was jailed until he pled guilty to wire fraud and computer fraud in 1999, and then spent an additional year in prison. As a condition of his supervised release in 2000, he was not permitted to use a computer or any type of wireless device for three years. The 2001 *USA Patriot Act* expands the government's authority to prosecute hacking activities and increases the penalties for unauthorized hacks.

In addition to unauthorized access, hacking may also involve unauthorized use, depending on what actions the hacker takes once he or she has gained access to the system. Usually the motivation for hacking is to steal information or to *sabotage* a computer system—two examples of unauthorized use. Sometimes hackers break into a system just to prove their computer expertise, to expand their knowledge, or to bring attention to a social cause, but don't steal information or sabotage the system. Regardless of the reason, unauthorized hacking is illegal. While the general public tends to use the term *hacker* to refer to any type of computer break-in regardless of what activities take place after the security breach, many hackers differentiate between types of hacking and they prefer the term *cracker* when referring to individuals who break into systems to be destructive or for material gain.

>**Unauthorized access.** Gaining access to a computer, network, file, or other resource without permission. >**Unauthorized use.** Using a computer resource for unapproved activities. >**Hacking.** Using a computer to break into a remote computer system.

One recent example of what some hackers consider hacking (not cracking) is the collection of attacks in 2002 by two hackers calling themselves the *Deceptive Duo*. These two individuals broke into secured databases and published selected information onto government Web sites. Some of the systems breached included a Midwest Express Airlines database containing flight schedules and passenger manifests, a NASA Ames Research Center employee database, a Union Bank database, and a U.S. Defense Department Defense Logistics Agency (DLA) database containing names and ID numbers of DLA employees. Selected information from the accessed databases was posted on Web sites belonging to such agencies as the U.S. Navy, the Federal Aviation Administration (FAA), and the Office of the Secretary of the Defense (OSD) to prove that the databases had been accessed. In their explanation regarding the motivation for the attack, the Deceptive Duo claimed that they hacked into the secure systems to bring attention to these systems' vulnerabilities. At the time of this writing, the case was under investigation by the FBI and the duo had been identified, but had not yet been formally charged.

Hacking is considered a very serious threat to our nation's security. With the increased number of computers and critical systems online and the improved abilities of hackers, some experts believe the risk of *cyberterrorism*—where terrorists attack via the Internet—has increased significantly. In response to this increased possibility, White House technology adviser Richard Clarke announced in early 2002 that the United States "reserves the right to respond in any way appropriate" to Internet warfare, including military action against cyberterrorists. Current concerns are attacks against the computers controlling such vital systems as the nation's power grids, banks, and water filtration facilities. Though unrelated to cyberterrorism, the widespread power blackout in the United States and Canada in August 2003 is viewed as a wake-up call by some, although the plans to update the electric grid may possibly make the system even more vulnerable than in the past, since the computers being used to monitor the grid could be hacker targets or become infected with *computer viruses*. Clarke has announced that the United States will spend billions of dollars in the next few years to prepare against cyberattacks; the government released a report titled "National Strategy to Secure Cyberspace" in 2003.

Unauthorized Wi-Fi Use: War Driving

Wireless networking standards, such as Wi-Fi, have opened up new opportunities for "bandwidth stealing" or using someone else's Internet access without permission. Because a Wi-Fi network is accessible up to about 300 feet of the wireless access point, unless the wireless access point is protected in some manner it is possible for people to use both public and private wireless networks without permission. Driving around neighborhoods looking for an unsecured Wi-Fi network to "borrow"—an action called *war driving*—has become a favorite pastime for some. In one recent example, a movie pirate used his neighbor's Wi-Fi home network to gain access to the neighbor's broadband Internet service to send a pirated movie over the Internet. The movie pirate was caught, and the incident sparked an educational campaign by at least one broadband provider to encourage customers to turn on security features built into their Wi-Fi networks to help protect against unauthorized sharing of their Internet connections.

Protecting Against Unauthorized Access and Use

A number of security risks can be reduced or eliminated by carefully controlling access to an organization's facilities and computer system. To prevent unauthorized access of these resources, an *identification* procedure can be used to verify that the person trying to access the facility or system is listed as an authorized user. An *authentication* system can be used to determine whether or not the person attempting access is actually who he or she claims to be. Some of the strongest access control systems include both identification and authentication procedures. *Firewalls* and other types of access prevention software can also protect against hackers and other unwanted intruders.

PASSWORD STRATEGIES

- Make the password at least 8 characters, if allowed by the application. A four- or five-character password can be cracked by a computer program in less than a minute. A 10-character password, in contrast, has about 3,700 trillion possible character permutations and could take a regular computer decades to crack.

- Choose an unusual sequence of characters to create a password that will not be in a dictionary—for instance, mix in numbers and special characters with abbreviations or unusual words you will remember. The password should be one that you can remember, yet one that doesn't conform to a pattern a computer can readily figure out.

- Keep a written copy of the password in a place where no one but you can find it. Many people place passwords on self-sticking notes that are affixed to their monitors or taped to their desks—a practice that's almost as bad as having no password at all.

- Don't use your name, your kids' or pets' names, your address, your birthdate, or other public information as your password.

- For Web site accounts that remember your settings or profile (such as online news, auction, shopping, or bookstore sites), use a different password than for your highly sensitive activities (such as online banking or stock trading). Computers storing passwords used on non-sensitive Web sites are usually easier to break into than on high-security sites and if a hacker determines your password on a low-security site, he or she can use it on your accounts containing sensitive data if you use the same password on those accounts.

- Change your passwords frequently.

FIGURE 8-27
Strategies for creating good passwords.

FIGURE 8-28
Picture PINs.

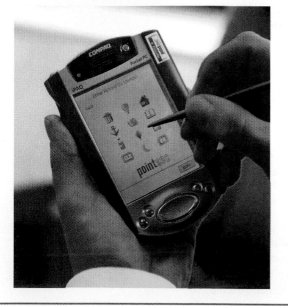

Possessed Knowledge Systems

A *possessed knowledge system* is an identification system that requires the individual requesting access to provide information only the authorized user is supposed to know. User names, PIN numbers, and passwords fall into this category.

Passwords, the most commonly used type of possessed knowledge, are secret words or character combinations associated with an individual. They can be used to restrict access to a facility, computer, network or a computing resource. For example, one password might be required for anyone requesting access to a corporate or school network, and then a different password may be required to access any drives, folders, or documents on that network containing sensitive or confidential information.

One of the biggest disadvantages of password-only systems is that passwords can be forgotten; another is that passwords can be guessed or deciphered by a hacker's PC easily if good password selection strategies are not applied. For example, it was discovered that the Deceptive Duo hackers were able to access the databases from which they retrieved information because the system administrator passwords for those databases had never been changed—they were still the default passwords (the ones assigned to the programs during manufacturing) and so were commonly known. As illustrated by this example, any individual possessing an authorized password will be granted access to the system because the system recognizes the password, regardless of whether or not the person using the password is the authorized user. Consequently, it is important to select good passwords and change them frequently. Some strategies for selecting good passwords are listed in Figure 8-27.

Two other types of possessed knowledge—*user names* (typically a variation of the person's first and/or last names) and *PIN* (*personal identification numbers*, such as those used with ATM cards)—are often used in conjunction with a password or other type of access control method (such as a *possessed object* or *biometric* characteristic, both of which are discussed shortly) to add another level of security. One new option is the *picture PIN*, where icons are selected on the screen in the proper order to replace a user name and password (see Figure 8-28). To prevent someone from guessing the proper sequence by looking over your shoulder or looking for wear marks on the PC's screen, the icons are displayed in random order each time.

>**Password.** A secret combination of characters used to gain access to a computer, computer network, or other resource.

Possessed Object Systems

Possessed objects are physical objects that are used for identification purposes. Common possessed objects used to access a facility or computer system are smart cards, encoded badges, and magnetic cards that are similar to credit cards (see Figure 8-29). One disadvantage of using possessed objects to restrict access to facilities or systems is that the object can be lost or, similar to passwords, used by an unauthorized individual. This latter disadvantage can be overcome by using a password or biometric characteristic in conjunction with the possessed object.

Biometric Systems

Biometrics is the study of identifying individuals based on measurable biological characteristics. **Biometric devices** are typically used to identify users by a particular unique physiological characteristic (such as a fingerprint, hand, face, or iris), although a personal trait (such as a voice or signature) can be used instead in some systems. Since the means of access (usually a part of the body) cannot be lost or forgotten and because it cannot be transferred to another individual or used by anyone other than the authorized individual, biometric access systems can perform both identification and authentication.

To grant access using biometric data, devices (such as *fingerprint scanners, hand geometry readers, face readers,* and *iris scanners*) are typically used in conjunction with software and a database to match a person's identity with his or her biometric characteristic that was previously stored in the database. In general, biometric systems are very accurate. According to IrisScan, a leading iris-recognition company, the odds of two different irises being declared a match is 1 in 10^{78}—even identical twins (who have the same DNA structure) have different fingerprints and irises. Systems based on physiological characteristics (traits that rarely change, such as a person's face, iris, hand geometry, or fingerprint) tend to be more accurate than those based on a personal trait (which may change, such as an individual's voice when he or she has a cold).

Biometric identification systems offer a great deal of convenience, because they require little effort on the part of the user and can completely replace both possessed knowledge and possessed objects. Consequently, biometric systems are increasingly being used to grant access to secure facilities (such as corporate headquarters, university residence halls, and prisons), to log onto computer systems and secure Web sites (by using an external reader or one built into the PC), to punch employees in and out of work, and to confirm consumers' identities at ATM machines and check-cashing services. Some examples of the most commonly used types of biometric systems are shown in Figure 8-30, along with their primary advantages and disadvantages. For a look at how fingerprint readers are being used for everyday activities, see the Trend box.

Firewalls and Other Protective Software

A **firewall** is a security system that acts as a protective boundary between a computer or network and the outside world, to protect against unauthorized access. *Personal firewalls* are typically software-based systems that are geared toward protecting home PCs from hackers attempting to access those computers through their Internet connections. Hackers who gain access to home PCs can access the information on them (such as passwords stored on the hard drive), as well as use those computers in *denial of service attacks* (discussed shortly) and other illegal activities. Consequently, all PCs with direct Internet connections (such as DSL, cable, or satellite) should use a firewall. (PCs using dial-up Internet access are relatively safe from hackers.) Firewalls designed to protect business networks may be software-based,

▷ FIGURE 8-29
Possessed objects, such as the magnetic card being used here, protect against unauthorized access.

N E T

TIP

To help users remember all their various passwords, *password utility programs* are available. All passwords are stored in an encrypted file; when they are needed, the user just unlocks the password file with a single password, and then can see all his or her user names and passwords.

>**Biometric device.** A device that uses the recognition of some unique physical characteristic (such as a person's fingerprint, face, or voice) to grant access to a computer network or physical facility. >**Firewall.** A collection of hardware and/or software intended to protect a computer or computer network from unauthorized access.

FINGERPRINT READER
Typically used to protect access to office PCs, to replace Web site passwords on home PCs, to pay for products or services, and to access resources such as Welfare benefits.

HAND GEOMETRY READER
Typically used to control access to facilities (such as government offices, prisons, and military facilities) and to punch in and out of work.

FACE READER
Typically used to control access to highly secure areas, as well as to identify individuals for law enforcement purposes.

IRIS SCANNER
Typically used to control access to highly secure areas, such as nuclear facilities and prisons; beginning to be used to authenticate users of ATMs and other banking facilities, as shown here.

BIOMETRIC CHARACTERISTIC	ADVANTAGES	DISADVANTAGES
Fingerprint	Easy to use; inexpensive.	Sometimes harder to read on older individuals; usually requires contact with scanner; negative social image.
Hand	Easy to use.	Usually requires contact with scanner; fairly expensive.
Face	Requires no direct contact with user; can be used without the person's cooperation.	Lighting, disguised appearance, and other factors may affect results; fairly expensive.
Iris	Requires no direct contact with user; easy to use.	Mirrored sunglasses and light conditions may affect results; expensive.

> **FIGURE 8-30**
> **Biometric devices.**

hardware-based, or a combination of the two. They can typically be used both to prevent network access from hackers and other outsiders, as well as to control employee Internet access.

Firewalls work by closing down all external *communication port addresses*—the electronic connections that allow a PC to communicate with other computers—to unauthorized computers and programs for both incoming and outgoing activities. While business firewalls are set up by the network administrator and those settings cannot typically be changed by end users, personal firewalls will usually notify the user when an application program on the PC wants Internet access. At that point, the user may either grant or deny access. Many personal firewall programs let users of a firewall-protected PC view all of the access attempts from outside computers that were blocked by the firewall. In addition to protecting your PC from outside access, firewall programs also protect against inside attacks from *computer viruses* and other malicious programs that may have slipped through your virus protection. If not blocked by a firewall, these programs can open ports and send data from your PC to a hacker at the hacker's request.

In addition to firewalls, many businesses and organizations use other software to protect the network, such as programs that record all attempts (both successful and unsuccessful) to access network resources by both outsiders and employees. This data is then analyzed to try to identify any potential problems, such as attempted network access by a hacker, access by employees to off-limit resources, or a possible *denial of service* attack.

For wireless networks, most have built-in security features to protect against unauthorized access. For instance, 802.11b networks use the *WEP* (*Wired Equivalent Privacy*) security protocol, which requires a *WEP key* (essentially a password) for access. Because wireless networks cannot be physically protected like wired networks located inside a private facility, they are inherently less secure than wired LANs. New improvements to wireless networking standards are expected to strengthen security features and reduce the ability to hack into a Wi-Fi network.

TREND

Personal Biometrics: Finger Payment Systems

Biometric devices are increasingly being used for more consumer applications, such as granting access to a gym or college dormitory. One of the newest consumer applications—in the test marketing stage by several companies at the time this book was written, and likely to be available in the very near future—is the use of fingerprint scanners to buy goods and services at restaurants, grocery stores, video stores, warehouse stores, and other types of retail establishments. One of the leading companies in this area is Solidus Networks. Their *Pay By Touch* finger payment system—whose 2002 test locations included some California McDonald's, Blockbuster, and Walgreens stores—uses a standard credit card point-of-sale reader with a small fingerprint scanner attached (see the accompanying photo). All consumers who would like the option of paying with this method simply enroll in the program by scanning in their fingerprint, entering their appropriate contact information, and adding the desired payment options (such as credit card or checking account information). Then, to pay for goods and services in the future, customers need only touch their finger to the fingerprint scanner, select the desired payment method from a list, and the transaction is finalized.

While fingerprint payment systems are convenient for consumers, reduce fraudulent transactions for merchants, and move customers through checkout lines faster, there are skeptics. Some individuals, worried about privacy and security, will likely never enter their fingerprint image into a payment database. And, though information entered into one brand of system (such as Pay By Touch or a competitive system from Biometric Access) is available at any other retailer using the same system, until one standard or clear winner in this market emerges, incompatibility between rival systems may become a frustration

for consumers. But consumer reaction so far seems to be positive. In one Pay By Touch pilot test, 65% of the 3,000 consumers offered the service were willing to enroll.

In an effort to alleviate privacy and security concerns, the Pay By Touch system includes an extensive privacy policy. Part of the policy states that the company will not sell, share, or rent consumers' information to others, except as needed to provide the Pay By Touch payment service; the biometric information gathered will not be used to uniquely identify users across other databases; and consumers can modify or delete their information at any time they desire. Whether or not consumers will trust fingerprint payment systems when they are widely introduced is still a question, but the outlook appears promising.

Fingerprint payment systems allow consumers to quickly pay for goods and services.

Computer Sabotage

Unfortunately, *sabotage*—acts of malicious destruction—is a common type of computer crime today. There are several forms computer sabotage can take, including launching a *computer virus* or *denial of service attack*, or changing data or programs located on a computer. Acts of sabotage can take place by employees of a company, as well as by outsiders, and are estimated to cost individuals and organizations billions of dollars per year. Just one incident can be extraordinarily expensive, averaging nearly $250,000 according to a 2003 study by the Computer Security Institute and the FBI. The most expensive computer virus to date—the LoveLetter computer virus released in 2000—was estimated to cost almost $9 billion, primarily for labor cost related to virus removal and lost productivity.

Computer Viruses and Other Types of Malware

Malware is the generic term used to refer to any type of malicious software. Malware programs are intentionally written to perform destructive acts, although some researchers believe that many young malware creators don't really realize the potential consequences of their actions and the huge amount of destruction and expense that can result from releasing this type of software into cyberspace. The most familiar type of malware is the **computer virus**—a small software program that is installed without the permission or knowledge of the computer user, is designed to alter the way a computer operates, and can replicate itself to infect any new media it is given access to. Viruses are embedded into program or data files and are spread whenever the infected file is downloaded from the Internet or another network, is transferred to a new computer via an infected removable disk, or is e-mailed to another computer (see Figure 8-31). Once a copy of the infected file reaches a new computer, it typically embeds itself into program, data, or system files on the new PC. After a computer is infected and the virus is stored on the computer, it remains there until it is discovered and removed.

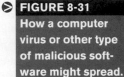

FIGURE 8-31
How a computer virus or other type of malicious software might spread.

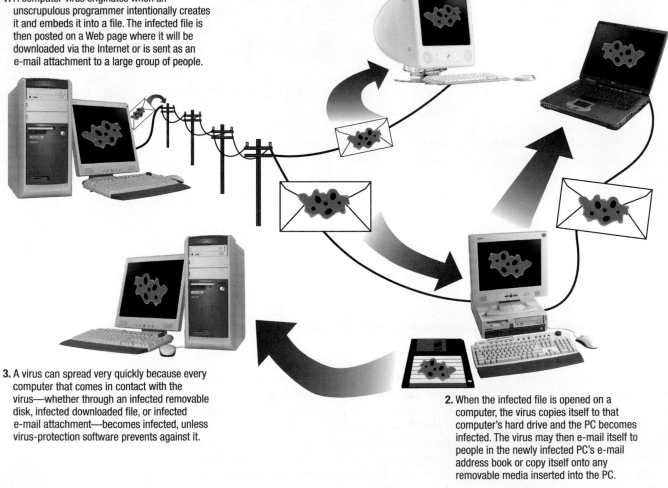

1. A computer virus originates when an unscrupulous programmer intentionally creates it and embeds it into a file. The infected file is then posted on a Web page where it will be downloaded via the Internet or is sent as an e-mail attachment to a large group of people.

3. A virus can spread very quickly because every computer that comes in contact with the virus—whether through an infected removable disk, infected downloaded file, or infected e-mail attachment—becomes infected, unless virus-protection software prevents against it.

2. When the infected file is opened on a computer, the virus copies itself to that computer's hard drive and the PC becomes infected. The virus may then e-mail itself to people in the newly infected PC's e-mail address book or copy itself onto any removable media inserted into the PC.

>**Malware.** Any type of malicious software. >**Computer virus.** A software program, installed without the user's knowledge, designed to alter the way a computer operates or to cause harm to the system.

Most computer viruses are programmed to harm the computers that they are transmitted to—such as by damaging programs, deleting files, making the computer not work properly, or completely erasing the entire hard drive. This damage can take place immediately after infection or it can begin when a particular condition is met. A virus that activates when it detects a certain condition, such as when a particular keystroke is pressed or an employee's name is deleted from an employee file, is called a *logic bomb*. A logic bomb whose trigger is a particular date or time is called a *time bomb*. In addition to destructive computer viruses, there are so-called "benign" viruses that aren't designed to do any permanent damage, but instead make their presence known by displaying a text or video message, or by playing a musical or audio message. Even though benign viruses may not cause any lasting harm (although some do unintentional damage because of programming errors), they are annoying, can require enormous amounts of time to get rid of, and can disrupt communications for the organizations involved.

Writing a computer virus or even posting the code for a computer virus on the Internet isn't illegal, but it is considered to be highly unethical and irresponsible behavior. Launching a computer virus, on the other hand, is illegal. David Smith, creator of the 1999 Melissa virus, is the first individual in the United States to receive jail time for unleashing a computer virus. This virus, released on Friday, March 26, 1999, infected over 100,000 computers by the end of the weekend. It eventually infected more than 1 million computers and caused an estimated $80 million of damage. Although originally facing up to 40 years in prison, Smith was sentenced in May 2002 to 20 months in federal prison—federal court documents unsealed in 2003 revealed that Smith worked undercover to help with FBI virus investigations during the nearly two-year period he was out on bail following his arrest in exchange for a lighter sentence.

There are other types of malware in addition to computer viruses. A **computer worm** is a malicious program designed to cause damage similar to a computer virus. Unlike a computer virus, however, a computer worm doesn't embed itself into other computer files to replicate itself; instead, it is usually embedded initially inside a document and spreads by creating copies of itself (by creating copies of the host document) and sending the copies to other computers via a network. Typically, the documents containing the worm are sent as e-mail attachments to other computers. After an infected attachment file is opened by an individual, the worm inflicts its damage, and then automatically sends copies of itself to other computers via the Internet or a private network, typically using addresses in the e-mail address book located on the newly infected PC. When those e-mail messages and their attachments are opened (and they frequently are because they usually look like they came from the person whose address book was used), those new computers become infected and the cycle continues. Because of its distribution method, a worm can spread very rapidly. For instance, the *Sobig.F* worm, released in 2003, spread so rapidly that within 72 hours, one out of every 17 e-mails contained the worm. Labeled the most pervasive worm to date at the time of this writing, it is estimated that the *Sobig.F* worm alone generated more than 100 million e-mail messages. Newer worms—such as *Blaster* released in mid-2003—are self propagating and so are spread over networks without any action by the users.

A **Trojan horse** is a malicious program that masquerades as something else—usually some type of application program. When the seemingly legitimate program (such as what appears to be a game, for example) is run, the destructive program executes instead. Unlike viruses and worms, Trojan horses can't replicate themselves and are usually spread by being downloaded from the Internet. A Trojan horse may also be sent as an e-mail attachment, either from the Trojan horse author or forwarded on by individuals not realizing the program is a Trojan horse.

FURTHER EXPLORATION

For links to further information about computer viruses, go to www.course.com/uc10/ch08

NET

>**Computer worm.** A malicious program designed to rapidly spread to a large number of computers by sending copies of itself to other computers. >**Trojan horse.** A malicious program that masquerades as something else.

Denial of Service Attacks

A **denial of service (DoS) attack** is an act of sabotage that attempts to flood a network or Web server with so many requests for action that it shuts down or simply cannot handle legitimate requests any longer, causing legitimate users to be denied service. For example, a hacker might set up one or more computers to continually *ping* a server (contact it with a request to send a responding ping back) with a false return address or to continually request non-existent information. If enough useless traffic is generated, the server has no resources left to deal with legitimate requests (see Figure 8-32).

During the past few years, many leading Web sites (such as those belonging to Microsoft, Yahoo!, eBay, CNET, Amazon.com, E*Trade, CNN, ABC News, and ESPN) have been the victims of DoS attacks. Most of these attacks utilized multiple computers (referred to as a *distributed denial of service* or *DDoS attack*). To perform DDoS attacks, hackers have begun more frequently to access and use unprotected PCs with direct Internet connections (such as those located in schools, businesses, or homes). These computers— referred to as *zombies*—participate in the attacks without the owners' knowledge. Because home PCs tend to be less protected than school and business PCs, hackers are increasingly targeting home PCs for use as zombie PCs. It is against the law to launch a denial of service attack in the United States and it can be very costly in terms of business lost, such as when an e-commerce site is shut down, as well as the time and expense required to bring the site back online.

Related to a DoS attack is *malicious spamming*, where enough bogus e-mail messages are sent to a mail server that it causes the mail server to shut down. Like a DoS attack, malicious spamming is targeted at a specific company, such as in the case of a former Southern California man who was convicted recently of maliciously bombarding the computer system of his ex-employer with thousands of e-mail messages; he was sentenced to 16 months in federal prison.

⊗ FIGURE 8-32
How a denial of service (DoS) attack might work.

1. Hacker's PC sends several simultaneous requests; each request asks to establish a connection to the server but supplies false return information. In a distributed DoS attack, multiple PCs send multiple requests at one time.

Hello? I'd like some info...

2. The server tries to respond to each request but can't locate the PC because false return information was provided. The server waits for a minute or so before closing the connection, which ties up the server resources and keeps others from connecting.

I can't find you, I'll wait and try again...

3. The hacker's PC continues to send in new requests, so as a connection is closed by the server a new request is waiting. This cycle continues, which ties up the server indefinitely.

Hello? I'd like some info...

HACKER'S PC

WEB SERVER

Hello? I'd like some info...

I'm busy, I can't help you right now.

LEGITIMATE PC

4. The server becomes so overwhelmed that legitimate requests can't get through and, eventually, the server usually crashes.

>**Denial of service (DoS) attack.** An act of sabotage that attempts to flood a network or network server with so much activity that it is unable to function.

Data or Program Alteration

Another type of computer sabotage occurs when a hacker breaches a computer system in order to delete or change data, modify programs, or otherwise alter the data and programs located there. For example, students have been caught changing grades in their schools' database and disgruntled or former employees have been caught after changing data on company computers, typically for revenge purposes—such as for being passed over for a promotion or for recently being terminated. Examples of employee alterations include changing programs so they work incorrectly; deleting important projects, customer records, or other critical data; and just randomly changed data in a company's database. Like hacking, data and program alteration is illegal.

Another example of data alteration that has become more common over the past few years is defacing or otherwise changing Web sites—sometimes classified as a type of *cybervandalism*. This has become a widely used method for hackers who want to draw attention to themselves or a specific cause. Sites modified by hackers in the last few years include those belonging to the Library of Congress, FBI, *New York Times*, CNN, Secretary of Defense, Sandia National Laboratories, NASA Jet Propulsion Laboratories, and Stanford University.

Protecting Against Computer Sabotage

A good firewall system can go a long way toward protecting against some types of sabotage, such as data and program alteration, worms, and Trojan horses. Although denial of service attacks are virtually impossible to prevent completely, good firewall and network security protections can lessen the chance of being a target, as well as prevent an individual PC from being enlisted as a zombie PC in a DoS attack.

As discussed in Chapter 6, antivirus software should be installed on all PCs in both homes and in offices to protect against computer viruses and other types of malware. Antivirus software should be set up to run continuously whenever the computer is on to check incoming e-mail messages and downloaded files, as well as to periodically run a complete scan of the entire PC. Antivirus software can protect against getting a virus in the first place (since it deletes or quarantines any suspicious e-mail attachments or downloaded files on their way in to your PC), and it can detect and remove any viruses or worms that may find their way onto your PC. If a known virus is found, the program will remove it and try to repair any damage caused by the virus. Antivirus software usually has an option to automatically download new virus definitions on a regular basis—this is an important precaution since new viruses are released all the time. According to McAfee Security, manufacturer of antivirus and security software, there are over 63,000 known viruses with new viruses being introduced at a rate of about 500 per month.

In addition to using up-to-date antivirus software, additional virus-prevention techniques include the following:

▼ Limit sharing disks and other removable storage media with others.

▼ Only download programs from reputable Web sites.

▼ Only open e-mail attachments from people that you know and that don't have an executable file extension (such as *.exe, .com*, or *.vbs*). If you think a file with an executable extension might be a legitimate attachment, double-check with the sender before opening the attachment.

▼ Regularly download and install the latest security patches available for your e-mail program to correct known security holes.

**N
E
T**

SUMMARY

NETWORKING AND COMMUNICATIONS APPLICATIONS

Chapter Objective 1:
Describe several uses for communications technology.

Communications, or *telecommunications*, refers to communications from one device to another over a distance—such as over long-distance phone lines, via privately owned cables, or by satellite. A wide variety of important business applications involve communications. Among these are **wireless phones**, *paging* or *messaging*, **global positioning systems (GPS)**, *satellite radio*, **online conferencing**, *collaborative computing*, **telecommuting**, and **telemedicine**.

WHAT IS A NETWORK AND HOW DOES IT TRANSMIT DATA?

Chapter Objective 2:
Understand characteristics about data and how it travels over a network.

A **computer network** is a collection of computers and other hardware devices that are connected together to share hardware, software, and data, as well as to facilitate electronic communications. Data that travels over a network can be *analog*—that is, sent as continuous waves. Computer hardware, however, are *digital* devices that handle data coded into 0s and 1s. Data transmissions can be characterized by their *bandwidth*, *speed*, whether they use **serial transmission** or **parallel transmission**, whether they transmit in *simplex, half-duplex, or full-duplex* directions, and how the transmissions are timed (namely, *synchronous, asynchronous,* or *isochronous transmission*).

Chapter Objective 3:
Name specific types of wired and wireless transmission media and explain how they transmit messages from one device to another.

Computer networks can be **wired networks** or **wireless networks**, depending on the type of transmission media used. Wired transmission media include **twisted-pair**, **coaxial**, and **fiber-optic cable**. Wireless networks typically send messages through the air in the form of *radio signals*. Wireless networks can use *broadcast radio*, **microwave stations**, **communications satellites**, **cellular radio**, and *infrared (IR)* technology.

TYPES OF NETWORKS

Networks can be classified in terms of their *topologies*, or geometrical patterns. Three common topologies are the **star network**, the **bus network**, and the **ring network**. Network topologies are often combined when smaller networks are connected to make a larger one. Networks are also either *client-server* networks, which consist of *server* devices that provide network services to *client* computers, or *peer-to-peer* networks, in which the user computers and the shared peripherals in the network communicate directly with one another instead of through a server.

Chapter Objective 4:
Explain the difference between local area, wide area, and other types of networks.

Network types correspond to their size and purpose. **Local area networks (LANs)** connect geographically close devices, such as within a single building. LANs fall into two categories. **Wide area networks (WANs)** span relatively wide geographical areas. Other possibilities include *metropolitan area networks (MANs)*; *personal area networks (PANs)*; **intranets** (private networks that implement the infrastructure and standards of the Internet and World Wide Web); **extranets** (intranets that are accessible to authorized outsiders); **virtual private networks (VPNs)** used to transfer private information over a public communications system, such as the Internet; and *storage area networks (SANs)*, networks consisting of high-speed, shared storage devices.

NETWORKING HARDWARE

Computer networks require a variety of hardware. PCs usually connect to a network through either a **network adapter**—called a **network interface card** (**NIC**) when it is in the form of an expansion card—or a **modem**. The type of modem depends on the type of connection to be used and will convert the signals between digital and analog mode as needed. Possibilities include *conventional dial-up, ISDN, DSL, cable,* and *satellite modems.* A **hub** is a device on a network that provides a central location where data arrives and then is transferred on. **Switches** and **routers** can also be used to pass network messages along to their destinations. A **wireless access point** is used to connect wireless devices to a network. Devices on two dissimilar networks can communicate with each other if the networks are connected by a *gateway.* Devices on two similar networks can communicate with each other if they are connected by a *bridge. Repeaters, multiplexers,* and *concentrators* are most commonly used with larger networks.

Chapter Objective 5:
List several types of networking hardware and explain the purpose of each.

COMMUNICATIONS PROTOCOLS

A communications *protocol* is a collection of procedures to establish, maintain, and terminate transmissions between devices. Because devices transmit data in so many ways, they collectively employ scores of different protocols. Three of the most commonly used protocols are **Ethernet**, **Token Ring**, and **TCP/IP**. Wireless networks typically use the **802.11** (**Wi-Fi**) protocol. Other possibilities include **Bluetooth** and *IrDA* (for very short-range wireless applications) and **Wireless Application Protocol** (**WAP**). For home networks, the *Phoneline, Powerline,* or *Ultra Wideband* (*UWB*) standards may be used instead.

Chapter Objective 6:
Identify the different protocols that can be used to connect the devices on a network.

NETWORK SECURITY ISSUES

Because computers and networks are so widespread, there is unprecedented opportunity for criminals and other individuals to commit acts that are not in the public interest. One important issue related to computer networks is **unauthorized access** and **unauthorized use**. **Hacking** is the term used for breaking into a computer system. There are many options for protecting a network against unauthorized access and use, including **passwords** and other types of *possessed knowledge, possessed objects* such as badges and cards, and **biometric devices** (devices that recognize some type of physical characteristic, such as a handprint or face). To protect a computer from being hacked, a **firewall** should be used. Common types of computer *sabotage* include **malware** (**computer viruses**, **computer worms**, and **Trojan horses**), **denial of service** (**DoS**) **attacks**, data and program alteration, and *cybervandalism.* Firewall and antivirus software can help prevent against some types of sabotage.

Chapter Objective 7:
Discuss some security issues involved with computer network usage and some security precautions that can be taken.

N E T

KEY TERMS

Instructions: Match each key term on the left with the definition on the right that best describes it.

a. biometric device

b. cellular radio

c. communications

d. communications satellite

e. computer network

f. computer worm

g. denial of service (DoS) attack

h. fiber-optic cable

i. hacking

j. hub

k. local area network (LAN)

l. network interface card (NIC)

m. password

n. TCP/IP

o. twisted-pair cable

p. unauthorized access

q. unauthorized use

r. virtual private network (VPN)

s. wide area network (WAN)

t. wireless network

1. _____ A collection of computers and other hardware devices that are connected together to share hardware, software, and data, as well as to communicate electronically with one another.

2. _____ A communications medium consisting of wire strands twisted in sets of two and bound into a cable.

3. _____ A communications medium that utilizes hundreds of hair-thin, transparent fibers over which lasers transmit data as light.

4. _____ A device that is a central location where data arrives and is then transferred in one or more directions.

5. _____ A device that uses the recognition of some unique physical characteristic (such as a person's fingerprint, face, or voice) to grant access to a computer network or physical facility.

6. _____ A form of broadcast radio that broadcasts using antennae located inside honeycomb-shaped cells.

7. _____ A group of secure paths over the Internet that provide authorized users a secure means of accessing a private network via the Internet.

8. _____ A malicious program designed to rapidly spread to a large number of computers by sending copies of itself to other computers.

9. _____ A network in which computers and other devices are connected to the network without physical cables.

10. _____ A network that connects devices located in a large geographical area.

11. _____ A network that connects devices located in a small geographical area, such as within a building.

12. _____ A secret combination of characters used to gain access to a computer, computer network, or other resource.

13. _____ An act of sabotage that attempts to flood a network or network server with so much activity that it is unable to function.

14. _____ An earth-orbiting device that relays communications signals over long distances.

15. _____ An expansion card through which a computer can connect to a network.

16. _____ Gaining access to a computer, network, file, or other resource without permission.

17. _____ The communications protocol that uses packet switching to facilitate the transmission of messages; the protocol used with the Internet.

18. _____ The transmission of data from one device to another.

19. _____ Using a computer resource for unapproved activities.

20. _____ Using a computer to break into a remote computer system.

REVIEW ACTIVITIES

Answers for the self-quiz appear at the end of the book in the References and Resources Guide.

True/False   SELF-QUIZ

Instructions: Circle **T** if the statement is true or **F** if the statement is false.

T   F   **1.** GPS systems are used only by the government.

T   F   **2.** With parallel transmissions, one byte of data is sent at one time.

T   F   **3.** The Internet is an example of a LAN.

T   F   **4.** The type of cable used inside most homes for telephone service is twisted-pair wire.

T   F   **5.** A computer virus can only be transferred to another computer via a disk.

Completion

Instructions: Supply the missing words to complete the following statements.

6. Telesurgery is an example of a(n) _____ application.

7. A(n) _____ orbits the earth to send and receive high-frequency, high-speed radio signals.

8. A(n) _____ is a network that transfers private information securely over the Internet or other public network.

9. A(n) _____ device uses some type of unique physiological characteristic of a person to identify or grant access to individuals.

10. A(n) _____ is used to protect a computer or network from unauthorized access by closing down external communication port addresses to unauthorized programs or requests.

---

1. Answer the following questions about the network below.   **EXERCISES**

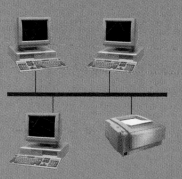

    a. What topology does the network use? _____
    b. How many nodes are connected to the network? _____
    c. Is this a wired or wireless network? _____
    d. Does this network use a hub? _____

2. Select the communications application from the numbered list below that best matches each of the following situations and write the corresponding number in the blank to the left of each description. Note that all communications applications will not be used.

   a. _____ To diagnose a patient from a distance.
   b. _____ To conduct a meeting between people located at a corporate headquarters in Los Angeles and a Miami-based clothing designer to decide which pieces to include in the final summer swimsuit line.
   c. _____ To notify a person giving a speech at a business luncheon about the change in time for an important meeting that evening.
   d. _____ To drive across the country listening to continuous music.
   e. _____ To receive telephone calls while you are out shopping.
   f. _____ To determine your physical location while hiking in the mountains.

   1. Satellite radio   5. Online conferencing
   2. Telecommuting   6. Telemedicine
   3. GPS   7. Web browsing
   4. Paging/messaging   8. Cellular phone

3. For each of the following modems, indicate whether or not they allow for data transmission over ordinary telephone lines.

Type of Modem	Transmits Over Telephone Lines?
a. Cable modem	_____
b. Conventional dial-up modem	_____
c. DSL modem	_____
d. ISDN modem	_____
e. Satellite modem	_____

4. Select the type of modem from the numbered list below that best matches each of the following communications situations and write the corresponding number in the blank to the left of each description. Note that all modem types will not be used.

   a. _____ Fast Internet access from a remote mountain cabin.
   b. _____ Access to the company network from a hotel room that doesn't have Internet service.
   c. _____ Access to the Internet from a car.

   1. Conventional dial-up modem   4. Cable modem
   2. ISDN modem   5. Satellite modem
   3. DSL modem   6. Wireless modem

5. If you need to download a 350 KB file and have a 56 Kbps conventional dial-up modem, how long should it take to download the file? What real-world conditions might affect this download time?

6. What communications protocol does the Internet use?

7. Is the password *john1* a good password? Why or why not?

PROJECTS

---

1. **Wi-Fi** As discussed in the chapter, Wi-Fi is hot right now. With the number of portable PC users approaching the number of desktop PC users, wireless networking in general is becoming increasingly important. Wireless home networking products abound, as do wireless networks in public locations, such as Starbuck's, McDonald's, parks, airports, libraries, college campuses, and more. Commuters in several areas of the United States, Canada, and Europe recently began having wireless Internet access available to them while riding the train.

   For this project, identify three locations where you think it would be valuable for you to have Wi-Fi access, assuming you had a portable PC that was Wi-Fi ready. Is Wi-Fi available at any of your listed locations? If so, is it free or is there a charge involved? If there isn't W-Fi access available, why isn't there? Would you be willing to pay for Wi-Fi access at any of your listed locations? At the conclusion of your research, prepare a one-page summary of your findings and submit it to your instructor.

HOT TOPICS

---

2. **Geocaching** *Geocaching* is a GPS application that has become popular with individuals and families alike. It is a worldwide phenomenon, taking place in over 180 countries. Geocaching is essentially a form of high-tech hide and seek—someone hides a water-tight container filled with a "treasure" (usually toys or cheap collectors' goodies) and posts the location of the cache (in GPS coordinates) on a geocaching Web site. Other individuals use their GPS equipment to find the cache and then can sign a log (if one is included in the cache), take an item from the cache, and put another object into the cache as a replacement. Many caches are stored in scenic locations that individuals and organizations would like others to experience.

   For this project, assume that you have decided you want to try your hand at geocaching. By searching online or visiting a geocaching Web site such as geocaching.com, find out what GPS equipment you would need, including approximate cost, features, size, weight, and the name of two potential products. Next, determine how you would go about informing others about a cache you have hidden and what types of items are considered appropriate to be included in a cache. Finally, find information about a cache currently hidden close to your city and describe what you would need to do in order to find it. At the conclusion of your research, prepare a one-page summary of your findings and submit it to your instructor.

**SHORT ANSWER/
RESEARCH**

3. **New Viruses** Unfortunately, new computer viruses and other types of malware are released all the time. At the time of this writing, the two most recent malware programs were the Sobig.F and Blaster worms, and the Klez worm was still making the rounds, despite being introduced nearly two years ago.

   For this project, either research one of the worms listed above or research a more recent example of malware and answer the following questions: When was it introduced? What did it do? How was it spread? How many computers were affected? Is there an estimated cost associated with it? Is it still in existence? At the conclusion of your research, prepare a one-page summary of your findings and submit it to your instructor.

**N
E
T**

HANDS ON

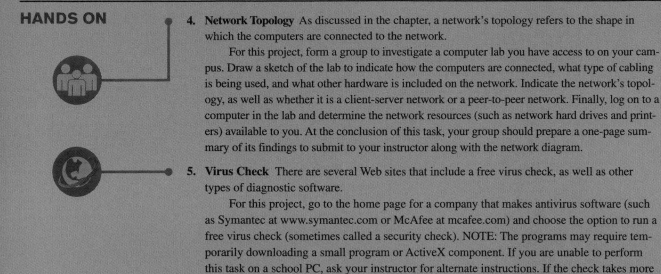

4. **Network Topology** As discussed in the chapter, a network's topology refers to the shape in which the computers are connected to the network.

   For this project, form a group to investigate a computer lab you have access to on your campus. Draw a sketch of the lab to indicate how the computers are connected, what type of cabling is being used, and what other hardware is included on the network. Indicate the network's topology, as well as whether it is a client-server network or a peer-to-peer network. Finally, log on to a computer in the lab and determine the network resources (such as network hard drives and printers) available to you. At the conclusion of this task, your group should prepare a one-page summary of its findings to submit to your instructor along with the network diagram.

5. **Virus Check** There are several Web sites that include a free virus check, as well as other types of diagnostic software.

   For this project, go to the home page for a company that makes antivirus software (such as Symantec at www.symantec.com or McAfee at mcafee.com) and choose the option to run a free virus check (sometimes called a security check). NOTE: The programs may require temporarily downloading a small program or ActiveX component. If you are unable to perform this task on a school PC, ask your instructor for alternate instructions. If the check takes more than 10 minutes and there is an option to limit the check to a particular drive and folder, redo the check just scanning part of the hard drive (such as the My Documents folder) to save time. After the virus scan is completed, print the page displaying the result. Did the program find any viruses or other security threats? At the conclusion of this task, submit your printout with any additional comments about your experience to your instructor.

WRITING ABOUT COMPUTERS

6. **Biometric Legalities** As discussed in the chapter, biometric devices can be used to limit individuals' access to a network or physical facility. This form of security is now being implemented on a wider scale than in the past, but may run into a few snags as these products become mainstream. For example, does taking a biometric measurement ever constitute a search? Can the information gathered for one purpose legally be used for another purpose? When does capturing biometric data violate personal privacy? If an iris reading device is used to punch employees in and out of work and the device is able to detect a potential drug or drinking problem, can this information be used against the employee?

   For this project, identify two types of biometric devices. Explain what they are typically used for and if their use has resulted in objections from individuals and privacy groups. If there have been objections, what are they and has the dispute entered the courts? Have you had any personal experience with biometric devices? If so, how did you feel in terms of security and your personal privacy? Would you be willing to work at a facility that used biometrics instead of time cards? What if the system was to provide access to a secure facility? Submit this project to your instructor in the form of a short paper, not more than two pages in length.

7. **Hacktivism** *Hacktivism* can be defined as the act of hacking into a computer system for a politically or socially motivated purpose. The individual who performs an act of hacktivism is said to be a *hacktivist*. While some view hacktivists no differently than other hackers, hacktivists contend that they break into systems in order to bring attention to political or social causes. Two recent examples of hacktivism include the Web defacements in 2002 by two individuals calling themselves the "Deceptive Duo" and the Web defacements following the death of a Chinese airman when his jet fighter collided with a U.S. surveillance plane in 2001.

   For this project, research one of the two examples of hacktivism mentioned above (or a more recent hacktivism example). Were the hackers identified or found guilty of a crime? What seemed to be the motivation behind the hacks? Form an opinion about hacktivism in general, such as whether or not this is a valid method of bringing attention to specific causes, and whether or not hacktivists should be treated any differently when caught than other types of hackers. Submit this project to your instructor in the form of a short paper, not more than two pages in length.

8. **Home Network** If you have two or more computers at home and want to share files, an Internet connection, or a printer, you will need to set up a home network. A few years ago this would have been a difficult and expensive task, but not today. There are a number of different options for connections and the necessary hardware is easily available, typically in both individual and kit form.

For this project, suppose that you want to set up a home network. Create a scenario (real or fictitious) that describes the number of PCs and other devices involved, where each item is located, and the tasks for which the network will be used. Identify two possible network setups (such as Wi-Fi, Ethernet, Powerline, or Phoneline) and the steps and equipment necessary to implement that network for your scenario. Be sure to include the cost and logistics involved. Share your findings (including a diagram of your proposed network) with your class in the form of a presentation. The presentation should not exceed 10 minutes and should make use of one or more presentation aids such as the chalkboard, handouts, overhead transparencies, or a computer-based slide presentation (your instructor may provide additional requirements). You may be asked to submit a summary of the presentation to your instructor.

9. **Virus Hoaxes** In addition to the valid reports about new viruses found in the news and on antivirus software Web sites, reports of viruses that turn out to be hoaxes abound on the Internet. In addition to being an annoyance, virus hoaxes waste time and computing resources. In addition, they may eventually lead some users to routinely ignore all virus warning messages, leaving them vulnerable to a genuine, destructive virus.

For this project, form a group to find information about recent virus hoaxes, as well as general guidelines for identifying virus hoaxes. Information about virus hoaxes can be found in computer journals, the newspaper, on Web sites for companies that make antivirus software (Symantec.com and mcafee.com, for example), and on the government Hoaxbusters site currently found at hoaxbusters.ciac.org. Share your findings with your class in the form of a presentation. The presentation should not exceed 10 minutes and should make use of one or more presentation aids such as the chalkboard, handouts, overhead transparencies, or a computer-based slide presentation (your instructor may provide additional requirements). Your group may be asked to submit a summary of the presentation to your instructor.

PRESENTATION/
DEMONSTRATION

N
E
T

10. **Imagine Tomorrow** Imagine yourself 10 years from now. The computer and communications industries have continued to offer new products and merge with each other in hopes of capturing more market share and ensuring their future. The capability of the Internet has increased 10-fold and everyone has access to a high-speed connection. Your personal computer has the capability and capacity of today's fastest supercomputers.

Select one of the following positions or create one of your own and express your point of view on the subject. Your instructor will indicate whether your response is to be posted to a class bulletin board, discussed in a class chat room, or discussed as an in-class activity. You may also be asked to submit a summary of your position and point of view to your instructor.

a. My life will not be much different in 10 years than it is right now, except that I will probably spend more time playing Web-based game software and watching TV and movies on my personal computer.

b. My life and lifestyle will change dramatically in the next 10 years. I will no longer drive to work each morning because my personal network communications device with holographic imaging capability allows me do my work from home or while I am traveling anywhere in the world.

INTERACTIVE
DISCUSSION

11. **Homeless Hacker** Hackers who try to gain access to business and government computers and networks are a growing problem. Some hackers do it for monetary gain; others supposedly to bring attention to system vulnerabilities or other, purportedly more noble, purposes (such as the hactivists discussed in Project 7). One example of a business and government network hacker is Adrian Lamo, a young freelance security consultant who regularly tries to hack into systems without authorization, looking for their security holes. If hackers like Lamo continue to use real networks and Web servers to practice and improve their hacking skills, what are the implications? Will it expose the data located on those networks to greater danger, or will it result in tightened security and, ultimately, a more secure system? Lamo says that, while he is an intruder, he is guided by a sense of curiosity and he is helping corporations and consumers understand the limits of Internet security. Should these types of hacks be treated any differently than hackers who break into systems to steal data or other resources? Are there varying degrees of criminal hacking or is a hack just a hack, regardless of the motivation? Lamo has begun publicizing his successful hacks through the media, instead of contacting the company directly. Does that make his motives more questionable? At the time of this writing, Lamo had just been arrested on federal charges for breaking into a database at the New York Times containing employee records for op-ed columnists. Does his arrest change your opinion at all about so-called "harmless hacking"?

For this project, form an opinion of the impact of hackers breaching the security of business and government computers and networks. Be sure to use the questions mentioned in the previous paragraph when forming your position. Your instructor will indicate whether your response is to be posted to a class bulletin board, discussed in a class chat room, or discussed as an in-class activity. You may also be asked to submit a summary of your position and point of view to your instructor.

STUDENT EDITION LABS

12. **Student Edition Labs** Reinforce the concepts you have learned in this chapter by working through the "Networking Basics" and "Wireless Networking" interactive Student Edition Labs, available online. To access these labs, go to www.course.com/uc10/ch08

If you have a SAM user profile, you have access to even more interactive content. Log in to your SAM account and go to your assignments page to see what your instructor has assigned for this chapter.

OUTLINE

Overview

Evolution of the Internet

    From ARPANET to Internet2

    The Internet Community Today

    Myths About the Internet

Getting Set Up to Use the Internet

    Type of Device

    Type of Connection and Internet Access

    Selecting an ISP and Setting Up Your PC

Searching the Internet

    Search Sites

    Search Strategies

    Evaluating Search Results

    Citing Internet Resources

Beyond Browsing and E-Mail

    Online Financial Transactions

    Online Entertainment

    Online News and Research

    Online Education

    Peer-to-Peer File Sharing

Censorship and Privacy Issues

    Censorship

    Web Browsing Privacy

    E-Mail Privacy

The Future of the Internet

The Internet and World Wide Web

LEARNING OBJECTIVES

After completing this chapter, you will be able to:

1. Discuss how the Internet evolved and what it is like today.

2. Identify the various types of individuals, companies, and organizations involved in the Internet community and explain their purposes.

3. Describe the device and connection options for connecting to the Internet, as well as some considerations to keep in mind when selecting an ISP.

4. Understand how to effectively search for information on the Internet and how to properly cite Internet resources.

5. List several useful things that can be done using the Internet, in addition to basic Web browsing and e-mail.

6. Discuss censorship and privacy, and how it is related to Internet use.

7. Speculate as to the format, structure, and use of the Internet in the future.

It's hard to believe that before 1990 few people outside the computer industry and academia had ever heard of the Internet, and even fewer had used it. Why? Because the hardware, software, and communications tools needed to unleash the power of the Internet as we know it today were not available then. In fact, it is only in the last few years that technology has evolved enough to allow multimedia applications, such as downloading audio and video files and viewing animated presentations, to become an everyday activity.

What a difference a few years can make. Today, the Internet and the World Wide Web are household words, and in many ways they have redefined how people think about computers and communications.

Despite the popularity of the Internet, however, many users cannot answer some important basic questions about it. What makes up the Internet? Is it the same thing as the World Wide Web? How did the Internet begin and where is it heading? What types of tools are available to help people make optimum use of the Internet? How can the Internet be used to find specific information? This chapter addresses questions such as these.

Chapter 9 begins with a discussion of the evolution of the Internet, from the late 1960s to the present. Then it looks into the many individuals, companies, and organizations that make up the Internet community. Next, the chapter covers the different options for connecting to the Internet, including the types of Internet access devices, Internet connections, and ISPs available. Then, it's on to one of the most important Internet skills you should acquire—efficient Internet searching. To help you appreciate the wide spectrum of resources and activities available through the Internet, we also take a brief look at some of the most common applications available via the Internet. The final sections of the chapter discuss a few of the important societal issues that apply to Internet use and take a look at the Internet's future. ■

EVOLUTION OF THE INTERNET

The **Internet** is a worldwide collection of interconnected networks that support personal and commercial communications and information exchange. It consists of thousands of separate, but interconnected, networks that are accessed daily by millions of people. Just as the shipping industry has simplified transportation by providing standard containers for carrying all sorts of merchandise via air, rail, highway, and sea, the Internet furnishes a standard way of sending messages and information across virtually any type of computer platform and transmission media. While *Internet* has become a household word only during the past few years, it has actually operated in one form or another for decades.

TIP

It is estimated that over 615 million people worldwide use the Internet.

>**Internet.** The largest and most well-known computer network, linking millions of computers all over the world.

From ARPANET to Internet2

The roots of the Internet began with an experimental project called *ARPANET.* Since then, the evolution of ARPANET plus the creation of the *World Wide Web* has resulted in the Internet with which we are familiar today.

ARPANET

The Internet began as an experimental network called **ARPANET**, which was created in 1969 by the U.S. Department of Defense's *Advanced Research Projects Agency* (*ARPA*). One objective of the ARPANET project was to create a computer network that would allow researchers located in different places to communicate with each other. Another objective was to build a computer network capable of sending data over a variety of paths to ensure that network communications could continue even if part of the network was destroyed, such as in a nuclear attack or by a natural disaster.

Initially, ARPANET connected four supercomputers. As it grew during its first few years, ARPANET enabled researchers at a few dozen academic institutions to communicate with each other and with government agencies on topics of mutual interest. However, the Department of Defense got much more than it bargained for. With the highly controversial Vietnam War in full swing, ARPANET's e-mail facility began to handle not only legitimate research discussions but also heated debates about U.S. involvement in Southeast Asia. As students began to access ARPANET, other unintended uses, such as playing computer games, began.

As the experiment grew during the next decade, hundreds of college and university networks were connected to ARPANET. These local area networks consisted of a mixture of DOS- and Windows-based computers, Apple Macintoshes, UNIX workstations, and so on. Over the years, *protocols* (standards) were developed for tying this mix of computers and networks together, for transferring data over the network, and for ensuring that data is transferred intact. Other networks soon connected to ARPANET, which eventually evolved into the present day Internet. The Internet infrastructure today can be used for a variety of purposes, such as exchanging e-mail and instant messages; participating in discussion groups, chat sessions, and videoconferences; downloading software and music; purchasing goods and services; and transferring files between Internet users. One of the most widely used Internet resources is the *World Wide Web*.

The World Wide Web

In its early years, the Internet was used primarily by the government, scientists, and educational institutions. Despite its popularity in academia and with government researchers, the Internet went virtually unnoticed by the general public and the business community for over two decades, primarily for two basic reasons—it was hard to use, and it was slow. Early Internet users had to type cryptic commands (see the first image in Figure 9-1), because the easy-to-use, attractive graphical user interfaces (GUIs) so commonplace today were still largely unknown.

As always, however, technology improved and new applications quickly evolved. First, communications hardware improved and computers gained speed and better graphics capabilities. Then, in 1989, a researcher named Tim Berners-Lee working at *CERN* (a physics laboratory in Europe), proposed the idea of the **World Wide Web**. He envisioned the World Wide Web as a way to organize information in the form of pages linked together through selectable text or images (today's hyperlinks) on the screen. Although the introduction of Web pages didn't replace other Internet resources (such as e-mail and

>**ARPANET.** The predecessor of the Internet, named after the Advanced Research Projects Agency (ARPA), which sponsored its development.
>**World Wide Web.** The collection of Web pages available through the Internet.

EARLY 1990s
Even at the beginning of the 1990s, using the Internet for most people meant learning how to work with a cryptic sequence of commands. Virtually all information was text-based.

TODAY
Today's Web pages organize much of the Internet's content into easy-to-read pages; instead of typing cryptic command sequences, users click hyperlinks to access the information they want. Web pages today can contain a wide variety of multimedia elements, such as the text, graphics, and animation used on the Web page shown above.

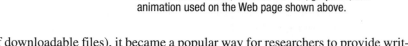

FIGURE 9-1
Using the Internet: Back in the "old days" versus now.

collections of downloadable files), it became a popular way for researchers to provide written information to others.

Things really got rolling with the arrival of the graphical user interface. In 1993, a group of professors and students at the University of Illinois *National Center for Supercomputing Applications* (*NCSA*) released *Mosaic*, the first graphically based Web browser. Mosaic used a graphical user interface and allowed Web pages to include graphical images in addition to text. Soon after, use of the World Wide Web began to increase dramatically because the graphical interface and graphical Web pages made using the World Wide Web both easier and more fun than in the past. Today's Web pages are a true multimedia experience. They can contain text, graphics, animation, sound, video, and three-dimensional virtual reality objects (refer to the second image in Figure 9-1).

Although the Web is only part of the Internet, it is by far one of the most popular and one of the fastest-growing parts. As interest in the Internet snowballed, companies began looking for ways to make it more accessible to customers, to make the user interface more functional, and to make more services available over it. Today, most companies regard their use of the Internet and World Wide Web as an indispensable competitive business tool and many individuals view the Internet as a vital research and communications medium.

One remarkable characteristic of both the Internet and World Wide Web is that they are not owned by any person or business, and no single person, business, or organization is in charge. Web pages are developed by individuals and organizations and hosted on Web servers owned by an individual; a school, business, or other organization; or a service provider. PCs and other devices used to access the Internet typically belong to individuals, organizations, or public facilities. Each network connected to the Internet is owned and managed individually by that network's network administrator, and the main communications media used as the *Internet backbone* are typically owned by telecommunications companies, such as telephone and cable companies. As a whole, the Internet has no owner or network administrator. The closest thing to an Internet governing body is a variety of organizations, such as the *Internet Society* (*ISOC*) and the *World Wide Web Consortium* (*W3C*). These organizations are involved with such issues as establishing the protocols used on the Internet, making recommendations for changes, and encouraging cooperation between and coordinating communication among the networks connected to the Internet.

Internet2

The next significant improvements to the Internet infrastructure may be a result of *Internet2*, a consortium of over 200 universities working together with industry and the government. Internet2 was created to develop and implement advanced Internet applications and technologies in hope of leading to improvements for tomorrow's Internet. One of the primary goals of the Internet2 project is to ensure that new network services and applications are quickly applied to the broader Internet community, not just to the Internet2 participants. It is important to realize that Internet2 does not refer to a new physical Internet that will eventually replace the Internet—it is simply a research and development project geared to ensuring that the Internet in the future can handle tomorrow's applications.

A complementary project is the *Next Generation Internet* (*NGI*). While Internet2 is university sponsored, NGI is a federal government-sponsored, multi-agency research and development program working to develop advanced networking technologies and revolutionary applications that require advanced networking capabilities. Internet2 is working in cooperation with the NGI project, as well as forming partnerships with similar projects in other countries, to ensure a cohesive and interoperable advanced networking infrastructure for the Internet of the future.

The Internet Community Today

The Internet community today consists of individuals, businesses, and a variety of organizations located throughout the world. Virtually anyone with a computer that has communications capabilities can be part of the Internet, either as a user or as a supplier of information or services. Most members of the Internet community fall into one or more of the following groups.

Users

Users are people who avail themselves of the vast amount of resources available through the Internet at work or in their personal lives. There are nearly 200 million Internet users in the United States alone and they come from all walks of life. The U.S. *digital divide*—the disproportionate higher level of Internet use for certain groups of individuals (typically the more affluent and more educated)—is beginning to lessen as free Internet access is becoming more commonplace in libraries, schools, and other public locations. That, combined with the availability of cheap PCs and Internet access in many areas today, has helped Internet use begin to approach the popularity and widespread use of phones and TVs.

Internet Service Providers

Internet service providers (**ISPs**)—often called *service providers* or *access providers*—are businesses or other organizations that provide Internet access to others, typically for a fee. Communications and media companies—such as conventional and wireless telephone companies and cable and satellite TV providers—typically offer Internet service over their respective media. In addition, a variety of other ISPs provide services over existing communications media (see Figure 9-2). Some, such as America Online and Earthlink, provide service nationwide; others have a more limited geographical area. ISPs act as an onramp to the Internet, providing their subscribers with access to the World Wide Web, e-mail, and other Internet resources. In addition to Internet access, some ISPs provide special online services available only to their subscribers. These ISPs are sometimes referred to as *online service providers*. A later section of this chapter covers ISPs in more detail, including factors to consider when selecting an ISP.

NET

FURTHER EXPLORATION

For links to further information about types of Internet access and ISPs, go to www.course.com/uc10/ch09

>**Internet service provider (ISP).** A business or other organization that provides Internet access to others, typically for a fee.

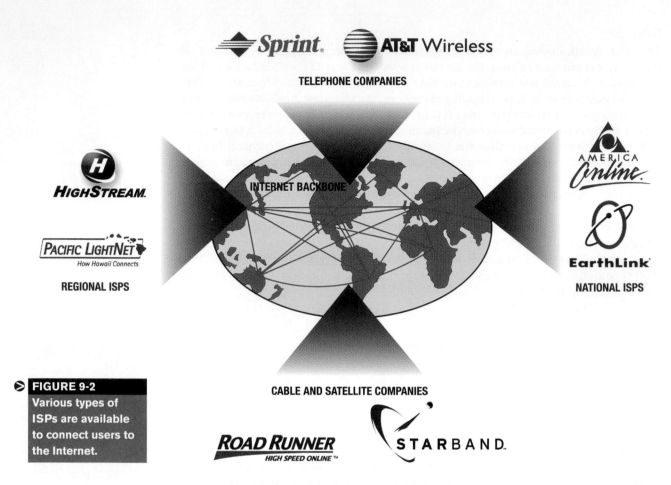

TELEPHONE COMPANIES

INTERNET BACKBONE

REGIONAL ISPS

NATIONAL ISPS

CABLE AND SATELLITE COMPANIES

> **FIGURE 9-2**
> Various types of
> ISPs are available
> to connect users to
> the Internet.

Internet Content Providers

Internet content providers supply the information that is available through the Internet. Internet content providers can be commercial businesses, non-profit organizations, educational institutions, individuals, and more. Some examples of content providers are listed next.

▼ A photographer who posts samples of her best work on a Web page.

▼ A political-action group that sponsors an online forum for discussions about topics that interest its members.

▼ A software company that creates a Web site to provide product information and software downloads.

▼ A national newspaper that maintains an online site to provide up-to-the-minute news, feature stories, and video clips.

▼ A television network that develops a site for its newest reality TV show, including statistics, photographs, and live video feeds.

▼ A music publisher that creates a site to provide song demos and to sell downloads of its artists' songs and albums.

▼ A film student who releases his original short movie to be viewed on the Web.

>**Internet content provider.** A person or an organization that provides Internet content.

Application Service Providers and Web Services

Application service providers (**ASPs**) are companies that manage and distribute software-based services to customers over the Internet. Instead of providing access to the Internet like ISPs do, ASPs provide access to software applications via the Internet. In essence, ASPs rent software access to companies or individuals—typically, customers pay a monthly or yearly fee to use the applications. One advantage to customers over buying software outright is less up-front money, which means small businesses may be able to afford the same state-of-the-art applications that larger companies use. Another advantage is that using ASP software may result in a reduction of computer support staffing, since the ASP can provide regular, automatic upgrades that all users see the next time they use the application; free or low-cost technical support and training may also be available from the ASP. Leasing applications in this manner also gives customers the flexibility of trying a different application whenever desired, without potentially wasting money purchasing software that may not fit the company's needs. Common ASP applications are office suites, collaboration and communications software, accounting programs, and e-commerce software. Some industry experts—such as the CEOs of Sun Microsystems and Microsoft—predict that within a relatively short period of time, software purchasing as we know it today will not exist. Instead, they believe software will be delivered as a service and the option to purchase software outright may not exist.

One type of special self-contained business application designed to work over the Internet or a company network is a **Web service**. Web services are programs written to strict specifications so that they can work together with other Web services and be used with many different computer systems. Unlike most other applications, Web services themselves don't have a user interface—they are simply a standardized way of allowing different applications and computers to share data and processes via a network. However, a Web service can be added to a Web page or application program to provide specific functionality to end users. For example, Web services can be used to facilitate communications between suppliers and customers, to provide a service via a Web site that was otherwise not feasible (such as the inclusion of mapping information on a Web site or Web application using Microsoft's MapPoint .NET Web service), or to add additional functionality to the end user via the Internet (such as a new Web service for Microsoft Office users expected to be available in the near future that allows them to print to any Kinko's locations from their program's File menu). A company that provides Web services is sometimes referred to as a *Web services provider*.

Infrastructure Companies

Infrastructure companies are the enterprises that own or operate the paths or "roadways" along which Internet data travel. Examples of infrastructure companies include telephone, satellite, and cable companies.

Hardware and Software Companies

A wide variety of hardware and software companies make and distribute the necessary products used with the Internet and Internet activities. The firms that supply Web browser, e-mail, Web server, and Web development software fall into this category. So, too, do the companies that make modems, cables, routers, servers, PCs, and other types of hardware used in conjunction with the Internet. The customers of software and hardware companies are users, service and content providers, and infrastructure companies.

>**Application service provider (ASP).** A company that manages and distributes software-based services over the Internet. >**Web service.** A self-contained business application that operates over the Internet.

The Government and Other Organizations

Many other organizations influence the Internet and its uses. Governments have among the most visible impact; their laws limit both information content and access in the Internet community. In the United States, rulings such as the 1968 *Carterfone Decision* (that allowed companies other than AT&T to utilize the AT&T infrastructure) and the 1996 *Telecommunications Act* (that deregulated the entire communications industry so that telephone companies, cable-TV and satellite operators, and firms in other segments of the industry were free to enter each other's markets), had a large impact on the communications industry in general. In addition, the ability of the government to block potential mergers between communications companies and to break apart companies based on antitrust law to prevent new monopolies also impacts the Internet and communications industry.

Key Internet organizations are responsible for many aspects of the Internet. For example, the Internet Society (ISOC) provides leadership in addressing issues that confront the future of the Internet and oversees the groups responsible for Internet infrastructure standards, such as which protocols can be used and how Internet addresses are constructed. *ICANN* (*Internet Corporation for Assigned Names and Numbers*) is charged with such responsibilities as IP address allocation and domain name management. The World Wide Web Consortium (W3C) is a group of over 450 organizations dedicated to developing new protocols and specifications to promote the evolution of the Web and to ensure its interoperability. In addition, many colleges and universities support Internet research and manage blocks of the Internet's resources.

Myths About the Internet

Because the Internet is so unique in the history of the world—and its content and applications keep evolving—several widespread myths about it have surfaced.

Myth 1: The Internet Is Free

This myth has been perpetuated largely by the fact that people can access Web pages from anywhere in the world and freely engage in long-distance e-mail or chat exchanges without paying additional fees, other than what they pay their ISPs for access to the Internet in general. It is also true that many people—such as students, employees, and consumers who opt for free Internet service or use free access available at public libraries or other public locations—pay nothing to use the Internet. Yet it should also be obvious that someone, somewhere, has to pay to keep the Internet up and running.

Businesses, schools, public libraries, and most home users pay Internet service providers flat monthly fees to connect to the Internet; businesses, schools, libraries, and other larger organizations may also have to lease high-capacity communications lines (such as from a telephone company) to support their high level of Internet traffic. ISPs, phone companies, cable companies, and other organizations who own part of the Internet infrastructure pay to keep their respective physical parts of the Internet running smoothly. ISPs also pay software and hardware companies for the resources they need to support their users. Eventually, most of these costs are passed along to end users through their ISP fees. Usually, free Internet access is supported by advertising revenue gained from onscreen ads (either ads displayed within the browser interface whenever Web pages or e-mail messages are being viewed, or *pop-up* ads that display in new browser windows), similar to regular TV broadcasting, or by selling personal or demographic data obtained from subscribers.

Another reason that this is a myth is the growing trend of subscription or per-use fees to access resources—such as journal or newspaper articles, music, games, and more—via the Internet. Typically, these fees are relatively small and many companies are working on ways to make the processing of small fees (sometimes called *micropayments*) practical. In lieu of a mandatory fee, some sites request donations for use of the site (see Figure 9-3). Many experts expect the use of fee-based Internet content to continue to grow at a rapid pace. In 2002 alone, subscriptions for Web site content surpassed $1 billion.

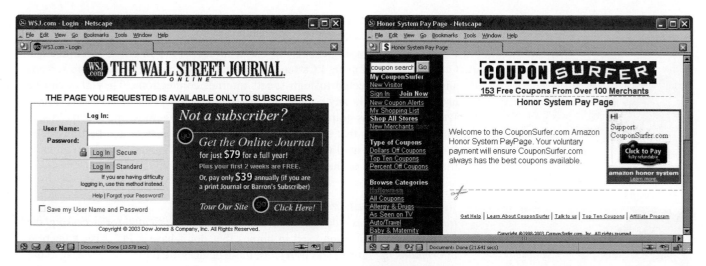

REQUIRED FEE
A subscription is required to view content on this site.

REQUESTED DONATION
A donation is requested for using this site.

Myth 2: Someone Controls the Internet

The popularity of conspiracy theories in recent years has contributed to the spread of this myth. In fact, as already discussed, no single group or organization controls the Internet. Governments in each country have the power to regulate the content and use of the Internet within their borders, as allowed by their laws. However, legislators often face serious obstacles getting legislation passed into law—let alone getting it enforced. Making governmental control even harder is the bombproof design of the Internet itself. If a government tries to block access to or from a specific country, for example, users can establish links between the two countries through a third country.

Guidelines by watchdog groups such as the Internet Society (ISOC) have sometimes folded under pressure from the tidal wave of people and organizations that have flocked to the Internet. For example, ISOC's policies that discouraged commercial use of the Internet fell by the wayside many years ago.

> **FIGURE 9-3**
> **Fee-based Web content.** Both required fees and requested donations for accessing Web content are becoming common.

Myth 3: The Internet and World Wide Web Are Identical

Since you can now use a Web browser to access most of the Internet's resources, many people think the Internet and the Web are the same thing. Although in everyday use many people use the terms *Internet* and *Web* interchangeably, they're not the same thing. Technically, the Internet is the physical network and the Web is the collection of Web pages accessible over the Internet. The majority of Internet activities today take place via Web pages, but there are Internet resources other than the Web, such as non-Web-based e-mail and collections of files accessed via *FTP* (*File Transfer Protocol*) programs.

GETTING SET UP TO USE THE INTERNET

Getting set up to use the Internet typically involves three decisions. The first is determining the type of device you will use to access the Internet. The second is selecting the type of connection desired. A final step is deciding on the Internet service provider to be used. Once these determinations have been made, your computer can be set up to access the Internet.

Type of Device

The Internet today can be accessed by a variety of devices. The type of device used depends on a combination of factors, including the amount of portability needed and the desired content to be retrieved from the Web. Some possible devices are shown in Figure 9-4 and discussed next.

DESKTOP, NOTEBOOK, OR TABLET PC

INTERNET APPLIANCE

HANDHELD PC OR SMART PHONE

> **FIGURE 9-4**
> A variety of devices
> can be used to
> access the Internet.

Desktop, Notebook, or Tablet PCs

Most users who have access to a desktop (see Figure 9-4), notebook, or tablet PC at home, work, or school will use it to access the Internet, when needed. One advantage of using PCs for Internet access is that they have large screens and can be connected to high-speed Internet connections. They also can be used with virtually any content that can be contained on or accessed from a Web page, such as graphics, animation, music files, games, and video clips. A final advantage is that they usually have access to a printer and hard drive, so Web pages and e-mail messages can be printed, and e-mail and downloadable files can be saved to the PC.

Internet Appliances

Internet appliances—devices that are designed specifically for accessing the Internet—are most often used in homes that don't have a PC. Also known as *information appliances* and *Web pads*, these devices are typically very easy to use and can access Web pages, e-mail, or both. Usually, Web page graphics can be displayed, although all multimedia content may not necessarily be accessible. Disadvantages of Internet appliances include little or no local storage space for saving e-mails or downloads (often everything must be stored online), possibly not being able to connect the device to a printer; and not being able to use the device for tasks other than Internet activities. In addition, many of these devices work only with a single specified provider, such as America Online, MSN, or a proprietary service designed just for that type of Internet appliance. Some Internet appliances are designed to be located in a kitchen or other central location (see Figure 9-4); others take the form of a set-top box located on or near a living room TV and can manage television viewing and recording, in addition to Internet access.

Mobile Devices

Mobile Web use—or *wireless Web*, as it is frequently called—is one of the fastest growing uses of the Internet today. Handheld PCs, mobile phones, and pagers increasingly have Internet connectivity built in and can be used to view Web page content and exchange e-mail and instant messages. Some devices, such as the handheld PC shown in Figure 9-4, include a keyboard for easier data entry; others utilize pen input instead.

Type of Connection and Internet Access

In order to use the Internet, your computer needs to be connected to it. Typically, this occurs by connecting your PC to another computer (usually belonging to an ISP, your school, or your employer) that is connected continually to the Internet. As discussed in Chapter 8, there are a variety of wired and wireless ways to connect to another computer. The following sections discuss the most common types of Internet connections. Some Internet connections are *dial-up connections*, which means your PC dials up and connects to your ISP's computer only when needed. Other Internet connections are *direct* or *always-on connections*, which means whenever your computer is on it is connected to your ISP on a continual basis. Within each of these two connection categories, there are Internet access alternatives.

Dial-Up Connections

Dial-up connections usually work over regular telephone lines. To connect to the Internet, your computer dials its modem and connects to a modem located at your ISP. While you are connected, your PC is assigned a temporary IP address for the current session and you can access Internet resources. At the end of each Internet session, you disconnect from your ISP's computer to allow another user to connect in your place. One advantage to a dial-up connection is security. Since you are not continually connected to the Internet, it is much less likely that anyone (such as a hacker) will gain access to your computer via the Internet, either to access the data located on your PC or, more commonly, to use your computer in some type of illegal or unethical manner.

One disadvantage of using a dial-up connection is the inconvenience of having to instruct your PC to dial up your ISP every time you want to check your e-mail or view a Web page. Also, your telephone line will likely be tied up while you are accessing the Internet, unless a second phone line is used. Some Internet call-waiting or call-forwarding services allow you to be notified when you get a telephone call while you are connected to the Internet. They are generally set up to allow the person to leave a short message; some newer systems give you a short window of time to disconnect from the Internet and pick up the telephone call, if desired. Newer dial-up modems help to facilitate some type of call-waiting service, as well. The two most common forms of dial-up Internet service are *conventional dial-up* and *ISDN*.

Conventional Dial-Up

Conventional (*standard*) **dial-up Internet access** uses a conventional dial-up modem connected to a standard telephone jack with twisted-pair telephone cabling. Conventional dial-up Internet service is commonly used with home PCs and Internet appliances; it can also be used with notebook PCs or other portable devices provided the device has a conventional dial-up modem. Conventional dial-up Internet access ranges from free to about $25 per month. Advantages of conventional dial-up include inexpensive hardware, ease of setup and use, and widespread availability. The primary disadvantage, in addition to the disadvantages pertaining to all types of dial-up connections discussed in the previous paragraph, is slow connection speeds—conventional dial-up connects to the Internet at a maximum of 56 Kbps.

One recent new application for conventional dial-up is *prepaid Internet*. Similar to prepaid long-distance telephone cards, prepaid Internet cards are purchased in advance (see Figure 9-5) and minutes are deducted from the card as Internet connection time is used. Some prepaid Internet services can be used with both local access numbers and toll-free numbers, although using a toll-free number typically consumes the prepaid minutes faster than a local number. Prepaid Internet service is useful for both infrequent Internet users and individuals who need to access the Internet periodically as they travel. Some travelers opt to connect to their dial-up Internet service providers using their cell phones instead (see Figure 9-6).

ISDN

ISDN (*integrated services digital network*) **Internet access** also transfers data over ordinary telephone lines, but it is faster than conventional dial-up and can use two phone lines to transfer data up to 128 Kbps—over twice as fast as conventional dial-up service. If your connection is set up to use one phone line for voice and one for data instead, your phone line won't be tied up during Internet use but your access speed will drop to 64 Kbps. Fairly expensive for the speed at about $70 per month, ISDN requires a special ISDN modem and is used more often in businesses than home connections.

> **FIGURE 9-5**
> **Prepaid Internet.**
> These prepaid conventional dial-up Internet cards can be used to connect to the Internet from anywhere the user has access to a telephone jack.

>Dial-up connection. A type of Internet connection in which the PC or other device must dial up and connect to a service provider's computer via telephone lines before being connected to the Internet. **>Conventional dial-up Internet access.** Dial-up Internet access via a conventional dial-up modem and standard telephone lines. **>ISDN Internet access.** Dial-up Internet access that is faster than conventional dial-up, but still uses standard telephone lines.

► FIGURE 9-6

Dial-up via cell phones. Some people choose to use their cell phones to connect to their dial-up ISP while on the go.

Direct Connections

Unlike dial-up connections that connect to your ISP only when you need to access the Internet, **direct** (*always-on*) **connections** keep you continually connected to your provider and, therefore, continually connected to the Internet. With a direct connection, your PC is typically issued a *static* (non-changing) IP address to be used to transfer data back and forth via the Internet and Internet access requires only opening a Web browser program, such as Internet Explorer or Netscape Navigator. Direct Internet connections are commonly used in homes and offices. In addition, they are often available at airports, coffee houses, libraries, and other public locations for travelers and other users on the go. Users can connect to direct Internet connections via either wired or wireless media.

Direct Internet connections are typically *broadband* connections; that is, connections for which more than one signal can be transferred at one time. Therefore, direct Internet connections are much faster than dial-up connections. In theory, they can be up to 100 times as fast as a dial-up connection, but actual speeds at the present time are closer to 25 to 50 times as fast. This discrepancy is due to outside factors such as the speed of the CPU and amount of memory in the PC being used, the condition of the transmission media being used, and the amount of traffic currently using the same transmission medium and Web server. *DSL* and *cable Internet* typically download data at about 1.5 Mbps; *satellite* and *fixed wireless Internet* usually download data between 500 Kbps to 1 Mbps; and the fast *T-1 lines* used by large businesses transfer data at about 1.5 Mbps. *Mobile wireless* speeds vary more, typically from 14.4 Kbps to about 400 Kbps, depending on the type of service used. Most direct Internet connections have slower upload speeds. The most significant characteristics of each of these types of direct Internet access are discussed next. For a look at another wireless alternative—the use of aircraft to transmit signals—see the Trend box.

T-1 Lines

Most schools or large businesses that offer a direct connection to the Internet for the PCs on their LANs lease a high-speed dedicated line, such as a *T-1 line*, from the telephone company or an Internet service provider. The speed of this type of Internet access for the end user depends on the speed of the connection between the school or office and the user's Internet service provider, as well as the speed of the LAN itself; however, T-1 lines are very fast (approximately 1.5 Mbps). Large businesses may choose to lease a faster *T-3 line* (which transmits data at speeds of about 43 Mbps), but these are used primarily for Internet backbone connections and connections from ISPs to the Internet. Smaller businesses may use DSL, cable, or satellite access to provide Internet to company employees through the company networks instead of a leased line.

DSL

As mentioned in Chapter 8, **DSL** (*digital subscriber line*) **Internet access** provides fast transmissions over telephone lines and uses a technology that doesn't tie up your telephone line. DSL is currently available only to users who are relatively close (three miles or less) to a telephone switching station with telephone lines capable of handling DSL, and the speed of the connection degrades as the distance gets closer and closer to the three-mile limit. DSL providers are looking for ways to overcome this limitation, such as by using some type of repeating system to boost the signal over longer distances. DSL is not available in all areas and each area with DSL service typically has a small number of DSL providers that can provide service to that area. DSL Internet service requires a DSL modem; typical monthly fees are around $50.

TIP

Because they are connected to the Internet at all times (as long as the PC is turned on), home and office PCs with a direct Internet connection should use a *firewall* program to protect against hackers and other types of unauthorized access.

>**Direct connection.** An always-on type of Internet connection in which the PC or other device is continually connected to the Internet.
>**DSL Internet access.** Fast, direct Internet access via standard telephone lines.

TREND

Aircraft-Based Internet: Broadband of the Future?

Instead of providing Internet access via cables, satellites, or radio towers, a new possibility is *aircraft-based Internet*, which uses aircraft to transmit signals between end users and their ISP. The aircraft—more officially called a *High Altitude Platform Station* (*HAPS*)—would fly over a specific area to provide service to that area.

One such service, expected to be available by the end of 2004, is AeroVironment's *SkyTower*, developed in conjunction with NASA. The SkyTower program uses solar-powered (with hydrogen fuel cell power backup) unmanned aircraft flying at 65,000 feet (see the accompanying photo). Each aircraft can remain airborne for up to 6 months and is expected to cover an area of about 50 miles in diameter. SkyTower service is predicted to be implemented at a much lower cost than cable, DSL, and satellite service since there are no cables to run to end user locations (like cable and DSL service) and the aircraft are much less expensive to deploy than satellites launched into space. The SkyTower platform is also scalable; that is, aircraft can be added or moved as needed to meet demand. Similar programs are being tested by other companies using manned aircraft and blimps. To receive fixed aircraft-based Internet

service, each end user needs a small outside-mounted transceiver dish. Mobile wireless services for both telephones and portable PCs are expected to also become available. Whether or not aircraft-based Internet becomes a viable alternative remains to be seen. It does, however, offer an intriguing solution to the "last-mile" problem of providing broadband access to each customer's location.

An unmanned SkyTower aircraft.

Cable

Cable Internet access is the most widely used type of home broadband connection. Cable connections are very fast and are available to anyone in a location with cable access and whose local cable provider supports Internet access. One disadvantage of cable Internet is that all users in an immediate geographical area share the bandwidth of their local cable. Although this may not prove to be a problem all the time, during high-use times of day— such as early evening—the speed of cable Internet service can slow down dramatically as you and your neighbors go online at the same time. Cable is also not widely available in rural areas. Cable Internet service requires a cable modem. Cost is about $45 per month just for Internet access; cable TV is optional and requires an additional fee.

Satellite

As discussed in Chapter 8, **satellite Internet access** is typically a little slower than cable or DSL, but it is often the only broadband option for rural areas. In addition to a satellite modem, it requires a *transceiver* satellite dish mounted outside the home or building to receive and transmit data to and from the appropriate satellite. Installation requires an unobstructed view of the southern sky (to have a clear line-of-site between the transceiver and appropriate satellite), and performance may degrade or stop altogether during very heavy rain or snowstorms. Typical cost is about $70 per month.

>**Cable Internet access.** Fast, direct Internet access via cable TV lines. >**Satellite Internet access.** Fast, direct Internet access via the airwaves using a satellite dish and satellite modem.

Fixed Wireless

Fixed wireless Internet access is similar to satellite Internet in that it requires a modem and an outside-mounted transceiver, but it uses radio transmission towers instead of satellites and is typically available only in large metropolitan areas. A clear line-of-sight is required between the transceiver and the provider's radio transmission tower; cost for service is about $50 per month.

Mobile Wireless

Mobile wireless (sometimes called *wireless Web*) **Internet access** is most commonly used with handheld PCs, smart phones, and other mobile devices to keep them connected to the Internet, even as you carry them from place to place. These devices are connected typically through a wireless network and wireless provider using a wireless modem or built-in Internet connectivity. The newest mobile communications devices are 3G devices, which support high-speed digital wireless transmissions. Just becoming available in limited areas in the United States, 3G is expected to operate at up to nearly 400 Kbps while on the go—fast enough to access multimedia content with portable PCs or mobile phones—and is viewed as a potentially huge breakthrough in mobile communications applications. Costs for wireless Internet vary widely, with some packages including unlimited Internet, some charging by the number of minutes of Internet use, and some charging by the amount of data transferred.

Public Hot Spots

Both free and fee-based wireless Internet are becoming available at *public hot spots*—public locations with a direct Internet connection that allow users to wirelessly connect to that Internet connection. Examples include the Internet service available at many Starbucks coffee houses and an increasing number of McDonald's restaurants; wireless access points at hotels, airports, and other locations frequented by business travelers; and free hot spots located in the vicinity of some larger metropolitan area libraries, subway stations, parks, and other public locations (see Figure 9-7).

> **FIGURE 9-7**
> **Public hot spots.**

FEE-BASED AND FREE HOT SPOTS
Public hot spots can offer fee-based Internet access (such as at the Starbucks location above) or free Internet access (such as outside the New York City public library, right).

>Fixed wireless Internet access. Fast, direct Internet access available in large metropolitan areas via the airwaves and a radio transceiver.
>Mobile wireless Internet access. Internet access via a wireless communications network, such as the ones used with cellular phones.

Selecting an ISP and Setting Up Your PC

Once the type of Internet access connection (such as dial-up or cable) is determined and the modem and hardware, if any, required by that type of connection are acquired, then the final steps to getting connected to the Internet are selecting an ISP and setting up your system.

Selecting an ISP

The type of device used (desktop PC or PDA, for example), the type of Internet connection and service desired (such as conventional dial-up or cable), and your geographical location will likely limit your ISP choices. Before choosing an ISP, compare the pricing and services available, since they may differ somewhat. For example some ISPs simply provide you with an onramp to the Internet; others may include additional content or services, such as instant messaging, music management, Web site hosting, personal online photo galleries, Web site filtering, spam filtering, and a personalized home page. Some ISPs are *regional ISPs* that provide access only to limited geographical areas; *national ISPs* usually offer a wider service area and may offer a higher level of services and support. To help you make your final selection, the questions listed in Figure 9-8 may be helpful.

TIP

It is becoming more common for ISPs to offer *tiered* pricing plans, in which subscribers can pay a lower fee for basic service, or pay a higher fee for faster access or other premium services.

Setting Up Your PC

The specific steps for setting up your PC to use your new Internet connection depend on the type of device, connection, and ISP you've chosen to use. Once your necessary hardware (your modem and any additional hardware, such as a satellite transceiver or set-top box) is in place, you will usually need to run installation software to set up your system to use your selected ISP. Usual tasks include downloading and installing any required

FIGURE 9-8
Choosing an ISP.
Some questions to ask before making your final selection.

Services	Can I use the browser of my choice?
	Does the e-mail service support attachments, spam filtering, multiple mailboxes, and any other features I'd like to have?
	How many e-mail addresses can I have?
	What is the size limit on incoming and outgoing e-mail messages and attachments?
	Is there dial-up service that I can use when I'm away from home (for both dial-up and broadband connections)?
	Are there any special member features or benefits?
	Is space available for posting a personal Web site or personal photos?
Speed	How fast are the maximum and usual downstream (ISP to my PC) speeds?
	How fast are the maximum and usual upstream (my PC to ISP) speeds?
	How much does the service slow down under adverse conditions (high traffic, poor weather, etc.)?
	If it's a dial-up connection, how often should I expect to get a busy signal? (A customer to modem ratio of about 10:1 or less is optimal.)
Support	Is 24/7 telephone technical support available?
	Is any technical support available through a Web site (e-mail support, online knowledge base, etc.)?
	What is the response time to answer my phone calls or e-mails when I have a problem?
	Is there ever a charge for technical support?
Cost	What is the monthly cost for the service? Is it lower if I prepay a few months in advance?
	If it's a dial-up connection, is there a local access telephone number to avoid long distance charges?
	Are there services that can be added or deleted (number of e-mail addresses, Web page hosting, etc.) to increase or decrease the monthly cost?
	Is there a set-up fee? If so, can it be waived with a 6-month or 12-month agreement?
	What is the cost of any additional hardware needed (modem, transceiver, etc.)? Can the fee be waived with a long-term service agreement?
	Are there any other services (conventional or wireless telephone service, or cable or satellite TV, for instance) available from this provider that I have or want and that can be combined with Internet access for a lower total cost?

software; setting up your telephone dialing software (for some conventional dial-up connections only); and walking through selecting a user name (usually used to log in and for your e-mail address), access number (for dial-up connections), and payment method. Some ISPs provide the installation program on CD; the installation programs for several common ISPs are also preinstalled on many new PCs. To sign up using an installation program on CD, insert the CD in your CD or DVD drive and the setup process should start automatically; to sign up using an installation program already installed on your PC, just use the mouse to open the appropriate desktop icon or Start menu item to launch the installation program. In either case, once the installation program begins, simply follow the onscreen instructions to complete the setup process. If you already have an Internet connection and are looking for a new ISP, the necessary installation program can typically be downloaded to your PC from the ISP's Web site and then run on your PC to begin the setup process. If your ISP doesn't have an installation program, follow its instructions to set up your Web browser and telephone-dialing software (if needed).

Selected screens of the installation process with one provider (America Online) are shown in Figure 9-9; the same general steps occur with most ISP installation programs, although they might occur in a different order.

> **FIGURE 9-9**
> **Setting up a PC for Internet access.**
> Most ISPs have an installation program that walks new subscribers through the setup process.

STEP 1: SELECT AN ACCESS NUMBER
For dial-up access, you will need to select a local access telephone number for your PC to call when you want to use the Internet.

STEP 2: PROVIDE YOUR CONTACT AND BILLING INFORMATION
The setup process will include specifying your contact and billing information.

STEP 3: SELECT A USER NAME AND PASSWORD
The user name (or screen name) and password you select may be used for logging on to the Internet, as well as for sending and receiving e-mail.

STEP 4: INSTALL AND SET UP BROWSER
The installation program will install and set up your browser, e-mail program, and dialing program to reflect the choices you made during the setup process.

SEARCHING THE INTERNET

While casual surfing is a popular Web pastime, people often turn to the Internet to find specific information. For instance, you might want to find out the price of the latest Tom Cruise DVD at a few online retailers, the flights available from Los Angeles to New York on a particular day, a recipe for clam chowder, the text of Martin Luther King's "I Had a Dream" speech, a map of hiking trails in the Grand Tetons, or Babe Ruth's home run average. The Internet is a storehouse of interesting and useful information, but that vast amount of information is useless if you can't find it when you need it. Consequently, one of the most important skills an Internet user can acquire today is how to successfully search for and locate information on the Internet. Basic searching was covered in Chapter 2, but to perform more successful Internet searches, you should also be familiar with the various types of search sites available and how they work, as well as some key searching strategies. These topics are discussed next.

Search Sites

There are many different **search sites**—Web sites that enable users to search for and find information on the Internet—available. As discussed in Chapter 2, many of the most popular search sites, such as Yahoo!, Google, AltaVista, HotBot, Excite, and so on, offer search services using both *keywords* and a *directory*; they may also include other search possibilities, such as searching for music files, image files, newsgroups, or news articles (see Figure 9-10). Since most search sites use some type of *search database* to locate appropriate Web pages as you search, it is important to understand a little about how such a database works.

> **FIGURE 9-10**
> **Search site options.**
> Many of the most widely used search sites allow you to search by keyword, directory categories, or more.

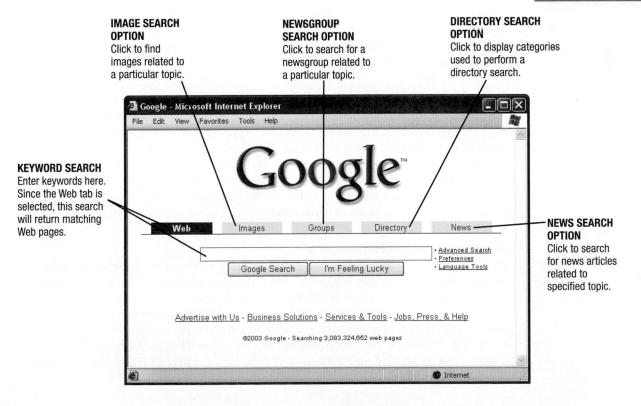

IMAGE SEARCH OPTION
Click to find images related to a particular topic.

NEWSGROUP SEARCH OPTION
Click to search for a newsgroup related to a particular topic.

DIRECTORY SEARCH OPTION
Click to display categories used to perform a directory search.

KEYWORD SEARCH
Enter keywords here. Since the Web tab is selected, this search will return matching Web pages.

NEWS SEARCH OPTION
Click to search for news articles related to specified topic.

>**Search site.** A Web site designed to help users search for Web pages that match specified keywords or selected categories.

Search Databases

While it may appear that a search site actually searches the Internet for you at the time you make a search request, in fact such a search would be entirely too time-consuming to perform in real time. Instead, virtually all search sites use a search database previously filled with millions or billions of URLs classified by various types of keywords or categories and a **search engine** program to retrieve a list of matching Web pages from the database. Since there isn't a single central database of all the Web pages located on the World Wide Web, each search site either creates and maintains its own database or has access to a search database created and maintained by another site. To maintain such a database, typically small, automated programs (often called *spiders* or *webcrawlers*) use the hyperlinks located on Web pages to jump continually from page to page on the Web. At each page, the program records important data about the page—such as its URL, page title, frequently used keywords, and descriptive information added to the page's code by the Web page author when the page was created—into the database. This information is used to find matching Web pages when the search site receives a search request. Spider programs can be tremendously fast, visiting more than 1 million pages per day. Search databases also obtain information when people who create Web sites submit URLs and keywords to them through an option on the search site, as discussed more in Chapter 11.

The size of the search database varies with each particular search site. For example, Google—one of the most popular search sites—has data on over 3 billion Web pages. Search sites also differ in how close a match has to be between the specified search criteria and a Web page before a link to that page (called a *hit*) is displayed. This can be good or bad, depending on the length of the list of matches the search returns and how much time you want to spend looking through the list of hits for something interesting enough to pursue further. To reduce the number of hits displayed, good search strategies (discussed shortly) can be used. Sites also differ regarding the order in which the hits are displayed. Some sites list the most popular sites (usually judged by the number of Web pages linked to it); others list Web pages belonging to organizations that pay a fee to receive a higher rank (sometimes called *sponsored links*) first.

Searching with Keywords

When you know generally what information you want to find but don't know the appropriate URL, one of your best options is to perform a *keyword search*. As shown in Figure 9-11, many different types of search sites allow the use of keyword searches. With a keyword search, you supply **keywords** (one or more key terms), and then the search engine uses those keywords to pull matching pages from its search database. Once one or more keywords are typed in the appropriate location on the search site's Web page and the Enter key is pressed, the search engine will retrieve and display a list of matching Web pages.

Searching with Directories

Directories are usually a good choice if you want information about a particular category, but don't have a very specific subject in mind. A directory also uses a database, but one that is typically screened by a human editor so it is much smaller, although often more accurate. For example, a spider program may classify a Web page about "computer chips" under the keyword "chips" together with information about potato chips, but a human editor wouldn't. One of the largest directories—the *Open Directory Project*, located at dmoz.org—has classified nearly 4 million Web pages using over 58,000 volunteer editors.

>Search engine. A software program used by a search site to retrieve matching Web pages from a search database. **>Keyword.** A word typed in a search box on a search site to locate information on the Internet. **>Directory.** A collection of categories that are used to locate appropriate Web pages from a search database.

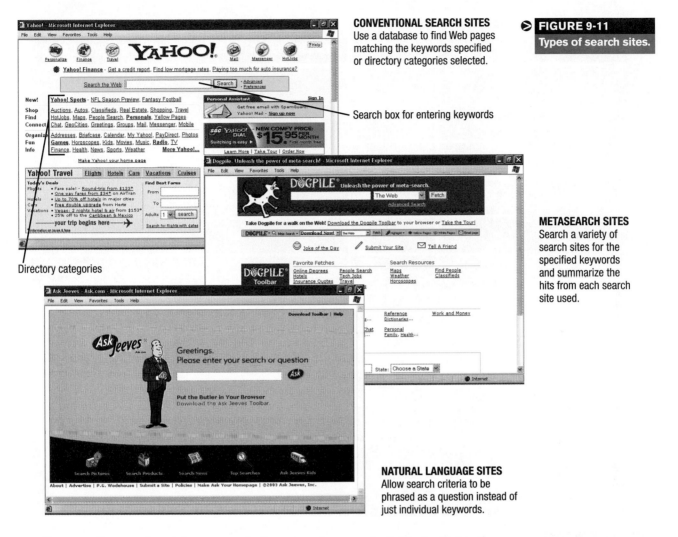

CONVENTIONAL SEARCH SITES
Use a database to find Web pages matching the keywords specified or directory categories selected.

Search box for entering keywords

Directory categories

METASEARCH SITES
Search a variety of search sites for the specified keywords and summarize the hits from each search site used.

NATURAL LANGUAGE SITES
Allow search criteria to be phrased as a question instead of just individual keywords.

To use a directory located on a search site, categories are selected instead of typing keywords (refer again to Figure 9-11). After selecting a main category, a list of more specific subcategories for the selected main category is displayed. Eventually, after selecting one or more subcategories, a list of appropriate Web pages is displayed.

Metasearch Sites

Some search sites are *metasearch sites*—that is, they search multiple search sites. Typically the metasearch site doesn't have its own search database. Instead, it acts as a middleman, passing on the specified keywords to a variety of search sites and then summarizing the results. One popular metasearch site is shown in Figure 9-11.

Natural Language Search Sites

A *natural language* search site, such as the Ask Jeeves search site shown in Figure 9-11, allows users to enter search criteria in full sentence form, instead of simply entering keywords. Some natural language sites include directory search capabilities or other search and reference tools, as well.

Search Strategies

There are a variety of strategies that can be employed to help whittle down a list of hits to a more manageable number (some searches can return millions of Web pages). Some search strategies can be employed regardless of the search site being used; others are available only on certain sites. Some of the most useful search strategies are discussed next.

SEARCH PHRASE USED	SEARCH SITE	NUMBER OF PAGES FOUND	TITLE OF FIRST TWO PAGES FOUND (HIGHLIGHTED ENTRIES INDICATE RELEVANT WEB PAGES)
dogs	AltaVista	4,619,341	I-Love-Dogs.com AKC - American Kennel Club for Purebred Dogs
	Google	9,120,000	I-Love-Dogs.com Guide Dogs for the Blind
	HotBot	5,145,352	I-Love-Dogs.com American Kennel Club
hand signals	AltaVista	627,659	Old Soccer Hand Signals Cree Hand Signals
	Google	1,470,000	Cree Hand Signals Soccer Officials' Hand Signals
	HotBot	539,617	Soccer Officials' Hand Signals Ann Arbor American H.O.G. Hand Signals
dog hand signals	AltaVista	52,341	Cree Hand Signals Why the Deaf Dog Barks
	Google	130,000	Dog Behavior Training, Teach Your Dog Hand Signals! PetsMart.com - Talking with hand signals
	HotBot	77,358	Training a Deaf Dog PetsMart.com - Talking with hand signals
"dog hand signals"	AltaVista	22	Pets with Disabilities - Dog Training Bunker Kennels
	Google	43	Dog Behavior Training, Teach Your Dog Hand Signals! PetsMart.com - Talking with hand signals
	HotBot	21	Training a Deaf Dog PetsMart.com - Talking with hand signals

> **FIGURE 9-12**
> **Examples of phrase searching.** Using different search phrases and different search sites can dramatically change the search results.

Using Phrases

One of the most straightforward ways to improve the quality of the hits returned is to use *phrase searching*—essentially typing more than one keyword in a keyword search. Most search engines automatically return the hits that include all the keywords typed first, followed by the hits matching most of the keywords, continuing down to the hits that fit only one of the keywords. To force this type of sorting, virtually all search engines allow some type of character—such as quotation marks—to be used to indicate that you want to search for all the keywords. On some sites, quotation marks can also be used to indicate that the keywords need to appear in the exact order they were typed. Because search options vary from site to site, it is best to look for a search tips link on the search site you are using; the search tips should explain the options available for that particular site. Examples of the results from using various search phrases at different sites to find Web pages about hand signals used with dogs are listed in Figure 9-12.

Using Boolean Operators

To further specify exactly what you want a search engine to find, *Boolean operators*—most commonly AND, OR, and NOT—can often be used in keyword searches. For example, if you want a search engine to find all documents that cover *both* the Intel and AMD microprocessor manufacturers, you can use the search phrase *Intel AND AMD*, if the search engine supports Boolean operators. If, instead, you want documents that discuss *either* (or both) of these companies, the Boolean phrase *Intel OR AMD* can be used. On the other hand, if you want documents about microprocessors that are cataloged with no

TIP

When searching, be efficient—if an appropriate Web page isn't included among the first page or two of hits, redo the search using more specific criteria or a different search strategy.

mention of Intel, *microprocessors NOT Intel* can be used. Just as with other operators, the rules for using Boolean operators may vary from search site to search site—check the search tips for the search site that you are using to see if that site supports Boolean operators. Some sites include an Advanced Search option using a fill-in form to walk you through using Boolean operators and other advanced search techniques; other sites use the characters + for AND and – for NOT.

Using Multiple Search Sites

As illustrated in Figure 9-12, different search sites can return surprisingly different results. Most users have a favorite search site that they are comfortable using. However, it's important to realize that sometimes a different search site may perform better. If you are searching for something and aren't making any progress with one search site, then try another search site. The "Web Guide" located in the References and Resources Guide at the end of this book includes the URLs of a number of different search sites.

Using Appropriate Keywords, Synonyms, Variant Word Forms, and Wildcards

When choosing the keywords to be used with a search site, it is important to select words that represent the key concept you are searching for. Unless you are using a natural language site, leave off any extraneous words, such as "the," "a," "in," and so forth. For example, if you want to find out about bed and breakfasts located in the town of Leavenworth, Washington, a keyword phrase such as *Leavenworth Washington bed and breakfast* should return appropriate results.

Another good strategy if your initial search didn't produce the results you were hoping for is to try the synonym approach. *Synonyms*—words that have meanings similar to other words—can be typed as keywords in addition to, or instead of, the original keywords. For example, you could replace *bed and breakfast* with *hotel* or *lodging*. To use synonyms in addition to the original keywords, Boolean operators can be used, such as the search phrase *"bed and breakfast" OR "hotel" OR "lodging" AND Leavenworth AND Washington*.

Variant—or alternate—word forms are another possibility. Try to think of a different spelling or form of your keywords, if your search still doesn't work as desired. For example, *bed and breakfast* could be replaced or supplemented with the variants *bed & breakfast* and *B&B*, and *hand signal* and *hand signaling* are variant word forms for the *hand signals* keywords used in Figure 9-12. Alternative spellings is a form of this strategy, as well.

Another strategy that is sometimes used with keywords is the *wildcard* approach. A wildcard is a special symbol that is used in conjunction with a part of a word to specify the pattern of the terms you want to search for. For instance, the asterisk wildcard (*) is used to represent any number of letters at the asterisk location, so on many sites searching for *hand sign** would search for *hand sign, hand signal, hand signals, hand signaling*, and any other keywords that fit this specific pattern.

Using Field Searches

A more advanced search strategy that can be used when basic searching isn't producing the desired results is *field searching*—a search limited to a particular search characteristic (or *field*), such as the page title, URL, page text, or domain. When a field search is performed, the specific text is searched for only in the specified field (see Figure 9-13 for some examples of field searching along with the results from performing those searches using the AltaVista search site). Many, but not all, search engines support some type of field searches. Check the search tips for the particular search site you are using to see if it has that option.

N
E
T

TIP

For more searching tips, see the "Web Searching Tips" section of the References and Resources Guide located at the end of this book.

SEARCH PHRASE USED	NUMBER OF PAGES FOUND	TITLE OF FIRST TWO PAGES FOUND	PAGE URL
title:"tax tips" (searches for Web pages containing "tax tips" in the page title)	7,014	UK Tax Tips Roger Kahan Tax Tips and Facts	www.ietaxguard.co.uk/uk-tax-tips.htm www.rak-1.com
url:taxtips (searches for Web pages containing "taxtips" in the page URL)	3,846	J A McNicholl & Co Tax Tips Table of Contents	www.mcnicholl.net/pages/taxtips.html www.fiorillo.com/Taxtips.htm
text:"tax tips" (searches for Web pages containing "tax tips" in the text of the page)	53,802	Yahoo! Tax Center IRS.gov Home	taxes.yahoo.com www.irs.gov
domain:gov (searches for Web pages located on government Web servers—domain ends in ".gov")	6,812,702	FirstGov – The U.S. Government's Official Web Portal National Science Foundation (NSF) - Home Page	www.firstgov.gov www.nsf.gov
title:"tax tips" domain:gov (searches for Web pages containing "tax tips" in the page title located on government Web servers—domain ends in ".gov")	5	CBA Consumer Tax Tips - California Department Of Consumer Affairs TAX TIPS	www.dca.ca.gov/press_releases/2003/taxtips.htm www.yorkcounty.gov/revenue/taxtips.htm

> **FIGURE 9-13**
> **Field searching.** Field searches limit search results to just those pages with a specific Web page title, URL, text, or top-level domain.

> **FIGURE 9-14**
> **Evaluating search results.** Before using information obtained from a Web page, use the following criteria to evaluate its accuracy and appropriateness.

Evaluating Search Results

Once a list of potentially matching Web sites is returned as a result of a search, it is time to evaluate the sites to determine their quality and potential for meeting your needs. Two things to look for before clicking on a link for a matching page are:

▼ Does the title and listed description sound appropriate for the information you are seeking?

▼ Is the URL from an appropriate company or organization? For example, if you want technical specifications about a particular product, you may want to start with information on the manufacturer's Web site. If you are looking for government publications, stick with government Web sites.

After an appropriate Web page is found, the evaluation process is still not complete. If you are using the information on the page for something other than idle curiosity, you want to be sure the information can be trusted. Some general guidelines are listed in Figure 9-14.

Evaluate the source.	Information from the company or organization in question is generally more reliable than information found on an individual's Web site. Government and educational institutions are usually good sources for historical or research data. If you clicked a link on a Web page to open a document, double-check the URL to make sure you still know what organization the page is from—it may be located on a completely different Web site than the page from which it was accessed.
Evaluate the author.	Does the author have the appropriate qualifications for the information in question? Does he or she have a bias or is the information supposed to be objective?
Check the timeliness of the information.	Web page content may be updated regularly or posted once and forgotten. Always look for the publication date on online newspaper and magazine articles; check for a "last updated" date on pages containing other types of information you'd like to use.
Verify the information.	When you will be using Web-based information in a report, paper, Web page, or other document where accuracy is important, try to locate the same information from other reputable Web sources to verify the accuracy of the information you plan to use.

TYPE OF RESOURCE	CITATION EXAMPLE
Web page article (magazine)	Naughton, Keith. (2003, September 29). Chrysler Shifts Gears. *Newsweek*. Retrieved March 13, 2004 from http://www.msnbc.com/news/969677.asp?0dm=s118k.
Web page article (journal)	Mion, L. (2003, May 31). Care Provision for Older Adults: Who Will Provide? *Online Journal of Issues in Nursing*, 8 no. 2. Retrieved March 1, 2004, from http://www.nursingworld.org/ojin/topic21/tpc21_3.htm.
Web page article (not appearing in a periodical)	Sullivan, Bob (2003, September 26). New Arrest in Internet Attacks case. MSNBC. Retrieved February 11, 2004, from http://msnbc.com/news/972467.asp?0dm=C14OT.
Web page content (not an article)	*Biography of Ronald Reagan.* (n.d). Retrieved March 5, 2003 from http://www.whitehouse.gov/history/presidents/rr40.html.
E-mail (cited in text, not reference list)	L.A. Chafez (personal communication, March 28, 2003).

Citing Internet Resources

According to the online version of the Merriam-Webster dictionary, the term *plagiarize* means "to steal and pass off the ideas or words of another as one's own" or to "use another's production without crediting the source." To avoid plagiarizing Web page content, Web pages—as well as any other Internet resources—need to be credited appropriately.

The citation guidelines for Web page content are similar to those for written material. Guidelines for crediting some Internet-based resources are listed next. Different style manuals may have different rules for citing Internet references—the following guidelines were obtained from the American Psychological Association Web site and some examples are listed in Figure 9-15. If in doubt when preparing a research paper, check with your instructor as to the style manual he or she prefers you follow and refer to that guide accordingly.

▼ *Web page article (journal, magazine, etc.).* List the author, date of publication, article title, and periodical information, similar to a print source, and then add a "Retrieved" statement and date with the appropriate URL of the Web page used.

▼ *Web page content (not an article).* List the author (if there is one), date of publication (if available; if not, use *n.d.*), and Web page title, followed by a "Retrieved" statement and date with the appropriate URL of the Web page used.

▼ *E-mail correspondence.* List the sender's name followed by a "personal communication" statement and the date received next to the reference in the text. This reference isn't included in the references section.

FIGURE 9-15
Citing Web sources. It is important to properly credit your Web sources. These examples follow the American Psychological Association citation guidelines.

FURTHER EXPLORATION

For links to further information about citing online references, go to www.course.com/uc10/ch09

BEYOND BROWSING AND E-MAIL

While some of the most common Internet activities are Web browsing and e-mail exchange (both discussed in Chapter 2), as well as searching for specific information (as previously discussed in this chapter), there are a host of other activities that can take place via the Internet. Chapter 8 discussed such applications as online conferencing, telecommuting, and telemedicine. Some additional Web-based applications are discussed next.

Online Financial Transactions

Online financial transactions—a type of *e-commerce*, discussed in greater detail in Chapter 11—are fast-growing Web activities. As more and more people have access to the Web from home and discover the convenience of shopping, banking, stock trading, and so forth on their home PCs, the popularity of performing these types of transactions online is likely to continue to grow. One of the major obstacles to online financial transactions is consumer concern for *online security*; some precautions a user can take are discussed next, followed by a look at some of the most common types of online financial transactions.

Online Security Considerations

Since *online fraud*, *credit card fraud*, and *identity theft* (in which someone gains enough personal information to order products or otherwise pose as another person) are growing problems, it is important to be cautious when participating in online financial activities. To protect yourself, use a credit card whenever possible when purchasing goods or services online so that any fraudulent activities can be disputed, and be sure only to enter your credit card number on a *secure Web page*. To identify a secure Web page, look for a locked padlock or a complete—non-broken—key at the bottom of your Web browser screen, a URL that begins with *https* instead of *http*, or some other indication that a secure server is being used. Secure Web pages should also be used to enter any other type of sensitive information (such as a bank account number or any information that you wouldn't want anyone else to see) and online access to financial accounts should be protected with good user passwords that are changed frequently.

Online Shopping

Online shopping is becoming very popular. With online shopping, products can be purchased directly from large companies—such as L.L. Bean, Dell Computer, Wal-Mart, Amazon.com, and Macy's—via their Web sites, as well as from a growing number of small retailers. Typically, shoppers locate the items they'd like to purchase by searching online retailer sites or browsing through online catalogs, and then adding the items to their online *shopping carts* or *shopping bags*. When a shopper is finished shopping, he or she follows the checkout procedures—such as supplying the appropriate billing and shipping information—to complete the sale (see Figure 9-16). After the payment is processed, the item is either shipped to the customer (if it is a physical product) or the customer is given instructions on how to download it (if it is a software program, electronic book or article, music, or some other product in electronic form).

Today, you can buy items online using any of several different payment methods. The method you use depends on where you shop. While most online stores accept credit cards, other options may or may not be allowed. Some possible payment methods are listed next (most are also discussed in more detail in Chapter 11).

▼ *Credit card.* You can usually pay for online purchases with a credit card just as you can when buying goods or services in person or over the phone. For online purchases, the credit card number is validated and the charge approved during the checkout process. On secure sites, your credit card data is encrypted (electronically scrambled) when it is sent, so it can't be intercepted by a third party. It is becoming increasingly common for credit card companies to also offer their customers one-time use *virtual credit card numbers* that can be used one time to charge an item to the customer's credit card, but are unusable for additional purchases. Typically, the customer obtains a virtual number online immediately prior to the online purchase.

▼ *Payment services.* Payment services, such as *PayPal*, enable individuals to exchange money via the Internet using their e-mail addresses. To send money, the individual needs to set up an account with an online payment service (such as PayPal), supplying the online payment service with the necessary information (such as a credit card or checking account number) and obtaining a user name and password. Typically, the individual either transfers money into the account before a purchase or sets up the account to automatically use a specified credit card or checking account when money is needed for transfers. The individual can then authorize the payment service to pay a participating merchant or individual a specific amount whenever needed. The recipient

>**Online shopping.** Buying products or services over the Internet.

ONLINE CATALOG
Contains pricing and descriptions of items for sale online; as items are selected, they are moved to an online shopping cart.

Can select a different section of the online catalog here.

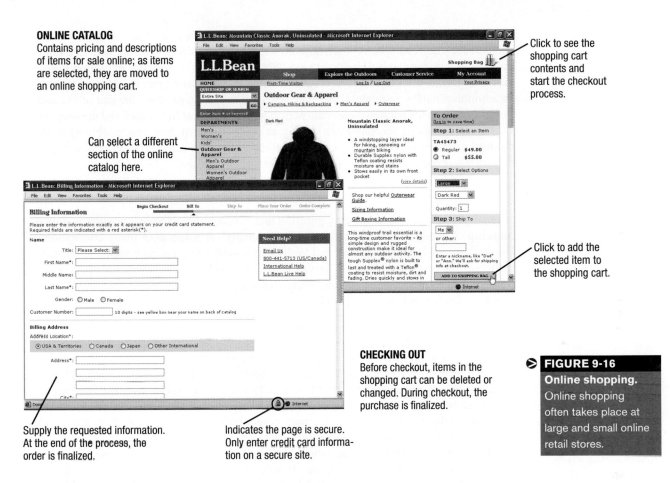

Click to see the shopping cart contents and start the checkout process.

Click to add the selected item to the shopping cart.

Supply the requested information. At the end of the process, the order is finalized.

Indicates the page is secure. Only enter credit card information on a secure site.

CHECKING OUT
Before checkout, items in the shopping cart can be deleted or changed. During checkout, the purchase is finalized.

> **FIGURE 9-16**
> **Online shopping.**
> Online shopping often takes place at large and small online retail stores.

is typically notified by e-mail that a payment has been received and then can retrieve the money via the payment services Web site. Some services require both parties to have payment services accounts; others require only the sender to have an account.

▼ *Smart card*. Smart cards containing a prepaid amount of money can be used like a debit card for online purchases. Many individuals feel more secure using a smart card instead of a credit card over the Internet because of the limited amount of spending power available on it, as opposed to a credit card. As discussed in Chapter 4, smart cards are inserted into a smart card reader to be used. Because of the proliferation of online shopping, some new keyboards and cell phones include a built-in smart card reader; external smart card readers are also available.

▼ *Conventional payment*. Some online merchants realize that consumers are wary of conducting business over the Internet and allow buyers to pay by conventional means. If this option is available on a site, it will usually appear on a checkout page, in the form of an option to request a representative to phone you to arrange payment by check or credit card, or there may be a toll-free phone number that can be used to place your order instead of using the online order form.

Online Auctions
Online auctions are the most common way to buy items online from other individuals. Sellers list items for sale on an auction site (such as eBay or Yahoo! Auctions) by paying a

>**Online auction.** An online activity for which bids are placed on items and the highest bidder purchases the item.

small listing fee and entering a description of the item and a length of time that the auction should run. They can specify a starting bid amount (that bidders see), as well as a minimum selling price (that bidders don't see—they just are told if there is a minimum selling price and if their bid has met or exceeded that price) that must be met in order for there to be a winning bidder. Individuals can enter bids on auction items until the end of the auction. At the time the auction closes, the person with the highest bid is declared the successful bidder (provided the minimum selling price was met, if one was established) and arranges payment and delivery for the item directly with the seller. The seller also pays a percentage of the sale price as a commission to the auction site.

Online Banking

A relatively new online financial application that is becoming extremely popular is **online banking**. Although it used to be available separately for a fee, now many conventional banks—such as Bank of America and Wells Fargo—offer free online banking services to their customers. Online banking services typically include reviewing account activity, sending electronic payments, transferring funds between accounts, and checking your credit card balances (see Figure 9-17).

Online Investing

Buying and selling stocks, bonds, and other types of securities is referred to as **online investing**. Although it is common to see stock quote capabilities on many search and news sites, trading stocks and other securities usually requires an *online broker*. The biggest advantage for using an online broker is the low transaction fee—often just $7 to $15 per trade, generally much less expensive than comparable offline services. It is also much more convenient for those investors who do a lot of trading.

Once an online brokerage account is set up, you can place stock buy and sell orders just as you would with an offline broker. Usually the history of your orders can be viewed online and open orders can be cancelled before they are executed, if desired. Many brokerage and financial sites also have convenient access to a variety of performance history, corporate news, and other useful information for investors. In addition, most online brokers allow you to set up an *online portfolio* that displays the status of the stocks you specify. On some sites, stock price data is delayed 20 minutes; on other sites, real-time quotes are available. Unless the quote or page is automatically refreshed for you on a regular basis, such as with a *Java applet* like the one shown in Figure 9-17, you must reload the Web page (using your browser's Refresh or Reload toolbar button) whenever you want to see updated quotes.

Online Entertainment

There are an ever-growing number of ways to use the Web for entertainment purposes, such as listening to music, watching videos, and playing online games. Some online entertainment options—such as listening to music and watching online videos—require a special media player program. Some common media players are *Windows Media Player*, *RealOne Player*, *WinAmp*, and *MusicMatch Jukebox* for Windows PCs; *RealOne Player* and *iTunes* are commonly used with Apple computers. All of these players are available as free downloads, although many have an optional fee-based service for premium Internet radio broadcasts. Some multimedia applications can be accessed with virtually any type of Internet connection; others require a broadband connection.

>**Online banking.** Performing banking activities over the Internet. >**Online investing.** Buying and selling stocks or other types of investments over the Internet.

ONLINE BANKING
Typically allows you to check your account balances, make electronic payments, view your transaction history, and more.

Click to switch to the Bill Pay or Transfer Funds options.

Click to change account or type of information displayed.

Checking account summary information is displayed here.

Click these options to get stock quotes, charts, news, and other information.

This portfolio uses a Java applet to continually update the quotes in real time.

Enter buy or sell information here to make a trade.

ONLINE INVESTING
Typically allows you to buy and sell stocks, view your portfolio, get real-time quotes, and more.

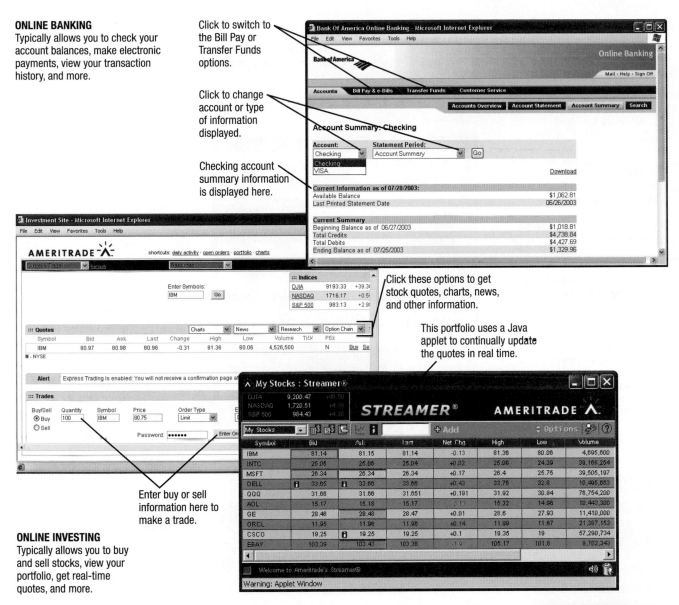

❯ **FIGURE 9-17**
Online banking and investing.

Online Music

Online music is perhaps one of the hottest Web-based entertainment activities today. Some of the most widely used possibilities are listening to online radio broadcasts and downloading songs to be played later on your PC or portable digital music player (such as an MP3 player). Online radio is broadcast from *online radio stations*, also called *Internet radio stations*. To listen to an Internet radio station, you typically open that Web page in your browser and click an appropriate hyperlink (see Figure 9-18). You will then begin to hear the broadcast via a media player program installed on your PC or a proprietary player that will open automatically. Many media players also have a tool to help you save your favorite radio stations in a list, so you can choose your desired radio station using the player's interface.

Although other formats are possible, most downloaded music is compressed using MP3 file compression to reduce its file size from about 10 MB per minute to less than 1 MB per minute, without a noticeable reduction in quality. To avoid copyright violations, all

>**Online music.** Music played or obtained via the Internet.

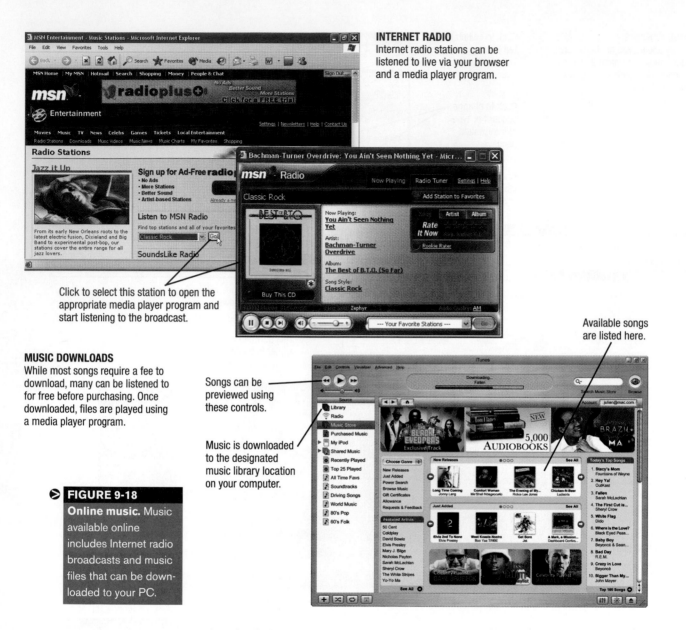

INTERNET RADIO
Internet radio stations can be listened to live via your browser and a media player program.

Click to select this station to open the appropriate media player program and start listening to the broadcast.

MUSIC DOWNLOADS
While most songs require a fee to download, many can be listened to for free before purchasing. Once downloaded, files are played using a media player program.

Songs can be previewed using these controls.

Music is downloaded to the designated music library location on your computer.

Available songs are listed here.

FIGURE 9-18

Online music. Music available online includes Internet radio broadcasts and music files that can be downloaded to your PC.

downloaded music should either be specified as free downloads (sometimes found on sites featuring new artists, for example) or the site should charge an appropriate fee (for royalties owed to the artist or record studio) for the download. Once downloaded, music files can be played from your PC's hard drive using a media player program installed on your PC. Provided the download agreement didn't preclude it, music files can also be copied to a CD to create a custom music CD (making a custom music CD was illustrated in the Chapter 7 How it Works box) or transferred to an MP3 player. For instance, the *iTunes Music Store* shown in the bottom part of Figure 9-18 allows both Mac and PC users to browse through over 200,000 songs, preview songs for free, and then download the ones they like for 99 cents each. Once downloaded, the songs can legally be played on up to three computers, transferred to a digital music player, and burned on an unlimited number of personal music CDs. Other sites, such as RealOne Rhapsody and MusicMatch Jukebox, offer similar services.

For a look at the controversy over the rights to distribute music via the Internet that has heated up since the introduction of the *Napster* file-sharing service in 1999, see the Inside the Industry box.

INSIDE THE INDUSTRY

The Napster Controversy

Chances are you've heard of Napster, a music-sharing service. It's been in the news the last several years because of lawsuits filed against it by the recording industry. Just in case you're not familiar with it, Napster was a file-sharing service for music. Its Web site didn't host any music files; instead, a user would log on to the service and would be put in touch (automatically, via the Napster software) with other online users who had the song (usually an MP3 file) on their PCs that the user was looking for. After being presented with a list of users, their connection speeds, and their reliability ratings, the user looking for the music file would select a host user and begin downloading the file from that individual's computer.

Because, theoretically, one user could rip a song from his or her CD and share it with an unlimited number of users via a music sharing service such as Napster, it's not surprising that the recording industry was not overjoyed by Napster's immense popularity. In fact Napster, as well as MP3.com and other sites involved with digital music downloads, have been the subject of a blizzard of lawsuits. Napster was eventually disbanded (although it reappeared in late 2003 as a legitimate service called *Napster 2.0* created by Roxio, the software company that purchased the Napster name in 2002), but other peer-to-peer sites remain and the controversy surrounding downloads of digital music and movies continues.

With the sale of CDs continuing to slip dramatically—most estimates place sales decreasing by roughly 60 million CDs during the past two years—the music industry has begun to take on the end user. Federal subpoenas have been issued to individuals suspected of sharing substantial amounts of copyright-protected material over peer-to-peer networks, and with fines for copyright infringement running as high as $150,000 per item, the upcoming suits are getting a great deal of attention. The hope of the music industry is that illegal peer-to-peer music file sharing will eventually be replaced by legitimate music download sites, such as Apple iTunes Music Store, RealOne Rhapsody, MusicMatch Jukebox, and Napster 2.0. With the risk of accidentally downloading spyware, a computer virus, or a corrupted file when downloading a file from another person's PC, plus the threat of prosecution, many peer-to-peer users may consider it worth their while to pay the roughly $1 per song for music downloads from a legitimate site instead of using a peer-to-peer service to obtain the song illegally.

That isn't to say that peer-to-peer file exchanges will become obsolete, however. Many expect the peer-to-peer model to continue to thrive, but with a different focus—for example, being used for legal music distribution or for facilitating document file sharing within a business. With at least 10 new Internet-based music services in the works and music downloads and subscription expected to hit nearly $300 million by the end of 2004, it looks like digital music is here to stay.

Online TV and Videos

Growing more slowly than online music, but still expected to be a significant entertainment option in the future, are television shows, movies, and video clips delivered through the Internet (see Figure 9-19). Some options at the present time are news clips, movie trailers, music videos, taped interviews, and similar short, prerecorded videos. These clips are usually found on Web sites dedicated to providing multimedia Web content; links to video clips are also widely found on news and entertainment sites. A few live online TV or video broadcasts exist, but they are fairly rare at the present time. Online video applications are expected to become much more common in the future as high-speed Internet use continues to grow and the convergence of television, computer, and Internet capabilities continues. Two emerging applications with a lot of potential are *interactive TV* and *video-on-demand*.

Interactive TV (*iTV*) allows the user to perform interactive activities during a television broadcast. Today, many interactive TV shows require the use of some type of set-top box, such as the ones used for cable or satellite television services. In fact, the

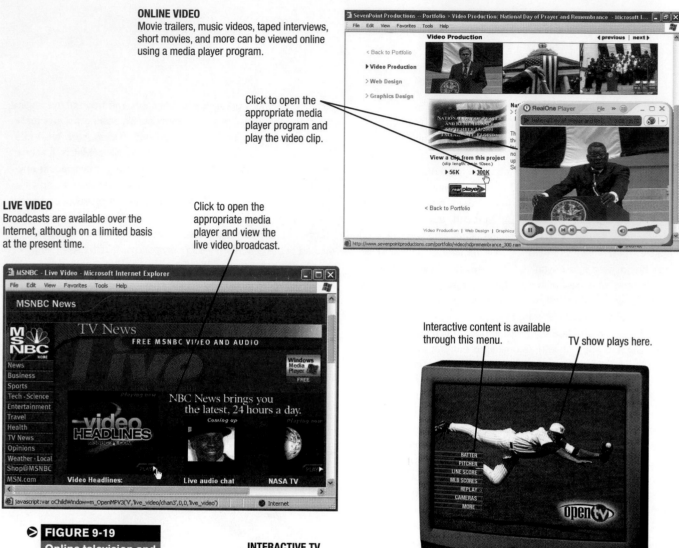

ONLINE VIDEO
Movie trailers, music videos, taped interviews, short movies, and more can be viewed online using a media player program.

Click to open the appropriate media player program and play the video clip.

LIVE VIDEO
Broadcasts are available over the Internet, although on a limited basis at the present time.

Click to open the appropriate media player and view the live video broadcast.

Interactive content is available through this menu.

TV show plays here.

INTERACTIVE TV
Brings the Web and broadcast television viewing together to make TV an interactive experience.

> **FIGURE 9-19**
> **Online television and videos.** Online video possibilities include viewing video clips, live video broadcasts, and interactive TV.

most common way of receiving iTV in the United States today is through a cable or satellite TV provider.

Video-on-demand (*VOD*) allows users to order movies and television shows, which are then typically sent to their PCs or *digital video recorder* (*DVR*). DVRs are similar to VCRs, but recordings are stored on a hard drive instead of on videotape. Because a hard drive is a direct-access medium (where data at any location on the drive can be immediately retrieved, like a CD or DVD) instead of a sequential-access medium (where data is stored and retrieved in a linear fashion, like a videotape), recorded shows can be located and played more easily. With video-on-demand, a portion of the movie usually downloads first, and then the movie can be played while the rest of the movie finishes downloading. This type of delivery—called *streaming media*—is commonly used with both audio and video distributed over the Internet to reduce the time needed to begin to view or hear the selection.

Today, video-on-demand is available primarily to cable and satellite TV subscribers in specific areas in a limited number of countries, but many predict the ability for virtually anyone to order video-on-demand through an Internet connection will be available in the near future. Available services include *Movielink* (sponsored by five Hollywood movie studios) and the privately owned *CinemaNow* and *MovieBeam*. Some movies are streamed from the server and must be watched in real time immediately after they begin playing; others are in downloadable form. Downloadable movies are typically "pay-per-view" movies that can only be viewed within a limited time period, such as within 24 hours after activation; at the end of that time, the movie becomes unusable. Other movies may be included in a monthly subscription fee and can be watched as many times as desired, as long as the viewer is an active subscriber. For a closer look at how video-on-demand works, see the How it Works box.

The increased use of broadband Internet, DVRs, and now video-on-demand has increased concerns about exchanging pirated copies of movies via the Internet. Some movies even make it on the Internet before they are released in theaters, such as the illegal copies of *The Hulk* which were uploaded to the Internet two weeks before the movie's release. And within just a few days of the theater release of *The Matrix Reloaded*, it is estimated that 200,000 people had downloaded or viewed the movie illegally via the Internet. The increased use of DVRs and the ability of some new digital video recorders to transmit recorded shows over the Internet to other compatible devices have fueled the ongoing controversy regarding the Internet being used for illegal distribution of copyrighted content. Just as with the music industry, the movie industry is looking into ways of fulfilling consumer demands for digital movie distribution balanced with copyright protection.

Online Gaming

Online gaming refers to games played over the Internet. Many sites—especially children's Web sites—include games for visitors to play. There are also sites whose sole purpose is hosting games that can be played online. Some of the games, such as Solitaire, are designed to be played alone. Other *multiplayer* games, such as Hearts, Backgammon, and Quake, can be played online against other online gamers. The Backgammon game featured in Figure 9-20 can be played free of charge without special software; other games (such as Quake) require you to have that program installed on your PC. Some gaming sites may offer additional premium games that are only available to paid subscribers. Online

> **FIGURE 9-20**
> **Online gaming.** Many online games are multiplayer games that are played against other gamers that are online at the moment.

N
E
T

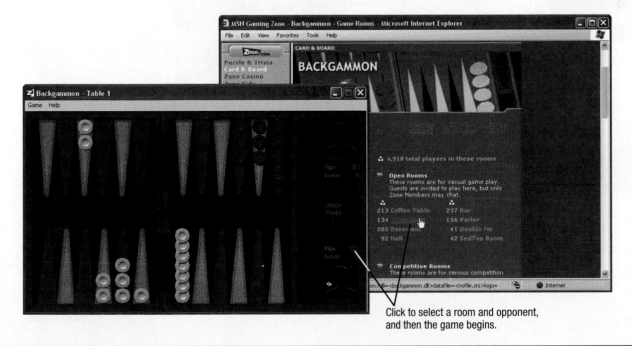

Click to select a room and opponent, and then the game begins.

>**Online gaming.** Playing games over the Internet.

HOW IT WORKS

Video-on-Demand

Most video-on-demand (VOD) services feature movie catalogs to help users find the movies they'd like to see (see Step 1 in the accompanying illustration). Depending on the site, all movies may be the same price, some movies could be included in a monthly fee, or the fees could vary from movie to movie. As movies are selected, they are typically placed in a shopping cart and then the transaction finalized after all movies to be downloaded have been selected. Movies are typically downloaded to a PC, although some services allow the movies to be downloaded directly to a DVR device, provided that the proper connections are in place. Regardless of where the movie is physically stored, it can be played on a PC monitor or a TV, if the display device is connected to the hard drive containing the movie or is accessible through a home network. Movies can

also be downloaded to notebook and tablet PCs to watch while traveling. Instead of downloading, some movies are available in a streaming format, which means they are watched in real-time when the movie is rented. Streaming video-on-demand is more similar to on-demand television than it is to digital movie rental.

For convenience, many VOD services allow users to download pay-per-view downloadable movies up to a month ahead of time, but once the movie has started to play, it only works for a 24-hour period. To watch the movie again after that point requires an additional fee, although the movie doesn't have to be re-downloaded, unless it was deleted from the user's hard drive. Typical fees for video-on-demand movies are comparable with conventional video rental services—about $3 to $5 each—but they provide end users the convenience of not having to leave their houses to pick up or return the movies, and they get movies faster than services that rent DVDs via regular mail.

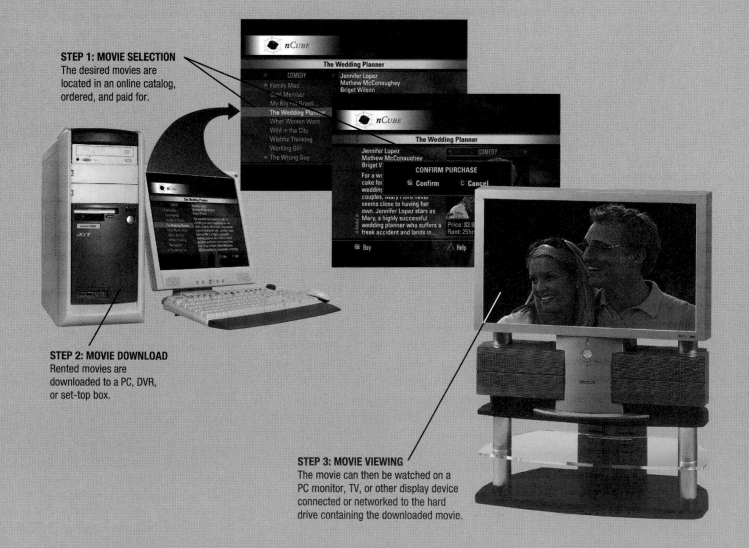

STEP 1: MOVIE SELECTION
The desired movies are located in an online catalog, ordered, and paid for.

STEP 2: MOVIE DOWNLOAD
Rented movies are downloaded to a PC, DVR, or set-top box.

STEP 3: MOVIE VIEWING
The movie can then be watched on a PC monitor, TV, or other display device connected or networked to the hard drive containing the downloaded movie.

multiplayer games are especially popular in countries, such as South Korea, with high levels of both high-speed Internet installations and Internet use in general. It has been estimated that about 70% of the homes in South Korea have broadband Internet access and a Korean online gaming network is the world's largest with over 3 million paid subscribers.

Online gaming is also involved quite often in *Internet addiction*—the inability to stop using the Internet or extensive use of the Internet interfering with other aspects of one's life. Internet addiction is a growing concern and is discussed in more detail in Chapter 16.

E-Books

E-books or *online books* are plentiful. From the entire works of Shakespeare to new best sellers, thousands of books can be read online or downloaded (see Figure 9-21). There are online libraries that host online books (many in HTML format so they can be displayed using a Web browser), and online bookstores where e-books can be purchased and downloaded. E-books are most commonly viewed using a handheld PC, but they can be viewed on a variety of other devices including desktop PCs and special devices designed for reading e-books. Depending on the format, one of several free e-book reader programs (such as *Microsoft Reader*, *Adobe Reader*, or *Palm Reader*) can be used to view e-books.

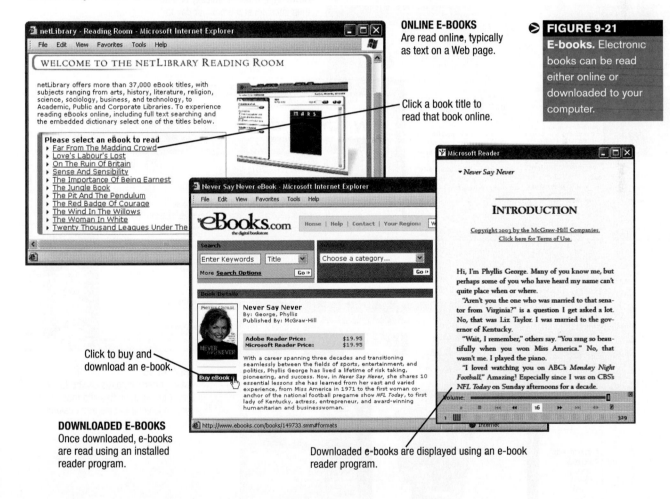

ONLINE E-BOOKS
Are read online, typically as text on a Web page.

Click a book title to read that book online.

FIGURE 9-21
E-books. Electronic books can be read either online or downloaded to your computer.

Click to buy and download an e-book.

DOWNLOADED E-BOOKS
Once downloaded, e-books are read using an installed reader program.

Downloaded e-books are displayed using an e-book reader program.

>**E-book.** A book obtained in electronic format.

Online News and Research

There is an abundance of news and research information available through the Internet. The following sections discuss a few of these resources.

News

Nearly every news organization continually updates its Web site to post current news (see Figure 9-22). Many also have searchable archives to look for past articles, although some newspaper and journal sites require a fee to view back articles. In addition to printed news, some news radio programs are broadcast over the Internet, similar to the music Internet radio station illustrated in Figure 9-18.

Reference

There are a number of *reference sites* on the Web, such as those used to generate maps, check the weather forecast, or provide access to encyclopedias, dictionaries, ZIP code

> **FIGURE 9-22**
>
> **News and research.**
> Up-to-the-minute news, reference tools, product information, and more abound on the Web.

NEWS
News organizations typically update their sites several times per day to provide access to the most current news and information.

REFERENCE
Many reference sites can be found on the Web, such as this site that enables you to look up people and businesses in an online telephone book.

PRODUCT INFORMATION
The Web is a good location for finding specifications, instruction manuals, and other types of product information.

directories, telephone directories (see Figure 9-22), and more. To find an appropriate reference site, type the information you are seeking (such as *ZIP code lookup* or *topographical map*) as keywords in a search site.

Portals

Links to news and reference tools are also found on **portal** pages—Web pages that include a variety of useful content (search and reference tools, news, weather, e-mail, calendars, stock quotes, and more) in hopes of enticing visitors to use the site as their browser's home page and return to the portal several times a day. Portal pages typically allow users to customize the page to display the news of their choice, such as sports, technology, weather, and national or local news so this information will be displayed each time the user visits the portal page. Popular portals include Yahoo!, AltaVista, MSN, AOL, and Bolt (the Yahoo! portal page was shown in Figure 9-11).

Product and Corporate Information

The Web is a very useful tool for locating product and corporate information. Before buying an item online (or in a conventional *brick-and-mortar store*, for that matter), many people research product options online. By going to manufacturers' Web sites, as in Figure 9-22, specifications can be viewed or downloaded; you can sometimes also obtain special offers, rebate forms, and instruction manuals online.

Investors frequently wish to research companies before making an investment decision. As mentioned in an earlier section, many brokerage sites contain links to corporate information. There are also separate sites that specialize in providing this type of information. Depending on the site, some or all of the information may be available free of charge. For example, the popular Hoover's Online site located at hoovers.com allows you to view company summaries (called *capsules*) free of charge, but requires a fee for more in-depth information.

Government Information

Government information is widely available on the Internet. Most state and federal agencies have Web sites to provide information to citizens, such as government publications, archived documents, forms, legislative bills, and so forth. You can also perform such tasks as downloading tax forms and filing your tax returns online—some cities and states allow you to pay your car registration, register to vote, or update your driver's license online, as well.

Online Education

Online education—using the Internet to facilitate learning—is a rapidly growing Internet application. The Internet can be used to deliver part or all of any educational class or program, such as in *Web-based training* (*WBT*) and *distance learning*; it can also be used to supplement or support traditional education, such as with *online testing* and *online writing*. In addition, many high school and college courses use Web content—such as online syllabi, schedules, chat rooms, discussion boards, study guides, and tutorials—as required or suggested supplements. For example, the Web site that accompanies this book contains an online study guide, online interactive labs, and other resources for students taking a course that uses this textbook. The next few sections take a look at some of the most widely used online education applications.

Web-Based Training and Distance Learning

There are more opportunities for Web-based learning today than ever before. Both businesses and schools commonly utilize Web-based training (WBT) for employee training or course materials and millions of people take classes via **distance learning** each year. With distance learning, students take classes from a location that is different from where the delivery of instruction takes place—for instance, from home or work. Distance learning (also called *online learning* and *e-learning*) is available through many colleges and universities; it is also used for corporate education and training. Distance learning can be used to train employees in just one task or new skill, as well as for an entire college course or degree program.

Typically the majority of distance learning coursework is completed over the Internet via class Web pages, discussion groups, chat rooms, and e-mail, although schools may require some in-person contact for credit courses, such as for orientation and testing. Instructors may develop their own course content, but it is becoming increasingly common for an online course environment to be available from an e-learning provider, such as the WebCT example shown in Figure 9-23. Distance learning classes often utilize Web-based training components.

Web-based training and distance learning are typically experienced individually and at the user's own pace. Online content for Web-based training components is frequently customized for each individual user, based on his or her mastery of the material already completed. Online content and activities (such as exercises, exams, and animations) are accessed in real-time, just as other Web pages are. Some advantages of Web-based training and distance learning include the following:

▼ *Self-paced instruction.* Students can usually work at their own pace and at their convenience, any time of day or night.

▼ *Flexible location.* Students do not need to live close to any particular facility to take part in the educational program. Web-based training can be accessed from home, while traveling, or basically anywhere the student has access to a computer with an Internet connection.

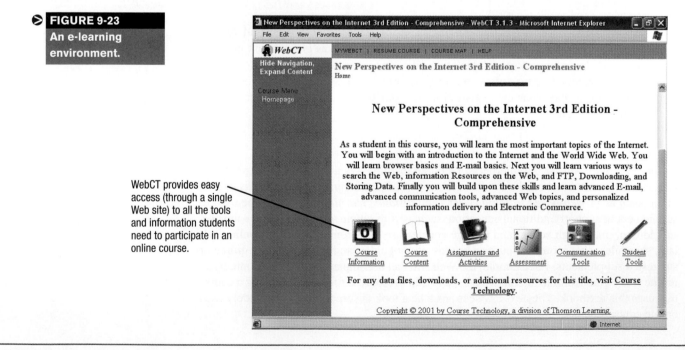

FIGURE 9-23
An e-learning environment.

WebCT provides easy access (through a single Web site) to all the tools and information students need to participate in an online course.

>**Distance learning.** A learning environment in which the student is physically located away from the instructor and other students; commonly instruction and communications take place via the Internet.

▼ *Up-to-date material.* Since all instructional material is hosted on a Web server, it can be updated whenever necessary simply by updating the server's content. Once updated, all users will see the newest version of the instructional material the next time they access the Web site.

▼ *Immediate feedback and customized content.* Web-based training components can be set up to provide immediate feedback for exercises, practice tests, simulations, and other online activities. The feedback can include automatically displaying supplementary material for any problem areas that are identified based on the user's responses. It can also require mastery of material before the student is allowed to move on to the next test or assignment, and can jump students to more advanced topics as appropriate. This flexibility can result in highly customized content, based on a student's progress and abilities.

While the advantages of Web-based training and distance learning are numerous, potential disadvantages include the following:

▼ *Technology requirements and problems.* In order to participate in Web-based training or distance learning, users must have access to a computer and the Internet. Slow PCs or Internet connections can be frustrating for students as they try to download materials or participate in online discussions. Technological problems—such as a computer crashing or Web server inaccessibility during a test day—can create significant problems for students and instructors.

▼ *Anonymity.* Because students are in remote locations, it can be difficult to ensure it is the actual student who is participating in online discussions and online exams. Some instructors choose to require face-to-face exams either at the school or an authorized testing center in the student's geographical area; newer authentication technology, such as smart cards, fingerprint scanners, and digital signatures, may help to alleviate this problem.

▼ *Lack of face-to-face contact.* Many educators view the interactive exchange of ideas as a very important part of the educational experience. Although interactivity can take place online via chat rooms and discussion groups, the lack of face-to-face contact for students to see, ask questions of, or have discussions with other students and their instructor is cited as a disadvantage by some educators.

Online Testing

In addition to being used with many distance learning classes, *online testing*, where students take quizzes or tests via the Internet, is also a growing trend. For large enrollment classes, online testing can make frequent, impromptu quizzes feasible, since they can be taken quickly via handheld PCs (either owned by the students or supplied to the students as they enter the lecture hall) and graded automatically for immediate feedback for both the students and the instructor. Objective tests (such as those containing multiple choice or true/false questions) and performance-based exams (such as those given in computer classes to test student mastery of software applications) can also be taken online. Typically these types of tests are automatically graded, freeing up instructor time for other activities, as well as providing faster feedback to the students. Some schools are even experimenting with giving final examinations via an online chat room. According to one instructor using this testing method in an International Business course, asking approximately three main questions during a 30-minute chat room final exam is sufficient to evaluate the student's understanding of the course material. In addition, this instructor states that this type of online testing has the added benefit of being able to interact with the student to ask follow-up questions or redirect the student if he or she is off track to more thoroughly evaluate the student's mastery of the material than is possible with a written exam.

NET

Online Writing

Online writing used in an educational setting today includes *blogs* and *wikis*, as well as *e-portfolios* (*electronic portfolios*).

Blog and Wikis

A **blog**—also called a *Web log*—is a Web page that contains short, frequently updated entries in chronological order. A blog is most often used as a personal journal for an individual, but can also be set up to have multiple authors—such as a group of employees collaborating on a project or all the students in a particular writing class. Blogs have been around for several years but couldn't be implemented on a wide scale because creating and publishing Web pages was fairly complicated. Today's new blogging tools and services make updating a blog as easy as typing in a new entry on a form and pressing a Publish or Submit button. Consequently, blog use is now on the rise. Today, blogs are used to express personal opinions on a variety of subjects, for work-related collaborations, and in conjunction with high school and college classes.

Originally used primarily in journalism and other types of writing classes, blogs are now used in a wide range of classes. For example, individual blogs can be used as electronic journals for writing or science classes, and group blogs can be used as a discussion medium or collaborative tool in practically any type of course. Blogs can be created and updated using a blogging site, such as the popular Blogger.com site (now owned by Google) which has over 1 million registered users. Some schools set up blogs on the school's Web site for the entire school to use; blogs also appear on course-specific sites, for course-specific blogs (see Figure 9-24).

Related to a blog is a *wiki*. From the Hawaiian phrase "wiki wiki" meaning "quick", a wiki is a way of creating and editing collaborative Web pages very quickly and easily. Once a wiki page has been selected (usually from a directory or by performing a search), the content on that page can be edited and republished to the Web. Similar to a blog, the page is republished just by pressing a Save or Submit button, but whereas a blog contribution is added to the existing content (and doesn't modify the previous content on that blog), any content posted to a wiki can be edited by anyone. In a nutshell, blogs are designed for primarily one-way running communications, while wikis are Web pages intended to be modified by others. In an educational setting, wikis can be used to easily create and access a shared workspace, such as for collaborating on a group or class project. They can also be used to easily create and publish Web pages for class projects or presentations. To protect the content of a wiki from sabotage, editing privileges can be password protected.

E-Portfolios

Student portfolios have been common in some educational programs—such as education and art—for many years. An **e-portfolio**, also called an *electronic portfolio* or *Webfolio*, is a collection of an individual's work accessible through a Web site. Today's e-portfolios are typically linked to a collection of student-related information, such as assessments, résumés, papers, projects, and other original works. For assessment purposes, the e-portfolio can be tied to a predetermined set of professional principles or standards, such as those required by a particular program or state. Some e-portfolios are used for just a single course; others are designed to be used and updated throughout a student's educational program, culminating in a comprehensive collection of information that can be used as a job-hunting tool, as well as an ongoing portfolio for professions commonly utilizing continuing education, such as teaching. An example of a student e-portfolio is shown in Figure 9-24.

>**Blog.** A Web page that contains short, frequently updated entries in chronological order, typically by just one individual; also called a *Web log*.
>**E-portfolio.** A collection of an individual's work accessible through a Web site.

BLOGS
Educational blogs can be course-specific (left) or intended for an entire school or program (below).

E-PORTFOLIOS
E-portfolios are a requirement in many educational programs today.

> **FIGURE 9-24**
> **Online writing tools.**
> Blogs and e-portfolios are writing tools commonly used in education today.

Peer-to-Peer File Sharing

One of the earliest widespread applications of *peer-to-peer file sharing*—sharing resources directly between users via the Internet—was Napster, the music-sharing service discussed in the Inside the Industry box. Unlike MP3.com and other Web sites that provided MP3 downloads, when a music file was downloaded using Napster, it wasn't downloaded from the Napster site's server; it was downloaded from another Napster user—from one peer to another.

Although the original Napster file sharing was shut down, peer-to-peer file sharing remains. Some services were shut down or are being legally pursued by the music and film industries for facilitating the illegal transfer of copyright-protected works; other peer-to-peer services are emerging in a legal environment. Many industry insiders believe peer-to-peer computing will have tremendous growth in the next few years. Companies such as CenterSpan, Intel, and Hewlett-Packard among others have joined the *Peer-to-Peer Working Group*, a consortium to create universal standards for peer-to-peer technologies.

CENSORSHIP AND PRIVACY ISSUES

There are many important societal issues related to the Internet. One—computer security—was touched on in Chapter 8. Two other important issues—*censorship* and *privacy*—are discussed next, in the context of Internet use. These and other societal issues and how they relate to computer use in general are discussed in further detail in Chapters 15 and 16.

Censorship

The First Amendment to the U.S. Constitution guarantees a citizen's right to free speech. This protection allows people to say or show things to others without fear of arrest. People must observe some limits to free speech, of course, such as the prohibition of obscenity over the public airwaves and of child pornography.

But how does the right to free speech relate to alleged patently offensive or indecent materials on the Internet, where they can be observed by children and the public at large? There have been some attempts at Internet content regulation—what some would view as *censorship*—in recent years, but the courts have had difficulty defining what is "patently offensive" and "indecent" as well as finding a fair balance between protection and censorship. For example, the *Communications Decency Act* was signed into law in 1996 and made it a criminal offense to distribute patently indecent or offensive material online. Although intended to protect children from being exposed to inappropriate Web content, the Supreme Court, in 1997, declared this law unconstitutional on the basis of free speech. The *Children's Online Privacy Protection Act of 1998*, which regulates how Web sites can collect information from minors and provides tax incentives for Web sites and ISPs that facilitate protecting minors from accessing materials deemed harmful to them, is one example of legislation that has held up under scrutiny. Another hotly debated law is the *Child Internet Protection Act* (*CIPA*) that went into effect in 2001 and required public libraries and schools to use *Internet filtering* to block Internet access to certain materials in order to receive public funds. Although intended to protect children, it was fought strenuously by free speech advocacy groups and some library associations and was ruled unconstitutional by a federal court in 2002. In a 6 to 3 ruling in 2003, however, the Supreme Court reversed the lower court decision and ruled that the law was constitutional because the need for libraries to prevent minors from accessing obscene materials outweighs the free speech rights of library patrons and Web site publishers.

Internet filtering—blocking access to particular Web pages or types of Web pages—can be used by individuals for their home computers (such as by individuals to protect themselves from material they would view as offensive or by parents to protect their children from material they feel is inappropriate). It is also commonly used by employers to try to keep non-work-related material out of the workplace, by some ISPs and search sites to block access to potentially objectionable materials, and by many schools and libraries. Available through both browser settings (see Figure 9-25) and stand-alone programs, Internet filtering typically restricts access to Web pages that contain specified keywords or that exceed a rating for potentially offensive categories, such as language, nudity, sex, or violence (the descriptions of the site and how these categories apply to its content are provided voluntarily by the content provider, not by an independent rating organization).

Web Browsing Privacy

Privacy, as it relates to the Internet, deals with what information about individuals is available, how it is used, and by whom. As more and more transactions and daily activities are being performed online, there is the potential for vast amounts of private information to be collected and distributed without the individual's knowledge or permission, if appropriate precautions are not taken. Thus, it is understandable that more public concern than ever exists regarding privacy and the Internet. Although privacy will be discussed in more detail in Chapter 15, a few issues that are of special concern to Internet users regarding Web browsing privacy and e-mail privacy are discussed in this and the following section.

One area of concern for many individuals who browse the Web on a regular basis is maintaining the *privacy* of where they go and what they do at Web sites. You may wonder: Does anyone keep track of which Web sites I visit, what hyperlinks I click on, how long I

> **Internet filtering.** Using a software program or browser option to block access to particular Web pages or types of Web pages.

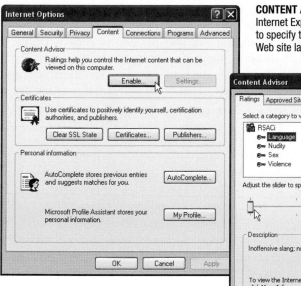

CONTENT ADVISOR
Internet Explorer's Content Advisor can be used to specify the maximum allowable levels of Web site language, nudity, sex, and violence.

> ▶ **FIGURE 9-25**
> **Internet filtering.**
> Browser settings can be changed to deny access to Web pages with objectionable content.

SUPERVISOR PASSWORD
A supervisor password can be used so that unauthorized individuals cannot change the Content Advisor settings.

N
E
T

stay on a Web site, and what things I download and buy? What about the information I provide to a Web site? Can I specify who gets to see it? The answer to each of these questions is "yes" to some extent, but it depends on the specific Web sites visited, the settings on your PC, and what other precautions you have taken to protect your privacy.

Cookies

Many Web pages today use **cookies**—small text files that are stored on your hard drive by a Web server, typically the one belonging to the Web page being viewed—to identify return visitors and their preferences. For example, if you visit Amazon.com and place

---

>**Cookie.** A small file stored on a user's hard drive by a Web server; commonly used to identify personal preferences and settings for that user.

items in your shopping cart, a cookie is sent from the Amazon.com Web server to your hard drive with information that will help the Amazon.com Web site retrieve your shopping cart at a later time. The cookie information can also be used to personalize the Amazon.com Web page based on your shopping preferences the next time you visit. The information stored in a cookie file typically includes the name of the cookie, its expiration date, the domain that the cookie belongs to, and either selected personal information that you have entered while visiting the Web site or an ID number assigned by the Web site that allows the Web site's server to retrieve your information from its database.

The database used in conjunction with a Web site is usually located on the Web site's server and may contain two types of information: *personally identifiable information* (*PII*) and *non-personally identifiable information* (*Non-PII*). Personally identifiable data is connected with a specific user's identity—such as his or her name, address, and credit card number provided to the site—that is typically given during the process of ordering goods or services. Non-personally identifiable information is anonymous data—such as which products were viewed or which advertisements located on the site were clicked—not directly associated with the visitor's name or another personally identifiable characteristic.

Some individuals view all cookies as a potentially dangerous invasion of privacy, but the use of cookies can provide some benefits to consumers. For example, cookies can enable a Web site to remember preferences for customized Web site content (such as displaying your local weather and your horoscope on your portal page), as well as retrieve a shopping cart containing items selected during a previous session, as illustrated in Figure 9-26. Other Web sites may use cookies to remember log-on information, although increasingly operating systems—such as recent versions of Windows—can also keep track of Web site passwords, for those users who prefer not to use cookies for that purpose. Some Web sites may also use cookies for marketing purposes to keep track of which pages on their Web site each person has visited, in order to display advertisements or products on return visits that match his or her interests.

Cookies are relatively safe from a privacy standpoint. Web sites can only read their own cookie files; they can't read other cookie files on your PC or any other data on your computer. A cookie also cannot track activity from one Web site to the next. Cookies are typically stored in a *Cookies* folder on a user's hard drive, and can be viewed—although sometimes deciphering the information contained in a cookie file is difficult. The middle part of Figure 9-26 shows the contents of the cookie file generated by shopping at the BestBuy.com site shown in the top part of Figure 9-26. Notice that the cookie file contains information about both the shopping cart contents and the signed-in user. Cookies can be deleted by the user, either directly from the hard drive or by using a browser option. Browser privacy settings can also be changed to specify which type cookies (if any) are allowed to be used, such as permitting the use of regular cookies, but not *third-party cookies* (cookies placed by companies other than the one related to the Web site the user is currently visiting, such as advertising firms who have placed ads on that page) or cookies using personally identifiable information (see the bottom part of Figure 9-26). *Cookie management software* is also available, and some firewall programs block the use of some cookies.

One of the factors that fueled objections to cookie use involved the practice of trying to track an individual's Web activity by using multiple cookies. The *DoubleClick* Internet advertising firm began this practice several years ago. Because DoubleClick places banner ads on literally thousands of different Web sites, that company was in the unique position of being able to place many cookies on a single user's hard drive—one for each site the user visited that contained a DoubleClick ad. DoubleClick then used all of the DoubleClick cookies located on that user's hard drive to get an idea of his or her overall Web activity. Although the data collected wasn't associated with the person's actual identity, privacy advocates and other individuals were concerned by the fact that the information was collected and analyzed, and then used to determine the most appropriate advertising to be displayed for each user. This issue came even more to the forefront in late 1999 when DoubleClick bought a catalog marketing company and announced plans to combine the previously anonymous consumers' online activity data with the newly acquired marketing company's information in order to track users' Web activity under their

COOKIE USE
Online stores frequently use cookies to remember the contents of your shopping cart (even if you close your browser between sessions) so you can continue shopping at a later time without starting over.

The user's identity and shopping cart contents are remembered when the site is revisited.

Cookie files are typically stored in a Cookies folder on the hard drive.

VIEWING COOKIES
Cookies are stored on the user's hard drive and can be viewed or deleted when desired.

This BestBuy.com cookie contains the identification and shopping cart contents shown on the BestBuy.com page above.

COOKIE SETTINGS
By choosing *Internet Options* from Internet Explorer's Tools menu (or *Preferences* from Netscape Navigator's Edit menu), you can specify your cookie settings.

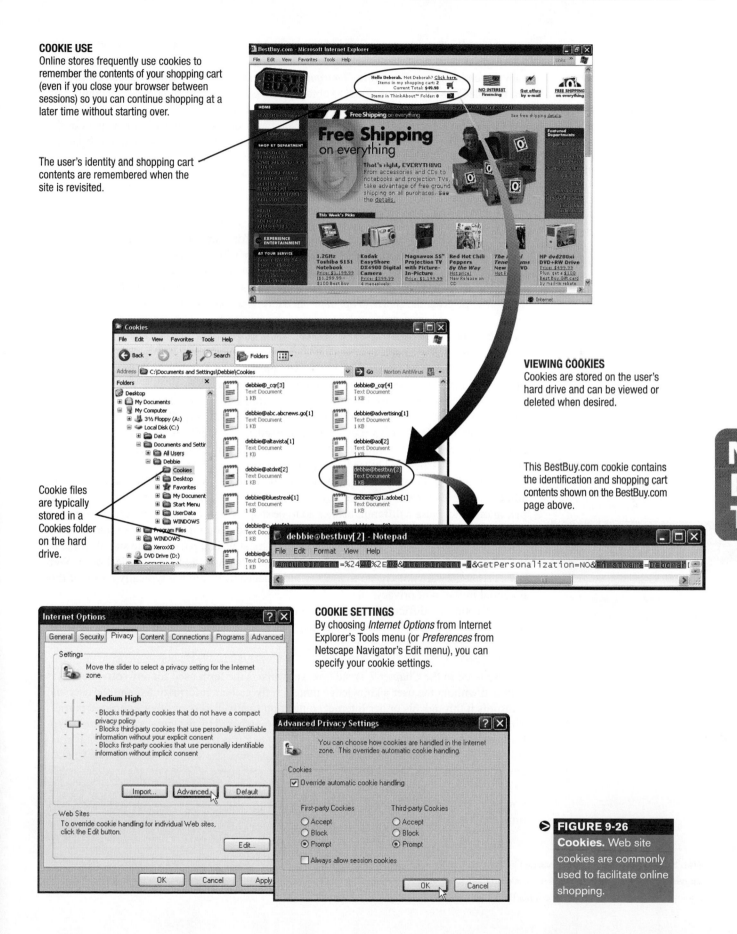

N E T

> **FIGURE 9-26**
> **Cookies.** Web site cookies are commonly used to facilitate online shopping.

actual identity. The announcement of DoubleClick's intent to sell the resulting information really caused an uproar. A flood of privacy lawsuits were filed, such as the one by the privacy watchdog group *EPIC* (the *Electronic Privacy Information Center*), which eventually led DoubleClick to agree, in 2002, to obtain permission from consumers before combining any personally identifiable data with Web surfing history.

As a result of the DoubleClick fiasco, there has been some demand for Congress or the Federal Trade Commission (FTC) to legislate how Web surfing data can be used. It is legal and generally accepted that cookies can be placed on a user's hard drive without direct permission by companies known to the user (such as by the site the user is visiting). Some people, however, believe that third-party cookies should not be able to be installed without direct permission from the user. Currently the advertising industry is pushing for voluntary adherence to usage standards, in lieu of legislation. It has formed the *Network Advertising Initiative* or *NAI* and is working with the FTC and the U.S. Department of Commerce to develop a self-regulatory process governing NAI members, which includes DoubleClick and several other large Internet advertising companies. These standards detail under what conditions non-personally identifiable information can be merged with personally identifiable information, as well as require that consumers be given the choice to opt out from data collection entirely.

Web Bugs

A **Web bug** is a very small (often 1 pixel by 1 pixel) image on a Web page that transmits data about a Web page visitor back to the Web page's server. Usually Web bug images are invisible because they are so tiny and typically match the color of the Web page's background. Web bugs can be used to retrieve information stored in cookies, if the Web bug and cookie are both from the same Web site or advertising company. Consequently, similar to the multiple-cookie scenario previously discussed, Web bugs can be used by third-party advertising companies to compile data about individuals. In fact, Web bugs are used extensively by DoubleClick and other Internet advertising companies.

In addition to being used in conjunction with cookies, Web bugs can also relay the IP address of the computer being used to view the Web page. This might be done, for example, in order to cause a different banner ad to be displayed for home users versus someone browsing on a company PC. Web bugs are also used to gather usage statistics about a Web site, such as the number of visitors to the site, the most visited pages on the site, the time of the visit, and the Web browser used for each visit. Perhaps the biggest objection to Web bugs is that they are not visible to users, which means users are not typically aware of this potential invasion of privacy.

Web bugs are difficult for users to identify, but programs—such as *Bugnosis*—can be used to make Web bugs visible on Web pages as you surf the Web.

Spyware

As discussed in the Chapter 7 Trend box, **spyware** is the term used for any software that is installed without the user's knowledge that secretly gathers information about the user and transmits it through his or her Internet connection to advertisers or other interested parties. Similar to cookies and Web bugs, the information gathered by the spyware software is typically not associated with a person's identity. Instead, it is usually used to provide advertisers with information to be used for marketing purposes, such as to help them select advertisements to display on each PC. Like Web bugs, people aren't normally aware when spyware is being used. Instead of being embedded into a Web page like a Web bug, however, spyware programs are usually installed without the user's knowledge at the same time another program is installed on the user's computer.

FURTHER EXPLORATION

For links to further information about Web bugs and spyware, go to www.course.com/uc10/ch09

>**Web bug.** A very small (usually invisible) image on a Web page that transmits data about the Web page visitor to a Web server.
>**Spyware.** Software programs often installed on a user's PC without the user's knowledge that secretly collect information and send it to an outside party via the user's Internet connection.

The inclusion of the spyware program is sometimes mentioned in the hosting software program's licensing agreement, but most spyware is installed without the user's knowledge. Once a spyware program is installed on a PC, it typically does not show up on any list of installed programs, making it difficult for users both to realize that the spyware program has been installed and to uninstall it.

Privacy advocates object to spyware because it collects and transmits data about individuals to others, as well as uses up a user's system resources and Internet bandwidth, all without the user's consent. As an additional annoyance, many spyware programs are not removed if the original hosting program is uninstalled. To remove spyware, programs—such as Ad-aware—can be used; there are also Web sites that can be used to check if a software program contains spyware before downloading it. Firewalls will also normally detect spyware if it attempts to access the Internet to transmit data back to advertisers.

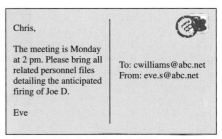

REGULAR (NON-ENCRYPTED E-MAIL) = POSTCARD

E-Mail Privacy

Many people mistakenly believe that the e-mail they send and receive is private and won't ever be read by anyone other than the intended recipient. Since it is transmitted over public media, however, only *encrypted* (electronically scrambled) e-mail can be transmitted safely. Although it is unlikely this will happen to your personal e-mail, *non-encrypted* e-mail can be intercepted and read by someone else. Consequently, it is wise to view non-encrypted e-mail correspondence as similar to a postcard rather than a letter, from a privacy standpoint (see Figure 9-27). It is also important to realize that your employer and your ISP have access to the e-mail you send through those organizations and they will often *archive* (keep copies of) it. There have been many cases in which e-mail sent by criminal suspects, such as computer hackers and stalkers, has been retrieved by law enforcement from the suspects' ISPs and used to prosecute them. One such e-mail interception system—*Carnivore*—is discussed in Chapter 15, along with encryption methods.

ENCRYPTED E-MAIL = SEALED LETTER

> **FIGURE 9-27**
> Unless e-mail messages are encrypted, do not assume they are private.

THE FUTURE OF THE INTERNET

The Internet has changed a great deal since its inception in 1969. From only four supercomputers, it has evolved into a vast network connecting virtually every type of computer. The use of the Internet has changed dramatically, as well. As the structure of the Internet evolves and improves, it can support new types of activities. New types of applications also drive the technological improvements necessary to support them.

The exact composition of the Internet of the future is anyone's guess. It will likely be a very high-speed optical network with virtually unlimited bandwidth. It will be accessed by the PC of the day, which will probably be much smaller and less obtrusive than the standard PC today—possibly built directly into desks, refrigerators, and other objects, or carried around on your body or as some type of portable device. The primary interface will likely be the voice and most network connections will be wireless.

Chances are the Internet will continue to be used for an ever-growing number of day-to-day activities, such as shopping, making voice or video phone calls, controlling home appliances, ordering and downloading TV shows or movies, ordering groceries, paying bills, telecommuting, and so forth. It will also continue to be widely used for business purposes, and high bandwidth will allow a much higher level of real-time video communications facilitating even more use of telecommuting, videoconferencing, and home-based offices. A universal payment system for micropayments is likely to facilitate paying small fees for Web content. Ideally, all of an individual's micropayments would be combined into a single monthly bill.

This is an exciting time for the Internet. It is already firmly embedded in our society, and it will be exciting to see what becomes of all the breathtaking new applications and technological improvements on the horizon and how the Internet will continue to evolve.

N E T

SUMMARY

EVOLUTION OF THE INTERNET

Chapter Objective 1:
Discuss how the Internet evolved and what it is like today.

The **Internet**—a worldwide collection of interconnected networks that is accessed by millions of people daily—dates back to the late 1960s. At its start and throughout its early years, the Internet was called **ARPANET**. It was not until the development of graphical user interfaces and the **World Wide Web** that public interest in the Internet began to soar. Most companies have Web sites today and consider the Web to be an indispensable business tool. While the Web is a very important and widely used Internet resource, it is not the only one. Over the years *protocols* have been developed to download files, send e-mail messages, and other tasks, in addition to using Web pages. Today, the term *Internet* has become a household word and, in many ways, has redefined how people think about computers and communications. The next significant improvement to the Internet infrastructure may be the result of projects such as *Internet2* and *Next Generation Internet (NGI)*.

Chapter Objective 2:
Identify the various types of individuals, companies, and organizations involved in the Internet community and explain their purposes.

The Internet community is made up of individual *users*, companies such as **Internet service providers (ISPs)**, **Internet content providers**, **application service providers (ASPs)**, *infrastructure companies*, a variety of software and hardware companies, the government, and other organizations. Virtually anyone with a computer with communications capability can be part of the Internet, either as a user or supplier of information or services. **Web services** are self-contained business functions that operate over the Internet.

Because the Internet is so unique in the history of the world—and it remains a relatively new phenomenon—several widespread myths about it have surfaced. Three such myths are that the Internet is free, that it is controlled by some central body, and that it is synonymous with the World Wide Web.

GETTING SET UP TO USE THE INTERNET

Chapter Objective 3:
Describe the device and connection options for connecting to the Internet, as well as some considerations to keep in mind when selecting an ISP.

When preparing to become connected to the Internet, three decisions must be made. The type of device (PC, *Internet appliance*, or mobile device) must be selected, and you need to decide whether to use a **dial-up connection** (**conventional dial-up** or **ISDN**) or a **direct connection** (through a *T-1*, **DSL**, **cable**, **satellite**, **fixed wireless**, or **mobile wireless Internet access**). Finally, you need to decide on the specific Internet service provider to be used. Once all these decisions are made, you can acquire the proper hardware and software and set up your system for Internet access.

SEARCHING THE INTERNET

Chapter Objective 4:
Understand how to effectively search for information on the Internet and how to properly cite Internet resources.

Search sites—Web sites that enable users to search for and find information on the Internet—typically locate pages using **keywords** or **directories**. Both types of searches use a *search database* that contains information about pages on the Web and a **search engine** to retrieve the list of matching Web pages from the database. Databases that search sites are generally maintained by automated *spider* programs; directory databases are typically maintained by human editors.

Keyword searches—where you type keywords in a search box and a list of links to Web pages matching the search criteria (*hits*) are displayed—are useful when you know generally what you want, but you don't know at which URL to find it. Directory searches—where you select categories until a list of links to Web pages matching the selected categories is displayed—can be used when you want information about a general topic, but you have less of a precise subject in mind. *Metasearch engines* use multiple search engines, some search sites are *natural language* sites, and many search sites use a combination of search options.

There are a variety of search strategies that can be used, including typing phrases instead of single keywords; using *Boolean operators*; trying the search at multiple search sites; and using *synonyms*, *variant word forms*, *wildcards*, and *field searches*. Once a list of links to Web pages matching the search criteria is displayed, the hits need to be evaluated for their relevancy; if the information found on a Web page is used in a paper, report, or other original document, the source should be credited appropriately.

BEYOND BROWSING AND E-MAIL

The Internet can be used for many different types of activities besides basic browsing and e-mail exchange. Common Web activities for individuals include a variety of consumer *e-commerce* activities, such as **online shopping, online auctions, online banking,** and **online investing**. When performing any type of financial transaction over the Internet, it is very important to use only *secure* Web pages.

Entertainment applications include downloading *MP3* files and other types of **online music**, *interactive TV* and *video-on-demand*, **online gaming**, and **e-books**. A wide variety of news, reference, government, product, and corporate information is available via the Web as well. News, reference, and search tools are commonly found on **portal** pages. Web-based training, **distance learning, blogs,** and **e-portfolios** are commonly used *online education* applications. *Peer-to-peer file sharing* is an additional Internet application.

Chapter Objective 5:
List several useful things that can be done using the Internet, in addition to basic Web browsing and e-mail.

CENSORSHIP AND PRIVACY ISSUES

Among the most important societal issues relating to the Internet are censorship and *privacy*. Web content is not censored as a whole, but **Internet filtering** can be used by parents, employers, educators, and anyone wishing to prevent access to sites they deem objectionable on computers for which they have control. *Privacy* is a big concern for individuals, particularly as it relates to their Web activity. **Cookies** are typically used by Web sites to save customized settings for that site and can also be used for advertising purposes. Other items of possible concern are **Web bugs** and **spyware**. Unless an e-mail message is *encrypted*, it should not be assumed to be completely private.

Chapter Objective 6:
Discuss censorship and privacy, and how it is related to Internet use.

THE FUTURE OF THE INTERNET

The Internet has evolved remarkably over the past few decades and will, no doubt, evolve in new ways that most people can't even dream of. The future Internet will likely be high-speed and accessed by wireless devices and appliances. Multimedia applications, such as real-time video communications and TV on demand, will likely be a reality in the near future.

Chapter Objective 7:
Speculate as to the format, structure, and use of the Internet in the future.

NET

KEY TERMS

Instructions: Match each key term on the left with the definition on the right that best describes it.

a. application service provider (ASP)

b. ARPANET

c. cookie

d. dial-up connection

e. direct connection

f. directory

g. distance learning

h. Internet

i. Internet content provider

j. Internet filtering

k. Internet service provider (ISP)

l. keyword

m. online auction

n. online investing

o. online shopping

p. search engine

q. search site

r. spyware

s. Web bug

t. World Wide Web

1. _____ A business or other organization that provides Internet access to others, typically for a fee.

2. _____ A collection of categories that are used to locate appropriate Web pages from a search database.

3. _____ A company that manages and distributes software-based services over the Internet.

4. _____ A learning environment in which the student is physically located away from the instructor and other students; commonly instruction and communications take place via the Internet.

5. _____ An always-on type of Internet connection in which the PC or other device is continually connected to the Internet.

6. _____ An online activity for which bids are placed on items and the highest bidder purchases the item.

7. _____ A person or an organization that provides Internet content.

8. _____ A small file stored on a user's hard drive by a Web server; commonly used to identify personal preferences and settings for that user.

9. _____ A software program used by a search site to retrieve matching Web pages from a search database.

10. _____ A type of Internet connection in which the PC or other device must dial up and connect to a service provider's computer via telephone lines before being connected to the Internet.

11. _____ A very small (usually invisible) image on a Web page that transmits data about the Web page visitor to a Web server.

12. _____ A Web site designed to help users search for Web pages that match specified keywords or selected categories.

13. _____ A word typed in a search box on a search site to locate information on the Internet.

14. _____ Buying and selling stocks or other types of investments over the Internet.

15. _____ Buying products or services over the Internet.

16. _____ Software programs often installed on a user's PC without the user's knowledge that secretly collect information and send it to an outside party via the user's Internet connection.

17. _____ The collection of Web pages available through the Internet.

18. _____ The largest and most well-known computer network, linking millions of computers all over the world.

19. _____ The predecessor of the Internet, named after the Advanced Research Projects Agency (ARPA), which sponsored its development.

20. _____ Using a software program or browser option to block access to particular Web pages or types of Web pages.

REVIEW ACTIVITIES

Answers for the self-quiz appear at the end of the book in the References and Resources Guide.

True/False

Instructions: Circle **T** if the statement is true or **F** if the statement is false.

T F 1. When the Internet was first developed, it was called Mosaic.

T F 2. On the Internet, an *access provider* and a *content provider* are essentially the same thing.

T F 3. With a direct connection, you need only open your browser to start your Internet session.

T F 4. All search sites allow you to type keywords.

T F 5. A locked padlock on the browser's status bar indicates that the Web page currently being viewed is secure.

Completion

Instructions: Supply the missing words to complete the following statements.

6. _____ is a type of always-on broadband Internet service that transmits data over standard telephone lines.

7. A(n) _____ is a software program used by a search site to retrieve matching Web pages from a search database.

8. With a(n) _____, people bid on products and the highest bidder is allowed to purchase the item.

9. A publicly-accessible Web page set up as an individual's personal online journal is called a(n) _____.

10. _____ deals with what information about an individual is available, how it is used, and by whom.

---

1. Assume you want to find an ISP for a home Internet connection. If you don't want to tie up your phone when you're online and you plan to download multimedia files frequently, list two types of Internet services you could use. For each type of service, state one situation in which that type of service might be the best option and why.

2. Suppose that you really like the Yahoo! home page found at www.yahoo.com and would like to make it your browser's home page so it will be the first page displayed when you open your browser and you can return there just by clicking the browser's Home button. Explain which menu would be used and the steps you would need to take to make this portal page your browser's home page using Internet Explorer.

3. List three different sets of keywords that could be used to search for information on how to maintain a trumpet.

4. What would each of the following searches look for?

    a. hot AND dogs _____

    b. snorkel* _____

    c. text:"Internet privacy" domain:gov _____

5. Select the Internet tool or application from the numbered list below that best matches each of the following situations and write the corresponding number in the blank to the left of each situation. Note that all tools and applications will not be used.

    a. _____ To communicate with a friend in a different state.

    b. _____ To pay a bill without writing a check.

    c. _____ To play cards with a friend in a different state.

    d. _____ To pay only as much as you specify for an item purchased through the Internet.

    e. _____ To post your original papers, résumé, and other original materials created for school classes.

    f. _____ To find Web pages containing information about growing your own Bonsai trees.

    1. Online banking   **5.** Searching

    2. E-mail   **6.** Interactive TV

    3. Online shopping   **7.** E-portfolio

    4. Online auction   **8.** Online gaming

6. Give one example of someone who might choose to use Internet filtering and explain why.

7. List one advantage and one disadvantage of the use of Web site cookies.

PROJECTS

1. **Internet Addiction** Computer and Internet addiction can happen to computer users of all ages, races, income levels, and occupations. As with other addictions, computer or Internet use is said to be a problem when it adversely affects your life, such as causing problems with your health, your family, or your job. According to experts, Internet addiction is growing at a very fast pace and it is a global problem—one study in North Korea found that about 40% of the nation's middle and high school students are addicted to the Internet to some extent.

    For this project, research Internet addiction. Locate two organizations that have information about Internet addiction, including its causes, symptoms, and treatment. Do the organizations agree? Contact either your local mental health organization or school health center and see if Internet addiction is considered an actual mental health condition and, if so, what types of treatment are available in your area. Have you ever noticed behavior exhibited by a friend or relative that might suggest the beginnings of an addiction to any type of technology? Are there precautions individuals can take to avoid becoming addicted to the Internet? Do you think Internet addiction will increase or decrease in the future? At the conclusion of your research, prepare a one-page summary of your findings and submit it to your instructor.

HOT TOPICS

2. **Auction Pirates** Pirated software being sold via online auctions is reaching epidemic proportions. One estimate by the Software and Information Industry Association was that over 90% of all software sold through online auctions is pirated. Pirated movies are prevalent as well, often available over the Internet before they are released on DVD— sometimes even before they are released worldwide in the theater.

    For this project, form a group to participate in the following scenario: While on an online auction site, you run across what looks like a great deal on a DVD movie that was just in the movie theater a few months ago. You win the item and, after receiving and cashing your personal check, the seller ships your DVD. When it arrives, the return address is in Thailand and the text on the cover of the DVD isn't English, so you realize that you have bought an Asian import DVD. When you contact the seller, he says that he buys his DVDs in the store in his country, so they can't be bootleg copies. Your group should research the legality of selling DVDs in the U.S. that are produced in other countries. If a DVD is available for retail sale in a foreign country, does that mean it can be bought there by an individual and then brought into the U.S., or imported for resale? Is there any way to check whether or not a DVD bought via an online auction is legitimate? Your group should also discuss the scenario explained above and determine how this problem might have been avoided in the first place, and what (if anything) could be done after the fact, if you weren't happy with your purchase. At the conclusion of your research, your group should submit its findings and opinions to your instructor in the form of a short paper, no more than two pages in length.

SHORT ANSWER/ RESEARCH

3. **Online Travel Planning** Planning and booking travel arrangements online is a very popular Internet activity today. There are a number of sites that claim to give discount rates on airplane tickets, hotel rooms, rental cars, and more. Some sites also offer information about weather, sites of interest, and more to help you plan your vacation.

    For this project, review two popular travel sites, such as Expedia.com and Travelocity.com, to see what services they offer and how easy, or difficult, it is to locate the information needed to plan and book a vacation via those sites. Select a destination and use the search facility located on one of the travel sites to obtain a quote for a particular flight on a particular day. Next, go to the Web site for the airline of the flight you were just quoted and use the site to obtain a quote for the same flight. Is there a difference in price or flight availability? Could you

NET

make a reservation online through both sites? Would you feel comfortable booking a vacation yourself online or are there other services that a travel agent could provide that you feel would be beneficial? Do you think these sites are most appropriate for making business travel plans or vacation plans, or are they suited to either? At the conclusion of your research, prepare a one-page summary of your findings and submit it to your instructor.

HANDS ON

4. **Wi-Fi Hot Spots** As discussed in the chapter, there are an increasing number of public locations offering Wi-Fi hot spots available for public use.

   For this project, find at least one location in your local area that offers public Wi-Fi access (possibilities include your public library; retail locations such as McDonald's, Starbucks, and Borders; and hot spots set up at phone booths, parks, and other public locations, often by a wireless Web provider for their subscribers). Once you have identified a public hot spot, either visit the location or call it on the phone to find out the following information.

   a. Is there a fee to use the hot spot? If so, do you have to subscribe on a regular basis or can you pay only when you want to use the hot spot? Where and how is payment made?

   b. Do you need any special software to access the hot spot? Do you need to be assigned a user name or WEP (Wired Equivalent Privacy) key before you can use the service?

   At the conclusion of your research, submit your findings to your instructor in the form of a short summary.

5. **Web Searching** As discussed in the chapter, search sites can be used to find Web pages containing specific information and there are strategies that can be used to make Web searching an efficient and useful experience.

   For this project, perform the following search tasks, answering the questions or printing the information as instructed below. After you have completed all four tasks, submit your results and printouts to your instructor. (Note: Some of the answers will vary from student to student.)

   a. Go to the Google search site located at www.google.com and Search for *rules*. How many pages were found? What is the name of the first page in the list of hits?

   b. Next, search for *backgammon rules*. How many pages were found? Click on the first page and look for a picture of how a backgammon board is initially set up. When you find one, print the page. If you can't find one on that site, select different pages in the hit list or perform another search until you find the proper illustration and then print the page.

   c. Perform a new search by clicking the link at the top of the Google page to go to the Advanced Search option. Use the form fields to perform a search for pages that contain all the words *hiking trails Sierra*, don't contain the word *horse*, and have the domain *.gov*. After the list of Web pages matching your search criteria is displayed, record the actual search phrase that is now listed in the search box along with the name and URL of the first page displayed in the list of hits.

   d. Use Google to search for a Web site that includes a telephone directory. Go to that site and supply the necessary information to search for yourself in the telephone directory. (If you are not currently listed in the phone book, search for a family member or friend that you know has a listed number.) Print the page displaying the requested information.

WRITING ABOUT COMPUTERS

6. **Cash, Credit Card, or Fingerprint?** The Trend box in Chapter 8 discussed using fingerprint biometric devices to pay for offline goods and services; biometric payment systems for online purchases are sure to follow if this type of payment is well received by consumers. Biometric payment methods raise some concerns about privacy and security, which are probably not much different than the concerns raised when credit cards were first introduced. For example: Could the goods and services I buy become public knowledge? Could someone else make charges on my account? However, this new payment method also raises new and potentially frightening

questions, such as: Once my fingerprints are in electronic format, could they be mixed up accidentally with someone else's fingerprints? Could someone trade my fingerprint image for another in a crime database to make it appear that I'm a criminal? Could my fingerprint image be used to make fraudulent purchases, as well as for voting and other applications that may soon use biometric identification? Some characteristics of biometric payment systems make them more secure than credit cards or cash—fingerprints can't be lost or used by another person, for example. Other characteristics of these systems may raise grave new concerns.

For this project, consider the questions mentioned in the previous paragraph and write a short essay expressing your opinion about the security of paying by cash, credit card, and fingerprints today for both offline and online purchases. Would you be willing to use a fingerprint payment system? Do you think such systems will be well received by consumers? List any additional pros and cons of these systems not covered in the Trend box or this project's instructions. Provide a concluding paragraph stating other possible uses for biometric ID systems and indicate whether or not you believe these systems would be useful. Submit your opinion on this issue to your instructor in the form of a short paper, not more than two pages in length.

7. **Online Job Hunting** There are a number of Web sites dedicated to online career planning, posting and reviewing résumés and job announcements, listing average salary information for various positions, and other useful job-hunting tools.

For this project, visit at least two career-oriented Web sites (such as Monster.com or CareerBuilder.com) and review the types of information and services available from the perspective of both a job seeker and an employer. Are there fees for any of the services? If you post a résumé, is it available for anyone to see or are there restrictions on access? When it comes time for you to look for a new job, would you want to use one of these sites? Are the sites useful from an employer's perspective? List any advantages and disadvantages you can think of for using one of these sites to find a new job. Submit your findings and opinions to your instructor in the form of a short paper, not more than two pages in length.

PRESENTATION/ DEMONSTRATION

8. **Free and Low-Cost Internet** There are several free and low-cost ($5 to $10 per month) ISPs. For example, Juno and NetZero (www.juno.com or www.netzero.net) offer users 10 hours of free dial-up access per month and Access4Less (access4less.net) offers unlimited dial-up service for about $5 per month.

For this project, research Juno or NetZero plus one other free or low-cost ISP and investigate their services. Do any of these offer unlimited Internet access for free? Is there still a 10-hour limit with Juno/NetZero? If so, what happens if you go over that limit? Are there any tradeoffs for using these free or low-cost ISPs? If you were looking for a dial-up provider, would you consider using either of your selected ISPs? Why or why not? Would these services be useful for other applications, such as for business travelers or for back up service for broadband subscribers? Share your findings and opinions with the class in the form of a short presentation. The presentation should not exceed 10 minutes and should make use of one or more presentation aids such as the chalkboard, handouts, overhead transparencies, or a computer-based slide presentation (your instructor may provide additional requirements). You may also be asked to submit a summary of the presentation to your instructor.

9. **Online Term Papers** There are a large number of Web sites from which term papers on a variety of subjects can be purchased and downloaded. Although many of these sites state that they provide the papers for research purposes only and do not support plagiarism, it is not surprising that some dishonest students turn in purchased online term papers as their own work.

For this project, form a group to discuss the availability and ethical use of online term papers. Has anyone in the group ever visited one of these sites? If so, what services were offered through the site? Was it clear to the student that there was a way of utilizing the site's services without encountering plagiarism problems? Do the members of your group believe it is ethical to use online term papers for research? Can your group think of any other valuable (and legal)

reasons for using these types of sites? If a term paper is purchased, instead of copying information without permission from a Web site, does turning it in as an original term paper still constitute plagiarism? Why or why not? What responsibility, if any, does your group feel the Web site has if its papers are used in an illegal or unethical manner? By referring to your course syllabus, student handbook, or school code of ethics, determine the penalties at your school for submitting a plagiarized term paper. Share your findings with the class in the form of a short presentation. The presentation should not exceed 10 minutes and should make use of one or more presentation aids such as the chalkboard, handouts, overhead transparencies, or a computer-based slide presentation (your instructor may provide additional requirements). Your group may also be asked to submit a summary of the presentation to your instructor.

INTERACTIVE DISCUSSION

10. **Your Privacy** When you surf the Web, you leave what is sometimes referred to as "click-stream data" or a "data trail." This information can be used to create a profile of your online activities. This profile, or collection of personal data, can then be sold to others and then used to target you with specific marketing materials in an effort to sell their products. Sometimes this data is collected through the use of cookies. After many years of relying on a self-regulatory approach to dealing with this problem, the FTC is investigating its authority for regulating online privacy and is exploring enacting legislation to protect consumer privacy.

    Select one of the following positions or create one of your own and express your point of view on the subject. Your instructor will indicate whether your response is to be posted to a class bulletin board, discussed in a class chat room, or discussed as an in-class activity. You may also be asked to submit a summary of your position and point of view to your instructor.
    a. We should avoid any sort of legislation with respect to the Internet. The companies that are guilty of collecting and using private information in an inappropriate way should be given additional time to amend their ways, and another chance to self-regulate their activities.
    b. Self-regulation is not the answer. If this were true, these companies would have resolved these problems several years ago. We have no choice but to enact legislation to deal with this issue.

11. **Rural Broadband** Citizens who live in rural areas typically have less access to broadband Internet than those in more highly populated areas. Maryland's Speaker of the House Casper R. Taylor views this as the real digital divide. Without broadband, he believes that "our kids are not going to have the advantage of urbanized society going into the future if we're disconnected from the rest of the world…If we don't accomplish this, we are clearly creating a second-class society." There are differing opinions regarding the importance of broadband Internet and whose responsibility it is to provide it. If a region has only 56K dial-up service, does that really put it at a disadvantage? Is the digital divide more about separating those who have access to technology such as the Internet and those who don't, or is it about the quality of that technology? What about the government's role—should it provide the necessary infrastructure to ensure an appropriate level of Internet access to all U.S. citizens? If not, how will the digital divide within the United States be eliminated? Will it ever be eliminated?

    For this project, form an opinion of the necessity of broadband Internet and the role of the government (if any) in providing broadband Internet access to its citizens. Be sure to use the questions mentioned in the previous paragraph when forming your position. Your instructor will indicate whether your response is to be posted to a class bulletin board, discussed in a class chat room, or discussed as an in-class activity. You may also be asked to submit a summary of your position and point of view to your instructor.

STUDENT EDITION LABS

12. **Student Edition Labs** Reinforce the concepts you have learned in this chapter by working through the "Connecting to the Internet" interactive Student Edition Lab, available online. To access this lab, go to www.course.com/uc10/ch09

    If you have a SAM user profile, you have access to even more interactive content. Log in to your SAM account and go to your assignments page to see what your instructor has assigned for this chapter.

REFERENCES AND RESOURCES

GUIDE

OUTLINE

Computer History Timeline R-2

A Look at Numbering Systems R-7

Coding Charts R-11

CPU Characteristics R-13

Guide for Buying a PC R-14

Web Guide R-19

Web Searching Tips: A Closer Look at
  Google R-23

Answers to Self-Quiz R-25

INTRODUCTION

When working on a PC, you often need to look up information related to computers. For instance, you may need to find out when the IBM PC was first invented, you may want tips on factors to consider when buying a PC, you may need a URL for an online dictionary, or you may want to learn new ways to search the Web. To help you with the tasks just mentioned and more, this References and Resources Guide brings together in one convenient location a collection of computer-related references and resources.

The earliest recorded calculating device, the abacus, is believed to have been invented by the Babylonians sometime between 500 B.C. and 100 B.C. It and similar types of counting boards were used solely for counting.

Blaise Pascal invented the first mechanical calculator, called the Pascaline Arithmetic Machine. It had the capacity for eight digits and could add and subtract.

Dr. John V. Atanasoff and Clifford Berry designed and built ABC (for Atanasoff-Berry Computer), the world's first electronic computer.

500 B.C.   1642   1937

Early Computers and Pre-Computers

1621   1804   1944

French silk weaver Joseph-Marie Jacquard built a loom that read holes punched on a series of small sheets of hardwood to control the pattern weaved. This automated machine introduced the use of punch cards and showed that they could be used to convey a series of instructions.

The Mark I, considered to be the first digital computer, was introduced by IBM. It was developed in cooperation with Harvard University, was more than 50 feet long, weighed almost five tons, and used electromechanical relays to solve addition problems in less than a second; multiplication and division took about six and twelve seconds, respectively.

The slide rule, a precursor to the electronic calculator, was invented. Used primarily to perform multiplication, division, square roots, and the calculation of logarithms, its wide-spread use continued until the 1970's.

Early Computers and Pre-Computers (before approximately 1945)

Most early computers and pre-computers were mechanical machines that worked with gears and levers. Electromechanical devices (using both electricity and gears and levers) were developed towards the end of this era.

First Generation (approximately 1946–1957)

Powered by vacuum tubes, these computers were faster than electromechanical machines, but they were large and bulky, generated excessive heat, and had to be physically wired and reset to run programs. Input was primarily on punch cards; output was on punch cards or paper. Machine and assembly languages were used to program these computers.

The UNIVAC 1, the first computer to be mass produced for general use, was introduced by Remington Rand. In 1952, it was used to analyze votes in the U.S. presidential election and correctly predicted that Dwight D. Eisenhower would be the victor only 45 minutes after the polls closed, though the results were not aired immediately because they weren't trusted.

The COBOL programming language was developed by a committee headed by Dr. Grace Hopper.

The first floppy disk (8 inches in diameter) was introduced.

Unix was developed at AT&T's Bell Laboratories; Advanced Micro Devices (AMD) was formed; and ARPANET (the predecessor of today's Internet) was established.

IBM unbundled some of its hardware and software and began selling them separately, allowing other software companies to emerge.

1951　　1960　　1967　　1969

First Generation　　　Second Generation　　Third Generation

1947　　1957　　1964　　1968

The FORTRAN programming language was introduced.

Robert Noyce and Gordon Moore founded the Intel Corporation.

John Bardeen, Walter Brattain, and William Shockley invented the transistor, which had the same capabilities as a vacuum tube but was faster, broke less often, used less power, and created less heat. They won a Nobel Prize for their invention in 1956 and computers began to be built with transistors shortly afterwards.

The first mouse was invented by Doug Engelbart.

The IBM System/360 computer was introduced. Unlike previous computers, System/360 contained a full line of compatible computers, making upgrading easier.

Second Generation (approximately 1958–1963)
Second-generation computers used transistors instead of vacuum tubes. They allowed the computer to be physically smaller, more powerful, more reliable, and faster than before. Input was primarily on punch cards and magnetic tape; output was on punch cards and paper; and magnetic tape and disks were used for storage. High-level programming languages were used with these computers.

Third Generation (approximately 1964–1970)
The third generation of computers evolved when integrated circuits (IC)—computer chips—began being used instead of conventional transistors. Computers became even smaller and more reliable. Monitors and keyboards were introduced for input and output; magnetic disks were used for storage. The emergence of the operating system meant that operators no longer had to manually reset relays and wiring.

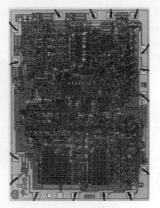

The first microprocessor, the Intel 4004, was designed by Ted Hoff. The single processor contained 2,250 transistors and could execute 60,000 operations per second.

Bill Gates and Paul Allen wrote a version of BASIC for the Altair, the first computer programming language designed for a personal computer. Bill Gates dropped out of Harvard to form Microsoft with Paul Allen.

Hailed as the first "personal computer," the Altair—allegedly named for a destination of the Starship Enterprise from a Star Trek TV episode—began to be sold as a kit for $395. Within months, tens of thousands were ordered.

Software Arts Inc.'s Visi-Calc, the first electronic spreadsheet and business program for PCs, was released. This program is seen as one of the reasons PCs first became widely accepted in the business world.

1971

1975

1979

Fourth Generation

1972

1976

1980

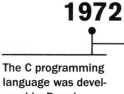

The C programming language was developed by Dennis Ritchie at Bell Labs.

Seymor Cray, called the "father of supercomputing," founded Cray Research, which would go on to build some of the fastest computers in the world.

Steve Wozniak and Steve Jobs founded Apple computer and released the Apple I (a single-board computer), followed by the Apple II (a complete PC that became an instant success in 1977). They originally ran the company out of Job's garage.

Sony Electronics introduced the 3.5-inch floppy disk and drive.

Seagate Technologies announced the first Winchester 5.25-inch hard disk drive, revolutionizing PC storage.

IBM chose Microsoft to develop the operating system for its upcoming PC. That operating system was PC-DOS.

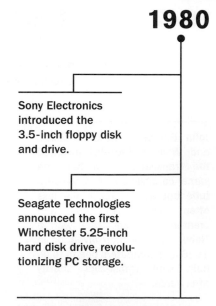

Fourth Generation (approximately 1971–present)

The fourth generation of computers began with large-scale integration (LSI)—chips that could contain thousands of transistors. Very large-scale integration (VLSI) resulted in the microprocessor and the resulting microcomputers. The keyboard and mouse are predominant input devices, though many other types of input devices are now available; monitors and printers provide output; storage is obtained with magnetic disks, optical discs, and memory chips.

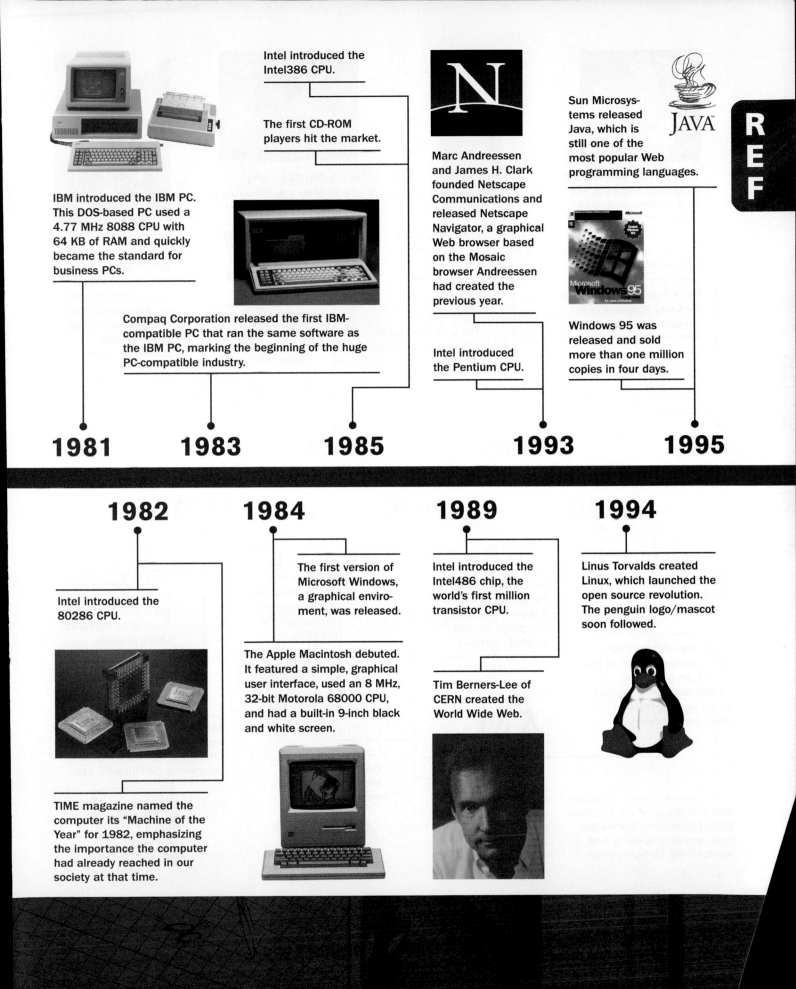

Intel introduced the Intel386 CPU.

The first CD-ROM players hit the market.

IBM introduced the IBM PC. This DOS-based PC used a 4.77 MHz 8088 CPU with 64 KB of RAM and quickly became the standard for business PCs.

Compaq Corporation released the first IBM-compatible PC that ran the same software as the IBM PC, marking the beginning of the huge PC-compatible industry.

Marc Andreessen and James H. Clark founded Netscape Communications and released Netscape Navigator, a graphical Web browser based on the Mosaic browser Andreessen had created the previous year.

Intel introduced the Pentium CPU.

Sun Microsystems released Java, which is still one of the most popular Web programming languages.

Windows 95 was released and sold more than one million copies in four days.

1981   1983   1985   1993   1995

1982   1984   1989   1994

Intel introduced the 80286 CPU.

The first version of Microsoft Windows, a graphical enviroment, was released.

The Apple Macintosh debuted. It featured a simple, graphical user interface, used an 8 MHz, 32-bit Motorola 68000 CPU, and had a built-in 9-inch black and white screen.

Intel introduced the Intel486 chip, the world's first million transistor CPU.

Tim Berners-Lee of CERN created the World Wide Web.

Linus Torvalds created Linux, which launched the open source revolution. The penguin logo/mascot soon followed.

TIME magazine named the computer its "Machine of the Year" for 1982, emphasizing the importance the computer had already reached in our society at that time.

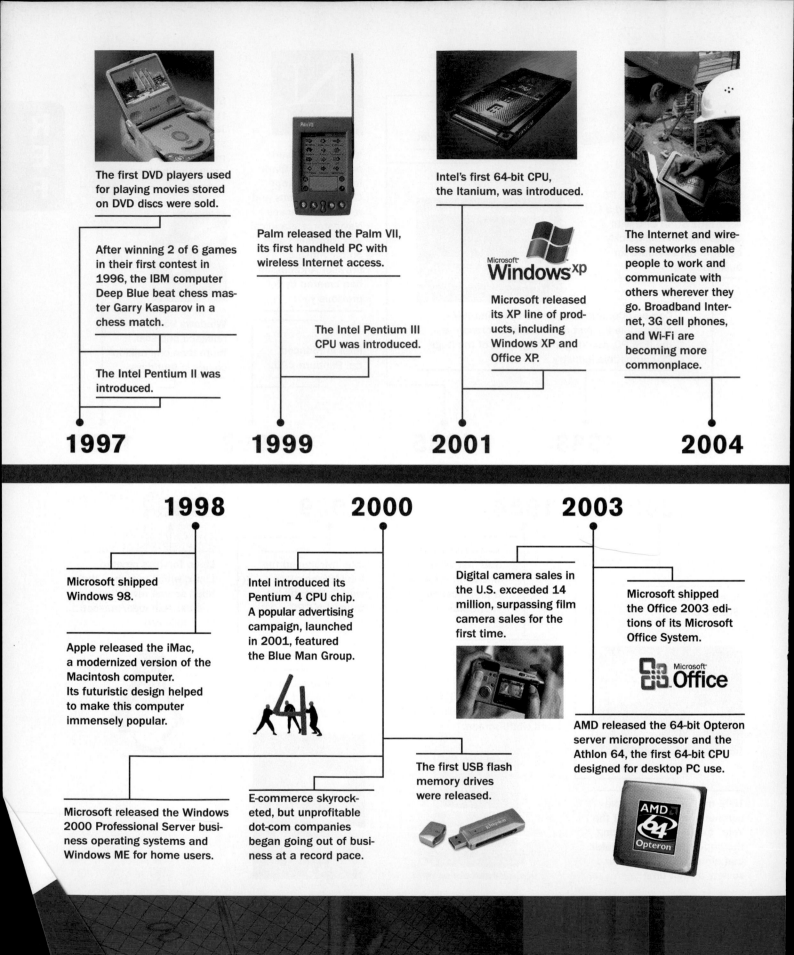

The first DVD players used for playing movies stored on DVD discs were sold.

After winning 2 of 6 games in their first contest in 1996, the IBM computer Deep Blue beat chess master Garry Kasparov in a chess match.

The Intel Pentium II was introduced.

1997

Palm released the Palm VII, its first handheld PC with wireless Internet access.

The Intel Pentium III CPU was introduced.

1999

Intel's first 64-bit CPU, the Itanium, was introduced.

Microsoft released its XP line of products, including Windows XP and Office XP.

2001

The Internet and wireless networks enable people to work and communicate with others wherever they go. Broadband Internet, 3G cell phones, and Wi-Fi are becoming more commonplace.

2004

1998

Microsoft shipped Windows 98.

Apple released the iMac, a modernized version of the Macintosh computer. Its futuristic design helped to make this computer immensely popular.

Microsoft released the Windows 2000 Professional Server business operating systems and Windows ME for home users.

2000

Intel introduced its Pentium 4 CPU chip. A popular advertising campaign, launched in 2001, featured the Blue Man Group.

E-commerce skyrocketed, but unprofitable dot-com companies began going out of business at a record pace.

The first USB flash memory drives were released.

Digital camera sales in the U.S. exceeded 14 million, surpassing film camera sales for the first time.

2003

Microsoft shipped the Office 2003 editions of its Microsoft Office System.

AMD released the 64-bit Opteron server microprocessor and the Athlon 64, the first 64-bit CPU designed for desktop PC use.

As discussed in Chapter 3 of this text, a numbering system is a way of representing numbers. People generally use the *decimal numbering system* explained in Chapter 3 and reviewed next; computers process data using the *binary numbering system*. Another numbering system related to computer use is the *hexadecimal numbering system*, which can be used to represent long strings of binary numbers in a manner more understandable to people than the binary numbering system. Following a discussion of these three numbering systems, this section of the References and Resources Guide takes a look at conversions between numbering systems and principles of computer arithmetic, and then closes with a look at how to perform conversions using a scientific calculator. ■

The Decimal and Binary Numbering System

The *decimal (base 10)*, numbering system uses 10 symbols—the digits 0, 1, 2, 3, 4, 5, 6, 7, 8, and 9—to represent all possible numbers and is the numbering system people use most often. The *binary (base 2)*, numbering system is used extensively by computers to represent numbers and other characters. This system uses only two digits—0 and 1. As illustrated in Figure 3-2 in Chapter 3, the place values (columns) in the binary numbering system are different from those used in the decimal system. For example, the right-most column has a value of 1, just like the decimal system, but the second column is the 2s column (instead of 10s), the third column is the 4s column (instead of 100s), and so on.

The Hexadecimal Numbering System

Computers often output diagnostic and memory-management messages to programmers and technically oriented users in *hexadecimal (hex)* notation. Hex is a shorthand method for representing the binary digits stored in a computer. Because large binary numbers—for example, 11010100010011101—can easily be misread by programmers, hexadecimal notation groups binary digits into units of four, which, in turn, are represented by other symbols.

The hexadecimal numbering system is also called the *base 16 numbering system* because it uses 16 different symbols. Since there are only 10 possible numeric digits, hex uses letters instead of numbers for the extra 6 symbols. The 16 hexadecimal symbols and their decimal and binary counterparts are shown in Figure R-1.

Hexadecimal is not itself a code that the computer uses to perform computations or to communicate with other machines. This numbering system does, however, have a special relationship to the 8-bit bytes of ASCII and EBCDIC that makes it ideal for displaying messages quickly. As you can see in Figure R-1, each hex character has a 4-bit binary counterpart, so any combination of 8 bits can be represented by exactly

> **FIGURE R-1**
> Hexadecimal characters and their decimal and binary equivalents.

HEXADECIMAL CHARACTER	DECIMAL EQUIVALENT	BINARY EQUIVALENT
0	0	0000
1	1	0001
2	2	0010
3	3	0011
4	4	0100
5	5	0101
6	6	0110
7	7	0111
8	8	1000
9	9	1001
A	10	1010
B	11	1011
C	12	1100
D	13	1101
E	14	1110
F	15	1111

The hexadecimal
number
4F6A

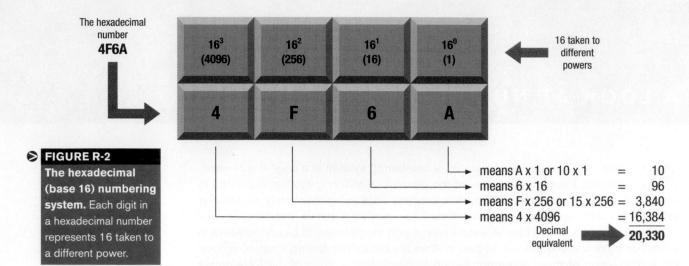

16 taken to
different
powers

> **FIGURE R-2**
> **The hexadecimal (base 16) numbering system.** Each digit in a hexadecimal number represents 16 taken to a different power.

means A x 1 or 10 x 1 = 10
means 6 x 16 = 96
means F x 256 or 15 x 256 = 3,840
means 4 x 4096 = 16,384
Decimal equivalent **20,330**

2 hexadecimal characters. For example, the letter N (represented in ASCII by 01001110) has a hex representation of *4E*.

Let's look at another example to see how to convert from hex to decimal. Suppose a programmer receives the following message on his or her monitor:

PROGRAM LOADED AT LOCATION 4F6A

This message tells the programmer the precise location in memory of the first byte of the program just loaded. To determine the decimal equivalent of a hexadecimal number such as 4F6A, you can use the procedure shown in Figure R-2.

Converting Between Numbering Systems

In Figure 3-2 in Chapter 3, we illustrated how to convert from binary to decimal; so far in this guide, we've shown how to convert from hexadecimal to decimal. Two other types of conversion are discussed next.

Hexadecimal to Binary and Binary to Hexadecimal

To convert from hexadecimal to binary, we convert each hexadecimal digit separately to 4 binary digits (using the table in Figure R-1). For example, to convert F6A9 to binary, we get

F	6	A	9
1111	0110	1010	1001

or 1111011010101001 in binary representation. To convert from binary to hexadecimal, we go through the reverse process. If the number of digits in the binary number is not divisible by 4, we add leading zeros to the binary number to force an even division. For example, to convert the binary number 1101101010011 to hexadecimal, we get

0001	1011	0101	0011
1	B	5	3

or 1B53 in hexadecimal representation. Note that three leading zeros were added to change the initial 1 to 0001 before making the conversion.

Decimal to Binary and Decimal to Hexadecimal

To convert from decimal to either binary or hexadecimal, we can use the *remainder method*. To use the remainder method, the decimal number is divided by 2 (to convert to a binary number) or 16 (to convert to a hexadecimal number). The *remainder* of the division operation is recorded and the division process is repeated using the *quotient* as the next dividend, until the quotient becomes 0. At that point, the collective remainders (written backwards) represent the equivalent binary or hexadecimal number (see Figure R-3).

R
E
F

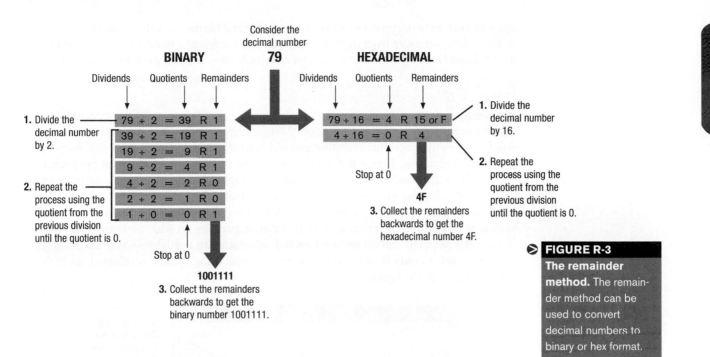

3. Collect the remainders backwards to get the binary number 1001111.

FIGURE R-3
The remainder method. The remainder method can be used to convert decimal numbers to binary or hex format.

A table summarizing all the numbering system conversion procedures covered in this text is provided in Figure R-4.

FROM BASE	TO BASE		
	2	10	16
2		Starting at right-most digit, multiply binary digits by 2^0, 2^1, 2^2, etc., respectively. Then add products.	Starting at right-most digit, convert each group of four binary digits to a hex digit.
10	Divide repeatedly by 2 using each quotient as the next dividend; then collect remainders in reverse order.		Divide repeatedly by 16 using each quotient as the next dividend; then collect remainders in reverse order.
16	Convert each hex digit to four binary digits.	Starting at right-most digit, multiply hex digits by 16^0, 16^1, 16^2, etc., respectively. Then add products.	

FIGURE R-4
Summary of conversions.

FIGURE R-5
Adding and subtracting with the decimal, binary, and hexadecimal numbering systems.

Computer Arithmetic

To most people, decimal arithmetic is second nature. Addition and subtraction using decimal numbers is introduced in kindergarten or first grade. Addition and subtraction using binary and hexadecimal numbers are not much harder than the same operations with decimal numbers, you just have to keep in mind the number of symbols used in each system.

Figure R-5 provides an example of addition and subtraction with decimal, binary, and hexadecimal numbers. Note that with binary and

	DECIMAL	BINARY	HEXADECIMAL
Addition	$\overset{1}{1}44$ $+\ \ 27$ $\overline{171}$	$\overset{111}{1}00101$ $+\ \ 10011$ $\overline{111000}$	$\overset{1}{8}E$ $+\ \ 2F$ $\overline{BD}$
Subtraction	$1\overset{3}{4}^{1}4$ $-\ \ 27$ $\overline{11\ 7}$	$\overset{0}{1}00\overset{0}{1}01$ $-\ \ 10011$ $\overline{10010}$	$\overset{7}{8}^{1}E$ $-\ \ 2\ F$ $\overline{5\ F}$

hexadecimal, as in decimal arithmetic, you carry to and borrow from the column to the left as needed as you move from right to left. Instead of carrying or borrowing 10, however—as you would in the decimal system—you carry or borrow 2 (binary) or 16 (hexadecimal).

Using a Scientific Calculator

A scientific calculator can be used to convert numbers between numbering systems, or to check conversions performed by hand. Many conventional calculators have different numbering system options; scientific calculator programs can be used for this purpose, as well. For example, Figure R-6 shows how to use the Windows Calculator program to double-check the hand calculations performed in Figure R-3 (the *Scientific* option must be selected using the View menu to display the options shown in the figure). Arithmetic can also be performed in any numbering system on a calculator, once that numbering system is selected on the calculator. Notice that, depending on which numbering system is currently selected, not all numbers on the calculator are available—only the possible numbers, such as only 0 and 1 when the binary numbering system is selected, as in the bottom screen in the figure.

FIGURE R-6

Using a scientific calculator. A physical calculator or calculator program can be used to convert between numbering systems, as well as to perform arithmetic in different numbering systems.

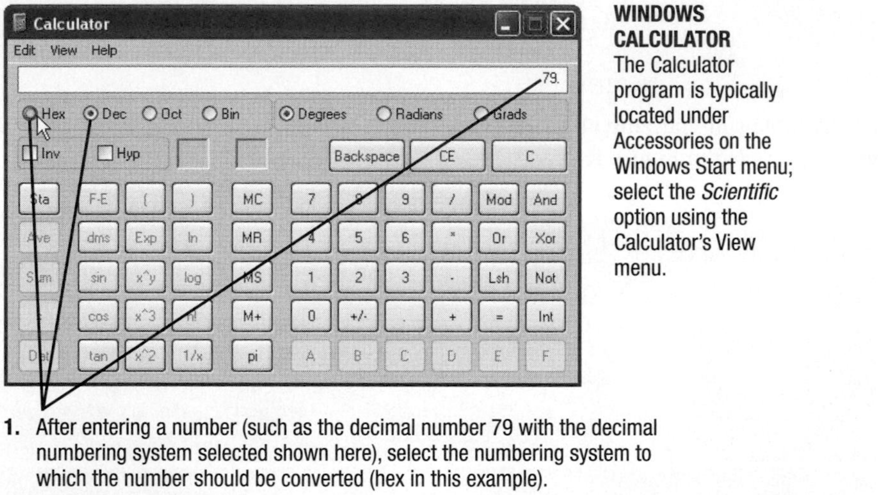

WINDOWS CALCULATOR
The Calculator program is typically located under Accessories on the Windows Start menu; select the *Scientific* option using the Calculator's View menu.

1. After entering a number (such as the decimal number 79 with the decimal numbering system selected shown here), select the numbering system to which the number should be converted (hex in this example).

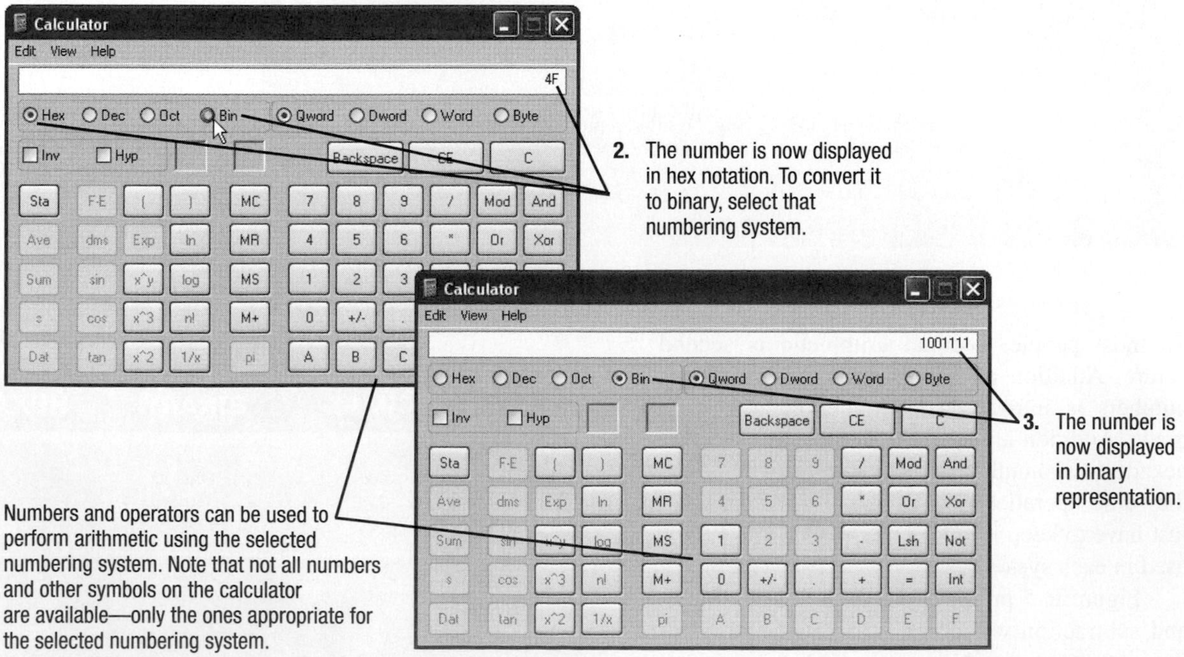

2. The number is now displayed in hex notation. To convert it to binary, select that numbering system.

3. The number is now displayed in binary representation.

Numbers and operators can be used to perform arithmetic using the selected numbering system. Note that not all numbers and other symbols on the calculator are available—only the ones appropriate for the selected numbering system.

As discussed in Chapter 3 of this text, coding systems for text-based data include *ASCII*, *EBCDIC*, and *Unicode*. ■

ASCII and EBCDIC

Figure R-7 provides a chart listing the ASCII and EBCDIC representations (in binary) for most of the symbols found on a typical keyboard.

> **FIGURE R-7**
> **ASCII and EBCDIC binary codes for typical keyboard symbols.**

SYMBOL	ASCII	EBCDIC	SYMBOL	ASCII	EBCDIC	SYMBOL	ASCII	EBCDIC
A	0100 0001	1100 0001	e	0110 0101	1000 0101	8	0011 1000	1111 1000
B	0100 0010	1100 0010	f	0110 0110	1000 0110	9	0011 1001	1111 1001
C	0100 0011	1100 0011	g	0110 0111	1000 0111	(	0010 1000	0100 1101
D	0100 0100	1100 0100	h	0110 1000	1000 1000	)	0010 1001	0101 1101
E	0100 0101	1100 0101	i	0110 1001	1000 1001	/	0010 1111	0110 0001
F	0100 0110	1100 0110	j	0110 1010	1001 0001	-	0010 1101	0110 0000
G	0100 0111	1100 0111	k	0110 1011	1001 0010	*	0010 1010	0101 1100
H	0100 1000	1100 1000	l	0110 1100	1001 0011	+	0010 1011	0100 1110
I	0100 1001	1100 1001	m	0110 1101	1001 0100	,	0010 1100	0110 1011
J	0100 1010	1101 0001	n	0110 1110	1001 0101	.	0010 1110	0100 1011
K	0100 1011	1101 0010	o	0110 1111	1001 0110	:	0011 1010	0111 1010
L	0100 1100	1101 0011	p	0111 0000	1001 0111	;	0011 1011	0101 1110
M	0100 1101	1101 0100	q	0111 0001	1001 1000	&	0010 0110	0101 0000
N	0100 1110	1101 0101	r	0111 0010	1001 1001	\	0101 1100	1110 0000
O	0100 1111	1101 0110	s	0111 0011	1010 0010	$	0010 0100	0101 1011
P	0101 0000	1101 0111	t	0111 0100	1010 0011	%	0010 0101	0110 1100
Q	0101 0001	1101 1000	u	0111 0101	1010 0100	=	0011 1101	0111 1110
R	0101 0010	1101 1001	v	0111 0110	1010 0101	>	0011 1110	0110 1110
S	0101 0011	1110 0010	w	0111 0111	1010 0110	<	0011 1100	0100 1100
T	0101 0100	1110 0011	x	0111 1000	1010 0111	!	0010 0001	0101 1010
U	0101 0101	1110 0100	y	0111 1001	1010 1000	|	0111 1100	0110 1010
V	0101 0110	1110 0101	z	0111 1010	1010 1001	?	0011 1111	0110 1111
W	0101 0111	1110 0110	0	0011 0000	1111 0000	@	0100 0000	0111 1100
X	0101 1000	1110 0111	1	0011 0001	1111 0001	_	0101 1111	0110 1101
Y	0101 1001	1110 1000	2	0011 0010	1111 0010	`	0110 0000	1011 1001
Z	0101 1010	1110 1001	3	0011 0011	1111 0011	{	0111 1011	1100 0000
a	0110 0001	1000 0001	4	0011 0100	1111 0100	}	0111 1101	1101 0000
b	0110 0010	1000 0010	5	0011 0101	1111 0101	~	0111 1110	1010 0001
c	0110 0011	1000 0011	6	0011 0110	1111 0110	[	0101 1011	0100 1010
d	0110 0100	1000 0100	7	0011 0111	1111 0111	]	0101 1101	0101 1010

A 0041	N 004E	a 0061	n 006E	0 0030	{ 007B	* 002A	■ 25A0	অ 0985
B 0042	O 004F	b 0062	o 006F	1 0031	| 007C	+ 002B	□ 25A1	গ 0997
C 0043	P 0050	c 0063	p 0070	2 0032	} 007D	, 002C	▲ 25B2	ে 09C7
D 0044	Q 0051	d 0064	q 0071	3 0033	~ 007E	- 002D	% 2105	৶ 09F6
E 0045	R 0052	e 0065	r 0072	4 0034	! 0021	. 002E	℞ 211E	č 0685
F 0046	S 0053	f 0066	s 0073	5 0035	" 0022	/ 002F	⅓ 2153	ڴ 06B4
G 0047	T 0054	g 0067	t 0074	6 0036	# 0023	£ 20A4	⅔ 2154	ਪ 06AA
H 0048	U 0055	h 0068	u 0075	7 0037	$ 0024	Σ 2211	♛ 2655	α 03B1
I 0049	V 0056	i 0069	v 0076	8 0038	% 0025	∅ 2205	☂ 2602	β 03B2
J 004A	W 0057	j 006A	w 0077	9 0039	& 0026	√ 221A	□ 2750	Δ 0394
K 004B	X 0058	k 006B	x 0078	[005B	' 0027	∞ 221E	☀ 2742	φ 03A6
L 004C	Y 0059	l 006C	y 0079	\ 005C	(0028	≤ 2264	➲ 27B2	Ω 03A9
M 004D	Z 005A	m 006D	z 007A	] 005D	) 0029	≥ 2265	♥ 2665	ÿ 03AB

Unicode

When consistent worldwide representation is needed, Unicode is typically used. Unicode can be used to represent every written language, as well as a variety of other symbols. Unicode codes are typically listed in hexadecimal notation—a sampling of Unicode is shown in Figure R-8.

Unicode notation is incorporated into many programs to refer to characters and other symbols. For instance, when the Symbol dialog box is opened using the Insert menu in Microsoft Office Word, the Unicode representation (as well as the corresponding ASCII code in either decimal or hexadecimal representation) can be viewed (see Figure R-9). Some programs allow you to enter a Unicode symbol using its Unicode hex value. For instance, in Microsoft Office programs you can use the Alt+X command when the insertion point is just to the right of a Unicode hex value to convert that hex value to the corresponding symbol. For example, the following keystrokes

2264Alt+X

results in the symbol corresponding to the Unicode code 2264 (the less than or equal sign ≤) being inserted into the document; entering 27B2 and then pressing Alt+X inserts the symbol shown in the Word screen in Figure R-9.

> **FIGURE R-8**
> **Selected Unicode codes.** Unicode can be used to represent all the world's written languages, as well as mathematical symbols, drawing symbols, punctuation marks, dingbats, and more.

> **FIGURE R-9**
> **Using Unicode.**

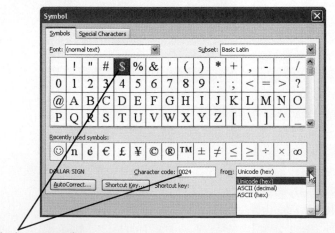

Unicode representation for $ symbol.

UNICODE REPRESENTATION
The Symbol dialog box shown here lists the Unicode representation of each symbol as it is selected. If preferred, the ASCII representation can be displayed.

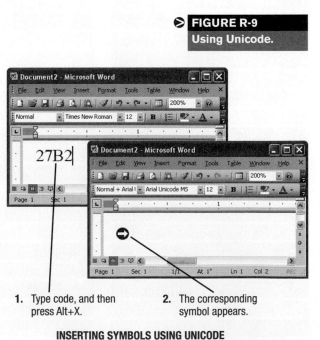

1. Type code, and then press Alt+X.

2. The corresponding symbol appears.

INSERTING SYMBOLS USING UNICODE
In Microsoft Office programs, typing the hexadecimal Unicode representation of a symbol and then pressing Alt+X displays the corresponding symbol.

CPU CHARACTERISTICS

As discussed in Chapter 3, CPUs have evolved over the years. An abbreviated summary of some of the most recent desktop and server CPUs was included in Chapter 3. The chart in Figure R-10 is a more comprehensive listing of some of the most significant processors since 1978. ▓

❯ **FIGURE R-10**
CPU characteristics.

Type of Processor	Year Introduced	CPU Name	Manu-facturer	Processing (clock) Speed	Word Size	Cache Memory			System Bus Width	System Bus Speed
						Level 1	Level 2	Level 3		
DESKTOP	2003	Athlon 64	AMD	2–2.2 GHz*	64 bit	128 KB	1 MB	n/a	64 bit	400 MHz
	2003	PowerPC G5	Apple/IBM	1.6–2 GHz*	64 bit	64 KB	512 KB	n/a	64 bit	1 GHz
	2003	Pentium M	Intel	900 MHz–1.7 GHz*	32 bit	64 KB	1 MB	n/a	64 bit	400 MHz
	2002	Celeron (Pentium 4-based)	Intel	1.7—2.8 GHz*	32 bit	20 KB	128 KB	n/a	64 bit	400 MHz
	2001	Athlon XP	AMD	1.33–2.25 GHz*	32 bit	128 KB	256–512 KB	n/a	64 bit	266–400 MHz
	2000	Pentium 4	Intel	1.3–3.2 MHz*	32 bit	20 KB	256–512 KB	n/a	64 bit	400–800 MHz
	2000	Duron	AMD	600 MHz–1.3 GHz	32 bit	128 KB	64 KB	n/a	64 bit	200 MHz
	2000	Celeron (Pentium III-based)	Intel	533 MHz—1.4 GHz	32 bit	32 KB	128–256 KB	n/a	64 bit	66–100 MHz
	1999	Athlon	AMD	500 MHz–1.4GHz	32 bit	128 KB	256–512 KB	n/a	64 bit	200–266 MHz
	1999	Pentium III	Intel	450 MHz–1.4GHz	32 bit	32 KB	256–512 KB	n/a	64 bit	100–133 MHz
	1999	PowerPC G4	Motorola	400—800 MHz	32 bit	32 KB	512 KB–2 MB	n/a	64 bit	133–167 MHz
	1998	Celeron (Pentium II-based	Intel	266–533 MHz	32 bit	32 KB	0–128 KB	n/a	64 bit	66 MHz
	1997	PowerPC 750(G3)	Motorola	200—400 MHz	32 bit	32 KB	256 KB–1 MB	n/a	64 bit	100 MHz
	1997	K6	AMD	166–550 MHz	32 bit	64 KB	256 KB	n/a	64 bit	66 MHz
	1997	Pentium II	Intel	233–450 MHz	32 bit	32 KB	512 KB–2 MB	n/a	64 bit	66–100 MHz
	1995	Pentium Pro	Intel	150–200 MHz	32 bit	16 KB	256 KB–1 MB	n/a	64 bit	60–66 MHz
	1993	Pentium	Intel	60–233 MHz	32 bit	16–32 KB	256 KB–1 MB	n/a	32–64 bit	50–66 MHz
	1989	80486	Intel	16–100 MHz	32 bit	8–16KB	128–256 KB	n/a	32 bit	16–33 MHz
	1985	80386	Intel	16–33 MHz	32 bit	n/a	16 KB	n/a	16–32 bit	16–12 MHz
	1982	80286	Intel	6–12.5 MHz	16 bit	n/a	n/a	n/a	16 bit	6–12 MHz
	1978/1979	8086/8088	Intel	4.77–10 MHz	16 bit	n/a	n/a	n/a	8–16 bit	5–12 MHz
SERVER	2003	Opteron	AMD	1.4–2.2 GHz*	64 bit	128 KB	1 MB	n/a	64 bit	667 MHz
	2002	Itanium 2	Intel	900 MHz–1.5GHz*	64 bit	32 KB	256 KB	1.5–6 MB	128 bit	400 MHz
	2001	Althon MP	AMD	1–2.13 GHz*	32 bit	128 KB	256–512 KB	n/a	64 bit	266 MHz
	2001	Xeon (Pentium4-based)	Intel	1.4–3.2 GHz*	32 bit	20 KB	256–512 KB	0–2 MB	64 bit	400–533 MHz
	2001	Itanium	Intel	733–800 MHz	64 bit	32 KB	96 KB	2–4 MB	64 bit	266 MHz
	1999	Xeon (PentiumIII-based)	Intel	500 MHz–1 GHz	32 bit	32 KB	256 KB–2 MB	n/a	64 bit	100–133 MHz
	1998	Xeon (PentiumII-based)	Intel	400–450 MHz	32 bit	32 KB	512 KB–2 MB	n/a	64 bit	100 MHz

* Higher speeds expected in the future.

Before buying a new PC, it is important to give some thought to what your needs are, including what software programs you wish to run, any other computers with which you need to be compatible, how you might want to connect to the Internet, and whether or not portability is important. This section of the References and Resources Guide explores topics related to buying and upgrading a PC. ■

Analyzing Needs

When referring to a computer system, a *need* refers to a functional requirement that the computer system must be able to meet. For example, at a video rental store, a computer system must be able to enter bar codes automatically from videos or DVDs being checked in and out, identify customers with overdue movies, manage movie inventories, and do routine accounting operations. Requiring portability is another example of a need. For example, sales personnel working out of the office can often justify purchasing a notebook computer simply on the basis of its usefulness as a sale-closing tool during presentations at their clients' offices.

Selecting a PC for home or business use must begin with the all-important question "What do I want the system to do?" Once you've determined what tasks the system will be used for, you can choose among the software and hardware alternatives available. Making a list of your needs in areas discussed in the next few sections can help you get a picture of what type of system you are shopping for. If you're not really sure what you want a system to do, you should think twice about buying one yet—you can easily make expensive mistakes if you're uncertain about what you want a system to do. Some common decision categories are discussed next; Figure R-11 provides a list of questions that can help you define the type of computer that will meet your needs.

> ◈ **FIGURE R-11**
>
> **Questions to consider when getting ready to buy a PC.**

What tasks will I be using the computer for (writing papers, accessing the Internet, graphic design, composing music, playing games, etc.)?

Do I prefer a Mac or PC-compatible? Are there any other computers I need my documents and storage media to be compatible with?

How fast do I need the system to be?

Do I need portability? If so, do I need the features of a conventional PC (notebook or tablet) or can I use a handheld PC?

What size and type of screen do I want?

What removable storage media will I need to use in the PC (such as standard floppy disks, Zip disks, CDs, DVDs, or flash memory drive)?

Do I need to be able to connect the PC to the Internet? If so, what type of Internet access will I be using (conventional dial-up, ISDN, DSL, cable, satellite, or wireless, for instance)?

Do I need to be able to connect the PC to a network? If so, is it a wired or wireless network?

What additional hardware do I need (scanner, printer, or digital camera, for example)?

When do I need the computer?

Do I want to pay extra for a better warranty (such as a longer time period or on-site service)?

Operating Systems and Application Software

Determining what functions you want the PC system to perform will help you decide which application software is needed. Most users start with an application suite containing a word processor, spreadsheet, and other programs. In addition, specialty programs, such as tax preparation, drawing, home publishing, reference software, games, and more may be needed or desired.

Not all software is available for all operating systems. Consequently, if a specific piece of software is needed, that choice may determine which operating system you need to use. Alternatively, if your documents need to be compatible with those of another computer (such as other office computers or between a home and an office PC), your operating system decision may already be made for you. The most widely used PC operating systems are Windows, Mac OS, and Linux.

Platforms and Configuration Options

If your operating system has already been determined, that is a good start in deciding the overall platform you will be looking for—most users will choose between the IBM-compatible and Apple Macintosh platform. IBM and compatible PCs usually run either Windows or Linux; Apple computers almost always use Mac OS.

Configuration decisions involve primarily determining the size of the machine desired. For non-portable systems, you have the choice between tower, desktop, or all-in-one configurations. For any of these PCs, you should determine how large a monitor is needed and if you want a CRT or flat-screen monitor. Portable, fully functioning PCs can be notebook or tablet PCs. If a powerful, fully functioning PC is not required, you may decide to go with a more portable option, such as a handheld or pocket PC.

You should also consider any other specifications that are important to you, such as the size of the hard drive, type of removable storage needed, amount of memory required, and so forth. As discussed in the next section, these decisions often require reconciling the features you want with the amount of money you're willing to spend.

Power vs. Budget Requirements

As part of the needs analysis, you should look closely at your need for a powerful system versus your budgetary constraints. Most users don't need a state-of-the-art system. Those who do should expect to pay more than the average user. A PC that was top of the line six months or a year ago is usually reasonably priced and more than adequate for most users needs. Individuals who just want a PC for basic tasks, such as using the Internet and word processing, can likely get by with an inexpensive PC designed for home use.

When determining your requirements, be sure to identify the features and functions that are absolutely essential for your primary PC tasks (such as a large hard drive and lots of memory for multimedia applications, a fast video card for gaming, a fast Internet connection for individuals with a high level of Internet use, and so forth).

Listing Alternatives

After you consider your needs and the questions mentioned in Figure R-11, you should have a pretty good idea of the hardware and software you'll need. You'll also know what purchasing options are available to you, depending on your time frame (while some retail stores have systems that can be purchased and brought home the same day, special orders or some systems purchased over the Internet may take a couple of weeks to arrive). The next step is to get enough information from possible vendors to compare and contrast a few alternative systems that satisfy your stated needs. Most often, these vendors are local stores (such as computer stores, warehouse clubs, and electronic stores) and/or online stores (such as manufacturer Web sites and e-tailers). To compare prices and specifications for possible computer systems, find at least three systems that meet or exceed your needs by looking through newspaper advertisements, configuring systems online via manufacturer and e-tailer Web sites, or calling or visiting local stores. A comparison sheet listing your criteria and the systems you are considering, such as the one in Figure R-12, can help you summarize your options. Although it is sometimes very difficult to compare the prices of systems, since they typically have somewhat different configurations, you can assign an approximate dollar value to each extra feature a system has (such as $100 for an included printer or $50 for a larger hard drive). Be sure to also include any sales tax and shipping charges when you compare the prices of each total system.

If your budget is limited, you will have to balance the system you need with extra features you may want. For example, unless you really need a digital camera for your coursework or job, that money might be better spent on a larger hard drive or extra memory, since hard drive space is consumed quickly and newer programs require more memory and processing speed. Often for just a few extra dollars, you can get a much faster system or larger hard drive—significantly cheaper than trying to upgrade to that level later. A good rule of thumb is to try to buy a little more computer than you think you'll need. On the other hand, don't buy a top-of-the-line system, unless you fall into the *power user* category and really

COMPONENT	EXAMPLE OF DESIRED SPECIFICATIONS	SYSTEM #1 VENDOR:	SYSTEM #2 VENDOR:	SYSTEM #3 VENDOR:
Operating System	Windows XP			
Manufacturer	HP or Compaq			
Style	Tower			
CPU	AMD 2 GHz or higher			
RAM	512 MB or higher			
Hard drive	80 GB or higher			
Removable storage	Floppy drive and flash memory card reader			
Optical drive	DVD-RW			
Monitor	Flat-panel 17-inch			
Video card and video RAM	must have at least 16 MB dedicated video RAM			
Keyboard	would like sleep key			
Mouse	optical with scroll wheel			
Sound card/speakers	Harmon-Kardon preferred			
Modem	Cable			
Network card	10/100Base-T Ethernet			
Printer	ink-jet if get deal on price with complete system			
Scanner	don't need			
Included software	Microsoft Office or Works			
Warranty	3 years min. (1 year onsite if not a local store)			
Other features	2 front USB ports			
Price				
Tax				
Shipping				
TOTAL COST				

> **FIGURE R-12**
> **Comparing PC alternatives.** A checklist such as this one can help to organize your desired criteria and evaluate possible systems.

need a state-of-the-art system. Generally, the second or third system down from the top of the line is a very good system for a much more reasonable price. Some guidelines for minimum requirements for most home users are as follows:

▼ 2.4 GHz Pentium 4 (or equivalent) CPU (generally, any CPU currently being sold today is fast enough for most users).

▼ 512 MB or more of memory (RAM).

▼ 80 GB or more hard drive space.

▼ CD or DVD drive plus a removable disk drive compatible with conventional floppy disks.

▼ Conventional dial-up modem plus a special modem, if needed, for an alternative type of Internet access.

▼ Sound card and external speakers.

▼ At least 2 USB ports.

System Troubleshooting and Upgrading

After your new system has been purchased and is up and running (refer to the Chapter 1 How it Works box for a review of how to set up a new PC), chances are at some point you will need to do some troubleshooting and upgrading.

Troubleshooting

Troubleshooting refers to actions taken to diagnose or solve a problem. Unfortunately, many problems are unique to specific types of hardware and software, so no simple troubleshooting remedy works all of the time. Nonetheless, the following simple steps and guidelines can help you to identify and correct a number of common problems.

▼ Try again. A surprising number of procedures work when you try a second or third time. You may have pressed the wrong keys the first time, not pressed the keys hard enough, or have a special function activated (such as by pressing the Caps Lock, Num Lock, or Insert key on the keyboard). If you've accidentally activated such a function, pressing the key again should turn the feature off and correct the problem.

▼ Check to see that all the equipment is plugged in and turned on and that none of the cables are detached or loose.

▼ Reboot the system. Many software problems are corrected after the computer is restarted and the program is opened again. Some operating systems—such as Windows—will also try to reconfigure problem devices when the system is restarted, as well as give you the option of temporarily disabling certain devices if your system crashed, to help you determine the problem device. If for some reason the system doesn't boot at all, use your system startup disk (most systems either come with one or suggest you make one using a system option).

▼ Recall exactly what happened between the time the system was operating properly and the time you began to encounter problems. You may have just deleted a large group of files or programs and possibly deleted a part of the system software by accident. Or perhaps you installed a new piece of hardware or software during your last session, and it is affecting the way your current application works.

▼ Be observant. If you heard a strange noise the last time you used your PC, it might be important. Even though solving the problem may be beyond your capabilities, the information may help the person who will assist you in figuring out the problem.

▼ Check the *documentation*, or descriptive instructions, that came with the system. Many products come with a hard-copy manual with a troubleshooting checklist; software programs usually have an online help feature that can help you solve many problems.

▼ Use diagnostic software. *Diagnostic utility programs* (discussed in Chapter 6) can be used to test your system to see if parts of it are malfunctioning or are just giving you poor performance. Sometimes when new equipment is added, problems arise with existing equipment or software. Also, hard drives can get fragmented with use over time and may need to be defragmented.

You should weigh the time that it takes to solve a problem yourself against the cost of outside help. It's not a personal failure to give up if the problem is more than you can handle. It is simply an admission that your time is valuable and that you are wise enough to know when to call in a professional for assistance. Options for technical assistance include:

▼ *Manufacturer*. Many manufacturers have toll-free phone numbers, fax numbers, e-mail addresses, and support information on their Web sites for users with technical assistance questions. If your system is still under warranty, you should contact the manufacturer before trying any other technical support options. Commonly, software manufacturers post *patches*—small software program updates that correct known bugs in the program—on their Web sites. These patches can usually be downloaded for free and typically are easy to install.

▼ *Third-party support.* If your system is out of warranty, you can get help from a third-party firm, such as a local computer repair company or a company that will provide assistance via the phone or Web. Typically you are charged by the minute or hour (with a minimum fee often assessed) for assistance acquired via a third party.

▼ *User Support.* You can also get suggestions from other users via online discussion groups. To find an appropriate group, check the manufacturer's Web site to see if it has a link to a discussion group for the product in question, or locate an appropriate group from a third-party technical support Web site. The message you post might be read by literally hundreds of other users, and there's a good possibility that someone out there has encountered and solved the problem you are now wrestling with. While you may get the answer you are seeking without paying a dime, don't be surprised if you have to wait for a few days or more to have your plea for help read by the right person.

Upgrading

Hardware and software generally need to be upgraded over time. *Upgrading* a computer system means buying new hardware or software components that extend the life of your current system. The question you must ask when considering an upgrade is the same one that you would ask when considering costly repairs to a car: Should I spend this money on my current system or start fresh and buy a completely new system?

Upgrading Hardware

Some common hardware upgrades include adding more RAM or an additional storage device to a system, installing a faster modem or additional memory, adding expansion boards to provide new types of functionality, and adding new peripheral equipment such as a scanner or color printer. Unless your system is powerful enough to handle growth, many upgrades are not possible. For example, if you have a computer that is more than three years old, it is usually not cost-effective to upgrade it, since some new PCs sell for $500 or less.

Upgrading Software

Many PC software vendors enhance their products in some major way every year or two, prompting users to upgrade. Each upgrade—called a *version*—is assigned a number, such as 1.0, 2.0, 3.0, and so on. The higher the number, the more recent and more powerful the software is. Minor versions, called *releases*, typically increase their numbers in increments of 0.1—such as 1.1, 1.2, and 1.3—or .01. For example, release 3.11 might follow release 3.1, and release 7.1 might follow 7.0. Releases are usually issued in response to bugs or shortcomings in the version and are often free.

When a free update is available for a program that you use, or when a patch to fix a known problem becomes available, typically these are downloaded via the software publisher's Web site (see Figure R-13). Many software publishers also offer free templates, clip art, and other downloaded resources via their Web sites—one example is shown in Figure R-13. Full software upgrades are more often purchased in physical form and they generally cost less than buying the full version. Before upgrading to a new version, be sure to weigh the benefits against its costs. Unless the new version has a feature that you require, it may not be necessary to upgrade to each and every new version.

◆ FIGURE R-13
Software updates.

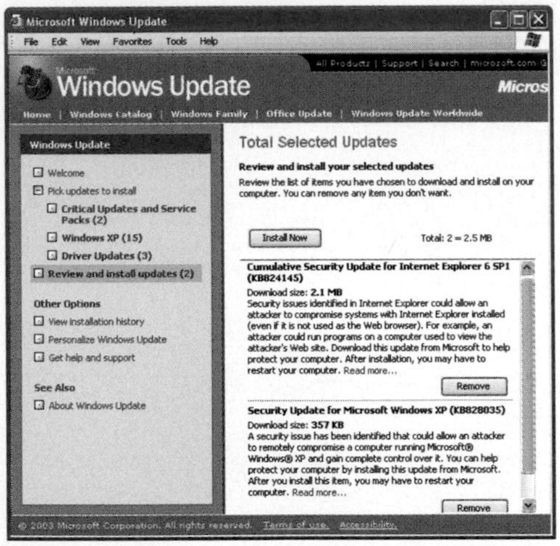

WINDOWS UPDATE
The Windows Update feature can be used to regularly locate and install patches and other updates for Windows and Internet Explorer.

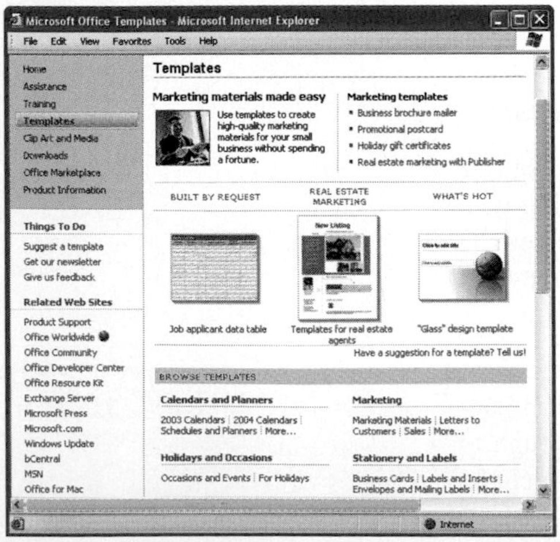

SOFTWARE WEB SITES
Support Web sites for specific software programs (such as the one for Microsoft Office shown here) can be used to locate free templates, clip art, and other resources to be used with that program.

WEB GUIDE

The World Wide Web has an enormous amount of useful and interesting information. This guide is a collection of useful sites, arranged into categories. Although these links were accurate at the time this book was published, URLs do change. For a more up-to-date list, visit the online Web Guide located at www.course.com/uc10/webguide.html ▪

BUSINESS AND PERSONAL FINANCE

Business Wire	www.businesswire.com	Current business news
CBS MarketWatch	www.cbsmarketwatch.com	Current news about business and financial markets
CNN Money	money.cnn.com	Current news about business and financial markets
Digital Daily	www.irs.gov	Current tax information on a wide variety of topics, including downloadable tax forms and publications from the IRS
FinanCenter	www.financenter.com	A variety of personal finance information, including loan and credit card information; and a variety of calculators, such as for loans, investments, savings, retirement, and life insurance
Fool.com	www.fool.com	Information on investing, retirement, and other personal finance topics
Forbes	www.forbes.com	Online version of the magazine containing articles and investment information
Fortune.com	www.fortune.com	Online articles and investment information
Hoover's Online	www.hoovers.com	Company capsules, stock quotes, charts, and other financial information
Morningstar.com	www.morningstar.com	Information on a variety of mutual funds
MSN MoneyCentral	moneycentral.msn.com/home.asp	Links to investing, stock tracking, and other financial information
Research	www.researchmag.com	Online broker magazine that includes free corporate profiles
Rutgers Accounting Web	accounting.rutgers.edu/raw/internet/internet1.html	Links to financial journals, accounting associations and organizations, SEC filings, tax information, and so forth
Securities & Exchange Commision	www.sec.gov	Access to government filings made by public companies
Silicon Investor	www.siliconinvestor.com	Free quotes, research information, and message boards related to technology stocks
USA Today Money	www.usatoday.com/money/front.htm	Online version of *USA Today's* Money *section*
Yahoo! Finance	finance.yahoo.com	Free stock quotes, news, and portfolio tracker

JOBS AND EMPLOYMENT

CareerBuilder	www.careerbuilder.com	Free job searching and resume posting, as well as helpful job-hunting tools and information
ComputerJobs.com	www.computerjobs.com	Search for computer-related jobs
Monster.com	www.monster.com	Free job searching and resume posting, as well as helpful tools and information
Sales Jobs, Inc.	www.salesjobs.com	Search for sales jobs and post online resumes
Talent Zoo	www.talentzoo.com	Find advertising-related jobs, such as art directors and copyeditors
Yahoo! HotJobs	hotjobs.yahoo.com	Search jobs and post online resumes

COMPUTERS

Business 2.0	www.business2.com	Online version of Business 2.0 magazine
Byte Online	www.byte.com	Online version of Byte magazine
CNET	www.cnet.com	News, articles, and reviews about computers
CNN Sci-Tech	cnn.com/TECH	CNN Technology page
Computer History Museum: Timeline of Computer History	www.computerhistory.org/ timeline	A thorough history of computers
Computerworld	www.computerworld.com	Online version of Computerworld magazine
eWEEK	www.eweek.com	Online version of eWEEK magazine
Free Email Address Directory	www.emailaddresses.com	Information about free e-mail service and other e-mail resources
The Free Graphics Store Archives	www.ausmall.com.au/ freegraf/freegrfa.htm	A collection of free GIF and JPEG images
MacCentral	maccentral.macworld.com	Information and news about Apple computers
Online Connection	www.barkers.org/online	Information about current pricing and services for a wide variety of national Internet providers
PC World Online	www.pcworld.com	Online version of PC World magazine
Shareware.com	www.shareware.com	A collection of downloadable shareware
Stroud's CWS Apps List	cws.internet.com	A collection of downloadable software
Tom's Hardware Guide	www.tomshardware.com	Articles, reviews, and other helpful information about hardware
ZD Net	www.zdnet.com	Computer news and reviews, plus links and searching capabilities for all ZDNet magazine

REFERENCE

Achoo Healthcare Online	www.achoo.com	Access to a wide range of health information
AnyWho Online Directory	www.tollfree.att.net/tf.html	Look up people, businesses, toll-free telephone numbers, maps, and so on
Bartleby.com—Great Books Online	www.bartleby.com	Access online reference books, including Columbia Encyclopedia and American Heritage College Dictionary, plus a collection of fiction and non-fiction books
Dictionary.com	www.dictionary.com	Search online dictionary; also access to online thesaurus
FindLaw	www.findlaw.com	Look up laws and access a variety of other legal information
HowStuffWorks	www.howstuffworks.com	Tutorials and explanations of how things work, such as computer, household, and electronic products
Internet Public Library	www.ipl.org	An online library with books, exhibits, and magazines
The Library of Congress	www.loc.gov	Look up books and historical papers, access Thomas for legislative information, and more
Merriam-Webster Online	www.m-w.com/netdict.htm	Online version of this dictionary; can search thesaurus, as well
Onelook Dictionaries	www.onelook.com	Online dictionary has access to over 6 million words in nearly 1,000 online dictionaries
SuperPages.com	superpages.com	Online white pages, yellow pages, reverse phone book, and more
Switchboard.com	www.switchboard.com	Online white pages, yellow pages, maps, and more
Thesaurus.com	www.thesaurus.com	Online thesaurus; also access to online dictionary
TopoZone.com	www.topozone.com	Free U.S. topographical maps
USPS—The United States Postal Service	www.usps.com	Includes a variety of services, such as looking up ZIP codes, checking postal rates, package tracking, and buying stamps online
WebMD	www.webmd.com	A collection of health information, including discussion boards and live chats with health experts
Webopedia	www.webopedia.com	Online dictionary for computer and Internet terms

ENTERTAINMENT AND SPORTS

Blue Mountain Arts	www1.bluemountain.com	Send free electronic greeting cards; the recipient is sent an e-mail link to view the card
ESPN.com	msn.espn.go.com	Sports news
Internet Movie Database	www.imdb.com	Comprehensive movie database—can search by title, actors, and more
iTunes Store	www.apple.com/itunes/store	Buy and download music singles
MLB.com	www.mlb.com	Official site of Major League Baseball
MSN Gaming Zone	zone.msn.com	Play over 20 free Internet-based games online against other Internet gamers; additional games can be played for a fee
Musicmatch Jukebox	musicmatch.com	Download free media player; buy and download music singles
Napster 2	napster.com	Buy and download music singles
National Gallery of Art	nga.gov	Take an online tour
NBA.com	www.nba.com	Official site of the National Basketball Association
NFL.com	www.nfl.com	Official site of the National Football League
Real.com	www.real.com	Download the free RealPlayer; sign up for paid radio and music downloads
Reel.com	www.reel.com	Movie previews and DVD movie information
Rock & Roll Hall of Fame	www.rockhall.com	Rock & Roll museum
Sports Illustrated.com	sportsillustrated.cnn.com	Sports news
Ticketmaster.com	www.ticketmaster.com	Book tickets for concerts, sporting events, and other live events
Trails.com	www.trails.com	Detailed information on more than 30,000 U.S. and Canadian skiing, biking, paddling, and hiking trails or other outdoor trips
TV Guide Online	www.tvguide.com	Includes TV news and gossip, as well as TV listings by time zone or ZIP code

NEWS AND WEATHER

ABC News.com	abcnews.go.com	Online version of ABC News
Accuweather	accuweather.com	National and international weather forecasts, maps, and satellite pictures
CNN.com	www.cnn.com	Online version of CNN
Intellicast	www.intellicast.com	National and international weather forecasts; weather planners for a variety of outdoor activities
Los Angeles Times	www.latimes.com	Online version of this newspaper
MSNBC	www.msnbc.com	Online version of MSNBC News
National Weather Service	www.nws.noaa.gov	National and international weather forecasts; weather hazard information
NewsDirectory.com	www.newsdirectory.com	Links to hundreds of online periodicals, by subject area; includes search capabilities
The New York Times on the Web	www.nytimes.com	Online version of this newspaper
USAToday.com	www.usatoday.com	Online version of this newspaper
WashingtonPost.com	www.washingtonpost.com	Online version of this newspaper
The Weather Channel	www.weather.com	National, international, and local weather forecasts
Weather Underground	www.wunderground.com	A variety of weather-related maps plus forecasts, ski reports, and more
Wired News	wired.com	News about technology, politics, culture, and so forth

SEARCH SITES

AskJeeves	www.ask.com	Natural language search site
Dogpile	dogpile.com	Metasearch site; search for Web pages, news, shopping, and more
Excite	www.excite.com	Keyword and directory searching; some reference tools, as well
Google	www.google.com	Keyword, directory, and news searching
Lycos	www.lycos.com	Keyword searching for Web pages and shopping
MSN Search	search.msn.com	Keyword and directory searching; some reference tools, as well
ODP–Open Directory Project	dmoz.org	Keyword and directory searching
Yahoo!	www.yahoo.com	Keyword and directory searching; lots of reference tools
Yahooligans!	www.yahooligans.com	Keyword and directory searching for kids

SHOPPING

Amazon.com	www.amazon.com	Buy books, music, DVDs and more; also features an online auction and goods from partner stores, such as Toys R Us and Target
Autoweb.com	www.autoweb.com	Information to help you research, buy, sell, finance, insure, and maintain your car
Barnes & Noble	www.barnesandnoble.com	Buy books, music, DVDs, videos, and more
Best Buy	www.bestbuy.com	Buy computers, electronics, movies, music, and more
Buy.com	www.us.buy.com	Buy movies, electronics, books, toys, and more
CircuitCity.com	circuitcity.com	Buy computers, electronics, movies, music, and more
CompUSA	www.compusa.com	Buy computers, electronics, movies, music, and more
Deep Discount CD	www.deepdiscountcd.com	Discount prices on CDs; free shipping
Deep Discount DVD	www.deepdiscountdvd.com	Discount prices on DVDs; free shipping
eBay	www.ebay.com	Online auction site where users can buy or sell goods
Epinions.com	www.epinions.com	Search for pricing and reviews for products
Homestore.com	homestore.com	Search for homes for sale, homes and apartments for rent, and lots of information on home-related topics and products
Land's End	landsend.com	Buy Land's End products online
OldNavy.com	www.oldnavy.com	Buy Old Navy products online
Schwan's: Fine Frozen Foods	www.schwans.com	Have frozen food delivered to your home
Walmart.com	www.walmart.com	Offers a variety of merchandise online

TRAVEL

Amtrak	www.amtrak.com	Check schedules and book your Amtrak trip online
Bed & Breakfast Inns Online	www.bbonline.com	Get information on more than 4,500 bed & breakfasts around the world
CitySearch	www.citysearch.com	City guides for the U.S. and abroad; search for restaurants, hotels, and more
Expedia Travel	expedia.com	Research and book flights, hotels, cars, cruises, and more
HostelWorld.com	www.hostelworld.com	Get information, pricing, and book stays at thousands of hostels worldwide
InfoHub Specialty Travel Guide	infohub.com	Search over 11,000 guided or self-guided specialty vacations offered by over 1,300 travel suppliers
Priceline.com	www.priceline.com	Bid prices for airline seats, hotel rooms, car rentals, and more
Study Abroad Programs	www.iiepassport.org	Search for college study abroad programs
Travelocity.com	www.travelocity.com	Check out and book flights, hotels, cars, cruises, and more

General search strategies, such as typing more than one keyword, and using synonyms, variant word forms, and multiple search sites, were discussed in Chapter 9. This guide takes a closer look at strategies for using one specific search site–*Google*. Google, one of the most widely used search sites, supports basic searching, advanced searching, plus a variety of reference tools. ■

Google Search Options

As illustrated in Figure 9-10 in Chapter 9, from the Google home page at www.google.com you can do a basic keyword search, or switch to an image, group, directory, or news search. In addition, there are other search options. For instance, the *Froogle Product Search* option enables you to search for products for sale online, and the *Glossary Search* option can be used to find definitions from dictionaries, medical and legal Web sites, and other sources. A complete list of Google search options is included in Figure R-14.

Google Advanced Search

The *Advanced Search* option accessed from the Google home page or by typing the appropriate URL is an easy-to-use, fill-in-the blank way of performing complex searches, such as those with Boolean operators and field searches. As shown in Figure R-15, entering the appropriate information and clicking the Search button results in the corresponding search terms being used and the matching Web pages displayed. Although many of the search operators that Google supports are available through the Advanced Search option, not all are. A list of some of the most commonly used Google search operators and their proper syntax is included in Figure R-16.

SEARCH OPTION	URL
Advanced search	www.google.com/advanced_search
Basic search	www.google.com
Catalog search	catalog.google.com
Directory search	directory.google.com
Discussion group search	groups.google.com
Glossary search	labs.google.com/glossary
Image search	images.google.com
Language tools	www.google.com/language_tools
News search	news.google.com
Product search (Froogle)	froogle.google.com

> **FIGURE R-14**
> Google search options.

> **FIGURE R-15**
> Advanced searching with Google.

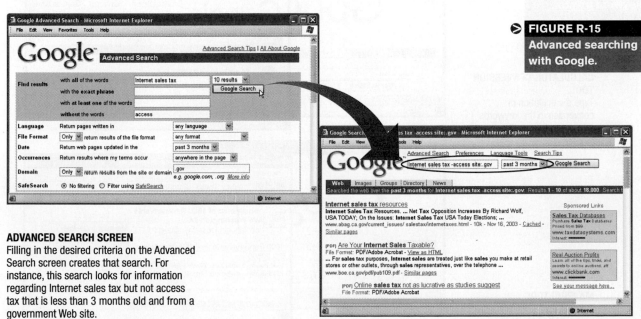

ADVANCED SEARCH SCREEN
Filling in the desired criteria on the Advanced Search screen creates that search. For instance, this search looks for information regarding Internet sales tax but not access tax that is less than 3 months old and from a government Web site.

COMMONLY USED GOOGLE SEARCH OPERATORS

Operator and Syntax	Purpose
cache:*URL*	Shows the cached version of the specified Web page.
link:*URL*	Lists all Web pages linked to the specified URL.
related:*URL*	Lists Web pages similar to the specified Web page.
define:*term*	Provides definition of specified word or phrase.
stocks:*symbol*	Shows stock information for specified stock ticker symbol.
keywords site:*URL*	Performs the specified keyword search on just the specified site.
Allintitle:*keywords*	Returns Web pages with specified keywords in their titles.
Allinurl:*keywords*	Returns Web pages with specified keywords in their URLs.
+*keyword*	Insures the specified keyword is not ignored in the search.
–*keyword*	Excludes the specified keyword from the search.
~*keyword*	Searches for Web pages matching the specified keyword plus its synonyms.
keyword OR *keyword*	Searches for Web pages matching either specified keyword.

> **FIGURE R-16**
> **Google search operators.**

> **FIGURE R-17**
> **Using the Google keyword box to access reference tools.**

Other Google Tools

Google is continually adding new features and reference tools. For instance, by simply entering the keywords or phrases in the keywords text box on the Google home page you can look up a phone number, map a location, or perform a conversion (see Figure R-17). In addition, Web pages written in Italian, French, Spanish, German, or Portuguese can be translated into English (look for a "Translate this page" option next to a page returned in a list of search results). Most Web pages are cached for a least a month, so that version of a Web page can be viewed using the "Cached" option listed next to the page in a list of hits, if the current version of the page no longer contains the information you need. Other searches (available at the time this book was published) that can be conducted using the keywords text box on the Google home page are:

▼ *Calculator:* Type a mathematical expression or a specific conversion (such as "10 pounds in kilograms") to see the result.

▼ *Phonebook:* Type a name and either city, area code, or ZIP code to look up that person's address and phone number; type a phone number to return the name and address of that person.

▼ *Stock quotes:* Type one or more ticker symbols to retrieve stock quotes.

▼ *Street maps:* Type an address to find a map to that location.

CALCULATOR/CONVERSION TOOL
Type a calculation or conversion in the keywords box to see the results.

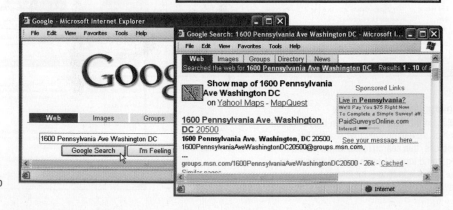

MAPPING TOOL
Type an address to get a link to a map of that location.

Chapter 1

1. F 2. T 3. F 4. T 5. F 6. Input 7. storage 8. tower 9. personal computer, PC 10. Internet appliance

Chapter 2

1. T 2. T 3. T 4. F 5. F 6. Start 7. hyperlink 8. servers 9. bookmark, favorite 10. telephony

Chapter 3

1. T 2. F 3. F 4. T 5. F 6. 13 7. 3 8. motherboard, system board 9. port 10. pipelining

Chapter 4

1. F 2. T 3. F 4. F 5. T 6. volatile 7. CD-R disc 8. magnetic tape 9. smart card 10. flash memory

Chapter 5

1. F 2. F 3. T 4. T 5. F 6. hard 7. pixels 8. scanner, optical scanner, flatbed scanner, handheld scanner 9. electronic pen, stylus 10. flat-panel, LCD; CRT

Chapter 6

1. F 2. T 3. F 4. F 5. T 6. path 7. operating system; utility 8. Linux 9. fragmented 10. compression

Chapter 7

1. T 2. F 3. T 4. T 5. F 6. shareware 7. font face, typeface; font 8. cell 9. record 10. slide show

Chapter 8

1. F 2. T 3. F 4. T 5. F 6. telemedicine 7. communications satellite 8. virtual private network (VPN) 9. biometric 10. firewall

Chapter 9

1. F 2. F 3. T 4. F 5. T 6. DSL 7. search engine 8. online auction 9. blog, Web log 10. Privacy, Information privacy

CREDITS

Throughout the modules: Screen shots of Microsoft Access®, Excel®, Paint®, PowerPoint®, Publisher®, Visual Basic®, Word®, and Windows® reprinted with permission from Microsoft Corporation. Internet Interfaces:

Netscape browser window© 2002 Netscape Communications Corporation. Used with permission. Netscape Communications has not authorized, sponsored, endorsed, or approved this publication and is not responsible for its content.

Copyright © Microsoft Explorer® reprinted with permission from Microsoft Corporation.

Chapter 1

Figure 1-1a, © Comstock Photography; **Figure 1-1b**, Courtesy of Microsoft Corporation; **Figure 1-1c**, Courtesy of the Electrolux Group; **Figure 1-1d**, © Comstock Photography; **Figure 1-2a**, © Eyewire; **Figure 1-2b**, Courtesy of Western Kentucky University; **Figure 1-2c**, Courtesy of Sony Electronics, Inc.; **Figure 1-3a**, Courtesy of International Business Machines Corporation. Unauthorized use not permitted.; **Figure 1-3b**, Courtesy of Hewlett-Packard Company; **Figure 1-3c**, Courtesy of Symbol Technologies, Inc.; **Figure 1-3d**, Courtesy of Intel Corporation; **Figure 1-4a**, Courtesy of Boingo Wireless, Inc.; **Figure 1-4b**, Courtesy of Kiosk Information Systems; **Figure 1-4c**, Courtesy of Garmin Ltd. or its subsidiaries; **Figure 1-4d**, Courtesy of The Internet Exchange; **Trend box**, Courtesy of Xybernaut Corporation; **Figure 1-6ace**, Courtesy of IBM Archives; **Figure 1-6b**, Courtesy U.S. Army; **Figure 1-6d**, Courtesy, Hewlett-Packard Company; **Figure 1-7a**, Courtesy of Gateway, Inc.; **Figure 1-7b**, Courtesy, Hewlett-Packard Company; **Figure 1-7c**, Courtesy of Lexar Media; **Figure 1-7d**, Courtesy of Telex Communications; **Figure 1-9b**, Courtesy of MUSICMATCH Inc.; **Figure 1-10a**, Courtesy MPC Computers; **Figure 1-10b**, Courtesy Acer America; **Figure 1-10c**, Courtesy of International Business Machines Corporation. Unauthorized use not permitted.; **Figure 1-11a**, Courtesy of Microsoft Corporation; **Figure 1-11b**, Courtesy of Research in Motion; **Figure 1-12a**, Courtesy Acer America; **Figure 1-12b**, Courtesy of @Xi Computer Corporation; **Figure 1-12c**, Courtesy of Apple Computer Corporation; **How box bd**, Courtesy Acer America; **How box c**, Courtesy Kensington Technology Group, www.kensington.com; **Inside box a**, Courtesy of CrazyModders.be; **Inside box b**, Courtesy of Kurt Villcheck; **Inside box c**, Courtesy of MNPCTECH.COM; **Figure 1-13a**, Courtesy of MPC Computers; **Figure 1-13b**, Courtesy of ViewSonic Corporation; **Figure 1-13c**, Courtesy of Palm, Inc.; **Figure 1-13def**, Courtesy Acer America; **Campus box**, Courtesy Stanford University Medical Center; **Figure 1-14a**, Courtesy of Sun Microsystems; **Figure 1-14b**, Courtesy Landel Telecom; **Figure 1-14c**, MSN TV Set Top Box from Microsoft; **Figure 1-15a**,© Comstock Photography; **Figure 1-15b**, Courtesy Acer America; **Figure 1-16**, © Corbis; **Figure 1-17**, Courtesy of Japan Marine Science and Technology Center.

Chapter 2

Figure 2-13be, Courtesy Opera Software ASA; **Figure 2-13c**, AOL screenshots © 2002 America Online, Inc. Used with permission.; **Figure 2-13d**, Courtesy Handspring Inc.; **Figure 2-14a**, Courtesy of The Internet Exchange **Figure 2-14b**, Courtesy of Dr. Martin Luther King, Jr. Library (San José, CA) **Figure 2-14c**, Courtesy Hewlett-Packard Company; **Figure 2-16a**, Courtesy Acer America; **Figure 2-16c**, ARTHUR Web site © 2003 WGBH; underlying ARTHUR TM/© Marc Brown.; **Figure 2-19b**, Netscape website © 2002 Netscape Communications Corporation. Screenshot used with permission.; **Figure 2-20**, BHG.com screen shot courtesy of Meredith Corporation; **Figure 2-21c**, The Survivor: Pearl Islands Logo is a registered trademark of Survivor Productions, LLC. CBS.com website contents © CBS Broadcasting Inc. Used by permission.; **Figure 2-24abcd**,Courtesy Acer America; **How box**, Courtesy of Talkway, Inc.; **Figure 2-26b**, Courtesy IRS.UStreas.gov.

Chapter 3

How box b, Courtesy MusicMatch; **Figure 3-5**, Courtesy Intuit; **Figure 3-7ac**, Courtesy of Intel Corporation; **Figure 3-7b**, © Advanced Micro Devices, Inc. Reprinted with permission. AMD, the AMD logo, AMD Athlon, and combinations thereof are trademarks of Advanced Micro Devices, Inc.; **Trend box**, Courtesy ChampionChip; **Inside box**, Courtesy: IBM Research, Almaden Research Center. Unauthorized use not permitted; **Figure 3-11a**, Courtesy of Netgear; **Figure 3-12a**, Courtesy of Sierra Wireless; **Figure 3-13**, Courtesy of Palm, Inc.; **Figure 3-14a**, Courtesy Acer America; **Figure 3-14b**, Courtesy of Belkin Corporation; **Figure 3-15**, Courtesy of Belkin Corporation; **Figure 3-16**, Courtesy Acer America; **Figure 3-17**, Courtesy of Palm, Inc.; **Figure 3-20b**, Courtesy SimpleTech, Inc.; **Figure 3-21**, Courtesy of Symantec; **Figure 3-24**, Courtesy: IBM Research, Almaden Research Center. Unauthorized use not permitted.; **Exercise 3-5a**, Courtesy of Intel Corporation.; **Exercise 3-5be**, Courtesy Acer America; **Exercise 3-5c**, Courtesy SimpleTech, Inc.; **Exercise 3-5df**, Courtesy of Netgear.

Chapter 4

Figure 4-1, Courtesy Acer America; **Figure 4-7**, Copyright © Iomega Corporation. All Rights Reserved. Iomega, the stylized "i" logo and all product images are property of Iomega Corporation in the United States and/or other countries. Zip is a registered trademark of Iomega Corporation in the United States and/or other countries.; **Figure 4-8**, Courtesy of Seagate Technology LLC; **Inside box**, Courtesy of DriveSavers, Inc. www.drivesavers.com; **Figure 4-11a**, Courtesy SimpleTech, Inc.; **Figure 4-11b**, Courtesy of Intel Corporation; **Figure 4-11c**, Courtesy of Seagate Technology LLC; **Figure 4-12a**, Courtesy Toshiba America, Inc.; **Figure 4-12b**, Copyright © Iomega Corporation. All Rights Reserved. Iomega, the stylized "i" logo and all product images are property of Iomega Corporation in the United States and/or other countries. Zip is a registered trademark of Iomega Corporation in the United States and/or other countries.; **Figure 4-12c**, Courtesy of CompuCable Corporation; **Figure 4-13**, Courtesy of International Business Machines Corporation. Unauthorized use not permitted.; **Figure 4-15bce**, Courtesy of CD Digital Card; **Figure 4-15d**, Courtesy of Citiscape Shapes, Ltd.; **How box**, Courtesy RosArt Multimedia, Inc.; **Figure 4-17ab**, Courtesy of Imation, Corp.; **Figure 4-17c**, Courtesy of Maxell Corporation of America; **Figure 4-17e**, Courtesy of Sony Electronics, Inc.; **Figure 4-18a**, Courtesy of Sony Electronics, Inc.; **Figure 4-18bcdf**, Courtesy SanDisk Corporation; **Figure 4-18e**, Courtesy of Palm, Inc.; **Figure 4-19ad**, Courtesy of Lexar Media; **Figure 4-19bc**, Courtesy SanDisk Corporation; **Figure 4-20**, Copyright © Iomega Corporation. All Rights Reserved. Iomega, the stylized "i" logo and all product images are property of Iomega Corporation in the United States and/or other countries. Zip is a registered trademark of Iomega Corporation in the United States and/or other countries.; **Figure 4-21**, Courtesy of Imation, Corp.; **Figure 4-23a**, Courtesy of Visa USA Inc.; **Figure 4-23b**, Courtesy Precise Biometrics; **Campus box**, Courtesy of Diebold, Incorporated; **Exercise 4-4b**, Courtesy of Seagate Technology LLC; **Exercise 4-4c**, Copyright © Iomega Corporation. All Rights Reserved. Iomega, the stylized "i" logo and all product images are property of Iomega Corporation in the United States and/or other countries. Zip is a registered trademark of Iomega Corporation in the United States and/or other countries.; **Exercise 4-4d**, Courtesy SanDisk Corporation; **Exercise 4-4e**, Courtesy of Visa USA Inc.; **Exercise 4-4f**, Courtesy of Imation, Corp.

Chapter 5

Figure 5-1, Courtesy of Logitech; **Figure 5-2a**, Courtesy of Logitech; **Figure 5-2b**, Courtesy of Seiko Instruments USA, Inc.; **Figure 5-3ab**, Courtesy of Logitech; **Figure 5-4a**, Copyright © 2002 Eclipsys Corporation. All rights reserved. Used with permission; **Figure 5-4b**, © Wacom Technology; **Figure 5-4c**, Courtesy Seiko Instruments, USA, Inc.; **Figure 5-4d**, Courtesy of NCR Corporation; **Figure 5-4e**, Courtesy of Symbol Technologies, Inc.; **Figure 5-4f**, Courtesy Fujitsu PC Corporation; **Figure 5-5b**, Courtesy Fujitsu PC Corporation; **Figure 5-6**, Courtesy of 3M, Inc.; **Figure 5-7ab**, Courtesy of Logitech; **Figure 5-7c**, Courtesy International Business Machines Corporation. Unauthorized use not permitted.; **Figure 5-7d**, Courtesy Fujitsu PC Corporation; **Figure 5-8a**, Courtesy Fujitsu PC Corporation; **Figure 5-8b**, Courtesy of Symbol Technologies, Inc.; **Figure 5-9a**, Courtesy, Hewlett-Packard Company; **Figure 5-9b**, Courtesy of C Technologies AB/Anoto Group AB (publ); **Figure 5-9c**, Courtesy of Visioneer, Inc.; **Figure 5-9d**, Courtesy ChampionChip; **Figure 5-10**, Courtesy Chatsworth Data Corporation; **Figure 5-11a**, Courtesy of Intermec Technologies Corporation; **Figure 5-11b**, Courtesy of NCR Corporation; **Figure 5-11cde**, Courtesy of Symbol Technologies, Inc.; **Figure 5-12**, Courtesy of Sierra Pacific; **Inside box**, Courtesy Texas Instruments RFID Systems; **Figure 5-13a**, Courtesy of NCR Corporation; **Figure 5-14a**, Courtesy Recognition Systems; **Figure 5-14b**, Courtesy Fujitsu PC Corporation; **How box a**, Courtesy of Logitech; **How box b**, Courtesy Acer America; **How box c**, Courtesy of Identix Inc. Minnetonka, MN, USA; **Figure 5-15a**, Courtesy of Lexar Media; **Figure 5-15b**, Courtesy of Sony Electronics Inc.; **Figure 5-15c**, Courtesy Veo, Inc.; **Figure 5-15d**, Courtesy of Motorola; **Figure 5-16a**, Courtesy of Sony Electronics, Inc.; **Figure 5-16b**, Courtesy of Apple Computer Corporation; **Figure 5-17a**, Courtesy ScanSoft, Inc. **Figure 5-17b**, Courtesy Acer America; **Figure 5-18**, Courtesy of Creative Labs, Inc.; **Figure 5-19b**, Courtesy Acer America; **Figure 5-20b**, Courtesy Acer

America; **Figure 5-21a**, Courtesy Fujitsu PC Corporation; **Figure 5-21b**, Courtesy Ceiva Logic, Inc.; **Figure 5-21c**, Courtesy of Hewlett-Packard Company; **Figure 5-21d**, Courtesy of Microsoft Corporation; **Figure 5-22**, Courtesy of Microsoft Corporation; **Figure 5-23**, Courtesy of Microsoft Corporation; **Figure 5-24ab**, Courtesy of InFocus Corporation; **Figure 5-25a**, Courtesy Captivate Network; **Figure 5-25b**, Courtesy Siemens AG; **Figure 5-25c**, Courtesy of Microsoft Corporation; **Campus box**, Courtesy of The Sextant Group, Inc.; **Figure 5-26a**, Courtesy Printek, Inc.; **Trend box**, Courtesy Gyricon LLC; **Figure 5-27**, Courtesy, Hewlett-Packard Company; **Figure 5-29b**, Courtesy, Hewlett-Packard Company; **Figure 5-30a**, Courtesy of Sony Electronics, Inc.; **Figure 5-30bc**, Courtesy Paxar; **Figure 5-30d**, Courtesy MacDermid ColorSpan, Inc.; **Figure 5-31**, Courtesy of Altec Lansing.

Chapter 6

Figure 6-1a, Courtesy of Hewlett-Packard Company; **Figure 6-7a**, Courtesy of Seagate Technology LLC; **Figure 6-7b**, Courtesy SimpleTech, Inc.; **Figure 6-10bd**, Courtesy Acer America; **Figure 6-10c**, Courtesy of IBM Corporation. Unauthorized use not permitted.; **Figure 6-13b**, Courtesy of Microsoft Corporation; **Figure 6-14**, Courtesy of Apple Computer Corporation; **Figure 6-15**, Courtesy SUSE Linux; **Figure 6-16**, Courtesy of Microsoft Corporation; **Trend box**, Photo courtesy of Visteon Corporation; **Figure 6-17a**, Courtesy of Sony Electronics, Inc.; **Figure 6-17b**, Courtesy Siemens AG; **How box ad**, Copyright 1991-2002 WinZip Computing, Inc. WinZip(R) is a registered trademark of WinZip Computing, Inc. WinZip is available from www.winzip.com. WinZip screen images reproduced with permission of WinZip Computing, Inc.; **Figure 6-19**, Courtesy Symantec.; **Figure 6-21**, Copyright 1991-2002 WinZip Computing, Inc. WinZip(R) is a registered trademark of WinZip Computing, Inc. WinZip is available from www.winzip.com. WinZip screen images reproduced with permission of WinZip Computing, Inc.; **Figure 6-23**, Courtesy Expertcity, Inc.

Chapter 7

Figure 7-3a, Courtesy Symantec; **Figure 7-3b**, Courtesy of onProject, Inc. www.onproject.com; **Figure 7-4a**, Courtesy Microsoft Corporation; **Figure 7-4b**, Box shot(s) reprinted with permission from Corel Corporation.; **Figure 7-4c**, Courtesy of IBM Corporation. Unauthorized use not permitted.; **Figure 7-4d**, Courtesy of Sun Microsystems; **Figure 7-7ad**, Courtesy DataViz, Inc.; **Figure 7-7bcef**, Courtesy of Microsoft Corporation; **Figure 7-19b**, Courtesy Fujitsu PC Corporation; **Figure 7-22b**, Copyright © 2004 Scholastic Library Publishing. All rights reserved.; **Figure 7-22c**, Courtesy Evans & Sutherland Computer Corporation; **Figure 7-22e**, SSX3 screenshot provided courtesy of Electronic Arts Inc. © 2003 Electronics Arts Inc. All Rights Reserved.; **Inside box**, Courtesy Jellyvision www.jellyvision.com; **Figure 7-23b**, Adobe product screen shot(s) reprinted with permission from Adobe Systems Incorporated.; **Figure 7-24a**, c. 2003. Sony Pictures Digital Inc. All rights reserved.; **Figure 7-24b**, Adobe product screen shot(s) reprinted with permission from Adobe Systems Incorporated.; **Figure 7-25**, Courtesy of Apple Computer Corporation; **Figure 7-26**, Copyright © 1995-2000 RealNetworks, Inc. All rights reserved. RealNetworks, Real.com, RealAudio, RealVideo, RealSystem, RealPlayer, RealJukebox and RealMedia are trademarks or registered trademarks of RealNetworks, Inc. **Trend box**, Courtesy Lavasoft; **Figure 7-27**, Courtesy of Steve Johnson; **Figure 7-28a**, Reprinted with permission of Quark, Inc. and its affiliates; **Figure 7-28b**, Courtesy Best Software; **Figure 7-28c**, © 2003 Riverdeep Interactive Learning Limited, and its licensors.; **Figure 7-28d**, Courtesy of Punch! Software, LLC; **Figure 7-28e**, Courtesy of Microsoft Corporation.

Chapter 8

Figure 8-1a, Courtesy Motorola.; **Figure 8-1b**, Courtesy of Globalstar; **Figure 8-2**, Courtesy of Motorola; **Figure 8-3**, Courtesy of Garmin International; **Figure 8-4**, Courtesy of WebEx; **Figure 8-5a**, Courtesy, University of Rochester; **Figure 8-5b**, Courtesy of Computer Motion, Inc.; **Figure 8-7b**, Courtesy of Panasonic; **Figure 8-7d**, Courtesy Acer America; **Figure 8-9a**, Courtesy of Logitech; **Figure 8-9bcd**, Courtesy Acer America; **Figure 8-9ef**, Courtesy International Business Machines Corporation. Unauthorized use not permitted.; **Figure 8-10bc**, Courtesy Acer America; **Figure 8-11ace**, Photos courtesy of The Siemon Company, www.siemon.com; **Figure 8-11bdf**, Courtesy of Belkin Components; **Figure 8-12ab**, Courtesy XM Satellite Radio Inc.; **Figure 8-12c**, Courtesy Starband; **Figure 8-12d**, Courtesy of @Xi Computer Corporation; **Figure 8-12e**, Courtesy Acer America; **Inside box**, Courtesy of Bantu, Inc.; **Figure 8-15a**, Courtesy Acer America; **Figure 8-15b**, Courtesy Linksys; **Figure 8-15c**, Courtesy International Business Machines Corporation. Unauthorized use not permitted.;

Figure 8-16abc, Courtesy Acer America; **Figure 8-16d**, Courtesy Linksys; **Figure 8-16e**, Courtesy International Business Machines Corporation. Unauthorized use not permitted.; **Figure 8-18a**, Courtesy Linksys; **Figure 8-18bd**, Courtesy NETGEAR; **Figure 8-18c**, Courtesy D-Link; **Figure 8-18e**, Courtesy Sierra Wireless Inc. **Figure 8-19ab**, Courtesy US Robotics; **Figure 8-19c**, Courtesy D-Link; **Figure 8-19d**, Courtesy Starband. **Figure 8-20abdgi**, Courtesy Acer America; **Figure 8-20ck**, Courtesy Linksys; **Figure 8-20e**, Courtesy D-Link; **Figure 8-20h**, Courtesy Juniper Networks; **Figure 8-20jm**, Courtesy of Apple Computer Corporation; **Figure 8-21bcd**, Courtesy Acer America; **How box a**, Courtesy NETGEAR; **How box b**, Courtesy D-Link; **How box c**, Courtesy Belkin Components; **Figure 8-22bcd**, Courtesy Acer America; **Figure 8-23ab**, Courtesy Acer America; **Figure 8-23c**, Courtesy Juniper Networks; **Figure 8-24a**, Courtesy Sony Ericsson Mobile Communications; **Figure 8-24b**, Courtesy International Business Machines Corporation. Unauthorized use not permitted.; **Figure 8-25**, Courtesy NETGEAR; **Figure 8-26**, Courtesy NETGEAR; **Figure 8-28**, Pointsec Mobile Technologies; **Figure 8-29**, Courtesy Diebold, Incorporated; **Figure 8-30ac**, Courtesy Identix; **Figure 8-30b**, Courtesy Recognition Systems; **Figure 8-30d**, Courtesy Diebold, Incorporated; **Trend box**, Courtesy VeriFone; **Figure 8-31acde**, Courtesy Acer America; **Figure 8-31b**, Courtesy of Apple Computer Corporation; **Figure 8-32ab**, Courtesy Acer America.

Chapter 9

Figure 9-1a, Courtesy Acer America; **Figure 9-1b**, The Survivor: Pearl Islands Logo is a registered trademark of Survivor Productions, LLC. CBS.com website contents © CBS Broadcasting Inc. Used by permission.; **Figure 9-2a**, Courtesy Sprint; **Figure 9-2b**, Courtesy AT&T Wireless; **Figure 9-2c**, America Online, AOL, and the AOL logo are registered trademarks of America Online, Inc. in the United States and other countries. Other AOL product and service names are also trademarks of America Online, which may be registered in some countries.; **Figure 9-2d**, Courtesy Earthlink; **Figure 9-2e**, Courtesy Starband; **Figure 9-2f**, Courtesy Time Warner Cable Inc.; **Figure 9-2g**, Courtesy Pacific Lightnet www.plni.net; **Figure 9-2h**, Courtesy Highstream.net; **Figure 9-4a**, Courtesy Acer America; **Figure 9-4b**, Courtesy of Salton, Inc.; **Figure 9-4c**, Courtesy Danger, Inc.; **Figure 9-5**, Courtesy Sprint; **Figure 9-6**, Courtesy of Motorola; **Figure 9-7a**, Courtesy of Hewlett-Packard Company; **Figure 9-7b**, Courtesy Intel Corporation; **Trend box**, Courtesy NASA; **Figure 9-9**, AOL screenshots © 2002 America Online, Inc. Used with permission; **Figure 9-11c**, Courtesy Ask Jeeves, Inc.; **Figure 9-18b**, Courtesy of Apple Computer Corporation; **Figure 9-19a**, Courtesy of SevenPoint Productions; **Figure 9-19b**, Copyright © 1995-2000 RealNetworks, Inc. All rights reserved. RealNetworks, Real.com, RealAudio, RealVideo, RealSystem, RealPlayer, RealJukebox and RealMedia are trademarks or registered trademarks of RealNetworks, Inc.; **Figure 9-19d**, Courtesy Panasonic; **Figure 9-19e**, Courtesy Open TV; **Inside box**, © Ken Krause/AP World Wide Photos; **How box a**, Courtesy Acer America; **How box bcd**, Courtesy Ncube; **How box e**, Courtesy Panasonic; **Figure 9-22a**, © 2003 CBS Broadcasting Inc. All Rights Reserved; **Figure 9-22b**, Courtesy Switchboard Incorporated.

References and Resources Guide: Computer History Timeline

1, 2, 5, 6, 9, 12, 19, Courtesy of IBM Archives; **3**, Courtesy Iowa State University; **4**, Courtesy Jim Bready; **7**, Courtesy Unisys Corporation ; **8**, Courtesy U.S. Navy; **10**, Courtesy AT&T; **11**, Courtesy Bootstrap Institute; **13, 23, 30, 33**, Courtesy of Intel Corporation; **14, 15**, Courtesy Microsoft Corporation; **16**, Courtesy Dan Bricklin; **17**, Courtesy Cray Inc.; **18, 24**, Courtesy Apple Computer, Inc.; **20**, Courtesy, Hewlett-Packard Development Company, L.P.; **21**, Netscape website © 2002 Netscape Communications Corporation. Screenshot used with permission.; **22**, Courtesy Microsoft Museum; **25**, Fabian Bachrach, courtesy W3C; **26**, Courtesy Larry Ewing lewing@isc.tamu.edu and The GIMP; **27**, Java and the Java Coffee Cup logo are trademarks or registered trademarks of Sun Microsystems, Inc.; **28**, Courtesy of Thomson, Inc.; **29**, Images of Palm handheld provided by Palm, Inc. Palm is a trademark of Palm, Inc.; **31, 34, 37**, Microsoft, Windows and the Windows logo are either registered trademarks or trademarks of Microsoft Corporation in the United States and/or other countries.; **32, 35**, Courtesy of Hewlett-Packard Company; **36**, Courtesy Kingston Technology Company Inc.; **38**, © Advanced Micro Devices, Inc. Reprinted with permission. AMD, the AMD logo, AMD Athlon, and combinations thereof are trademarks of Advanced Micro Devices, Inc.

* wildcards, 383
/ symbol, 57
@ sign, 57

A

abbreviations, 72, 73, 74
ABS function, 278
absolute cell references, 279
Accelerated Graphics Port (AGP) bus, 105, 106
accelerator boards, 107
Access. *See* Microsoft Access
access providers. *See* Internet access; Internet service
   provider (ISP); *specific access devices*
accessing networks, 18
accounting software, 297, 298
Acer, 20
acronyms, 72, 74
active desktop, 235
Active Service Pages (.asp), 55
active windows, 43, 48
adapter boards. *See* expansion card; *specific card names*
Ad-Aware, 299
add-in boards. *See* expansion card; *specific card names*
address book, 68
addressable media. *See* random access storage
addresses. *See specific address types*
Adobe® AfterEffects®, 296
Adobe® Encore DVD®, 294
Adobe® Illustrator®, 292
Adobe® LiveMotion®, 296
Adobe® PhotoDeluxe®, 293
Adobe® Photoshop®, 293
Adobe® Premiere®, 293
advanced intelligent tape (AIT), 158
Advanced Micro Devices CPUs. *See* AMD CPUs
Advanced Mobile Phone Service (AMPS) standard, 325
Advanced Research Projects Agency (ARPA), 365
adware, 299
AeroVironment, 375
AGP (Accelerated Graphics Port) bus, 105, 106
AIT (advanced intelligent tape), 158
AIX (IBM) operating system, 242
alignment, of documents, 274
All Programs option, 47
all-in-one desktop PCs, 20
Altair computer, R-4
AltaVista, 379, 382, 397
ALU. *See* arithmetic/logic unit (ALU)
always-on connections. *See* direct connection; *specific
   connection types*
AMD CPUs
   characteristics, 96–97, 98, 114, 121, 232, R-13
   search example, 382–383
   64-bit Opteron, 97, 98, 103, 121, 232, R-13, R-6
America Online (AOL), 52, 53, 378, 397
American Standard Code for Information Interchange.
   See ASCII
AMPS (Advanced Mobile Phone Service) standard, 325
analog networks, 317
animated GIF A group of GIF images stored in a special
   animated GIF file that is inserted in a Web page; the individual images are displayed one after another to simulate
   movement, 62, 294–296
animated GIF programs, 294–296

animation The process by which a series of graphical
   images are displayed one after the other to simulate
   movement.
   animated GIFs, 62, 294–296
   illustrated, 61
   slide shows, 287
   Web page, 62
animation software Application software used to create
   animation to be used on Web pages or other multimedia
   applications, 294–296
anonymity concerns, 73–75
antispam programs, 251
antivirus program Software used to detect and eliminate
   computer viruses, 72–73, 246, 353
AOL. *See* America Online (AOL)
AOL Instant Messenger, 71
Apple computers, 20
   evolution, R-4–6
   FireWire/IEEE 1394 bus, 105, 106
   iBook notebook computer, 20
   iMac desktop computer, 20
   Macintosh computers, 20
   media players, 388
   operating system. *See* Mac OS; Mac OS X
   PC-compatible vs., 20
   PowerPC CPUs, 97, 98, 114, 228, 232, R-13
Apple DVD Studio Pro, 294
Apple Final Cut Express, 293
application service provider (ASP) A company that manages and distributes software-based services over the
   Internet, 14, 369
   evolution, 369
   packaged software vs., 266
   Web service, 369
   Web-based software, 265–266, 369
application software Programs that enable users to perform
   specific tasks on a computer, such as writing a letter or
   playing a game, 14, 15, 222–223, 262–299. *See also* software suite; *specific application types, names*
   analyzing needs, R-14
   commercial, 264
   delivery methods, 263, 264–266
   downloading, 5, 245
   examples, 15
   freeware, 264, 265
   further exploration, 270
   for handheld PCs, 269–270
   Help systems, 270–271
   installed vs. Web-based, 265–266
   installing, 14, 245
   licenses. *See* ownership rights; software license
   OLE, 268–269
   ownership rights, 263–265
   packaged vs. downloaded, 266
   public domain software, 265
   representation. *See* machine language
   shareware, 264–265
   starting, 47
   system software vs., 222–223
   types, 262–263, 264
   uninstalling, 115–117, 247–248
   upgrading, R-18
   Windows PC vs. Mac, 95
application-based Help, 270, 271

arithmetic (computer), R-9–10
arithmetic/logic unit (ALU) The part of the CPU that performs arithmetic and logical operations, 112, 114, 115
ARPANET The predecessor of the Internet, named after the
   Advanced Research Projects Agency (ARPA), which
   sponsored its development, 365, R-3
arrows
   keyboard, 175
   menus, 45
   scroll bars, 50
artificial intelligence system A system in which a computer performs actions that are characteristic of human
   intelligence, 12
ASCII A fixed-length, binary coding system widely used to
   represent text-based data for computer processing on
   many types of computers, 90, 91, R-11
Ask Jeeves, 63
asleep mode, 41, 51
ASP. *See* application service provider (ASP)
.asp (Active Service Pages), 55
asterisk wildcards (*), 383
asynchronous transmission, 319
at (@) sign, 57
AT&T WorldNet, 52
ATA drives, 146
ATA/100 drives, 146
ATA-2 drives, 146
Athlon CPUs, 96–97, 98, 103, 114, R-13
auctions. *See* online auction
audio Sound, such as music, spoken voice, and sound effects.
   codec, 94
   data coding, 92–94
   editing software, 293
   file extensions, 226
   input devices, 193–194
   media players, 294, 388
   MP3-encoded. *See* MP3 (MPEG Audio Layer 3)
   samples, 92–94
   streaming, 392
   voice-input systems, 12, 193–194
   waveform, 92–94
authentication systems, 345
AVERAGE function, 278

B

backbone network, 52, 366
backside bus (BSB), 100
Backspace key, 175
backup A duplicate copy of data or other computer contents
   in case the original version is destroyed.
   automatic, 250
   devices, 147
   hard disk crashes and, 143, 144
   illustrated, 249
   manual, 249, 250
   media, 135, 248
   before partitioning hard drives, 145
   portable hard drives, 147
   procedures, 249–250
   removable-media advantages, 135
   storage locations, 144
   system restore, 249, 250
   utility programs, 248–250
bandwidth, 317–318

banking online. *See* online banking

bar code A machine-readable code that represents data as a set of bars, 185–187, 188

bar-code printer An output device that prints bar-coded documents, 206–207

bar-code reader An input device that reads bar codes, 185–187

base numbers, 89–90

base 16. *See* hexadecimal numbering system

base 10. *See* decimal numbering system

base 2. *See* binary numbering system

BASIC An easy-to-learn, high-level programming language that was developed to be used by beginning programmers, 14

basic input/output system (BIOS), 104

Berners-Lee, Tim, 365, R-5

binary digits (bits), 88

binary numbering system The numbering system that represents all numbers using just two symbols (0 and 1), 88–95

  ASCII, 90, 91, R-11

  audio data coding, 92–94

  base number, 89–90

  bits (binary digits), 88

  byte equivalents, 91

  bytes, 91

  computer arithmetic, R-9–10

  decimal conversions, R-7, R-8–10

  decimal system vs., 89–90, R-7

  EBCDIC, 90, 91, R-11

  examples, 90

  graphics data coding, 92, 93

  hexadecimal conversions, R-7, R-8–10

  illustrated, 89, 90

  natural language system, 89

  non-text coding systems, 92–95

  overview, 89–90

  representing, options, 89

  scientific calculators for, R-10

  text-based data coding system, 90–91

  Unicode, 90, 91, R-12

  video data coding, 95

biometric data, 159

biometric device A device that uses the recognition of some unique physical characteristic (such as a person's fingerprint, face, or voice) to grant access to a computer network or physical facility, 189, 190, 347

  face recognition, 189, 190, 347, 348

  finger payment systems, 349

  fingerprint readers, 189, 347, 348, 349

  hand geometry readers, 189, 347, 348

  illustrated, 161, 189

  iris scanners, 347, 348

  pros/cons summary, 348

  reading smart cards, 159, 161

  security effectiveness, 347

BIOS (basic input/output system), 104

biotechnology, 122

bit depth, 196

bitmap, 92

bitmapped images, 92, 93

bits (binary digits), 88

.biz file extension, 55

blade, 96

blade servers, 96

Blaster worm, 351

blocks, 104

blog A Web page that contains short, frequently updated entries in chronological order, typically by just one individual; also called a Web log, 400, 401

blue laser discs, 154

Bluetooth A communications standard used to facilitate an automatic connection between devices once they get within the allowable range, 341–342

  analog signals, 317

  cards, 108

  devices, 177

  features, 341–342

  illustrated, 342

  master devices, 341–342

  slave devices, 342

  specifications, 341–342

  voice command feature, 241

body PCs. *See* wearable PCs

bold font, 273

Bolt portal, 397

bookmarks, 62–63

books online. *See* e-book

Boolean operators, 382–383, R-23

boot To start up a computer, 40–41

  common problems, 41

  power-on self-test (POST), 103, 104

  process, 40–41, 224

  troubleshooting, 41, R-17–18

bottom margins, 274

bridges, 334

broadband Internet service, 118, 374–376. *See also specific service types*

broadcast radio transmissions, 322

brokerage site A type of Web site used to bring buyers and sellers together to facilitate transactions, such as online stock trading and exchanging goods, services, and commodities, 389

BSB (backside bus), 100

buddy lists, 71

buffer An area in RAM or on the hard drive designated to hold input and output on their way in or out of the system, 229–230

burning

  CD/DVD discs, 153, 294, 295

  custom music CDs, 295, 390

  software, 294

bus An electronic path on the motherboard or within the CPU or other computer component along which data is transferred, 104–106. *See also* expansion bus

  backside, 100

  frontside, 100

  illustrated, 105

  internal, 100, 105

  speed, 97, 100, 118, R-13

  system, 100, 105, R-13

  width, 97, 100, 118, R-13

bus interface unit The part of the CPU where instructions and data flow in and out of the CPU, 112, 113

bus network A network consisting of a central cable to which all network devices are attached, 327

business card discs, 150, 151

business presentations, 289

business Web site list, R-19

buttons. *See specific button names*; task button

buying computers, 107, R-14–18

  analyzing needs, R-14–15

  comparing alternatives, R-15–16

  configuration options, R-15

  platform options, R-14, R-15

  power vs. budget requirements, R-15

  system troubleshooting, 41, R-17–18

byte A group of 8 bits; in ASCII and EBCDIC, it holds a single character of data, 91

C

C A high-level structured programming language that has the executional efficiency of an assembly language, R-4

C++ A newer, object-oriented version of the C programming language, 14

cable Internet access Fast, direct Internet access via cable TV lines, 317, 375

  download speed, 374

  features, 375

  modems, 333, 335

cable types. *See* wired network

cache memory A group of fast memory chips located on or near the CPU to help speed up processing, 98–99

  disk cache vs., 145–146

  external cache, 99, 105

  internal cache, 99, 105, 112, 113, 116

  Levels, 98, 99, 113, R-13

CAD. *See* computer-aided design (CAD)

cameras. *See* digital camera; PC video cameras

campus close-ups

  smart cards, 162

  smart classrooms, 201

  wired med students, 24

Caps Lock key, 175

captive marketing, 199, 200

cards. *See* expansion card; *specific card names*

careers

  brief descriptions, 16

  Web sites, R-19

Carrier Sense Multiple Access/Collision Detection (CSMA/CD), 336, 337

cars, smart, 241

Carterfone Decision (1968), 370

cartridge tapes, 158

Category 3 cable, 320

Category 5 cable, 320, 340

Category 6 cable, 320

cathode-ray tube monitor. *See* CRT (cathode-ray tube) monitor

CBT. *See* computer-based training (CBT)

CCD (charge-coupled device), 192

CD burner, 154. *See also* CD/DVD drives

CD discs, 14. *See also specific disc types*

  advantages, 152

  audio data coding, 92–94

  burning, 153, 294, 295

  capacities, 152, 153

  caring for, 151–152

  characteristics, 150–152

  custom music, creating, 295, 390

  digital copy protection, 155

  illustrated, 13, 150, 151, 153, 154

  injection molding, 152

  mass-producing, 152

  recordable, 153, 154, 163

  rewritable, 154

  ripping, 293, 295

CD/DVD drives, 14, 163

  alternative names for, 154

  CD-ROM drive, 152, 153, 154

  compatibility, 154

  illustrated, 13, 96

  inserting media, 151–152

  random access storage, 135–136

  recordable, 153, 154, 163

  rewritable, 154

  speed, 151

CDMA (Code Division Multiple Access), 325

CD-R disc A recordable CD, 117, 153, 163

CD-ROM disc An optical disc, usually holding about 650 MB, that can be read, but not written to, by the user, 152

CD-ROM drive, 152, 153, 154

CD-RW A rewritable CD, 154, 163

Celeron CPUs, 96–97, 98, R-13

cell The location at the intersection of a row and column on a worksheet into which data can be typed, 276

  absolute references, 279

  address, 276

  block/range, 276, 277

  components, illustrated, 277

  content types, 276, 277–278

  copying, 278–279

  current, 276

  editing contents, 278

  formatting, 279–280

  moving, 278–279

  pointer, 276, 277

  range, 276

  relative references, 279

  word processing tables, 275

cells (wireless transmission), 324–325

cellular phone. *See* wireless phone
cellular radio A form of broadcast radio that broadcasts using antennae located inside honeycomb-shaped cells, 324–325
  evolution, 325
  generations, 325
  mechanics of, 324–325
  presence technology, 325, 326
  standards, 325
cellular towers, 324–325
censorship, 402, 403
center alignment, 274
central processing unit (CPU) The chip located inside the system unit of a computer that performs the processing for a computer, 13, 96–100. *See also specific chip names; specific components*
  buses. *See* bus
  cache memory, 98–99, 105, 113, 116, R-13
  characteristics, 97–100, R-13
  chipset, 104, 105
  clock speed, 97, 113–114
  components, 112–113
  concurrent processing, 228, 229
  cooling, 118
  desktop PCs, 96–97
  environmentally friendly, 97
  evolution, R-4–6
  further exploration, 97
  heat sinks, 118
  illustrated, 96, 97, 105, 112
  instruction set, 95, 113, 121
  machine cycles, 114–115, 116
  manufacturers, 96–97
  materials improvement, 119
  mechanics of, 111–115
  microprocessors, 96
  multiprocessing, 119–120
  parallel processing, 119–120, 121, 228, 229
  pipelining, 119, 120
  portable computers, 97
  processing example, 115, 116
  processing speed, 97, 98, 113–114, R-13
  registers, 100, 102–103, 112, 113
  simultaneous processing, 228, 229
  supported types, 232
  system clock, 97, 113–115
  transistors, 11–12, 111, R-3
  upgrading, 118, R-18
  wearable PCs, 9
  word sizes, 97
  workstations, 97
ceramic superconductors, 119
ChampionChip, 99
character formatting, 273–274
characters per second (cps), 204
charge-coupled device (CCD), 192
charts, 280
chat room An Internet service that allows multiple users to exchange written messages in real time, 71
chat sessions, 58, 71
check boxes, 46
check marks, 45
check reading, 187–189
Child Internet Protection Act (CIPA) (2001), 402
Children's Online Privacy Protection Act (COPPA) (1998), 402
chips, 12
  CPUs. *See* central processing unit (CPU); *specific CPU components; specific CPU names*
  unusual uses, 99
chipset, 104, 105
CinemaNow, 392
CIPA (Child Internet Protection Act) (2001), 402
circuit boards. *See* motherboard; *specific motherboard components*
CISC (complex instruction set computing), 121
citing Internet resources, 385

Clark, Richard, 345
classrooms, smart, 199, 201
clean rooms, 144
clients
  client-server networks, 17, 328
  software, 231, 232, 240
client-server networks, 328
  components, 17, 328
  illustrated, 328
clip art images, 273, 275
cloaking services, 75
clock speed The number of ticks of the system clock that occurs per second, 97, 113–114. *See also* system clock
Close button, 48, 49
Close command, 267
closing windows, 48, 49
cluster The part of a track on a disk that crosses a fixed number of contiguous sectors; it is the smallest addressable area of a disk, 138–139
  floppy disks, 138, 139
  hard drives, 141, 142, 145
  illustrated, 139
Coatue, 101
coaxial cable A communications medium consisting of a center wire inside a grounded, cylindrical shield, capable of sending data at high speeds, 321
COBOL A high-level programming language developed for transaction processing applications, 12, 14
Code Division Multiple Access (CDMA), 325
codec, 94
codes of conduct, 344
coding charts, R-11–12
coding systems
  ASCII, 90, 91, R-11
  audio data, 92–94
  charts, R-11–12
  EBCDIC, 90, 91, R-11
  examples, 91, 92
  graphics data, 92, 93
  Huffman coding, 94
  perceptual coding, 94
  text-based data, 90–91
  Unicode, 90, 91, R-12
  video data, 95
collaborative computing, 315
collisions, 336, 337
color images, 92, 93, 184–185
column In a spreadsheet program, a vertical group of cells on a worksheet. In a database, a field, 276
  database. *See* field
  deleting, 278
  formatting, 280
  illustrated, 277
  inserting, 278
  word processing tables, 275
combination topologies, 328
.com file extension, 55, 72
command buttons, 46, 47
command line interfaces, 231, 233
commands (DOS), 233
commercial software Copyrighted software that is developed, usually by a commercial company, for sale to others, 264. *See also specific software names*
communications The transmission of data from one device to another, 10, 312. *See also specific communication methods*
  applications, 312–316
  computers for, 7
  devices, 13
  online vs. traditional, 73
Communications Decency Act (1996), 402
communications devices, 13, 14. *See also specific devices*
communications protocols, 336–343
  Bluetooth. *See* Bluetooth
  cards supporting, 332
  802.11 (Wi-Fi). *See* 802.11 (Wi-Fi)
  Ethernet, 331, 336–337

  IrDA, 342
  Phoneline networks, 342–343
  Powerline networks, 343
  TCP/IP, 337, 339
  Token Ring, 337, 338
  UWB, 343
  WAP, 342
communications satellite An earth-orbiting device that relays communications signals over long distances, 323–324
CompactFlash cards, 156, 157
complex instruction set computing (CISC), 121
compressed files
  file compression programs, 248
  file extensions, 226
computer A programmable, electronic device that accepts data input, performs operations on that data, and presents and stores the results, 9. *See also specific computer types, topics*
  categories summary, 19
  early computers, 4–5, 11, R-2
  fifth generation, 12
  first generation, 11, R-2–3
  fourth generation, 11, 12, R-4–6
  primary operations, 10
  second generation, 11–12, R-3
  social impact, 28–29
  speed. *See* increasing computer speed; system clock
  third generation, 11, 12, R-3
computer arithmetic, R-9–10
computer crime Any illegal act involving a computer, *See also* security issues; security measures
  cyberterrorism, 345
  identity theft. *See* identity theft
  sabotage, 344, 349–353
  writing virus software. *See* computer virus
computer history, 4–5, 10–12, R-2–6
  computer generations, 10–12, R-2–6
  further exploration, 12
  information age, 28
  information revolution, 28
  pre-1945, 11
  timelines, 11, R-2–6
computer hoax An inaccurate statement or story spread through the use of computers, 57
computer information Web sites, R-20
computer literacy The knowledge and understanding of basic computer fundamentals, 5
computer network A collection of computers and other hardware devices that are connected together to share hardware, software, and data, as well as to communicate electronically with one another, 17–18, 312, 317–353
  accessing, 18
  analog, 317
  architectures, 328–329
  asynchronous transmission, 319
  bandwidth, 317–318
  bus networks, 327
  client-server networks, 17, 328
  codes of conduct, 344
  data transmission characteristics, 317–320
  digital, 317
  extranets, 330
  full-duplex transmission, 318
  half-duplex transmission, 318
  hardware. *See* modem; networking hardware
  home networks, 335, 340
  identity management programs, 250–251
  illustrated, 17, 335
  intranets, 330
  isochronous transmission, 319–320
  LANs, 329
  logging on, 18
  MANs, 329
  origin, 12
  PANs, 330
  parallel transmission, 318

peer-to-peer. *See* peer-to-peer networks
performance monitors, 250
protocols. *See* communications protocols; *specific protocols*
ring networks, 327
SANs, 148, 330
security. *See* security issues; security measures
serial transmission, 318
servers, 17
simplex transmission, 318
software, 18
speed, 317–318
star networks, 327
synchronous transmission, 319
throughput, 318
topologies, 327–328
transmission directions, 318
transmission timing, 319–320
types, 17–18, 327–330
uses, 317
utilities, 250–251
VPNs, 330
WANs, 329
wired. *See* wired network
wireless. *See* wireless network
computer operations personnel, 16
computer professionals, 16. *See also* careers; programmer
computer user A person who uses a computer, 16
computer virus A software program, installed without the user's knowledge, designed to alter the way a computer operates or to cause harm to the system, 72–73, 246, 350–351
antivirus software, 72–73, 246, 353
cyberterrorism, 345
examples, 349, 351
firewall protection, 348
further exploration, 351
hoaxes, 57
legal ramifications, 351
logic bombs, 351
mechanics of, 350–351
protecting against, 72–73, 246, 353
spreading, illustrated, 350
statistics, 349, 351
time bombs, 351
Trojan Horses vs., 351
worms vs., 351
computer worm A malicious program designed to rapidly spread to a large number of computers by sending copies of itself to other computers, 351
computer-aided design (CAD) A general term applied to the use of computer technology to automate design functions, 297, 298
computer-based training (CBT) Individualized instruction delivered via a computer, 289
concentrators, 335
concurrent processing, 228, 229
conductive e-ink, 202
connector types, 109, 320, 321, 322
constant value A numerical entry in a worksheet cell, 277
Control Panel option, 47
control unit The part of the CPU that coordinates its operations, 112, 113
conventional dial-up Internet access Dial-up Internet access via a conventional dial-up modem and standard telephone lines, 373
features, 373
modems, 332, 333, 373
prepaid access, 373
convergence, defined, 6
convertible tablet PCs, 23
cookie A small file stored on a user's hard drive by a Web server; commonly used to identify personal preferences and settings for that user, 403–406
features, 403–404
illustrated, 405
managing, 404, 405

PII vs. Non-PII information, 404
privacy issues, 404
tracking browsing activity, 404–406
viewing, 405
Web bugs vs., 406
cooling CPUs, 118
COPPA (Children's Online Privacy Protection Act) (1998), 402
coprocessing, 228
Copy command, 233, 244, 267, 272
copying
files, 243–244
folders, 243–244
spreadsheet cells, 278–279
word processing content, 272
copyright The legal right to sell, publish, or distribute an original artistic or literary work; is held by the creator of a work as soon as it exists in physical form.
digital copy protection, 155
movie download violations, 393
music file considerations, 329, 389–390, 391
Napster controversy, 390, 391, 401
peer-to-peer networking and, 329, 390, 391, 401
of UNIX, 239
Corel Paradox, 282
Corel Presentations, 285
Corel Quattro Pro, 276
Corel WordPerfect, 272
Corel WordPerfect Office, 266
CorelDRAW, 292
corporate information online, 397
COUNT function, 278
cps (characters per second), 204
CPU. *See* central processing unit (CPU); *specific CPU components*; *specific CPU names*
crackers, 344
Cray, Seymour, R-4
credit cards, 386
CRT (cathode-ray tube) monitor A display device that projects images onto a display screen using a technology similar to the one used with conventional TVs, 197
CSMA/CD (Carrier Sense Multiple Access/Collision Detection), 336, 337
current command, 44
cursor. *See* insertion point
Cut command, 267, 272
cyber crime. *See* computer crime; computer virus; security issues; security measures
cyberterrorism, 345
cybervandalism, 353
cylinder The collection of tracks located in the same location on a set of hard disk surfaces, 142, 143

D

DAT (digital audio tape), 158
data Raw, unorganized facts, 16
information and, 16
data alteration sabotage, 353
data movement time, 143
data projector A display device that projects all computer output to a wall or projection screen, 13, 199
data recovery firms, 143, 144
data representation. *See* binary numbering system; digital data representation
database A collection of related data that is stored in a manner enabling information to be retrieved as needed; in a relational database, a collection of related tables, 281–285. *See also* database software
fields. *See* field
relational. *See* relational database management system (RDBMS)
tables. *See* table
for Web, 285
database management system (DBMS) A type of software program used to create, maintain, and access databases, 281. *See also* database software; see also relational database management system (RDBMS)

database software Application software that allows the creation and manipulation of an electronic database, 262, 281–285. *See also* relational database management system (RDBMS)
common programs, 282
concepts, 281–285
creating databases, 282–283, 284
deleting records, 283–284
editing records, 283–284
fields (columns), 281, 282–283
further exploration, 285
illustrated, 282
inserting records, 283–284
modifying databases, 283–284
objects, 282, 283
overview, 281–282
paper-based database vs., 282
queries, 284
records (rows), 281, 283–284
reports, 285
tables, 281, 282–283
Web sites and, 285
data/video projectors. *See* data projector
DB-9 connectors, 109
DB-25 connectors, 109
DDR (double-data rate) SDRAM, 102
DDR-II (double-data rate-II) SDRAM, 102
Deceptive Duo, 345
decimal numbering system
binary conversions, R-7, R-8–10
binary vs., 89–90, R-7
hexadecimal conversions, R-7, R-8–10
decode unit The part of the CPU that translates instructions into a form that can be processed by the ALU, 113
functions, 113, 114, 115
illustrated, 112, 116
Deep Blue, R-6
Delete command (DOS), 233
Delete key, 175, 283
deleting
accidentally, 244
columns, 278
e-mail messages, 68
files, 245
folders, 245
records (rows), 283–284
rows, 278
temporary files, 117
unnecessary files, 117
Dell, 20
demo version software, 264
denial of service (DoS) attack An act of sabotage that attempts to flood a network or network server with so much activity that it is unable to function, 347, 348, 352, 353
Dense WDM (DWDM), 335
design software, 297, 298
desktop computer A PC designed to fit on or next to a desk, 19, 20–21
buying, 107, R-14–18
case styles, 20
expansion slots/cards, 106–107, 331–332
illustrated, 20
ports, 108–110
setting up, 21
system unit. *See specific system unit components*; system unit
desktop publishing software, 297–298
desktop The background work area displayed on the screen when using Microsoft Windows or another operating system with a graphical user interface, 42
features, 42
icons, 42, 43–44, 45, 47
illustrated, 42
showing, 49
destination documents, 269
device driver A program that enables an operating system to communicate with a specific hardware device, 224

DeviceLogics, 233

DHTML. *See* dynamic HTML (DHTML)

diagnostic programs, 246–247

dialog box A window that requires the user to supply information to the computer about the task being requested, 44, 46–47
  check boxes, 46
  command buttons, 46, 47
  drop-down list boxes, 46, 47
  elements, 44, 46–47
  ellipses indicating, 44, 45, 47
  illustrated, 43, 46
  list boxes, 46, 47
  option buttons, 46
  radio buttons, 46
  scroll bars, 47
  simple list boxes, 46, 47
  sliders, 46
  spin boxes, 46
  text boxes, 46

dial-up connection A type of Internet connection in which the PC or other device must dial up and connect to a service provider's computer via telephone lines before being connected to the Internet, 52, 373. *See also* conventional dial-up Internet access; ISDN Internet access
  establishing connection, 58
  features, 373
  illustrated, 335
  modems, 332, 333, 373

digital audio tape (DAT), 158

digital camera An input device that takes pictures and records them as digital data (instead of film or video-taped) images, 13, 191–193
  advantages, 192
  costs, 192
  disposable, 192
  illustrated, 191
  kiosks, 8
  media, 192
  photo management, 192
  resolutions, 192
  still, 191–192
  video, 191, 192–193
  watches, 191

digital computers, 88

digital copy protection, 155

digital data representation, 88–95
  binary numbering. *See* binary numbering system
  digital, defined, 88
  further exploration, 90
  non-text coding systems, 92–95
  text-based data coding system, 90–91

digital divide The gap between those who have access to technology and those who don't, 6, 367

digital linear tape (DLT), 158

digital media units, 26

Digital Millennium Copyright Act (DMCA), 155

digital networks, 317

digital pens, 178, 179

digital portfolios, 179

digital projectors. *See* data projector

digital video recorders (DVRs), 143, 392, 394

digital writing tools, 178, 179

digitizing tablet. *See* graphics tablet

dimmed items, 45

DIMMs (dual in-line memory modules), 100

direct connection An always-on type of Internet connection in which the PC or other device is continually connected to the Internet, 52, 68, 372, 374–376. *See also specific connection types*

directory (folder). *See* folder; *specific folder names*

directory A collection of categories that are used to locate appropriate Web pages from a search database, 65, 379, 380–381

directory services, 250–251

discs vs. disks, 150

discussion group An Internet communications medium that enables individuals to post messages on a particular topic for others to read and respond to, 58, 70, 72

disk, diskette. *See* floppy disk

disk access time The time it takes to locate and read data from (or position and write data to) a storage medium, 143

disk cache A dedicated part of RAM used to store additional data adjacent to data retrieved during a disk fetch to improve system performance, 145–146

Disk Cleanup, 117, 247

disk controller cards, 107

Disk Defragmentor, 247

disk mirroring, 149

disk optimizer programs, 247

disk striping, 149

disks vs. discs, 150

display device An output device that contains a viewing screen, 195–200. *See also* monitor
  characteristics, 195–196
  color vs. monochrome, 195
  data projectors, 199
  emerging technologies/applications, 199–200
  flat-panel displays, 197–198
  flexible, 199, 200
  gas plasma, 198
  graphics standards, 196
  illustrated, 13, 195, 196, 197, 198, 199, 200
  integrated PCs, 199, 200
  LCD, 198
  screen resolution, 196
  size, 195–196
  smart classrooms, 199, 201
  smart displays, 198
  viewable image size (VIS), 196, 197

distance learning A learning environment in which the student is physically located away from the instructor and other students; commonly instruction and communications take place via the Internet, 7, 397, 398–399

distributed processing systems, 120

dithering, 92

DLT (digital linear tape), 158

DMCA. *See* Digital Millennium Copyright Act (DMCA)

DNS server, 340

.doc, 226

docking station A device that connects a portable PC to conventional hardware, such as a keyboard, mouse, monitor, and printer, 25, 111

document formatting, 274

documents. *See also* file
  defined, 136
  file extensions, 226
  new, command, 267
  opening, 47
  storing, 136

Documents to Go, 270

domain name A text-based Internet address used to uniquely identify a computer on the Internet, 54–55
  components, 55
  determining availability, 54
  examples, 55
  formats, 55
  registering, 54
  restrictions, 55
  standards organization, 55
  TLDs, 55

DOS (Disk Operating System) The operating system designed for and widely used on early IBM and IBM-compatible PCs, 227, 231, 233, R-4

DoS attacks. *See* denial of service (DoS)

dot (.), 57

dot pitch, 197

dot-matrix printers, 203

dots per inch (dpi), 184, 201

DoubleClick browser tracking, 404–406

double-data rate (DDR) SDRAM, 102

double-data rate-II (DDR-II) SDRAM, 102

Dow Chemical, 122

downloading
  movies, 198, 392–393, 394
  music, 5, 389–390, 394
  software, 5, 245

downward compatibility, 140

dpi (dots per inch), 184, 201

dragging/dropping objects, 177

Dragon NaturallySpeaking software, 193

DRAM (dynamic RAM), 102

drawing programs, 292

DR-DOS, 233. *See also* DOS (Disk Operating System)

driver. *See* device driver

drives, 14. *See also specific drive types*

DriveSavers, 144

drop-down list boxes, 46, 47

drum scanners, 184

DSL Internet access Fast, direct Internet access via standard telephone lines, 332–333, 374

dual in-line memory modules (DIMMs), 100

dual processors, 228, 232

dumb terminals, 25

DVD burner, 154. *See also* DVD drives

DVD discs. *See also specific disc types*
  advantages, 152
  authoring software, 294
  burning, 153, 294
  capacities, 152, 153
  caring for, 151–152
  digital copy protection, 155
  further exploration, 141
  illustrated, 13, 14, 150, 153
  recordable, 153, 154
  rewritable, 154

DVD drives, 14, 163
  alternative name for, 154
  compatibility, 154
  further exploration, 141
  illustrated, 13
  inserting media, 151–152
  origin, R-6
  recordable, 153, 154, 163
  speed, 151

DVD-R/DVD+R discs Recordable DVDs, 153, 163

DVD-ROM disc An optical disc, usually holding 4.7 GB, that can be read, but not written to, by the user, 153

DVD-RW/DVD+RW/ DVD-RAM discs Rewritable DVDs, 117, 153, 154, 163

Dvorak keyboards, 175

DVR. *See* digital video recorders (DVRs)

DWDM (Dense WDM), 335

Dynamic HTML (DHTML) A form of HTML used to add dynamic capabilities and interactivity to Web pages, 296

dynamic RAM (DRAM), 102

E

early computers, 4–5, 11, R-2

Earth Simulator supercomputer, 27, 28, 120, 242

Earthlink, 52

EB (exabyte), 91

EBCDIC A fixed-length, binary coding system widely used to represent text-based data on IBM mainframe computers, 90, 91, R-11

e-book A book obtained in electronic format, 395

e-commerce The act of doing business transactions over the Internet or similar technology, 7
  cookies and, 403–406
  corporate information, 397
  product information, 397
  security issues, 386
  shopping Web sites, R-22
  smart cards for, 160, 161

ECP (Extended Capabilities Port), 110

EDI. *See* electronic data interchange (EDI)

editing
  cell contents, 278
  database records (rows), 283–284
  word processing documents, 272, 273
  worksheets, 278–279

editing software
  audio files, 293
  graphic images, 292–293
education computers, 6–7
  colleges, universities, 7
  digital divide, 6, 367
  illustrated, 6
  K-12 schools, 6
  software use, 6
  statistics, 6
  uses, 6–7
educational software, 297, 298
.edu file extension, 55
edutainment software, 298
EIDE (enhanced integrated drive electronics) drives, 146
802.11 (Wi-Fi) A widely used communications protocol for
  wireless networks, 338–341
  analog signals, 317
  features, 338–339, 341
  network adapters, 331–332
  public hot spots, 54, 320, 322, 324, 338–339, 376
  smart displays, 198
  specifications, 339–341
  unauthorized use, 345
  versions, 339–341
  war driving, 345
802.20 (Mobile-Fi), 341
e-learning. *See* Web-based training (WBT)
electronic data interchange (EDI) The transfer of data
  between different companies using the Internet or another
  network, 7
electronic ink, 202. *See also* electronic paper (e-paper)
electronic mail (e-mail) Electronic messages sent from
  one user to another over the Internet or other network,
  5, 65–69
  abbreviations, 72, 73, 74
  acronyms, 72, 74
  addresses. *See* e-mail address
  antispam programs, 251
  citing correspondence guidelines, 385
  deleting, 68
  emoticons, 72, 74
  encrypted, 407
  filtering programs, 251
  flame mail, 72
  hoaxes, 57
  hyperlinks, 61
  illustrated, 66, 69
  Inbox folders, 68
  managing, 68
  mechanics of, 65–66
  netiquette, 71–72
  non-encrypted, 407
  privacy, 407
  programs, 15, 65
  receiving, 68, 69
  sending, 68, 69
  setting up, 65
  SHOUTING, 72
  spam, 72, 75
  storing, 68
  video e-mail, 67
  viruses. *See* computer virus
  Web-based, 65–66
electronic paper (e-paper), 199, 202
electronic pen An input device that resembles an ordinary
  pen, 177–180
  digital pens, 178, 179
  digital portfolios, 179
  graphics tablet, 177, 178
  handwriting recognition, 177, 179–180
  pen-based PCs, 177, 178, 179
  signature capture devices, 178, 179
electronic postage (e-stamps), 207
electronic product code (ePC), 188
ellipses, 44, 45, 47

e-mail. *See* electronic mail (e-mail)
e-mail address An Internet address consisting of a user
  name and computer domain name that uniquely identifies
  a person on the Internet, 56
  address book, 68
  formats, 56
  pronouncing, 57
  sending messages, 68, 69
  user names, 56
embedded computers, 4
embedded operating systems, 231, 240
embedding objects, 269
emoticons, 72, 74
encryption A method of scrambling e-mail or files to make
  them unreadable if they are intercepted by an unauthorized user.
  e-mail, 407
  programs, 250
  secure Web pages, 55, 386, 387
  smart cards, 160
  URLs, 55
  VPNs, 330
end users. *See* computer user
end-user licensing agreement (EULA), 299
end-user programs. *See* application software; software suite;
  specific application types, names
enhanced 911 (e911), 326
enhanced integrated drive electronics (EIDE) drives, 146
Enhanced Parallel Port (EPP), 110
ENIAC, 11
e911 (enhanced 911), 326
Enter key, 175
enterprise storage systems, 148
enterprise-class servers. *See* mainframe computer
entertainment software, 289–291, 298. *See also* games
entertainment Web sites, R-21
e-paper (electronic paper), 199, 202
ePC (electronic product code), 188
EPIC (explicitly parallel computing), 121
EPOC operating system, 242
e-portfolio A collection of an individual's work accessible
  through a Web site, 400–401
EPP (Enhanced Parallel Port), 110
e-retailers. *See* e-commerce
ergonomic hardware Hardware, typically input and output
  devices, that are designed to be more ergonomically-
  correct than their non-ergonomic counterparts, 176
error messages, 60
e-signs, 202
E-stage (execution stage), 114
e-stamps (electronic postage), 207
Ethernet A widely used communications protocol for a
  LAN, 331, 336–337
ethics Overall standards of moral conduct.
  citing resources, 385
  computer hoaxes, 57
etiquette. *See* netiquette
EULA (end-user licensing agreement), 299
EUV (extreme ultraviolet) light, 122
evaluating search results, 384
exabyte (EB), 91
Excel. *See* Microsoft Excel
Excite search site, 63, 379
executable file extensions, 72, 248
execute cycle, 114, 115
execution stage (E-stage), 114
.exe file extension, 72
expansion bus A bus that connects the CPU to peripheral
  devices, 104–106
  AGP bus, 105, 106
  FireWire/IEEE 1394 bus, 105, 106
  ISA bus, 104, 105
  PCI bus, 104–106
  types, 104–106
  USB. *See* Universal Serial Bus (USB)

expansion card A circuit board that can be inserted into an
  expansion slot on a PC's motherboard to add additional
  functionality or to attach a peripheral device, 106–108.
  See also specific card names
  common types/purposes, 107
  desktop PCs, 106–107
  handheld PCs, 108
  illustrated, 96, 107
  mobile devices, 108
  network adapters, 14, 240, 331–332, 343
  NIC cards, 107, 108, 331–332
  notebook computers, 107–108
  PC cards, 107–108
  for ports, 96, 107, 108, 109
  tablet PCs, 107–108
expansion slot A location on the motherboard into which
  expansion cards are inserted, 106–108
  desktop PCs, 106–107
  handheld PCs, 108
  illustrated, 96, 105
  mobile devices, 108
  notebook computers, 107–108
  portable computers, 107–108
  tablet PCs, 107–108
  unique configurations, 106
explicitly parallel computing (EPIC), 121
Explorer (browser). *See* Microsoft Internet Explorer
Explorer (file management program). *See* Windows
  Explorer
Extended Binary-Coded Decimal Interchange Code.
  See EBCDIC
Extended Capabilities Port (ECP), 110
Extensible Markup Language (XML). *See* XML (Extensible
  Markup Language)
external cache, 99, 105
external hard drives. *See* portable hard drives
external storage, 134. *See also specific media*
extranet An intranet that is at least partially accessible to
  authorized outsiders, 330
extreme ultraviolet (EUV) light, 122
EZ-D disc, 154

F
face recognition, 189, 190, 347, 348
fans, 96, 118
FAQs (frequently asked questions), 72
Fast ATA drives, 146
Fast Ethernet (100Base-T), 337
Fast IDE drives, 146
FAT. *See* file allocation table (FAT)
fault tolerance, 149
favorites, 62–63
fax machines, 208
FDM (Frequency Division Multiplexing), 335
female connectors, 108
FeRAM (ferroelectric RAM), 101
ferroelectric RAM (FeRAM), 101
fetch cycle, 114, 115
fiber-optic cable A communications medium that utilizes
  hundreds of hair-thin, transparent fibers over which lasers
  transmit data as light, 321–322
  connectors, 109, 321, 322
  transmission speed, 322
Fibre Channel interface card, 146
Fibre Channel storage, 146, 148
field A single category of data to be stored in a database,
  such as a person's name or telephone number; also called
  a column, 281
  creating, 282–283, 284
  default values, 282
  required, 282
  size, 282
field searching, 383–384
field-programmable gate arrays (FPGAs), 119
fifth-generation computers, 12

file Something stored on a storage medium, such as a program, document, or image, 136
copying, 243–244
deleting, 245
moving, 243–244
naming. *See* filename
opening, 243
pasting, 244
paths, 225–226
retrieving deleted, 244
viewing contents, 243
file allocation table (FAT), 138–139
FAT32 file system, 145
NTFS file system, 145
file compression programs, 248
file extensions. *See also specific extension names*
commonly used, 226
defined, 72
executable, 72
URLs, 55
file management, 225–226. *See also* folder; *specific folder names*
defined, 225
illustrated, 226
logical vs. physical representation, 136–137
paths, 225–226
root directory, 225, 226
file management program A utility program that enables the user to perform file management tasks, such as copying and deleting files, 226, 243–245
file server, 328
file systems. *See* file allocation table (FAT)
File Transfer Protocol (FTP), 55, 371
filename A name given to a file by the user that is used to retrieve the file at a later time, 136
assigning, 226, 244
extensions. *See* file extensions; *specific file extension names*
long, 226
rules, 226
special characters, 226
financial brokerage sites, 389
finger payment systems, 349
fingerprint readers, 189, 347, 348, 349
firewall A collection of hardware and/or software intended to protect a computer or computer network from unauthorized access, 347–348, 353
direct Internet connection need, 347–348, 374
features, 347–348
mechanics of, 348
programs, 251
FireWire/IEEE 1394
buses, 105, 106
cards, 108
hubs, 110
ports, 110, 111
first-generation cell phones, 325
first-generation computers, 11, R-2–3
fixed wireless Internet access Fast, direct Internet access available in large metropolitan areas via the airwaves and a radio transceiver, 322, 374, 376
fixed-media storage, 135. *See also specific media*
flame mail, 72
Flash, 62
flash memory A type of non-volatile memory that can be erased and reprogrammed; commonly implemented in the form of sticks or cards, 100, 104
ports, 156–157
storage comparison chart, 163
uses, 155, 156
flash memory card A small, rectangular type of flash memory media, such as a CompactFlash or Secure Digital card, 13, 108, 156–157, 163. *See also specific card names*
flash memory card reader, 156, 163
external device, 13, 14
illustrated, 13, 111, 156, 157
notebook computers, 111

flash memory drive A small drive that usually plugs into a PCs USB port and contains flash memory media, 13, 109, 158, 162, 163, R-6
flash memory media Memory-chip-based storage media commonly implemented in the form of sticks or cards, 104, 155–158, 163
adapter cards, 108
for digital cameras, 192
flash memory stick A type of flash memory media about the size of a stick of gum, 156, 163
flash RAM. *See* flash memory
flatbed scanner An input device that scans flat objects one at a time, 183, 184
flat-panel display A slim type of display device, 197–198
flexible displays, 199, 200
flexible organic light-emitting diodes (FOLEDs), 199
floppy disk A low-capacity, removable magnetic disk made of flexible plastic permanently sealed inside a hard plastic cover, 14, 137, 138–140
anatomy of, 138
characteristics, 138–139
clusters, 138, 139
comparison chart, 163
evolution, R-3, R-4
file directory/FAT, 138–139
formatting, 139–140
illustrated, 13, 138, 139
reading disks, 140
sectors, 138, 139
storage capacity, 139
tracks, 138, 139
using, 139–140
floppy disk drive A storage device that reads from and writes to floppy disks, 14, 138, 163
ejecting disks, 139
illustrated, 13, 96
inserting disks, 139
random access storage, 135–136
reading disks, 140
read/write heads, 140
writing (storing) data, 140
flowlines, 296
foldable keyboards, 176
folder A named place on a storage medium into which files can be stored to keep the medium organized, 136. *See also specific folder names*
copying, 243–244
creating new, 243
deleting, 245
hierarchy, 225–226
moving, 243–244
naming, 243, 244
organizing, 136–137
pasting, 244
paths, 225–226
retrieving deleted, 244
subfolders within, 136
URLs for, 55–56
viewing contents, 243
FOLEDs (flexible organic light-emitting diodes), 199
F1, F2, F3... keys (function keys), 175
font
faces, 273–274
formatting, 273–274
illustrated, 273, 274
sizes, 273–274
styles, 273–274
footers, 273, 274
form fields, 61, 62
formatting
floppy disks, 139–140
hard drives, 143–145
spreadsheets, 277, 279–280
word processing documents, 273–274
forms, 284
formula An entry in a worksheet cell that performs computations on worksheet data and displays the results, 277–278, 279

formula bar, 278
FORTRAN A high-level programming language used for mathematical, scientific, and engineering applications, 12, R-3
48-bit color, 184–185
forward slash (/), 57
4G (fourth-generation) cellular devices, 325
four-bit memory, 101
fourth-generation (4G) cellular devices, 325
fourth-generation computers, 11, 12, R-4–6
FPGAs (field-programmable gate arrays), 119
fragmented files, 115–117, 247
frames (Web page), 61, 62
fraud, 386
freeware Copyrighted software that may be used free of charge, 264, 265
Frequency Division Multiplexing (FDM), 335
frontside bus (FSB), 100
FSB. *See* frontside bus (FSB)
FTP (File Transfer Protocol), 55, 371
full-duplex transmission, 318
fulleride, 119
function A named formula that can be entered into a worksheet cell to perform some type of calculation or to extract information from other cells in the worksheet, 278, 279
function keys, 175
function lock (F lock) key, 175
further exploration topics
application software, 270
citing Web resources, 385
computer history, 12
CPUs, 97
database software, 285
digital data representation, 90
DVD discs, 141
DVD drives, 141
GPS systems, 314
graphics, 296
hard drives, 141
Internet access, 367
ISPs, 367
memory, 104
multimedia, 296
Napster controversy, 390
operating systems, 241
PCs, 23
peer-to-peer file sharing, 390
presentation graphics software, 287
scanners, 185
search sites, 63
spreadsheet software, 281
utility programs, 251
viruses, 351
Web browsers, 52
Web bugs/spyware, 406
wired networks, 326
wireless networks, 326
word processing software, 275
future trends
Internet, 407
nanotechnology, 122
operating systems, 251
optical computers, 12, 123
organic computers, 122
quantum computing, 123
speed enhancement, 122–123
FV function, 278

G
G5. *See* Power Mac G5
Gaidano, Scott, 144
game ports, 109, 110
gamepads, 181
games, 15
devices, 13, 181, 182
online, 393–395
software, 289–291, 298
gas plasma displays, 198

Gateway, 20, 28
gateways, 334, 335, 340
GB. *See* gigabyte (GB)
General Packet Radio Service (GPRS), 325
General Public License (GPL), 239
general-purpose computers, 4
generations
    cellular technology, 325
    computer, 10–12, R-2–6
geosynchronous (geostationary) orbits, 323–324
gesture recognition, 181
GHz (gigahertz), 97
GIF, animated, 62, 294–296
gigabyte (GB) Approximately 1 billion bytes, 91
gigaglops, 114
gigahertz (GHz), 97
global positioning system (GPS) A system that uses satel-
    lites and a receiver to determine the exact geographic
    location of the receiver, 314. *See also* communications
    satellite
    further exploration, 314
    illustrated, 8, 314
    orbit cycles, 324
    receivers, 314
    satellites, 314, 324
    smart cars, 241
    wearable PCs, 9
Global System for Mobile Communication (GSM), 325
GNOME environment, 238
GNU General Public License (GPL), 239
Google, 63, 64, 379, 380, 382, R-23–24
government
    information, 397
    Internet participation, 370
.gov file extension, 55
GPL (General Public License), 239
GPRS (General Packet Radio Service), 325
GPS systems. *See* global positioning system (GPS)
graphic A digital representation of a photograph, drawing,
    chart, or other visual image, *See also* multimedia; multi-
    media software; *specific multimedia elements*
    bitmapped images, 92, 93
    clip art images, 273, 275
    color images, 92, 93
    data, 92, 93
    dithering, 92
    file extensions, 226
    further exploration, 296
    grayscale images, 92, 93
    illustrated, 93
    monochrome images, 92, 93
    photographic (true color), 92, 93
    pixels, 92, 93
    standards, 196
    vector-based images, 92
    word processing software, 273, 275
graphical user interface (GUI) A graphically based inter-
    face that allows a user to communicate instructions to the
    computer easily, 41, 231, 365, 366
graphics coprocessors, 228
graphics software Application software used to create or
    modify images, 291-296. *See also* multimedia software;
    specific application names
    common programs, 292, 293
    drawing programs, 292
    image-editing programs, 292–293
    layering images, 292
    optimizing images, 292–293
    painting programs, 292
    presentation graphics. *See* presentation graphics software
    raster-based, 292, 293
    vector-based, 292, 293
    Web and, 296
graphics tablet A flat, rectangular input device that is used
    in conjunction with a stylus to transfer drawings,
    sketches, and anything written on the device to a PC in
    graphic form, 177, 178

graphing, 280
grayed-out items, 45
grayscale images, 92, 93
grid computing, 27–28, 120
GSM (Global System for Mobile Communication), 325
GUI. *See* graphical user interface (GUI)

H
hacking Using a computer to break into a remote computer
    system, 344–345
    data alteration, 353
    examples, 344, 345
    legal ramifications, 344
    program alteration, 353
half-duplex transmission, 318
hand geometry readers, 189, 347, 348
handheld computer A portable PC about the size of a
    paperback book or pocket calculator, 19, 24–25
    add-on devices, 111
    alternative names for, 24–25
    application software, 269–270
    desktop-compatible software, 270
    digital portfolios, 179
    docking stations, 25
    expansion slots/cards, 108, 331–332
    features, 24–25
    handwriting recognition, 179-180
    illustrated, 23, 111
    infrared capabilities, 25
    keyboards, 176
    operating systems, 240–242
    options available, 25
    Palm PCs, 111, 179–180, R-6
    pen-based, 177, 178, 179
    ports, 108, 111
    Springboard modules, 111
    Universal Connectors, 111
handheld scanner A small, handheld optical scanner,
    183, 184
handshaking, 336
handwriting recognition The ability of a device to identify
    handwritten characters, 177, 179–180
HAPS (High Altitude Platform Station), 375
hard copy, 174
hard disk drive A storage system consisting of one or more
    metal magnetic disks permanently sealed with an access
    mechanism inside its drive, 134, 137, 140–149
    adding second drive, 117
    alternative names for, 141
    anatomy of, 141, 142
    capacities, 141, 147
    characteristics, 141–143
    in consumer products, 143
    cylinders, 142, 143
    damage, 142–143
    data movement time, 143
    data recovery, 143, 144, 249, 250
    disk access time, 143
    disk cache, 145–146
    disk management programs, 246–247
    FAT32 file systems, 145
    file systems, 145
    formatting, 143–145
    fragmented, 115–117, 247
    further exploration, 141
    head crashes, 142–143
    illustrated, 13, 96, 141, 142, 143, 247
    increasing efficiency, 145
    large computer systems, 147–149
    maintaining, 115–117, 246–247
    multiple operating systems on, 145
    NAS devices, 148
    networks, 147–149
    partitioning, 143–145
    PC cards, 108
    Pixie Dust technology, 141
    portable systems, 146–147, 163

RAID designs, 149
    random access storage, 135–136
    read/write heads, 142–143
    removable cartridges, 141, 146–147, 163
    rotational delays, 143
    SAN devices, 148
    seek time, 143
    shared, 231, 232
    speeds, 142, 143
    spinning, 142
    standards, 146
    storage comparison chart, 163
    surface obstacles, 143
    upgrading, 117, R-18
    virtual memory, 228–229, 230
hardware The physical parts of a computer system, such as
    the keyboard, monitor, printer, and so forth, 12–14. *See
    also specific hardware*
    external, 12
    illustrated, 13
    input devices, 13
    internal, 12
head crashes, 142–143
headers, 273, 274
headphone jacks, 209
heat sinks, 118
Help command, 47
Help systems, 270–271
    application-based, 270, 271
    illustrated, 271
    index, 270
    offline, 270
    search, 270
    table of contents, 270
    Web-based, 270
Hewlett-Packard, 20, 122, 239
hexadecimal numbering system, R-7–9
hierarchy (folders), 225–226
High Altitude Platform Station (HAPS), 375
high-capacity removable disks/drives, 140. *See also specific
    media, drives*
high-end servers. *See* mainframe computer
highlighted items, 45
high-tech pets, 99
History list, 62–63
Hitachi, 141
hits (search), 380
Hoaxbusters, 57
hoaxes. *See* computer hoax
Hollerith, Herman, 11
holographic storage An emerging type of storage technol-
    ogy that uses multiple laser beams to store data in three
    dimensions, 161
home computers, 5–6
    networks, 335, 340
    smart homes, 6
    statistics, 5, 6
    uses, 5–6
home page The designated starting page for a Web site,
    52, 58
Home Phoneline Networking Association (Home PNA),
    342–343
HomePlug AV, 343
HomePlug Powerline Alliance, 343
Hopper, Grace, R-3
hot spots. *See* public hot spots
HotBot search site, 379, 382
Hotmail, 65–66
hot-swappable devices, 110
how it works features
    business card CDs, 151
    creating custom music CDs, 295
    downloading programs, 245
    face recognition, 190
    installing programs, 245
    MP3 compression, 94
    setting up home network, 340

setting up PCs, 21
video e-mail, 67
video-on-demand, 394
HTML (Hypertext Markup Language) A markup language widely used for creating Web pages, 55
http (Hypertext Transfer Protocol), 55
hub A device that is a central location where data arrives and is then transferred in one or more directions, 334
FireWire/IEEE 1394 hub, 110
illustrated, 335
USB hub, 110
Huffman coding, 94
hybrid mobile devices (PDAs), 24–25
hyperlink Text or an image located on a Web page or other document that is linked to a Web page or other type of document, 44
e-mail, 61
features, 44, 51
illustrated, 43, 45, 60
using, 60
word processing documents, 275
Hypertext Markup Language. *See* HTML (Hypertext Markup Language)
Hypertext Transfer Protocol (http), 55
hyperthreading A technique used in some Intel CPUs to enable software to treat the CPU as two processors to complete processing more quickly, 120–121

I

IBM, 20, 122, 123
Deep Blue, R-6
evolution, R-3–6
large computer operating systems, 242
Lotus SmartSuite, 266
Microdrive, 141
Pixie Dust technology, 141
UNIX copyright challenge, 239
ViaVoice, 193
IBM PC, 20
compatibles. *See* PC-compatible computers; personal computer (PC)
history, R-5
illustrated, 11
iBook notebook computer, 20
ICANN (Internet Corporation for Assigned Names and Numbers), 55, 370
iCi (Interactive Conversation Interface), 291
icon A small picture or other type of graphical image that represents a program, command, or document and invokes some action when selected, 43–44
desktop icon, 42, 43–44, 45, 47
features, 43–44
illustrated, 42, 43
icon-based authoring programs, 296
ICs. *See* integrated circuits (ICs)
ID cards, 159, 162
identification procedures, 345
identity management programs, 250–251
identity theft Using someone else's identity to purchase goods or services, obtain new credit cards or bank loans, or otherwise illegally masquerade as that individual, 73, 386
IEEE. *See* Institute of Electrical and Electronics Engineers (IEEE)
IEEE 1394. *See* FireWire/IEEE 1394
IF function, 278
illegal operations, 223
ILP (instruction-level parallelism), 121
IM. *See* instant messaging (IM)
iMac desktop computer, 20
image-editing programs, 292–293
Imation, 140
impact of computers, 4–8
in education, 6–7
on the go, 8
at home, 5–6
social impact, 28–29
why learn computers, 4–5
in workplace, 7

Inbox folders, 68
increasing computer speed, 115–123
adding memory, 115
adding second hard drive, 117
bus speed, 97, 100, 118
CPU upgrade, 118, R-18
future trends, 122–123
hyperthreading, 120–121
instruction set design, 121
Internet connection upgrade, 118
materials improvement, 119
moving circuits together, 118
multiprocessing, 119–120
nanotechnology, 122
optical computers, 12, 123
organic computers, 122
parallel processing, 119–120, 121, 228, 229
pipelining, 119
production strategies, 118–121
quantum computing, 123
RAM, 102, 115
system maintenance, 115–117, 246–247
3-D chips, 123
today, 115–118
video card upgrade, 118
Industry Standard Architecture (ISA) bus, 104, 105
.info file extension, 55
information Data that has been processed into a meaningful form, 16
integrity, 75
IPOS cycle, 10
kiosks, 291
processing, 16
information age, 28
information appliances. *See* Internet appliance
information processing (IPOS) cycle, 10
information revolution, 28
information system types
artificial intelligence, 12
CAD, 297, 298
infrared (IR) transmissions, 326
infrared capabilities
handheld computers, 25
IrDA ports, 110
IrDA protocol, 342
Infrared Data Association (IrDA)
ports, 110
protocol, 342
infrastructure companies, 369
ink-jet plotters, 207–208
ink-jet printer An output device that sprays droplets of ink to produce images on paper, 205–206
bubble-jet technology, 205, 206
costs, 205
emerging technologies, 205
features, 205
illustrated, 206, 207
ink cartridges, 205, 206
mechanics of, 206
wide-format (plotters), 207–208
input device A piece of hardware that supplies input to a computer, 13, 174. *See also specific devices*
input The process of entering data into a computer; can also refer to the data itself, 10
inserting columns/rows, 278
insertion point An onscreen character that indicates the current location in a document, which is where the next change will be made to the document, 176, 272, 273
inside industry features
data recovery firms, 144
emoticons/acronyms, 74
Jellyvision iCi, 291
Linux desktops, 239
Napster controversy, 391
non-volatile memory, 101
PC modding, 22
presence technology, 326
installed software, 265

installing software, 14, 245
instant messaging (IM) A form of private chat set up to allow users to easily and quickly exchange real-time typed messages with the individuals they specify, 71
buddy lists, 71
features, 70
illustrated, 70
programs, 71
Institute of Electrical and Electronics Engineers (IEEE), 341
instruction set, 95, 113
instruction stage (I-stage), 114
instruction-level parallelism (ILP), 121
integrated circuits (ICs)
chips, 96
moving close together, 118
origin, 12
integrated services digital network. *See* ISDN Internet access
integrated software programs, 267–268. *See also* software suite; *specific software names*
Intel CPUs
characteristics, 96–97, 98, 113, 114, R-13
evolution, R-4–6
search example, 382–383
Interactive Conversation Interface (iCi), 291
interactive TV (iTV), 198, 391–392
interface cards. *See* expansion card; *specific card names*
interfaces. *See* operating system; *specific operating systems*; user interfaces
internal bus, 100, 105
internal cache, 99, 105, 112, 113, 116
internal storage, 134. *See also specific media*
Internet The largest and most well-known computer network, linking millions of computers all over the world, 4, 18, 51–65. *See also specific online services*
addresses, 54–57
backbone, 52, 366
citing resources, 385
community today, 367–370
control, 366, 371
costs, 370
early images, 365, 366
evolution, 364–371
fees, 370, 371
future trends, 407
governing body, 366, 370, 371
government participation, 370
hardware companies, 369
infrastructure companies, 369
mobile access, 8
myths, 370–371
netiquette, 71–72
network ownership, 366
origin, 12
overview, 51–52
searching. *See* search engine; search site
software companies, 369
standards evolution, 365
URLs. *See* uniform resource locator (URL)
users, 367
World Wide Web vs., 18, 51, 365–366, 371
Internet access. *See also* Internet service provider (ISP); *specific access devices*; Web browser
aircraft-based, 375
broadband service, 118, 374–376
connection types, 372–376
desktop PCs, 372
devices, 5–6, 25, 26, 371–372
dial-up connections, 52, 58, 335, 373
direct connections, 52, 68, 372, 374–376
DSL, 332–333, 374
fees, 373, 374, 375, 376, 377
fixed wireless access, 322, 374, 376
further exploration, 367
hot spots. *See* public hot spots
mobile wireless, 372, 374, 376
notebook computers, 372
public hot spots, 54, 320, 322, 324, 338–339, 376

setting up connections, 371–378
speed, 373, 374, 375, 376
tablet PCs, 372
T-1 lines, 374
Internet address What identifies a computer, person, or Web page on the Internet, such as an IP address, domain name, or e-mail address, 54–57. *See also* uniform resource locator (URL)
Internet appliance A specialized network computer designed primarily for Internet access and/or e-mail exchange, 26, 372
convergence, 6
digital media units, 26
features, 5–6, 26, 372
illustrated, 25
set-top boxes, 25, 26
Internet cafés, 8, 53, 54
Internet content provider A person or an organization that provides Internet content, 368
Internet Corporation for Assigned Names and Numbers (ICANN), 55, 370
Internet Explorer. *See* Microsoft Internet Explorer
Internet filtering Using a software program or browser option to block access to particular Web pages or types of Web pages, 402, 403
Internet peer-to-peer computing, 329
Internet Protocol address. *See* IP address
Internet radio, 389, 390
Internet service provider (ISP) A business or other organization that provides Internet access to others, typically for a fee, 52–53, 367–368. *See also* Internet access; *specific access devices*
alternative names for, 367
connection types, 372–376
e-mail service, 65, 66
fees, 52–53
further exploration, 367
networks, 52
online storage, 159, 160
provider options, 52–53, 367–368
public locations, 8, 53, 54
questions, 377
selecting, 377
types, 367, 368
upgrading connection, 118
Internet Society (ISOC), 366, 370, 371
Internet telephony The process of placing telephone calls over the Internet, 71, 337
Internet2, 367
interpolated (enhanced) resolution, 185, 192
intranet A private network that is set up similar to the World Wide Web, 330
investing. *See* online investing
IP address A numeric Internet address used to uniquely identify a computer on the Internet, 54–55
IPOS (information processing) cycle, 10
IR (infrared transmissions), 326
IrDA. *See* Infrared Data Association (IrDA)
iris scanners, 347, 348
ISA (Industry Standard Architecture) bus, 104, 105
ISDN Internet access Dial-up Internet access that is faster than conventional dial-up, but still uses standard telephone lines.
features, 373
modems, 332
ISOC (Internet Society), 366, 370, 371
isochronous transmission, 319–320
I-stage (instruction stage), 114
Itanium (Intel) CPUs, 97, 98, 103, 113, 121, 232, R-6
iTunes, 388
iTunes Music Store, 390

J

Jasc Paint Shop Pro, 292
Java A high-level, object-oriented programming language frequently used for Web-based applications, 14, R-5
Java applet A small program inserted into a Web page that performs a specific task, such as changing the values in a

stock portfolio or scrolling text across the screen, 62, 388, 389
Java Desktop System, 238
JavaScript animation, 296
Jellyvision Interactive Conversation Interface (iCi), 291
jobs. *See* careers
joystick An input device that resembles a car's gear shift and is often used for gaming, 13, 181, 182
.jp file extension, 55
justifying documents, 274

K

K-12 schools, 7
Kasparov, Garry, R-6
KB. *See* kilobyte (KB)
Kbps (thousands of bits per second), 318
KDE environment, 238
KDE Internet project, 238
kernel, 224
key drives. *See* flash memory drive
keyboard An input device containing numerous keys, arranged in a configuration similar to that of a typewriter, that can be used to input letters, numbers, and other symbols, 174–176
anatomy of, 175
buffer, 230
connectors, 109, 110
ergonomic, 176
foldable, 176
illustrated, 13, 175
keys, 175
layouts, 175
notebook computers, 175
portable, 176
ports, 109, 110
wireless, 176
keyboard shortcuts, 45, 250, 267
keyword A word typed in a search box on a search site to locate information on the Internet, 379, 380
illustrated, 381
Internet filtering, 402, 403
searching on, 64, 380, 383, R-23–24
special operators, 64, R-24
kilobyte (KB) 1,024 bytes, 91
kiosks, 8, 291

L

label A text-based entry in a worksheet cell that identifies data on the worksheet, 277
label printers, 206–207
LAN. *See* local area network (LAN)
lands, 152
landscape orientation, 274
lane-departure systems, 241
language translator A software program that converts program code to machine language, 95
laptop computer. *See* notebook computer
laser printer An output device that uses toner powder and technology similar to that of a photocopier to produce images on paper, 204–205
costs, 204
illustrated, 205
mechanics of, 205
specifications, 204
toner powder/cartridges, 204, 205
laser servo (LS) drives, 140
layering images, 292
leaking memory, 228
left margins, 274
legacy drive, 138
legacy port, 109
LEO (low earth orbit) satellites, 324
Level 1 cache, 98, 99, 113, R-13
Level 3 cache, 98, 99, R-13
Level 2 cache, 98, 99, 113, R-13
light pens, 177, 178
line printers, 204
line spacing, 274

linear tape-open (LTO), 158
line-of-sight, 177
linking objects, 269
Linux A version of UNIX that is available without charge over the Internet and is increasingly being used with PCs, servers, mainframes, and supercomputers, 14, 238–239
cost comparison, 239
desktops, 238, 239
development, 238–239
GNOME environment, 238
illustrated, 238
KDE environment, 238
large computer operating system, 242
origin, 238, R-5
personal vs. network versions, 231–232
supercluster, 242
user interface, 42, 231
liquid crystal display (LCD), 198
list boxes, 46, 47
literacy. *See* computer literacy
lithography, 122
local area network (LAN) A network that connects devices located in a small geographical area, such as within a building, 329
logging on, 18
logic bombs, 351
logical file representation, 136–137
long filenames, 226
Lotus 1-2-3, 276
Lotus Approach, 282
Lotus Freelance Graphics, 285
Lotus SmartSuite, 266
Lotus WordPro, 272
LoveLetter virus, 349
low earth orbit (LEO) satellites, 324
LS (laser servo) drives, 140
LS-120 disks, 140
LS-240 disks, 140, 163
LTO (linear tape-open), 158
lurking, 72

M

Mac OS The operating system for Apple's Macintosh line of computers, 14, 237
illustrated, 237
personal vs. network versions, 231–232
user interface, 42
Mac OS X The most recent version of Mac OS, 237
machine cycle The series of operations involved in the execution of a single machine-level instruction, 114–115, 116
machine language A low-level programming language in which the program code consists of 1s and 0s, 95
instruction set, 95, 113, 121
translating into, 95
Macintosh computers. *See* Apple computers
Macintosh Operating System. *See* Mac OS; Mac OS X
Macromedia Authorware, 296
Macromedia Director, 296
Macromedia Fireworks, 296
Macromedia Flash, 296
Macromedia Freehand, 292
Macs. *See* Apple computers
magnetic disk A storage medium that records data using magnetic spots on disks made of flexible plastic or rigid metal, 137–149
clusters, 138, 139, 141, 142, 145
floppy disks. *See* floppy disk
hard drives. *See* hard disk drive
high-capacity removable, 140
illustrated, 137, 139
sectors, 138, 139, 141, 142, 150
storage comparison chart, 163
tracks, 138, 139, 141, 142, 150, 152
magnetic ink character recognition (MICR) readers, 187–189
magnetic RAM (MRAM), 101
magnetic stripe technology, 159

magnetic tape A plastic tape with a magnetizable surface that stores data as a series of magnetic spots; typically comes as a cartridge, 158
magnetic tape drives, 136, 158
magneto-optical (M-O) storage, 154
mail server, 328
mainframe computer A computer used in large organizations (such as hospitals, large businesses, and colleges) that need to manage large amounts of centralized data and run multiple programs simultaneously, 27
  operating systems, 242
  user interfaces, 231
maintenance (hard drives), 115–117, 246–247. *See also* utility program
male connectors, 108
malicious spam, 352
malware Any type of malicious software, 350–351. *See also* computer virus
MAN (metropolitan area network), 329
managing e-mail, 68
manipulating windows, 48–50
  active windows, 43, 48
  closing windows, 48, 49
  maximizing windows, 48
  minimizing windows, 48
  mouse pointer changes, 49
  moving windows, 49
  restoring windows, 49
  scroll bars, 50
  showing desktop, 49
  sizing windows, 48–49
margins, 274
massively parallel processing (MPP)
  processing mechanics, 119–120
  super computer, 27, 120
master devices, 341–342
math coprocessors, 228
mathematical operators, 277
Matrix Semiconductors, 123
MAX function, 278
Maximize button, 48
maximizing windows, 48
MB. *See* megabyte (MB)
Mbps (millions of bits per second), 318
mechanical mice, 176
media players, 294, 388
medical students
  handheld PC use, 24
  technology benefits, 24, 29
  virtual surgery, 29
medium earth orbit (MEO) satellites, 324
megabyte (MB) Approximately 1 million bytes, 91
megaflops, 114
megahertz (MHz), 97
Melissa virus, 351
memory, 13, 100–104. *See also* register; *specific memory types*
  blocks, 104
  further exploration, 104
  leaking, 228
  management, 228–229
menu A set of options (usually text-based) that can be displayed on the screen to enable the user to issue commands to the computer, 44–46
  arrows, 45
  bar, illustrated, 43, 45
  check marks, 45
  current command, 44
  dimmed items, 45
  elements, 44–46
  ellipses, 44, 45, 47
  highlighted items, 45
  keyboard shortcuts, 45
  option (radio) buttons, 45
  personalized, 45, 46
  submenus, 45

MEO (medium earth orbit) satellites, 324
message boards. *See* discussion group
messaging, 313
metasearch sites, 381
metropolitan area network (MAN), 329
MHTML (MIME Hypertext Markup Language), 275
MHz (megahertz), 97
microbrowser A special type of Web browser used with handheld PCs and mobile devices, 52, 53, 342
microcode, 113
microcomputer A computer system based on a microprocessor, designed to be used by one person at a time; also called a personal computer or PC, 5, 20. *See also* microprocessor; personal computer (PC)
microdisplays, 9
Microdrive (IBM), 141
microns, 122
microphone
  illustrated, 13, 194
  voice-input systems, 194
microprocessor A CPU for a microcomputer, 96
  origin, 12, R-4
  transistors, 11–12, 111, R-3
  uses, 19–20
Microsoft Access, 282
  Microsoft Office 2003, 266
  using, 282–285
Microsoft Corporation, 233, R-4
Microsoft Excel, 276
  Microsoft Office 2003, 266
  using, 276–281
Microsoft Internet Explorer, 52
  buttons, 59
  commands, 59
  cookie settings, 405
  deleting temporary files, 117
  as freeware, 265
  illustrated, 59
Microsoft Office
  commands summary, 267
  contents, 266
  cost comparison, 239
  keyboards, 175
  OLE, 268–269
  versions, 266
Microsoft Outlook, 65, 266
Microsoft Outlook Express, 65, 69
Microsoft Photo Editor, 293
Microsoft PowerPoint, 285
  Microsoft Office 2003, 266
  using, 285–288
Microsoft Publisher, 266
Microsoft Windows The most common operating system for IBM and IBM-compatible PCs, *See specific Windows system names*; Windows
Microsoft Word, 272
  file extensions, 226
  Microsoft Office 2003, 266
  using, 272–275
Microsoft Works, 267
microwave antenna, 323
microwave station An earth-based device that sends and receives high-frequency, high-speed radio signals, 322–323
MIDI. *See* Musical Instrument Digital Interface (MIDI)
midrange server A medium-sized computer used to host programs and data for a small network.
  features, 19, 26
  illustrated, 26
.mil file extension, 55
MIME Hypertext Markup Language (MHTML), 275
MIN function, 278
minicomputers (minis). *See* midrange server
Minimize button, 48
minimizing windows, 48, 49
MiniSD cards, 157
mips (millions of instructions per second), 114

mirroring, 149
Mitnick, Kevin, 344
MMC. *See* MultiMedia cards (MMC)
MMX (Multimedia Extensions), 121
M-O discs. *See* magneto-optical (MO) storage
mobile computers. *See specific computer type*
mobile device A very small device, usually based on a wireless phone or pager, that has some type of computing or Internet capability built in, 8, 19. *See also specific devices*
  expansion slots/cards, 108
  features, 19
  flat panel technology, 197–198
  hybrid devices, 24–25
  illustrated, 19
  operating systems, 240–242
mobile wireless Internet access Internet access via a wireless communications network, such as the ones used with cellular phones, 372, 374, 376
Mobile-Fi, 341. *See also* 802.20 (Mobile-Fi)
modding PCs, 22
modem A communications device that enables digital computers to communicate over analog media, such as connecting to the Internet via telephone lines, 13, 14, 317, 332–333
  cable modem, 333, 335
  cards, 107, 108, 332, 333
  dial-up, 332, 333, 373
  DSL, 332–333
  illustrated, 333
  ISDN, 332
  PC cards, 108, 333
  ports, 109, 110, 111
  types, 14, 332–333
monitor A display device for a desktop PC, 195. *See also* display device
  color vs. monochrome, 195
  connector, 109
  CRT, 195, 196, 197
  dot pitch, 197
  flat-panel displays, 197–198
  HDTV, 198
  illustrated, 13, 195, 196
  ports, 109, 110, 111
  refreshing, 197
  screen resolution, 196
  size, 195–196
  viewable image size (VIS), 196, 197
monochrome images, 92, 93
Mosaic, 366
motherboard The main circuit board of a computer, located inside the system unit, to which all computer system components connect, 96. *See also specific motherboard components*
Motorola, 122
mouse A common pointing device that the user slides along a flat surface to move a pointer around the screen and clicks its buttons to make selections, 176–177
  Bluetooth-compliant, 177
  clicking, 177
  connector types, 109, 110
  dragging/dropping objects, 177
  gesture recognition vs., 181
  illustrated, 13
  invention, R-3
  mechanical, 176
  operations, 44, 176–177
  optical, 176, 177
  pointer, 42, 49, 176
  ports, 109, 110
  right-click shortcut menus, 243
  scroll button, 177
  scroll wheel, 177
  wireless, 177
mouse pad, 176
MovieBeam, 392
Movielink, 392

movies
  copyright violations, 393
  downloading, 198, 392–393, 394
moving
  files, 243–244
  folders, 243–244
  spreadsheet cells, 278–279
  word processing content, 272
Moving Pictures Experts Group (MPEG), 94. *See also* MP3
  (MPEG Audio Layer 3)
MPEG. *See* MPEG (Moving Pictures Experts Group); MP3
  (MPEG Audio Layer 3)
MPP. *See* massively parallel processing (MPP)
MP3 (MPEG Audio Layer 3)
  compression, 94, 389
  custom music CDs, 295, 390
MRAM (magnetic RAM), 101
MS-DOS, 233. *See also* DOS (Disk Operating System)
MSN, 397
MSN Explorer, 53
MSN Messenger, 71
MT-RJ connectors, 321, 322
multifunction devices, 208
multimedia The integration of a variety of media, such as
  text, graphics, video, animation, and sound, 62. *See also*
  graphic; *specific multimedia elements*
  applications. *See* graphics software; multimedia software;
    specific application names
  further exploration, 296
  illustrated, 61
  input devices, 191–194
  output devices, 208–209
  presentation graphics. *See* presentation graphics software
  projectors, 13, 199
  speakers, 13, 208–209
  voice-output systems, 209
multimedia authoring software Application software
  designed to create stand-alone multimedia applications to
  be delivered via CD, DVD, or the Web, 296
MultiMedia cards (MMC), 156, 157
Multimedia Extensions (MMX), 121
multimedia site development, 296
multimedia software, 15, 288–296. *See also* graphics software; presentation graphics software
  authoring software, 296
  business presentations, 289
  computer-based training, 289
  defined, 263
  entertainment, 289–291, 298
  illustrated, 290
  information kiosks, 291
  Interactive Conversation Interface, 291
  reference materials, 289, 290
  virtual reality, 289, 290
  Web-based training, 289, 290
multiplexers, 334–335
multiprocessing The capability of an operating system to
  use multiple processors simultaneously in a single computer, usually to process multiple jobs at one time faster
  than could be performed with a single processor,
  119–120, 228, 229
multiprogramming, 227
multitasking The capability of an operating system to execute two or more programs or program tasks concurrently
  for a single user, 227, 235, 238
multithreading, 227
.museum file extension, 55
music
  custom CDs, 295, 390
  input systems, 110, 194
  online. *See* online music
Musical Instrument Digital Interface (MIDI)
  audio editing software, 293
  devices, 110, 194
  ports, 110
  sharing files, 329
MusicMatch Jukebox, 294, 388

My Documents folder, 47
myths, Internet, 370–371

N

.name file extension, 55
naming files. *See* file extensions; filename; *specific file*
  extension names
naming folders, 243, 244
nanocrystals, 101
nanometers, 122
nanotechnology The science of creating tiny computers
  and components by working at the individual atomic and
  molecular levels, 122
Napster 2.0, 391
Napster controversy, 390, 391, 401
NAS. *See* network attached storage (NAS)
National Center for Supercomputing Applications
  (NCSA), 366
National Nanotechnology Research Program, 122
natural language system A system in which the computer
  can understand natural languages, 89, 381
navigation systems (cars), 241
NCSA (National Center for Supercomputing
  Applications), 366
NEC, 20, 27, 120, 242
Nero 6: The Ultimate CD/DVD Burning Suite, 294
netiquette An etiquette for guiding online behavior, 71–72
.net file extension, 55
Netscape Mail, 65, 69
Netscape Navigator, 52
  buttons, 59
  commands, 59
  cookie settings, 405
  deleting temporary files, 117
  as freeware, 265
  illustrated, 59
  origin, R-5
NetWare A widely used operating system for PC-based
  networks, 231, 232, 239
network adapter A network interface, such as an expansion card or external network adapter, 14, 331–332, 340,
  343. *See also* network interface card (NIC)
network attached storage (NAS) A high-performance storage server individually connected to a network to provide
  storage for computers on that network, 148
network computer (NC) A PC designed to access a network for processing and data storage, instead of performing those tasks locally, 25–26
  alternative name for, 25
  dumb terminals vs., 25
  illustrated, 25
  NAS devices, 148
  SAN devices, 148
  storage systems, 147–149
network interface card (NIC) An expansion card through
  which a computer can connect to a network, 107, 108,
  331–332
network licenses, 264
network operating system A type of operating system
  designed to support multiple users over a network,
  231–232. *See also specific operating systems*
network ports, 109, 110, 111, 331, 332
network servers, 17
network storage. *See* remote storage
networking hardware, 331–335
  adapters, 14, 331–332, 340, 343
  bridges, 334
  concentrators, 335
  connectors, 109
  gateways, 334, 335
  hubs, 334, 335
  modems. *See* modem
  multiplexers, 334–335
  NICs, 107, 108, 331–332
  printers, 203–204
  repeaters, 334
  routers, 334

  switches, 334
  wireless access points, 334
networking protocol, 332. *See also specific protocols*
networks. *See* computer network
New document command, 267
news online, 396, 397, R-21
newsgroups. *See* discussion group
newsreaders, 70
Next Generation Internet (NGI), 367
NGI (Next Generation Internet), 367
non-impact printers, 203. *See also* ink-jet printer; laser
  printer
non-personally identifiable information (Non-PII), 404
non-volatile Describes a storage medium that retains its
  contents when the power is shut off, 135
  memory, 100, 101
  storage media, 135
notebook computer A fully functioning portable PC that
  opens to reveal a screen and keyboard, 19, 23
  add-on devices, 111
  docking station. *See* docking station
  features, 23
  flat panel technology, 197–198
  illustrated, 23, 111
  keyboards, 175
  PC cards, 107–108, 331–332, 333
  universal drive bays, 107
Novell
  Linux, 238, 239
  Netware, 231, 232, 239
NOW function, 278
NTFS file system, 145
numbering systems, 89–90. *See also* binary
  numbering system
  computer arithmetic, R-9–10
  converting between, R-7, R-8–10
  decimal, 89–90, R-7, R-8–9
  hexadecimal, R-7–9
numeric formatting, 277, 280
numeric keypad, 175

O

object linking and embedding (OLE), 268–269
object-based authoring programs, 296
OCR. *See* optical character recognition (OCR)
OCR-A font, 187
office software suites. *See* software suite; *specific*
  suite names
offline, defined, 18
offline Help systems, 270
OLE (object linking and embedding), 268–269
OLEDs (organic light-emitting diodes), 199
OMRs (optical mark readers), 185
100Base-T standard, 337
online, defined, 18
online auction An online activity for which bids are placed
  on items and the highest bidder purchases the item, 16,
  387–388
online banking Performing banking activities over the
  Internet, 18, 298, 388, 389
online brokers, 388
online communications. *See also specific communications*
  methods
  anonymity concerns, 73–75
  differences, 73
  information integrity, 75
  privacy. *See* privacy concerns
online conferencing A real-time meeting that takes place
  between people in different locations via computers and
  communications media, 314–315
online conferencing service providers, 315
online education, 397–401
  blogs, 400, 401
  distance learning, 7, 397, 398–399
  e-portfolios, 400–401
  online writing, 397, 400–401
  testing online, 399
  WBT, 289, 290, 397, 398–399

online entertainment, 388–395. *See also specific activities*
online forums. *See* discussion group
online gaming Playing games over the Internet, 393–395
online investing Buying and selling stocks or other types of investments over the Internet, 388, 389
online learning. *See* Web-based training (WBT)
online music Music played or obtained via the Internet, 389–391
  copyright laws, 329, 389–390, 391
  custom CDs, 295, 390
  downloading, 5, 389–390, 391
  formats, 389
  Internet radio, 389, 390
  media players, 294, 388
  Napster controversy, 390, 391, 401
online news, 396, 397
online payment account A type of payment account accessed via the Internet and used to make electronic payments to others, either from funds deposited into the account or by charging the appropriate amount to a credit card, 386–387
online payment methods, 386–387
online portfolio management, 298, 388, 389
online services providers. *See* Internet access; Internet service provider (ISP); *specific access devices*
online shopping Buying products or services over the Internet, 386–387. *See also* e-commerce
online stock trading, 18
online testing, 399
online TV/video. *See* television; video
online writing, 397, 400–401
Open command, 267, 272, 276
Open Directory Project, 380
open source software, 238
opening
  files/documents, 47, 243, 267
  folders, 47, 243
OpenOffice.org, 238, 239, 266
Opera, 53
operating system The main component of system software that enables the computer to manage its activities and the resources under its control, run application programs, and interface with the user, 14, 223–242, 251. *See also specific operating systems*
  analyzing needs, R-14
  boot process, 40–41, 224
  buffering, 229–230
  command line interfaces, 231, 233
  coprocessing, 228
  CPUs supported, 232
  device drivers, 224
  differences, 230–232
  file management. *See* file management
  functions, 224–226
  further exploration, 241
  future trends, 251
  GUI interfaces, 41, 231, 365, 366
  handheld computers, 240–242
  illegal operations, 223
  intermediary role, 223–224
  kernel, 224
  larger computers, 242
  managing resources/jobs, 225
  memory management, 228–229
  mobile devices, 240–242
  monitoring resources/jobs, 225
  multiple, on hard drive, 145
  multiple users, 226, 227
  multiprocessing, 119–120, 228, 229
  multitasking, 227, 235, 238
  multithreading, 227
  origin, 12
  overview, 223–224
  parallel processing, 119–120, 121, 228, 229
  passwords, 226, 227
  personal vs. network, 231–232
  processing efficiency, 227–230
  registry files, 224

  resources, 225
  scheduling routines, 225
  security, 226, 227
  spooling, 229–230
  time-sharing, 227–228
  user interface, 41, 223–225
  virtual memory, 228–229, 230
operations personnel, 16
operators
  Boolean, 382–383, R-23
  keyword search, 64, R-23–24
  mathematical, 277
Opteron (AMD) CPUs, 97, 98, 103, 121, 232, R-13, R-6
optical character recognition (OCR) The ability of a scanning device to recognize handwritten or typed characters and convert them to electronic form as text, not images, 183
  benefits, 183
  devices, 187
  handwriting recognition vs., 180
  optical fonts, 187
  software, 183
  turnaround documents, 187
optical characters, 187
optical chips, 123
optical computers, 12, 123
optical disc A type of storage medium read from and written to using a laser beam, 150–154. *See also specific disc/drive types*
  burning, 153
  characteristics, 150–152
  illustrated, 150
  read-only (ROM) discs, 152–153
  recording, 153
  rewritable discs, 154
  sectors, 150
  storage comparison chart, 163
  tracks, 150, 152
optical fonts, 187
optical mark readers (OMRs), 185
optical marks, 185
optical mice, 176, 177
optical resolution, 185
optical scanner. *See* scanner
optimizing images, 292–293
option buttons
  dialog boxes, 46
  illustrated, 46
  menus, 45
optoelectronic computers, 123
Oracle Corporation, 282
Oracle database software, 282
organic computers, 122
organic light-emitting diodes (OLEDs), 199
.org file extension, 55
OS/2, 240
OS/2 Warp, 240
OUM (Ovonyx unified memory), 101
Outlook. *See* Microsoft Outlook
Outlook Express. *See* Microsoft Outlook Express
output device A piece of hardware that accepts output from the computer and presents it in a form the user can understand, 13, 174. *See also specific devices*
output The process of presenting the results of processing; can also refer to the results themselves, 10
Ovonyx unified memory (OUM), 101
ownership rights, 263–265. *See also* software license
  categories, 263, 264
  commercial software, 264
  freeware, 264, 265
  public domain software, 264, 265
  shareware, 264–265

P

packet switching, 337, 339
packets, 337, 339
Page Down (PgDn) key, 175
page formatting, 274

page printers, 204
Page Setup (word processing), 274
Page Up (PgUp) key, 175
pages per minute (ppm), 204
paging, 229, 313
painting programs, 292
Palm Graffiti alphabet, 179
Palm handheld PCs, 111, 179–180, R-6
Palm OS The operating system designed for Palm handheld PCs, 242, 269
PANs (personal area networks), 330
Panther. *See* Mac OS X
paper
  electronic, 199, 202
  size, 274
paragraph formatting, 274
parallel connector, 109
parallel ports, 109–110, 111
parallel processing A processing technique that uses multiple processors simultaneously in a single computer, usually to process a single job as fast as possible, 119–120, 121, 228, 229
parallel transmission Data transmission in which an entire byte of data is transmitted at the same time, 318
partitioning hard disks, 143–145
partitions, 143–145
Pascal A structured, high-level programming language often used to teach structured programming; especially appropriate for use in math and science applications, 14
password A secret combination of characters used to gain access to a computer, computer network, or other resource, 346
  identity management programs, 250–251
  operating system, 226, 227
  strategies, 346
  utility programs, 347
Paste command, 244, 267, 272
Paste Special command, 268
pasting files/folders, 244
Pay By Touch finger payment system, 349
PayPal, 386
PC Buyer's Guide, R-14–18
PC cams. *See* PC video cameras
PC card A small card that fits into a slot located on the exterior of a computer to provide new functionality or to attach a peripheral device, 107–108, 331–332, 333
PC card bus, 107
PC card slot A slot on the exterior of a computer into which a PC card is inserted, 107–108, 111
PC cards. *See* expansion card
PC postage (electronic postage), 207
PC video cameras, 192, 193
PC-compatible computers, 20. *See also* personal computer (PC)
PC-DOS, 233. *See also* DOS (Disk Operating System)
PCI (Peripheral Component Interconnect) bus, 104–106
PCMCIA card slot. *See* PC card slot
PDAs (personal digital assistants). *See* handheld computer
peer-to-peer networks
  features, 328–329
  file sharing issues, 329, 390, 391, 401
  illustrated, 328
  Napster controversy, 390, 391, 401
Peer-to-Peer Working Group, 401
pen-based PCs, 177, 178, 179
Penn State ID+ cards, 162
Pentium 4 (P4) CPUs, 96, 97, 98, 114, R-13
Pentium M CPUs, 97, 98, R-13
perceptual coding, 94
Peripheral Component Interconnect (PCI) bus, 104–106
peripheral devices, 25. *See also specific devices*
personal area networks (PANs), 330
Personal Computer Memory Card International Association, 107
personal computer (PC) Another name for microcomputer, 19–26
  back panel illustrated, 21
  backing up, 21

buying guide, R-14–18
costs, 20
expansion slots/cards, 106–107, 331–332
further exploration, 23
Internet setup, 372, 377–378
manufacturers, 20
microprocessors. *See* microprocessor
modding, 22
operating. *See* Windows
operating systems. *See* operating system; *specific operating systems*
overview, 19–26
"PCs" vs. "Macs", 20
phone calls, 71
remote access programs, 251
standards, 20
personal digital assistants (PDAs). *See* handheld computer
personal finance. *See also* online banking; online investing
software, 298
Web sites, R-19
personal firewalls, 347
personal identification numbers (PINs), 346
personal impact. *See* impact of computers
personal operating system A type of operating system designed for single users, 231
personal printers, 203–204
personal publishing software, 297–298
personalized menu, 45, 46
personally identifiable information (PII), 404
pervasive computing, 4
pet identification chips, 99
petabyte (PB), 91
PFRAM (polymeric ferroelectric RAM), 101
PgDn (Page Down) key, 175
PgUp (Page Up) key, 175
phase-change technology, 154
phone ports, 109, 110
Phoneline networks, 342–343
phonemes, 194
photo printer An output device designed for printing digital photographs, 206
photographs
cameras for. *See* digital camera
photo editing software, 293
sharing online, 159, 160, 192
true color, 92, 93
phrase searching, 382
physical file representation, 137
PII (personally identifiable information), 404
PINs (personal identification numbers), 346
pipelining A CPU feature designed to begin processing a new instruction as soon as the previous instruction completes the first stage of the machine cycle, 119, 120
piracy (movie), 393
pits, 152
pixel The smallest colorable area in an electronic image, such as a scanned document, digital photograph, or image displayed on a display screen, 185. *See also* resolution
bit depth, 196
coding, 92
graphics standards, 196
illustrated, 195, 196
Pixie Dust technology, 141
plagiarism Presenting someone else's work as your own, 385
plotters, 207–208
PMT function, 278
pocket computers. *See* handheld computer
Pocket Office, 270
pointing device An input device that moves an onscreen pointer, such as an arrow or insertion point, to allow the user to select objects on the screen, 176–181. *See also* mouse
digital pens, 178, 179
digital portfolios, 179
electronic pens, 177–180
graphics tablet, 177, 178

handwriting recognition, 177, 179–180
joy sticks, 13, 181, 182
pen-based PCs, 177, 178, 179
pointing sticks, 181, 182
signature capture devices, 178, 179
steering wheels, 181
touch pads, 181, 182
touch screens, 12, 180, 181
pointing stick An input device shaped like a pencil eraser that appears in the middle of some notebook computer keyboards and is used as a pointing device, 181, 182
point-of-sales systems, 7, 186
points, 273–274
polymer memory (polymeric ferroelectric RAM), 101
polymeric ferroelectric RAM (PFRAM), 101
pop-up ads, 370
port A connector on the exterior of a PC's system unit to which a device may be attached, 12, 108–111. *See also specific port names*
connecting instructions, 108–109
connector types, 109, 320, 321, 322
desktop PCs, 108–110
expansion cards, 96, 107, 108, 109
female connectors, 108
flash memory, 156–157
genders, 108
illustrated, 21, 109, 111
legacy port, 109
male connectors, 108
network ports, 109, 110, 111, 331, 332
notebook computers, 111
types, 109–111
port replicator connection, 111
portable bar-code readers, 185, 186
portable hard drives, 146–147
capacities, 147
illustrated, 147
interfaces, 146–147
portable PC A small personal computer, such as notebook, tablet, or handheld PC, designed to be carried around easily, 22–25. *See also specific portable PC types*
add-on devices, 111
CPUs, 97
expansion slots/cards, 107–108
flat panel technology, 197–198
illustrated, 8, 23
increasing popularity, 22–23
keyboards, 175–176
overview, 22–25
system unit. *See specific system unit components*; system unit
portable printers, 207
portal A Web site that supplies timely or useful content in hopes of enticing visitors to use the site several times a day, 63–64, 397. *See also* search site
portrait orientation, 274
possessed knowledge systems, 346
possessed object systems, 347
POST (power-on self-test), 103, 104
PostNet bar codes, 186, 187
power connectors, 109
Power Mac G5, 228, 237
power supply, illustrated, 96
Powerline networks, 343
power-on self-test (POST), 103, 104
PowerPC CPUs, 97, 98, 114, 228, 232, R-13
PowerPoint. *See* Microsoft PowerPoint
ppm (pages per minute), 204
pre-computers, 11, R-2
prefetch unit The part of the CPU that attempts to retrieve data and instructions before they are needed for processing, in order to avoid delays, 113
prepaid Internet, 373
presence technology, 325, 326
presentation graphic An image, such as a graph or text chart, designed to visually enhance a presentation, 285, 286. *See also* presentation graphics software

presentation graphics software Application software used to create presentation graphics and online slide shows, 6, 262, 285–288
animation, 287
common programs, 285
creating presentations, 286–287
enhancing presentations, 287–288
features, 286–287
further exploration, 287
graphic elements, 286
illustrated, 286, 287
overview, 285
slide shows, 287, 288
transitions, 287–288
Web presentations, 288
primary operations, 10. *See also specific operations*
print buffer, 230
Print command, 267
print queue, 230
print resolution, 201
print server, 328
printer An output device that produces output on paper, 200–208. *See also* ink-jet printer; laser printer
bar-code printer, 207–208
characteristics, 200–204
color vs. black/white, 203
fax machines, 208
illustrated, 13, 203, 204, 205, 206, 207
impact vs. non-impact, 203
label printer, 207–208
multifunction devices, 208
personal vs. network, 203–204
photo printer, 206
plotters, 207–208
portable, 207
resolution, 201
special purpose, 206–208
speed, 204
spooling jobs, 229–230
privacy concerns
anonymity concerns, 73–75
"Big Brother", 29, 190
cookies and, 403–406
e-mail, 407
social concerns, 29, 73, 190
spyware, 299, 406–407
video surveillance, 71
Web browsing, 402–406
processing Performing operations on data that has been input into a computer to convert that input to output, 10
concurrent, 228, 229
cycle, 10
efficiency techniques, 227–230
simultaneous, 228, 229
speed, 97, 113–114, R-3
processing devices, 13
product information online, 396, 397
productivity software, 7. *See also* software suite; *specific suite names*
professionals, 16. *See also* careers; programmer
program alteration sabotage, 353
programmability, 9
programmer A person whose primary job responsibility is to write, maintain, and test computer programs, 16
programming language A set of rules, words, symbols, and codes used to write computer programs, 12, 14, 89, 381. *See also specific languages*
programs. *See* software; *specific program names, types*
project management software, 297, 298
pronouncing Internet addresses, 57
protocols. *See* communications protocols; *specific protocols*
proxy server, 340
PS/2 connectors, 109, 110
public domain software Software that is not copyrighted and may be used without restriction, 264, 265
public hot spots, 54, 320, 322, 324, 338–339, 376

Publisher. *See* Microsoft Publisher
Punch Card Tabulating Machine and Sorter, 11

Q

QIC (quarter-inch-cassette), 158
quantum computing A technology that applies the principles of quantum physics and quantum mechanics to computers to direct atoms or nuclei to work together as quantum bits (qubits), which function simultaneously as the computer's processor and memory, 123
quarter-inch-cassette (QIC), 158
qubits, 123
query A request to see information from a database matching specified criteria, 284
Quick Launch toolbar, 42, 43, 49
QWERTY keyboards, 175

R

radio (Internet), 389, 390
radio buttons, 45, 46
radio frequency identification (RFID), 188
radio waves, 177
RAID A storage method that uses several small hard disks in parallel to do the job of a larger disk, 149
RAM. *See* random access memory (RAM)
Rambus DRAM (RDRAM), 102, 118
Rambus in-line memory modules (RIMMs), 100
random access memory (RAM) Chips located on the motherboard that provide a temporary location for the computer to hold data and program instructions while they are needed, 100–103
   adding, 115
   addressing, 102, 103
   capacities, 101–102
   DDR SDRAM, 102
   DIMMs, 100
   DRAM, 102
   FeRAM, 101
   illustrated, 96, 105
   increasing speed, 115, 118
   module types, 100–101
   MRAM, 101
   non-volatile, 100, 101
   RDRAM, 102, 118
   RIMMs, 100
   SDRAM, 102
   SIMMs, 100
   speed, 102
   SRAM, 102
   storage systems vs., 134
   types, 101, 102
   volatility, 100, 135
   VRAM, 196
random access storage, 135–136
raster-based programs, 292, 293
RDRAM (Rambus DRAM), 102, 118
read-only (ROM) discs, 152–153. *See also specific discs*
read-only memory (ROM) Non-erasable chips located on the motherboard into which data or programs have been permanently stored, 100, 103
read/write heads, 140, 142–143
RealOne Player, 294, 388
receiving e-mail, 68, 69
recharging ink/toner cartridges, 204
record A collection of related fields in a database; also called a row, 281, 283–284
recordable CD/DVD. *See specific media names*
recovery utilities, 249, 250
Recycle Bin
   emptying, 117
   retrieving file/folder from, 244
red, green, blue (RGB), 192
Red Hat, 238, 239
reduced instruction set computing (RISC), 121
redundant arrays of independent disks. *See* RAID
reference material software, 289, 290
reference sites, 63, 65, 396–397, R-20

reference software, 298
register High-speed memory built into the CPU that temporarily stores data during processing, 100, 102–103, 112, 113
registry files, 224
relational database management system (RDBMS) A type of database system in which data is stored in tables related by common fields; the most widely used database model today, 281, 282
   common programs, 282
   creating, 282–283, 284
   deleting records, 283–284
   editing records, 283–284
   fields (columns), 281, 282–283
   general concepts, 281–285
   illustrated, 282
   inserting records, 283–284
   modifying databases, 283–284
   objects, 282, 283
   paper-based database vs., 282
   queries, 284
   records (rows), 281, 283–284
   reports, 285
   table relationships, 281, 282–283
   Web sites and, 285
relative cell references, 279
remote PC access software, 251
remote storage A storage device that is not directly a part of the PC being used, such as network storage or online storage, 134, 159
removable flash drives. *See* flash memory drive
removable-media, 135. *See also specific media*
repeaters, 334
report A formatted means of looking at a database table or the results of a query, 285
resolution
   digital cameras, 192
   dot pitch vs., 197
   interpolated (enhanced), 185, 192
   monitors, 196
   optical, 185
   printers, 201
   scanners, 184–185
resources (computer), 225
resources (Internet), citing, 385
Restore button, 49
restore points, 21
restoring system software, 249, 250
retrieving deleted files, 244
RFID (radio frequency identification), 188
RGB (red, green, blue), 192
right margins, 274
RIMMs (Rambus in-line memory modules), 100
ring network A network that connects devices in a closed loop, 327
ripping software, 293, 295
RISC (reduced instruction set computing), 121
RJ-11 connector, 320
RJ-45 connector, 109, 110, 320, 331, 340
RoadRunner, 53
robot-assisted surgery, 316
ROM. *See* read-only memory (ROM)
root directory, 225, 226
rotational delays, 143
router A device on a network that sends data via the most efficient route to travel to a specific location, 334
row A collection of related fields located in a single table in a database. In a spreadsheet program, a horizontal group of cells on a worksheet, 276
   database. *See* record
   deleting, 278
   formatting, 280
   illustrated, 277
   inserting, 278
   word processing tables, 275
Roxio Easy CD and DVD Creator, 294

S

sabotage, 344, 349-353. *See also* computer virus
   data alteration, 353
   DoS attacks, 347, 348, 352, 353
   program alteration, 353
   protecting against, 353
   statistics, 349
safety systems (smart cars), 241
S-AIT (Super advanced intelligent tape), 158
samples, audio, 92–94
SAN. *See* storage area network (SAN)
satellite Internet access Fast, direct Internet access via the airwaves using a satellite dish and satellite modem, 317, 374, 375
satellite radio, 314
satellite transmissions, 314, 322, 323–324
Save command, 250, 267
saving
   files, 51, 250
   keyboard shortcut for, 250
SC connectors, 322
scanner An input device that reads printed text and graphics and transfers them to a computer in digital form, 13, 181–189
   bar-code, 185–187
   drum, 184
   evaluating, 185
   flatbed, 183, 184
   further exploration, 185
   handheld, 183, 184
   illustrated, 184
   MICR readers, 187–189
   OCR devices, 187
   OMRs, 185
   resolution, 184–185
   sheetfed, 183, 184
   source data automation, 7, 182–183
   source documents, 182
   three-dimensional, 184
scientific calculators, R-10
SCO Group, 238, 239
scroll bar A horizontal or vertical bar that appears along an edge of a window when the window is not large enough to display its entire content; scroll bars are used to view the rest of the information in the window, 50
   components, 50
   dialog boxes, 47
   illustrated, 50
   windows, 50
scroll button, 177
scroll wheel, 177
SCSI. *See* Small Computer System Interface (SCSI)
SD cards. *See* secure digital (SD) cards
SDIO. *See* Secure Digital Input/Output (SDIO)
SDRAM (synchronous DRAM), 102
search engine A software program used by a search site to retrieve matching Web pages from a search database, 63–65, 380. *See also* search site
   databases, 379, 380
   search strategies, 63–65, 381–384, R-23–24
   using phrases, 382
search site A Web site designed to help users search for Web pages that match specified keywords or selected categories, 63–65, 379–381
   advanced searches, R-23
   Boolean operators, 382–383, R-23
   companies, 63–64, 379
   directories, 65, 379, 380–381
   evaluating results, 384
   example search, 382–383
   field searching, 383–384
   further exploration, 63
   Google search tips, R-23–24
   guide, R-22
   hits, 380
   illustrated, 64

keywords. See keyword
metasearch sites, 381
natural language, 381
portals, 63–64, 397
reference sites, 63, 65, 396–397, R-20
results example, 382
search strategies, 63–65, 381–384, R-23–24
selecting categories, 64, 65
special operators, 64, R-24
using, 63–65, 381–384
using multiple, 382, 383
variant word forms, 383
Web-based Help systems, 270, 271
wildcards, 383
search tool utility, 243
searching Internet. See search engine; search site
second-generation (2G) cell phones, 325
second-generation computers, 11–12, R-3
sector A pie-shaped area on a disk surface.
floppy disks, 138, 139
hard drives, 141, 142
illustrated, 139
optical discs, 150
Secure Digital Input/Output (SDIO) devices, 108
Secure Digital (SD) cards, 108, 156, 157
secure Web pages, 55, 386, 387
security issues, 344–349. See also computer crime; security
measures
anonymity concerns, 73–75
crackers, 344
DoS attacks, 347, 348, 352, 353
fraud, 386
identity theft. See identity theft
online transactions, 386
operating system, 226, 227
spyware, 299, 406–407
unauthorized access, 344–349, 353
unauthorized use, 344–349
viruses. See computer virus
war driving, 345
security measures, 345–349
antivirus software, 72–73, 246, 353
firewalls. See firewall
identity management programs, 250–251
passwords. See password
PINs, 346
possessed knowledge systems, 346
possessed object systems, 347
presence technology, 325, 326
removable-media advantages, 135
video surveillance, 71
seek time, 143
self-service kiosks. See kiosks
sending e-mail, 68, 69
September 11, 2001, 315
sequential access, 135–136
serial ATA drives, 146
serial cards, 108
serial connectors, 109
serial ports, 109
serial transmission Data transmission in which every bit in
a byte must travel down the same path in succession, 318
servers, 328. See also client-server networks; specific
server types
service providers. See Internet access; Internet service
provider (ISP); specific access devices
set-top boxes, 25, 26
shared hard disks, 231, 232
shareware Copyrighted software that is distributed on the
honor system; should be either paid for or uninstalled
after the trial period, 264–265
sharing files/photos, 159, 160, 192
sheetfed scanners, 183, 184
shielded cable, 320
shipping industry bar codes, 186–187
Shockwave, 62
shopping Web sites, R-22

shortcuts
keyboard shortcuts, 45, 250, 267
menus, 243
Show Desktop button, 49
Shut Down option, 51
shutting down PCs, 51
signature capture devices, 178, 179
silicon on insulator (SOI) chips, 119
SIMMs (single in-line memory modules), 100
simple list boxes, 46, 47
simplex transmission, 318
simultaneous processing, 228, 229
single in-line memory modules (SIMMs), 100
single-user licenses, 264
site licenses, 264
64-bit
buses, 100, 104, 105
Mac OS, 237
operating systems, 232, 236, 237, 240
processors, 102, 103, 121, 232, R-6
registers, 103
Solaris, 240, 242
Windows XP, 236
words, 98
sizing windows, 48–49
SkyTower platform, 375
slash (/), 57
slate tablet PCs, 23
slave devices, 342
sleep mode, 41, 51
slide A one-page presentation graphic that can be displayed
in a group with others to form an online slide show, 285,
286, 287, 288
slide shows, 288
sliders, 46
Small Computer System Interface (SCSI)
drives, 146
interface cards, 146
ports, 110
smart appliances
defined, 6
illustrated, 5
smart bar codes, 187, 188
smart bullets, 99
smart card A credit-card-sized piece of plastic containing a
chip and other circuitry into which data can be stored,
159–161, 162, 387
capacities, 159
characteristics, 159–160
encryption, 160
illustrated, 161
magnetic disk combination, 160
reading devices, 160
student IDs, 159, 162
uses, 159, 160, 161
using, 160
smart cars, 241
smart classrooms, 199, 201
smart display A portable display device that connects wirelessly to its associated system unit, 198
smart homes
defined, 6
illustrated, 5
smart pagers, 19
smart phones, 19, 176
smart tennis shoes, 99
SmartMedia cards, 157
Smith, David, 351
SMP (symmetric multiprocessing), 119–120
Sobig.F worm, 351
social impact
anonymity concerns, 73–75
computers, 28–29
cyberspace, 72–75
face recognition technology, 190
information age, 28
information integrity, 75

information revolution, 28
online communications differences, 73
privacy. See privacy concerns
soft copy, 174
software The instructions, also called computer programs,
that are used to tell a computer what it should do, 14–15.
See also application software; software suite; specific
software names; system software; utility program
ASPs. See application service provider (ASP)
CD key code, 245
delivery methods, 263, 264–266
downloading, 5, 245
in education, 6
installing, 14, 245
licenses. See ownership rights; software license
networking, 18
open source, 238
types, 14–15
upgrading, R-18
software license An agreement, either included in a software package or displayed on the screen during installation, that specifies the conditions under which a buyer of
the program can use it, 263. See also ownership rights
EULA, 299
GPL, 239
illustrated, 263
reading/accepting terms, 245, 299
single-user, 264
site/network, 264
software suite A collection of software programs bundled
together and sold as a single software package, 266–268
commands summary, 267
common suites, 266, 267
cost comparison, 239
handheld PCs, 270
integrated software programs vs., 267–268
keyboard shortcuts, 267
manufacturers, 266
OLE, 268–269
SOI (silicon on insulator) chips, 119
Solaris (Sun Microsystems), 240, 242
solid-state storage system, 155
Solidus Networks, 349
Sony Pictures DigitalACID® Pro, 293
Sony Pictures DigitalSound Forge®, 293
Sony Pictures DigitalVegas®, 293
sound cards, 107
sound ports, 109, 111
sound recorders, 293
source data automation, 7, 182–183. See also scanner
source documents, 181–182, 269
source module. See source code
spam Unsolicited, bulk e-mail sent over the Internet, 72, 75
antispam programs, 251
malicious, 352
speakers Output devices that produce sound, 13, 208–209
speed
buses, 97, 100, 118, R-13
CD/DVD drives, 151
increasing. See increasing computer speed
Internet access, 373, 374, 375, 376
networks, 317–318
printers, 204
processing, 97, 113–114, R-3
RAM, 102
supercomputers, 27
system clock, 97, 113–114
spelling/grammar check, 267, 272
spin boxes, 46
spooling The process of placing items in a buffer so they
can be retrieved by the appropriate device (such as a
printer) when needed, 229–230
sports Web sites, R-21
spreadsheet A group of values and other data organized
into rows and columns, 276. See also cell; spreadsheet
software

spreadsheet software Application software used to create spreadsheet documents, which typically contain a great deal of numbers and mathematical computations and are organized into rows and columns, 262, 276–281. *See also* cell
  absolute cell references, 279
  autoformatting styles, 280
  charts, 280
  columns, 276, 277, 278, 280
  common programs, 276
  components, illustrated, 277
  concepts, 276–281
  constant values, 277
  creating worksheets, 276–278
  deleting rows/columns, 278
  editing, 278–279
  formatting, 277, 279–280
  formulas, 277–278, 279
  functions, 278, 279
  further exploration, 281
  graphing, 280
  inserting rows/columns, 278
  labels, 277
  mathematical operators, 277
  menus, 277
  numeric formatting, 277, 280
  origin, R-4
  overview, 276
  relative cell references, 279
  rows, 276, 277, 278, 280
  toolbars, 277
  Web and, 281
  what-if analysis, 280–281
  workbooks, 276
  worksheets. *See* worksheet
Springboard modules, 111
spyware Software programs often installed on a user's PC without the user's knowledge that secretly collect information and send it to an outside party via the user's Internet connection, 299, 406–407
spyware detectors, 299
SRAM (static RAM), 102
SSEs (streaming SIMD extensions), 121
SSE2 (streaming SIMD extensions), 121
ST connectors, 321, 322
Standby option, 51
star network A network that uses a host device connected directly to several other devices, 327
StarBand, 53
StarOffice (Sun), 239, 266
Start button, 42, 51, 235, 240
Start menu The main Windows menu that is used to start programs, 42–43
  features, 42–43
  illustrated, 42, 47
starting
  computer, 40–41
  programs, 47
  Web browsers, 58
static RAM (SRAM), 102
stealthware. *See* spyware
steering wheels (games), 181
stock trading online, 18
storage The operation of saving data, programs, or output for future use, 10. *See also specific storage systems/devices/media*
  adding second drive, 117
  alphabetic names, 134–135
  comparison chart, 162–163
  device names, 134–135
  drive selection, 162–163
  e-mail, 68
  fragmented files, 115–117, 247
  holographic, 161
  IPOS cycle perspective, 10
  logical vs. physical representation, 136–137
  magnetic systems. *See* floppy disk; hard disk drive; magnetic disk
  magnetic tape systems, 158

magneto-optical (MO) systems, 154
  memory vs., 100
  online, 159, 160
  optical systems, 150–154
  organizing data, 136–137
  random vs. sequential access, 135–136
  remote systems, 134, 159
  smart cards. *See* smart card
  system properties, 134–137
  transportability, 135
  unlimited capacity, 135
storage area network (SAN) A network of hard drives or other storage devices that provide storage for another network of computers, 148, 330
storage bays, 96, 117
storage cycle, 114, 115
storage device A piece of hardware, such as a floppy drive or CD drive, into which a storage medium is inserted to be read from or written to, 134. *See also specific devices*
  examples, 13, 14
  external, 134
  internal, 134
  remote. *See* remote storage
storage medium The part of a storage system where data is stored, such as a floppy disk or CD disc, 14, 134. *See also specific media*
  hard drives. *See* hard disk drive
  non-volatile, 135
  optical systems, 150–154
  removable vs. fixed, 135
storage server A hardware device containing multiple high-speed hard drives, 148
StorCard, 160
streaming media, 392, 394
streaming SIMD extensions (SSEs), 121
streaming SIMD extensions 2 (SSE2), 121
striping, 149
StuffIt program, 248
styles
  font, 273–274
  paragraph formatting, 274
stylus A cordless electronic pen often used with pen-based PCs, 177
subdirectory. *See* subfolders
subfolders, 136
submenus, 45
subnet mask, 340
SUM function, 278
Sun Microsystems
  Java. *See* Java
  large computer operating system, 242
  Solaris, 240, 242
  StarOffice, 239, 266
Super advanced intelligent tape (S-AIT), 158
super VGA (SVGA) standard, 196
supercomputer The fastest, most expensive, and most powerful type of computer, 27–28
  costs, 27
  example, 27, 28
  features, 19, 27–28
  grid computing, 27–28, 120
  illustrated, 28
  MPPs, 27, 120
  processing speed, 27
superconductive materials, 119
SuperDisk drives, 140
superdiskettes, 140. *See also* Zip disks
SuperDisks, 140, 163
superscaler computers, 114
SUPER-UX operating system, 242
surfing Web, 58–62
surgery technology
  robot-assisted, 316
  telesurgery, 316
  virtual surgery, 29
SVGA (super VGA) standard, 196
S-video ports, 111
swap file, 228

swapping, 229
switch A device on a network to which data is sent so it can be forwarded on to the appropriate network node, 334
Symbian OS A leading operating system for smart phones, 242
symmetric multiprocessing (SMP), 119–120
synchronous DRAM (SDRAM), 102
synchronous transmission, 319
system board Another name for motherboard, 96. *See also specific motherboard components*
system bus, 100, 105
system clock The timing mechanism within the computer system that synchronizes the computer's operations, 113–115
  clock speed, 97, 113–114
  measurements, 114
  mechanics of, 113–115
system maintenance (routine), 115–117, 246–247
System Restore, 249, 250
system software Programs, such as the operating system, that control the operation of a computer and its devices, as well as enable application software to run on the PC, 14, 222–251. *See also* operating system; *specific operating systems*; utility program
  application software vs., 222–223
  categories, 222
  common systems, 14
  overview, 222
system unit The main box of a computer that houses the CPU, motherboard, memory, and other devices, 95–111
  CD/DVD drives, 13, 96
  cooling, 118
  CPUs. *See* central processing unit (CPU); *specific CPU components*; *specific CPU names*
  expansion card. *See* expansion card
  expansion slot. *See* expansion slot
  fans, 96, 118
  floppy drives, 13, 96
  hard drives. *See* hard disk drive
  illustrated, 13, 96
  internal components, 12
  memory. *See specific memory types*
  motherboards, 96
  power supply, 96, 115
  RAM. *See* random access memory (RAM)
  registers, 100, 102–103, 112, 113
  restoring, 249, 250
  ROM, 100, 103
  storage bays, 96, 117
  troubleshooting, R-17–18
  Zip drives, 96, 163
systems analyst A person who studies systems in an organization in order to determine what work needs to be done and how this work may best be achieved, 16

T

table In a relational database, a collection of related records (rows), 281
  creating, 282–283, 284
  modifying structure, 283
tables (word processing), 273, 275
tablet PC A portable PC about the size of a notebook that is designed to be used with an electronic pen, 19, 23
  convertible tablet PC, 23
  design styles, 23
  features, 23
  operating system, 236
  PC cards, 107–108
  pen-based, 177, 178, 179
  slate tablet PC, 23
tabs, 274
tape drives, 136, 158
task, defined, 227
task button A button displayed on the taskbar to represent an open window; using this button, the window can be minimized, restored, or closed, 43
  features, 43, 48
  illustrated, 42, 48

Task Manager (Windows), 224
taskbar The bar located at the bottom of the Windows desktop that contains the Start button, task buttons, and the system tray, 42–43
   features, 42–43
   illustrated, 42, 47, 240
   toolbar, 42, 43, 47
   Windows Mobile, 240
TCP/IP The communications protocol that uses packet switching to facilitate the transmission of messages; the protocol used with the Internet, 337, 339
telecommunications, 312, 370
Telecommunications Act (1996), 370
telecommuting The use of computer and electronic devices to enable an individual to work from his or her home, 6, 316
teleconferencing. *See* videoconferencing
telemedicine The use of communications technology to provide medical information and services, 316
telephone. *See also* wireless phone
   connectors, 109
   ports, 109, 110
   smart phones, 19, 176
   video calls, 193
telesurgery, 316
television. *See also* video
   digital media units, 26
   HDTV monitors, 198
   interactive, 198, 391–392
   online, 391–393
   S-video ports, 111
   TV tuner cards, 107
   video-on-demand, 198
templates (word processing), 275
temporary files, 117
10Base-T protocol, 336–337
terabyte (TB) Approximately 1 trillion bytes, 91
teraflops, 114
terrorism
   cyberterrorism, 345
   September 11, 2001, 315
testing online, 399
text boxes, 46
text-based user interface, 41
thin client Another name for network computer, 25–26. *See also* network computer (NC)
third-generation (3G) cellular devices, 325
third-generation computers, 11, 12, R-3
32-bit processors, 232
threads, 70, 227
3G (third-generation) cellular devices, 325
three-dimensional (3-D) chips, 123
three-dimensional (3-D) scanners, 184
throughput, 318
thumb pads, 176
time bombs, 351
timelines, 11, R-2–6
time-sharing, 227–228
TLDs (top-level domain names), 55
Token Ring A communications protocol that uses token passing to control the transmission of messages, 337, 338
tokens, 337, 338
T-1 lines, 374
toner powder/cartridges, 204, 205
toolbar A set of icons or buttons displayed horizontally or vertically on the screen that can be used to issue commands to the computer, 44
   features, 44
   illustrated, 42, 43
   Linux operating system, 238
toolbar button A button on a toolbar that is clicked to issue a command to the computer, 43, 44
top margins, 274
top-level domain names (TLDs), 55
topologies (network), 327–328
   bus networks, 327
   combination, 328
   ring networks, 327
   star networks, 327

Torvalds, Linus, 238, R-5
touch pad A small rectangular-shaped input device, often found on notebook computers, that is touched with the finger or thumb to control an onscreen pointer and make selections, 181, 182
touch screen A display device that is touched with the finger to issue commands or otherwise generate input to the connected PC, 13, 180, 181
tower cases, 20
track A concentric path on a disk where data is recorded, 138
   floppy disks, 138, 139
   hard drives, 141, 142
   illustrated, 139
   optical discs, 150, 152
trackball An input device, similar to an upside-down mouse, that can be used to control an onscreen pointer and make selections, 181, 182
tracking browsing activity, 404–406
transceivers, 322, 375
transistors, 11–12, 111, R-3
transitions, 287–288
Transmeta Crusoe CPU, 97
Transmission Control Protocol/Internet Protocol. *See* TCP/IP
transmission directions, 318
transmission speed, 318
transmission timing, 319–320
   asynchronous transmission, 319
   isochronous transmission, 319–320
   synchronous transmission, 319
Trash, 117. *See also* Recycle Bin
Travan, 158
travel Web sites, R-22
trends. *See also* future trends
   aircraft-based Internet, 375
   digital copy protection, 155
   electronic paper, 199, 202
   e-mail hoaxes, 57
   finger payment systems, 349
   optical computers, 12, 123
   smart cars, 241
   spyware, 299
   unusual chip uses, 99
   wearable PCs, 8, 9, 22
trial version software, 264
Trojan Horse A malicious program that masquerades as something else, 351
troubleshooting, 41, R-17–18
true color images, 92, 93
tubes, vacuum, 11
tunneling, 330
Turn Off Computer dialog box, 51
turnaround documents, 187
TV tuner cards, 107
twisted-pair cable A communications medium consisting of wire strands twisted in sets of two and bound into a cable, 320–321
2G (second-generation) cell phones, 325
typeface. *See* font

U
ubiquitous computing, 4
Ultra Wideband (UWB) communications, 343
UltraSPARC processors, 97
UMTS (Universal Mobile Telecommunications System), 325
unauthorized access Gaining access to a computer, network, file, or other resource without permission, 344–349
   hacking, 344–345, 353
   protecting against, 345–349
   unauthorized use vs., 344
unauthorized use Using a computer resource for unapproved activities, 344–349
   protecting against, 345–349
   unauthorized access vs., 344
   Wi-Fi war driving, 345
Undo command, 267
Unicode A coding system for text-based data using any written language, 90, 91, R-12

uniform resource locator (URL) An Internet address, usually beginning with http://, that uniquely identifies a Web page, 55–56
   error messages, 60
   example, 55–56
   file extensions, 55
   illustrated, 56, 60
   pronouncing, 57
   reloading, 60
   secure Web pages, 55, 386, 387
   typing, 60
   using, 60
uninstall utilities, 117, 247–248
uninstalling programs, 115–117, 247–248
UNIVAC, 11, R-3
Universal Connectors, 111
Universal Mobile Telecommunications System (UMTS), 325
Universal Product Code (UPC) code, 186–187, 188
Universal Serial Bus (USB), 106, 107
   connectors, 109
   flash memory drives, 158
   hot-swappability, 110
   hubs, 110
   illustrated, 105, 109
   locations, 109
   PC cards, 108
   ports, 109, 110, 111
   quantities, 107, 109
   specifications, 106
   storage system comparisons, 162–163
UNIX A multiuser, multitasking operating system developed in the 1970s for midrange servers and mainframes, 237–238. *See also* Linux
   copyright challenge, 239
   flavors, 237–238
   flexibility, 237
   large computer operating systems, 242
   origin, R-3
   personal vs. network versions, 231–232
   user interface, 231
Up toolbar button, 243
UPC (Universal Product Code) code, 186–187, 188
upgrading
   computer systems, 117, 118, R-18
   CPUs, 118, R-18
   hard drives, 117, R-18
   software, R-18
   video cards, 118
USA Patriot Act (USAPA), 344
USB. *See* Universal Serial Bus (USB)
USB mini-drives. *See* flash memory drive
user interfaces, 41, 223–225. *See also* operating system; *specific operating systems*
   command line, 231, 233
   defined, 41
   GUI, 41, 231, 365, 366
   text-based, 41
user name A name that uniquely identifies a user on a particular network, 18, 346
   anonymity concerns, 73
   e-mail, 56
   identity management programs, 250–251
users, Internet, 367
.us file extension, 55
utility program A type of software that performs a specific task, usually related to managing or maintaining the computer system, 117, 222, 243–251
   antivirus software, 72–73, 246, 353
   deleting unnecessary files, 117
   diagnostic programs, 246–247
   disk management programs, 246–247
   downloading, 5, 245
   encryption. *See* encryption
   file compression programs, 248
   file management, 226, 243–245
   further exploration, 251
   installing, 14, 245
   Internet, 250–251

network, 250–251
recovery programs, 249, 250
remote PC access software, 251
uninstalling programs, 115–117, 247–248
UWB (Ultra Wideband) communications, 343

V

vacuum tubes, 11
variant word forms, 383
.vbs file extension, 72
vector-based images, 92
vector-based programs, 292, 293
VGA (video graphics array) standard, 196
ViaVoice (IBM) software, 193
video A continuous stream of visual information broken
  into separate images or frames to be displayed one after
  the other to simulate the original visual event, *See also*
  television
  analog, transferring to PCs, 193
  cameras, 191, 192–193
  capture boards, 107, 193
  cards, 107, 108, 118, 196
  data coding, 95
  on demand, 198, 391, 392–393, 394
  displays. *See* display device; monitor
  downloading movies, 198, 392–393, 394
  DVRs, 143, 392, 394
  editing software, 293
  e-mail, 67
  file extensions, 226
  graphics boards, 107
  media players, 294, 388
  online, 391–393
  output cards, 108
  PC cameras, 192, 193
  phone calls, 193
  pirated movies, 393
  RAM (VRAM), 196
  streaming, 392
  S-video ports, 111
  TV tuner cards, 107
  upgrading cards, 118
  Web cams, 193
video graphics array (VGA) standard, 196
video RAM (VRAM), 196
video surveillance, 71
videoconferencing The use of computers, video cameras,
  microphones, and other communications technologies to
  conduct face-to-face meetings over the Internet, 70, 71,
  193, 314–315
video-on-demand (VOD), 198, 391, 392–393, 394
viewable image size (VIS), 196, 197
viewing PC contents, 243
virtual memory A memory-management technique that
  uses hard drive space as an extension to a PC's RAM,
  228–229, 230
virtual private network (VPN) A group of secure paths
  over the Internet that provide authorized users a secure
  means of accessing a private network via the Internet, 330
Virtual Reality Modeling Language (VRML), 296
virtual reality (VR) The use of a computer to create three-
  dimensional environments that look like they do in the
  real world, 51, 289, 290
viruses. *See* computer virus
VIS (viewable image size), 196, 197
Visual Basic An object-oriented, fourth-generation version
  of the BASIC programming language, 14
VOD (video-on-demand), 198, 391, 392–393, 394
Voice over IP (VoIP), 71, 337
voice recognition. *See* voice-input system
voice-input system A system that enables a computer to
  recognize the human voice, 193–194
  components, 193, 194
  fifth-generation computers, 12
  mechanics of, 194
  phoneme use, 194
  software, 193
  uses, 194

voice-output system A system that enables a computer to
  play back or imitate the human voice, 209
VoIP (voice over IP), 71, 337
volatile Describes a medium whose contents are erased
  when the power is shut off, 100, 135
VPN. *See* virtual private network (VPN)
VRAM (video RAM), 196
VRML (Virtual Reality Modeling Language), 296
VSE/ESA (IBM) operating system, 242

W

WAN. *See* wide area network (WAN)
WAP. *See* Wireless Application Protocol (WAP)
war driving, 345
WAV format, 295
Wave Division Multiplexing (WDM), 335
waveform audio, 92–94
WBT. *See* Web-based training (WBT)
WCDMA (Wideband Code Division Multiple Access), 325
WDM (Wave Division Multiplexing), 335
wearable PCs, 8, 9, 22
weather Web sites, R-21
Web browser A program used to view Web pages, 15, 18,
  52. *See also specific browsers*
  address/location bar, 56
  bookmarks, 62–63
  common programs, 52, 53, 58–59
  deleting temporary files, 117
  error messages, 60
  favorites, 62–63
  features, 58–59
  first graphics-based, 366
  further exploration, 52
  History list, 62–63
  illustrated, 53
  microbrowsers, 52, 53
  setting up, 378
  starting, 58
  tracking activity of, 404–406
Web browsing
  cookies tracking, 404–406
  privacy, 402–406
  surfing Web, 58–62
Web bug A very small (usually invisible) image on a Web
  page that transmits data about the Web page visitor to a
  Web server, 406
Web cams, 193
Web conferencing. *See* videoconferencing
Web databases, 63, 65, 285, 396–397, R-20
Web Guide, R-19–22
Web pads. *See* Internet appliance
Web page A document, typically containing hyperlinks to
  other documents, located on a Web server and available
  through the World Wide Web, 51, 60–62
  animation, 61, 62, 296
  citing, 385
  colors, coding, 92, 93
  components, 60–62
  development, 296
  e-mail hyperlinks, 61
  error messages, 60
  form fields, 61, 62
  frames, 61, 62
  home pages. *See* home page
  illustrated, 61
  presentation graphics software generating, 288
  reloading, 60
  searching strategies/tips, 389–394, R-23–24
  secure pages, 55, 386, 387
  spreadsheets and, 281
  text/images, 61
  URLs. *See* uniform resource locator (URL)
  word processing for, 275
Web searching strategies/tips, 391–394, R-23–24
Web server A computer that is continually connected to the
  Internet and hosts Web pages that are accessible through
  the Internet, 51, 328

Web service A self-contained business application that
  operates over the Internet, 369
Web site A collection of related Web pages usually belonging to an organization or individual, 52
  databases, 285
  development, 296
  e-commerce. *See* e-commerce
  guide, R-19–22
  home pages. *See* home page
  online storage, 159, 160
  video cameras, 193
  visiting. *See* surfing Web
Web surfing, 58–62
Web-based e-mail, 65–66
Web-based Help, 270, 271
Web-based software, 265–266, 369. *See also* application
  service provider (ASP)
Web-based training (WBT) Instruction delivered on an
  individual basis via the World Wide Web, 289, 290, 397,
  398–399
  advantages, 398–399
  disadvantages, 399
  testing online, 399
Webfolio. *See* e-portfolio
WECA (Wireless Ethernet Compatibility Alliance), 338
WEP (Wired Equivalency Privacy) security protocol, 348
what-if analysis, 280
Whois domain name search function, 54
why learn computers, 4–5
wide area network (WAN) A network that connects
  devices located in a large geographical area, 329
Wideband Code Division Multiple Access (WCDMA), 325
wide-format printers, 207–208
Wider-Fi, 341
Wi-Fi, 338–341. *See also* 802.11 (Wi-Fi)
wiki, 400
wildcards, 383
Wi-Max, 341
WinAmp, 388
Wincom Systems, 119
window A rectangular area in which programs, documents,
  and other content are displayed, 43–44. *See also specific
  window elements*
  active, 43, 48
  closing, 48, 49
  elements, 43–44
  illustrated, 42, 43, 48, 49, 235
  manipulating, 48–50
  maximizing, 48
  minimizing, 48, 49
  moving, 49
  opening, 47
  restoring, 49
  scroll bars, 50
  sizing, 48–49
Windows The primary PC operating system developed by
  Microsoft Corporation; the most recent version is Windows XP, 14, 41–51, 234–236. *See also specific versions*
  cost comparison, 239
  desktop. *See* desktop
  dialog boxes. *See* dialog box
  evolution, R-5–6
  interface, 42–47
  menus. *See* menu
  registry files, 224
  scientific calculator, R-10
  shutting down, 51
  starting programs, 47
  task buttons, 42, 43
  Task Manager, 224
  taskbar, 42–43, 47
  versions, 41–42, 234–236
  windows. *See specific window elements*; window
Windows CE .NET, 240
Windows Embedded A family of operating systems based
  on Windows and designed for non-personal computer
  devices, such as cash registers and consumer electronic
  devices, 240

Windows Explorer, 226, 243, 244
Windows Me (Millennium Edition), 234
Windows Media Player, 294, 295, 388
Windows Messenger, 71
Windows Mobile A family of operating systems based on Windows and designed for handheld PCs, smart phones, and other mobile devices, 240, 241–242, 269, 270
Windows 98, 234
Windows 95, 234
Windows NT An earlier version of the Windows network operating system designed for both high-end single-user and network applications that was replaced by Windows 2000, 234, 235
Windows Paint, 292
Windows PCs, 20. *See also* personal computer (PC)
Windows Server 2003 The most recent version of Windows designed for server use, 236
Windows Sound Recorder, 293
Windows 3.x, 234
Windows 2000 The upgrade to Windows NT, 235
Windows XP The latest version of Windows; designed to replace both Windows Me and Windows 2000, 235–236
  cost comparison, 239
  features, 235–236
  illustrated, 236
  System Restore, 249, 250
  versions, 236, 240
WinZip program, 248
Wired Equivalency Privacy (WEP) security protocol, 348
wired network A network in which computers and other devices are connected to the network via physical cables, 320–322
  Category 3 cable, 320
  Category 5 cable, 320, 340
  Category 6 cable, 320
  coaxial cable, 321
  connector types, 109, 320, 321, 322
  further exploration, 326
  hardware. *See* modem; networking hardware
  microwave transmissions, 322–323
  transmission media, 320–322
  twisted-pair cable, 320–321
  wireless vs., 320
wireless access point A device used to connect wireless devices to a wired network, 334
Wireless Application Protocol (WAP) A standard for delivering content, such as Web pages, to mobile devices, 342
wireless Ethernet. *See* 802.11 (Wi-Fi)
Wireless Ethernet Compatibility Alliance (WECA), 338
wireless fidelity (Wi-Fi). *See* 802.11 (Wi-Fi)
wireless Internet service providers (WISPs), 376. *See also* mobile wireless Internet access
wireless keyboards, 176
wireless mice, 177
wireless monitors. *See* smart display
wireless network A network in which computers and other devices are connected to the network without physical cables, 320, 322–326
  adapter cards, 331–332
  broadcast radio transmissions, 322
  cellular radio, 324–325, 326
  further exploration, 326
  handheld computers, 25
  illustrated, 323, 324

infrared transmissions, 326
  microwave transmissions, 322–323
  presence technology, 325, 326
  satellite transmissions, 322, 323–324
  wired vs., 320
wireless phone A cellular or satellite phone, 313
  generations, 325
  Internet accessible, 8
  statistics, 325
  technology evolution, 325
  transmissions, 324–325, 326
wireless WANs, 329
WISPs. *See* mobile wireless Internet access; wireless Internet services providers (WISPs)
wizards, 275
Word. *See* Microsoft Word
word processing Using a computer and word processing software to create, edit, save, and print written documents, such as letters, contracts, and manuscripts, 271–272. *See also* word processing software
word processing software Application software used to create, edit, save, and print written documents, 271–275
  character formatting, 273–274
  common programs, 272
  concepts, 271–275
  creating documents, 272
  document formatting, 274
  editing documents, 272, 273
  features, illustrated, 273
  formatting documents, 273–274
  further exploration, 275
  graphics, 273, 275
  hyperlinks, 275
  insertion point, 272
  overview, 271–272
  page formatting, 274
  paragraph formatting, 274
  software, 6, 15, 262
  spelling/grammar check, 267, 272
  tables, 273, 275
  templates, 275
  Web and, 275
  wizards, 275
  word wrap, 272, 273
word sizes, 97
word wrap The feature found in a word processing program that automatically returns the insertion point to the next line when the end of the screen line is reached, 272, 273
workbook A collection of worksheets saved in a single spreadsheet file, 276. *See also* cell; spreadsheet software; worksheet
workplace computers
  illustrated, 7
  impact, 7
  wearable PCs, 9
Works. *See* Microsoft Works
worksheet A document in a spreadsheet program, 276. *See also* cell; spreadsheet software
  absolute cell references, 279
  autoformatting styles, 280
  constant values, 277
  creating, 276–278
  deleting rows/columns, 278
  editing, 278–279

  formatting, 277, 279–280
  formulas, 277–278, 279
  functions, 278, 279
  inserting rows/columns, 278
  labels, 277
  mathematical operators, 277
  multiple, 276, 277
  relative cell references, 279
  tabs, 277
workstation CPUs, 97
World Wide Web The collection of Web pages available through the Internet, 51–65, 365–366
  browsers. *See specific browsers*; Web browser
  chat sessions, 58
  databases, 285
  discussion groups, 58
  evolution, 365–366
  Internet vs., 18, 51, 365–366, 371
  network ownership, 366
  origin, 365–366, R-5
  overview, 51–52
  presentations on, 288
  searches. *See* search engine; search site
  site guide, R-19–22
  spreadsheets and, 281
  surfing, 58–62
  URLs. *See* uniform resource locator (URL)
World Wide Web Consortium (W3C), 366
worms. *See* computer worm
wrapping text. *See* word wrap
writing (storing) data, 140, 142–143
writing online, 397, 400–401
W3C (World Wide Web Consortium), 366

X

xD cards, 157
Xeon (Intel) CPUs, 97, 98, R-13
Xerox, 122
XML (Extensible Markup Language) A set of rules used for exchanging data over the Web; addresses only the content, not the formatting, so the device being used displays the content in an appropriate format, 275

Y

Yahoo!, 63, 379, 381, 397
Yahoo! Mail, 65–66
Yahoo! Messenger, 71
YB. *See* yottabyte (YB)
yottabyte (YB), 91
You Don't Know Jack program, 291

Z

ZB. *See* zettabyte (ZB)
zettabyte (ZB), 91
Zip disks, 117, 140, 163
Zip drives, 96, 140, 163
.zip file extension, 226, 248
zombies, 352, 353
Z/OS (IBM) operating system, 242
Z/VM (IBM) operating system, 242